M

Ireland in Quotes

Conor O'Clery

Born in Belfast and educated at Queen's University, Belfast, Conor O'Clery has worked for the *Irish Times* for 27 years in various positions, including news editor and resident correspondent in Belfast, London, Moscow, Washington and currently Beijing. He has won several awards for his work, including Journalist of the Year in Ireland in 1987, and is the author of four books: *Phrases Make History Here*; *America, A Place Called Hope?*; *Melting Snow* and *The Greening of the White House*, published in the United States as *Daring Diplomacy*.

IRELAND
QUOTES

Conor O'Clery

THE O'BRIEN PRESS
DUBLIN

For Zhanna

First published 1999 by The O'Brien Press Ltd.,
20 Victoria Road, Dublin 6, Ireland
Tel. +353 1 4923333; Fax. +353 1 4922777
email: books@obrien.ie
website: http://www.obrien.ie

ISBN: 0-86278-592-8

British Library Cataloguing-in-publication Data
O'Clery, Conor
Ireland in quotes : a history of the 20th century
1.Ireland - Politics and government -
20th century - Quotations, maxims, etc.
I.Title
320.9'417

1 2 3 4 5 6 7 8 9 10
99 00 01 02 03 04 05 06 07

The O'Brien Press receives
assistance from

The Arts Council
An Chomhairle Ealaíon

Layout and design: The O'Brien Press Ltd.
Colour separations: C&A Print Services Ltd.
Printing: MPG Books Ltd.

CONTENTS

LIST OF ABBREVIATIONS

AOH	Ancient Order of Hibernians
BBC	British Broadcasting Corporation
DL	Democratic Left
DUP	Democratic Unionist Party
EC	European Communities
EEC	European Economic Community
FF	Fianna Fáil
FG	Fine Gael
GAA	Gaelic Athletic Association
HC	House of Commons
HL	House of Lords
IRA	Irish Republican Army
INLA	Irish Nationalist Liberation Army
ITGWU	Irish Transport and General Workers' Union
KLA	Kosovo Liberation Army
LVF	Loyalist Volunteer Force
MEP	Member of the European Parliament
MP	Member of Parliament
NATO	North Atlantic Treaty Organisation
NI	Northern Ireland
NILP	Northern Ireland Labour Party
NORAID	Irish Northern Aid
PD	Progressive Democrats
PUP	Progressive Unionist Party
RIC	Royal Irish Constabulary
RTÉ	Radio Teilifís Éireann
RUC	Royal Ulster Constabulary
SAS	Special Air Services
SDLP	Social, Democratic Labour Party
SF	Sinn Féin
TCD	Trinity College, Dublin
TD	Teachta Dála (member of the Irish Parliament)
UCD	University College, Dublin
UDA	Ulster Defence Association
UDP	Ulster Democratic Party
UDR	Ulster Defence Regiment
UFF	Ulster Freedom Fighters
UK	United Kingdom
UN	United Nations
UNIFIL	United Nations Interim Force in Lebanon
US	United States
UUP	Ulster Unionist Party
UVF	Ulster Volunteer Force
UWC	Ulster Workers' Council

INTRODUCTION

This book is an oral political history of Ireland in the twentieth century. Historians have written of what people did in Ireland in the last, turbulent hundred years. This is what they said.

Irish people love words. They admire eloquence. They relish a colourful turn of phrase, a clever riposte, a wicked insult. They treasure a *bon mot*; they love a good malapropism and a splendidly outrageous mixed metaphor. They fling the phrases of long-dead politicians about in argument. They quote poets in political battle. Ireland is one of the few countries in the world where newspapers carry long columns of 'This Week They Said'. The reader will find the best, the most memorable and the most oft-quoted phrases of the century in the pages of this book.

We can, of course, exaggerate the power of the spoken word. British Prime Minister, David Lloyd George, cautioned the House of Commons in December 1921, during debate on the Anglo-Irish Treaty, that 'you do not settle great complicated problems, the moment you utter a good phrase about them'. But words can have great force in Ireland. In December 1996, futureNobel Laureate John Hume defined political leadership as being about 'changing the language of others'. The powerful rhetoric used against Home Rule during the earlier part of the century furnished Ireland, in the words of Herbert Asquith in 1912, with a 'grammar of anarchy'. Around the same time, Arthur Griffith complained that if Home Rule was liberty, then 'the lexicographers have deceived us'. In 1945 we find the UK Representative in Dublin, Sir John Maffey, warning his government that 'phrases make history here'. Phrases, remembered or half-forgotten, often misquoted, sometimes a line from a ballad or a catch-cry from an election, often a slip of the tongue or words spoken in anger, are a major part of the intellectual and emotional baggage of every generation in Ireland. The good, the telling, the rhetorical, the funny, the belligerent, the treacherous, the short-sighted, the visionary, the shocking, the bitter, the poignant, the eloquent – all such phrases have inspired, inflamed and coloured Irish political and social life. Every statement is in itself a small confession. Each quotation recorded here touches on the great issues and the political, religious and social preoccupations of the time or the passing distractions of the day. Many bear out the conclusion of English writer Ernest Benn that 'politics is the art of looking for trouble, finding it whether it exists or not, diagnosing it incorrectly, and applying the wrong remedy'. Some confirm the wisdom of Seamus Heaney's advice as a northerner: 'Whatever you say, you say nothing'.

Nor are political phrases the preserve of politicians. Poets and playwrights have produced highly political quotations. Yeats wondered in his declining years if some words of his might have sent out 'certain men the English shot'. Bishops and clerics of every stripe have never ceased preaching, cajoling, dictating (and of late apologising) to people and politicians in their century-long attempt to bend political and social Ireland to their will. Gunmen and victims, athletes and academics, mistresses and minders, people from all walks of life have contributed to the oral history of the century. Children have uttered some of the most poignant truths.

The quotations in this book are arranged in chronological order so that the reader can follow the course of the debates which shaped the country as it passed through rebellion and division, through times of high drama and great national events, to a final climactic decade packed with argument, discourse, scandal and constitutional upheavals. The selection is subject to my own judgement, ignorance and prejudices as to what is worthy of inclusion. Generally I have sought to convey the flavour of debate, using the telling phrases of the time, and not excluding quotations from figures outside Ireland who influenced our fate in different ways. I have largely avoided the common abuse of political debate; most of it is not worth recording. I have, as you will perceive, a weakness for the accidental double entendre.

Where possible, the quotations have been obtained from primary sources such as newspapers, in particular *The Irish Times*, Ireland's paper of record, and from parliamentary records, contemporary history books and original writings. Most quotations have been uttered or written in the public domain, a few have been taken from private papers which have become public with the passing of time. Each quotation is placed in context and the source identified. In my research, I have developed a strong appreciation of the writers of history who give the precise dates of quotations they use, and an antipathy to those who carelessly repeat common misquotations. I have attempted to record every quotation in its original form.

Ireland in Quotes will, I hope, be consulted for reference or pleasure, or read from beginning to end as a transcript of a remarkable century, with plot, dialogue and a multitude of colourful characters.

I would like to thank all those who helped me in my research, especially Jill Russell, Deaglán de Breadún, Joan O'Clery, Judy Loy, Joe Hayes, Deirdre Hayes, Andrew Stephen, Richard Ryan, Mairead Carr, Ken Gray, Don Lavery, Patrick Comerford, Niall O'Dowd, Jim Cantwell, Gerry Donnelly, the staff of the *Irish Times* library, especially Esther Murnane, and of the National Library of Ireland, and the staff of The O'Brien Press, in particular Íde ní Laoghaire, Rachel Pierce and Ivan O'Brien. Without the long hours and editing skills of my wife, Zhanna O'Clery, in helping prepare the text, this book might never have met its pre-millennium deadline.

ACKNOWLEDGEMENTS

The publishers have made every reasonable effort to contact the copyright holders of the material reproduced in this book. If any involuntary infringement of copyright has occurred, the owners of such copyright should contact the publishers immediately. For permission to reproduce the following copyright material, the publishers acknowledge the following:

Extracts from the work of W.B. Yeats courtesy of A.P. Watts Ltd, on behalf of Michael B. Yeats. Extract from the work of Paul Durcan courtesy of the poet. Extracts from the work of Patrick Kavanagh by kind permission of the Trustees of the Estate of Patrick Kavanagh, c/o Peter Fallon, Literary Agent, Loughcrew, Oldcastle, Co Meath, Ireland. Extracts from the work of James Joyce reproduced by permission of the Estate of James Joyce © Estate of James Joyce. Extracts from the work of Seamus Heaney reproduced by permission of Faber and Faber, London, and Farrar, Straus and Giroux, Llc. Extracts from the work of John Montague by kind permission of the author and The Gallery Press. Extracts from the work of Louis MacNeice reproduced with permission. Extracts from the work of Brendan Behan reproduced with permission. Extracts from the work of Seán Ó Faoláin reproduced with permission.

COVER IMAGES

Photos of Bernadette Devlin, Gerry Adams, Ian Paisley and David Trimble by permission of *The Irish Times*. Photos of Winston Churchill (Poole IMP 1630) and W.B. Yeats (R22, 092) courtesy of The National Library of Ireland. Photos of Bertie Ahern and Bill Clinton by permission of Pacemaker, Belfast. Photo of Margaret Thatcher by permission of Derek Spiers. All other photos taken from The O'Brien Press archives.

HISTORICAL SUMMARY

The twentieth century began with Ireland under Direct Rule from London and attitudes towards the Union the major political issue on the island. All of Ireland was then an integral part of the United Kingdom and had been since the Act of Union in 1800 which abolished the independent Irish Parliament. This assembly had been controlled by the mainly Protestant Anglo-Irish landowners who had settled in Ireland in the sixteenth and seventeenth centuries, seizing most of the good land and depriving the native Catholic Irish of their civil and property rights. The Catholics had welcomed the Act of Union, but their lot had not substantially improved, and they now sought a new 'Home Rule' parliament which the reform of the franchise would allow Irish nationalists to dominate. Irish politics therefore, as the new century dawned, had three major groupings: (1) The Catholic Irish who wanted Home Rule, and who held the large majority of the 105 Irish seats and occasionally the balance of power at Westminster; (2) Separatist nationalists, many of whom belonged to the secret Irish Republican Brotherhood, prepared to use violence but attracting little support as faith in constitutional nationalism was still strong; and (3) Protestant Unionists living mainly in the north and forming a quarter of the population, and who regularly returned about 20 MPs to Westminster. But by 1900 constitutional nationalism was facing a crisis. The first Home Rule Bill fourteen years earlier had been defeated in the House of Commons, and a second had been blocked by the House of Lords. The Irish Party at Westminster was in disarray following a bitter split over their leader, Charles Stewart Parnell, who had brilliantly fought for Home Rule but was disgraced because of his affair with Kitty O'Shea and had died a broken man. The action of the Roman Catholic Bishops in helping bring Parnell down was a forerunner of a century-long struggle by the Catholic Church to shape Irish politics, which only waned in the 1990s as the Church itself was wracked by scandal. Conservative governments in London were, by the start of the twentienth century, trying to 'kill Home Rule with kindness' by passing laws to allow tenants to buy out their holdings. But in all spheres of life, Irish nationalism was entering a resurgent phase. A literary revival was in full swing. The Irish Literary (later the Abbey) Theatre had been established by W. B. Yeats and Lady Gregory in 1899. The Gaelic League had been set up in 1893 to revive the Irish language, and the Gaelic Athletic Association established in 1884 to promote Gaelic games. Socialist movements had also begun to mobilise under the leadership of such figures as James Connolly and James Larkin. In the northern counties, unionist opposition to Home Rule, hardening at the prospect of 'Rome Rule' through an all-Ireland Catholic parliament, had united behind Randolph Churchill's 1886 slogan, 'Ulster will fight and Ulster will be right'. The scene was set for a showdown over the introduction of a third Home Rule Bill which would lead to a century-long struggle to shape modern Ireland, which continued right to the final days of 1999.

1900-1910

1901   (February) John Redmond elected leader of Irish Party.

1903   (July) King Edward VIII visited Dublin.
(June) Independent Orange Order founded in Belfast.

1904   (January) Pogrom against Jews in Limerick.
(August) Landlords formed Irish Reform Association.

1905   Arthur Griffith founded Sinn Féin.
(March) Ulster Unionist Council formed to oppose Home Rule.

1907   (January) Disturbances in Abbey Theatre over Synge play.
Dock strike in Belfast united Catholics and Protestants.

1909   James Larkin founded Irish Transport and General Workers' Union (ITGWU).
British Liberal Party adopted Home Rule policy.

1910-1920

1911   British Liberal Government introduced Home Rule Bill.

1912   (June) Irish Labour Party founded.
(September) 218,000 unionists signed Covenant to oppose Home Rule.

1913   (January) UVF founded to resist Home Rule.
(August) Dublin Lock-Out began.
(November) James Connolly founded Citizens' Army.
(November) Irish Volunteers founded.

1914   (March) Curragh mutiny of British officers who refused to move against UVF.
(April) UVF guns brought into Larne, County Antrim.
(July) Irish Volunteers' guns brought into Howth, County Dublin.
(August) First World War began.
(August) 36th Ulster Division formed from UVF volunteers to fight in France.
(September) Third Home Rule Bill passed but suspended until end of war.
(September) National Volunteers split from Irish Volunteers and refused to join British Army.

1916   (April) Easter Rising in Dublin.
(May) Leaders of Rising executed by British.
(August) Battle of Somme began, decimating Ulster Division.

(August) Sir Roger Casement hanged for role in Rising.

1917   (June) British staged convention on Ireland's future.

1918   (April) Anti-conscription campaign launched in Dublin.
(August) National Volunteers became Irish Republican Army (IRA).
(November) First World War ended.
(December) Sinn Féin won majority of Irish seats in election and withdrew from Westminster.

1919   (January) War of Independence began.
(January) First meeting of Dáil Éireann in Dublin formed by Sinn Féin MPs.

The 1920s

1920   (January) Black and Tans deployed in Ireland.
(March) Mayor of Cork, Tomás MacCurtain, killed by Crown forces.
(November) Fourteen British agents shot dead in Dublin.
(November) Black and Tans killed 12 people in Croke Park on Bloody Sunday.
(December) Black and Tans burned centre of Cork.
(December) NI Parliament set up under Government of Ireland Act.

1921   (May) Customs House destroyed by fire in Dublin.
(June) King George V opened NI Parliament.
(June) James Craig became first NI prime minister.
(July) Truce agreed by IRA and British Government pending peace treaty.
(July) Pogrom against Catholics in Belfast.
(August) Second Dáil met after election. Eamon de Valera elected President.
(October) Cork mayor, Terence MacSwiney, died on hunger strike.
(December) Anglo-Irish Treaty signed, setting up Free State and NI Boundary Commission.

1922   (January) Dáil approved Treaty. Michael Collins became Provisional Government chairman.
(June) Civil War broke out between pro- and anti-Treaty forces.
(August) Michael Collins killed in ambush in Béal na mBláth, County Cork.
(November) Free State Government began execution of 77 prisoners.
(November) Republican leader, Erskine Childers, executed.
(December) W. T. Cosgrave elected leader of Free State Government.

1923   (March) Pro-Treaty Sinn Féin became Cumann na nGaedheal.
(May) Civil War ended with call by IRA to dump arms.

1924   (March) Attempted mutiny in Free State Army.

1925   (December) Boundary Commission dissolved without changing NI borders.

1926   (May) Fianna Fáil founded by Eamon de Valera.

1927   (July) Justice Minister Kevin O'Higgins assassinated.
(August) Eamon de Valera led Fianna Fáil into Dáil.

1929   (July) Censorship Board established.

The 1930s

1931 (September) *Irish Press* newspaper founded by Eamon de Valera.

1932 (February) Eamon de Valera elected leader of Fianna Fáil Government.
(February) 'Blueshirts', later National Guard, founded.
(May) NI nationalist MPs began abstentionist policy at Stormont.
(June) Economic war with Britain began with non-payment of land annuities to London.
(October) Protestants and Catholics rioted together in Belfast over living conditions.

1933 (July) General Eoin O'Duffy became leader of 'Blueshirts'.
(July) Unionist leaders urged employers not to hire Catholics.
(September) Fine Gael formed from Cumann na nGaedheal, 'Blueshirts' and Centre Party.

1936 (June) IRA declared illegal organisation.
(November) Irish Brigade joined Franco forces in Spanish Civil War.
(December) References to Crown removed from Irish Constitution.

1937 (July) Revised Constitution, including claim to NI, established by referendum.
(December) Eamon de Valera elected leader of Fianna Fáil Government.

1938 (April) Economic war ended and Britain agreed to return Treaty Ports.

1939 (January) IRA announced bombing campaign in England.
(August) IRA bomb killed 5 people in Coventry.
(September) Eamon de Valera announced Irish neutrality in war.

The 1940s

1940 (June) Britain offered united Ireland in principle for participation in war.
(April) Two IRA prisoners died on hunger strike.
(November) J. M. Andrews became NI Prime Minister on death of James Craig.

1941 (April) Blitz began in Belfast, killing over 1,000 people.
(May) German bombs fell on Dublin, killing 34 people.
(June) James Dillon resigned deputy leadership of Fine Gael in protest at neutrality.
(December) Britain again offered united Ireland for participation in war.

1942 American troops arrived in Northern Ireland.

1943 (April) Basil Brooke succeeded Andrews as NI Prime Minister.

1944 (February) US and Britain demanded Ireland close German and Japanese legations.

1945 (May) Eamon de Valera paid condolences at German embassy on death of Hitler.
(May) Eamon de Valera and Churchill in radio recriminations over Irish neutrality.
(June) Seán T. Ó Ceallaigh elected President of Ireland.

1948 (March) John A. Costello (FG) elected Taoiseach of Inter-Party Government.

(July) Ireland decided to stay out of NATO.

(September) Inter-Party Government decided to declare Republic.

1949 (April) Free State became Republic of Ireland.

(May) Ireland Act at Westminster confirmed NI would remain part of UK.

The 1950s

1951 (April) Catholic hierarchy opposed free health scheme. Minister for Health, Dr Noel Browne, resigned.

(June) Eamon de Valera elected Taoiseach of Fianna Fáil Government.

1954 (May) John A. Costello (FG) re-elected Taoiseach of Inter-Party Government.

(October) IRA introduced rule forbidding any action in Republic.

1955 (December) Republic of Ireland admitted to UN.

1956 (December) IRA border campaign launched.

1957 (March) Eamon de Valera re-elected Taoiseach of Fianna Fáil Government.

(July) Boycott of Protestant businesses in Fethard-on-Sea, County Wexford.

(July) Internment introduced in Republic after IRA killed RUC man in County Armagh.

1959 (June) Eamon de Valera elected President.

(June) Sean Lemass elected Taoiseach of Fianna Fáil Government.

The 1960s

1961 (October) Fianna Fáil retained power in election.

(December) *RTÉ* television launched.

1963 (April) Terence O'Neill became NI Prime Minister.

(June) President John F. Kennedy visited Ireland.

1964 (September) Riots in Belfast over display of tricolour.

1965 (January) Taoiseach Sean Lemass and NI Prime Minister Terence O'Neill met at Stormont.

(February) Derry lost battle for New University of Ulster.

(April) Fianna Fáil retained power in election.

1966 (March) Nelson's Pillar in Dublin blown up by saboteur.

(June) UVF shot Catholic barman in Belfast.

(June) Eamon de Valera re-elected President.

(November) Jack Lynch elected Taoiseach of Fianna Fáil Government.

1967 (January) NI Civil Rights Association formed.

(December) Taoiseach Jack Lynch and Terence O'Neill met at Stormont.

1968 (October) NI Civil Rights march in Derry.

1969 (January) People's Democracy march attacked at Burntollet by loyalists.

(April) James Chichester-Clark became NI Prime Minister on resignation of Terence O'Neill.

(June) Jack Lynch elected Taoiseach of Fianna Fáil Government.

(August) Battle of Bogside. British Army deployed in Derry and Belfast.

(October) B Specials ordered to disband.

(December) Ulster Defence Regiment established.

(December) IRA split, leading to formation of Provisional IRA.

The 1970s

1970 (May) Taoiseach Jack Lynch sacked Charles Haughey and Neil Blaney in arms crisis.

(April) NI Alliance Party founded.

(July) SDLP founded.

(July) Curfew imposed on Falls Road, Belfast.

(October) Charles Haughey and Neil Blaney acquitted on arms charges.

1971 (March) Brian Faulkner became NI Prime Minister on resignation of James Chichester-Clark.

(July) SDLP withdrew from Stormont after British army killings in Derry.

(August) Internment introduced in Northern Ireland.

(September) DUP founded by Rev Ian Paisley.

(September) UDA founded in Belfast.

1972 (January) British soldiers killed 13 civilians in Derry's 'Bloody Sunday'.

(February) British Embassy in Dublin burned down.

(March) NI Parliament abolished; Direct Rule imposed.

(May) Official IRA ceasefire.

(May) Republic's entry into EEC approved by referendum.

(July) Provisional IRA members met British Government ministers in London.

(July) IRA bombs killed 11 people in Belfast's 'Bloody Friday'.

(July) British army 'Operation Motorman' removed NI 'no-go' areas.

(November) Taoiseach Jack Lynch sacked *RTÉ* authority over Sinn Féin interview.

(December) Bombs in Dublin panicked Dáil into passing emergency legislation.

(December) Special role of Catholic Church removed from Constitution.

(February) Liam Cosgrave (FG) elected Taoiseach of FG-Labour Government.

1973 (May) Erskine Childers elected President of Ireland.

(June) Elections to NI power-sharing Assembly.

(December) Sunningdale Agreement on power-sharing and Council of Ireland.

1974 (May) Loyalist car bombs in Dublin killed 22 people.

(May) Loyalist strike brought down NI power-sharing executive.

(December) Cearbhall Ó Dálaigh installed as President after death of Erskine Childers.

(December) IRA bombs killed 21 people in Birmingham.

(December) Britain introduced Prevention of Terrorism Act with deportation powers.

1975   (February) IRA truce.
(May) Elections to NI Convention.
(September) IRA truce ended.

1976   (March) NI Convention recommended return to majority rule.
(July) British ambassador killed in Dublin.
(August) Peace People formed in Belfast.
(November) Nobel Peace Prize awarded to Peace People.
(December) Patrick Hillery became President of Ireland on resignation of
Cearbhall Ó Dálaigh.

1977   (March) Special category status removed from NI paramilitary prisoners.
(July) Jack Lynch elected Taoiseach of Fianna Fáil Government.

1979   (March) British Labour Government fell on vote of Gerry Fitt.
(March) Conservative MP, Airey Neave, killed by INLA bomb at Westminster.
(August) Lord Mountbatten killed in Sligo, 18 British soldiers killed at Warrenpoint.
(September) Pope visited Republic and pleaded with IRA to end campaign.
(December) Charles Haughey elected Taoiseach of Fianna Fáil Government.

The 1980s

1981   (May) Hunger striker Bobby Sands died in Maze prison.
(June) Garret FitzGerald (FG) elected Taoiseach of FG-Labour Coalition
Government.
(November) Unionist MP, Robert Bradford, killed by IRA.

1982   (March) Charles Haughey elected Taoiseach of Fianna Fáil Government.
(December) Garret FitzGerald elected Taoiseach of FG-Labour Coalition
Government.
(December) 17 people killed by INLA bomb at pub in Derry.

1983   (May) New Ireland Forum of nationalist parties met.
(September) Anti-abortion amendment to Constitution approved in referendum.

1984   (May) New Ireland Forum recommended options for future Ireland.
(June) US President Ronald Reagan visited Ireland.
(October) IRA bombed Conservative Party hotel in Brighton.
(November) British Prime Minister, Margaret Thatcher, rejected Forum options.

1985   (November) Anglo-Irish Agreement signed at Hillsborough.
(December) Progressive Democrats founded after Fianna Fáil split.

1986   (June) Divorce rejected in referendum in Republic.

1987   (March) Charles Haughey elected Taoiseach of Fianna Fáil Government.
(November) IRA bomb killed 11 people at Enniskillen Remembrance Day service.

1988   (March) Three IRA members killed by SAS in Gibraltar.
(October) British Government banned broadcasting of voices of Sinn Féin or IRA
members.

1989   (June) Charles Haughey became Taoiseach of FF-PD Coalition Government.

(October) Guildford Four released after convictions quashed.

The 1990s

1990   (November) Fianna Fáil presidential candidate Brian Lenihan sacked as Minister.

(November) Mary Robinson elected President.

1991   (March) Birmingham Six released after convictions quashed.

1992   (February) Albert Reynolds elected Taoiseach of FF-PD Coalition Government.

(February) Supreme Court overturned injunction preventing 14-year-old girl travelling to England for abortion.

(May) Bishop Eamonn Casey resigned over disclosure he had a son.

(November) Charles Haughey became Taoiseach of FF-Labour Coalition Government.

(November) Abortion referendum gave right to travel and information.

1993   (January) Albert Reynolds became Taoiseach of FF-Labour Coalition Government.

(March) IRA bomb in Warrington killed two children.

(June) President Mary Robinson shook hands with Gerry Adams in Belfast.

(October) IRA bomb killed 10 people on Shankill Road, Belfast.

(October) Loyalist gunmen killed seven at Greysteel, County Derry.

(December) British and Irish governments signed joint declaration on NI's future.

1994   (January) Gerry Adams given visa to visit US.

(January) Irish Government lifted broadcasting ban on Sinn Féin.

(June) UVF killed 6 Catholics in pub in Loughinisland, County Down.

(August) IRA ceasefire began.

(October) Loyalist ceasefire began.

(December) John Bruton elected Taoiseach of FG-Labour Coalition Government.

1995   (May) President Clinton hosted NI investment conference in Washington.

(May) *Irish Press* shut down.

(November) Referendum in Republic legalised divorce.

(November) President Clinton visited NI and Republic.

1996   (February) IRA ceasefire ended with bomb in London.

(June) All-party talks began under chairmanship of former US Senator George Mitchell.

(July) Widespread violence across NI as Orange parade forced through Garvaghy Road, Portadown.

1997   (May) Labour won British general election. Mo Mowlam appointed NI Secretary of State.

(May) Gerry Adams and Martin McGuinness of Sinn Féin won seats in Westminster election.

(June) Bertie Ahern elected Taoiseach of FF-PD Coalition Government.

(July) Police again forced Orange parade through Garvaghy Road, Portadown.

(July) Charles Haughey admitted he received £1.3 million from Ben Dunne.

(July) IRA ceasefire resumed.

(October) Minister for Foreign Affairs, Ray Burke, resigned over political donations.

(November) Mary McAleese elected President.

1998 (April) Good Friday Agreement signed in Belfast.

(May) Good Friday Agreement approved in referenda in NI and Republic.

(July) Widespread violence in north as police blocked Orange parade on Garvaghy Road, Portadown.

(August) 'Real IRA' bomb killed 28 people in Omagh.

(September) President Clinton visited NI and Republic.

(October) Nobel Peace Prize awarded to John Hume and David Trimble.

(November) British Prime Minister Tony Blair addressed Oireachtas.

(December) Labour and Democratic Left merged.

1999 (January) Flood Tribunal began hearings on payments to politicians.

(March) NI solicitor, Rosemary Nelson, killed by car bomb.

(May) Gay Byrne retired as host of The Late Late Show.

(May) Terry Keane revealed 27-year affair with Charles Haughey.

(June) Negotiations to implement Good Friday Agreement failed over decommissioning.

(July) Seamus Mallon resigned as NI deputy chief executive.

THE QUOTATIONS

1900

John Ingram

I have no sympathy with those who preach sedition in our own day, when all the circumstances are radically altered. In my opinion no real popular interest can now be furthered by violence.

As author of the popular 1843 ballad 'Who Fears to Speak of '98', which praised the rising of 1798. Robinson, Lennox, *Lady Gregory's Journal*, Putnam, 1946, p. 243.

1900

Hanna Sheehy Skeffington

[I] was amazed and disgusted to learn that I was classed among criminals, infants and lunatics – in fact, that my status as a woman was worse than any of these.

As new member of women's suffrage movement. Cullen Owens, Rosemary, *Smashing Times*, Attic, 1984, p. 39.

February 9, 1900

Irish Party

In the name of Ireland, we declare at an end the divisions which hitherto separated the Irish nationalist representatives, and we hereby form ourselves into one united party.

As Irish MPs in House of Commons, bringing about end of Parnellite split in Irish Parliamentary Party and election of John Redmond as leader. Gwynn, Dennis, *The Lady of John Redmond*, Harrap, 1932, p. 94.

July 7, 1900

James Connolly

Ireland without her people is nothing to me, and the man who is bubbling over with love and enthusiasm for 'Ireland' and yet can pass unmoved through our streets and witness all the wrong and suffering, the shame and degradation wrought upon the people of Ireland, aye, wrought by Irishmen upon Irish men and women, without burning to end it, is in my opinion a fraud and a liar in his heart.

As labour organiser, writing against romantic nationalism, in *Workers' Republic*. Carty, James, *Ireland 1851-1921*, Fallon, 1951, p. 168.

1901

Pioneer Total Abstinence Association

Ireland sober, Ireland free.

Slogan used to discourage abuse of alcohol by nationalists. Bardon, Jonathan, *A History of Ulster*, Blackstaff Press, 1992, p. 423.

1901

George Russell ('AE')

If the stupefying influence of foreign control is removed, if we had charge of our own national

affairs, it would mean the starting up into sudden life of a thousand dormant energies, spiritual, intellectual, artistic, social, economic and human.

As writer and commentator, in letter to Lady Gregory. Lee, J. J., *Ireland 1912-1985*, Cambridge University Press, 1990, p. 172.

January 7, 1901

Douglas Hyde

It is equally true, though, that the Gaelic League [aims] at stimulating the old peasant, Papist, aboriginal population.

As founder of Gaelic League, in letter to Lady Gregory. Hepburn, A. C., *The Conflict of Nationality in Modern Ireland*, Arnold, 1980, p. 65.

May 12, 1902

John Morley

Dublin Castle [is] the best machine that has ever been invented for governing a country against its will.

As Liberal Party MP, speaking in Manchester. Macardle, Dorothy, *The Irish Republic*, Irish Press, 1951, p. 53.

September 3, 1902

Captain John Shawe-Taylor

The land war in this country has raged fiercely and continuously...producing hatred and bitterness...an honest, simple and practical suggestion will be submitted.

As Galway landowner, inviting politicians and landlords to conference from which emerged 1904 Act allowing peasants to buy land and repay by annuities. Gwynn, Denis, *The Life of John Redmond*, Harrap, 1932, p. 99.

October 26, 1902

Arthur Griffith

We call upon our countrymen abroad to withdraw all assistance from the promoters of a useless, degrading and demoralising policy [Home Rule] until such time as the members of the Irish Parliamentary Party substitute for it the policy of the Hungarian deputies of 1861, and, refusing to attend the British parliament or recognise its right to legislate for Ireland, remain at home to help in promoting Ireland's interests.

As member of Cumann na nGaedheal, forerunner of Sinn Féin. Lyons, F. S. L., *Ireland Since the Famine*, Fontana, 1985, p. 251.

1903

George Bernard Shaw

An Englishman thinks he is moral when he is only uncomfortable.

As playwright, in words spoken by character in 'Man and Superman', Act III.

July 21, 1903
George Wyndham

For three miles to Trinity one roar of cheers and frenzy of handkerchiefs...they lift their hands to Heaven to imprecate 'God bless the King' as if adjuring the Deity to fulfil their most ardent desire...the people became nearly delirious. They worked themselves into an ecstasy.

As Chief Secretary for Ireland, on reception given to King Edward on visit to Dublin. Robinson, Lennox, *Lady Gregory's Journal*, Putnam, 1946, p. 239.

October 17, 1903
Arthur Griffith

All of us know that Irish women are the most virtuous in the world...no country is so faithful to the marriage bond.

As member of Cumann na nGaedheal, forerunner of Sinn Féin. *United Irishman*, October 17, 1903.

1904
George Bernard Shaw

The people of England have done the people of Ireland no wrong whatever...the most distressful country...has borne no more than her fair share of the growing pains of human society.

As playwright, in words spoken by character in play, 'John Bull's Other Island'. Kiberd, Declan, *Inventing Ireland*, Jonathan Cape, 1995, p. 54.

January 1904
Rev Creagh

Have no dealings of any kind with them [Jews].

As Redemptorist priest, in Limerick sermon which resulted in attacks on Jewish-owned businesses. *The Irish Times*, April 13, 1904.

January 18, 1904
Michael Davitt

The Jews have never done any injury to Ireland. Like our own race, they have endured a persecution, the records of which will forever remain a reproach to the 'Christian' nations of Europe. Ireland has no share in this black record.

As founder of United Irish League, writing in *Freeman's Journal* about anti-Semitism in Limerick. Hyman, Louis, *The Jews in Ireland*, Keter, 1972, p. 213.

April 10, 1904
Marcus Joseph Blond

All of a sudden, like a thunderstorm [they] spoke hatred and animosity against the Jews, how they crucified Lord Jesus, how they martyred St Simon, and gradually in one month's time I have none of my previous customers.

As Limerick shopkeeper, originally from Lithuania, and victim of anti-Jewish boycott which drove 80 of 140 Jews out of city, in letter to *Times*. Hyman, Louis, *The Jews in Ireland*, Keter, 1972, p. 217.

May 7, 1904
Standish O'Grady

If there were no Jews in Ireland, our own Irish Christian usurers...would be at just the same bad work, only without competitors.

As editor of *All-Ireland Review*. Hyman, Louis, *The Jews in Ireland*, Keter, 1972, p. 213.

August 25, 1904
Irish Reform Association

We believe that [the] Union is compatible with the devolution to Ireland of a larger measure of self-government than she now possesses.

Manifesto from body which included leading Irish landlords. Gwynn, Denis, *The Life of John Redmond*, Harrap, 1932, p. 105.

August 25, 1904
John Dillon

[It is an attempt] to kill Home Rule with kindness.

As Irish Party MP, on manifesto from Irish Reform Association suggesting limited devolution. Gwynn, Denis, *The Life of John Redmond*, Harrap, 1932, p. 106.

September 1904
John Redmond

The announcement is of the utmost importance. It is simply a declaration for Home Rule and is quite a wonderful thing.

As leader of Irish Party, reacting, from America, to manifesto from Irish Reform Association. Gwynn, Denis, *The Life of John Redmond*, Harrap, 1932, p. 106.

March 3, 1905
George Wyndham

I must insist on resigning...because my policy – which is not the policy of the Reform Association – cannot proceed now.

As Chief Secretary for Ireland, resigning under pressure from Ulster Unionist MPs who believed he was behind manifesto from Irish Reform Association suggesting limited devolution. Gwynn, Denis, *The Life of John Redmond*, Harrap, 1932, p. 109.

April 27, 1905
Pope Pius X

To my beloved son, John Redmond...with a wish that he...using all legal and peaceful means, may win that liberty which makes for the welfare of the whole country.

Inscription on photograph presented to Redmond in Rome which ended strained relations between Vatican and Irish Party over papal rescript of 1888. Gwynn, Denis, *The Life of John Redmond*, Harrap, 1932, p. 113.

July 13, 1905
Lindsay Crawford
The anniversary of the Battle of the Boyne seems to us a fitting opportunity to address our countrymen – both Protestant and Catholic...not as victors in the fight, not to applaud the noble deeds of our ancestors, but to bridge the gulf that has so long divided Ireland into hostile camps, and to hold out the right hand of fellowship to those who, while worshipping at other shrines, are yet our countrymen, bone of our bone, flesh of our flesh.

As Grand Master of Independent Orange Order, in 'Magheramourne Manifesto'. Gray, John, *City in Revolt*, Blackstaff Press, 1985, p. 48.

September 11, 1905
William Walker
Protestantism means protesting against superstition and hence true Protestantism is synonymous with Labour.

As Labour candidate, replying in *Northern Whig* to Belfast Protestant Association asking if he put Protestantism before Labour Party. Gray, John, *City in Revolt*, Blackstaff Press, 1985, p. 37.

September 11, 1905
Ramsay MacDonald
I was never more sick of an election than that at North Belfast, and the religious replies at the back of it knocked everything out of me.

As British Labour Party leader, acting as election agent for Labour candidate William Walker who was publicly questioned about his Protestanism by Belfast Protestant Association. Gray, John, *City in Revolt*, Blackstaff Press, 1985, p. 37.

September 23, 1906
John Redmond
The Irish Party and I have no responsibility whatever, direct or indirect, for the proposal of any such makeshift [arrangement]...nothing short of a complete scheme of Home Rule can ever be accepted as a settlement of the Irish question.

As leader of Irish Party, speaking at Limerick on new government proposal for form of administrative Home Rule. Gwynn, Denis, *The Life of John Redmond*, Harrap, 1932, p. 133.

January 28, 1907
John Millington Synge
...it's Pegeen I'm seeking only, and what'd I care if you brought me a drift of chosen females, standing in their shifts itself...

As playwright, in words spoken by character in 'The Playboy of the Western World', which caused riots at Abbey Theatre, Dublin, over use of word 'shift' to indicate female attire. Kiberd, Declan, *Inventing Ireland*, Jonathan Cape, 1995, p. 183.

January 28, 1907
Lady Gregory
Audience broke up in disorder at word 'Shift'.

As founder of National Theatre Company, in telegram to William Butler Yeats in Scotland, after disturbances at Abbey Theatre, Dublin, during Synge's 'The Playboy of the Western World', over use of word 'shift' to indicate female attire. Hogan & Kilroy, *The Abbey Theatre: The Years of Synge*, Dolmen, 1978, p. 126.

January 29, 1907
William Butler Yeats
If it is a play that is bad it will die without your help. If the play is good your hindrance cannot mar it. What you can mar very greatly is the reputation of the country for fair play.

As poet and playwright, appealing for calm from Abbey Theatre stage before second-night performance of Synge's 'The Playboy of the Western World', Hogan & Kilroy, *The Abbey Theatre: The Years of Synge*, Dolmen, 1978, p. 128.

May 18, 1907
James Larkin
Although St Patrick was credited with banishing the snakes, there was one he forgot and that was Gallagher – a man who valued neither country, God nor creed.

As trade union organiser, quoted in *Northern Whig*, about Thomas Gallagher of Gallagher's Tobacco, during industrial dispute in Belfast organised by Larkin. Gray, John, *City in Revolt*, Blackstaff Press, 1985, p. 63.

June 26, 1907
Alex Boyd
It is now war to the knife.

As trade union leader, to striking dockers in Belfast. Bardon, Jonathan, *A History of Ulster*, Blackstaff Press, 1992, p. 427.

July 12, 1907
Lindsay Crawford
Stand firm, out of this movement will spring not only the strength of organised labour but also...the unity of all Irishmen.

As Grand Master of Independent Orange Order, to strikers in Belfast. Bardon, Jonathan, *A History of Ulster*, Blackstaff Press, 1992, p. 428.

July 17, 1907
Alex Boyd
He was proud of the fact that he could come to Clonard Gardens and address a meeting in his official capacity as the representative of Sandy Row...his friend Lindsay Crawford [Grand Master of Independent Orange Order] and a few others had set about to unite the people of Ireland in one strong bond of friendship.

As Protestant leader of Municipal Employees' Association, in newspaper report of his speech, at strike meeting in

Catholic area of Belfast. Gray, John, *City in Revolt*, Blackstaff Press, 1985, p. 92.

July 27, 1907
James Sexton

We do not recognise any distinction in the labour movement between the man who works with a baton and the man who works with a spade.

As dockers' leader at meeting in Belfast in support of striking RIC (Royal Irish Constabulary) men. Gray, John, *City in Revolt*, Blackstaff Press, 1985, p. 126.

August 3, 1907
Constable William Barrett

Down with blacklegs and cheap labour, say I, whether in civilian or constabulary life...we should have struck out for more pay at the time of the Boer War when there was no military force available in this country.

As striking policeman, addressing workers, including other RIC men, at meeting at Belfast's Customs House called to support police strike for more pay. Gray, John, *City in Revolt*, Blackstaff Press, 1985, p. 132.

August 4, 1907
Assistant Inspector General Alexander Gambell

...for the good of the city and for the purposes of showing the turbulent classes how easily we can cover the city with military pickets, it would be very advisable.

As senior RIC officer, on proposed use of troops to restore order in Belfast during dock strike. Gray, John, *City in Revolt*, Blackstaff Press, 1985, p. 144.

August 12, 1907
James Larkin

It was a scandalous thing that they should disgrace a broken bottle by using it on an officer of the British Army.

As strike leader, after troops brought into Belfast to break dock strike. Gray, John, *City in Revolt*, Blackstaff Press, 1985, p. 149.

August 12, 1907
James Larkin

Not as Catholics or Protestants, as nationalists or unionists, but as Belfastmen and workers, stand together and don't be misled by the employers' game of dividing Catholic and Protestant.

As strike leader, in handbill co-signed by other leaders, after rioting during Lock-Out and strike in Belfast. Berresford Ellis, Peter, *A History of the Irish Working Class*, Pluto, 1985, p. 180.

August 18, 1907
Rev P. Convery

It was a scandal and a shame that the police should have been attacked in such an outrageous way... They were the best Catholics in the city; they were steady, respectable, and sober men... When [I] was in financial difficulties in regard to the completion of the church, the men in Cullingtree Road and Roden Street barracks had responded nobly.

As priest at St Paul's Church, Belfast, after riots in Falls Road area when police helped to break dock strike. Gray, John, *City in Revolt*, Blackstaff Press, 1985, pp. 165-166.

1908
William Butler Yeats

It is of such as these Goethe thought when he said 'The Irish seem to me always like a pack of hounds dragging down some noble stag'.

As director of Abbey Theatre, on critics of J. M. Synge (in famous misquotation of 19th century poet, Goethe who said 'the Catholics...are always prepared to make common cause against a Protestant. They are like a pack of hounds, snapping at one another, but the moment they catch sight of a stag, they herd together and attack.') Tuohy, Frank, *Yeats*, Macmillan, 1976, p. 141.

January 4, 1909
Sean O'Casey

In a room in a tenement in Townsend Street, with a candle in a bottle for a torch, and a billycan of tea, with a few buns for a banquet, the Church militant here on earth, called the Irish Transport and General Workers' Union, was founded.

As playwright and social activist, on occasion of formation by James Larkin of ITGWU in Dublin. Curriculum Development Unit, *Dublin 1913*, O'Brien, 1984, p. 62.

July 1, 1909
Countess Markievicz

...the first step on the road to freedom is to realise ourselves as Irishwomen – not as Irish or merely as women, but as Irishwomen doubly enslaved and with a double battle to fight.

As President of Cumann na mBan (b. Constance Gore-Booth), writing in *Bean na hÉireann* on suffrage issue. Cullen Owens, Rosemary, *Smashing Times*, Attic, 1984, p. 104.

c. August 1, 1909
Countess Markievicz

A good nationalist should look upon slugs in a garden much in the same way as she looks upon the English in Ireland, and only regret that she cannot crush the Nation's enemies as she can the garden's, with one tread of her dainty foot.

As president of Cumann na mBan, in celebrated gardening feature in *Bean na hÉireann*. Kiberd, Declan, *Inventing Ireland*, Jonathan Cape, 1995, p. 399.

November 27, 1909
John Redmond
The political conditions in Ireland are such that, unless an official declaration on the question of Home Rule be made, not only will it be impossible for us to support Liberal candidates in England, but we will most unquestionably have to ask our friends to vote against them.

As leader of Irish Party, in letter to Lord Morley of Liberal Party. Gwynn, Denis, *The Life of John Redmond*, Harrap, 1932, pp. 166-167.

December 10, 1909
Herbert Asquith
The solution of the [Irish] problem can be found only in one way, by a policy which, while explicitly safeguarding the supremacy and indefectible authority of the Imperial Parliament, will set up in Ireland a system of full self-government in regard to purely Irish affairs.

As British Prime Minister, in Albert Hall, London, committing Liberal Party again to Home Rule. Gwynn, Denis, *The Life of John Redmond*, Harrap, 1932, p. 169.

January 1910
Arthur Griffith
The 103 Irishmen are faced with 567 foreigners [in the House of Commons]... Ten years hence, the majority of Irishmen will marvel they once believed that the proper battleground for Ireland was one chosen and filled by Ireland's enemies.

As President of Sinn Féin, writing in *United Irishman*. Mansergh, Nicholas, *The Irish Question*, Unwin University Books, 1968, p. 226.

July 1, 1910
James Connolly
Only the Irish working class remain as the incorruptible inheritors of the fight for freedom in Ireland.

As labour organiser, writing in *Labour in Irish History*, Dudley Edwards, Ruth, *James Connolly*, Gill & Macmillan, 1981, p. 78.

1911
Gilbert Keith Chesterton
For the great Gaels of Ireland
Are the men that God made mad,
For all their wars are merry,
And all their songs are sad.

As poet, in *The Ballad of the White Horse*, Book II.

January 9, 1911
James Craig
There is a spirit spreading abroad which I can testify to from my personal knowledge that Germany and the German Emperor would be preferred to the rule of John Redmond, Patrick

Ford, and the Molly Maguires [i.e. the Ancient Order of Hibernians].

As Ulster Unionist MP, speaking against Home Rule. Reported in *Morning Post*. Horgan, J. J., *The Complete Grammar of Anarchy*, Nisbet, 1919, p. 19.

July 1, 1911
Irish Party
Our people will receive the King on his coming visit to Ireland with the generosity and hospitality which are traditional with the Irish race; and when the day comes that the King will enter the Irish capital to reopen the ancient Parliament of Ireland we believe he will obtain from the Irish people a reception as enthusiastic as ever welcomed a British monarch in any of his dominions.

As Irish MPs in House of Commons, after coronation of King George V. Gwynn, Denis, *The Life of John Redmond*, Harrap, 1932, p. 189.

July 12, 1911
King George V
Without effort and without restraint, and in obedience to what seemed a natural impulse of goodwill, the entire populace, men, women and children, came out into the streets and parks to give us a true Irish welcome.

As British monarch, in letter to the Irish people after visit to Dublin. Curriculum Development Unit, *Dublin 1913*, O'Brien, 1984, p. 18.

September 23, 1911
Edward Carson
We must be prepared...the morning Home Rule passes, ourselves to become responsible for the government of the Protestant Province of Ulster.

As Ulster Unionist leader, addressing rally at Strandtown. Bardon, Jonathan, *A History of Ulster*, Blackstaff Press, 1992, p. 432.

September 25, 1911
Council of Unionist Clubs and Orange Lodges
It is resolved...to take immediate steps in consultation with Sir Edward Carson to frame and submit a constitution for a Provisional Government for Ulster...to come into operation on the day of the passage of any Home Rule bill.

At meeting in Belfast as British Prime Minister, Herbert Asquith, prepared to introduce third Home Rule bill. Horgan, J. J., *The Complete Grammar of Anarchy*, Nisbet, 1919, pp. 20-21.

September 30, 1911
Éamonn Ceannt
You appear to see Larkin at the bottom of all trouble. Sufficient for you is that Larkin is the agitator causing troubles between employer and employed. In similar manner the English Tory and

his Irish allies described Irish politicians as vile agitators who caused trouble between the good and kind landlords and their willing slaves, the tenant farmers of Ireland.

As Sinn Féin member (executed in 1916) attacking Arthur Griffith for his opposition to James Larkin. Berresford Ellis, Peter, *A History of the Irish Working Class*, Pluto, 1985, p. 191.

October 1911
Winston Churchill
We must not attach too much importance to these frothings of Sir Edward Carson. I daresay when the worst comes to the worst, we shall find that civil war evaporates in uncivil words.

As First Lord of the Admiralty, on warnings by Unionist leader of rejection of Home Rule. Bardon, Jonathan, *Belfast*, Blackstaff Press, 1983, p. 178.

October 7, 1911
Arthur Griffith
In Dublin the wives of some men that Larkin has led out on strike are begging in the streets. The consequences of Larkinism are workless fathers, mourning mothers, hungry children and broken homes.

As President of Sinn Féin, replying to Éamonn Ceannt's defence of Larkin on September 30, 1911. Berresford Ellis, Peter, *A History of the Irish Working Class*, Pluto, 1985, p. 191.

1912
Rev J. B. Armour
...the secret disciples of Home Rule are not only large but an increasing number... The belief that democracy in Ireland would become a persecutor of Protestants...can only arise in the minds of those who hate democracy and all its works.

As Presbyterian minister, arguing case for Home Rule from Presbyterian viewpoint. Armour, J. B., *The New Irish Constitution*, Hodder and Stoughton. *The Irish Times*, September 9, 1969.

1912
John Dillon
Women's suffrage will, I believe, be the ruin of our western civilisation. It will destroy the home, challenging the headship of man laid down by God. It may come in your time, I hope not in mine.

As Irish Party MP, in conversation with suffragettes, as recalled by Hanna Sheehy Skeffington. Cullen Owens, Rosemary, *Smashing Times*, Attic, 1984, p. 48.

1912
Rudyard Kipling
Before an Empire's eyes,
the traitor claims his price.

What need for further lies?
We are the sacrifice...

As poet, expressing unionist opposition to Home Rule. *Morning Post*, 1912.

January 8, 1912
Jennie Wyse Power
As an Irish nationalist I cannot see why there should be any antagonism between the Irish women's demand for citizenship and the demand for a native parliament. Our claim is that we shall not be debarred merely by sex from the rights of citizens.

As Vice President of Sinn Féin, on agitation for female suffrage. Cullen Owens, Rosemary, *Smashing Times*, Attic, 1984, p. 52.

January 15, 1912
Augustine Birrell
I don't see how I could remain in a Cabinet which has adopted *en bloc* female suffrage, married and single – and if I couldn't, how could [Prime Minister Herbert Asquith]? I believe the wire-pullers are satisfied that no such amendment can pass.

As Chief Secretary for Ireland to John Dillon of Irish Party, on move to allow vote for women. Cullen Owens, Rosemary, *Smashing Times*, Attic, 1984, p. 47.

January 22, 1912
Frederick Smith
There was no length to which Ulster would not be entitled to go, however desperate or unconditional, in carrying the quarrel, if the quarrel was wickedly fixed upon them.

As Conservative MP, in Liverpool speech against Home Rule. Gwynn, Denis, *The Life of John Redmond*, Harrap, 1932, p. 200.

January 22, 1912
Edward Carson
If they [Ulster Unionists] did anything else, they would have been false to the position in which they were placed. If that is inciting to riot, here I am.

As Ulster Unionist leader, in Liverpool speech, on action taken to prevent Winston Churchill using Ulster Hall to speak in favour of Home Rule. Gwynn, Denis, *The Life of John Redmond*, Harrap, 1932, p. 200.

February 8, 1912
Winston Churchill
What harm could Irish ideas and sentiment, and Irish dreams, if given free play in an Irish parliament, do to the strong structure of British power? Was it not worthwhile for the English statesmen to try to make their life-long partner happy and contented and free? Let [Protestant

Ulster] fight for the spread of charity, tolerance and enlightenment among men. Then indeed, gentlemen, Ulster will fight, and Ulster will be right.

As First Lord of the Admiralty, at Home Rule rally to mostly Catholic crowd in Belfast's Celtic Park, after Ulster Unionist Council had refused use of Ulster Hall. *The Irish Times*, February 9, 1912.

March 31, 1912
Padraic Pearse

The Bill which we support today will be for the good of Ireland... But if we are tricked this time... Let the Gall understand that if we are cheated once more there will be red war in Ireland.

As editor of Gaelic League newspaper, speaking at Dublin rally with John Redmond, leader of Irish Party, on third Home Rule Bill. Macardle, Dorothy, *The Irish Republic*, Irish Press, 1955, p. 82.

April 9, 1912
Andrew Bonar Law

Once again you hold the pass, the pass for the Empire. You are a besieged city. The timid have left you; your Lundys have betrayed you; but you have closed your gates. The Government by their Parliament Act have erected a boom against you, a boom to cut you off from the help of the British people. You will burst that boom.

As leader of Conservative Party, addressing mass anti-Home Rule demonstration at Balmoral, near Belfast. Buckland, Patrick, *Ulster Unionism*, Gill & Macmillan, 1983, p. 54.

April 11, 1912
Arthur Griffith

If this is liberty, the lexicographers have deceived us.

As President of Sinn Féin, on Home Rule Bill. Bardon, Jonathan, *A History of Ulster*, Blackstaff Press, 1992, p. 436.

April 11, 1912
Cardinal Michael Logue

...a skeleton on which to hang restrictions.

As Primate of Ireland, on Home Rule Bill. Bardon, Jonathan, *A History of Ulster*, Blackstaff Press, 1992, p. 436.

April 16, 1912
John Redmond

Ireland today is peaceful beyond record. She has almost entirely, I believe, cast aside her suspicions and her rancour toward this country; and England, on her side, is, I believe, today more willing than ever she was in her past history to admit Ireland on terms of equality,

liberty and loyalty into that great sisterhood of nations that makes up the British Empire.

As leader of Irish Party, in House of Commons, on first reading of third Home Rule Bill. Gwynn, Denis, *The Life of John Redmond*, Harrap, 1932, p. 203.

April 29, 1912
Major Fred Crawford

If they [unionists] were put out of the Union...he [Major Crawford] would infinitely prefer to change his allegiance right over to the Emperor of Germany.

As director of ordnance for Ulster Unionists, responsible for Ulster gun-running, speaking in Bangor. Horgan, J. J., *The Complete Grammar of Anarchy*, Nisbet, 1919, p. 23.

May 10, 1912
Edward Carson

Assuming...that the people of this country [Britain] would allow the coercion of their kith and kin [unionists] – what would be the effect upon the army? Many officers would resign; no army could stand such a strain upon them.

As Ulster Unionist leader, speaking after second reading of third Home Rule Bill. Horgan, J. J., *The Complete Grammar of Anarchy*, Nisbet, 1919, p. 24.

June 11, 1912
T. G. Agar-Robartes

I have never heard that orange bitters will mix with Irish whiskey.

As Liberal MP in House of Commons, proposing Home Rule Bill exclude Antrim, Armagh, Down and Londonderry. Coogan, Tim Pat, *The IRA*, Fontana, 1980, p. 27.

June 14, 1912
Edward Carson

The Government last night declared war against Ulster and have announced that the only solution to this question is to drive them out of a community in which they are satisfied, into a community which they loathe, hate and detest. We will accept the declaration of war. We are not altogether unprepared.

As Ulster Unionist leader, in London, after defeat of Home Rule Bill amendment to exclude Antrim, Armagh, Down and Londonderry. Horgan, J. J., *The Complete Grammar of Anarchy*, Nisbet, 1919, p. 25.

June 18, 1912
Andrew Bonar Law

If Ulster does resist by force...no Government would dare to use their troops to drive them out...the Government which gave the order to employ troops for that purpose would run a greater risk of being lynched in London than the loyalists of Ulster would run of being shot in Belfast.

As Conservative leader, in House of Commons. Gwynn, Denis, *The Life of John Redmond*, Harrap, 1932, p. 208.

July 20, 1912
Katherine Tynan
The women were hunted like rats in the city.

As Dublin poet and novelist, recalling mob violence in Dublin against women after English suffragettes had thrown a hatchet into a carriage carrying Herbert Asquith and John Redmond through Dublin. Cullen Owens, Rosemary, *Smashing Times*, Attic, 1984, p. 60.

July 27, 1912
Frederick Smith
Should it happen that Ulster is threatened with a violent attempt to incorporate her in an Irish parliament with no appeal to the English electors, I say to Sir Edward Carson, appeal to the young men of England.

As Conservative MP, at anti-Home Rule rally in Blenheim Palace. Horgan, J. J., *The Complete Grammar of Anarchy*, Nisbet, 1919, p. 27.

July 27, 1912
Andrew Bonar Law
If an attempt were made to deprive these men of their birthright – as part of a corrupt parliamentary bargain – they would be justified in resisting such an attempt by all means in their power, including force... I can imagine no length of resistance to which Ulster can go in which I would not be prepared to support them.

As Conservative Party leader addressing anti-Home Rule rally at Blenheim Palace. Lyons, F. S. L., *Ireland Since the Famine*, Fontana, 1982, p. 303.

July 31, 1912
Herbert Asquith
What answer are you going to make to the vast majority of the Irish people when they [Ulster Unionists] resist the considered determination of parliament and appeal to the language of the right honourable gentlemen to justify their action?

As British Prime Minister, in House of Commons, responding to Conservative leader's speech at Blenheim Palace on July 27, 1912. Horgan, J. J., *The Complete Grammar of Anarchy*, Nisbet, 1919, p. 27-28.

August 14, 1912
Hanna Sheehy Skeffington
Hunger-strike was then a new weapon – we were the first to try it out in Ireland – had we but known we were the pioneers in a long line.

As woman activist, recalling hunger strikes by English and Irish suffragettes in Dublin after being refused political prisoner status. Cullen Owens, Rosemary, *Smashing Times*, Attic, 1984, p. 63.

August 15, 1912
Augustine Birrell
Personally I am dead against forcible feeding which always ends with the release of the prisoner long before her time. I want to keep these ladies under lock and key for five years and I am willing to feed them with Priests' [sic] Champagne and Michaelmas Geese all the time, if it can be done... These wretched hags...are obstinate to the point of death.

As Chief Secretary of Ireland, on suffragettes, in letter to John Dillon of Irish Party. Cullen Owens, Rosemary, *Smashing Times*, Attic, 1984, p. 64.

September 12, 1912
Dr William McKean
The Irish Question is at bottom a war against Protestantism; it is an attempt to establish a Roman Catholic ascendancy in Ireland...

As former Presbyterian Moderator, preaching in Ulster Hall. *Belfast News Letter*, September 13, 1912.

September 21, 1912
Edward Carson
In the event of this proposed parliament being thrust upon us, we solemnly and mutually pledge ourselves not to recognise its authority... I do not care twopence whether it is treason or not.

As Ulster Unionist leader, speaking against Home Rule in Coleraine. Horgan, J. J., *The Complete Grammar of Anarchy*, Nisbet, 1919, p. 29.

September 24, 1912
Lord Willoughby de Broke
Peaceable methods would be tried first, but if the last resort was forced on them by the radical Government, the latter would find that they had not only Orangemen against them, but that every white man in the British Empire would be giving support, either moral or active, to one of the most loyal populations that ever fought under the Union Jack.

As British opponent of Home Rule, at rally in Dromore, Co Down. Horgan, J. J., *The Complete Grammar of Anarchy*, Nisbet, 1919, p. 29.

September 28, 1912
Ulster Covenant
We...do hereby pledge ourselves in Solemn Covenant throughout this our time of threatened calamity to stand by one another in defending for ourselves and our children our cherished position of equal citizenship in the United Kingdom, and in using all means which may be found necessary to defeat the present conspiracy to set up a Home Rule Parliament in Ireland...and mutually pledge ourselves to refuse to recognise its authority.

From Ulster Covenant, signed at Belfast and other centres, as demonstration against Home Rule, by 474,414 people. Harbinson, John F., *The Ulster Unionist Party*, Blackstaff Press, 1973, p. 28.

October 1, 1912
Edward Carson

The Attorney General has been reading me a lecture upon what is a serious matter, because I myself once or twice had the honour of being a law officer of the Crown. He says that my doctrines and the course I am taking lead to anarchy. Does he not think I know that?

As Ulster Unionist leader, speaking in Glasgow on his opposition to Home Rule. Horgan, J. J., *The Complete Grammar of Anarchy*, Nisbet, 1919, p. 32.

October 5, 1912
Herbert Asquith

The reckless rodomontade at Blenheim [against Home Rule] in the early summer as developed and amplified in this Ulster campaign, furnishes for the future a complete grammar of anarchy.

As British Prime Minister, speaking in Ladybank. Horgan, J. J., *The Complete Grammar of Anarchy*, Nisbet, 1919, p. 33.

1913
Rt Rev Samuel Prenter

In an Irish parliament civil allegiance to the Holy See would be the test of membership, and would make every Roman Catholic member a civil servant of the Vatican.

As Moderator of the General Assembly of the Presbyterian Church, speaking against Home Rule. Lee, J. J., *Ireland 1912-1985*, Cambridge University Press, 1990, p. 9.

1913
John Redmond

Nobody denies that a riot may be attempted in Belfast and one or two other towns, but nobody in Ulster, outside a certain number of fanatics and leaders, believes in any organised rebellion, active or passive.

As leader of Irish Party, on prospects of resistance to Home Rule. Lee, J. J., *Ireland 1912-1985*, Cambridge University Press, 1990, pp. 15-16.

February 22, 1913
Sean O'Casey

The delivery of Ireland is not in the Labour Manifesto, good and salutary as it may be, but in the strength, beauty, nobility and imagination of the Gaelic ideal.

As writer and playwright. *The Irish Worker*, February 22, 1913.

June 22, 1913
Padraic Pearse

We pledge ourselves to follow in the steps of Tone, never to rest, either by day or by night, until his work be accomplished, deeming it the proudest of all privileges to fight for freedom, to fight, not in despondency, but in great joy, hoping for the victory in our day, but fighting on whether victory seem far or near...accounting ourselves base as long as we endure the evil thing against which he testified with his blood.

As revolutionary, in address at grave of Wolfe Tone in Bodenstown churchyard. Pearse, Padraic H., *Political Writings and Speeches*, Talbot, 1952, p. 63.

July 12, 1913
Edward Carson

The Government know perfectly well that they could not tomorrow rely upon the army to shoot down the people of Ulster... The army are with us.

As Ulster Unionist leader, speaking in Belfast on prospect of army being used to enforce Home Rule. Horgan, J. J., *The Complete Grammar of Anarchy*, Nisbet, 1919, p. 40.

July 19, 1913
William Martin Murphy

I would think there is talent enough amongst the men in the [tramways] service to form a union of their own, without allying themselves to a disreputable organisation, and placing themselves under the feet of an unscrupulous man who claims the right to give you the word of command and to issue his orders to you and to use you as tools to make him the labour dictator of Dublin.

As leader of Dublin employers, asking Tramways Company employees not to join Irish Transport and General Workers' Union at urging of James Larkin. Curriculum Development Unit, *Dublin 1913*, O'Brien, 1984, pp. 74-75.

July 29, 1913
James Connolly

I don't think I can stand Larkin as a boss much longer... He is consumed with jealousy and hatred of anyone who will not cringe to him and beslaver all over him.

As labour organiser, in letter to friend, William O'Brien, about bad relations between Connolly and Larkin. Dudley Edwards, Ruth, *James Connolly*, Gill & Macmillan, 1981, p. 101.

August 4, 1913
James Craig

According to the Government programme, we may look for Home Rule in May, Civil War in June, the Union Jack being hauled down and being tramped upon in July and the smash up of the Empire in August.

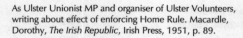
As Ulster Unionist MP and organiser of Ulster Volunteers, writing about effect of enforcing Home Rule. Macardle, Dorothy, *The Irish Republic*, Irish Press, 1951, p. 89.

August 26, 1913
James Larkin

This is not a strike, it is a lock-out... We are fighting for bread and butter.

As strike leader in address to striking tramway workers on first day of the Dublin Lock-Out. Curriculum Development Unit, *Dublin 1913*, O'Brien, 1984, p. 78.

August 31, 1913
Winston Churchill

Something should be done to afford the characteristically Protestant and Orange counties the option of a moratorium of several years before acceding to the Irish parliament... Much is to be apprehended from a combination of the rancour of a party in the ascendant and the fanaticism of these stubborn and determined Orangemen.

As First Lord of the Admiralty, in letter to John Redmond. Hepburn, A. C., *The Conflict of Nationality in Modern Ireland*, Arnold, 1980, p. 77.

September 1913
William Butler Yeats

What need you, being come to sense,
But fumble in a greasy till...
Romantic Ireland's dead and gone,
It's with O'Leary in the grave.

As poet, on death of Fenian, John O'Leary, in 'September 1913'. Tuohy, Frank, *Yeats*, Macmillan, 1976, p. 145.

September 7, 1913
Edward Carson

We will set up a government. I am told it will be illegal. Of course it will. Drilling is illegal. I was reading an Act of Parliament forbidding it. The [Ulster] Volunteers are illegal, and the Government know they are illegal, and the Government dare not interfere with them. Don't be afraid of illegalities.

As Ulster Unionist leader, speaking in Newry on consequences of Home Rule. Horgan, J. J., *The Complete Grammar of Anarchy*, Nisbet, 1919, pp. 41-42.

September 11, 1913
V. I. Lenin

The police have gone positively wild; drunken policemen assault peaceful workers, break into homes, torment the aged, women and children... People are thrown into prison for making the most peaceful speeches. The city is like an armed camp.

As Russian revolutionary leader, writing in *Severnaya Pravda*, on attack by police on strikers in Dublin during

Lock-Out. Berresford Ellis, Peter, *A History of the Irish Working Class*, Pluto, 1985, pp. 195-196.

September 20, 1913
Frederick Smith

[Conservatives] would say to their followers in England: 'To your tents, Oh Israel!' and would stand side by side with loyal Ulster refusing to recognise any law, and prepared with them to risk the collapse of the whole body politic to prevent this monstrous crime.

As Conservative MP, at anti-Home Rule rally in Ballyclare. Horgan, J. J., *The Complete Grammar of Anarchy*, Nisbet, 1919, p. 43.

October 4, 1913
James Larkin

We are determined that Christ will not be crucified in Dublin by these men... My suggestion to the employers is that if they want peace we are prepared to meet them, but if they want war then war they will have.

As spokesman for workers addressing Tribunal of Inquiry during Dublin Lock-Out. McLoughlin, Michael, *Great Irish Speeches of the Twentieth Century*, Poolbeg, 1996, pp. 20-23.

October 7, 1913
George Russell ('AE')

I address this warning to you, the aristocracy of industry in this city... The men whose manhood you have broken will loathe you, and will always be brooding and scheming to strike a fresh blow. The children will be taught to curse you...your class will be cut off from humanity as the surgeon cuts the cancer and alien growth from the body. Be warned ere it is too late.

As writer and commentator, in open letter to Dublin employers during 1913 Lock-Out. *The Irish Times*, October 7, 1913.

October 9, 1913
Dr Patrick O'Donnell

There is no length to which any of us would refuse to go to satisfy the Orangemen at the start of our new Government [in Dublin], provided Ireland did not suffer seriously.

As Bishop of Raphoe, in letter to Redmond as rumours of partition gained ground. Gwynn, Denis, *The Life of John Redmond*, Harrap, 1932, p. 231.

October 12, 1913
John Redmond

Ireland is a unit. It is true that within the bosom of a nation there is room for diversities of the treatment of government and of administration but... The two-nation theory is to us an abomination and a blasphemy.

As leader of Irish Party, speaking in Limerick. Gwynn, Denis, *The Life of John Redmond*, Harrap, 1932, p. 232.

October 20, 1913
Dr William Walsh
They can be no longer held worthy of the name of Catholic mothers if they so far forget that duty as to send away their little children to be cared for in a strange land, without [ascertaining] that those to whom the poor children are to be handed over are Catholics, or indeed persons of any faith at all.

As Archbishop of Dublin, in letter to newspapers about proposal to send children of impoverished strikers to homes in England. Curriculum Development Unit, *Dublin 1913*, O'Brien, 1984, p. 94.

November 1913
Augustine Birrell
It certainly was an outrage. For the first place, there are no starving children in Dublin, and in the second place, the place swarms with homes for them.

As Chief Secretary for Ireland in report to British Prime Minister on proposal to send children of impoverished strikers to homes in England. Curriculum Development Unit, *Dublin 1913*, O'Brien, 1984, p. 96.

November 1913
William Butler Yeats
I charge the Dublin nationalist newspapers with deliberately arousing religious passion to break up the organisation of the working man, with appealing to mob law day by day... And I charge the unionist press of Dublin and those who directed the police with conniving in this conspiracy.

As poet, in letter to *Irish Worker* during Dublin Lock-Out. Tuohy, Frank, *Yeats*, Macmillan, 1976, p. 144.

November 1913
Padraic Pearse
I am glad that the Orangemen have armed, for it is a goodly thing to see arms in Irish hands. I should like to see the AOH [Ancient Order of Hibernians] armed. I should like to see any and every body of Irish citizens armed. We must accustom ourselves to the thought of arms, to the sight of arms, to the use of arms. We may make mistakes in the beginning and shoot the wrong people; but bloodshed is a cleansing and a sanctifying thing, and the nation which regards it as the final horror has lost its manhood. There are many things more horrible than bloodshed; and slavery is one of them.

As revolutionary, in pamphlet *The Coming Revolution*. Pearse, Padraic H., *Political Writings and Speeches*, Talbot, 1952, pp. 98-99.

November 1913
Padraic Pearse
I think the Orangeman with a rifle a much less ridiculous figure than a nationalist without a rifle.

As revolutionary, writing in *Irish Freedom*. Pearse, Padraic H., *Political Writings and Speeches*, Talbot, 1952, p. 185.

November 9, 1913
J. P. Convery
Under no circumstances [will we] allow Ulster or any portion of it to be taken from the map of Ireland.

As organiser of United Ireland League, at meeting of nationalists in Donaghmore, Co Tyrone. Bardon, Jonathan, *A History of Ulster*, Blackstaff Press, 1992, p. 446.

November 13, 1913
James Connolly
I am going to talk sedition. The next time we are out for a march I want to be accompanied by four battalions of trained men with their corporals and sergeants. Why should we not drill and train men as they are doing in Ulster?

As labour organiser, speaking at Dublin meeting to celebrate release of James Larkin from prison. Boyle, John W., *The Making of 1916: Studies in the History of the Rising*, Stationery Office, 1969, p. 55.

November 14, 1913
Irish Churchman
We have the offer of aid from a powerful continental monarch [German Kaiser]...should our King sign the Home Rule Bill, the Protestants of Ireland will welcome this continental deliverer as their forefathers under similar circumstances did once before.

As Protestant journal, in comment on meeting in Hamburg between Edward Carson and the German Kaiser. Berresford Ellis, Peter, *A History of the Irish Working Class*, Pluto, 1985, p. 205.

November 25, 1913
Eoin MacNeill
The more genuine and successful the local volunteer movement in Ulster becomes, the more completely does it establish the principle that Irishmen have the right to decide and govern their own national affairs.

As chairman at inaugural meeting in Dublin of Irish Volunteers set up in response to creation of Ulster Volunteers. Macardle, Dorothy, *The Irish Republic*, Irish Press, 1951, p. 96.

November 28, 1913
Andrew Bonar Law
King James had behind him the letter of the law just as completely as Mr Asquith...the King had the largest army which had ever been seen in England.

What happened? There was no Civil War. There was a revolution, and the King disappeared. Why? Because his own army refused to fight for him.

As Conservative leader, in Dublin speech regarded as incitement to British Army to mutiny if ordered against Ulster Unionists. Gwynn, Denis, *The Life of John Redmond*, Harrap, 1932, p. 239.

December 1913
Padraic Pearse

A citizen without arms is like a priest without religion, like a woman without chastity, like a man without manhood... I say to each one of you who read this that it is your duty to arm...if you cannot arm otherwise than by joining Carson's Volunteers, join Carson's Volunteers. But you can, for instance, start Volunteers of your own.

As revolutionary, writing in *Irish Freedom*. Pearse, Padraic H., *Political Writings and Speeches*, Talbot, 1952, pp. 196-197.

December 5, 1913
Lt-Colonel Pretyman Newman

If...by any chance he should bring bloodshed in Ulster by means of Imperial troops, then...any man would be justified in shooting Mr Asquith in the streets of London.

As Conservative MP, speaking at anti-Home Rule meeting in Potter's Bar, referring to British Prime Minister Herbert Asquith. Horgan, J. J., *The Complete Grammar of Anarchy*, Nisbet, 1919, p. 46.

1914
William Butler Yeats

In dreams begin responsibilities

As poet, in 'Responsibilities, epigraph (from an old play)', 1914. Yeats, W. B., *Collected Poems*, Macmillan, 1965.

1914
Thomas Clarke

Joe, it is worth living in Ireland these times... There is an awakening. Wait till they get their fist clutching the steel barrel of a business rifle, and then Irish instincts and Irish manhood can be relied upon.

As Irish Volunteer, in letter to Joe McGarrity, Clan na nGael leader in Philadelphia. Bardon, Jonathan, *A History of Ulster*, Blackstaff Press, 1992, p. 443.

January 30, 1914
James Larkin

We are beaten. We make no bones about it; but we are not too badly beaten still to fight.

As strike leader, in speech in Dublin on end of Dublin Lock-Out. Curriculum Development Unit, *Dublin 1913*, O'Brien, 1984, p. 102.

February 7, 1914
Padraic Pearse

The Gaelic League will be recognised in history as the most revolutionary influence that has ever come into Ireland. The Irish revolution really began when the seven proto-Gaelic Leaguers met in O'Connell Street... The germ of all future Irish history was in that back room.

As Volunteer leader, writing in *Irish Volunteer*. Macardle, Dorothy, *The Irish Republic*, Irish Press, 1951, p. 61.

February 9, 1914
James Connolly

And so we Irish workers must again go down into hell, bow our backs to the lash of the slave driver, let our hearts be seared by the iron of his hatred, and instead of the sacramental wafer of brotherhood and common sacrifice, eat the dust of defeat and betrayal. Dublin is isolated.

As labour organiser, writing in *Forward* on workers' defeat in Dublin Lock-Out. Dudley Edwards, Ruth, *James Connolly*, Gill & Macmillan, 1981, p. 110.

February 11, 1914
Edward Carson

I say to the leader of the Nationalist Party, if you want Ulster, go and take her, or go and win her. You have never wanted her affections, you have wanted her taxes.

As Ulster Unionist leader, in House of Commons, on Home Rule. McLoughlin, Michael, *Great Irish Speeches of the Twentieth Century*, Poolbeg, 1996, p. 28.

February 25, 1914
Edward Carson

Crawford, I'll see you through this business, if I should have to go to prison for it.

As Ulster Unionist leader, giving Major Fred Crawford go-ahead to run guns to Ulster Volunteers. Gwynn, Denis, *The Life of John Redmond*, Harrap, 1932, p. 303.

February 25, 1914
Major Fred Crawford

Sir Edward, this is all I want. I leave tonight. Good-bye.

As organiser of gun-running to Ulster Volunteers, replying to Edward Carson, above. Gwynn, Denis, *The Life of John Redmond*, Harrap, 1932, p. 303.

March 1, 1914
John Redmond

The rights and interests of the nationalists of Ulster will not be neglected or betrayed by us.

As leader of Irish Party, in letter to Bishop McHugh of Derry after he had persuaded him to call off Home Rule rally in Derry because of possible disorder. Gwynn, Denis, *The Life of John Redmond*, Harrap, 1932, p. 267.

March 2, 1914
John Redmond
We are ready to give our acquiescence to the solution of the standing out for three years by option of the countries of Ulster as the price of peace.

As leader of Irish Party, in memorandum to British Prime Minister, Herbert Asquith offering compromise on Home Rule Bill. Gwynn, Denis, *The Life of John Redmond*, Harrap, 1932, p. 269.

March 9, 1914
Edward Carson
We do not want sentence of death, with a stay of execution for six years.

As Ulster Unionist leader, responding to publication of British Prime Minister, Herbert Asquith's proposal to allow individual counties to opt out of Home Rule for six years. Gwynn, Denis, *The Life of John Redmond*, Harrap, 1932, p. 274.

March 9, 1914
Herbert Asquith
The best, and indeed the only practical way – at any rate for the simplest and fairest plan – is to allow the Ulster counties themselves to determine, in the first instance, whether or not they desire to be excluded [for] a term of six years...to test, by experience, the actual working of the Irish Parliament.

As British Prime Minister, in House of Commons, proposing that individual counties could temporarily opt out of Home Rule. McLoughlin, Michael, *Great Irish Speeches of the Twentieth Century*, Poolbeg, 1996, p. 34.

March 12, 1914
V. I. Lenin
Lord Carson has threatened rebellion, and has organised armed Black Hundred gangs for this purpose. This is an empty threat of course. There can be no question of rebellion by a handful of hooligans.

As Russian revolutionary leader, writing in *Put Pravdy*. Berresford Ellis, Peter, *A History of the Irish Working Class*, Pluto, 1985, p. 205.

March 14, 1914
Winston Churchill
They [Ulster Unionists] denounce all violence except their own...if all the loose, wanton and reckless chatter is in the end to disclose a sinister and revolutionary purpose then...put these grave matters to the proof.

As First Lord of the Admiralty, in speech at Bradford. Gwynn, Denis, *The Life of John Redmond*, Harrap, 1932, p. 274.

March 14, 1914
War Office, London
[As] attempts may be made in various parts of Ireland by evil-disposed persons to obtain possession of arms, ammunition and other Government stores, it is considered advisable that you should at once take special precautions for safeguarding depots... It appears from the information received that Armagh, Omagh, Carrickfergus and Enniskillen are insufficiently guarded, being specially liable to attack.

As order to General Sir Arthur Paget, General Officer Commanding in Ireland, to move British troops at Curragh to northern towns in anticipation of Unionist revolt against Home Rule. Horgan, J. J., *The Complete Grammar of Anarchy*, Nisbet, 1919, p. 48.

March 17, 1914
General Sir Arthur Paget
Any such move of troops would create intense excitement in Ulster, and possibly precipitate a crisis. For these reasons I do not consider myself justified in moving troops.

As General Officer Commanding in Ireland, to War Office, after being ordered to send troops to north. Gwynn, Denis, *The Life of John Redmond*, Harrap, 1932, p. 288.

March 19, 1914
Colonel J. E. B. Seely
Officers actually domiciled in Ulster would be exempted from taking part in any operations that might take place. They would be permitted to 'disappear' and when all was over would be allowed to resume their place without their career or their position being affected.

As War Minister, in concession to try to prevent Curragh mutiny. Gwynn, Denis, *The Life of John Redmond*, Harrap, 1932, p. 289.

March 20, 1914
General Sir Arthur Paget
Officer commanding 5th Lancers states that all officers, except two and one doubtful, are resigning their commissions today. I much fear same conditions in the 16th Lancers. Fear men will refuse to move. Regret to report Brigadier-General Gough and 57 officers 3rd Cavalry Brigade prefer to accept dismissal if ordered North.

As General Officer Commanding in Ireland, in telegrams to War Office after new orders received to move army units from Curragh to north. Horgan, J. J., *The Complete Grammar of Anarchy*, Nisbet, 1919, p. 48.

March 23, 1914
Colonel J. E. B. Seely
His Majesty's Government must retain the right to use all the forces of the Crown in Ireland to maintain law and order and to support the civil

power in the ordinary execution of its duty. But they have no intention whatever of taking advantage of this right to crush political opposition to the policy or principles of the Home Rule Bill.

As War Minister, sanctioning reinstatement of officers who rebelled at Curragh. Gwynn, Denis, *The Life of John Redmond*, Harrap, 1932, pp. 296-297.

March 25, 1914
Brigadier-General Hubert Gough

I got a signed guarantee [from the Government] that in no circumstances shall we be used to force Home Rule on the Ulster people. If it came to civil war, I would fight for Ulster rather than against her.

As Commander of 3rd Cavalry Brigade at Curragh, in statement issued after consultations with War Office over his refusal to move north against Ulster Unionists. *Daily Telegraph*, March 25, 1914.

March 26, 1914
Morning Post

The Army has killed the Home Rule Bill.

As British newspaper, commenting on Curragh mutiny. Gwynn, Denis, *The Life of John Redmond*, Harrap, 1932, p. 297.

March 27, 1914
Roger Casement

...the 'Union' means the military occupation of Ireland as a conquered country, that the real headquarters of Irish Government, on the Unionist principle, is the Curragh Camp...the cat is out of the Irish bag.

As former colonial administrator, in letter to *Irish Independent* on Curragh mutiny. Casement, Roger, *The Crime Against Europe: The Writings and Poetry of Roger Casement*, Fallon, 1958, pp. 110-111.

April 18, 1914
James Connolly

The time has long since gone when Irish men and Irish women could be kept from thinking by hurling priestly thunder at their heads.

As labour organiser, writing in *Labour, Nationality and Religion*, April 18, 1914.

April 24, 1914
Ulster Volunteers

'Gough.'

Password used by Ulster Volunteers during gun-running at Larne, after Brigadier-General Hubert Gough, a leading figure in Curragh mutiny. *Daily Mail*, April 28, 1914.

May 6, 1914
Hanna Sheehy Skeffington

The proposed 'Ladies' Auxiliary Committee' has apparently no function beyond that of a conduit

pipe to pour a stream of gold into the coffers of the male organisation [the Irish Volunteers], to be turned off automatically as soon as it had served this mean and subordinate purpose.

As representative of women's suffrage movement, writing in *Freeman's Journal*, following formation of Cumann na mBan or Women's Volunteer Force. Owens, Rosemary Cullen, *Smashing Times*, Attic, 1984, p. 110.

May 8, 1914
Mary Colum and Louise Gavan Duffy

We consider at the moment that helping to equip the Irish Volunteers is the most necessary national work. We may mention that many of the members of our Society are keen suffragists, but as an organisation we must confine ourselves within the four walls of our constitution.

As members of Cumann na mBan, Cullen Owens, Rosemary, *Smashing Times*, Attic, 1984, p. 111.

May 25, 1914
William O'Brien

This Act will be born with a rope around its neck. It is not even intended to be enforced... We regard this Bill as no longer a Home Rule Bill but as a Bill for the murder of Home Rule.

As Irish Party MP for Cork, in House of Commons, after Government announced plans to exclude parts of Ulster from Home Rule Bill. Macardle, Dorothy, *The Irish Republic*, Irish Press, 1951, p. 107.

June 9, 1914
John Redmond

The effect of Sir Edward Carson's threats upon public opinion in England, the House of Commons and the Government, the occurrences at the Curragh Camp, and the successful gun-running in Ulster vitally altered the position, and the Irish Party took steps about six weeks ago to inform their friends...it was desirable to support the [Irish] Volunteer movement.

As leader of Irish Party, in letter to Irish newspapers, announcing that Irish Party would join governing committee of Irish Volunteers. Gwynn, Denis, *The Life of John Redmond*, Harrap, 1932, p. 317.

June 16, 1914
John Dillon

You do not put down Irishmen by coercion. You simply embitter them and stiffen their backs.

As Irish Party MP, on why party leaders did not demand the prosecution of Unionists for incitement or treason. Gwynn, Denis, *The Life of John Redmond*, Harrap, 1932, p. 225.

July 12, 1914
Edward Carson

Give us a clean cut.

As Ulster Unionist leader, after House of Lords voted on July 8 to make exclusion of six counties from Home Rule permanent. Dudley Edwards, Ruth, *The Making of 1916: Studies in the History of the Rising*, Stationery Office, 1969, p. 130.

July 21, 1914
King George V
...the cry of civil war is on the lips of the most responsible and sober-minded of my people. We have in the past endeavoured to act as a civilising example to the world, and to me it is unthinkable, as it must be to you, that we should be brought to the brink of fratricidal strife upon issues apparently so capable of adjustment as those you are now asked to consider.

As British monarch, in speech at first meeting of conference on Ulster question called by king at Buckingham Palace. Gwynn, Denis, *The Life of John Redmond*, Harrap, 1932, p. 337.

July 24, 1914
John Redmond
[Let's] have a good shake-hands for the sake of the old days together on circuit.

As leader of Irish Party, to Ulster Unionist leader, Edward Carson, as Buckingham Palace Conference on Ulster broke up in disagreement. Gwynn, Denis, *The Life of John Redmond*, Harrap, 1932, p. 343.

July 24, 1914
Winston Churchill
[It] toiled round the muddy byways of Fermanagh and Tyrone.

As First Lord of the Admiralty, on breakdown of Buckingham Palace Conference on Ulster. Bardon, Jonathan, *A History of Ulster*, Blackstaff Press, 1992, p. 447.

July 24, 1914
Herbert Asquith
Nothing could have been more amicable in tone or more desperately fruitless in result.

As British Prime Minister, on breakdown of Buckingham Palace Conference on Ulster. Gwynn, Denis, *The Life of John Redmond*, Harrap, 1932, p. 343.

July 25, 1914
James Larkin
Oh Irishmen, dear countrymen,
take heed of what we say,
for if you do England's dirty work,
you will surely rue the day.

As trade union organiser, in article opposing Irish recruitment to the British Army at outbreak of war. *The Irish Worker*, July 25, 1914.

August 1, 1914
James Connolly
Governments in a capitalist society are but committees of the rich to manage the affairs of the capitalist class.

As labour organiser. *The Irish Worker*, August 1914.

August 1, 1914
James Connolly
Should a German army land in Ireland tomorrow, we should be perfectly justified in joining it, if by doing so we could rid this country once and for all from its connection with the Brigand Empire that drags us unwillingly to war.

As labour organiser, writing in *Irish Worker* on outbreak of war in Europe. Greaves, Desmond, C., *The Life and Times of James Connolly*, Lawrence and Wishart, 1961, p. 284.

August 3, 1914
John Redmond
I say that the coast of Ireland will be defended from foreign invasion by her armed sons, and for this purpose armed nationalist Catholics in the South will be only too glad to join arms with the armed Protestant Ulstermen in the North. Is it too much to hope that out of this situation there may spring a result which will be good, not merely for the Empire, but good for the future welfare and integrity of the Irish nation?

As leader of Irish Party, in House of Commons, on outbreak of war. Hepburn, A. C., *The Conflict of Nationality in Modern Ireland*, Arnold, 1980, p. 84.

August 5, 1914
Winston Churchill
I have called the new battleship *Erin* on account of your memorable speech, the echoes of which will long linger in British ears.

As First Lord of the Admiralty, in letter to John Redmond on promise of Irish support in war. Gwynn, Denis, *The Life of John Redmond*, Harrap, 1932, p. 362.

August 6, 1914
UVF Member and Irish Volunteer
Bless the good fortune that brings us together...
Townsmen and countrymen, Irishmen all;
Ulstermen, Munstermen, Connachtmen, Leinstermen,
Faithful to Eirin, we answer her call!

As recruits, one from Belfast, the other from the Glens of Antrim, on enlisting to fight Germany. Bardon, Jonathan, *A History of Ulster*, Blackstaff Press, 1992, pp. 448-449.

August 7, 1914
Lord Kitchener
Give me five thousand men and I will say thank you. Give me ten thousand and I will take off my hat to you.

As War Secretary, declining John Redmond's offer to use Irish Volunteers as home guard. Gwynn, Denis, *The Life of John Redmond*, Harrap, 1932, p. 366.

August 8, 1914
Arthur Griffith
Ireland is not at war with Germany...we are Irish nationalists and the only duty we can have is to stand for Ireland's interests... If Irishmen are to defend Ireland they must defend it for Ireland, under Ireland's flag, and under Irish officers.

As President of Sinn Féin, on outbreak of war. *Sinn Féin*, August 8, 1914.

August 21, 1914
Herbert Asquith
The old bother about Tyrone and those infernal snippets of Fermanagh and Derry etc. popped up again.

As British Prime Minister, on further negotiations over Home Rule Bill. Gwynn, Denis, *The Life of John Redmond*, Harrap, 1932, p. 373.

September 1914
Herbert Asquith
The Irish on both sides are giving me a lot of trouble just at a difficult moment. I sometimes wish we could submerge the whole lot of them and their island for say ten years under the waves of the Atlantic.

As British Prime Minister, in diary. Bardon, Jonathan, *A History of Ulster*, Blackstaff Press, 1992, p. 450.

September 3, 1914
Edward Carson
Our country and our Empire are in danger. I say to our Volunteers without hesitation, go and help to save your country.

As Ulster Unionist leader, in speech at meeting of Ulster Unionist Council following which Ulster Volunteers joined the British Army 36th (Ulster) Division en masse. Bardon, Jonathan, *Belfast*, Blackstaff Press, 1983, p. 184.

September 12, 1914
Herbert Asquith
We must all recognise...that employment of force, any kind of force, for what you call the coercion of Ulster, is an absolutely unthinkable thing...the Home Rule Bill will not, and cannot, come into operation until Parliament has had the fullest opportunity, by an Amending Bill, of altering, modifying or qualifying its provisions in such a way as to secure the general consent both of Ireland and of the United Kingdom.

As British Prime Minister, in House of Commons, suspending Home Rule Bill until end of war. Gwynn, Denis, *The Life of John Redmond*, Harrap, 1932, pp. 380-381.

September 15, 1914
John Redmond
Just as Botha and Smuts have been able to say...that the concession of free institutions to South Africa has changed the men who but ten or a little more years ago were your bitter enemies in the field into your loyal comrades and fellow citizens in the Empire, just as truthfully can I say to you that...Ireland has been transformed from what George Meredith described a short time ago as 'the broken arm of England' into one of the strongest bulwarks of the Empire.

As leader of Irish Party, in House of Commons, on passing of Home Rule Bill. *HC Debates: Vol. 55: Col. 912.*

September 20, 1914
John Redmond
The war is undertaken in defence of the highest principles of religion and morality and right, and it would be a disgrace for ever to our country, and a reproach to her manhood, and a denial of the lessons of her history, if young Ireland confined their efforts to remaining at home to defend the shores of Ireland from an unlikely invasion, and shrunk from the duty of proving on the field of battle that gallantry and courage which has distinguished our race all through its history.

As leader of Irish Party, urging Irish Volunteers at Woodenbridge, Co Wicklow to join British Army. Hepburn, A. C., *The Conflict of Nationality in Modern Ireland*, Arnold, 1980, p. 84.

September 24, 1914
Provisional Committee of Irish Volunteers
Mr Redford [is] no longer entitled, through his nominees, to any place in the administration and guidance of the Irish Volunteer organisation.

As majority of Irish Volunteers, including Padraic Pearse, repudiating Redmond's Woodenbridge speech of September 20 promoting recruitment to British Army. Gwynn, Denis, *The Life of John Redmond*, Harrap, 1932, p. 392.

September 28, 1914
Edward Carson
When the War is over and we have beaten the Germans, as we are going to do, I tell you what we will do; we will call our Provisional Government together, and we will repeal the Home Rule Bill, so far as it concerns us, in ten minutes.

As Ulster Unionist leader, at Ulster Day rally in Belfast. Gwynn, Denis, *The Life of John Redmond*, Harrap, 1932, p. 395.

October 1914
Louie Bennett
I suppose when the necessity of knitting socks [for soldiers] is over, the order will be 'Bear sons!' And

those of us who can't will feel we had better get out of the way as quickly as we can.

As co-founder of Irish Women's Suffrage Federation, in letter to Hanna Sheehy Skeffington. Cullen Owens, Rosemary, *Smashing Times*, Attic, 1984, p. 98.

October 5, 1914
Roger Casement
Ireland has no blood to give to any land, to any cause, but that of Ireland.

As former colonial administrator, in letter published in Ireland and United States. *Irish Independent*, October 5, 1914.

October 29, 1914
General Sir Lawrence Parsons
To establish special recruiting centres where Mr Crilly suggests would mean filling us with Liverpool and Glasgow and Cardiff Irish who are slum-birds that we don't want. I want to see the clean, fine, strong, temperate, hurley-playing country fellows such as we used to get in the Munsters, Royal Irish, Connaught Rangers.

As officer in charge of recruitment to Irish Division, rejecting request from F. L. Crilly, secretary of the United Irish League of Great Britain, to open recruiting centres in Britain for Irish division. Gwynn, Denis, *The Life of John Redmond*, Harrap, 1932, p. 400.

1915
Padraic Pearse
O wise men, riddle me this: what if the dream come true?
What if the dream come true? and if millions unborn shall dwell
In the house that I shaped in my heart, the noble house of my thought?

As Volunteer leader, in 'The Fool', about a dream of an independent Ireland. *Collected Works of Padraic H. Pearse*, Phoenix, p. 336.

February 1, 1915
General Sir Lawrence Parsons
Politicians are apt to forget that I alone am responsible that I get my division fit to take its place in the field, and that when it gets there it will not disgrace the British Army and its country, and that I therefore cannot go on sacrificing military to political interests.

As British officer, in letter refusing John Redmond's request for a commission for his son in Irish division and considered by Irish Party leader to be extremely offensive. Gwynn, Denis, *The Life of John Redmond*, Harrap, 1932, p. 411.

February 3, 1915
Hugh Lane
This is a Codicil to my last Will to the effect that the group of pictures now at the London National Gallery, which I had bequeathed to that institution, I now bequeath to the city of Dublin, providing that a suitable building is provided for them within five years of my death.

As art collector, in amendment to will not recognised by British Government, despite Irish protests, because it was not witnessed. Robinson, Lennox, *Lady Gregory's Journal*, Putnam, 1946, p. 285.

May 18, 1915
Herbert Asquith
The Ministry is about to be reconstructed on a broad national basis... I am most anxious you should join. The Opposition are anxious that Carson, whose administrative gifts they value, should be included.

As British Prime Minister, inviting John Redmond to join wartime Coalition Government. Gwynn, Denis, *The Life of John Redmond*, Harrap, 1932, p. 423.

May 19, 1915
John Redmond
The principles and history of the party I represent make the acceptance of your offer impossible... I think most strongly Carson should not be included.

As leader of Irish Party, rejecting British Prime Minister Herbert Asquith's offer of inclusion in wartime Coalition Government, in which Unionist leader Edward Carson was made Attorney General. Gwynn, Denis, *The Life of John Redmond*, Harrap, 1932, p. 423.

June 7, 1915
John Redmond
Sir Edward Carson, the leader of the small Unionist Party in Ireland, who had constituted himself the apostle of physical force against law, [is] to be included in the new Cabinet. I was offered...by you a place in the Cabinet...I was not offered a place in the government of my country.

As leader of Irish Party, in letter to British Prime Minister Herbert Asquith opposing Edward Carson's post in wartime Coalition Government. Gwynn, Denis, *The Life of John Redmond*, Harrap, 1932, pp. 430-431.

August 1, 1915
Padraic Pearse
They think that they have pacified Ireland. They think that they have purchased half of us and intimidated the other half. They think that they have foreseen everything, think that they have provided against everything; but the fools, the fools, the fools! – they have left us our Fenian dead, and while Ireland holds these graves, Ireland unfree shall never be at peace.

As Volunteer leader, in oration at funeral in Glasnevin of Fenian Jeremiah O'Donovan Rossa. Pearse, Padraic H., *Political Writings and Speeches*, Talbot, 1952, p. 137.

c. *September 1, 1915*
Douglas Hyde

We were doing the only business that really counted, we were keeping Ireland Irish, and that in a way that the Government and Unionists, though they hated it, were powerless to oppose. So long as we remained non-political, there was no end to what we could do.

As founder of Gaelic League, resigning after convention in Dundalk over adoption of nationalist policies. Kiberd, Declan, *Inventing Ireland*, Jonathan Cape, 1995, p. 153.

November 15, 1915
Roger Casement

If conscription is applied to Ireland, it will be met, and instead of recruits for the British Army in Flanders, England will have to greatly increase her garrison in Ireland. Already we have kept 200,000 Irishmen out of the ranks of the British Army in this war... This act of mine is termed treason in England. In Ireland men call it by another name.

As former colonial administrator. Casement, Roger, *The Crime Against Europe: The Writings and Poetry of Roger Casement*, Fallon, 1958, p. 137.

November 23, 1915
John Redmond

Ireland would for ever be disgraced in the history of the world if, having sent these men to the front, she did not raise the necessary reserves to fill every gap that may arise in their ranks.

As leader of Irish Party, on return from visit to Irish regiments on continent. Gwynn, Denis, *The Life of John Redmond*, Harrap, 1932, p. 453.

December 1915
Padraic Pearse

Ireland has not known the exhilaration of war for over a hundred years. Yet who will say that she has known the blessings of peace? When war comes to Ireland, she must welcome it as she would welcome the Angel of God. And...we must not faint at the sight of blood. Winning through it, we (or those of us who survive) shall come unto great joy.

As Volunteer leader, in pamphlet *Peace and the Gael*. Pearse, Padraic H., *Political Writings and Speeches*, Talbot, 1952, pp. 217-218.

1916
James Joyce

–Do you know what Ireland is? asked Stephen with cold violence. Ireland is the old sow that eats her farrow.

As author, from *A Portrait of the Artist as a Young Man*. Bartlett, John, *Familiar Quotations*, Little, Brown, 1992, p. 647.

January 1, 1916
Padraic Pearse

I have spent the greater part of my life in immediate contemplation of the most grotesque and horrible of the English inventions for the debasement of Ireland. I mean their education system... They have planned and established an education system which more wickedly does violence to the elementary human rights of Irish children than would an edict for the general castration of Irish males.

As Volunteer leader, and teacher, in pamphlet *The Murder Machine*. Pearse, Padraic H., *Political Writings and Speeches*, Talbot, 1952, pp. 6-7.

February 1, 1916
Eoin MacNeill

I am certain that the only possible basis for successful revolutionary action is deep and widespread popular discontent. We have only to look around us in the streets to realise that no such condition exists in Ireland.

As Chief of Staff of Irish Volunteers. Wall, Maureen, *The Making of 1916: Studies in the History of the Rising*, Stationery Office, 1969, p. 160.

April 8, 1916
James Connolly

We are out for Ireland for the Irish. But who are the Irish? Not the rack-renting, slum-owning landlord; not the sweating, profit-grinding capitalist; not the sleek and oily lawyer; not the prostitute pressmen – the hired liars of the enemy...but the Irish working class... The cause of labour is the cause of Ireland. The cause of Ireland is the cause of labour. They cannot be dissevered... Therefore, on Sunday, April 16, the Green Flag of Ireland will be solemnly hoisted over Liberty Hall.

As commander of Citizen Army, writing in *Workers' Republic* to alert members of imminent Rising. Berresford Ellis, Peter, *A History of the Irish Working Class*, Pluto, 1985, pp. 191-226.

April 17, 1916
James Connolly

In the event of victory, hold on to your rifles, as those with whom we are fighting may stop before our goal is reached. We are out for economic as well as political liberty.

As commander of Citizen Army. Dudley Edwards, Ruth, *James Connolly*, Gill & Macmillan, 1981, p. 145.

April 22, 1916
Irish Volunteer Executive

Arrangements are now nearing completion in all the more important brigade areas for the holding of a very interesting series of manoeuvres at

Easter...the Dublin programme may well stand as a model for other areas.

As leadership of Volunteers, in announcement in *Irish Volunteer* signalling planned Rising. Wall, Maureen, *The Making of 1916: Studies in the History of the Rising*, Stationery Office, 1969, p. 203.

April 22, 1916
Eoin MacNeill

Owing to the very critical position, all orders given to Irish Volunteers for tomorrow, Easter Sunday, are hereby rescinded, and no parades, marches or other movements of Irish Volunteers will take place.

As Chief of Staff of the Irish Volunteers, in newspaper notice trying to call off Easter Rising after failure to land German arms in Kerry. *Sunday Independent*, April 23, 1916.

April 23, 1916
Eoin MacNeill

As Chief of Staff I have ordered and hereby order that no movement whatsoever of Irish Volunteers is to be made today.

As Chief of Staff of Irish Volunteers, in message sent to Eamon de Valera, Adjutant of Dublin Brigade. Macardle, Dorothy, *The Irish Republic*, Irish Press, 1951, p. 163.

April 24, 1916
Thomas MacDonagh

The four City Battalions will parade for inspection and route march at 10 a.m. today.

As founder member of IRB, in message, countersigned by Padraic Pearse, signalling start of Rising, against wishes of Volunteer leader, Eoin MacNeill. Macardle, Dorothy, *The Irish Republic*, Irish Press, 1951, p. 165.

April 24, 1916
James Connolly

We are going out to be slaughtered.

As commander of Citizen Army, on leaving Liberty Hall to participate in Rising. Hayes-McCoy, G. A., *The Making of 1916: Studies in the History of the Rising*, Stationery Office, 1969, p. 263.

April 24, 1916
James Connolly

Thanks be to God, Pearse, we have lived to see this day.

As commander of Citizen Army, when taking Padraic Pearse's hand after tricolour had been hoisted over General Post Office. Dudley Edwards, Ruth, *James Connolly*, Gill & Macmillan, 1981, p. 139.

April 24, 1916
The Provisional Government of the Irish Republic

Irishmen and Irishwomen: In the name of God and of the dead generations from which she received her old tradition of nationhood, Ireland, through us, summons her children to her flag and strikes for her freedom... We declare the right of the people of Ireland to the ownership of Ireland... Standing on that fundamental right and again asserting it in arms in the face of the world, we hereby proclaim the Irish Republic as a sovereign independent state.

As leaders of Easter Rising, in Proclamation, signed by Thomas J. Clarke, Sean MacDiarmada, Thomas MacDonagh, Padraic Pearse, Éamonn Ceannt, James Connolly, Joseph Plunkett. Hepburn, A. C., *The Conflict of Nationality in Modern Ireland*, Arnold, 1980, pp. 94-95.

April 25, 1916
Padraic Pearse

The country is rising in answer to Dublin's call and the final achievement of Ireland's freedom is now, with God's help, only a matter of days... Such looting as has already occurred has been done by hangers-on of the British Army. Ireland must keep her new honour unsmirched.

As leader of Easter Rising, in war communiqué circulated in Dublin. Macardle, Dorothy, *The Irish Republic*, Irish Press, 1951, pp. 171-172.

April 27, 1916
James Connolly

Courage, boys, we are winning, and in the hour of our victory let us not forget the splendid women who have everywhere stood by us and cheered us on. Never had man or woman a grander cause, never was a cause more grandly served.

As commander of Citizen Army, in message dictated to his secretary, Winifred Carney, after he had been wounded by rifle fire. Dudley Edwards, Ruth, *James Connolly*, Gill & Macmillan, 1981, p. 140.

April 27, 1916
The Irish Times

How many citizens of Dublin have any real knowledge of the works of Shakespeare? Could any better occasion for reading them be afforded than the coincidence of enforced domesticity with the poet's tercentenary?

As pro-Union newspaper, in emergency edition, giving celebrated advice to readers on how to pass the time during Easter Rising. *The Irish Times,* April 26, 1916.

April 28, 1916
Padraic Pearse

If they do not win this fight, they will at least have deserved to win it. But win it they will, although they may win it in death. Already they have won a great thing. They have redeemed Dublin from many shames, and made her name splendid among the names of cities.

As leader of Easter Rising, in manifesto issued as British troops besieged General Post Office. Macardle, Dorothy, *The Irish Republic*, Irish Press, 1951, p. 174.

April 28, 1916
General Sir John Maxwell
If necessary, I shall not hesitate to destroy all buildings within any area occupied by the rebels.

As newly appointed supreme commander of British Army in Ireland, in proclamation. Macardle, Dorothy, *The Irish Republic*, Irish Press, 1951, pp. 173-174.

April 28, 1916
Joseph Plunkett
It is the first time it has happened since Moscow, the first time that a capital has been burnt since then.

As one of leaders of Easter Rising, later executed, in General Post Office. Hayes-McCoy, G. A., *The Making of 1916: Studies in the History of the Rising*, Stationery Office, 1969, p. 325.

April 28, 1916
Padraic Pearse
I am satisfied that we should have accomplished more...had our arrangements for a simultaneous rising of the whole country, with a combined plan as sound as the Dublin plan has proven to be, been allowed to go through on Easter Sunday.

As leader of Easter Rising, in final bulletin from General Post Office. Wall, Maureen, *The Making of 1916: Studies in the History of the Rising*, Stationery Office, 1969, p. 188.

April 28, 1916
Louis Botha
Accept my heartfelt sympathy. Regret that small section in Ireland are jeopardising the great cause.

As South African leader in telegram from Cape Town to John Redmond. Gwynn, Denis, *The Life of John Redmond*, Harrap, 1932, p. 474.

April 29, 1916
Padraic Pearse and James Connolly
In order to prevent further slaughter of Dublin citizens, and in the hope of saving the lives of our followers now surrounded and hopelessly outnumbered, the members of the Provisional Government present at Headquarters have agreed to an unconditional surrender, and the Commandants of the various districts in the City and Country will order their commands to lay down arms.

As leaders of Easter Rising, in Order signed at 3.45 p.m. after Padraic Pearse had surrendered his sword to Brigadier-General Lowe of the British Army. Macardle,

Dorothy, *The Irish Republic*, Irish Press, 1951, pp. 176-177.

May 1, 1916
The Irish Times
The State has struck but its work is not yet finished. The surgeon's knife has been put to the corruption in the body of Ireland and its course must not be stayed until the whole malignant growth has been removed... The rapine and bloodshed of the past week must be finished with a severity which will make any repetition of them impossible for generations to come.

As pro-Union newspaper, in editorial calling for executions after Easter Rising. *The Irish Times*, edition dated April 28 and 29 and May 1.

May 2, 1916
Padraic Pearse
We seem to have lost. We have not lost. To refuse to fight would have been to lose; to fight is to win. We have kept faith with the past, and handed on a tradition to the future.

As leader of Easter Rising, at court-martial on day before his execution. Dudley Edwards, Ruth, *Patrick Pearse – The Triumph of Failure*, Gollancz, 1977, p. 318.

May 2, 1916
General Sir John Maxwell
I am going to punish the offenders, four of them are to be shot tomorrow morning. I am going to ensure that there will be no treason whispered, even whispered, in Ireland for a hundred years.

As British Army commander, in response to plea from John Dillon of Irish Party against executions. Robinson, Lennox, *Lady Gregory's Journal*, Putnam, 1946, p. 170.

May 3, 1916
German Army
Irishmen! Heavy uproar in Ireland! English guns are firing on your wives and children!

Message on board erected on German lines facing Royal Irish Regiment in France. Gwynn, Denis, *The Life of John Redmond*, Harrap, 1932, p. 495.

May 3, 1916
John Redmond
I would most earnestly beg of you to prevent any wholesale trials of this kind – wholesale executions would destroy our last hope. The precedent of Botha's [South African Leader] treatment of the rebels in S. Africa is the only wise and safe one to follow.

As leader of Irish Party, in letter sent to British Prime Minister Herbert Asquith after first executions of leaders of Rising. Gwynn, Denis, *The Life of John Redmond*, Harrap, 1932, p. 482.

May 3, 1916
Thomas MacDonagh
We do not profess to represent the mass of the people of Ireland. To Ireland's soul and intellect the inert mass, drugged and degenerate by ages of servitude, must, in the distant day of resurrection, render homage and free service.

As signatory to Easter Proclamation, at court-martial at which he was sentenced to death. Sullivan, T. D., A. M. and D. B., *Speeches from the Dock*, Gill & Macmillan, 1968, p. 339.

May 9, 1916
Herbert Asquith
I sent a strong telegram to [General] Maxwell yesterday, and I hope that the shootings – unless in some quite exceptional case – will cease.

As British Prime Minister, replying to John Redmond's pleas that execution of leaders of Easter Rising should cease. Gwynn, Denis, *The Life of John Redmond*, Harrap, 1932, p. 488.

May 9, 1916
James Connolly
Irishmen are ready to die endeavouring to win for Ireland those national rights which the British Government has been asking them to die to win for Belgium. As long as that remains the case, the cause of Irish freedom is safe.

As commander of Citizen Army, at court-martial which sentenced him to death for his part in Easter Rising. Dudley Edwards, Ruth, *James Connolly*, Gill & Macmillan, 1981, p. 142.

May 10, 1916
George Bernard Shaw
My own view is that the men who were shot in cold blood, after their capture or surrender, were prisoners of war, and that it was therefore entirely incorrect to slaughter a man in this position without making him a martyr and a hero, even though the day before the rising he may have been only a minor poet.

As playwright, in letter to *Daily News*, May 10, 1916. Macardle, Dorothy, *The Irish Republic*, Irish Press, 1951, pp. 185-187.

May 10, 1916
Irish Independent
Certain of the leaders remain to be dealt with, and the part they played was worse than that of some of those who have paid the extreme penalty.

As Dublin newspaper, in editorial encouraging execution on May 12 of James Connolly, who opposed newspaper's owner William Martin Murphy in the 1913 Lock-Out. Coogan, Tim Pat, *De Valera*, Hutchinson, 1993, pp. 75-76.

May 10, 1916
Herbert Asquith
So far as the great body of insurgents is concerned I have no hesitation in saying in public that they conducted themselves with great humanity... They were young men; often lads. They were misled, almost unconsciously, I believe, into this terrible business. They fought very bravely and did not resort to outrage.

As British Prime Minister, in House of Commons, about 1916 Rising. Macardle, Dorothy, *The Irish Republic*, Irish Press, 1951, pp. 187-188.

May 11, 1916
John Dillon
But it is not murderers who are being executed. It is insurgents who have fought a clean fight, however misguided, and it would be a damn good thing for you if your soldiers were able to put up as good a fight as did these men in Dublin – three thousand men against twenty thousand with machine guns and artillery.

As Irish Party MP, in House of Commons. Reid, George, *Great Irish Voices*, Irish Academic Press, 1999, p. 50.

c. May 20, 1916
Captain David Platt
The Irish ought to be grateful to us. With a minimum of casualties to the civilian population, we have succeeded in removing some third-rate poets.

As British officer, in letter to wife Jane on aftermath of Easter Rising. Kiberd, Declan, *Inventing Ireland*, Jonathan Cape, 1995, p. 225.

May 30, 1916
Cecil Spring Rice
They have blood in their eyes when they look our way... Our cause for the present among the Irish here is a lost one.

As British Ambassador to Washington, on effect on Irish Americans of executions in Ireland. Coogan, Tim Pat, *Michael Collins*, Arrow Books, 1991, p. 60.

June 30, 1916
Roger Casement
Ireland has seen her sons – aye, and her daughters, too! – suffer from generation to generation, always for the same cause, meeting always the same fate, and always at the hands of the same power. Still, always a fresh generation has passed on to withstand the same opposition...the Unionist champions chose a path which they felt would lead to the woolsack, while I went a road I knew must lead to the dock, and the event proved we were both right.

As leading participant in Easter Rising, in speech from dock during trial in London for treason, for which he was executed on August 3, 1916. Casement, Roger, *The Crime Against Europe: The Writings and Poetry of Roger Casement*, Fallon, 1958, pp. 152-156.

July 4, 1916
Leon Trotsky

The experiment of an Irish national rebellion...is over. But the historical role of the Irish proletariat is only beginning. Already it has brought into this revolt, even though under an archaic flag, its class indignation against militarism and imperialism. This indignation will not now subside.

As Russian revolutionary, writing in journal *Nashe Slovo*, on implications of 1916 Rising. Berresford Ellis, Peter, *A History of the Irish Working Class*, Pluto, 1985, p. 233.

July 20, 1916
Dr Edward O'Dwyer

I have very little pity for you or yours. You have ceased to be men; your leaders consequently think they can sell you like chattels.

As Bishop of Limerick, in letter to Belfast nationalists about Irish Party's acquiescence in scheme to exclude six counties from Home Rule. Macardle, Dorothy, *The Irish Republic*, Irish Press, 1951, p. 195.

July 20, 1916
Dr Charles McHugh

Irishmen, calling themselves representatives of the people, are prepared to sell their brother Irishmen into slavery to secure a nominal freedom for a section of the people... Was coercion of a more objectionable or despicable type ever resorted to by England in its dealings with Ireland than that now sanctioned by the men whom we elected to win us freedom?

As Bishop of Derry, in letter protesting against Irish Party's agreement to exclude six counties from Home Rule. Macardle, Dorothy, *The Irish Republic*, Irish Press, 1951, p. 195.

July 22, 1916
George Bernard Shaw

Casement should be treated as a prisoner of war... In Ireland he will be regarded as a national hero if he is executed, and quite possibly as a spy if he is not. For that reason it may well be that he would object very strongly to my attempt to prevent his canonisation.

As playwright, on trial of Roger Casement, in letter published by *The Manchester Guardian*, July 22, 1916.

September 14, 1916
Dr Edward O'Dwyer

Ireland will never be content as a province. God has made her a nation, and while grass grows and water runs there will be men in Ireland to dare and die for her.

As Bishop of Limerick, on being conferred with freedom of city of Limerick. Sullivan, T. D., A. M. and D. B., *Speeches from the Dock*, Gill & Macmillan, 1968, p. 318.

September 25, 1916
William Butler Yeats

All changed, changed utterly:
A terrible beauty is born.

* * *

Too long a sacrifice
Can make a stone of the heart.

* * *

Was it needless death after all?
For England may keep faith
For all that is done and said.

As poet, in 'Easter 1916'. Yeats, W. B., *Collected Poems*, Macmillan, 1965, p. 205.

October 10, 1916
Cardinal Michael Logue

The Bishops...joyfully approve and bless the project...for the training of Irish missionaries for China, who in a spirit worthy of our missionary race, offer their lives for the propagation of the faith in a pagan country.

As Primate of Ireland, approving Maynooth Mission to China. Smyth, Bernard, *The Chinese Batch*, Four Courts Press, 1994, pp. 71-72.

November 30, 1916
John Redmond

The condition of Ireland, though still far from satisfactory, has vastly improved within the last two months...due, amongst other causes, to the release of over a thousand of the interned prisoners, and the confident expectation, which has been spread by us, that the Government contemplated...the release of the remainder of the interned prisoners.

As leader of Irish Party, to British Prime Minister Herbert Asquith. Hepburn, A. C., *The Conflict of Nationality in Modern Ireland*, Arnold, 1980, pp. 98-99.

c. 1917
Eoin MacNeill

There is no body of people in the world more free from intolerance in matters of religion than the Catholics of Ireland.

As Chief of Staff of Irish Volunteers, dismissing Unionist fears that Ulster Protestants would be suppressed. Lee, J. J., *Ireland 1912-1985*, Cambridge University Press, 1990, p. 19.

March 7, 1917
Willie Redmond

In the name of God, we here who are about to die, perhaps, ask you to do that which largely induced us to leave our homes...make our country happy and contented, and enable us, when we meet the Canadians and the Australians and the New Zealanders...to say to them 'Our country, just as yours, has self-government within the Empire.'

As MP and son of Irish Party leader John Redmond, in House of Commons, shortly before being killed in the war as major in Royal Irish Regiment. Gwynn, Denis, *The Life of John Redmond*, Harrap, 1932, p. 541.

March 7, 1917
David Lloyd George
In the north-eastern portion of Ireland, you have a population as hostile to Irish rule as the rest of Ireland is to British rule, yea, and as ready to rebel against it as the rest of Ireland is against British rule – as alien in blood, in religious faith, in traditions, in outlook – as alien from the rest of Ireland in this respect as the inhabitants of Fife or Aberdeen.

As British Prime Minister, in House of Commons. Macardle, Dorothy, *The Irish Republic*, Irish Press, 1951, p. 211.

April 13, 1917
Cecil Spring-Rice
The fact that the Irish question is still unsettled is continually quoted against us, as a proof that it is not wholly true that the fight is one for...the independence of small nations.

As British Ambassador in Washington to British Government on American arguments against coming into war. Macardle, Dorothy, *The Irish Republic*, Irish Press, 1951, p. 212.

May 6, 1917
Joe Devlin
The electors had to decide...whether they were in favour of a self-governed Ireland or a hopeless fight for an Irish Republic.

As Belfast MP, for Irish Party candidate in South Longford by-election, which resulted in Sinn Féin's victory. Macardle, Dorothy, *The Irish Republic*, Irish Press, 1951, p. 214.

May 8, 1917
Bishops' Manifesto
To Irishmen of every creed and class and party, the very thought of our country partitioned and torn as a new Poland must be one of heart-rending sorrow.

As group of three Catholic archbishops, 15 Catholic bishops, three Church of Ireland bishops and county council chairmen, in protest against partition proposals. Macardle, Dorothy, *The Irish Republic*, Irish Press, 1951, p. 214.

May 9, 1917
Sinn Féin
Put him in to get him out.

As pro-independence party, in election slogan which helped win Longford by-election for republican Joe McGuinness in Lewes Prison. Coogan, Tim Pat, *Michael Collins*, Arrow Books, 1991, p. 67.

May 23, 1917
David Lloyd George
We must make it clear that at the end of the provisional period, Ulster does not, whether she wills it or not, merge in the rest of Ireland.

As British Prime Minister, in letter to unionist leader, Edward Carson. Coogan, Tim Pat, *De Valera*, Hutchinson, 1993, p. 90.

June 2, 1917
Arthur Griffith
He [Lloyd George] summons a Convention and guarantees that a small minority of people will not be bound by its decision, and thus, having secured its failure, he is armed to assure the world that England left the Irish to settle the question of government for themselves and that they could not agree.

As President of Sinn Féin, writing in *Nationality* about convention summoned by Lloyd George to discuss future government of Ireland. Macardle, Dorothy, *The Irish Republic*, Irish Press, 1951, p. 217.

June 18, 1917
Peader Kearney
Soldiers are we whose lives are pledged to Ireland, Some have come, from a land beyond the wave... In Erin's cause, come woe or weal; 'Mid cannon's roar and rifle's peal, We'll chant a soldiers' song

As Irish volunteer; in song first sung to welcome De Valera home from prison, and which later became Irish National Anthem. Coogan, Tim Pat, *De Valera*, Hutchinson, 1993, p. 91.

July 5, 1917
Eamon de Valera
Let Ulster Unionists recognise the Sinn Féin position which has behind it justice and right. It is supported by nine tenths of the Irish people and if those Unionists do not come in on their side, they will have to go under.

As Sinn Féin candidate in Clare by-election, which he won from Irish Party. Macardle, Dorothy, *The Irish Republic*, Irish Press, 1951, p. 224.

July 9, 1917
T. P. O'Connor
I feel almost like James II – a new desertion every day.

As Irish Party envoy, in letter to John Redmond from United States where he had been sent to rally Irish American support for Irish Party. Hepburn, A. C., *The*

Conflict of Nationality in Modern Ireland, Arnold, 1980,
p. 103.

September 25, 1917
Thomas Ashe

Let me carry your cross for Ireland, Lord!
For the cause of Roisin Dubh.

As Volunteer, shortly before his death on hunger strike in
Mountjoy Jail. Coogan, Tim Pat, *De Valera*, Hutchinson,
1993, p. 101.

September 30, 1917
Michael Collins

Nothing additional remains to be said. That
volley which we have just heard is the only
speech which it is proper to make above the
grave of a dead Fenian.

As Volunteer leader, in oration at burial of Thomas Ashe
who died on hunger strike. Mitchell and Ó Snodaigh,
Irish Political Documents 1916-1949, Irish Academic
Press, 1985, p. 31.

October 15, 1917
Eamon de Valera

We are not doctrinaire republicans.

As President of Sinn Féin. Coogan, Tim Pat, *De Valera*,
Hutchinson, 1993, p. 97.

October 23, 1917
David Lloyd George

I have read the speeches of the honourable
member for East Clare [de Valera]. They are not
excited, and so far as language is concerned they
are not violent. They are plain, deliberate, and I
might also say, cold-blooded incitements to
rebellion.

As British Prime Minister, in House of Commons.
Macardle, Dorothy, *The Irish Republic*, Irish Press, 1951,
p. 236.

October 25, 1917
Eamon de Valera

England pretends it is not by the naked sword,
but by the good will of the people of the country
that she is here. We will draw the naked sword
to make her bare her own naked sword.

As President of Sinn Féin, after election. Macardle,
Dorothy, *The Irish Republic*, Irish Press, 1951, p. 917.

c. December 1, 1917
David Lloyd George

The Irish are now paralysing the war activities of
America...this is the opportunity to show that it
places the Empire above everything... If America
goes wrong we are lost.

As British Prime Minister, in letter to his Chancellor of
Exchequer, Bonar Law, urging Unionist compromise on
Home Rule. Bardon, Jonathan, *A History of Ulster*,
Blackstaff Press, 1992, pp. 458-459.

c. December 10, 1917
George Russell ('AE')

You who have fought on fields afar,
That other Ireland did you wrong
Who said you shadowed Ireland's star,
Nor gave you laurel wreath nor song.

As writer and commentator, replying to Yeats's 'Easter
1916', on Irish who fell in Great War. *The Irish Times*,
December 1917.

January 4, 1918
John Redmond

My modest ambition would be to serve in some
quite humble capacity under the first Unionist
prime minister of Ireland.

As leader of Irish Party, addressing all-party Irish
Convention in Dublin. Gwynn, Denis, *The Life of John
Redmond*, Harrap, 1932, p. 582.

January 14, 1918
Dr Patrick O'Donnell

A parliament in Dublin two months hence,
without customs...will not bear examination. The
principle is given away. If Ulster had come in, or
had promised to come in, we could have given
something away.

As Bishop of Raphoe, in letter to John Redmond which
forced end of Redmond's last attempt at compromise on
Home Rule and collapse of Irish Convention. Gwynn,
Denis, *The Life of John Redmond*, Harrap, 1932,
pp. 584-585.

January 27, 1918
Eamon de Valera

[The Unionists are] a rock in the road...they must
make up their minds not to be peddling with this
rock. They must if necessary blast it out of their
path.

As President of Sinn Féin, in speech in south Armagh.
Bowman, John, *De Valera and the Ulster Question*, 1982,
p. 35.

April 16, 1918
Field-Marshal Lord French

Home Rule will be offered and declined, then
conscription will be enforced. If they will leave me
alone I can do what is necessary. I shall notify a
date before which recruits must offer themselves in
the various districts. If they do not come we will
fetch them.

As Lord Lieutenant of Ireland, on Bill passed by House of
Commons on April 16 for conscription in Ireland.
Macardle, Dorothy, *The Irish Republic*, Irish Press, 1951, p.
252.

April 18, 1918
Mansion House Conference
The passing of the Conscription Bill by the British House of Commons must be regarded as a declaration of war on the Irish nation.

From resolution passed at anti-conscription meeting presided over by Lord Mayor of Dublin and attended by de Valera, Griffith, Dillon and other nationalist leaders. Mitchell and Ó Snodaigh, *Irish Political Documents 1916-1949*, Irish Academic, 1985, p. 42.

April 18, 1918
Catholic Hierarchy
We consider that conscription forced in this way upon Ireland is an oppressive and inhuman law which the Irish people have a right to resist by every means that are consonant with the law of God.

As Irish Bishops, in manifesto issued after visit by deputation from Mansion House Conference opposing Conscription Bill. Mitchell and Ó Snodaigh, *Irish Political Documents 1916-1949*, Irish Academic, 1985, pp. 42-43.

May 1, 1918
Ernest Blythe
A Conscription campaign will be an unprovoked onslaught by an army upon the civilian population...anyone, civilian or soldier, who assists directly or by connivance in this crime against us, merits no more consideration than wild beasts, and should be killed without mercy or hesitation as opportunity offers.

As member of Sinn Féin Executive, in statement smuggled from prison and printed in *An tÓglach*, Volunteer journal. Macardle, Dorothy, *The Irish Republic*, Irish Press, 1951, p. 260.

May 18, 1918
Field-Marshal Lord French
Certain subjects of His Majesty the King, domiciled in Ireland, have conspired to enter into and have entered into treasonable communication with the German enemy...drastic measures must be taken to put down this German plot.

As Lord Lieutenant, in proclamation from Dublin castle announcing internment without trial. Mitchell and Ó Snodaigh, *Irish Political Documents 1916-1949*, Irish Academic Press, 1985, pp. 44-45.

June 25, 1918
Edward Short
Ireland – I mean the great, true heart of the Irish people – is not responsible for what the Germans do and is not responsible for what the two or three hundred extremists in Ireland do. Ireland, I believe, is sound at the core today.

As new Chief Secretary for Ireland, in House of Commons. Escouflaire, R. G., *Ireland, an Enemy of the Allies?* Murray, 1919, p. 230.

August 1, 1918
An tÓglach
The Irish Volunteers are the Army of the Irish Republic.

As Volunteer magazine, announcing the birth of the IRA. Coogan, Tim Pat, *The IRA*, Fontana, 1980, p. 42.

November 11, 1918
Belfast Telegraph
For those lonely ones, the gladness of this hour is chastened by the thought of the vacant chair.

As Belfast newspaper, on celebrations of end of war, in which tens of thousands of Ulster and Irish volunteers were killed. *Belfast Telegraph*, November 11, 1918.

November 16, 1918
William O'Brien
It is because a degenerate parliamentarianism spent all its precious years of power in misrepresenting and thwarting the principles now clung to in desperation that opportunities such as never occurred before, and are not likely soon to occur again, were madly sacrificed.

As Irish Party MP for Cork, in letter to press regarded as prophecy of downfall of Irish Party. Macardle, Dorothy, *The Irish Republic*, Irish Press, 1951, p. 262.

November 25, 1918
Sinn Féin
Sinn Féin gives Ireland the opportunity of vindicating her honour and pursuing with renewed confidence the path of national salvation by rallying to the flag of the Irish Republic. Sinn Féin aims at securing the establishment of that Republic (1) By withdrawing the Irish representation from the British Parliament... (2) By making use of any and every means available to render impotent the power of England to hold Ireland in subjection by military force or otherwise.

As pro-independence party, in manifesto for December 14 election. Mitchell and Ó Snodaigh, *Irish Political Documents 1916-1949*, Irish Academic Press, 1985, p. 48.

December 1, 1918
Michael Collins
Any scheme of government which does not confer upon the people of Ireland the supreme, absolute and final control of all of this country, external as well as internal, is a mockery and will not be accepted.

As (successful) Sinn Féin candidate for South County Cork. Macardle, Dorothy, *The Irish Republic*, Irish Press, 1951, p. 264.

January 1, 1919
William Butler Yeats
Things fall apart; the centre cannot hold;
Mere anarchy is loosed upon the world...

* * *

The best lack all conviction, while the worst
Are full of passionate intensity...

* * *

And what rough beast, its hour come round at last,
Slouches towards Bethlehem to be born?

As poet, in 'The Second Coming', believed inspired by events in Ireland and Russia. Tuohy, Frank, *Yeats*, Macmillan, 1976, p. 168.

January 21, 1919
Dáil Éireann
We, the elected representative of the ancient Irish people in National Parliament assembled, do, in the name of the Irish nation, ratify the establishment of the Irish Republic and pledge ourselves and our people to make this declaration effective by every means at our command.

As Assembly (Dáil) of pro-independence Irish MPs, in Declaration of Independence read at first meeting in Dublin after winning 73 of 105 Irish seats in general election. Mitchell and Ó Snodaigh, *Irish Political Documents 1916-1949*, Irish Academic Press, 1985, pp. 57-58.

January 21, 1919
Cathal Brugha
Deputies, you understand from what is asserted in this Declaration that we are now done with England. Let the world know it and those who are concerned bear it in mind.

As Sinn Féin member, at first meeting of Dáil. Macardle, Dorothy, *The Irish Republic*, Irish Press, 1951, p. 274.

January 21, 1919
Dan Breen
Our only regret was that the police escort had consisted of only two peelers instead of six. If there had to be dead peelers at all, six would have created a better impression than a mere two.

As IRA man, on the killing of two RIC men in ambush at Soloheadbeg which signalled start of War of Independence. Breen, Dan, *My Fight for Irish Freedom*, Anvil Press, 1981, p. 32.

January 23, 1919
Dr Michael Fogarty
The fight for Irish freedom has passed into the hands of the young men of Ireland...and when the young men of Ireland hit back at their

oppressors it is not for an old man like me to cry 'foul'.

As Bishop of Killaloe, in statement taken as approving armed action against British forces. Macardle, Dorothy, *The Irish Republic*, Irish Press, 1951, pp. 289-290.

February 3, 1919
Eamon de Valera
Study economics and read *The Prince*.

As President of Sinn Féin, giving advice on a political career to Richard Mulcahy, referring to Machiavelli. Coogan, Tim Pat, *De Valera*, Hutchinson, 1993, p. 118.

March 1919
Michael Collins
...the sooner fighting was forced and a general state of disorder created throughout the country the better it would be for the country.

As IRA Director of Organisation at Sinn Féin meeting, quoted by Darrell Figgis. Colum, Padraig, *Arthur Griffith*, Browne & Nolan, 1959, p. 193.

March 4, 1919
United States Congress
It is the earnest hope of the Congress of the United States of America that the Peace Conference now sitting in Paris and passing upon the rights of the various people will favourably consider the claims of Ireland to self-determination.

Resolution moved by Thomas Gallagher of Illinois and passed by House of Representatives by 261 to 41. Macardle, Dorothy, *The Irish Republic*, Irish Press, 1951, p. 280.

June 6, 1919
United States Senate
The Senate of the United States earnestly requests the American Peace Commission at Versailles to endeavour to secure for Eamon de Valera, Arthur Griffith and George Noble Count Plunkett, a hearing before the Peace Conference...and further the Senate of the United States expresses its sympathy with the aspirations of the Irish people for a government of their own choice.

Resolution passed with only one vote against. Macardle, Dorothy, *The Irish Republic*, Irish Press, 1951, pp. 296-297.

June 11, 1919
Woodrow Wilson
You have touched on the great metaphysical tragedy of today.

As US President, explaining to Irish delegation why he could not stand by his earlier support for liberation movements or for Irish place at post-war Paris Peace Conference. Coogan, Tim Pat, *De Valera*, Hutchinson, 1993, p. 143.

July 17, 1919
General Jan Smuts

The most pressing of all constitutional problems is the Irish question. It has become a chronic wound, the septic effects of which are spreading to our whole system.

As South Africa representative at Paris Peace Conference. Macardle, Dorothy, *The Irish Republic*, Irish Press, 1951, p. 299.

August 30, 1919
Woodrow Wilson

Ireland's case, from the point of view of interest it has excited in the world, and especially among our own people, whom I am anxious to serve, is the outstanding case of a small nationality. You do not know and cannot appreciate the anxieties I have experienced as the result of these many millions of peoples having their hopes raised by what I said.

As US President, telling Frank Walsh of American Friends of Irish Freedom that he regretted saying every nation had a right to self-determination, and he would not support giving a voice to Ireland at Paris Peace conference because of English opposition. Macardle, Dorothy, *The Irish Republic*, Irish Press, 1951, p. 297.

December 8, 1919
Herbert Samuel

If what is now going on in Ireland had been going on in the Austrian Empire, all England would be ringing with denunciation of the tyranny of the Hapsburghs and of denying people the right to rule themselves.

As former British Cabinet Minister. Macardle, Dorothy, *The Irish Republic*, Irish Press, 1951, p. 319.

December 22, 1919
David Lloyd George

...any attempt at secession will be fought, with the same determination, with the same resources, with the same resolve, as the Northern States of America put into the fight against the Southern States. It is important that this should be known not merely throughout the world, but in Ireland itself.

As British Prime Minister, in House of Commons. Mitchell and Ó Snodaigh, *Irish Political Documents 1916-1949*, Irish Academic Press, 1985, p. 68.

January 23, 1920
Field-Marshal Lord French

The principal cause of the trouble is that for five years emigration has practically stopped. In this country there are from one hundred thousand to two hundred thousand young men from eighteen to twenty-five years of age who in normal times would have emigrated.

As Lord Lieutenant of Ireland, in interview with *Le Journal* of Paris. Macardle, Dorothy, *The Irish Republic*, Irish Press, 1951, p. 333.

February 3, 1920
Walter Long

The people in the inner circle hold the view that the new province should consist of the Six Counties, the idea being that the inclusion of Donegal, Cavan and Monaghan would provide such an access of strength to the Roman Catholic party that the supremacy of the Unionists would be seriously threatened.

As First Lord of the Admiralty, in report to British Cabinet. Arthur, Paul, *Government and Politics of Northern Ireland*, Longman, 1980, p. 69.

February 6, 1920
Eamon de Valera

The United States by the Monroe Doctrine...safeguarded itself from the possible use of the island of Cuba as a base for an attack by a foreign power... Why doesn't Britain declare a Monroe doctrine for the two neighbouring islands? The people of Ireland so far from objecting would cooperate with their whole soul.

As President of Dáil Éireann, in interview in US. *Westminster Gazette*, February 6, 1920.

February 14, 1920
John Devoy

If the present movement should be metamorphosed into a demand for a free Ireland under an English Protectorate [rather than an independent Republic], there would be a sudden waning, if not complete collapse, of the present enthusiasm in America.

As Clan na nGael leader in US, responding to Eamon de Valera's proposal of Cuba-type association of Ireland with Britain. Mitchell and Ó Snodaigh, *Irish Political Documents 1916-1949*, Irish Academic Press, 1985, p. 69.

February 15, 1920
Dr Robert Browne

The [law and order] policy of the British Government seems to be to make use of every means and every opportunity to exasperate the people and drive them to acts of desperation.

As Bishop of Cloyne, in Lenten pastoral after widespread arrests throughout Ireland. Macardle, Dorothy, *The Irish Republic*, Irish Press, 1951, p. 330.

February 20, 1920
Eamon de Valera

The Friends of Irish Freedom Organisation is an association of American citizens, founded to assist the Irish people in securing the freedom the Irish people desire... I am convinced it is ready to cooperate to the full with [me as] the responsible head of the Republic...

As President of Dáil Éireann, in letter to Daniel Cohalan, head of Irish Freedom Organisation, insisting it take directions from de Valera. Coogan, Tim Pat, *De Valera*, Hutchinson, 1993, p. 162.

February 22, 1920
Daniel Cohalan

We have no law of *lese-majeste* here.

As head of Irish Freedom Organisation in US, rejecting as an American, Eamon de Valera's demand of February 20 that it take its lead from him. Coogan, Tim Pat, *De Valera*, Hutchinson, 1993, p. 163.

March 4, 1920
Erskine Childers

Lincoln...fought to abolish slavery, you fight to maintain it.

As member of Dáil, replying to claim by British Prime Minister, Lloyd George, on December 22, 1919, that Ireland was attempting to secede like southern states in US. Macardle, Dorothy, *The Irish Republic*, Irish Press, 1951, p. 322.

March 18, 1920
United States Senate

When self-government is attained by Ireland, a consummation it is hoped is at hand, it should promptly be admitted as a member of the League of Nations.

Resolution passed during debate on Treaty of Versailles. Macardle, Dorothy, *The Irish Republic*, Irish Press, 1951, pp. 366-367.

March 18, 1920
Edward Carson

The truth is that we came to the conclusion after many anxious hours and anxious days of going into the whole matter almost parish by parish and townland by townland that you would have no chance of successfully starting a parliament in Belfast which was to be responsible for the government of Donegal, Cavan and Monaghan...you would bring from these three counties into the Northern province an additional two hundred and sixty thousand Roman Catholics.

As Ulster Unionist leader, in House of Commons, on why Unionists demanded only six counties of Ulster. Macardle, Dorothy, *The Irish Republic*, Irish Press, 1951, pp. 339-339.

March 20, 1920
Cork Coroner's Jury

[Tomás Mac Curtáin] was wilfully murdered under circumstances of most callous brutality...the murder was organised and carried out by the Royal Constabulary, officially directed by the British Government.

As jury in inquest on Lord Mayor of Cork, assassinated by Crown forces, returning verdict of wilful murder against Lloyd George and others. Macardle, Dorothy, *The Irish Republic*, Irish Press, 1951, p. 334.

March 30, 1920
Terence MacSwiney

...it is not they who can inflict most, but they who can suffer most, will conquer.

As Lord Mayor of Cork in address on succeeding Tomás Mac Curtáin, assassinated by Crown forces on March 19. Sullivan, T. D., A. M. and D. B., *Speeches from the Dock*, Gill & Macmillan, 1968, p. 327.

June 6, 1920
Eamon de Valera

The [US] Republicans must promise to recognise the Irish Republic... All of Chicago wants this.

As President of Dáil Éireann, at Republican Convention in Chicago, which rejected demand. Coogan, Tim Pat, *De Valera*, Hutchinson, 1993, p. 179.

June 6, 1920
Dr Pat McCartan

There was no chance of offending America that we did not take.

As Sinn Féin member on Eamon de Valera's failure to influence Republic Convention in Chicago. Coogan, Tim Pat, *De Valera*, Hutchinson, 1993, p. 179.

June 17, 1920
Lt-Colonel Bruce Smyth

Now, men, Sinn Féin has had all the sport up to the present, and we are going to have the sport now...you may make mistakes occasionally, and innocent persons may be shot, but that cannot be helped, and you are bound to get the right parties sometime. The more you shoot, the better I will like you, and I assure you, no policeman will get into trouble for shooting any man.

As RIC Divisional Police Commander, Munster, addressing RIC men at Listowel. Macardle, Dorothy, *The Irish Republic*, Irish Press, 1951, p. 360.

June 17, 1920
RIC Officer

By your accent I take it you are an Englishman and in your ignorance forget that you are addressing Irishmen. These too [cap, belt and bayonet] are English. Take them as a present from me and to hell with you – you are a murderer.

As police officer, responding to invitation from Colonel Smyth to shoot whoever they liked, without fear of official retribution, in war against IRA. Macardle, Dorothy, *The Irish Republic*, Irish Press, 1951, pp. 361-362.

June 28, 1920
Henry Wilson
I really believe that we shall be kicked out [of Ireland].

As Chief of Imperial Staff at British War Office, in private note. Macardle, Dorothy, *The Irish Republic*, Irish Press, 1951, p. 377.

July 5, 1920
Lord Monteagle
The Sinn Féin courts are steadily extending their jurisdiction and dispensing justice even-handed between man and man, Catholic and Protestant, farmer and shopkeeper, grazer and cattle driver, landlord and tenant.

As landlord, on collapse of British judicial system. *The Irish Times*, July 5, 1920.

July 5, 1920
Hugh Martin
Ireland is taking pleasure in law and order for the first time within the memory of man.

As English correspondent, writing in *Daily News* on popularity of Sinn Féin courts. Macardle, Dorothy, *The Irish Republic*, Irish Press, 1951, p. 350.

August 1920
Michael Collins
England will give us neither as a gift. The same effort that would get us Dominion Home Rule will get us a Republic.

As IRA Director of Organisation, in interview with syndicated columnist Carl W. Ackerman. Coogan, Tim Pat, *Michael Collins*, Arrow Books, 1991, p. 192.

August 11, 1920
Henry Grattan Bellew
I hope my colleagues will follow my example so that the wrecking of Irish towns and the ruin of Irish industry [by Crown forces] may be proceeded with without any camouflage or appearance of approval by Irishmen of the sabotage of their country.

As Cork magistrate, announcing his resignation to Lord Chancellor. Macardle, Dorothy, *The Irish Republic*, Irish Press, 1951, p. 363.

August 13, 1920
Dr John Harty
It seems futile to demand justice from the British Government in Ireland... They speak of outrages attributed to Sinn Féin, but they do not call attention to the murder of a nation, or the depopulation of the country...or the protection afforded to the criminal [Edward Carson] who taught the grammar of anarchy.

As Archbishop of Cashel, in open letter to British authorities after killing in his diocese of James Mulcahy by military. Sullivan, T. D., A. M. and D. B., *Speeches from the Dock*, Gill & Macmillan, 1968, pp. 335-336.

August 17, 1920
Terence MacSwiney
I will put a limit to any term of imprisonment you may impose as a result of the action I will take. I have taken no food since Thursday, therefore...I shall be free, alive or dead, within a month.

As Lord Mayor of Cork before being sentenced for possession of secret code, and embarking on hunger strike from which he died. Sullivan, T. D., A. M. and D. B., *Speeches from the Dock*, Gill & Macmillan, 1968, pp. 331-332.

September 24, 1920
General Sir Nevil Macready
Punishment for such acts [reprisals] is a delicate matter, inasmuch as it might be interpreted as setting at naught the hoped-for effect of the training the officers had given their men.

As British Army commander, in interview with American correspondents after sacking by military of Balbriggan and other reprisals. Macardle, Dorothy, *The Irish Republic*, Irish Press, 1951, p. 389.

October 4, 1920
Herbert Asquith
Its only logical sequence is to take in hand the task of reconquering Ireland and holding her by force – a task which, though not perhaps beyond their powers, will never be sanctioned by the will or the conscience of the British people.

As former Liberal prime minister, in letter about reprisals in Ireland. *The Times*, October 4, 1920.

October 14, 1920
James Craig
Do I approve of the action you boys have taken in the past? I say yes.

As Ulster Unionist MP, speaking in Belfast shipyard after expulsion of Catholics. Farrell, Michael, *Northern Ireland: The Orange State*, Pluto, 1983, p. 34.

October 20, 1920
Hamar Greenwood
I cannot in my heart of hearts...condemn in the same way those policemen who lost their heads as I condemn the assassins who provoked this outrage.

As Chief Secretary of Ireland, in House of Commons, claiming he could not identify Crown forces who sacked Balbriggan and killed two inhabitants. *HC Debates:* Vol. 133: Col. 947.

October 20, 1920
Lord Curzon
It is not guerrilla warfare. It is the warfare of the red Indian, of the Apache. It is the warfare, which

nearly a hundred years ago the Government of India had to suppress, and which was known as 'Thuggee'...this is not rebellion by rising; this is not freedom by fighting; this is rebellion by murder.

As Foreign Secretary, in House of Lords, on IRA campaign in Ireland. Mitchell and Ó Snodaigh, *Irish Political Documents 1916-1949*, Irish Academic, 1985, p. 85.

October 25, 1920
Joe Devlin
The Chief Secretary is going to arm pogromists to murder the Catholics... Instead of paving stones and sticks, they are to be given rifles.

As Belfast nationalist MP, in House of Commons, in debate on setting up of Ulster Special Constabulary. Farrell, Michael, *Arming the Protestants*, Brandon, 1983, pp. 48-49.

October 29, 1920
Colonel Wilfrid Spender
The Government has definitely recognised that there are two distinct elements among the population – those who are loyal to the British Crown and Empire and those who are not... There is no reason why the UVF should not furnish all the numbers required.

As commander of Ulster Volunteer Force, urging members to join newly formed 'A', 'B'and 'C' Specials as reserves to Royal Ulster Constabulary. Mitchell and Ó Snodaigh, *Irish Political Documents 1916-1949*, Irish Academic Press, 1985, pp. 86-89.

November 1920
Eoin MacNeill
In prison we are their jailers;
On trial their judges,
Persecuted their punishers,
Dead their conquerors.

As founder of Irish Volunteers, on effect of executions and deaths from hunger strike. Coogan, Tim Pat, *Michael Collins*, Arrow Books, 1991, p. 156.

November 1, 1920
Kevin Barry
During the twisting of my arm, the first officer continued to question me as to the names and addresses of my companions, and also asked me for the name of the company commander and any other officer I knew... He informed me that if I gave all the information I knew I could get off.

As IRA Volunteer, in sworn statement before his execution for taking part in ambush in Dublin – read at later date to House of Commons by J. H. Thomas. *HC Debates:* Vol. 1341: Col. 708.

November 1, 1920
Anonymous
In Mountjoy Jail, one Monday morning,
High upon the gallows tree,
Kevin Barry gave his young life
For the cause of liberty...
Another martyr for old Ireland
Another murder for the Crown.

Ballad to commemorate execution of IRA Volunteer Kevin Barry. Loesberg, John, *Songs and Ballads of Ireland*, Ossian Publications, 1993, p. 36.

November 4, 1920
Hamar Greenwood
I have never associated the majority of the Irish people with this campaign of murder. I believe they loathe it... We have every information that they welcome the increasing energy of soldiers and the police in stamping out this campaign.

As Chief Secretary for Ireland, in House of Commons, in debate on reprisals by Crown forces in Ireland. *HC Debates:* Vol. 134: Col. 722.

November 9, 1920
David Lloyd George
We have murder by the throat...we struck the terrorists and now the terrorists are complaining of terror.

As British Prime Minister, at Guildhall banquet in London. Coogan, Tim Pat, *De Valera*, Hutchinson, 1993, p. 183.

November 11, 1920
David Lloyd George
Neither for the sake of Britain nor for the sake of Ireland can we contemplate anything which would set up in Ireland an independent sovereign state... We cannot consent to anything which will enable Ireland to organise an army and a navy of her own.

As British Prime Minister, in House of Commons. Mitchell and Ó Snodaigh, *Irish Political Documents 1916-1949*, Irish Academic Press, 1985, p. 89.

November 11, 1920
Joe Devlin
...they plead in the most tender way, almost with tears in their voice, for the acceptance of this Bill, that it may end religious rancour [but] my friends and myself, 340,000 Catholics...are to be left permanently and enduringly at the mercy of the Protestant Parliament in the North of Ireland.

As Belfast Nationalist MP, in House of Commons, opposing Government of Ireland Bill partitioning Ireland. *HC Debates:* Vol. 134: Col. 1447.

November 11, 1920
Edward Carson

I hope with all my heart that in the long run it will lead to unity and peace in Ireland, and that in the long run it will lead the Honourable Gentleman opposite and myself to see Ireland one and undivided, loyal to this country and loyal to the Empire.

As Ulster Unionist leader, in House of Commons, on Government of Ireland Bill partitioning Ireland, referring to Belfast MP Joe Devlin. *HC Debates:* Vol. 134: Col. 1442.

November 21, 1920
Michael Collins

I found out that those fellows [British agents] we put on the spot were going to put a lot of us on the spot, so I got in first.

As IRA Director of Organisation, explaining (after Truce) to General Crozier of British Army why IRA shot dead 14 British agents in Dublin on that date. Lyons, F. S. L., *Ireland Since the Famine*, Fontana, 1985, p. 419.

November 24, 1920
Hamar Greenwood

They are not always innocent institutions, allied with gaily caparisoned dairy maids, spreading beneficient light and humour in the neighbourhood. They are sometimes the headquarters of the assassins.

As Chief Secretary for Ireland, in House of Commons, on official reprisals against creameries. *HC Debates:* Vol.135: Cols. 499-500.

November 24, 1920
Joe Devlin

It was when [Edward Carson] made a speech in which he said 'I am not sorry for the armed drilling of those who are opposed to me in Ireland. I have certainly no right to complain of it. I started it myself...' There is the root of it. There is where treason started.

As Belfast Nationalist MP, in House of Commons, in debate on 'murders and reprisals' in Ireland. *HC Debates:* Vol. 135: Col. 534.

November 29, 1920
Tom Barry

Keep close to them should be our motto... There are no good or bad shots at ten yards' range.

As IRA leader in Cork, after leading ambush at Kilmichael, in which 17 Auxiliaries and three Volunteers were killed. Barry, Tom, *Guerilla Days in Ireland*, Irish Press, 1949, p. 47.

December 7, 1920
Michael Collins

Let us drop talking and get on with our work.

As IRA Director of Organisation, in phrase that became his hallmark, in article written by him for *Irish Independent*. Coogan, Tim Pat, *Michael Collins*, Arrow Books, 1991, p. 197.

December 12, 1920
Dr Daniel Cohalan

Anyone, be he a subject of this diocese or an extern, who within the diocese of Cork, shall organise or take part in ambushes or kidnappings, or shall otherwise be guilty of murder or attempted murder, shall incur by the very fact the censure of excommunication.

As Bishop of Cork, in anti-IRA decree. Coogan, Tim Pat, *Michael Collins*, Arrow Books, 1991, p. 201.

December 22, 1920
Eamon de Valera

Big Fellow! We'll see who's the Big Fellow!

As President of Dáil Éireann, on return from US and hearing praise of the 'Big Fellow' – Michael Collins. Coogan, Tim Pat, *Michael Collins*, Arrow Books, 1991, p. 204.

December 24, 1920
Eamon de Valera

You are going too fast. This odd shooting of a policeman here and there is having a bad effect, from the propaganda point of view, on us in America. What we want is one good battle about once a month with about 500 men on each side.

As President of Dáil Éireann, in comment to IRA Chief of Staff, Richard Mulcahy. Valiulis, Maryann, *De Valera and His Times*, Cork University Press, 1983, p. 94.

1921
George Bernard Shaw

You see things; and you say, 'Why?' But I dream things that never were, and I say, 'Why not?'

As playwright, in words spoken by character in 'Back to Methusalah', Part I, Act I.

1921
Konstantine Gamsakhurdia

Georgia is not as politically evolved as Ireland but Georgia will have its own Casements and MacSwineys until it gains full independence.

As nationalist leader of Soviet-occupied Georgia, in prophesy to Soviet leader Lenin which came about in 1989 when son Zviad Gamsakhurdia organised hunger strikes to win independence for Georgia in 1991. O'Clery, Conor, *Melting Snow, An Irishman in Moscow*, Appletree Press, 1991, p. 272.

January 1921
Dr Joseph Clune

When Mr Lloyd George, the Prime Minister, in my presence, spoke of them [IRA] as assassins, I corrected him saying, 'No sir, not assassins, but the cream of their race.'

As Archbishop of Perth, in conversation with Sean T. Kelly, Dáil representative in Paris. Coogan, Tim Pat, *Michael Collins*, Arrow Books, 1991, p. 200.

January 18, 1921
Michael Collins

The long whore won't get rid of me that easily.

As IRA Director of Organisation, on refusing request by Eamon de Valera to go to the US. Coogan, Tim Pat, *Michael Collins*, Arrow Books, 1991, p. 205.

March 1, 1921
Brigadier-General Hubert Gough

Law and order have given place to a bloody and brutal anarchy, in which the armed agents of the Crown violate every law in aimless and vindictive and insolent savagery. England has departed further from her own standards even of any nation in the world, not excepting the Turk and Zulu, than has ever been known in history before.

As British Army commander, and leader of Curragh mutiny in 1914, after Crown forces murdered three leading Limerick citizens. Macardle, Dorothy, *The Irish Republic*, Irish Press, 1951, p. 432.

March 30, 1921
Eamon de Valera

If they [the British] may use their tanks and steel-armoured cars, why should we hesitate to use stone walls and ditches? Why should the use of the element of surprise be denied to us?

As President of Dáil Éireann, taking responsibility for actions of IRA, and justifying use of ambush tactics. Macardle, Dorothy, *The Irish Republic*, Irish Press, 1951, pp. 437-438.

April 2, 1921
Michael Collins

When I saw you before I said that the same effort that would get us Dominion Home Rule would get us a Republic. I am still of that opinion... Compromises are difficult and settle nothing.

As IRA Director of Organisation, in interview with American reporter. Mitchell and Ó Snodaigh, *Irish Political Documents 1916-1949*, Irish Academic Press, 1985, pp. 102-103.

c. May 1, 1921
Herbert Asquith

Things are being done in Ireland which would disgrace the blackest annals of the lowest despotism in Europe.

As former British Prime Minister. Bardon, Jonathan, *A History of Ulster*, Blackstaff Press, 1992, p. 480.

May 4, 1921
David Lloyd George

I will meet Mr de Valera, or any of the Irish leaders, without condition on my part.

As British Prime Minister, in remark conveyed to Eamon de Valera on May 11 by American journalist. Macardle, Dorothy, *The Irish Republic*, Irish Press, 1951, p. 450.

May 4, 1921
Eamon de Valera

The blossoms are not the fruit but the precursors of the fruit – beware how you pluck them.

As President of Dáil Éireann, on British approaches for talks. Macardle, Dorothy, *The Irish Republic*, Irish Press, 1951, p. 933.

May 11, 1921
Henry Wilson

We are having more success than usual in killing rebels and now is the time to reinforce and not to parley.

As Chief of Imperial Staff, advising against negotiations with Sinn Féin. Macardle, Dorothy, *The Irish Republic*, Irish Press, 1951, p. 450.

May 22, 1921
Pope Benedict XV

Unflinching even in the shedding of blood in her devotion to the ancient Faith and in her reverence for the Holy See [Ireland] is subjected today to the indignity of devastation and slaughter...property and home are being ruthlessly and disgracefully laid waste...on both sides a war resulting in the deaths of unarmed people...is carried on. We exhort English as well as Irish to calmly consider...some means of mutual agreement.

As Pontiff, in statement on Irish question. Coogan, Tim Pat, *Michael Collins*, Arrow Books, 1991, pp. 203-204.

May 24, 1921
James Craig

The Union Jack must sweep the polls. Vote early, work late.

As Ulster Unionist leader, in first NI elections. Bardon, Jonathan, *A History of Ulster*, Blackstaff Press, 1992, p. 479.

June 22, 1921
King George V

I appeal to all Irishmen to pause, to stretch out the hand of forbearance and conciliation, to forgive and forget, and to join in making for the land which they love a new era of peace, contentment and goodwill.

As British monarch, opening Northern Ireland Parliament, in speech setting atmosphere for Anglo-Irish negotiations. Mitchell and Ó Snodaigh, *Irish Political Documents 1916-1949*, Irish Academic Press, 1985, p. 112.

June 22, 1921
David Lloyd George
The British Government are deeply anxious that, as far as they can assure it, the King's appeal for reconciliation in Ireland shall not have been made in vain. Rather than allow yet another opportunity of settlement in Ireland to be cast aside, they feel it incumbent on them to make a final appeal, in the spirit of the King's words, for a conference between themselves and the representatives of Southern and Northern Ireland.

As British Prime Minister, in letter to Eamon De Valera which led to truce on July 11 and initiated Anglo-Irish negotiations. Mitchell and Ó Snodaigh, *Irish Political Documents 1916-1949*, Irish Academic, 1985, p. 112.

June 26, 1921
Michael Collins
Once a truce is agreed and we come out in the open it is extermination for us if the truce should fail... We shall be like rabbits coming out from their holes.

As IRA Director of Organisation, in discussion with de Valera. Coogan, Tim Pat, *Michael Collins*, Arrow Books, 1991, p. 217.

June 28, 1921
Eamon de Valera
We most earnestly desire to help in bringing about a lasting peace between the peoples of these two islands, but see no avenue by which it can be reached if you deny Ireland's essential unity and set aside the principle of national self-determination.

As President of Dáil Éireann, in reply to invitation from Lloyd George to begin negotiations. Mitchell and Ó Snodaigh, *Irish Political Documents 1916-1949*, Irish Academic Press, 1985, p. 113.

c. July 1, 1921
Cardinal Michael Logue
If we are to judge by the public utterance of those into whose hands power is fallen, we have times of persecution before us.

As Archbishop of Armagh, on formation of NI Government. Keogh, Dermot, *Twentieth-Century Ireland*, Gill & Macmillan, 1994, p. 2.

July 5, 1921
Eamon de Valera
If the status of Dominion rule is offered, I shall use all our machinery to get the people to accept it.

As President of Dáil Éireann, to Prime Minister of South Africa, Jan Smuts, in Dublin. Coogan, Tim Pat, *De Valera*, Hutchinson, 1993, p. 228.

July 12, 1921
Orangeman
Ye never heard of the Twelfth? Away home, man, and read your bible.

As Ulster Protestant, in remark to foreigner, as recounted in diaries of Lady Spender. Buckland, Patrick, *The Factory of Grievances*, Gill & Macmillan, 1979, p. 185.

August 4, 1921
General Jan Smuts
I believe that...the force of community of interests will, over a period of years, prove so great and compelling that Ulster will herself decide to join the Irish State.

As unofficial South African mediator, in letter to Eamon de Valera. Macardle, Dorothy, *The Irish Republic*, Irish Press, 1951, p. 488.

August 10, 1921
Eamon de Valera
...we do not contemplate the use of force [to prevent partition]. If your Government stands aside we can effect a complete reconciliation.

As President of Dáil Éireann, in letter to Lloyd George. Moynihan, Maurice, *Speeches and Statements by Eamon de Valera, 1917-1973*, Gill & Macmillan, 1980, p. 52.

August 13, 1921
David Lloyd George
We are profoundly glad to have your agreement that Northern Ireland cannot be coerced.

As British Prime Minister, replying to Eamon de Valera, above. Macardle, Dorothy, *The Irish Republic*, Irish Press, 1951, p. 494.

August 19, 1921
David Lloyd George
The Government...are sincerely desirous that peace should ensue, that the mischievous, long misunderstandings...should be brought to an end. I hope that...Irish leaders will not reject the largest measure of freedom ever offered to their country.

As British Prime Minister, in House of Commons, on attempt to begin Anglo-Irish negotiations. *HC Debates:* Vol. 146: Col. 1877.

August 20, 1921
Michael Collins
Bring me into the spotlight of a London conference and quickly will be discovered the common clay of which I am made. The glamour of the legendary figure will be gone.

As IRA Director of Organisation, arguing with Eamon de Valera against going to London for Treaty negotiations. Coogan, Tim Pat, *Michael Collins*, Arrow Books, 1991, p. 227.

August 22, 1921
Eamon de Valera
Dáil Éireann had not the power and some of
them had not the inclination to use force with
Ulster... For his part, if the Republic were
recognised, he would be in favour of giving each
county power to vote itself out of the Republic if
it so wished.

As President of Dáil Éireann, speaking in Dáil during
private session. Quoted by Conor Cruise O'Brien in *The
Irish Times*, October 3, 1972.

August 26, 1921
Seán Mac Eóin
Eamon de Valera first met the English as a
soldier and beat them as a soldier. He has been
meeting them now as a statesman and he will
beat them as a statesman.

As commander of IRA in Longford, proposing Eamon de
Valera as President of Irish Republic at Dáil meeting in
Mansion House. Macardle, Dorothy, *The Irish Republic*,
Irish Press, 1951, p. 502.

August 30, 1921
Eamon de Valera
We have proposed the principle of government
by consent of the governed...on this basis we are
ready at once to appoint plenipotentiaries.

As President of Dáil Éireann, in reply to Lloyd George
proposal for negotiations. Macardle, Dorothy, *The Irish
Republic*, Irish Press, 1951, pp. 509-511.

September 4, 1921
Eoin O'Duffy
They would have to put on the screw – the
boycott. They would have to tighten that screw
and, if necessary, they would have to use the lead
against them [Unionists].

As Sinn Féin speaker, at Armagh rally after which he
became known among Unionists as 'Give-them-the-lead'
O'Duffy. Farrell, Michael, *Northern Ireland: The Orange
State*, Pluto, 1983, p. 43.

September 7, 1921
David Lloyd George
Her Majesty's Government [asks] whether you
are prepared to enter a conference to ascertain
how the association of Ireland with the
community of nations known as the British
Empire can best be reconciled with Irish national
aspirations.

As British Prime Minister, in reply to Eamon de Valera's
letter of August 30. Macardle, Dorothy, *The Irish
Republic*, Irish Press, 1951, pp. 512-513.

September 20, 1921
James Craig
We here are prepared to work in friendly rivalry
with our fellow countrymen in the South and
West... We are prepared to work for the
betterment of the people of Ireland, not to quarrel,
not to continue political strife.

As NI Prime Minister, on effects of Truce. Bardon,
Jonathan, *A History of Ulster*, Blackstaff Press, 1992, p. 482.

September 23, 1921
Winston Churchill
A lasting settlement with Ireland would not only
be a blessing in itself but with it would also be
removed the greatest obstacle which has ever
existed to Anglo-American unity and...far across
the Atlantic Ocean we should reap a harvest sown
in the Emerald Isle.

As Dominions Secretary, speaking in Dundee on how a
settlement would improve British-US relations. Macardle,
Dorothy, *The Irish Republic*, Irish Press, 1951, p. 522.

September 30, 1921
Eamon de Valera
We have received your letter of invitation to a
conference in London on October 11, 'with a view
to ascertaining how the association of Ireland with
the community of nations known as the British
Empire may best be reconciled with Irish national
aspirations'. We accept...

As President of Dáil Éireann, replying to Lloyd George.
Macardle, Dorothy, *The Irish Republic*, Irish Press, 1951,
p. 524.

October 7, 1921
Eamon de Valera
It is understood before decisions are finally
reached on the main question, that a despatch
notifying the intention to make these decisions will
be sent to members of the Cabinet in Dublin, and
that a reply will be awaited by the
plenipotentiaries before final decision is made.

As President of Dáil Éireann, in instructions given to
Griffith, Collins, Barton, Duggan, and Gavan Duffy before
travelling to London to negotiate Anglo-Irish Treaty.
Mitchell and Ó Snodaigh, *Irish Political Documents
1916-1949*, Irish Academic Press, 1985, p. 116.

October 19, 1921
Pope Benedict XV
We rejoice at the resumption of the Anglo-Irish
negotiations and pray to the Lord, with all our
heart, that He may bless them and grant to your
Majesty the great joy and imperishable glory of
bringing to an end the age-old dissension.

As Pontiff, in telegram to King George V. Macardle,
Dorothy, *The Irish Republic*, Irish Press, 1951, p. 535.

October 21, 1921
Arthur Griffith

The Truce does not mean that your military forces should prepare during the period of the Truce for the end of it and that we should not.

As Vice President of Sinn Féin, replying to British allegations of breaches of Truce in importing arms and drilling. Macardle, Dorothy, *The Irish Republic*, Irish Press, 1951, p. 540.

October 24, 1921
Eamon de Valera

There can be no question of our asking the Irish people to enter an arrangement which would make them subject to the British king. If war is the alternative, we can only face it.

As President of Dáil Éireann, in message to Treaty negotiators in London. Coogan, Tim Pat, *Michael Collins*, Arrow Books, 1991, p. 247.

October 31, 1921
Lt-Colonel Croft

I would remind him of the liquor legislation in Ireland, where preference has always been given; the land legislation for which this country poured out its millions for the peasants of Ireland; conscription, from which Ireland was exempt; the rationing of food which did not apply to Ireland, and when we were tightening our belts Ireland got fat... Far from being oppressed or downtrodden, Ireland seems to have been the spoilt darling of the Empire.

As MP, in House of Commons, on Anglo-Irish negotiations. *HC Debates:* Vol. 147: Cols. 1434-1435.

October 31, 1921
Lt-Colonel Sir Samuel Hoare

The Irish administration of the last twelve months has been deplorable...politics adopted one day and abandoned the next...a war that has not been a war, peace that has not been peace.

As MP, in House of Commons, on Anglo-Irish negotiations. *HC Debates:* Vol. 147: Cols. 1393-1394.

October 31, 1921
Colonel Gretton

If we have a British Government...submitting to negotiations with a gang of gunmen, what a vista is opened! A British Government brought to heel here may be brought to heel elsewhere than in Ireland by methods of this kind. They are beginning in India. We hear of something in Egypt.

As leader of Conservative Unionist Party, in House of Commons, criticising Anglo-Irish negotiations. *HC Debates:* Vol. 147: Col. 1378.

November 11, 1921
Arthur Griffith

You are my Chief, and if you tell me to go, I'll go. But I know, and you know, that I can't bring back a Republic.

As Vice President of Sinn Féin, on being asked by Eamon de Valera to join Irish delegation to Treaty negotiations. Coogan, Tim Pat, *De Valera*, Hutchinson, 1993, p. 249.

c. November 20, 1921
Winston Churchill

It was a good price, £5,000. Look at me: £25 dead or alive! How would you like that?

As Dominions Secretary, in conversation in his London home with Michael Collins for whose capture a £5,000 reward had been offered in Dublin, compared to £25 Boers had offered for Churchill in South Africa. Pelling, Henry, *Winston Churchill*, Pan Books,1977, p. 169.

November 29, 1921
James Craig

By Thursday next either the negotiations will have broken down or the Prime Minister will send me new proposals for consideration by the Cabinet. In the meantime the rights of Ulster will be in no way sacrificed or compromised.

As NI Prime Minister, speaking in Belfast. Macardle, Dorothy, *The Irish Republic*, Irish Press, 1951, p. 574.

c. December 1, 1921
Michael Collins

I stand for that!

As member of Irish Treaty delegation (and devotee of rural Ireland), on spotting a donkey and cart in a London street. Kiberd, Declan, *Inventing Ireland*, Jonathan Cape, 1995, p. 487.

December 5, 1921
David Lloyd George

I have to communicate with Sir James Craig tonight: here are the alternative letters I have prepared, one enclosing the Articles of Agreement reached by His Majesty's Government and yourselves, the other saying that the Sinn Féin representatives refuse the oath of allegiance and refuse to come within the Empire. If I send this [second] letter it is war – and war in three days! Which letter am I to send? ...we must know your answer by 10pm tonight. You can have until then but no longer to decide whether you will give peace or war to your country.

As British Prime Minister, addressing Irish delegation at end of Treaty negotiations in London. Owen, Frank, *Tempestuous Journey: Lloyd George, His Life and Times*, Hutchinson, 1954, p. 587.

December 5, 1921
Winston Churchill
Michael Collins rose looking as though he were going to shoot someone, preferably himself. In all my life I have never seen so much pain and suffering in restraint.

As Dominions Secretary, on reaction of Michael Collins to Lloyd George ultimatum, above. Coogan, Tim Pat, *Michael Collins*, Arrow Books, 1991, p. 274.

December 5, 1921
Arthur Griffith
I personally will sign this Agreement and recommend it to my countrymen.

As Vice President of Sinn Féin, responding, before final conference of Irish delegates, to Lloyd George request that Treaty be signed almost immediately. Owen, Frank, *Tempestuous Journey: Lloyd George, His Life and Times*, Hutchinson, 1954, p. 587.

December 6, 1921
Anglo-Irish Treaty
The oath to be taken by Members of the Parliament of the Irish Free State shall be in the following form:
I...do solemnly swear the faith and allegiance to the Constitution of the Irish Free State as by law established and that I will be faithful to H. M. King George V, his heirs and successors by law, in virtue of the common citizenship of Ireland with Great Britain and her adherence to and membership of the group of nations forming the British Commonwealth of Nations.

From Paragraph 4 of Articles of Agreement signed by British and Irish delegations. Macardle, Dorothy, *The Irish Republic*, Irish Press, 1951, p. 953.

December 6, 1921
Anglo-Irish Treaty
[A] Commission consisting of three persons, one to be appointed by the Government of the Irish Free State, one to be appointed by the Government of Northern Ireland, and one who shall be Chairman to be appointed by the British Government, shall determine in accordance with the wishes of the inhabitants, so far as may be compatible with economic and geographical conditions, the boundaries between Northern Ireland and the rest of Ireland.

From Paragraph 12 of Articles of Agreement signed by British and Irish delegations. Coogan, Tim Pat, *De Valera*, Hutchinson, 1993, p. 739.

December 6, 1921
Frederick Smith (Lord Birkenhead)
I have signed my political death warrant.

As British Cabinet member, after signing Treaty. *Eamon de Valera*, The Irish Times Ltd., 1976, p. 100.

December 6, 1921
Michael Collins
I may have signed my actual death warrant.

As member of Irish Treaty delegation, responding to Lord Birkenhead, above. Coogan, Tim Pat, *Michael Collins*, Arrow Books, 1991, p. 276.

December 6, 1921
James Craig
There's a verse in the Bible which says Czecho-Slovakia and Ulster are born to trouble as the sparks fly upward.

As NI Prime Minister, emerging from Downing Street after Irish delegation signed Treaty. Bardon, Jonathan, *A History of Ulster*, Blackstaff Press, 1992, p. 495.

December 6, 1921
Michael Collins
Think – what have I got for Ireland? Something which she has wanted these past seven hundred years. Will anyone be satisfied at the bargain? Will anyone? I tell you this – early this morning I signed my death warrant.

As member of Irish Treaty delegation, in letter written immediately after signing Treaty. Ó Broin, Leon, *Michael Collins*, Gill & Macmillan, 1980, p. 113.

December 8, 1921
Eamon de Valera
The terms of this agreement are in violent conflict with the wishes of the majority of this nation... I cannot recommend the acceptance of this Treaty... The greatest test of our people has come.

As President of Dáil Éireann, in statement to press after seeing text of Treaty. Coogan, Tim Pat, *Michael Collins*, Arrow Books, 1991, p. 296.

December 10, 1921
James Larkin
We pledge ourselves now and in the future, to destroy this plan of a nation's destruction. We propose carrying on the fight until we make the land of Erin a land fit for men and women – a Workers' Republic or death.

As trade union organiser, writing about the Treaty. Berresford Ellis, Peter, *A History of the Irish Working Class*, Pluto, 1985, p. 263.

December 14, 1921
Lord Edward Carson
What a fool I was! I was only a puppet, and so was Ulster, and so was Ireland, in the political game that was to get the Conservative Party into power... Ulster is not for sale. Her loyalty does not depend upon taxes.

As Ulster Unionist leader, in House of Lords, opposing Treaty. *HL Debates*: Vol. 48: Deb. 5: Cols. 44-50.

December 14, 1921
David Lloyd George

You do not settle great complicated problems the moment you utter a good phrase about them.

As British Prime Minister, in debate on Treaty, *HC Debates*: Vol. 149: Col. 31.

December 15, 1921
Winston Churchill

Whence does this mysterious power of Ireland come? It is a small, poor, sparsely populated island, lapped about by British sea power, accessible on every side, without iron or coal. How is it that she sways our councils, shakes our parties and infects us with her bitterness, convulses our passions and deranges our action. How is it that she has forced generation after generation to stop the whole traffic of the British Empire in order to debate her domestic affairs? Ireland is not a daughter race. She is a parent nation.

As Dominions Secretary, in House of Commons. *HC Debates:* Vol. 149: Col. 182.

December 15, 1921
R. S. Gwynn

What effect must this surrender, or Treaty, or whatever you like to call it, have on other parts of our Empire? It is a direct inducement to the rebels in India to go on and shoot more.

As MP, in House of Commons. *HC Debates:* Vol. 149: Cols. 165-166.

December 15, 1921
Colonel Gretton

We are inviting everybody throughout the world to come to the British Government with sufficient violence and persistence in outrage to insist on getting what they want, and we shall be told of another great act of statesmanship.

As MP, in House of Commons. *HC Debates:* Vol. 149: Col. 155.

December 15, 1921
Herbert Asquith

Are we or are we not prepared to welcome...this new compact between two peoples, giving as it does to Ireland complete local autonomy, and at the same time, what is equally important, preserving for Irishmen a full share of free citizenship throughout the British Empire?

As former British Prime Minister, in House of Commons. *HC Debates:* Vol. 149: Col. 138.

December 15, 1921
William Davison

Is not the bitterness of Ulster as the bitterness of gall?
You have:
Jeered at her loyalty
Trod on her pride,
Scorned her, repulsed her –
Great-hearted Ulster –
Flung her aside.
That is the feeling of Ulster today.

As pro-Union MP, in House of Commons. *The Irish Times*, November 26, 1985.

December 17, 1921
David Lloyd George

We cannot consent to any abandonment...of the principle of allegiance to the King.

As British Prime Minister, in telegram to Eamon de Valera turning down request for further Anglo-Irish conference. Macardle, Dorothy, *The Irish Republic*, Irish Press, 1951, p. 519.

December 17, 1921
Liam Mellowes

We who stand by the Republic still will I presume rebel against the new government that would be set up if this Treaty is passed.

As IRA leader and Dáil member, rejecting Treaty. Lee, J. J., *Ireland 1912-1985*, Cambridge University Press, 1990, p. 56.

December 19, 1921
Arthur Griffith

We have come back from London with that Treaty – Saorstát na hÉireann recognised – the Free State of Ireland. We have brought back the flag; we have brought back the evacuation of Ireland after 700 years by British troops and the formation of an Irish army. We have brought back to Ireland her full rights and powers of fiscal control. We have brought back to Ireland equality with England... If the Irish people say 'we have got everything else but the name Republic and we will fight for it' I would say to them that they are fools.

As signatory to Treaty, proposing that Dáil Éireann 'approves of the Treaty between Great Britain and Ireland, signed in London on December 6, 1921.' *DÉ Debates, pp. 21-23.*

December 19, 1921
Seán Mac Eóin

To me this Treaty gives me what I and my comrades fought for; it gives us for the first time in 700 years the evacuation of Britain's armed forces out of Ireland.

As IRA leader and Dáil member, seconding the motion that Dáil Éireann approve the Treaty. *DÉ Debates*, p. 23.

December 19, 1921
Eamon de Valera
We were elected by the Irish people, and did the Irish people think we were liars when we said that we meant to uphold the Republic... I am against this Treaty because it does not reconcile Irish national aspirations with association with the British Government.
As President of Dáil Éireann, opposing the motion that Dáil Éireann approve the Treaty. *DÉ Debates*, p. 24.

December 19, 1921
Austin Stack
Has any man here the hardihood to stand up and say that it was for this our fathers suffered, that it was for this our comrades have died in the field and in the barrack yard?
As member of Republic 'Cabinet' for Home Affairs, in Dáil. *DÉ Debates*, p. 28.

December 19, 1921
Michael Collins
In my opinion it gives us freedom, not the ultimate freedom that all nations desire and develop to, but the freedom to achieve it.
As signatory to Treaty, in Dáil. Coogan, Tim Pat, *Michael Collins*, Arrow Books, 1991, p. 301.

December 19, 1921
Erskine Childers
Irish Ministers will be King's Ministers; the Irish Provisional Government that under this Treaty is going to be set up, within a month would be the King's Provisional Government. Every executive Act in Ireland, every administrative function in Ireland would be performed – you cannot get away from it – in the name of the King.
As secretary to Treaty delegation, in Dáil. *DÉ Debates*, p. 40.

December 19, 1921
Kevin O'Higgins
We sent these men to London, trusting them, and they have brought back a document which they believe represents the utmost that can be got for the country, short of the resumption of war against fearful odds...you are not entitled to reject it without being able to show them you have a reasonable prospect of achieving more...
As Minister of Republic, in Dáil debate. *DÉ Debates*, pp. 42-45.

December 19, 1921
Sean MacSwiney
I have sworn an oath to the Republic, and for that reason I could not vote for the Treaty.
As Sinn Féin deputy, in Dáil. *DÉ Debates*, p. 49.

December 19, 1921
Robert Barton
The English Prime Minister with all the solemnity and the power of conviction that he alone, of all men I met, can impart by word and gesture...declared that the signature and recommendation of every member of our delegation was necessary, or war would follow immediately.
As signatory to Treaty, in Dáil. *DÉ Debates*, p. 49.

December 20, 1921
Sean Etchingham
I say to you, finally, if you do vote for this thing...it will be a renunciation of your principles... Nay, it is more, it is the burial service over the grave of the Irish nation, and there is to be no firing party.
As Minister of Republic, in Dáil debate. *DÉ Debates*, p. 57.

December 20, 1921
Finian Lynch
The bones of the dead have been rattled indecently in the face of this assembly... I stand for this Treaty...if this Treaty is rejected...you are going to bring the people back to war, and make no mistake about it.
As Sinn Féin deputy, in Dáil. *DÉ Debates*, pp. 57-59.

December 20, 1921
Sean T. O'Kelly
The two great principles for which so many have died, and for which they would still gladly die – no partition of Ireland and no subjugation of Ireland to any foreign power – have gone by the board in this Treaty.
As Sinn Féin deputy, in Dáil. *DÉ Debates*, p. 65.

December 20, 1921
Sean Milroy
Reject this Treaty, you bring confusion and chaos throughout the whole of Ireland, and the sign to the bigots in Ulster to start with renewed vigour pogroms on the helpless minority.
As Sinn Féin deputy, in Dáil. *DÉ Debates*, p. 74.

December 20, 1921
Dr Patrick McCartan
It would take five years' fighting at the very least on the part of the Irish Republican Army, with all their gallantry, to get back to the position we were in two or three months ago. Therefore, I submit, as a political factor the Republic is dead... We are presented with a *fait accompli* and asked to endorse it. I as a republican will not endorse it, but will not vote for chaos.

As Sinn Féin representative in Washington, in Dáil. *DÉ Debates*, p. 81.

December 21, 1921
Sean Hayes
If we owe a duty to the dead, we also owe a duty to the living, and I, for one, cannot see how I could cast a vote that would expose the Irish people to the risk of war.

As Sinn Féin deputy, in Dáil. *DÉ Debates*, p. 82.

December 21, 1921
George Gavan Duffy
The complaint is...that the alternative to our signing that particular Treaty was immediate war; that we who were sent to London as the apostles of peace...were suddenly to be transformed into the unqualified arbiters of war; that we had to make this choice within three hours... And that monstrous iniquity was perpetrated by the man [Lloyd George] who had invited us under his roof in order, moryah, to make a friendly settlement.

As signatory to Treaty, in Dáil. *DÉ Debates*, pp. 85-87.

December 21, 1921
David Ceannt
There will be shadows haunting the men of this assembly who will try to filch away the nation's rights.

As Sinn Féin member, in Dáil. *DÉ Debates*, p. 95.

December 21, 1921
William T. Cosgrave
This instrument [the Treaty] gives us an opportunity of capturing the northern unionists and that is the proposition worthy of our best consideration... They are great citizens of this nation, even though they differ from us.

As Minister of Republic, in Dáil. *DÉ Debates*, pp. 106-107.

December 21, 1921
Mary MacSwiney
...to many of the young men of this Dáil, 'what is good enough for Michael Collins is good enough for me'. If Mick Collins went to hell in the morning would you follow him there?

As one of five women Sinn Féin deputies, all five of whom opposed Treaty, in Dáil. *DÉ Debates*, pp. 109-114.

December 21, 1921
Richard Mulcahy
We are told that the alternative to the acceptance of the Treaty is war...we have not been able to drive the enemy from anything but a fairly good-sized police barracks.

As Chief of Staff of the IRA, in Dáil. *DÉ Debates*, pp. 142-143.

December 21, 1921
Sean Moylan
If there is a war of extermination waged on us...I may not see it finished, but by God, no loyalist in North Cork will see its finish, and it is about time somebody told Lloyd George that.

As Sinn Féin deputy, in Dáil. *DÉ Debates*, p. 146.

December 21, 1921
Sean MacEntee
...the provisions of this Treaty mean this: that in the North of Ireland, certain people differing from us somewhat in tradition, and differing in religion...are going to be driven, in order to maintain their separate identity, to demarcate themselves from us, while we, in order to preserve ourselves against the encroachment of English culture, are going to be driven to demarcate ourselves as far as ever we can from them.

As Sinn Féin deputy, in Dáil. *DÉ Debates*, pp. 152-156.

December 21, 1921
Fermanagh County Council
We...do not recognise the partition parliament in Belfast and do hereby direct our secretary to hold no further communications with either Belfast or British local government departments, and we pledge our allegiance to Dáil Éireann.

As pro-nationalist councillors, in motion passed on day local government powers were transferred from London to Belfast. The council was dissolved. Farrell, Michael, *Northern Ireland: The Orange State*, Pluto, 1983, p. 82.

December 25, 1921
Dr Michael Fogarty
Let the people have no mistake about it; the rejection of this Treaty must lead inevitably to war of such a destructive character as would lay Ireland out dead in a very short time.

As Bishop of Killaloe, in Ennis cathedral. Macardle, Dorothy, *The Irish Republic*, Irish Press, 1951, p. 624.

December 27, 1921
George Bernard Shaw
Any practical statesman will, under duress, swallow a dozen oaths to get his hand on the driving wheel.

As playwright, on Treaty. *Manchester Guardian*, December 27, 1921.

December 29, 1921
Sean Hales
I agree with Mick [Michael Collins]. He says the British broke the Treaty of Limerick, and we'll

break this Treaty too when it suits us, when we have our own army.

As IRA leader from Cork, on why he supported the Treaty. Coogan, Tim Pat, *Michael Collins*, Arrow Books, 1991, p. 339.

c. *December 31, 1921*
Mahatma Gandhi

...it is not the blood that the Irishmen have taken which has given them what appears to be their liberty. But it is the gallons of blood they have willingly given themselves... It is the magnitude of the Irish sacrifice which has been the deciding factor.

As pacifist Indian leader, on Treaty. Kiberd, Declan, *Inventing Ireland*, Jonathan Cape, 1995, p. 259.

c. *January 1, 1922*
David Lloyd George

Arguing with de Valera [is] like trying to catch a man on a merry-go-round, or picking up mercury with a fork.

As British Prime Minister, in conversation. McMahon, Deirdre, *Republicans and Imperialists: Anglo-Irish Relations in the 1930s*, Yale University Press, 1984, p. 30.

c. *January 1, 1922*
Eamon de Valera

Why doesn't he try a spoon?

As President of Dáil Éireann, on hearing of Lloyd George's comment, above. *The Irish Times*, April 10, 1998.

c. *January 1, 1922*
Michael Collins

No one is going to shoot me in my own country.

As signatory to Treaty. Lee, J. J., *Ireland 1912-1985*, Cambridge University Press, 1990, p. 56.

c. *January 1, 1922*
Winston Churchill

The Irish have a genius for conspiracy rather than government.

As Dominions Secretary. Lee, J. J., *Ireland 1912-1985*, Cambridge University Press, 1990, p. 91.

January 3, 1922
Piaras Béaslaí

Think of the evacuation of Ireland by foreign troops. Why, it seems like a fairy vision. All the old Gaelic poets sang of the going of the foreign hosts out of Ireland as an unreal dream of far off happiness. They did not sing of a Republic.

As Sinn Féin deputy, in resumed Dáil debate on Treaty. *DÉ Debates*, p. 178.

January 3, 1922
Countess Markievicz

These anti-Irish Irishmen [Southern Unionists] are to be given some select way of entering this House, some select privileges – privileges that they have earned by their cruelty to the Irish people and the working classes of Ireland... That is one of the biggest blots on this Treaty...

As Minister of Republic, in Dáil, on prospect of appointed Senate. *DÉ Debates*, pp. 181-182.

January 3, 1922
Ernest Blythe

I also believe that they [Ulster Unionists] might be coerced [into a united Ireland], and I would stand for it, that we have the right to coerce them, if we thought fit, and if we have the power to do so.

As Vice President of Sinn Féin, in Dáil. *DÉ Debates*, p. 194.

January 4, 1922
Alec McCabe

I am prepared to take the Treaty for what it is worth, and as a stepping stone to getting more.

As Sinn Féin deputy, in Dáil. *DÉ Debates*, p. 215.

January 4, 1922
Margaret Pearse

It has been said here on several occasions that Padraic Pearse would have accepted the Treaty... Padraic Pearse would not have accepted a Treaty like this with only two-thirds of his country in it.

As mother of Padraic Pearse, and Sinn Féin deputy, in Dáil. *DÉ Debates*, pp. 221-223.

January 4, 1922
Eamon de Valera

One of the reasons why I did not go to London was that I wanted to keep that symbol of the Republic [its President] pure – even from insinuation – lest any word across the table from me would, in any sense, give away the Republic.

As President of Dáil Éireann, in Dáil. *DÉ Debates*, p. 258.

January 4, 1922
Eoin O'Duffy

Let us consider for a moment what will happen our unfortunate people in the north-east if this Treaty is rejected. My opinion is that there will be callous, cold-blooded murder there again.

As IRA leader in Ulster, in Dáil. *DÉ Debates*, p. 225.

January 4, 1922
Liam Mellowes

We would rather have this country poor and indignant, we would rather have the people of Ireland eking out a poor existence on the soil; as long as they possessed their souls, their minds and their honour. This fight has been for something more than the fleshpots of Empire.

As IRA Director of Purchases, in Dáil. *DÉ Debates*, p. 231.

January 6, 1922
Eamon de Valera

I was reared in a labourer's cottage here in Ireland...and whenever I wanted to know what the Irish people wanted, I had only to examine my own heart and it told me straight off what the Irish people wanted.

As President of Dáil Éireann, offering to resign after emergence of divisions in Irish Cabinet over Treaty. *DÉ Debates*, p. 274.

January 6, 1922
Seamus Robinson

[Is there] any authoritative record of his having ever fired a shot for Ireland at an enemy of Ireland?

As Sinn Féin deputy, in Dáil, on Michael Collins. Coogan, Tim Pat, *Michael Collins*, Arrow Books, 1991, p. 305.

January 7, 1922
Harry Boland

I respectfully suggest that this conference was called because England found it impossible to carry on her work in Ireland and to preserve and carry on her Empire; and having failed to force British sovereignty on the Irish nation for 750 years, she has done it now by diplomacy.

As Secretary to de Valera, in Dáil. *DÉ Debates*, p. 302.

January 7, 1922
Cathal Brugha

If...our last cartridge has been fired, our last shilling had been spent, and our last man were lying on the ground and his enemies howling round him and their bayonets raised, ready to plunge them into his body, that man should say – true to the traditions handed down – if they said to him 'Now, will you come into our Empire?' he should say, and he would say 'No! I will not.

As Minister of Republic, in Dáil. *DÉ Debates*, p. 330.

January 7, 1922
Arthur Griffith

We went there to London, not as Republican doctrinaires, but looking for the substance of freedom and independence... I say now to the people of Ireland that it is their right to see that this Treaty is carried into operation, when they get, for the first time in seven centuries, a chance to live their lives in their own country and take their place among the nations of Europe.

As signatory to Treaty, summing up debate on Treaty, which was approved by the Dáil by 64-57 votes. *DÉ Debates*, pp. 340-344.

January 7, 1922
Michael Collins

...when countries change from peace to war, or war to peace, there are always elements that make for disorder and that make for chaos...if we could form some kind of joint committee to carry on... I think that is what we ought to do.

As signatory to Treaty, after its approval by Dáil. *DÉ Debates*, p. 346.

January 7, 1922
Eamon de Valera

We have had a glorious record for four years; it has been four years of magnificent discipline in our nation. The world is looking to us now.

As President of Dáil Éireann, before breaking down in tears after Dáil approved Treaty. *DÉ Debates*, p. 347.

January 7, 1922
Mary MacSwiney

This is a betrayal and a gross betrayal...that majority is not united; half of them are looking for a gun and the other half are looking for the fleshpots of the Empire.

As Sinn Féin deputy, after Dáil approved Treaty. Coogan, Tim Pat, *Michael Collins*, Arrow Books, 1991, p. 307.

January 10, 1922
Michael Collins

Every Irishman here who has lived amongst them knows very well that the plain people of England are much more objectionable towards us than the upper classes...they are always making jokes about Paddy and the pig and that sort of thing.

As signatory to Treaty, in Dáil. *DÉ Debates*, p. 394.

January 10, 1922
Arthur Griffith

I will not reply to any damned Englishman in this Assembly.

As newly elected President of Dáil Éireann, responding to a question from Erskine Childers, who was born in England. *DÉ Debates*, p. 416.

January 10, 1922
Richard Mulcahy

If any assurance is required – the Army [IRA] will remain the Army of the Irish Republic.

As Chief of Staff of the IRA, after Arthur Griffith elected President of Dáil Éireann. *DÉ Debates*, p. 424.

January 16, 1922
Michael Collins

We've been waiting 700 years, you can have the seven minutes.

As Chairman of Provisional Government, on being told by Viceroy he was seven minutes late in arriving to take over Dublin Castle. (Anecdotal.) Coogan, Tim Pat, *Michael Collins*, Arrow, 1991, p. 310.

January 16, 1922
Michael Collins

How could I ever have expected to see Dublin Castle itself – that dread Bastille of Ireland – formally surrendered into my hands by the lord lieutenant in the brocade-hung council chamber, on my producing a copy of the London Treaty?

As Chairman of Provisional Government. Fanning, Ronan, *Independent Ireland*, Helicon, 1983, p. 1.

January 25, 1922
James Craig

I will never give in to any rearrangement of the boundary that leaves our Ulster area less than it is under the Government of Ireland Act [comprising total area of six counties].

As NI Prime Minister, speaking in Belfast. Macardle, Dorothy, *The Irish Republic*, Irish Press, 1951, p. 658.

c. February 1, 1922
Patrick Hogan

One more cow, one more sow, and one more acre under the plough.

As Minister for Agriculture, in slogan to promote farming growth. Lee, J. J., *Ireland 1912-1985*, Cambridge University Press, 1990, p. 302.

February 1, 1922
Irish Vigilance Association

Immoral stories, immoral situations, nude figures, indecently dressed figures – in a word everything contrary to Christian purity and modesty – should be banned mercilessly. All films and performances which are used for propaganda purposes alien to Irish and Catholic ideals must be turned down, also...pictures and performances that assume the lawfulness of divorce.

As pressure group, in proposals endorsed by Irish Catholic Directory. Fanning, Ronan, *Independent Ireland*, Helicon, 1983, p. 57.

February 1, 1922
Michael Collins

Our claim [under the Boundary Commission] is clear; majorities must rule; in any map marked on that principle...we secure immense anti-Partition areas [from Northern Ireland's six counties].

As Chairman of Provisional Government. Macardle, Dorothy, *The Irish Republic*, Irish Press, 1951, p. 660.

February 2, 1922
James Joyce

–History, Stephen said, is a nightmare from which I am trying to awake.

As author, in words of character in *Ulysses*. Joyce, James, *Ulysses*, Oxford World Classics, 1998, p. 34

February 15, 1922
Winston Churchill

If the Irish people accept his [Arthur Griffith's] advice and guidance and ratify the Treaty...he will be able to disestablish the Irish Republic...is it not a desirable thing that upon the authority of the Irish people recorded at an election, the Republican idea should be definitely, finally and completely put aside?

As Dominions Secretary, in House of Commons. Macardle, Dorothy, *The Irish Republic*, Irish Press, 1951, pp. 662-663.

February 16, 1922
Winston Churchill

Then came the Great War. Every institution, almost, in the world was strained. Great empires had been overturned. The whole map of Europe has been changed. The position of countries has been violently altered. The modes of thought of men, the whole outlook on affairs, the grouping of parties, all have encountered violent and tremendous change in the deluge of the world, but as the deluge subsides and the waters fall short we see the dreary steeples of Fermanagh and Tyrone emerging once again. The integrity of their quarrel is one of the few institutions that has been unaltered in the cataclysm which has swept the world.

As Dominions Secretary, in House of Commons, in debate on Irish Free State Bill. *HC Debates:* Vol. 150: Col. 1270.

February 16, 1922
Winston Churchill

Let us assume that the [Boundary] Commission...were to reduce Ulster to its preponderatingly Orange areas...would not that be a fatal and permanent obstacle to the unity and cooperation of Ireland?

As Dominions Secretary, in House of Commons. Macardle, Dorothy, *The Irish Republic*, Irish Press, 1951, p. 663.

March 3, 1922
Frederick Smith (Lord Birkenhead)

Northern Ireland...is regarded as a creature already constituted, having its own Parliament and its own defined boundaries... I have no doubt that the tribunal, not being presided over by a lunatic, will take a rational view of the limits of its own jurisdiction and will reach a rational conclusion.

As member of British Cabinet, in letter to Conservative leader, Lord Balfour, on work of Boundary Commission. Macardle, Dorothy, *The Irish Republic*, Irish Press, 1951, p. 685.

March 7, 1922
Winston Churchill

It is up to the Provisional Government not to allow themselves to be defied in public by lawless persons... I am supplying to them means to assert their authority.

As Dominions Secretary, in House of Commons, on arms supplies to Provisional Government after attacks on former RIC members in Tipperary. *The Irish Times*, March 8, 1922.

March 14, 1922
James Craig

Come and see for yourselves. Come and ask the loyalists to go out of the Empire into the Free State... When the Free Staters had got all they possibly could from the British Government, the republicans would say: 'Thank you very much, and now we will take charge of the machine.'

As NI Prime Minister, addressing British critics of partition, at opening of NI Parliament in Belfast. *The Irish Times*, March 14, 1922.

March 16, 1922
Eamon de Valera

It was only by civil war after this that they [Republicans] could get their independence.

As President of Sinn Féin, speaking at Dungarvan. Moynihan, Maurice, *Speeches and Statements by Eamon de Valera 1917-1973*, Gill & Macmillan, 1980, p. 98.

March 16, 1922
Frederick Smith (Lord Birkenhead)

If someone had presented Queen Elizabeth with this alternative: 'Would you rather send Lord Essex and British troops to put down the turbulent population of the South of Ireland, or would you rather deal with a man who is prepared, with Irish troops, to do it for you...would [she] have hesitated?'

As member of British Government, in House of Lords, on role of Michael Collins. Macardle, Dorothy, *The Irish Republic*, Irish Press, 1951, p. 688.

March 17, 1922
Eamon de Valera

If they accepted the Treaty, and if the Volunteers of the future tried to complete the work the Volunteers of the last four years had been attempting, they would have to complete it, not over the bodies of foreign soldiers, but over the dead bodies of their countrymen. They would have to wade through, perhaps, the blood of some of the members of the Irish government in order to get Irish freedom.

As President of Sinn Féin, speaking at Thurles. *Irish Independent*, March 18, 1922.

March 22, 1922
J. W. Dulanty

The people...regard it as an intolerable burden, a relic of mediaevalism, a test imposed from outside under threat of immediate and terrible war.

As Irish High Commissioner in London, in note to British Government on oath of allegiance in Treaty. Mitchell and Ó Snodaigh, *Irish Political Documents 1916-1949*, Irish Academic Press, 1985, p. 195.

March 24, 1922
John MacMahon

When we got down they lined us up in the room below, my father, my four brothers, Edward McKinney and myself, against the wall. The leader said: 'You boys say your prayers!'

As survivor of Belfast Catholic family of publicans, killed by murder gang led by police. Coogan, Tim Pat, *Michael Collins*, Arrow Books, 1991, p. 352.

March 25, 1922
Joe Devlin

If Catholics have no revolvers to protect themselves they are murdered. If they have revolvers they are flogged and sentenced to death.

As Belfast Nationalist MP, in House of Commons, after murder of MacMahon family in Belfast on March 23 by men in uniform. Macardle, Dorothy, *The Irish Republic*, Irish Press, 1951, p. 683.

March 29, 1922
James Craig

No stone should be left unturned to try to stop the murdering that is going on in Ireland.

As NI Prime Minister, on eve of meeting Michael Collins. *The Irish Times*, April 2, 1994.

March 30, 1922
Michael Collins and James Craig

Peace is today declared. From today the two Governments undertake to cooperate in every way in their power with a view to the restoration of peaceful conditions in the unsettled areas.

As leaders of two parts of Ireland, in (short-lived) peace agreement signed in London. Mitchell and Ó Snodaigh, *Irish Political Documents 1916-1949*, Irish Academic Press, 1985, pp. 130-131.

April 3, 1922
Michael Collins

I am in sympathy with the majority of the IRA... The 'big' businessmen and the politicians will come forward when peace is established and perhaps after some years gain control. Their methods will never demand a renewal of war.

As Chairman of Provisional Government, in note to friend. Fanning, Ronan, *Independent Ireland*, Helicon, 1983, p. 13.

April 5, 1922
David Lloyd George
A point might come when it would be necessary to tell Mr Collins that if he was unable to deal with the situation the British Government would have to do so.

As British Prime Minister, in Cabinet, on republican opposition to Provisional Government. Younger, Calton, *Ireland's Civil War*, Fontana, 1979, p. 265.

April 8, 1922
Winston Churchill
It is possible that things will get worse before they get better. It is possible that Irishmen will kill and murder each other, and destroy Irish property and cripple Irish prosperity.

As Dominions Secretary, speaking at Dundee. Macardle, Dorothy, *The Irish Republic*, Irish Press, 1951, p. 702.

April 9, 1922
Michael Collins
If the so-called government in Belfast has not the power nor the will to protect its citizens, the Irish Government must find means to protect them.

As Chairman of Provisional Government, responding in Wexford speech to murders of Catholics in Northern Ireland. Coogan, Tim Pat, *Michael Collins*, Arrow Books, 1991, p. 341.

April 11, 1922
Arthur Griffith
[We are] unable to protect our people in Belfast... These people are being murdered. We can always make reprisals, you can burn [unionist] property. That does not save the lives of the people.

As President of Dáil at meeting with northern nationalists. Fanning, Ronan, *Independent Ireland*, Helicon, 1983, p. 31.

April 11, 1922
Michael Hayes
Can nationalists in the North recognise a Northern government temporarily in certain matters? [If not] then the position is clear. It means great financial liability on our side.

As Chairman of the Dáil, at meeting with northern nationalists, at which it was decided Dáil should continue temporarily to pay teachers' salaries in Northern Ireland. Fanning, Ronan, *Independent Ireland*, Helicon, 1983, p. 27.

April 11, 1922
Seamus Woods
When we were fighting in the war [of independence] the men had the hope that even if they were sentenced to 15 years they had a chance of getting out soon. The men arrested now are sentenced to 15 years and there is very little hope of their getting out inside of 15 years... Some of them say they are ready to fight but I know them and there was not one of them ready to fight.

As northern IRA commander at meeting with Dáil, on demoralisation of Belfast IRA. Fanning, Ronan, *Independent Ireland*, Helicon, 1983, p. 30.

April 13, 1922
Rory O'Connor
I am safe in saying that if the [Republican] Army were ever to follow a political leader, Mr de Valera is the man.

As head of anti-Treaty IRA, after its occupation of Four Courts, Dublin. *The Irish Republic*, Irish Press, 1951, p. 695.

April 16, 1922
Eamon de Valera
Young men and young women of Ireland, the goal is at last in sight. Steady all together; forward, Ireland is yours for the taking. Take it.

As President of Sinn Féin, in proclamation after seizure of Four Courts by anti-Treaty IRA. Coogan, Tim Pat, *Michael Collins*, Arrow Books, 1991, p. 320.

April 26, 1922
Catholic Hierarchy
The best and wisest course for Ireland is to accept the Treaty and make the most of the freedom it undoubtedly brings us...the young men connected with this military revolt...when they shoot their brothers on the opposite side they are murderers.

As Irish Bishops, in statement opposing anti-Treaty IRA. Younger, Calton, *Ireland's Civil War*, Fontana, 1979, pp. 277-278.

April 29, 1922
Michael Collins
I suppose we are two of the Ministers whose blood is to be waded through?

As Chairman of Provisional Government (referring to Eamon de Valera's March 17 speech in Thurles) arriving with Arthur Griffith for meeting with Eamon de Valera and Cathal Brugha – who replied 'Yes'. Coogan, Tim Pat, *De Valera*, Hutchinson, 1993, p. 315.

May 20, 1922
Michael Collins and Eamon de Valera
We are agreed... That a National Coalition panel for this Third Dáil, representing both parties in the Dáil and in the Sinn Féin Organisation, be sent forward, on the ground that the national position

requires the entrusting of the Government of the country into the joint hands of those who have been the strength of the national situation during the last few years, without prejudice to their present respective positions.

As Chairman of Provisional Government and President of Sinn Féin, in agreement that election to new Dáil should not be fought on Treaty. Macardle, Dorothy, *The Irish Republic*, Irish Press, 1951, p. 712.

May 25, 1922
Henry Wilson
The surrender of the Provisional Government to de Valera [in agreeing to election pact, is] one of the most pitiful, miserable and cowardly stories in history...the Union must be re-established.

As military adviser to NI Government, speaking in Liverpool. Macardle, Dorothy, *The Irish Republic*, Irish Press, 1951, p. 714.

June 1, 1922
Lionel Curtis
[Negotiating with Collins is like] trying to write on water.

As British civil servant, on talks involving Michael Collins in London. Coogan, Tim Pat, *Michael Collins*, Arrow Books, 1991, p. 327.

June 1, 1922
Winston Churchill
We must act like a sledgehammer so to cause bewilderment and consternation among the people in southern Ireland.

As Dominions Secretary, to Committee of Imperial Defence, on anti-IRA measures along Border, including sending troops to Beleek-Pettigo triangle. Coogan, Tim Pat, *Michael Collins*, Arrow Books, 1991, p. 368.

June 2, 1922
Winston Churchill
The more the fear of renewed warfare is present in the minds of the electors, the more likely are they to get to the polls and support the Treaty.

As Dominions Secretary, in Cabinet. Younger, Calton, *Ireland's Civil War*, Fontana, 1979, p. 305.

June 14, 1922
Michael Collins
I am not hampered now by being on a platform where there are coalitionists, and I can make a straight appeal to you to vote for the candidates you think best of.

As Chairman of Provisional Government, in Cork speech regarded as derogation from election pact with Eamon de Valera. Younger, Calton, *Ireland's Civil War*, Fontana, 1979, p. 312.

June 16, 1922
Constitution of the Irish Free State
Such oath [as in the Treaty] shall be taken and subscribed by every member of the Parliament [Oireachtas] before taking his seat therein before the Representative of the Crown or some person authorised by him.

From Constitution of Free State, published on morning of polling day. Macardle, Dorothy, *The Irish Republic*, Irish Press, 1951, p. 723.

June 22, 1922
David Lloyd George
The ambiguous position of the Irish Republican Army can no longer be ignored by the British Government. Still less can Mr Rory O'Connor be permitted to remain with his followers and his arsenal in open rebellion in the heart of Dublin in possession of the Courts of Justice, organising and sending out from this centre enterprises of murder... His Majesty's Government [is] prepared to place at your disposal the necessary pieces of artillery.

As British Prime Minister, in letter sent to Michael Collins following IRA assassination in London of Henry Wilson. Mitchell and Ó Snodaigh, *Irish Political Documents 1916-1949*, Irish Academic Press, 1985, p. 137.

June 23, 1922
Eamon de Valera
I do not approve, but I must not pretend to misunderstand.

As President of Sinn Féin, on assassination of Henry Wilson, military adviser to NI Government. Moynihan, Maurice, *Speeches and Statements by Eamon de Valera 1917-1973*, Gill & Macmillan, 1980, pp. 105-106.

June 23, 1922
Diarmuid O'Hegarty
My Government have been profoundly shocked by the tragic and untimely death of Sir Henry Wilson and they hasten to place on record their condemnation of the assassination by whomsoever it was perpetrated.

As spokesman for Provisional Government, whose leader, Michael Collins, ordered the assassination of Henry Wilson. Coogan, Tim Pat, *Michael Collins*, Arrow Books, 1991, p. 374.

June 26, 1922
Winston Churchill
If it [the IRA occupation of the Four Courts] does not come to an end; if through weakness, want of courage, or some other even less creditable reason it is not brought to an end, and a speedy end, then it is my duty to say...that we shall regard the Treaty as having been formally violated.

As Dominions Secretary, in House of Commons, after assassination of Henry Wilson on June 22. Macardle, Dorothy, *The Irish Republic*, Irish Press, 1951, p. 741.

June 28, 1922
Eamon de Valera

At the bidding of the English, Irishmen are today shooting down, on the streets of our capital, brother-Irishmen, old comrades-in-arms, companions in the recent struggle for Ireland's independence and its embodiment – the Republic... England's threat of war – that, and that alone – is responsible for the present situation.

As President of Sinn Féin, after Provisional Government forces attacked anti-Treaty IRA in Four Courts. Moynihan, Maurice, *Speeches and Statements by Eamon de Valera 1917-1973*, Gill & Macmillan, 1980, p. 107.

June 28, 1922
Liam Lynch

The fateful hour has come. At the dictation of our hereditary enemy our rightful cause is being treacherously assailed by recreant Irishmen... Gallant soldiers of the Irish Republic stand vigorously firm... The sacred spirits of the Illustrious Dead are with us in this great struggle...rally to the support of the Republic.

As leader of anti-Treaty IRA executive (killed in Civil War in 1923). Macardle, Dorothy, *The Irish Republic*, Irish Press, 1951, pp. 74-46.

June 29, 1922
Richard Mulcahy

Today having driven the tyranny of the stranger from our land...you are called upon to serve her still in arms to protect her from a madness from within.

As Minister for Defence, in message to Army attacking anti-Treaty IRA. Mitchell and Ó Snodaigh, *Irish Political Documents 1916-1949*, Irish Academic, 1985, p. 139.

June 29, 1922
Michael Collins

The safety of the nation is the first law and henceforth we shall not rest until we have established the authority of the people of Ireland in every square mile under their jurisdiction.

As Commander-in-Chief of Army, signalling offensive against IRA. Coogan, Tim Pat, *Michael Collins*, Arrow Books, 1991, p. 386.

June 30, 1922
Oscar Traynor

To help me to carry on the fight outside you must surrender forthwith. I would be unable to fight my way through to you even at terrific sacrifice... If the Republic is to be saved, your surrender is a necessity.

As Officer Commanding Dublin Brigade, anti-Treaty IRA, ordering surrender of Four Courts. Macardle, Dorothy, *The Irish Republic*, Irish Press, 1951, p. 751.

June 30, 1922
Michael Collins

There can be no question of forcing Ulster into union with the 26 Counties. I am absolutely against coercion of that kind. If Ulster is to join us it must be voluntarily. Union is our final goal, that is all.

As Commander-in-Chief of Army, in *Daily Mail* interview. Coogan, Tim Pat, *Michael Collins*, Arrow Books, 1991, p. 384.

July 1, 1922
Winston Churchill

The archives of the Four Courts may be scattered, but the title deeds of Ireland are safe.

As Dominions Secretary, on destruction of Public Records Office in explosion as Four Courts garrison surrendered. Coogan, Tim Pat, *Michael Collins*, Arrow Books, 1991, p. 332.

July 4, 1922
Frank Aiken

Are you prepared to carry on a war with your own people to enforce that Oath of Allegiance to England, while you have a splendid opportunity of uniting the whole nation to fight against it with success?

As leading member of IRA, in letter to Minister for Defence, Richard Mulcahy, asking for removal of Article 17 from the Free State Constitution to avoid civil war. Macardle, Dorothy, *The Irish Republic*, Irish Press, 1951, pp. 761-762.

July 5, 1922
Winston Churchill

Better a state without archives than archives without a state.

As Dominions Secretary, in House of Commons, on loss of Irish records in destruction of Four Courts. Younger, Calton, *Ireland's Civil War*, Fontana, 1979, p. 333.

July 7, 1922
Winston Churchill

Of course, from the imperial point of view, there is nothing we would like better than to see the South and the North join hands in an all-Ireland assembly without prejudice to the existing rights of Irishmen. Such ideas could be vehemently denied in many quarters at the moment, but events in the history of nations sometimes move very quickly.

As Dominions Secretary, in letter to Michael Collins. Quoted by John Hume in House of Commons on June 28, 1983. Routledge, Paul, *John Hume*, Harper Collins, 1998, p. 193.

July 12, 1922
William Butler Yeats

We had fed the heart on fantasies,
The heart's grown brutal from the fare.

As poet, in 'Meditations in Time of Civil War'. Yeats, W. B., *Collected Poems*, Macmillan, 1965, pp. 230-231.

July 18, 1922
Reginald Dunne

The same principles for which we shed our blood on the battle-field of Europe led us to commit the act we are charged with...we will go to the scaffold justified by the verdict of our own consciences.

As former British Army soldier, in speech prepared for trial with fellow ex-serviceman Joseph O'Sullivan, for IRA murder of Henry Wilson in London on June 22, for which they were found guilty and hanged. *Irish Independent*, July 21, 1922.

c. August 1, 1922
George Gavan Duffy

Ministers must feel some diffidence about championing against their own justices the judges of the old regime, most of whom, a year or two ago, would have welcomed an opportunity of lodging our present rulers in jail.

As member of Provisional Government, resigning because of decision to abolish Republican courts set up in 1920 and retain former British courts. Macardle, Dorothy, *The Irish Republic*, Irish Press, 1951, p. 770.

August 3, 1922
Michael Collins

I'd send a wreath but I suppose they'd return it torn up.

As Commander-in-Chief of Army, on death of political and personal rival Harry Boland, a former close friend, in letter to fiancée Kitty Kiernan. Coogan, Tim Pat, *Michael Collins*, Arrow Books, 1991, p. 389.

August 7, 1922
Ernest Blythe

The...one logical and defensible line is full acceptance of the Treaty. This undoubtedly means recognition of the Northern government and implies that we shall influence all those within the Six Counties who look to us for guidance to acknowledge its authority, and refrain from any attempt to prevent it working.

As member of Provisional Government, in report on northern policy. Fanning, Ronan, *Independent Ireland*, Helicon, 1983, p. 35.

August 16, 1922
Dr Michael Fogarty

Michael, you should be prepared – you might be next.

As Bishop of Killaloe, to Michael Collins, at funeral of Arthur Griffith in Glasnevin cemetery. Coogan, Tim Pat, *Michael Collins*, Arrow Books, 1991, p. 399.

August 18, 1922
Michael Collins

Ah, whatever happens, my own fellow countrymen won't kill me.

As Commander-in-Chief of Army, before setting out on journey to Cork. Coogan, Tim Pat, *Michael Collins*, Arrow Books, 1991, p. 400.

August 20, 1922
Rev Corbett

The poor man is in a hurry to meet his death.

As Archdeacon of Mallow, in comment to member of Michael Collins's convoy en route to Cork. Younger, Calton, *Ireland's Civil War*, Fontana, 1979, p. 430.

August 23, 1922
Eamon de Valera

I told them not to do it, even pleaded with them, but they wouldn't listen to me, and now what will become of us all.

As President of Sinn Féin, talking to himself in distress, after leaving area where Michael Collins was shot dead at Béal na Bláth. Coogan, Tim Pat, *Michael Collins*, Arrow Books, 1991, pp. 426-427.

August 23, 1922
Richard Mulcahy

To the men of the Army: Stand calmly by your posts. Bend bravely and undaunted to your work. Let no cruel act of reprisal blemish your bright honour. Every dark hour that Michael Collins met since 1916 seemed but to steel that bright strength of his and temper his gay bravery. You are left each inheritors of that strength and of that bravery. To each of you falls his unfinished work.

As Chief of General Staff of Army, after death of Michael Collins in IRA ambush at Béal na Bláth. *The Irish Times*, December 17, 1971.

c. September 1, 1922
Rev Jeremiah Cohalan

The day Michael Collins was shot, where was de Valera? Ask the people of Béal na Bláth and they will tell you. There was a scowling face at a window looking out over that lovely valley and de Valera could tell you who it was.

As Canon of Bandon, Co Cork. Coogan, Tim Pat, *De Valera*, Hutchinson, 1993, p. 332.

September 9, 1922
William T. Cosgrave

If elected to this position it is my intention to implement the Treaty...to enact a Constitution, to assert the authority and supremacy of parliament.

As (successful) candidate for leadership of Provisional Government. Macardle, Dorothy, *The Irish Republic*, Irish Press, 1951, pp. 782-783.

September 9, 1922
Kevin O'Higgins

We had very good reasons to believe that [by attacking Four Courts] we anticipated by a couple of hours the creation of conditions...which would have brought back the British power – horse, foot, artillery and navy.

As incoming Minister for Justice at first meeting of Dáil elected on June 16. Macardle, Dorothy, *The Irish Republic*, Irish Press, 1951, p. 785.

September 9, 1922
Cathal O'Shannon

There is not a county in the 26 Counties, there is not a barracks or jail out of which has not come information which is a disgrace to any Irish Government.

As Labour Party Chairman, complaining in Dáil about ill-treatment of prisoners. Macardle, Dorothy, *The Irish Republic*, Irish Press, 1951, p. 784.

September 11, 1922
William T. Cosgrave

The nation which has struggled so long against the most powerful aggression will not submit to an armed minority which makes war upon its liberties, its institutions, its representation and its honour.

As head of Provisional Government, in Dáil. McLoughlin, Michael, *Great Irish Speeches of the Twentieth Century*, Poolbeg, 1996, pp. 120-121.

September 12, 1922
Richard Mulcahy

If any young men in the army brush up against individuals here and there in a rough or in an untactful way, well it is a very great credit to the army as a whole, and to the young men of this country who form it, that there is not a greater volume of complaint along that line.

As Minister for Defence, in Dáil, on allegations of ill-treatment of Republican prisoners. Macardle, Dorothy, *The Irish Republic*, Irish Press, 1951, p. 786.

September 24, 1922
Dr Daniel Cohalan

The killing of National soldiers is murder.

As Bishop of Cork, in pastoral letter. Macardle, Dorothy, *The Irish Republic*, Irish Press, 1951, p. 801.

September 27, 1922
Kevin O'Higgins

I do know that the able Englishman [Erskine Childers] who is leading those who are opposed to this Government has his eye quite definitely

on one objective, and that that is the complete breakdown of the economic and social fabric, so that this thing that is trying so hard to be an Irish nation will go down in chaos, anarchy and futility.

As Minister for Justice, in Dáil, on setting up of military courts with powers to impose the death penalty. Macardle, Dorothy, *The Irish Republic*, Irish Press, 1951, pp. 802-803.

September 27, 1922
William T. Cosgrave

We are not going to treat rebels as prisoners of war.

As leader of Provisional Government, in Dáil. Macardle, Dorothy, *The Irish Republic*, Irish Press, 1951, p. 804.

September 29, 1922
Seamus Woods

Recognition of the Northern government, of course, will mean the breaking up of our [IRA 3rd Northern] Division... The breaking up of this organisation is the first step to making partition permanent. If this must come, then there is very little hope of organising in Ulster along Gaelic lines for a long time.

As northern IRA commander, in letter to Minister for Defence, Richard Mulcahy. Fanning, Ronan, *Independent Ireland*, Helicon, 1983, p. 37.

October 10, 1922
Catholic Hierarchy

A section of the community, refusing to acknowledge the Government set up by the Nation, have chosen to attack their own country as if she were a foreign power...the guerilla warfare now being carried on by the Irregulars is without moral sanction, and, therefore, the killing of National soldiers in the course of it is murder before God.

As Irish Bishops, in pastoral letter. Younger, Calton, *Ireland's Civil War*, Fontana, 1979, p. 482.

October 26, 1922
Liam Lynch

We, on behalf of the soldiers of the Republic...have called upon the former President, Eamon de Valera, and the faithful members of Dáil Éireann, to form a Government, which they have done.

As Chief of Staff of IRA, after signing proclamation along with twelve other IRA officers at secret meeting of anti-Treaty deputies in Dublin. Macardle, Dorothy, *The Irish Republic*, Irish Press, 1951, p. 808.

c. November 1, 1922
Maud Gonne MacBride

If I did not renounce the Government, she renounced my society for ever.

As widow of executed 1916 leader, John MacBride, and supporter of anti-Treaty forces, to William Butler Yeats. Tuohy, Frank, *Yeats*, Macmillan, 1976, p. 182.

November 12, 1922
Winston Churchill

I have seen with satisfaction that the mischief-making murderous renegade, Erskine Childers, has been captured. No man has done more harm or shown more genuine malice, or endeavoured to bring a greater curse upon the common people of Ireland, than this strange being, actuated by a deadly and malignant hatred for the land of his birth [England]. Such as he is, may all who hate us be.

As Dominions Secretary, speaking at Dundee. Macardle, Dorothy, *The Irish Republic*, Irish Press, 1951, p. 811.

November 17, 1922
Kevin O'Higgins

If they took as their first case [for execution] some man who was outstandingly active and outstandingly wicked in his activities, the unfortunate dupes throughout the country might say that he was killed because he was a leader, because he was an Englishman, or because he combined with others to commit rape.

As Minister for Justice in Dáil after first four executions of Republican prisoners, and taken as indication that Government planned execution of Erskine Childers, who was born in England. Younger, Calton, *Ireland's Civil War*, Fontana, 1979, p. 485.

November 19, 1922
Erskine Childers

I was bound by honour, conscience and principle to oppose the Treaty by speech, writing and action, both in peace and, when it came to the disastrous point, in war... Some day we shall be justified when the nation forgets its weakness.

As leading opponent of Treaty, in statement published after his execution on November 24 for possession of a miniature pistol. *The Irish Times*, November 27, 1922.

November 24, 1922
Erskine Childers

Come closer, boys. It will be easier for you.

As leading opponent of Treaty, to firing squad at execution. Wilkinson, Burke, *The Zeal of the Convert*, 1976.

November 27, 1922
Liam Lynch

Every member of your body who voted for this resolution by which you pretend to make legal the murder of soldiers, is equally guilty. We therefore give you and each member of your body due notice that unless your army recognises the rules of warfare in future, we shall adopt very drastic measures to protect our forces.

As Chief of Staff of IRA, in letter to Speaker of Dáil threatening to kill Dáil members in retaliation for execution of IRA prisoners. Younger, Calton, *Ireland's Civil War*, Fontana, 1979, p. 491.

November 30, 1922
Richard Mulcahy

We are people who realise that man is made in the image and likeness of God...when a man is going to his death, he does get a priest.

As Minister for Defence, in Dáil, after execution of three IRA prisoners. Macardle, Dorothy, *The Irish Republic*, Irish Press, 1951, p. 816.

December 8, 1922
Liam Mellowes

Though unworthy of the greatest human honour that can be paid an Irishman or woman, I go to join Tone and Emmet, the Fenians, Tom Clarke, Connolly, Pearse, Kevin Barry and Childers. My last thoughts will be on God, and Ireland and on you.

As Minister for Defence in underground government set up by de Valera, in letter to his mother from Mountjoy Prison before his execution. Coogan, Tim Pat, *The IRA*, Fontana, 1980, p. 53.

December 8, 1922
Free State Government

[This was] a reprisal for the assassination of Brig. Hales, TD, as a solemn warning to those associated with them who are engaged in the conspiracy of assassination against the Representatives of the Irish people.

In official proclamation after execution of Liam Mellowes, Rory O'Connor, Joseph McKelvey and Richard Barrett in retaliation for IRA killing of Dáil member Sean Hales. Macardle, Dorothy, *The Irish Republic*, Irish Press, 1951, p. 823.

December 8, 1922
William T. Cosgrave

Terror will be struck into them [IRA].

As leader of Free State Government after execution of IRA prisoners. Macardle, Dorothy, *The Irish Republic*, Irish Press, 1951, p. 823.

December 8, 1922
Kevin O'Higgins

Personal spite, great heavens! Vindictiveness! One of these men was a friend of mine.

As Minister for Justice, in Dáil, about execution of four Republican prisoners, one of whom, Rory O'Connor, had been best man at O'Higgins's wedding the previous year. Younger, Calton, *Ireland's Civil War*, Fontana, 1979, p. 494.

December 10, 1922
Dr Edward Byrne
That one man should be punished for another's crimes seems to me to be absolutely unjust. Moreover such a policy is bound to alienate many friends of the Government and it requires all the sympathy it can get.

As Archbishop of Dublin after execution of four IRA prisoners as a reprisal for assassination of Dáil member Sean Hales. Keogh, Dermot, *Twentieth-Century Ireland*, Gill & Macmillan, 1994, p. 15.

December 27, 1922
George Russell ('AE')
There is no dishonour in raising the conflict from the physical to the intellectual plane.

As writer and commentator, in letter to newspaper appealing to Republicans to lay down their arms. *The Irish Times*, December 27, 1922.

December 31, 1922
Kevin O'Higgins
The Provisional Government was simply eight young men in the City Hall standing amidst the ruins of one administration, with the foundation of another not yet laid and with wild men screaming through the keyhole.

As Minister for Justice, on first months of existence of Free State Government (paraphrasing keyhole metaphor used in 1919 by David Lloyd George about the Versailles peace conference). Coogan, Tim Pat, *The IRA*, Fontana, 1980, pp. 52-53.

1923
William Magennis
You cannot be a good Catholic if you allow divorce even between Protestants.

As professor and Dáil member, in debate on divorce legislation. Keogh, Dermot, *Twentieth-Century Ireland*, Gill & Macmillan, 1994, p. 31.

c. January 1, 1923
William Butler Yeats
The Government of the Free State has been proved legitimate by the only effective test: it has been permitted to take life.

As poet, on executions of republican prisoners. Tuohy, Frank, *Yeats*, Macmillan, 1976, p. 191.

January 11, 1923
Kevin O'Higgins
There should be executions in every county [because] local executions would tend considerably to shorten the struggle.

As Minister for Justice, in memo on war against IRA. Lee, J. J., *Ireland 1912-1985*, Cambridge University Press, 1990, p. 98.

February 7, 1923
Eamon de Valera
We can best serve the nation at this moment by trying to get the constitutional way adopted.

As President of Sinn Féin, in letter to Liam Lynch suggesting end of armed struggle. Moynihan, Maurice, *Speeches and Statements by Eamon de Valera 1917-1973*, Gill & Macmillan, 1980, p. 118.

April 23, 1923
Sean O'Casey
I believe in the freedom of Ireland and that England has no right to be here, but I draw the line when I hear the gunmen blowin' about dyin' for the people, when it's the people that are dyin' for the gunmen.

As playwright, in words spoken by character in 'The Shadow of a Gunman', first perfomed in Abbey Theatre on this date. Kiberd, Declan, *Inventing Ireland*, Jonathan Cape, 1995, p. 221.

c. May 1, 1923
Kevin O'Higgins
They may not handle a cup of tea as gracefully as the deputy, but they have served the state at a time when the deputy's effort was in a rather contrary direction.

As Minister for Justice, in Dáil, defending CID from charges of brutality. Brady, Conor, *Guardians of the Peace*, Gill & Macmillan, 1974, p. 127.

May 13, 1923
James Larkin
I ask all Republicans to give up the armed struggle and take up the political, constitutional struggle. Give up your arms. There is no disgrace in peace. There can never be dishonour in peace.

As trade union organiser, urging end to Civil War at Republican meeting in Dublin to honour James Connolly. *The Irish Times*, January 20, 1976.

May 15, 1923
C. J. Gregg
Do not hanker after a mullet if you have only the price of a dudgeon in your pocket.

As organiser of Free State civil service, invoking Juvenal, in memo to Attorney General, Hugh Kennedy, on unacceptable cost of reforming legal system. Lee, J. J., *Ireland 1912-1985*, Cambridge University Press, 1990, p. 128.

May 24, 1923
Eamon de Valera
Soldiers of the Republic, Legion of the Rearguard: The Republic can no longer be defended successfully by your arms. Further sacrifice of life would now be vain, and continuance of the struggle in arms unwise in the national interest and prejudicial to the future of our cause. Military

victory must be allowed to rest for the moment with those who have destroyed the Republic. Other means must be sought to safeguard the nation's right.

As President of Sinn Féin, in message to anti-Treaty forces after defeat in Civil War. Moynihan, Maurice, *Speeches and Statements by Eamon de Valera 1917-1973*, Gill & Macmillan, 1980, p. 114.

May 24, 1923
Frank Aiken

Comrades! The arms with which we fought the enemies of our country are to be dumped. The foreign and domestic enemies of the Republic have for the moment prevailed.

As Commander-in-Chief of IRA, signalling end of Civil War. Coogan, Tim Pat, *De Valera*, Hutchinson, 1993, p. 354.

October 5, 1923
Hugh Kennedy

[Protestants] will resent any cutting down of the existing facilities that were open to non-Catholics as an invasion of their rights, and of the position of the minority, which they were told would be protected.

As Attorney General, in submission to Government on proposal to ban divorce. Fanning, Ronan, *Independent Ireland*, Helicon, 1983, p. 55.

October 9, 1923
Cardinal Michael Logue

The Bishops of Ireland have to say that it would be altogether unworthy of an Irish legislative body to sanction concession of such divorce, no matter who the petitioners may be.

As Primate of Ireland, replying to request for Bishops' views on divorce from leader of Free State Government, W. T. Cosgrave. Fanning, Ronan, *Independent Ireland*, Helicon, 1983, p. 56.

1924
Eoin MacNeill

You might as well be putting wooden legs on hens as trying to restore Irish through the school system.

As Minister for Education. Lee, J. J., *Ireland 1912-1985*, Cambridge University Press, 1990, p. 133.

1924
Desmond FitzGerald

England is our most important external affair.

As Minister for External Affairs. Fanning, Ronan, *Independent Ireland*, Helicon, 1983, p. 110.

January 24, 1924
Catholic Bulletin

It is common knowledge that the line of recipients of the Nobel Prize shows that a reputation for paganism in thought and word is a very considerable advantage in the sordid annual race for money, engineered as it always is by clubs, coteries, salons and cliques.

As Catholic newspaper, on award of Nobel Prize for Literature to William Butler Yeats. Brown, Terence, *Ireland, A Social and Cultural History 1922-1979*, 1982, p. 72.

c. February 1, 1924
Oliver St John Gogarty

[There is in Ireland] a regular wave of destruction...led by a few ferocious and home-breaking old harridans.

As Senator, in speech praising William Butler Yeats for winning Nobel Prize for Literature, believed to refer to Maude Gonne and Countess Markiewicz. Tuohy, Frank, *Yeats*, Macmillan, 1976, p. 183.

March 3, 1924
Sean O'Casey

Sacred heart o'Jesus, take away our hearts o'stone, and give us hearts o'flesh! Take away this murdherin' hate an' give us Thine own eternal love!

As playwright, in words spoken by Mrs Boyle, or Juno, on death of her son in the Troubles, in first performance of 'Juno and the Paycock' at Abbey Theatre, Dublin, on March 3, 1924. O'Casey, Sean, *Juno and the Paycock and The Plough and the Stars*, Macmillan, 1969, p. 72.

March 6, 1924
Major-General Liam Tobin and Colonel Charles Dalton

...we can no longer be party to the treachery that threatens to destroy the aspirations of the nation.

As Free State Army officers in ultimatum demanding that Government move towards setting up Republic or face mutiny. Valiulis, Maryann, *Almost a Rebellion*, Tower Books, 1985, p. 51.

March 10, 1924
Richard Mulcahy

Two army officers have attempted to involve the army in a challenge to the authority of the Government. This is an outrageous departure from the spirit of the Army. It will not be tolerated.

As Defence Minister, reacting to threatened mutiny of old IRA demanding speedy move towards goal of Republic. Valiulis, Maryann, *Almost a Rebellion*, Tower Books, 1985, p. 53.

March 11, 1924
William T. Cosgrave

The attempt [by army officers to challenge the Government]...is a challenge to the democratic foundations of the State, to the very basis of parliamentary representation and of responsible Government.

As leader of Free State Government responding in Dáil to threatened mutiny of old IRA officers. Valiulis, Maryann, *Almost a Rebellion*, Tower Books, 1985, p. 54.

March 12, 1924
Kevin O'Higgins
We were told that these men, while they might have written a foolish, an almost criminally foolish document, were not really taking up the position of challenging the fundamental right of the people to decide political issues.

As Minister of Home Affairs, informing Dáil that old IRA army officers had backed down in their threatened mutiny. Valiulis, Maryann, *Almost a Rebellion*, Tower Books, 1985, p. 54.

c. April 1, 1924
Department of Education
Irish is dying because the people of the Gaeltacht think that Irish and poverty, Irish and social inferiority are inextricably connected. They will continue to think so until the government proves conclusively...that Irish pays.

In analysis of Irish language. Lee, J. J., *Ireland 1912-1985*, Cambridge University Press, 1990, p. 133.

May 19, 1924
Joe McGrath
[I] would not be a party to taking action against a body of men who were responsible very largely for the birth of the Free State and for its life since.

As Minister for Industry and Commerce, on his resignation in sympathy with army officers who threatened mutiny on March 6. Valiulis, Maryann, *Almost a Rebellion*, Tower Books, 1985, p. 52.

August 15, 1924
Eamon de Valera
I would disappoint a number here if I were not to start by saying, 'Well, as I was saying to you when we were interrupted.'

As President of Sinn Féin, in Ennis, where he was arrested a year previously at public meeting. Moynihan, Maurice, *Speeches and Statements by Eamon de Valera 1917-1973*, Gill & Macmillan, 1980, p. 115.

October 15, 1924
William T. Cosgrave
Had those pronouncements been made at the time [of the Treaty negotiations], there would not have been Irish signatories to the Treaty.

As leader of Free State Government in Dáil debate, on British assurances to Unionists that Boundary Commission would not make significant changes to Border. Farrell, Michael, *Arming the Protestants*, Brandon, 1983, p. 225.

October 17, 1924
William Butler Yeats
I have no hope of seeing Ireland united in my time, or of seeing Ulster won in my time; but I believe it will be won in the end, and not because we fight it, but because we govern this country well.

As Senator, in Senate. Pearce, Donald R., *The Senate Speeches of W. B. Yeats*, Faber and Faber, 1961, p. 87.

October 30, 1924
Patrick McGilligan
There are certain limited funds at our disposal. People may have to die in this country and may have to die through starvation.

As Minister for Industry and Commerce, on precarious state of economy. McCullagh, David, *A Makeshift Majority*, IPA, 1998, p. 49.

November 1, 1924
Justice Richard Feetham
If the Commission were to make a change in the boundary...simply in order to gratify one thousand of such inhabitants at the cost of offending the other nine hundred and ninety-nine, such a proceeding would obviously be unreasonable.

As Chairman of Boundary Commission, in memorandum on limitations of possible change. *The Irish Times*, January 29, 1970.

January 3, 1925
George Russell ('AE')
Ireland has not only the unique Gaelic tradition, but it has given birth, if it accepts all its children, to many men who have influenced European culture and science; Berkeley, Swift, Goldsmith, Burke, Sheridan, Moore, Hamilton, Kelvin, Tyndall, Shaw, Yeats, Synge and many others of international repute. If we repudiate the Anglo-Irish tradition, if we say these are aliens, how poor does our life become?

As writer and commentator. *Irish Statesman*, January 3, 1925.

January 25, 1925
Eamon de Valera
No decent Republican should ever enter the present Dáil.

As President of Sinn Féin. Browne, Vincent, *The Magill Book of Irish Politics*, Magill Publications, 1981, p. 56.

March 13, 1925
Sean Lemass
Whenever the Irish people came within sight of achieving their national independence the full political power of the Church was flung against them, and forced them back. That political power

must be destroyed if our national victory is ever to be won.

As leading Sinn Féin member, in by-election speech. *Irish Independent*, March 14, 1925.

March 31, 1925
Sir Edward Archdale

A man in Fintona asked him how it was he had over fifty percent Catholics in his ministry. He thought that too funny. He had 109 on his staff and as far as he knew there were four Roman Catholics. Three of these were civil servants turned over to him, whom he had to take when he began.

As NI Minister for Agriculture, at Stormont, reported in *Northern Whig*. Bardon, Jonathan, *A History of Ulster*, Blackstaff Press, 1992, p. 498.

April 1925
James Craig

Not an inch!

As NI Prime Minister, in election slogan, referring to Border still to be ratified by British and Irish Governments. Younger, Calton, *A State of Disunion*, Muller, 1972, p. 212.

April 1925
Joe Devlin

Permanent abstention means permanent disfranchisement.

As nationalist MP for West Belfast, announcing intention to enter NI Parliament. Bardon, Jonathan, *A History of Ulster*, Blackstaff Press, 1992, p. 507.

April 1925
Cahir Healy

We will only intervene when we feel we can expose injustice. But we reserve the right to come in or stay outside as and when our people may decide.

As nationalist MP for Fermanagh, on participation in NI Parliament. Bardon, Jonathan, *A History of Ulster*, Blackstaff Press, 1992, p. 510.

June 11, 1925
William Butler Yeats

If you show that this country, Southern Ireland, is going to be governed by Catholic ideas and by Catholic ideas alone, you will never get the North.

As Senator, in Senate, on Government measure against divorce. Pearce, Donald R., *The Senate Speeches of W. B.Yeats*, Faber and Faber, 1961, p. 99.

June 11, 1925
William Butler Yeats

We against whom you have done this thing are no petty people. We are one of the great stocks of Europe. We are the people of Burke; we are

the people of Grattan; we are the people of Swift, the people of Emmet, the people of Parnell. We have created the most of the modern literature of this country. We have created the best of its political intelligence.

As Senator, in Senate, on discrimination against southern Protestants. Pearce, Donald R., *The Senate Speeches of W. B. Yeats*, Faber and Faber, 1961, p. 99.

June 12, 1925
D. P. Moran

Mr Yeats has divorced Kathleen Ní Houlihan and formed an alliance with Dolly Brae.

As editor of *Leader*, on W. B. Yeats's speech on divorce, above. Fallon, Brian, *An Age of Innocence*, Gill & Macmillan, 1998, p. 43.

June 21, 1925
Eamon de Valera

For our part, we are content to rest for the moment, if it must be so, simply faithful.

As President of Sinn Féin, in speech at grave of Wolfe Tone at Bodenstown. Moynihan, Maurice, *Speeches and Statements by Eamon de Valera 1917-1973*, Gill & Macmillan, 1980, p. 121.

October 6, 1925
Catholic Hierarchy

To say nothing of the special danger of drink, imported dances of an evil kind, the surroundings of the dance hall, withdrawal from the hall for intervals, and the dark ways home have been the destruction of virtue in every part of Ireland.

As Irish Bishops, in joint pastoral on occasions of sin. Keogh, Dermot, *Twentieth-Century Ireland*, Gill & Macmillan, 1994, p. 29.

November 25, 1925
Sam Patterson

While the people of Belfast are starving, we have rogues, vagabonds, thieves and murderers in Sir James Craig and his Government...by the aid of rifle, revolver and bomb we can blow the Government to hell.

As NI Labour Party member, in speech for which he was sentenced to six months hard labour for sedition. Farrell, Michael, *Northern Ireland: The Orange State*, Pluto, 1983, p. 123.

November 28, 1925
Kevin O'Higgins

The Commission took the line of least resistance; where the special police were thick in the North, the Commission sheered away...influenced by specials standing with their fingers on the trigger.

As Minister for Justice, speaking at tripartite conference of Dublin, London and Belfast at Chequers, which ratified boundary of Northern Ireland. Farrell, Michael, *Arming the Protestants*, Brandon, 1983, p. 248.

December 4, 1925
William T. Cosgrave

I want you to put on record my belief that this situation will tend more surely and more speedily towards bringing about the ultimate political unity of the two sections of the country than any other course that could have been adopted.

As leader of Free State Government, in *Belfast Telegraph* interview, on ratification of boundaries of Northern Ireland. Mitchell and Ó Snodaigh, *Irish Political Documents 1916-1949*, Irish Academic, 1985, p. 169.

December 5, 1925
Cahir Healy

John Redmond was driven from public life for even suggesting Partition for a period of five years. The new leaders agree to a Partition forever.

As nationalist MP for Fermanagh and Tyrone, on ratification of boundaries of Northern Ireland. Mitchell and Ó Snodaigh, *Irish Political Documents 1916-1949*, Irish Academic Press , 1985, p. 170.

December 6, 1925
Eamon de Valera

The worst of this bargain is the complexion that will be put upon it, for it will be said that we have sold our countrymen for the meanest of all considerations – a money consideration.

As President of Sinn Féin, in Dublin, on Boundary Agreement releasing Free State from obligation to service the public debt of the former United Kingdom. Moynihan, Maurice, *Speeches and Statements by Eamon de Valera 1917-1973*, Gill & Macmillan, 1980, pp. 122-123.

December 9, 1925
James Craig

I believe that a new era will be opened in Irish history and that...much may be accomplished to smooth over those small but irritating difficulties that are bound to arise from time to time between two neighbouring States.

As NI Prime Minister, on ratification of boundaries of Northern Ireland. Mitchell and Ó Snodaigh, *Irish Political Documents 1916-1949*, Irish Academic Press, 1985, pp. 166-167.

January 22, 1926
Sean Lemass

...there are some who would have us sit by the roadside and debate abstruse points about a *de jure* this and a *de facto* that, but the reality we want is away in the distance – and we cannot get there unless we move.

As member of Sinn Féin, writing in *An Phoblacht*. Farrell, Brian, *De Valera and His Times*, Cork University Press, 1983, p. 36.

February 11, 1926
William Butler Yeats

Fallon, I'm sending for the police; and this time it'll be their own police. (To audience) You have disgraced yourselves again.

As director of Abbey Theatre, to actor Gabriel Fallon, as nationalists rushed stage during scenes they disliked in Sean O'Casey's 'The Plough and the Stars'. Tuohy, Frank, *Yeats*, Gill & Macmillan, 1976, p. 192.

March 3, 1926
Winston Churchill

Neither by threats or violence or by intrigues, not yet by unfair economic pressure, shall the people of Ulster be compelled against their wishes to sever the ties which bind them to the United Kingdom, or be forced, unless by their own free and unfettered choice, to join another system of government.

As Chancellor of the Exchequer, in words engraved 12 years later on a silver cup presented to Churchill by James Craig, then Lord Craigavon. Fisk, Robert, *In Time of War*, Paladin, 1985, pp. 61-62.

March 10, 1926
Eamon de Valera

...once the admission oaths of the 26-county and six-county assembles are removed, it becomes a question not of principle but of policy whether or not Republican representatives should attend these assemblies.

As President of Sinn Féin, on eve of resignation to form Fianna Fáil. Moynihan, Maurice, *Speeches and Statements by Eamon de Valera 1917-1973*, Gill & Macmillan, 1980, p. 127.

May 16, 1926
Eamon de Valera

Another objection raised is that entering a 26-county assembly would be an acceptance of partition. I deny that. To recognise the existence of facts, as we must, is not to acquiesce in them.

As leader of Fianna Fáil, at inaugural meeting in La Scala Theatre, Dublin. Moynihan, Maurice, *Speeches and Statements by Eamon de Valera 1917-1973*, Gill & Macmillan, 1980, p. 139.

June 14, 1926
Samuel Patterson

Here are the police coming. They are always on the alert when revolution is spoken of. Run like hell!

As leader of Unemployed Workers' Association at rally on Belfast's Shankill Road, following which he was jailed for six months. Bardon, Jonathan, *A History of Ulster*, Blackstaff Press, 1992, p. 525.

November 1926
J. J. Walsh
A country without a language was not a country at all. This country had for centuries been dosed with compulsory English to the entire exclusion of their native tongue, and the people who now complain of compulsory Irish were whole-hog backers of that English policy.

As Minister for Posts and Telegraphs, defending language policy. Brown, Terence, *Ireland, A Social and Cultural History, 1922-1979*, Fontana, 1982, p. 62.

November 1926
Douglas Hyde
It will save the historic Irish nation, for it will preserve for all time the fountain source from which future generations can draw forever.

As President of Gaelic League, on creation of Gaeltacht areas. Brown, Terence, *Ireland, A Social and Cultural History, 1922-1979*, Fontana, 1982, p. 93.

December 8, 1926
Dr Thomas Gilmartin
Company keeping under the stars had succeeded in too many places to the good old Irish custom of visiting, chatting and story-telling from one house to another, with the Rosary to bring all home in due time.

As Archbishop of Tuam, on effects of modern dancing. Keogh, Dermot, *Twentieth-Century Ireland*, Gill & Macmillan, 1994, p. 29.

1927
Catholic Hierarchy
Since there are within the Irish Free State three university colleges sufficiently safe in regard to faith and morals, we, therefore, strictly inhibit, and under pain of grave sin, we forbid priests and all clerics by advice or otherwise, to recommend parents or others having charge of youth to send the young persons in their charge to Trinity College.

As Irish Bishops, ruling that no Catholics could attend 'Protestant' Trinity College, Dublin. Whyte, J. H., *Church & State in Modern Ireland*, Gill & Macmillan, 1980, p. 305.

March 10, 1927
Oliver St John Gogarty
As long as there is English spoken in the home, whatever is taught in the morning will be undone in the evening by the parents, and the greatest enthusiast has not suggested the shooting of mothers of English-speaking children.

As Senator, in Senate, on Gaeltacht Commission report. *SED*, March 10, 1927.

May 23, 1927
Charles Lindbergh
I flew down almost touching the craft and yelled at them, asking if I was on the right road to Ireland. They just stared. Maybe they just didn't hear me. Maybe I didn't hear them. Or maybe they thought I was just a crazy fool. An hour later I saw land.

As first person to fly solo across Atlantic, describing encounter with Irish fishermen. *The New York Times*, May 23, 1927.

June 3, 1927
Tom Johnson
No country can be strong and healthy on a diet of revolution. A revolution is an emetic, not a food.

As Labour Party leader. Coogan, Tim Pat, *De Valera*, Hutchinson, 1993, p. 402.

June 6, 1927
Mary MacSwiney
Mistake not, sir, potatoes for principles; and worse, do not exalt potatoes and attempt to pass them off as the highest and noblest principles of nationhood.

As Sinn Féin activist, addressing leader of Labour Party. *An Phoblacht*, June 6, 1927.

June 23, 1927
Kevin O'Higgins
The party that was to end partition, the party that was to halve taxation, the party that was to have every man sitting down under his own vine tree smoking a pipe of Irish-grown tobacco, are not here today.

As Minister for Justice, on failure of Fianna Fáil to take their seats after election. *DÉ Debates*, June 23, 1927.

June 27, 1927
Eamon de Valera
Unionists [who] have wilfully assisted in mutilating their motherland can justly be made to suffer for their crime.

As leader of Fianna Fáil, in interview with *Manchester Guardian*. Bowman, John, *De Valera and the Ulster Question*, Clarendon, 1982, p. 99.

July 12, 1927
Kevin O'Higgins
I forgive my murderers. [I'm going to play a harp] on a damp cloud with Mick.

As Minister for Justice, among last words after being shot by IRA men. Coogan, Tim Pat, *De Valera*, Hutchinson, 1993, p. 400.

July 12, 1927
William T. Cosgrave
We shall meet this form of terrorism as we met other forms of terrorism and we shall not falter till every vestige of it is wiped from our land.

As leader of Free State Government, on assassination of Minister for Justice, Kevin O'Higgins. Keogh, Dermot, *Twentieth-Century Ireland*, Gill & Macmillan, 1994, p. 46.

August 10, 1927
Eamon de Valera
The required declaration is not an oath...it is merely an empty political formula which deputies can conscientiously sign without becoming involved, or without involving their nation, in obligations of loyalty to the English Crown.

As leader of Fianna Fáil, in anticipation of entering Dáil Éireann and taking seats. Moynihan, Maurice, *Speeches and Statements by Eamon de Valera 1917-1973*, Gill & Macmillan, 1980, p. 150.

August 11, 1927
Eamon de Valera
I am putting my name here merely as a formality to get the permission necessary to enter among the other Teactaí that were elected by the people of Ireland... You must remember that I am taking no oath.

As leader of Fianna Fáil, addressing, in Irish, clerk of the chamber in Dáil Éireann, after leaving aside the Bible and signing book containing Oath of Allegiance to Crown. Coogan, Tim Pat, *De Valera*, Hutchinson, 1993, pp. 404-405.

c. August 12, 1927
Dr Mannix
[They] no more told a falsehood than I would, if I sent down word to an unfortunate visitor that I was not at home.

As Cork-born Australian archbishop, on Fianna Fáil TDs' assertion they were not taking an Oath of Allegiance to the British Crown when they signed book containing oath. Lee, J. J., *Ireland 1912-1985*, Cambridge University Press, 1990, p. 133.

March 14, 1928
Eamon de Valera
Very well, there must be somebody in charge to keep order in the community, and by virtue of your *de facto* position you are the only people in a position to do it... I say you have not come by that position legitimately. You brought off a *coup d'état* in the summer of 1922.

As leader of Fianna Fáil, in Dáil, addressing Free State Government on legitimacy of State. Coogan, Tim Pat, *The IRA*, Fontana, 1980, p. 81.

March 21, 1928
Sean Lemass
I think it would be right that Fianna Fáil is a slightly constitutional party. We are perhaps open to the definition of a constitutional party, but, before anything, we are a Republican party... Five years ago we were on the defensive and perhaps in time we may recoup our strength sufficiently to go on the offensive. Our object is to establish a Republican Government in Ireland. If this can be done by the present methods we have, we would be very pleased. If not, we would not confine ourselves to them.

As Fianna Fáil TD, in Dáil. *DÉ Debates*: Vol. 22: Col. 1615.

July 12, 1928
Eamon de Valera
A servant in a big mansion must give up the luxuries of a certain kind which were available to him by being in that mansion... If he goes into the cottage he has to make up his mind to put up with the frugal fare of that cottage.

As leader of Fianna Fáil, on hardships of Irish independence. Lee, J. J., *Ireland 1912-1985*, Cambridge University Press, 1990, pp. 379-380.

August 8, 1928
Belfast Board of Guardians
Faced with such sloth, fecklessness and iniquity, the Guardians' duty [is] to discourage idleness and create a spirit of independence since much of the money given to the poor was wasted.

As charity administrators, in minutes of meeting, on recipients of outdoor relief payments. Bardon, Jonathan, *A History of Ulster*, Blackstaff Press, 1992, p. 525.

c. August 31, 1928
Lily Coleman
There is no poverty under the blankets.

As chairman of Belfast Board of Guardians, in celebrated remark criticising the poor. Bardon, Jonathan, *A History of Ulster*, Blackstaff Press, 1992, p. 525.

September 22, 1928
William Butler Yeats
Our zealot's idea of establishing the Kingdom of God upon earth is to make Ireland an island of moral cowards.

As poet, protesting against proposal to establish censorship board. *Manchester Guardian*, September 22, 1928.

c. September 22, 1928
George Russell ('AE')
It is a real peril in a country where there are vast numbers of semi-literates who can be roused to help in the denunciation of books which they have never read...[its] triumph would be to place genius in servitude to mediocrity...

As writer and commentator, on proposal to establish a censorship board. Fallon, Brian, *An Age of Innocence*, Gill & Macmillan, 1998, p. 88.

November 17, 1928
George Bernard Shaw

If, having broken England's grip of her, she slips back into the Atlantic as a little grass patch in which a few million moral cowards cannot call their souls their own...then the world will let 'these Irish' go their own way into insignificance without the smallest concern.

As playwright, speaking from his home in England, on Catholic influence on legislation in Free State. *Irish Statesman*, November 17, 1928, p. 208.

June 5, 1929
Sean T. O'Kelly

We of the Fianna Fáil party believe that we speak for the big body of Catholic opinion. I think I could say, without qualification of any kind, that we represent the big element of Catholicity.

As Fianna Fáil TD, in Dáil. Whyte, J. H., *Church & State in Modern Ireland*, Gill & Macmillan, 1980, p. 41.

1930
Kinematographs Renters' Society of Great Britain and Ireland Ltd.

He [film censor, James Montgomery] is intolerant of one-piece bathing costumes or what is properly known as the university costume, as used in swimming and during competitions.

As film distributors, at meeting with Department of Justice to protest at severity of censorship of films. *The Irish Times*, January 2, 1991.

1930
James Montgomery

I don't cut bathing or diving but I do cut exhibitions of beauty parades, where men are seen pawing girls in bathing suits, or vetting them, as it is elegantly described.

As film censor, responding to complaint of film distributors above. *The Irish Times*, January 2, 1991.

1930
W. C. Sellar and R. J. Yeatman

Gladstone spent his declining years trying to guess the answer to the Irish Question; unfortunately whenever he was getting warm, the Irish secretly changed the question.

As British authors, writing in *1066 and All That*. Jay, Anthony, *The Oxford Dictionary of Political Quotations*, Oxford, 1997, p. 323.

1931
J. H. Thomas

...the Spanish onion in the Irish stew.

As Dominions Secretary, describing de Valera. McMahon, Deirdre, *Republicans and Imperialists: Anglo-Irish Relations in the 1930s*, Yale University Press, 1984, p. 32.

1931
Michael Conway

I'm telling ye, that fella will be as bad as Cosgrave, he'll hang you when he gets in, mark my words, he'll hang you.

As IRA man, later sentenced to death (commuted), on Eamon de Valera. *The IRA*, Fontana, London, 1986, p. 86.

January 1931
Rev E. A. D'Alton

We are not appointing a washerwoman or a mechanic, but an educated girl who ought to know what books to put into the hands of the Catholic boys and girls of this country...is it safe to entrust a girl who is not a Catholic, and is not in sympathy with Catholic views, with their handling?

As Dean of Tuam, on decision of library committee of Mayo County Council not to approve appointment of Protestant librarian, Miss Letitia Dunbar-Harrison. Whyte, J. H., *Church & State in Modern Ireland*, Gill & Macmillan, 1980, pp. 44-45.

January 3, 1931
J. T. Morahan

Trinity culture is not the culture of the Gael; rather it is poison gas to the kindly Celtic people.

As councillor in Mayo County Council debate, opposing appointment of Trinity-educated Protestant librarian. *Connaught Telegraph*, January 3, 1931.

June 17, 1931
Eamon de Valera

If it is a mere passive position of handing down books that are asked for, then the librarian has no particular duty for which religion should be regarded as a qualification, but if...it is active work of a propagandist educational character...then I say the people of Mayo, in a county where...over 98 percent of the population is Catholic, are justified in insisting upon a Catholic librarian.

As leader of Fianna Fáil, on decision of library committee of Mayo County Council not to approve appointment of Protestant librarian. Whyte, J. H., *Church & State in Modern Ireland*, Gill & Macmillan, 1980, pp. 45-46.

June 20, 1931
Peadar O'Donnell

...all the powers in their hands we must take into our hands and in the final phase we must be prepared to meet force with force.

As Republican spokesman, addressing IRA volunteers at Wolfe Tone commemoration at Bodenstown. Keogh, Dermot, *Twentieth-Century Ireland*, Gill & Macmillan, 1994, p. 53.

August 28, 1931
William Butler Yeats
Out of Ireland have we come.
Great hatred, little room,
Maimed us at the start.
I carry from my mother's womb
A fanatic heart.

As poet, in 'Remorse for Intemperate Speech'. Jeffares, A. Norman, *W.B. Yeats, Selected Poetry*, Macmillan, 1970, p. 159.

October 4, 1931
William T. Cosgrave
Young men are being taught that murder is a legitimate instrument for the furtherance of communist or political aims...the new patriotism based on Muscovite teachings with a sugar coating of Irish extremism is completely alien to Irish tradition.

As leader of Free State Government, in Dáil, on need for special powers to combat Saor Éire (Socialist Republican Party). Mitchell and Ó Snodaigh, *Irish Political Documents 1916-1949*, Irish Academic, 1985, p. 186.

October 19, 1931
Catholic Hierarchy
Surely the ranks of the communist revolution are no place for an Irish boy of Catholic instincts.

As Irish Bishops, in pastoral condemning the IRA and Saor Éire (Socialist Republican Party). Mitchell and Ó Snodaigh, *Irish Political Documents 1916-1949*, Irish Academic Press, 1985, pp. 187-188.

December 1931
Cardinal Joseph MacRory
The Protestant Church in Ireland...is not only not the rightful representative of the early Irish Church, but it is not even a part of the Church of Christ.

As Primate of Ireland, in public statement. Bardon, Jonathan, *A History of Ulster*, Blackstaff Press, 1992, p. 536.

January 1932
Frank Ryan
While we have fists, hands and boots to use, and guns if necessary, we will not allow speech to traitors.

As left-wing Republican leader, at public meeting in Dublin against Cumann na nGaedheal and 'Blueshirts' (neo-fascist National Guard). Coogan, Tim Pat, *The IRA*, Fontana, 1980, p. 91.

January 30, 1932
Alfie Byrne
The disciples of paganism [will] never again find either Dublin city or any part of Ireland an easy prey to their anti-God preaching.

As Lord Mayor of Dublin, attacking left-wing elements at launch of Cumann na nGaedheal manifesto. Keogh, Dermot, *Twentieth-Century Ireland*, Gill & Macmillan, 1994, p. 59.

February 5, 1932
William T. Cosgrave
[The IRA] are whining. Gallant, patriotic Irishmen never whined in difficulties; they took their medicine like men.

As leader of Free State Government, on setting up of military tribunals to deal with outbreak of IRA violence with aim of all-Ireland Republic. Keogh, Dermot, *De Valera and His Times*, Cork University Press, 1983, p. 154.

March 1932
Joseph Devlin
We were willing to help but you rejected all friendly offers... You went on on the old political lines, fostering hatreds, keeping one third of the population as if they were pariahs in the community.

As nationalist MP for West Belfast, shortly before leading nationalists out of NI Parliament for decade of intermittent abstentionism. Bardon, Jonathan, *A History of Ulster*, Blackstaff Press, 1992, p. 511.

March 9, 1932
Sean Moylan
[A triumph for] the owners of the donkey and cart over the pony-and-trap class.

As Fianna Fáil TD for North Cork, on victory of Fianna Fáil in election. Keogh, Dermot, *Twentieth-Century Ireland*, Gill & Macmillan, 1994, p. 64.

March 12, 1932
IRA
Fianna Fáil declares its intention to chop off some of the imperial tentacles; every such achievement is of value and will be welcomed. Notwithstanding such concessions, the Irish Republican Army must continue its work, and cannot escape its role as the vanguard of the freedom movement.

Statement in *An Phoblacht,* after Fianna Fáil victory in election. Coogan, Tim Pat, *The IRA*, Fontana, 1980, p. 90.

March 15, 1932
Eamon de Valera
We heard of frightful things that would happen the moment the Fianna Fáil government came into power. We have seen no evidence of these things. We have had a peaceful change of government.

As leader of Free State Government, to Dáil, on assuming office. Fanning, Ronan, *Independent Ireland*, Helicon, 1983, p. 109.

March 23, 1932
J. H. Thomas
The Free State Government are bound by the most formal and explicit undertaking to continue to pay the land annuities to the National Debt Commissioners, and the failure to do so would be a manifest violation of an engagement which is binding in law and honour on the Irish Free State.

As Dominions Secretary, to leader of Free State Government, Eamon de Valera, on his demand for abolition of Oath of Allegiance and right to withhold land annuities from British Government. Mitchell and Ó Snodaigh, *Irish Political Documents 1916-1949*, Irish Academic Press, 1985, p. 196.

April 5, 1932
Eamon de Valera
The elimination of the oath is a measure required for the peace, order and good government of the State.

As leader of Free State Government, to Dominions Secretary. Mitchell and Ó Snodaigh, *Irish Political Documents 1916-1949*, Irish Academic, 1985, p. 198.

April 9, 1932
J. H. Thomas
What is actually raised is nothing less than a repudiation of the Settlement of 1921 as a whole.

As Dominions Secretary, replying to Eamon de Valera above. Mitchell and Ó Snodaigh, *Irish Political Documents 1916-1949*, Irish Academic Press, 1985, pp. 199-201.

April 22, 1932
Eamon de Valera
If there are to be hair shirts at all, it will be hair shirts all round. Ultimately I hope the day will come when the hair shirt will give way to the silk shirt all round.

As leader of Free State Government, after cutting own salary and those of ministers. Coogan, Tim Pat, *De Valera*, Hutchinson, 1993, p. 438.

April 27, 1932
William T. Cosgrave
Two of the greatest Irishmen that ever lived...signed that agreement [the Treaty]... They never contemplated, never imagined, that this country would repudiate or make any attempt to repudiate the signatures appended to that instrument.

As leader of Cumann na nGaedheal, in Dáil, on Fianna Fáil's intention to remove Oath of Allegiance to British Crown. Mitchell and Ó Snodaigh, *Irish Political Documents 1916-1949*, Irish Academic, 1985, p. 202.

April 29, 1932
Eamon de Valera
The thing that was most heartbreaking in this Dáil since I came into it was to find the two parties, who should have stood side by side trying to secure freedom in order that they might have power to order their own policy, divided. I am speaking of the Fianna Fáil Party and the Labour Party.

As leader of Free State Government, in Dáil debate on unemployment. Moynihan, Maurice, *Speeches and Statements by Eamon de Valera 1917-1973*, Gill & Macmillan, 1980, p. 203.

June 7, 1932
J. H. Thomas
Don't think, Mr President, that the day you declare a Republic you will be met by British guns and battleships; you will be faced with the possibility of your people in England being aliens – with the return to your country of thousands of civil servants and thousands of unemployed people.

As Dominions Secretary, to Eamon de Valera, in Dublin. Coogan, Tim Pat, *De Valera*, Hutchinson, 1993, p. 450.

July 7, 1932
James McNeill
I do not think I should resign any office because other office-holders think I am a suitable target for ill-conditioned bad manners.

As Governor General of Free State, writing to de Valera, after series of snubs from Fianna Fáil ministers because he represented the Crown. The correspondence was published and McNeill forced to resign three months later. McMahon, Deirdre, *Republicans and Imperialists: Anglo-Irish Relations in the 1930s*, Yale University Press, 1984, p. 64.

July 12, 1932
James Craig
Ours is a Protestant Government and I am an Orangeman.

As NI Prime Minister, at Orange demonstration at Poyntzpass, Co Armagh. Bardon, Jonathan, *A History of Ulster*, Blackstaff Press, 1992, p. 538.

July 22, 1932
Ramsay MacDonald
So long as de Valera is there, there is no way out. He begins somewhere about the birth of Christ and wants a commission...to explore the past centuries... It makes one sick.

As British Prime Minister, in letter after breakdown of talks with Eamon de Valera in London on land annuities. McMahon, Deirdre, *Republicans and Imperialists: Anglo-Irish Relations in the 1930s*, Yale University Press, 1984, p. 68.

August 5, 1932
Thomas Inksip
It is not money that stands in the way of peace. There is something bigger and deeper. Does Mr de Valera want to be a partner in the Empire, or is he pursuing the will-o'-the-wisp of a republic?

As British Attorney General, about Fianna Fáil ending of annuity payments to Britain. *The Times*, August 5, 1932.

August 29, 1932
Frank Aiken
We have refrained from coercion because we believe it is a bad father who always uses the rod.

As Minister for Defence, explaining tolerant Government attitude to IRA. Brady, Conor, *Guardians of the Peace*, Gill & Macmillan, 1974, p. 172.

September 24, 1932
Sean MacEntee
...there are, unfortunately, reactionary and imperialist elements in the country...spreading the spirit of faction among us, and in this connection I recall the old saying: 'It never was Sassenach that beat us; it was the Gael that beat us... Knaves and traitors stand aside.'

As Minister for Finance, about alleged collusion between Opposition and British Government. McMahon, Deirdre, *Republicans and Imperialists: Anglo-Irish Relations in the 1930s*, Yale University Press, 1984, pp. 79-80.

September 30, 1932
Tommy Henderson
We have not met for four months and we are going to adjourn for another two months; in the meantime the starving people of Northern Ireland are to continue starving. The unemployed will have to beg in the streets. I condemn the way the Government have treated the unemployed. It is a disgrace to civilisation.

As Shankill Ulster Unionist MP, during last sitting of NI Parliament in Belfast City Hall before moving to Stormont. Bardon, Jonathan, *Belfast*, Blackstaff Press, 1983, p. 218.

September 30, 1932
Jack Beattie
I am going to put this out of action... The House indulges in hypocrisy while there are starving thousands outside.

As NI Labour MP, before throwing mace on floor at last sitting of NI Parliament in Belfast City Hall. Bardon, Jonathan, *Belfast*, Blackstaff Press, 1983, p. 218.

October 1, 1932
Hugh Pollock
[Stormont is] the outward and visible proof of the permanence of our institutions; that for all time we are bound indissolubly to the British Crown.

As NI Minister of Education, on opening of Stormont Parliament Building. Bardon, Jonathan, *A History of Ulster*, Blackstaff Press, 1992, p. 513.

October 10, 1932
Tommy Geehan
For many years the workers of Belfast had been divided by artificial barriers of religion and politics but the past two months had witnessed a wonderful spectacle because the workers were now united on a common platform demanding the right to live.

As Revolutionary Workers' Group organiser, during agitation uniting Protestants and Catholics in Belfast over low levels of outdoor relief pay. Farrell, Michael, *Northern Ireland: The Orange State*, Pluto, 1983, p. 127.

October 12, 1932
James Craig (Lord Craigavon)
If they [nationalists] have any designs by the trouble they have created in our city, if they have it at the back of their minds that this is one step towards securing a Republic for all Ireland... I say they are doomed to bitter disappointment.

As NI Prime Minister, after rioting in Protestant and Catholic areas of Belfast during agitation over low levels of outdoor relief pay. Farrell, Michael, *Northern Ireland: The Orange State*, Pluto, 1983, p. 130.

c. November 1, 1932
Sean Lemass
We have reached the point where a collapse of our economic system is in sight. By a collapse I mean famine conditions for a large number of our people.

As Minister for Industry and Commerce, in memo to Eamon de Valera on economic war with Britain. Fanning, Ronan, *Independent Ireland*, Helicon, 1983, p. 145.

November 8, 1932
Eamon de Valera
If the British Government should succeed in beating us in this fight, then you could have no freedom, because at every step they could threaten you again and force you again to obey the British. What is involved is whether the Irish nation is going to be free or not.

As leader of Free State Government and of Fianna Fáil, to party árd fheis, on economic war with British over refusal to pay London Irish land annuities. Fanning, Ronan, *Independent Ireland*, Helicon, 1983, p. 113.

December 21, 1932
Fianna Fáil, New York
Plays such as 'The Playboy of the Western World', 'Juno and the Paycock', 'The Shadow in the Glen', and others are anything but elevating to the Irish

character...with their filthy language, their drunkenness, murder and prostitution, and holding up the Irish character generally to be scoffed at and ridiculed by people of other races.

As NY party branch, objecting to state-subsidised Abbey Theatre tour in US. Coogan, Tim Pat, *De Valera*, Hutchinson, 1993, p. 500.

February 6, 1933
Eamon de Valera

You sometimes hear Ireland charged with a narrow and intolerant nationalism, but Ireland today has no other hope than this; that, true to her holiest traditions, she should humbly serve the truth and help by truth to save the world.

As leader of Free State Government, opening radio transmitter in Athlone. *Catholic Bulletin*, March 3, 1933.

March 1, 1933
William Butler Yeats

Your Minister may have it in his power to bring our theatre to an end but as long as it exists it will retain its freedom.

As director of Abbey Theatre, refusing to drop plays by O'Casey and Synge from repertoire at request of government official, after protests from New York. Coogan, Tim Pat, *De Valera*, Hutchinson, 1993, p. 502.

April 17, 1933
Eamon de Valera

All three [plays by Mr Sean O'Casey] touch upon the struggle for national independence in a manner which tends to create a false and unfavourable opinion of the motives and character of men who during the struggle risked their lives in the service of their country...their production abroad is likely to injure the reputation of the country and would certainly arouse feelings of shame and resentment among Irish exiles.

As leader of Free State Government, in (unsuccessful) attempt to persuade Abbey Theatre to drop O'Casey and Synge from its repertoire. Coogan, Tim Pat, *De Valera*, Hutchinson, 1993, p. 504.

April 23, 1933
Eamon de Valera

Let us remove these forms one by one, so that this state that we control may be a republic in fact and that when the time comes, the proclaiming of the Republic may involve no more than a ceremony, the formal confirmation of a status already attained.

As leader of Free State Government, on symbolic links with Britain, at Arbour Hill, Dublin. Moynihan, Maurice, *Speeches and Statements by Eamon de Valera 1917-1973*, Gill & Macmillan, 1980, p. 237.

May 27, 1933
King Alfonso

I have just seen that rascal, de Valera. I cut him, of course. Wouldn't you have done the same?

As Spanish monarch, to British Ambassador to Holy See, after encountering Eamon de Valera in Rome. McMahon, Deirdre, *Republicans and Imperialists: Anglo-Irish Relations in the 1930s*, Yale University Press, 1984, p. 114.

July 12, 1933
Basil Brooke

There was a great number of Protestants and Orangemen who employed Roman Catholics. He [Brooke] felt he could speak freely on this subject as he had not a Roman Catholic about his own place... There was a definite plot to overpower the vote of unionists in the North. He would appeal to loyalists therefore, wherever possible to employ good Protestant lads and lassies.

As NI Minister, speaking at Newtownbutler, Co Fermanagh. *Fermanagh Times*, July 13, 1933.

July 12, 1933
Captain T. T. Verschoyle

He who sows the wind shall reap the whirlwind...it remains to be seen whether the Colebrook Hitler will receive a well-merited rebuke from a responsible member of the Government.

As Protestant landlord in Co Fermanagh, condemning speech by Basil Brooke, above. (There was no rebuke.) Bardon, Jonathan, *A History of Ulster*, Blackstaff Press, 1992, p. 538.

July 12, 1933
J. M. Andrews

Another allegation made against the Government, which is untrue, is that of 31 porters at Stormont, 28 are Roman Catholic. I have investigated the matter and I have found that there are 30 Protestants and only one Roman Catholic, there only temporarily.

As NI Minister of Labour, at Orange demonstration. Farrell, Michael, *Northern Ireland: The Orange State*, Pluto, 1983, p. 136.

July 12, 1933
Major McCormick

Too many Protestants were giving employment to Roman Catholics...the Protestant who did so was a traitor to his country and his Protestantism was virtually lost. Rome would be in power in twenty years both inside Parliament and outside it.

As Belfast Ulster Unionist MP, speaking at Orange demonstration at Newtownbutler, Co Fermanagh. *The Irish Times*, July 13, 1933.

July 12, 1933
Rev W. J. Mitchell
Speakers [who urged Protestants not to employ Catholics] seemed to have little or no consideration for their Protestant brethren across the Border [in the South] where many of their lads and lassies were depending for their livelihood on Roman Catholic employers.

As Co Cavan rector, in letter to newspaper, following call by Ulster Unionist MPs not to employ Catholics. *The Irish Times*, August 14, 1933.

July 20, 1933
Eoin O'Duffy
Blue is adopted as the organisation colour for flags, shirts, ties, badges etc., just as sports clubs adopt a distinctive blazer or jersey.

As leader of neo-fascist Army Comrades Association or National Guard, known as 'Blueshirts', at meeting in Dublin hotel. *The Irish Times*, July 21, 1933.

August 13, 1933
Basil Brooke
Mr Mitchell was probably correct when he said [on July 12] that Protestants in the Free State were getting a square deal [but]... Ninety-seven percent of the Roman Catholics in Ireland politically were disloyal and disruptive and if they in the North would increase their power by employing such people, in a very few years Ulster would be voted into the Free State.

As Ulster Unionist MP, responding at Enniskillen Orange demonstration to criticism by Rev W. J. Mitchell of effect his statement had south of Border. *The Irish Times*, August 14, 1933.

September 1933
Thomas O'Higgins
If the other side broke gobs, they [Blueshirts] would also break gobs. They had the material and they would use it.

As President of neo-fascist 'Blueshirts' (and brother of assassinated minister, Kevin Higgins), about Republican attempts to break up their paramilitary meetings. Browne, Vincent, *The Magill Book of Irish Politics*, Magill Publications, 1981, p. 67.

September 8, 1933
Eoin O'Duffy
The people are being brought to beggary and defrauded of all hope of getting rid of partition by sham republicanism, which only uses the name republic as a pretext for self-glorification, for claiming a monopoly of patriotism, and for perpetuating discord.

As former general and leader of 'Blueshirts', in manifesto as President of United Ireland Party, formed from Cumann na nGaedheal, Centre Party and General

O'Duffy's National Guard (Blueshirts). *The Irish Times*, September 9, 1933.

October 2, 1933
Joseph McGarrity
To be frank, it is apparent that an agreement between your forces and the forces of the IRA is a national necessity. They will do things you will not care to do or cannot do in the face of public criticism, while the IRA pay no heed to public clamour as long as they feel they are doing a national duty.

As Clan na nGael leader in US, in proposal (rejected January 31, 1934) to leader of Free State Government, Eamon de Valera. Coogan, Tim Pat, *De Valera*, Hutchinson, 1993, p. 483.

November 11, 1933
United Ireland Party
[The party seeks] the voluntary reunion of all Ireland in a single independent state as a member, without any abnegation of Irish sovereignty, of the British Commonwealth in free and equal partnership.

As party formed by coalition of Cumann na nGaedheal, Centre Party and General O'Duffy's National Guard (Blueshirts), in policy statement. Browne, Vincent, *The Magill Book of Irish Politics*, Magill Publications, 1981, p. 47.

December 20, 1933
Catholic Hierarchy
During the intervals [between dances] the devil is busy; yes very busy, as sad experience proves, and on the way home in the small hours of the morning he is busier still.

As Irish Bishops, in statement on morality. *Irish Catholic*, December 23, 1933.

c. January 1, 1934
Victor Fiorentini
We are the smallest Fascist club in the United Kingdom.

As Italian-born secretary of Fascist Party in Derry, in Rome, to Mussolini. Fisk, Robert, *In Time of War*, Paladin, 1985, p. 461.

c. January, 1 1934
Benito Mussolini
Then grow!

As Italian Duce, replying to Victor Fiorentini, above. Fisk, Robert, *In Time of War*, Paladin, 1985, p. 461.

January 31, 1934
Eamon de Valera
You talk about coming to an understanding with the IRA. You talk of the influence it would have both here and abroad. You talk as if we were fools and didn't realise this. My God! Do you know that

ever since 1921 the main purpose in everything I have done has been to try and secure a base for national unity.

As leader of Free State Government, replying to letter of Joe McGarrity of October 2, 1933. McMahon, Deirdre, *Republicans and Imperialists: Anglo-Irish Relations in the 1930s*, Yale University Press, 1984, p. 126.

February 2, 1934
John A. Costello
The Blueshirts will be victorious in the Free State; the Blackshirts were victorious in Italy; the Hitlershirts were victorious in Germany.

As TD and future Fine Gael Taoiseach, on neo-fascist movement. Manning, Maurice, *Blueshirts*, Gill & Macmillan, 1970, p. 215.

March 20, 1934
Basil Brooke
I recommend those people who are Loyalists not to employ Roman Catholics, 99 percent of whom are disloyal... I want you to realise that, having done your bit, you have got your Prime Minister behind you.

As NI Minister, to Derry Unionist Association. Farrell, Michael, *Northern Ireland: The Orange State*, Pluto, 1983, pp. 90-91.

March 21, 1934
James Craig (Lord Craigavon)
There is not one of my colleagues who does not entirely agree with him, and I would not ask him to withdraw one word he said.

As NI Prime Minister, at Stormont, when asked to repudiate statement by Brooke recommending employers not to hire Catholics. Farrell, Michael, *Northern Ireland: The Orange State*, Pluto, 1983, p. 91.

April 8, 1934
IRA
A Republic of a united Ireland will never be achieved except through a struggle which uproots capitalism on its way.

Resolution passed by IRA officers meeting in Athlone. Moody, Martin, Byrne (Eds), *A New History of Ireland*, Vol. VIII, Oxford, 1982, p. 418.

April 24, 1934
James Craig (Lord Craigavon)
I have always said that I am an Orangeman first and a politician and member of this Parliament afterwards... They still boast of Southern Ireland being a Catholic State. All I boast of is that we are a Protestant Parliament and a Protestant State.

As NI Prime Minister, at Stormont, speaking in favour of motion condemning employment of 'disloyalists' from Republic. Hepburn, A. C., *The Conflict of Nationality in Modern Ireland*, Arnold, 1980, p. 165.

April 24, 1934
James Craig (Lord Craigavon)
It would be rather interesting for historians of the future to compare a Catholic State launched in the South with a Protestant State launched in the North and see which gets on the better and prospers the more.

As NI Prime Minister, at Stormont. Hepburn, A. C., *The Conflict of Nationality in Modern Ireland*, Arnold, 1980, p. 165.

April 24, 1934
Cahir Healy
You will notice he makes no distinction between Catholics in this declaration. The ex-Service man who risked his life in the Great War is put on a level with people like myself, who believe that the best thing for all Irishmen is a united Ireland... Hitler has not prosecuted the Jews nearly so much nor so subtly, nor so long...

As nationalist MP, at Stormont, criticising NI Prime Minister Lord Craigavon for advising unionists not to employ Catholics. McLoughlin, Michael, *Great Irish Speeches of the Twentieth Century*, Poolbeg, 1996, p. 159.

August 25, 1934
Lord Granard
He is on the border line between genius and insanity. I have met men of many countries and have been governor of a lunatic asylum, but I have never met anybody like [him] before.

As Irish Senator, on Eamon de Valera, in private report to London. McMahon, Deirdre, *Republicans and Imperialists: Anglo-Irish Relations in the 1930s*, Yale University Press, 1984, p. 143.

September 25, 1934
Eoin O'Duffy
Hitler had done more for Germany than any other leader in the world had done for his country.

As leader of National Guard, or 'Blueshirts'. Keogh, Dermot, *Twentieth-Century Ireland*, Gill & Macmillan, 1994, p. 83.

November 8, 1934
Wilfrid Spender
If the Prime Minister is dissatisfied with our present system [of recruitment], I think the only course would be for the Government to come out in the open and to say that only Protestants are admitted to our service.

As permanent head of NI civil service, in memo to Cabinet Secretary, after NI Prime Minister Lord Craigavon disapproved of employing Catholic workers at Stormont. Buckland, Patrick, *James Craig*, Gill & Macmillan, 1980, p. 111.

November 21, 1934
James Craig (Lord Craigavon)
Regarding public appointments, these were given by the Government as far as possible to loyal men and women. We have our own means of finding out [their loyalty]. That was behind [the] whole idea of carrying on a Protestant Government for a Protestant people.

As NI Prime Minister, at Stormont, replying to charge by nationalist MP Cahir Healy that Catholic minority were denied their rights. *The Irish Times*, November 22, 1934.

December 19, 1934
Eamon de Valera
No longer shall our children, like our cattle, be brought up for export.

As leader of Free State Government, in Dáil, on determination to end emigration. Murphy, John A., *De Valera and His Times*, Cork University Press, 1983, p. 10.

March 17, 1935
Eamon de Valera
Since the coming of St Patrick, fifteen hundred years ago, Ireland has been a Christian and a Catholic nation. All the ruthless attempts made through the centuries to force her from this allegiance have not shaken her faith. She remains a Catholic nation.

As leader of Free State Government, in radio broadcast to United States. *The Irish Press*, March 18, 1935.

March 22, 1935
IRA
The Army Council offers the services of the Army to assist in mobilising the maximum support for the Dublin transport workers in their struggle, and is prepared to send representatives to meet the strike committee for this purpose.

Statement issued after Free State Government used army lorries during transport strike, following which police arrested 44 IRA members. Coogan, Tim Pat, *The IRA*, Fontana, 1980, p. 114.

July 11, 1935
Rt Rev John MacNeice
Forget the things that are behind. Forget the unhappy past. Forget the story of the old feuds, the old triumphs, the old humiliations... One should understand the past the better to forget it.

As Church of Ireland Bishop of Down and father of poet Louis MacNeice, on eve of Orange celebrations. Bardon, Jonathan, *A History of Ulster*, Blackstaff Press, 1992, p. 540 (final phrase, undated, was published in *The Irish Times*, March 3, 1998).

July 12, 1935
Joseph Davison
Are we to forget that the aim of these people is to establish an all-Ireland Roman Catholic state, in which Protestantism will be crushed out of existence?

As Orange Grand Master, replying at Orange celebrations in Belmont 'Field' to Dr John MacNeice, above. Bardon, Jonathan, *A History of Ulster*, Blackstaff Press, 1992, p. 540.

August 28, 1935
Brinsley McNamara
The audience shows a wholly uncritical...almost insane admiration for the vulgar and worthless plays of Mr O'Casey.

As director of Abbey Theatre, before resigning over alleged anti-Catholic bias in Sean O'Casey's 'Silver Tassie'. Hunt, Hugh, *The Abbey*, Gill & Macmillan, 1979, p. 151.

September 16, 1935
Eamon de Valera
Make no mistake, if on any pretext whatever we were to permit the sovereignty of even the weakest state amongst us to be unjustly taken away, the whole foundation of the League [of Nations] would crumble into dust.

As President of the Council of League of Nations, addressing assembly on eve of Italian invasion of Abyssinia. Keogh, Dermot, *Twentieth-Century Ireland*, Gill & Macmillan, 1994, p. 87.

1936
J. W. Dulanty
[I] felt like a whore at a christening.

As Irish High Commissioner in London, describing to Canadian High Commissioner his meetings with Commissioners from other Commonwealth countries. McMahon, Deirdre, *Republicans and Imperialists: Anglo-Irish Relations in the 1930s*, Yale University Press, 1984, p. 171.

June 18, 1936
Gerald Boland
We smashed them [Blueshirts] and we are going to smash the others.

As Fianna Fáil Minister for Justice, in Dáil, after declaring IRA illegal following series of shootings. Coogan, Tim Pat, *The IRA*, Fontana, 1980, p. 123.

August 14, 1936
Sean Russell
Our air force may be small, but it is reasonably efficient.

As IRA leader, quoted in *Daily Mirror*. (The IRA had no air force but once hired a small aircraft in abortive attempt to rescue prisoners in British jail.) Coogan, Tim Pat, *The IRA*, Fontana, 1980, pp. 154-155.

September 16, 1936
Joseph McGarrity
[Eamon de Valera is] selling out his former
friends and repressing all freedom of thought in
Ireland with the ruthlessness of a dictator.

As head of Clan na nGael, on anti-IRA crackdown.
Coogan, Tim Pat, *De Valera*, Hutchinson, 1993, p. 484.

December 11, 1936
Eamon de Valera
...we are retaining the King for those purposes
for which he was used hitherto...as the symbol of
cooperation in the States of the Commonwealth.

As leader of Free State Government, in Dáil, on External
Relations Act removing references to Crown from
constitution. Chubb, Basil, *Source Book of Irish
Government*, Institute of Public Administration, 1983,
p. 14.

April 1, 1937
Michael Tierney
Our course, above all in war-time, must be one
of 'sacred egoism'.

As professor and former Fine Gael TD, advocating
neutrality. *Ireland Today*, April 1937.

May 9, 1937
Mary Kettle
No woman who works will have any security
whatsoever.

As chairwoman of Joint Committee of Women's
Societies, on effect of Eamon de Valera's proposed
Constitution, which elevated women 'within the home'.
Coogan, Tim Pat, *De Valera*, Hutchinson, 1993, p. 496.

May 11, 1937
The Irish Constitution
Article 2. The National territory consists of the
whole island of Ireland, its islands and the
territorial seas.
Article 3. Pending the reintegration of the
national territory, and without prejudice to the
right of the Parliament and Government
established by this Constitution to exercise
jurisdiction over the whole of that territory, the
laws enacted by that Parliament shall have the
like area and extent of application as the laws of
Saorstát Éireann and the like extraterritorial
effect.

As territorial articles in revised Constitution presented to
Dáil by Eamon de Valera, and established by
referendum. Mitchell and Ó Snodaigh, *Irish Political
Documents 1916-1949*, Irish Academic, 1985, p. 216.

May 11, 1937
Eamon de Valera
If it [the Northern Ireland problem] was not there,
in all probability there would be a flat, downright
proclamation of the Republic in this.

As leader of Free State Government, in Dáil debate on
Constitution. Chubb, Basil, *Source Book of Irish
Government*, Institute of Public Administration, 1983,
p. 16.

June 27, 1937
Eamon de Valera
My reply is get a copy of the new Constitution.
There is in it an assertion that the national
territory is the whole of Ireland, not part of it.

As Taoiseach, replying to heckler in Monaghan who asked
'What about the Six Counties?' Bardon, Jonathan, *A History
of Ulster*, Blackstaff Press, 1992, p. 542.

August 29, 1937
German Foreign Ministry
The German Government will refrain from all
hostile activity towards Irish territory and will
respect Ireland's integrity provided that for her
part, Ireland will observe strict neutrality towards
Germany.

As Nazi Government ministry, in letter to German Minister
in Dublin, Eduard Hempel. Coogan, Tim Pat, *The IRA*,
Fontana, 1980, p. 262.

c. September 30, 1937
J. B. Whelehan
What matters political freedom if our finest lads
must still slave for the foreigner and return,
caskets of ashes?

As professor and author, on death of 10 Achill youths in
hostel fire in Scotland. Keogh, Dermot, *Twentieth-Century
Ireland*, Gill & Macmillan, 1994, p. 93.

October 6, 1937
Malcolm MacDonald
[De Valera] had been in favour of the Irish
declaring a Republic, and so breaking with the
Empire, but afterwards coming back into
association with it. He had thought that process
necessary in order to establish Irish independence.

As Dominions Secretary, in memo after meeting Taoiseach,
Eamon de Valera. Lee, J. J., *Ireland 1912-1985*, Cambridge
University Press, 1990, p. 213.

November 17, 1937
Eduard Hempel
[The Irish] say agreeable things without meaning
everything that is said.

As German Minister in Ireland. Lee, J. J., *Ireland
1912-1985*, Cambridge University Press, 1990, p. 247.

November 27, 1937
William T. Cosgrave

The war in Spain is a war for the victory or defeat of communism and all it stands for, with its denial of Christian principles, individual liberty, and democracy. I do not see how a country with our history, our beliefs, our traditions and our ideals, moral, religious and political, can fail to withdraw recognition from a government which stands for everything we abhor.

As Fine Gael leader, urging Dáil (unsuccessfully) to recognise Franco Government. McLoughlin, Michael, *Great Irish Speeches of the Twentieth Century*, Poolbeg, 1996, p. 176.

February 9, 1938
Franklin D. Roosevelt

I am not convinced that any intervention – no matter how direct – on our part would be wise, or for that matter accomplish the effect we had in mind.

As US President, replying to message from US minister in Ireland, John Cudahy, urging US intervention to end partition. Coogan, Tim Pat, *De Valera*, Hutchinson, 1993, p. 515.

March 14, 1938
Neville Chamberlain

Is Mr de Valera trying to make it appear that we are thrusting a burden upon Éire in making her take over the defended ports? I am lost in admiration of Mr de Valera's skill in dialectics.

As British Prime Minister, on request by Taoiseach, Eamon de Valera, for return of 'Treaty' ports of Cobh, Berehaven and Lough Swilly, still occupied by Britain under 1921 Treaty. Coogan, Tim Pat, *De Valera*, Hutchinson, 1993, p. 518.

April 27, 1938
Eamon de Valera

It is far better for Britain, far more advantageous for Britain, to have a free Ireland by its side than an Ireland that would be unfriendly because of liberties which Britain denied.

As Taoiseach, in Dáil on agreement with Britain to return 'Treaty' ports. McLoughlin, Michael, *Great Irish Speeches of the Twentieth Century*, Poolbeg, 1996, p. 181.

May 5, 1938
Winston Churchill

These ports are in fact the sentinel towers of the western approaches, by which the forty-five million people in this island so enormously depend on foreign food for their daily bread... Now we are to give them up, unconditionally, to an Irish Government led by men – I do not want to use harsh words – whose rise to power has

been proportionate to the animosity with which they have acted against this country.

As Conservative MP, in House of Commons, on return of 'Treaty' ports. *HC Debates:* Vol. 355; Cols. 1094-1105.

May 5, 1938
Neville Chamberlain

We came to the conclusion that a friendly Ireland was worth far more to us both in peace and in war than those paper rights that could only be exercised at the risk of maintaining and perhaps increasing their sense of grievance.

As British Prime Minister, in House of Commons, about end of economic war with Ireland and handing over of 'Treaty' ports to Free State. *HC Debates:* Vol. 355; Cols. 1072-1078.

June 14, 1938
Eamon de Valera

We are going to get them in the right way. We want not the physical territory as much as the hearts of the people.

As Taoiseach, in election speech in Dun Laoghaire, on how to get the Six Counties. *The Irish Times*, June 15, 1938.

July 1, 1938
William Butler Yeats

Did that play of mine send out
Certain men the English shot?

As poet, in 'The Man and the Echo', reflecting on his 1902 play 'Cathleen ni Houlihan', in which Ireland, as a poor old woman, summoned hero to fight for the cause. Tuohy, Frank, *Yeats*, Macmillan, 1976, p. 129.

September 30, 1938
Eamon de Valera

[Neville Chamberlain] is a knight of peace [who has] attained the highest peak of human greatness, and a glory greater than that of all the conquerors.

As President of the Council of the League of Nations, on British Prime Minister's appeasement of Hitler at Munich. Coogan, Tim Pat, *De Valera*, Hutchinson, 1993, p. 530.

October 13, 1938
Eamon de Valera

It is possible to visualise a critical situation arising in the future in which a united free Ireland would be willing to cooperate with Britain to resist a common attack. Let me say clearly that the chances of such cooperation in the event of a European war are very, very slight, while partition remains.

As Taoiseach, in interview in *The Evening Standard*. Moynihan, Maurice, *Speeches and Statements by Eamon de Valera 1917-1973*, Gill & Macmillan, 1980, p. 361.

1939
Louis MacNeice
Castles are out of date,
The tide flows round the children's sandy fancy;
Put up what flag you like, it is too late
To save your soul with bunting.

As Belfast-born poet, on Northern Ireland, in 'Autumn Journal'. Longley, Michael (Ed.), *Louis MacNeice, Selected Poems*, Faber and Faber, 1988, p. 64.

1939
Louis MacNeice
Why do we like being Irish? Partly because
It gives us a hold on the sentimental English
As members of a world that never was,
Baptized with fairy water.

As Belfast-born poet, in 'Autumn Journal'. Longley, Michael (Ed.), *Louis MacNeice, Selected Poems*, Faber and Faber, 1988, p. 62.

January 12, 1939
Sean Russell
I have the honour to inform you that the Government of the Irish Republic...herewith demand the withdrawal of all British armed forces stationed in Ireland... The Government of the Irish Republic believe that a period of four days is sufficient...

As leader of IRA, which claimed to be real Irish Government on basis of support from survivors of Second Dáil, in letter to London, Berlin and Rome governments, preceding bombing campaign in England. Coogan, Tim Pat, *The IRA*, Fontana, 1980, pp. 164-165.

February 7, 1939
Eamon de Valera
If I were told tomorrow, 'You can have a united Ireland if you give up your idea of restoring the national language to be the spoken language of the majority of the people', I would for myself say no.

As Taoiseach, in Dáil. Moynihan, Maurice, *Speeches and Statements by Eamon de Valera 1917-1973*, Gill & Macmillan, 1980, p. 372.

April 28, 1939
Adolf Hitler
He...asks for a statement that Germany will not attack Ireland. Now I have just read a speech by de Valera, the Irish Taoiseach, in which, strangely enough, and contrary to Mr Roosevelt's opinion, he does not charge Germany with oppressing Ireland, but he reproached England with subjecting Ireland to continuous aggression.

As German dictator, in speech to Reichstag after US President Roosevelt had publicly asked Hitler for assurances he would not attack 31 specified countries,

including Free State. Shirer, William L., *The Rise and Fall of the Third Reich*, Pan, 1960, p. 577.

May 1939
Neville Chamberlain
If you really want to help us, *don't* press for conscription. It will only be an embarrassment.

As British Prime Minister, recalling Irish reaction to conscription in 1918, in meeting with NI Prime Minister Lord Craigavon in London. Bardon, Jonathan, *A History of Ulster*, Blackstaff Press, 1992, p. 554.

September 2, 1939
Dáil Éireann
Arising out of armed conflict now taking place in Europe, a national emergency exists affecting the vital interests of the State.

As Irish parliament, in declaration of emergency at outbreak of war (it remained in effect until August 31, 1976). Chubb, Basil, *Source Book of Irish Government*, Institute of Public Administration, 1983, p. 38.

September 2, 1939
Eamon de Valera
As long as our own country or any part of it is subjected to force, the application of force, by a stronger nation, it is only natural that our people, whatever sympathies they might have in a conflict like the present, should look at their own country first...

As Taoiseach, in Dáil, announcing policy of Irish neutrality. McLoughlin, Michael, *Great Irish Speeches of the Twentieth Century*, Poolbeg, 1996, p. 190.

September 2, 1939
James Craig (Lord Craigavon)
As an additional precaution against sedition and attacks in our midst, we took into our care last night forty-five of the IRA... Who are these men? I can describe them in a sentence. They are the King's enemies.

As NI Prime Minister, at Stormont, on security measures on outbreak of war with Germany. McLoughlin, Michael, *Great Irish Speeches of the Twentieth Century*, Poolbeg, 1996, pp. 194-195.

September 4, 1939
Winston Churchill
If they throw bombs in London, why should they not supply fuel to U-boats?

As First Lord of the Admiralty, calling for report on 'so-called neutrality of the so-called Éire'. Coogan, Tim Pat, *De Valera*, Hutchinson, 1993, p. 536.

October 28, 1939
IRA
England's difficulty – Ireland's opportunity has ever been the watchword of the Gael... Now is the time for Irishmen to take up arms and strike a

blow for our Ulster people. By destroying the Orange ascendancy, by expelling the British Army, by abolishing the Border, we shall cut away the cancer that is gnawing away at the heart of Ireland.

In appeal in IRA *War News*. Dwyer, Thomas Ryle, *Irish Neutrality and the USA 1939-1947*, Rowman and Littlefield & Gill & Macmillan, 1977, p. 21.

November 9, 1939
Eamon de Valera

The Government have been faced with the alternative of two evils. We have had to choose the lesser, and the lesser evil is to see men die, rather than that the safety of the whole community should be endangered.

As Taoiseach, in Dáil, on refusal to release IRA prisoners on hunger strike. Moynihan, Maurice, *Speeches and Statements by Eamon de Valera 1917-1973*, Gill & Macmillan, 1980, pp. 421-422.

1940
Nicholas Monsarrat

As they [British convoys] sailed past this smug coastline, past people who did not give a damn how the war went as long as they could live on in their fairy-tale world, they had time to ponder a new aspect of indecency. In the list of people you were prepared to like when the war was over, the man who stood by and watched while you were getting your throat cut could not figure very high.

As British author, on Ireland. Monsarrat, N., *The Cruel Sea*, Cassell, 1951, p. 151.

January 23, 1940
Frank Aiken

Instead of earning the respect and goodwill of both belligerents it [neutrality] is regarded by both with hatred and contempt; 'He who is not with me is against me.'

As Minister for Coordination of Defence Measures, in memo to Cabinet justifying censorship of Irish newspapers during war. Fisk, Robert, *In Time of War*, Paladin, 1985, p. 165.

February 10, 1940
Paul Woermann

By reason of its militant attitude towards England, the IRA is a natural ally of Germany.

As Divisional Director, German Foreign Ministry, to German Foreign Minister von Ribbentrop after Sean Russell of IRA had made contact with German Government. Fisk, Robert, *In Time of War*, Paladin, 1985, p. 340.

May 12, 1940
Eamon de Valera

Today these two small nations are fighting for their lives, and I think it would be unworthy of this small nation if, on an occasion like this, I did not utter our protest against the cruel wrong that has been done them.

As Taoiseach, in first criticism of Nazi Germany, after German invasion of Belgium and Holland. Coogan, Tim Pat, *De Valera*, Hutchinson, 1993, p. 547.

May 28, 1940
Edmond Warnock

I am no longer a member of the Government. I have heard speeches about Ulster pulling her weight but they have never carried conviction.

As NI Parliamentary Secretary for Home Affairs, resigning in protest at lack of urgency shown by NI Government in war effort. Kennedy, David, *Ireland in the War Years and After*, Gill & Macmillan, 1969, p. 55.

June 16, 1940
Jan Smuts

The Irish Atlantic ports should be seized at once, even in the face of Irish opposition, to prevent them suffering the same fate as the Norwegian ports [seized by Germany].

As South African Minister, in message to British War Cabinet. Dwyer, Thomas Ryle, *Irish Neutrality and the USA 1939-1947*, Rowman and Littlefield & Gill & Macmillan, 1977, p. 73.

June 21, 1940
Malcolm MacDonald

That there should be a declaration of a United Ireland in principle, the constitutional and other practical details of the Union to be worked out in due course: Ulster to remain a belligerent, Éire to remain neutral at any rate for the time being; if both parties desired it, a Joint Defence Council to be set up at once; at the same time, in order to secure Éire's neutrality against violation by Germany, British naval ships to be allowed into Éire ports, British troops and aeroplanes to be stationed at certain agreed points in the territory.

As British Minister for Health, conveying British offer of united Ireland to Taoiseach Eamon de Valera, at meeting in Dublin. Fisk, Robert, *In Time of War*, Paladin, 1985, p. 197.

June 21, 1940
Eamon de Valera

That Éire and Ulster should be merged in a United Ireland, which should at once become neutral; its neutrality to be guaranteed by Great Britain and the United States of America; since Britain was a belligerent, its military and naval forces should not take any active part in guaranteeing that neutrality, but American ships should come into the Irish ports, and perhaps American troops into Ireland, to effect this guarantee.

As Taoiseach, in counter-offer to British Government's offer, above. (At time US was also not a belligerent.) Fisk, Robert, *In Time of War*, Paladin, 1985, p. 198.

June 25, 1940
Neville Chamberlain
I do not believe that the Ulster Government would refuse to play their part in bringing about so favourable a development.

As British Prime Minister, to War Cabinet, on British proposal to de Valera of united Ireland in principle in return for use of Free State territory. Fisk, Robert, *In Time of War*, Paladin, 1985, p. 201.

June 26, 1940
Malcolm MacDonald
If the authorities in Éire missed this opportunity of reaching their great goal, the opportunity might never present itself again...on the assumption that Éire had carried out its part of the plan and come into the war, it was unthinkable that the promise [of a united Ireland] should be broken.

As British Minister of Health, at meeting with Eamon de Valera in Dublin. Fisk, Robert, *In Time of War*, Paladin, 1985, p. 202.

June 26, 1940
Neville Chamberlain
You will observe that the document takes the form of an inquiry only, because we have not felt it right to approach you officially with a request for your assent unless we had first a binding assurance from Éire that they would, if the assent were given, come into the war.

As British Prime Minister, in letter to NI Prime Minister Lord Craigavon on proposal of united Ireland made to Irish Government. Fisk, Robert, *In Time of War*, Paladin, 1985, p. 207.

June 27, 1940
James Craig (Lord Craigavon)
Am profoundly shocked and disgusted by your letter making suggestions so far-reaching behind my back and without any preconsultation with me. To such treachery to loyal Ulster I will never be a party.

As NI Prime Minister, in telegram to Chamberlain on British proposal of united Ireland made to Irish Government. Fisk, Robert, *In Time of War*, Paladin, 1985, p. 207.

June 27, 1940
Neville Chamberlain
Little likelihood of progress with Éire, but you can be assured that you will have every

opportunity of making your views known before any decision affecting Ulster is taken. Meanwhile please remember the serious nature of the situation which requires that every effort be made to meet it.

As British Prime Minister, replying in telegram to Craigavon, above. Fisk, Robert, *In Time of War*, Paladin, 1985, pp. 207-208.

June 29, 1940
James Craig (Lord Craigavon)
De Valera is under German dictation and far past reasoning with. He may purposely protract negotiations till enemy has landed. Strongly advocate immediate naval occupation of harbours and military advance south.

As NI Prime Minister, in telegram to Chamberlain in response to telegram, above. Fisk, Robert, *In Time of War*, Paladin, 1985, p. 210.

July 5, 1940
Eamon de Valera
The plan would commit us definitely to an immediate abandonment of our neutrality. On the other hand it gives no guarantee that in the end we would have a united Ireland.

As Taoiseach, rejecting British Government proposal for united Ireland. Fisk, Robert, *In Time of War*, Paladin, 1985, p. 212.

July 11, 1940
Joachim von Ribbentrop
As long as Ireland conducts herself in a neutral fashion it can be counted on with absolute certainty that Germany will respect her neutrality unconditionally...it is an utterly unreasonable suspicion that we might have the intention to prepare to use Ireland as a military base against England through a so-called 'fifth column' which besides does not exist.

As German Foreign Minister in message to Eduard Hempel, German Minister in Dublin. Fisk, Robert, *In Time of War*, Paladin, 1985, p. 333.

August 15, 1940
Franklin D. Roosevelt
[The Irish] must realise that in the end they will have to fish or cut bait.

As US President, in message to US Minister in Dublin on Irish refusal to join Allies. Lyle Dwyer, Thomas, *Irish Neutrality and the USA 1939-1947*, Rowman and Littlefield & Gill & Macmillan, 1977, p. 81.

November 6, 1940
Winston Churchill
The fact that we cannot use the south and west coasts of Ireland to refuel our flotillas and aircraft, and thus protect the trade by which Ireland as well

as Great Britain lives, is a most heavy and
grievous burden, and one which should never
have been placed on our shoulders, broad though
they may be.

As British Prime Minister, in House of Commons. Fisk,
Robert, *In Time of War*, Paladin, 1985, p. 287.

November 7, 1940
Eamon de Valera

There can be no question of the handing over of
these ports so long as this State remains neutral...
Any attempt to bring pressure to bear on us by
any side – by any of the belligerents – by Britain
– could only lead to bloodshed.

As Taoiseach, in Dáil, replying to Churchill, above.
Moynihan, Maurice, *Speeches and Statements by Eamon
de Valera 1917-1973*, Gill & Macmillan, 1980,
pp. 451-452.

November 10, 1940
David Gray

[De Valera is] probably the most adroit politician
in Europe and he honestly believes that all he
does is for the good of the country. He has the
qualities of martyr, fanatic and Machiavelli. No
one can outwit him, frighten him or brandish
him.

As US Minister in Dublin, in message to President
Roosevelt. Lyle Dwyer, Thomas, *Irish Neutrality and the
USA 1939-1947*, Rowman and Littlefield & Gill &
Macmillan, 1977, pp. 90-91.

December 3, 1940
Adolf Hitler

A landing in Ireland can be attempted only if
Ireland requests help... The occupation of
Ireland might lead to the end of the war.

As German dictator, at conference with German naval
staff. Fisk, Robert, *In Time of War*, Paladin, 1985, p. 225.

December 12, 1940
George Bernard Shaw

The [Treaty] ports do not belong to Ireland, they
belong to Europe, to the world, to civilisation, to
the Most Holy Trinity as you might say, and are
only held in trust by your Government in
Dublin. In their names we must borrow the ports
from you for the duration.

As playwright, in advice to Churchill on what to say to
justify taking back Treaty ports. *The Irish Press*, December
12, 1940.

December 13, 1940
Winston Churchill

Our merchant seamen...take it much amiss that
we should have to carry Irish supplies through
air and U-boat attacks and subsidise them

handsomely, when de Valera is quite content to sit
happy and see us strangle.

As British Prime Minister, in message to President Roosevelt
on Britain's reduction of shipments to Ireland. Lyle Dwyer,
Thomas, *Irish Neutrality and the USA 1939-1947*, Rowman
and Littlefield & Gill & Macmillan, 1977, p. 99.

1941
Marianne Moore

I am troubled, I'm dissatisfied, I'm Irish.

As poet, in last line of 'Spencer's Ireland'. Bartlett, John,
Familiar Quotations, Little, Brown, 1992, p. 664.

January 1, 1941
Adolf Hitler

Éire's neutrality must be respected. A neutral Irish
Free State is of greater value to us than a hostile
Ireland.

As German dictator, in discussion with officer about
possible invasion of Britain. Fisk, Robert, *In Time of War*,
Paladin, 1985, p. 263.

January 1, 1941
Joseph Walsh

Small nations like Ireland do not and cannot
assume the role of defenders of just causes except
their own.

As Secretary of Department of External Affairs, on policy of
neutrality. Keogh, Dermot, *Twentieth-Century Ireland*, Gill
& Macmillan, 1994, p. 108.

c. January 14, 1941
Irish Independent

[James Joyce] reviled the religion in which he had
been brought up and fouled the nest which was his
native city.

As Dublin newspaper, on death of James Joyce on January
13, 1941. Gray, Tony, *The Lost Years, The Emergency in
Ireland 1939-1945*, Warner Books, 1998, p. 169.

January 20, 1941
John Maffey

Éire is a bog with a petty leader raking over old
muck-heaps.

As UK Representative in Dublin, in report to London. Fisk,
Robert, *In Time of War*, Paladin, 1985, p. 297.

January 31, 1941
Winston Churchill

No attempt should be made to conceal from Mr de
Valera the depth and intensity of feeling against
the policy of Irish neutrality. We have tolerated
and acquiesced in it, but juridically we have never
recognised that southern Ireland is an independent
sovereign state.

As British Prime Minister, in letter to Dominions Secretary.
Fisk, Robert, *In Time of War*, Paladin, 1985, pp. 298-299.

February 4, 1941
David Gray

The Dáil makes me think of the Supervision meetings that I used to report in Monroe County when I worked on the *Rochester Union and Advertiser*.

As US Minister in Ireland, in message to President Roosevelt on quality of Irish politics. Lyle Dwyer, Thomas, *Irish Neutrality and the USA 1939-1947*, Rowman and Littlefield & Gill & Macmillan, 1977, p. 104.

February 10, 1941
James Dillon

We are living under a sword of Damocles that might fall to destroy freedom and man's right to adore God... It may be policy of this Government to stand neutral, but I am not neutral. The issue at stake means whether I want to live or die.

As deputy Fine Gael leader, in address attacking neutrality and supporting allies at Fine Gael árd fheis. Fisk, Robert, *In Time of War*, Paladin, 1985, p. 303.

March 17, 1941
Eamon de Valera

A small country like ours that had for centuries resisted imperial absorption, and that still wished to preserve its separate national identity, was bound to choose the course of neutrality in this war... The continued existence of partition, that unnatural separation of six of our counties from the rest of Ireland, added, in our case, a further decisive reason.

As Taoiseach, in St Patrick's Day radio broadcast to United States. Moynihan, Maurice, *Speeches and Statements by Eamon de Valera 1917-1973*, Gill & Macmillan, 1980, p. 454.

c. April 1, 1941
Sean O Faolain

No sooner does any man attempt, or achieve here anything fine, than the rats begin to emerge from the sewers, bringing with them a skunk-like stench of envy and hatred, worse than the drip of a broken drain.

As writer, on cultural deficiencies of Dublin. Brown, Terence, *Ireland, A Social and Cultural History, 1922-1979*, Fontana, 1982, pp. 174-175.

April 7, 1941
Franklin D. Roosevelt

Preposterous! What you have to fear is German aggression... I have never heard anything so preposterous in all my life!

As US President, in White House, to Minister for Coordination of Defensive Measures, Frank Aiken, who suggested Ireland also had to fear British aggression. Lyle Dwyer, Thomas, *Irish Neutrality and the USA 1939-1947*,

Rowman and Littlefield & Gill & Macmillan, 1977, p. 113.

May 5, 1941
Ernst von Kuhren

When we approached the target at half past two we stared silently into a sea of flames such as none of us had seen before...in Belfast there was not just a large number of conflagrations, but just one enormous conflagration which spread over the entire harbour and industrial area.

As German radio reporter, broadcasting eye-witness account of blitz on Belfast. Fisk, Robert, *In Time of War*, Paladin, 1985, p. 500.

May 13, 1941
Tommy Henderson

Will the right honourable member come with me to the hills and to Divis Mountain? Will he go to the barns and sheughs throughout Northern Ireland to see the people of Belfast, some of them lying on damp ground? Will he come to Hannahstown and the Falls Road? The Catholics and Protestants are going up there mixed and they are talking to one another... They all say the same thing, that the Government is no good.

As Shankill MP, at Stormont, about flight of Belfast's population from German air raids. Bardon, Jonathan, *A History of Ulster*, Blackstaff Press, 1992, p. 573.

May 15, 1941
Dawson Bates

There are in the country [NI] probably about 5,000 unbilletable persons. They are unbilletable owing to personal habits which are sub-human.

As Home Affairs Minister in NI Government, in memorandum about refugees from German blitz. Fisk, Robert, *In Time of War*, Paladin, 1985, p. 507.

May 21, 1941
Robert (Bertie) Smyllie

Whenever I have appealed to Caesar [Eamon de Valera] – and I have done so more than once – I have found the Long Fellow more than anxious to be fair.

As editor of *Irish Times*, to Richard Mulcahy, of Fine Gael, after censor deleted much of Mulcahy's speech. Fisk, Robert, *In Time of War*, Paladin, 1985, pp. 167-168.

May 24, 1941
Cardinal Joseph MacRory

...An ancient land, made one by God, was partitioned by a foreign power against the vehement protests of its people, and...conscription would now seek to compel those who still writhe under this grievous wrong to fight on the side of its perpetrators.

As Primate of Ireland, on prospect of conscription in Northern Ireland. Fisk, Robert, *In Time of War*, Paladin, 1985, p. 513.

May 25, 1941
Eamon de Valera
The conscription of the people of one nation by another revolts the human conscience... The Six Counties...are part of Ireland, they have always been part of Ireland, and their people, Catholic and Protestant, are our people.

As Taoiseach, in message to Churchill after Unionist Government recommended conscription. Moynihan, Maurice, *Speeches and Statements by Eamon de Valera 1917-1973*, Gill & Macmillan, 1980, p. 459.

May 25, 1941
Frank Aiken
[Britain has] no right to occupy six counties of Ireland and then go on to commit the monstrous outrage of conscripting men into an army they allege is fighting for freedom and democracy.

As Minister for Coordination of Defensive Measures, interviewed in *The New York Times*. Lyle Dwyer, Thomas, *Irish Neutrality and the USA 1939-1947*, Rowman and Littlefield & Gill & Macmillan, 1977, p. 119.

May 25, 1941
Captain Denis Ireland
After one hundred and fifty years, Catholics and Protestants are once more united on the fundamental issue.

As leader of Protestant Ulster Union Club, at anti-conscription rally in Belfast. *The Irish Press*, May 26, 1941.

May 27, 1941
Winston Churchill
[Conscription] would be more trouble than it was worth to enforce.

As British Prime Minister, deferring conscription in Northern Ireland. Lyle Dwyer, Thomas, *Irish Neutrality and the USA 1939-1947*, Rowman and Littlefield & Gill & Macmillan, 1977, p. 127.

June 2, 1941
Rt Rev J. B. Woodburn
If something is not done now to remedy this rank inequality there will be a revolution after the war.

As retiring Moderator of Presbyterian Assembly, on wretchedness of bomb victims in Belfast. Bardon, Jonathan, *Belfast*, Blackstaff Press, 1983, p. 248.

July 9, 1941
Hans Hartmann
The fate of Russia under Bolshevik rule is comparable to the fate of Ireland under English

sovereignty, and it is to be noticed that these two powers have now entered into an alliance.

As Nazi propagandist, broadcasting in Irish from Berlin. O'Donoghue, David, *Hitler's Irish Voices*, Beyond the Pale Publications, 1998, p. 64.

July 17, 1941
James Dillon
I say today that the German Nazi Axis seeks to enforce on every small nation in Europe the same beastly tyranny that we successfully fought for 700 years.

As deputy leader of Fine Gael, in Dáil speech challenging Irish neutrality for which he had to resign from party. McLoughlin, Michael, *Great Irish Speeches of the Twentieth Century*, Poolbeg, 1996, pp. 197-200.

August 21, 1941
Franklin D. Roosevelt
If factories close in Ireland and there is a great deal more suffering there, there will be less general sympathy in the United States than if it happened six months ago. People are, frankly, getting pretty fed up with my old friend Dev.

As US President, writing to US Minister in Dublin. Lyle Dwyer, Thomas, *Irish Neutrality and the USA 1939-1947*, Rowman and Littlefield & Gill & Macmillan, 1977, p. 134.

November 1941
Eamon de Valera
I wish there was some way of knowing who will win this war. It would make decisions much easier.

As Taoiseach, in private conversation. Coogan, Tim Pat, *De Valera*, Hutchinson, 1993, p. 522.

December 8, 1941
Winston Churchill
Most immediate. Prime Minister to Mr de Valera. Personal, private and secret. Now is your chance. Now or never. A nation once again. Am very ready to meet you at any time. Ends.

As British Prime Minister, in telegram to Eamon de Valera after Japanese bombing of Pearl Harbour, suggesting end of partition for immediate Irish participation in war. Fisk, Robert, *In Time of War*, Paladin, 1985, p. 323.

December 14, 1941
Eamon de Valera
...for a divided nation to fling itself into this war would be to commit suicide.

As Taoiseach, in Cork, on Churchill's offer above. Moynihan, Maurice, *Speeches and Statements by Eamon de Valera 1917-1973*, Gill & Macmillan, 1980, p. 462.

December 17, 1941
The Irish Times
The many friends of Mr John A. Robinson, who was involved in a recent boating accident, will be pleased to hear that he is alive and well... He is a

particularly good swimmer, and it is possible that he owes his life to this accomplishment.

As Dublin newspaper, in celebrated report under the headline 'Accident in the Pacific' getting around censor's ban on news of Irishmen serving in the British forces. *The Irish Times*, December 17, 1941.

January 1942
George Gavan Duffy

On ascertaining that Mr Gros was a Jew, she refused consent explaining: 'Their principles are not ours; they are anti-Christian and I could not have an anti-Christian living in the house where I live.'

As justice, upholding in court right of Catholic landlady to refuse tenancy to Jewish dentist. Carroll, Joseph T., *Ireland in the War Years*, David & Charles, 1975, p. 137.

May 20, 1942
David Gray

...a few well-placed bombs on the Irish barracks at the Curragh and in the Dublin area would be the most merciful way of shutting off opposition.

As US Minister in Ireland, advising President Roosevelt on what to do if US invaded Free State and met opposition. Coogan, Tim Pat, *De Valera*, Hutchinson, 1993, p. 595.

August 1942
Tom Williams

Well may England quake, Ireland's awake, Ireland's awake. After twenty years of slumber our nation will once against strike, please God, at the despoilers who have infringed the nation's liberty, freedom, and murdered her sons, her daughters, who have given us a foreign tongue...

As IRA member, in letter from Crumlin Road Prison, Belfast, before his execution on September 2 for shooting policemen in Belfast, written to Hugh McAteer, IRA Chief of Staff. Coogan, Tim Pat, *The IRA*, Fontana, 1980, pp. 234-235.

August 5, 1942
Francis Stuart

To those comparative few who not only love Ireland but who are ready to sacrifice all for the freedom of Irish soil...I will only say this. The past has belonged to the politicians and the financiers. The future is going to be yours.

As Berlin-based commentator, addressing IRA in broadcast to Ireland on German radio. O'Donoghue, David, *Hitler's Irish Voices*, Beyond the Pale Publications, 1998, p. 101.

August 27, 1942
David Gray

Governments, especially in war time, do not like to be coerced, and fear that clemency exercised under pressure will be interpreted as weakness.

As US Minister in Ireland, warning Eamon de Valera against campaign to save six IRA men sentenced to death in Belfast for murder of RUC man. Five were reprieved. Coogan, Tim Pat, *The IRA*, Fontana, 1980, p. 233.

September 1942
Louis MacNeice

But then look eastwards from your heart, there bulks
A continent, close, dark, as archetypal sin,
While to the west of your own shores the mackerel
Are fat – on the flesh of your kin.

As Belfast-born poet, writing from Britain on Irish neutrality, in 'Neutrality'. Longley, Michael (Ed.), *Louis MacNeice, Selected Poems*, Faber and Faber, 1988, p. 95.

October 1942
United States Army

Éire's neutrality is a real danger to the Allied cause. There, just across the Irish Channel from embattled England, and not too far from your own billets in Ulster, the Axis nations maintain large legations and staffs. These Axis agents send out weather reports, find out by espionage what is going on in Ulster.

As US force in NI, in *Pocket Guide to Northern Ireland*, issued to American soldiers. Lyle Dwyer, Thomas, *Irish Neutrality and the USA 1939-1947*, Rowman and Littlefield & Gill & Macmillan, 1977, pp. 155-156.

October 10, 1942
Myles na gCopaleen [Flann O'Brien]

The picture is executed in the modern manner and could not be expected to please persons whose knowledge of sacred art is derived from the shiny chromo-lithograph bondieuserie of the Boulevard Saint Sulpice, examples of which are to be found in every decent Irishman's bedroom.

As columnist, protesting at refusal by Municipal Gallery to accept gift of Georges Rouault painting 'Christ and the Soldier'. *The Irish Times*, October 10, 1942.

November 4, 1942
T. J. Campbell

Were they to be the only community of white ones with no representation anywhere?

As nationalist MP explaining why he was taking his seat at Stormont despite Nationalist Party abstentionist policy. Farrell, Michael, *Northern Ireland: The Orange State*, Pluto, 1983, p. 171.

December 18, 1942
Franklin D. Roosevelt

During all these years it has been a pity that Ireland has lived in a dream under the rule of a dreamer. They do not know the facts of life and it will take a rude awakening to teach them.

As US President, in message to US Minister in Dublin. Coogan, Tim Pat, *De Valera*, Hutchinson, 1993, p. 546.

February 25, 1943
John Maffey

[David Gray] had the temerity to make it plain to Irish nationalists that they were no longer the darling Playboy of the Western World, and to point out that the audience were bored.

As UK Representative in Dublin, in memo to Dominions Office in London on unpopularity of US Minister in Dublin. Lyle Dwyer, Thomas, *Irish Neutrality and the USA 1939-1947*, Rowman and Littlefield & Gill & Macmillan, 1977, p. 216.

March 17, 1943
Eamon de Valera

Let us turn aside for a moment to that ideal Ireland that we would have. That Ireland which we dreamed of would be the home of a people who valued material wealth only as the basis of right living, of a people who were satisfied with frugal comfort and devoted their leisure to the things of the spirit – a land whose countryside would be bright with cosy homesteads, whose fields and villages would be joyous with the sounds of industry, with the romping of sturdy children, the contests of athletic youths and the laughter of comely maidens, whose firesides would be forums for the wisdom of serene old age. It would, in a word, be the home of a people living the life that God desires that man should live.

As Taoiseach, in St Patrick's Day radio broadcast. Moynihan, Maurice, *Speeches and Statements by Eamon de Valera 1917-1973*, Gill & Macmillan, 1980, p. 466.

April 1, 1943
Irish Press

There is no kind of oppression visited on any minority in Europe which the Six County nationalists have not endured.

As pro-Fianna Fáil newspaper, in editorial. *Irish Press*, April 1, 1943.

April 24, 1943
The IRA

This cinema has been commandeered by the Irish Republican Army for the purpose of holding an Easter commemoration for the dead who died for Ireland.

Message flashed on screen of Broadway cinema, Falls Road, Belfast, after it had been taken over by IRA. Coogan, Tim Pat, *The IRA*, Fontana, 1980, p. 241.

May 15, 1943
Francis Stuart

If the worst should come to the worst and any of you be conscripted and be sent to one of the battlefields, you only have to wait for a suitable opportunity and go over to the Germans.

As Berlin-based commentator in broadcast on German radio directed to Northern Ireland. O'Donoghue, David, *Hitler's Irish Voices*, Beyond the Pale Publications, 1998, p. 120.

c. June 1, 1943
Brendan Bracken

The public would be horrified if they heard anything from the BBC about de Valera and those lousy neutrals; people of Irish stock overseas are heartily ashamed of Éire's attitude.

As British Minister for Information, banning BBC from covering general election in Ireland. O'Donoghue, David, *Hitler's Irish Voices*, Beyond the Pale Publications, 1998, p. 118.

June 22, 1943
Fianna Fáil

Don't change horses while crossing the stream.

Slogan for general election, which Fianna Fáil won. Fanning, Ronan, *Independent Ireland*, Helicon, 1983, p. 126.

July 9, 1943
Oliver J. Flanagan

How is it that we do not see any of these [Emergency] Acts directed against the Jews who crucified Our Saviour nineteen hundred years ago and who are crucifying us every day of the week?... There is one thing that Germany did and that was to rout the Jews out of their country. Until we rout the Jews out of this country it does not matter a hair's breadth what orders you make. Where the bees are there is the honey and where the Jews are there is the money.

As Fine Gael TD, in Dáil. *DÉ Debates*, Vol. 91, Col. 569.

February 21, 1944
David Gray

Axis agents enjoy almost unrestricted opportunity for bringing military information of vital importance from Great Britain and Northern Ireland and from there transmitting it by various routes and methods to Germany... We request therefore that the Irish Government take appropriate steps for the recall of German and Japanese representatives in Ireland.

As US Minister in Dublin, in formal note presented to Taoiseach Eamon de Valera on behalf of US Government. Lyle Dwyer, Thomas, *Irish Neutrality and the USA 1939-1947*, Rowman and Littlefield & Gill & Macmillan, 1977, pp. 183-184.

February 21, 1944
Eamon de Valera

Éire will not grant this request; we have done everything to prevent Axis espionage, going beyond what we might reasonably be expected to do...the German Minister, I am satisfied, has behaved very correctly and decently and as a neutral we will not send him away.

As Taoiseach, to US Minister in Dublin, refusing US Government request to close German and Japanese legations in Dublin. Lyle Dwyer, Thomas, *Irish Neutrality and the USA 1939-1947*, Rowman and Littlefield & Gill & Macmillan, 1977, p. 185.

February 27, 1944
Eamon de Valera

At any monent the war may come upon us and we may be called upon to defend our rights and our freedoms with our lives. Should the day come we will all face our duty with the traditional courage of our race.

As Taoiseach, speaking in Co Cavan after putting army on alert in anticipation of Allied invasion because of rejection of US demand to close German and Japanese legations in Dublin. Coogan, Tim Pat, *De Valera*, Hutchinson, 1993, p. 603.

March 7, 1944
Eamon de Valera

...the removal of representatives of a foreign state on the demand of the government to which they are accredited is universally recognised as the first step towards war.

As Taoiseach, in message to US President Roosevelt rejecting American proposal to close German and Japanese legations in Dublin. Coogan, Tim Pat, *De Valera*, Hutchinson, 1993, p. 605.

March 14, 1944
Winston Churchill

If a catastrophe were to occur to the Allied armies which could be traced to the retention of the German and Japanese representatives in Dublin, a gulf would be opened between Britain on the one hand and Southern Ireland on the other which even generations could not bridge.

As British Prime Minister, in House of Commons, following refusal by Irish Government of American request to close German and Japanese legations in Dublin. Carroll, Joseph T., *Ireland in the War Years*, David & Charles, 1975, p. 150.

March 24, 1944
Winston Churchill

To keep them guessing for a while would be much better in my opinion. I think we should let fear work its healthy process.

As British Prime Minister, in letter to US president Roosevelt advising that Eamon de Valera should not be told that Allies had no plan to invade Free State. Coogan, Tim Pat, *De Valera*, Hutchinson, 1993, p. 606.

March 31, 1944
George Bernard Shaw

I tried hard before the United States entered the war to get de Valera to abandon neutrality and join in. I told him he would not get away with it...but de Valera did get away with it... Howbeit, that powerless little cabbage garden called Ireland wins in the teeth of all the mighty powers. Erin go Bragh!

As playwright. *The Irish Press*, March 31, 1944.

c. *April 1, 1944*
Dr John Charles McQuaid

Any Catholic who disobeys this law is guilty of mortal sin, and while he persists in disobedience is unworthy to receive the Sacraments.

As Archbishop of Dublin, reinforcing 1927 ruling that no Catholics could attend 'Protestant' Trinity College. Keogh, Dermot, *Twentieth-Century Ireland*, Gill & Macmillan, 1994, p. 146.

April 27, 1944
Basil Brooke

Before 1939, Ulster was too often in the position of reminding Great Britain that she also was one of the great family of the British Commonwealth and Empire. During this war Great Britain and the Allies have had reason to be grateful for our insistence on remaining in the family group.

As NI Prime Minister, in Derry, on NI role in war. Fisk, Robert, *In Time of War*, Paladin, 1985, p. 474.

November 7, 1944
Dr Bernard Griffin

Today Roman Catholics are being persecuted in Germany and Poland – and I need hardly mention the persecution that is going on even at the present day in Northern Ireland.

As Catholic Archbishop of Westminster, speaking to meeting of Christians and Jews in London. Fisk, Robert, *In Time of War*, Paladin, 1985, p. 469.

April 1945
Seán O Faolain

...mainly a lot of well-meaning, good hearted, good humoured, not unidealistic, cute chancers with about as much cultivation as the heel of your boot.

As author, on new middle class being created by Fianna Fáil. *The Bell*, April 1945.

May 2, 1945
Eamon de Valera

...to have failed to call upon the German representative would have been an act of unpardonable discourtesy to the German nation and to [German representative] Hempel himself. During the whole of the war, Dr Hempel's conduct was invariably correct – in marked contrast with [US representative] Gray. I certainly was not going to add to his humiliation in the hour of defeat.

As Taoiseach, in letter to Robert Brennan, Irish envoy to Washington, defending much-criticised decision to pay condolences at German Legation on death of Hitler. Longford and O'Neill, *Eamon de Valera*, Arrow, 1974, p. 411.

May 2, 1945
John Maffey
[His] condolences took on a smear of turpitude.

As UK Representative in Dublin, on Eamon de Valera's visit to German Legation on death of Hitler. Bardon, Jonathan, *A History of Ulster*, Blackstaff Press, 1992, p. 583.

May 13, 1945
Winston Churchill
Owing to the action of Mr de Valera, so much at variance with the temper and instinct of thousands of southern Irishmen, who hastened to the battle-front to prove their ancient valour, the approaches which the southern Irish ports and airfields could so easily have guarded were closed by the hostile aircraft and U-boats. This was indeed a deadly moment in our life, and if it had not been for the loyalty and friendship of Northern Ireland, we should have been forced to come to close quarters with Mr de Valera, or perish forever from the earth. However, with a restraint and poise, to which I venture to say, history will find few parallels, His Majesty's Government...left the de Valera Government to frolic with the German and later with the Japanese representatives to their heart's content.

As British Prime Minister, in victory broadcast at end of war. *Eamon de Valera*, The Irish Times Ltd., 1976, p. 110.

May 17, 1945
Eamon de Valera
Mr Churchill is proud of Britain's stand alone, after France had fallen and before America entered the war. Could he not find in his heart the generosity to acknowledge that there is a small nation that stood alone, not for one year or two, but for several hundred years, against aggression; that endured spoliations, famines, massacres in endless succession; that was clubbed many times into insensibility, but that each time, on returning consciousness, took up the fight anew; a small nation that could never be got to accept defeat and had never surrendered her soul?

As Taoiseach, in radio broadcast replying to attack on Irish neutrality by Churchill, above. Moynihan, Maurice,

Speeches and Statements by Eamon de Valera 1917-1973, Gill & Macmillan, 1980, pp. 475-476.

May 18, 1945
The Irish Times
The Taoiseach's broadcast reply to Mr Churchill was as temperate as it was dignified. Mr de Valera has his faults as a statesman and as a politician; but he has one outstanding quality. He is a gentleman.

As Dublin newspaper, in editorial on Eamon de Valera's radio broadcast at end of war. Coogan, Tim Pat, *De Valera*, Hutchinson, 1993, p. 612.

May 18, 1945
John Kearney
We had him on a plate. We had him where we wanted him. But look at the papers this morning!

As Canadian High Commissioner in Dublin, on success of Eamon de Valera's broadcast reply to Churchill. Coogan, Tim Pat, *De Valera*, Hutchinson, 1993, p. 612.

May 21, 1945
John Maffey
Phrases make history here.

As UK Representative in Dublin, warning London of drawbacks in taking on Eamon de Valera in radio exchanges. Fisk, Robert, *In Time of War*, Paladin, 1985, pp. 540-541.

c. June 1, 1945
H. G. Wells
God of course is Minister without Portfolio in whatever cabinet happens to be in power... Awkward problems can always be referred back to Christ or Cromwell.

As writer, on Ireland under Eamon de Valera. Fallon, Brian, *An Age of Innocence*, Gill & Macmillan, 1998, p. 211.

July 17, 1945
Eamon de Valera
Look up...any standard book of reference and get from any of them any definition of a republic or any description of what a republic is, and judge whether our state does not possess every characteristic mark by which a republic can be distinguished or recognised.

As Taoiseach, in Dáil, in 'Dictionary Republic' speech claiming Free State was republic in everything but name. Chubb, Basil, *Source Book of Irish Government*, Institute of Public Administration, 1983, pp. 16-17.

November 1945
John Maffey
Dark Rosaleen has a sex appeal, whereas Britain is regarded as a maiden aunt.

As UK Representative in Dublin, on likely support abroad for Anti-Partition league set up in Dungannon. Bardon, Jonathan, *A History of Ulster*, Blackstaff Press, 1992, p. 598.

November 28, 1945
William Magennis

Is Ireland to be Irish, or is it to be subjugated again by a foreign printing press by means of a spiritual defeat? [Cheap foreign books are designed] to teach all the secrets of sex to young children and to instruct the adults in the full technique of marital relations.

As chairman of censorship board, in Senate, justifying censorship of books. Brown, Terence, *Ireland, A Social and Cultural History, 1922-1979*, Fontana, 1982, p. 198.

February 5, 1946
Richard Mulcahy

Ireland's political liberties, its military security and its hope of ending partition are firmly bound up with our membership of the British Commonwealth.

As TD and future Fine Gael leader. *Irish Press,* February 6, 1946.

May 28, 1946
Sean MacBride

If you had a dog would you treat it in that fashion?

As lawyer for next-of-kin in celebrated question at inquest on IRA hunger striker, Sean McCaughey, to prison doctor, who replied 'No.' Coogan, Tim Pat, *De Valera*, Hutchinson, 1993, p. 625.

June 9, 1946
William Norton

[De Valera] can throw a somersault on the edge of a razor blade and, when you express amazement, he will say there is heaps of room for everybody to do it.

As leader of Labour Party, in Dáil. Keogh, Dermot, *Twentieth-Century Ireland*, Gill & Macmillan, 1994, p. 163.

September 25, 1946
S. A. Roche

They do not assimilate with our own people but remain a sort of colony of a world-wide Jewish community. This makes them a potential irritant in the body politic and has led to disastrous results from time to time in other countries.

As Secretary of Department of Justice, in memo, on discouraging Jewish immigrants. Keogh, Dermot, *Twentieth-Century Ireland*, Gill & Macmillan, 1994, p. 129.

c. 1947
Sam Hume

Because you can't eat a flag.

As father of John Hume, advising son why he should not get involved in republican politics. Routledge, Paul, *John Hume*, Harper Collins, 1998, p. 25.

1947
Drs Walsh, Dignan and Browne

It has been contended...that Catholic farmers ought to admit over their lands whatever person the hunt committee may select as Master. Such a contention shows gross ignorance or contempt for the religious convictions and feelings of a Catholic people.

As Bishops of Tuam, Clonfert and Galway respectively, endorsing decision by Catholic farmers not to allow Galway Blazers to hunt over their lands because hunt master was divorced Protestant. Whyte, J. H., *Church & State in Modern Ireland*, Gill & Macmillan, 1980, p. 172.

September 27, 1947
Harry Midgley

I have now reached the conclusion that there is no room for division among those...who are anxious to preserve the constitutional life and spiritual heritage of our people.

As leader of NI Commonwealth Labour Party, in letter applying to join Ulster Unionist Party. Farrell, Michael, *Northern Ireland: The Orange State*, Pluto, 1983, p. 192.

October 7, 1947
Catholic Hierarchy

Our young are leaving Ireland to take up employment in circumstances, and under conditions, which, in many cases, are full of danger to their religious and moral well-being.

As Irish Bishops, on emigration to Britain. *The Irish Press*, October 8, 1947.

November 17, 1947
Andrei Vishinsky

It is impossible to recognise as peace-loving such states as Ireland and Portugal which supported fascism in its struggle against peace and peace-loving peoples...and which are even now maintaining particularly friendly relations with Franco Spain.

As Soviet Foreign Minister, at United Nations, on Soviet veto on Ireland joining UN. *The Irish Times*, January 3, 1981.

c. January 1, 1948
George Bernard Shaw

I have lived for twenty years in Ireland and for seventy-two in England but the twenty came first, and in Britain I am still a foreigner and shall die one.

As playwright. Fallon, Brian, *An Age of Innocence*, Gill & Macmillan, 1998, p. 92.

January 1, 1948
Fianna Fáil

The Dev you know is better then the devil you don't.

Slogan for election, which Fianna Fáil lost. McCullagh, David, *A Makeshift Majority*, IPA, 1998, p. 19.

January 1, 1948
Fine Gael
Put them out!

Slogan for election. McCullagh, David, *A Makeshift Majority*, IPA, 1998, p. 7.

January 28, 1948
Richard Mulcahy
Any final form for the Irish State or description of it can be settled only when partition has passed away and the Irish people as a whole, from Fair Head to Mizen head, wish to decide.

As TD and future Fine Gael leader, promising the party would not declare a Republic in office. McCullagh, David, *A Makeshift Majority*, IPA, 1998, p. 23.

February 5, 1948
Patrick Lindsay
I pulled in diagonally and lowered my window. 'Guard, is there any news from Dublin?'
'At ten past five this afternoon, Mr John Aloysius Costello was elected Taoiseach of this country.'
'Guard, would you like a drink?'
'We'll have two.'
'Will you wait a minute, until I park this car?'
'Leave it where it is. We have freedom for the first time in sixteen years.'

As former Master of High Court, in Tuam, on reaction of police officer to defeat of Fianna Fáil Government. Lindsay, Patrick, *Memories*, Blackwater Press, 1992, p. 152.

February 18, 1948
Seán MacBride
Mr Boland, give me a list of all the British agents working in your department.

As incoming Minister for external affairs, to secretary of department, Mr Frederick Boland. Keogh, Dermot, *Twentieth-Century Ireland*, Gill & Macmillan, 1994, p. 186.

February 18, 1948
James Dillon
...we may see a sovereign, independent and united Ireland delivered from the nauseating frauds of a dictionary republic sooner than we anticipate.

As Minister for Agriculture, referring to July 17, 1945 comment by Eamon de Valera. McCullagh, David, *A Makeshift Majority*, IPA, 1998, p. 75.

February 23, 1948
John A. Costello
On the occasion of our assumption of office and our first cabinet meeting, my colleagues and myself desire to repose at the feet of Your Holiness the assurance of our filial loyalty and of our devotion, as well as our firm resolve to be guided in all our work by the teaching of Christ and to strive for the attainment of a social order in Ireland based on Christian principles.

As Taoiseach in inter-party government, in message to Pope Pius XII. McCullagh, David, *A Makeshift Majority*, IPA, 1998, p. 199.

February 25, 1948
Pope Pius XII
Ireland is the only place I could go – only there would I have the atmosphere and the sense of security to rule the Church as Christ wants me to rule it.

As Pontiff, replying to Irish offer of refuge in Free State if communists took over Italy. Keogh, Dermot, *Twentieth-Century Ireland*, Gill & Macmillan, 1994, p. 188.

March 1948
Basil Brooke
They may bid as high as they please. Ulster is not for sale.

As NI Prime Minister, on offer by all-party government in Dublin of 'any reasonable constitutional guarantees' to end partition. Bardon, Jonathan, *A History of Ulster*, Blackstaff Press, 1992, p. 599.

April 13, 1948
E. C. Ferguson
I would ask the meeting to authorise their executive to adopt whatever plans and take whatever steps, however drastic, to wipe out this nationalist majority.

As Ulster Unionist MP, disclosing, at unionist meeting, that nationalist majority in Fermanagh stood at 3,604. Farrell, Michael, *Northern Ireland: The Orange State*, Pluto, 1983, pp. 88-89.

July 20, 1948
Seán MacBride
Our sympathies lie clearly with Western Europe, but the continuance of Partition precludes us from taking our rightful place in the affairs of Europe.

As Minister for External Affairs, on why Free State would not join new European military alliance which became NATO in 1949. Mansergh, Nicholas, *Ireland in the War Years and After*, Gill & Macmillan, 1969, pp. 136-137.

September 7, 1948
John A. Costello
There was no reason why Éire should not continue in association with Britain but not as a formal member of the British Commonwealth...the External Relations Act was full of inaccuracies and infirmities and the only thing to do was to scrap it.

As Taoiseach, revealing decision to declare Republic, during press conference in Ottawa, Canada. *The Irish Times*, September 8, 1948.

September 11, 1948
John A. Costello
As you will know, I very nearly, if not actually, 'declared' the Republic – in Ottawa above all places. I will explain when I return why I decided to state publicly that we intended to repeal the External Relations Act. It was really the article in the *Sunday Independent* [predicting this course] that decided me.

As Taoiseach, in letter from Canada to Labour Party leader William Norton. *The Irish Times*, January 3, 1979.

October 21, 1948
Lord Rugby
[Fine Gael] had a sudden brainwave that they could steal the Long Fellow's [Eamon de Valera's] clothes...and must now find high-sounding phrases to justify it.

As UK Representative in Ireland, in note to London on declaration of Republic. McCullagh, David, *A Makeshift Majority*, IPA, 1998, p. 81.

November 14, 1948
John A. Costello
The repeal of the External Relations Act will take the gun out of Irish politics and will give us complete independence with a republic form of government.

As Taoiseach, on decision to proclaim Republic. *The Irish Times*, November 15, 1948.

November 24, 1948
John A. Costello
No people can be expected willingly and permanently to accept as part of their political institutions the symbol of the British Crown, when fidelity to the Catholic faith, the faith of the vast majority of our Irish people, was throughout the years regarded as disaffection and disloyalty to the British Crown...

As Taoiseach, in Dáil, introducing Bill to proclaim Republic. *Dáil Debates:* Vol. CXIII: Cols. 347-390.

November 25, 1948
Clement Attlee
Accordingly, the United Kingdom Government will not regard the enactment of this legislation by Éire as placing Éire in the category of foreign countries or Éire citizens in the category of foreigners.

As British Prime Minister, in House of Commons, on Irish Government decision to recognise special relationship with Britain despite declaring Republic. Chubb, Basil, *Source Book of Irish Government*, Institute of Public Administration, 1983, pp. 19-20.

December 18, 1948
Locke Tribunal
The charge is an extremely grave one. We are satisfied that it is wholly untrue, that it is entirely without foundation and that it was made with a degree of recklessness amounting to complete irresponsibility.

Report of High Court judges dismissing claim by independent TD, Oliver J. Flanagan, that Eamon de Valera, Sean Lemass and others profitted from sale of Locke's Distillery in Kilbeggan, Co Cork. Lee, J. J., *Ireland 1912-1985*, Cambridge University Press, 1990, p. 297.

1949
Arland Ussher
Irishmen have sung for so long the line of Thomas Davis 'for righteous men must make our land a nation once again' that they have forgotten that *cultured* men should also have a say. And righteousness without culture has a tendency to turn rancid.

As commentator and writer. Ussher, Arland, *The Face and Mind of Ireland*, Victor Gollancz, 1949, pp. 99-100.

January 24, 1949
Basil Brooke
Give an answer to our opponents at the polls that will resound around the world. No surrender! We are King's men!

As NI Prime Minister, after calling election. *The Irish Times*, January 25, 1949.

February 15, 1949
John A. Costello
We have brought the partition question up to the international plane as we intended to bring it, and on that plane we will succeed in ending partition.

As Fine Gael leader, at party árd fheis. *The Irish Times*, February 16, 1949.

April 9, 1949
Northern Ireland Labour Party
[The party pledges itself] to maintain unbroken the connection between Great Britain and Northern Ireland as a part of the Commonwealth and to...seek the closest possible means of cooperation with the British Labour Party.

As Belfast-based party, in response to Free State leaving Commonwealth. Moody, Martin, Byrne (Eds), *A New History of Ireland*, Vol. VIII, Oxford, 1982, p. 432.

April 17, 1949
Micheál Mac Liammóir
Irish Republic tonight at midnight. H. piously thanked God that England was free at last from seven hundred years of Irish domination.

As leading Dublin actor and producer, writing in diary ('H.' referred to friend Hilton Edwards). *Put Money in Thy Purse*, Methuen, 1952.

April 18, 1949
RTÉ

Our listeners will join us in seeking God's blessing on the Republic and praying that it will not be long before the sovereignty of the Republic extends over the whole of our national territory.

As national broadcasting body, announcing at one minute past midnight that Ireland had became republic. McCullagh, David, *A Makeshift Majority*, IPA, 1998, p. 100.

May 3, 1949
Clement Attlee

It is hereby declared that Northern Ireland remains part of Her Majesty's Dominions of the United Kingdom and it is hereby affirmed that in no event will Northern Ireland or any part thereof cease to be part of Her Majesty's Dominions and the United Kingdom without the consent of the Parliament of Northern Ireland.

As British Prime Minister, in House of Commons, citing Ireland Act introduced in response to declaration of Republic by Government in Dublin. Coogan, Tim Pat, *The IRA*, Fontana, 1980, p. 324.

May 9, 1949
John A. Costello

[We] protest against the introduction by the British parliament of legislation purporting to endorse and continue the existing partition of Ireland...and the present occupation of our six north-eastern counties.

As Taoiseach, in Dáil on Ireland Act. Coogan, Tim Pat, *The IRA*, Fontana, 1980, p. 324.

July 7, 1949
Dr P. Moran

There is a real danger that it will pauperise the people and prostitute the profession... Pregnancy certainly should not be raised or lowered to the status of a dangerous disease.

As President of Irish Medical Association, on doctors' opposition to Mother and Child scheme to provide free medical care. *The Irish Times*, July 8, 1949.

August 17, 1949
William Norton

The intolerable dictatorship in the Six Counties [wields a] veto, as strong as Molotov often wielded, over the right of the Irish people to national self determination.

As Tánaiste and Labour leader. *The Irish Times*. August 18, 1949.

September 18, 1949
Inter-Party Government

[It is] the course of least disadvantage.

As Irish Government, announcing devaluation of Irish pound from $4.03 to $2.80, following British devaluation. McCullagh, David, *A Makeshift Majority*, IPA, 1998, p. 166.

December 1949
Sean O Faolain

God smiles, the priest beams and the novelist groans.

As Irish author, in article 'The Dilemma of Irish Letters'. *The Mouth*, December 1949.

1950
James Deeny

One day I was walking up to Bewley's for a coffee and a bun lunch and as usual I was accompanied by J. D. McCormack... I said to J. D. quite suddenly, 'I've got to name this thing. We'll call it the Mother and Child service; that should sell it. No one could oppose a scheme with a name like that.'

As Chief Medical Officer, Department of Health. Deeny, James, *To Cure and to Care: Memoirs of a Chief Medical Officer*, Glendale Press, 1989, p. 116.

c. January 1950
Eddie McAteer

Should it happen that you have the leisure to go to the department, act stupid, demand explanations, object, anything at all that will clog the department machinery.

As vice chairman of Anti-Partition League, recommending passive resistance by nationalists visiting NI government offices. Farrell, Michael, *Northern Ireland: The Orange State*, Pluto, 1983, pp. 203-204.

February 4, 1950
Peadar Cowan

Action, not talk, will end partition. A strong volunteer movement determined to end partition is needed and must be organised now. Further delay is dangerous.

As ex-army captain and former member of Clann na Poblachta, in advertisement for Dublin meeting to plan invasion of Northern Ireland, which attracted 800 people. *Irish Press*, February 4, 1950.

June 20, 1950
Catholic Hierarchy

...where there has been no existing and longstanding custom, to open public houses on Sundays even for a few hours would be a serious violation of this ecclesiastical law [and] it would be sinful to agitate for their opening.

As Irish Bishops, (successfully) opposing legislation to allow pubs to open on Sunday. Whyte, J. H., *Church & State in Modern Ireland*, Gill & Macmillan, 1980, p. 178.

July 11, 1950
Dr Noel Browne

[It is] unworthy of members of the medical profession to try to confuse the simple matter of pounds, shillings and pence with questions of high principles and morality.

As Minister for Health, on doctors' opposition to his Mother and Child scheme. *The Irish Times*, July 12, 1950.

October 10, 1950
Catholic Hierarchy

The powers taken by the State in the proposed Mother and Child Health Service are in direct opposition to the rights of the family and of the individual and are liable to very great abuse... If adopted in law, they would constitute a ready-made instrument for future totalitarian aggression.

As Irish Bishops, in letter to Taoiseach John A. Costello after consultation about proposed free health scheme. *The Irish Times*, April 12, 1951.

c. 1951
Eamon de Valera

After all, Peadar, if you had been in power, a million would have had to emigrate as well.

As Taoiseach, to left wing republican Peadar O'Donnell, quoted by Professor Tom Garvin. *The Irish Times,* April 4, 1998.

c. 1951
Peadar O'Donnell

Yes Dev, but it would have been a different million.

As left wing republican, responding to Eamon de Valera above. *The Irish Times,* April 4, 1998.

February 13, 1951
Charles Casey

How can any Catholic logically demand or permit any legislation which would endanger the soul of a single child?... Take the case of a Catholic girl who...hands her child over to kindly people not of her faith. When that mother has rehabilitated herself and become more normal, she will know that she has done wrong...

As Attorney General, defending refusal of Government to introduce legal adoptions. Whyte, J. H., *Church & State in Modern Ireland*, Gill & Macmillan, 1980, pp. 189-190.

February 13, 1951
Sean MacEoin

I don't want to get a belt of the crozier.

As Minister for Justice, on fear of criticism by Catholic bishops. McCullagh, David, *A Makeshift Majority*, IPA, 1998, p. 46.

March 14, 1951
John A. Costello

Whatever about fighting the doctors, I will not fight the bishops, and whatever about fighting the bishops, I will not fight the doctors and the bishops together.

As Taoiseach, privately warning Minister for Health Dr Noel Browne that he would not support his Mother and Child scheme. McCullagh, David, *A Makeshift Majority*, IPA, 1998, p. 222.

March 23, 1951
Harry Truman

Outsiders intervening in family issues always suffered and the issue was rarely settled.

As US President, refusing to discuss partition in Washington with Minister for Foreign Affairs, Seán MacBride. McCullagh, David, *A Makeshift Majority*, IPA, 1998, p. 138.

April 5, 1951
Catholic Hierarchy

The Hierarchy cannot approve of any scheme which, in its general tendency, must foster undue control by the State in a sphere so delicate and so intimately concerned with morals as that which deals with gynaecology or obstetrics and with the relations between doctor and patient.

As Irish Bishops, in private letter to Taoiseach John A. Costello opposing Minister for Health Dr Noel Browne's proposed Mother and Child scheme. Whyte, J. H., *Church & State in Modern Ireland*, Gill & Macmillan, 1980, p. 446.

April 6, 1951
Dr Noel Browne

I reflected that one Judas was bad enough, but twelve of them must be some kind of record, even in Ireland.

As Minister for Health, on refusal, one by one, of inter-party government cabinet members to back his Mother and Child scheme. Browne, Noel, *Against the Tide*, Gill & Macmillan, 1986, p. 177.

April 9, 1951
John A. Costello

That decision expresses the complete willingness of the Government to defer to the judgement so given by the Hierarchy.

As Taoiseach, notifying bishops that Government would drop Minister for Health Dr Noel Browne's scheme for limited health service. Whyte, J. H., *Church & State in Modern Ireland*, Gill & Macmillan, 1980, p. 232.

April 10, 1951
Seán MacBride
The creation of a situation where it is made to appear that a conflict exists between the spiritual and temporal authorities is always undesirable; in the case of Ireland, it is highly damaging to the cause of national unity.

As leader of Clann na Poblachta, requesting resignation from Government of party colleague and Minister for Health Dr Noel Browne, after conflict between Browne and Catholic Church over Mother and Child scheme. *The Irish Times*, April 12, 1951.

April 10, 1951
Dr Noel Browne
On the other side is your envenomed attack on me at the executive meeting last Sunday because...I had allowed myself to be photographed with the Protestant Archbishop of Dublin. This puerile bigotry is scarcely calculated to assist the cause of national reunification which you profess to have at heart.

As Minister for Health, in reply to Seán MacBride, above. *The Irish Times*, April 12, 1951.

April 12, 1951
The Irish Times
The most serious revelation, however, is that the Roman Catholic Church would seem to be the effective government of this country.

As Dublin newspaper, in editorial on disclosure of role of Catholic Church in opposing Mother and Child scheme. *The Irish Times*, April 12, 1951.

April 12, 1951
John A. Costello
I as a Catholic continue to obey my Church authorities and will continue to do so in spite of *The Irish Times* or anything else.

As Taoiseach, in Dáil, on resignation of Minister for Health, Dr Noel Browne. McLoughlin, Michael, *Great Irish Speeches of the Twentieth Century*, Poolbeg, 1996, pp. 233-234.

April 12, 1951
Dr Noel Browne
While, as I have said, I as a Catholic accept unequivocally and unreservedly the views of the Hierarchy on this matter, I have not been able to accept the manner in which this matter has been dealt with by my former colleagues in the government.

As Minister for Health, in Dáil, on resigning after his Mother and Child scheme was blocked by intervention of the Catholic Church. McLoughlin, Michael, *Great Irish Speeches of the Twentieth Century*, Poolbeg, 1996, p. 241.

April 12, 1951
Seán MacBride
For the last year, in my view, the Minister for Health has not been normal.

As leader of Clann na Poblachta, in Dáil, after requesting resignation of party colleague, Dr Noel Browne, from Government. Whyte, J. H., *Church & State in Modern Ireland*, Gill & Macmillan, 1980, p. 229.

April 12, 1951
Eamon de Valera
I think we have heard enough.

As Fianna Fáil leader, in only contribution to Dáil debate on controversy over Mother and Child scheme. Murphy, John A., *De Valera and His Times*, Cork University Press, 1983, p. 8.

April 12, 1951
Harry Midgley
Read, mark and inwardly digest.

As NI Minister for Education, on Catholic Church's role in influencing legislation in Republic by blocking Mother and Child scheme. *The Irish Times*, April 13, 1951.

April 17, 1951
Dr Neil Farren
The power and the spirit behind practically all social legislation at the present time is taken from the worst principles of both Nazi and Russian materialism.

As Bishop of Derry, defending Catholic Church's opposition to Dr Noel Browne's Mother and Child scheme. *The Irish Press*, April 18, 1951.

c. April 20, 1951
John A. Costello
I am an Irishman second; I am a Catholic first. If the Hierarchy give me any direction with regard to Catholic social teaching or Catholic moral teaching, I accept without qualification in all respects the teaching of the Hierarchy and the Church to which I belong.

As Taoiseach, on his role in opposing Mother and Child scheme. Fanning, Ronan, *Independent Ireland*, Helicon, 1983, p. 185.

April 30, 1951
Dr Michael Browne
The establishment of this scheme [Mother and Child] would soon eliminate the free medical practitioner and create a monopoly of socialised medical services under complete state control – a terrible weapon to put into the hands of men who might not have received instruction in Catholic principles, or who might repudiate such principles.

As Bishop of Galway, defending Catholic Church's opposition to Dr Noel Browne's Mother and Child scheme. *The Irish Times*, May 1, 1951.

May 13, 1951
John A. Costello
I could never understand...why anybody should stand over a scheme which involved the old age pensioner in Connemara and the agricultural labourer in Laois-Offaly paying for the rich lady in Foxrock when she was having her children.

As Taoiseach, on Mother and Child scheme which his government rejected. *The Irish Times*, May 14, 1951.

June 1, 1951
Sean O Faolain
The Dáil proposes; Maynooth disposes.

As author, on Mother and Child controversy. Fallon, Brian, *An Age of Innocence*, Gill & Macmillan, 1998, p. 191.

July 18, 1951
Sean O'Casey
Keep the home fires burning.

As playwright, in last lines spoken in 'The Plough and the Stars', in Abbey Theatre, Dublin, staged on evening before it burned down. Hunt, Hugh, *The Abbey*, Gill & Macmillan, 1979, p. 175.

November 7, 1951
Sean Lemass
The efforts we have made firmly to establish freedom here will be unavailing if we cannot secure our financial freedom as well.

As Minister for Industry and Commerce, in Dáil. Lee, J. J., *Ireland 1912-1985*, Cambridge University Press, 1990, p. 373.

c. March 1, 1952
Patrick Kavanagh
A wake is what is going on in this country...and at the moment we are trying to get the family to remove the corpse – the corpse of 1916, the Gaelic language, the inferiority complex – so that the house may be free for the son to bring in a wife.

As poet, writing in *Kavanagh's Weekly*, No 5. Keogh, Dermot, *Twentieth-Century Ireland*, Gill & Macmillan, 1994, p. 222.

c. January 1, 1953
Paul Blanshard
Like Spain's inquisition under Torquemada, the Irish book censorship is not so much famous as infamous. It is probably the best known feature of the Irish clerical republic.

As American writer, on contemporary Ireland. Lenihan, Brian, *For the Record,* Blackwater Press, 1991, p. 214.

February 14, 1953
Department of Education
There is bound to be comment and a degree of unhealthy curiosity in mixed schools and even in schools for girls only, during the latter months of pregnancy of married women teachers.

In memo to Cabinet on why women teachers must retire on marriage. Keogh, Dermot, *Twentieth-Century Ireland*, Gill & Macmillan, 1994, p. 281.

November 21, 1953
Liam Kelly
I do not believe in constitutional methods. I believe in the use of force; the more the better, the sooner the better.

As leader of Saor Éire (Free Ulster) and (successful) candidate for mid-Tyrone in NI election. Farrell, Michael, *Northern Ireland: The Orange State*, Pluto, 1983, p. 205.

April 16, 1954
G. B. Hanna
Were I to ban a Republican...procession or meeting in one part of the country and not only to permit an Orange procession in a nationalist district, but to provide police protection for that procession, I would be holding up our entire administration up (sic) to ridicule and contempt.

As NI Minister of Home Affairs, announcing ban on Orange parade along Longstone Road, Co Down (lifted in 1955 to allow parade led by Brian Faulkner). Farrell, Michael, *Northern Ireland: The Orange State*, Pluto, 1983, p. 208.

October 1954
IRA
Volunteers are strictly forbidden to take any militant action against 26-County Forces under any circumstance whatsoever.

From Standing Order Number Eight, incorporated into IRA's 'General Army Orders' after raid on Omagh barracks, and remaining in force ever since. Coogan, Tim Pat, *The IRA*, Fontana, 1980, p. 328.

April 12, 1955
Dr Cornelius Lucey
When the bishops in this country took a stand not so long ago on the health bill...their position was that they were the final arbiters of right and wrong, even in political matters.

As Bishop of Cork and Ross, on Catholic Church's opposition to Dr Noel Browne's Mother and Child scheme. *The Irish Times*, April 13, 1955.

November 27, 1955
Thomas Leonard
There is no name [on the death certificate]. I could not say if the man was married or single, what occupation he had. In the age column I wrote 'about 30', that was all.

As coroner for North East Monaghan, on signing death certificate for Connie Green, killed during republican raid on Rosslea RUC barracks and buried secretly by Irish Government. Coogan, Tim Pat, *The IRA*, Fontana, 1980, p. 364.

November 30, 1955
Basil Brooke (Lord Brookeborough)

It is unbelievable that any civilised country which has outlawed the IRA is yet afraid to take action which any civilised country would take to prevent blackguards and scoundrels coming here to commit murder and create antagonism among the people.

As NI Prime Minister, at Stormont, criticising Republic after raid on Rosslea RUC barracks. Coogan, Tim Pat, *The IRA*, Fontana, 1980, p. 365.

November 30, 1955
John A. Costello

...there can be no question of our handing over, either to the British or to the Six-County authorities, persons whom they may accuse of armed political activities in Britain or in the Six Counties.

As Taoiseach, in Dáil after republican raid on Rosslea RUC barracks. Coogan, Tim Pat, *The IRA*, Fontana, 1980, p. 367.

January 18, 1956
Catholic Hierarchy

We declare that it is a mortal sin for a Catholic to become or remain a member of an organisation or society, which arrogates to itself the right to bear arms or to use them against its own or another state; that it is also sinful for a Catholic to cooperate with, express approval of, or otherwise assist any such organisation or society, and that if the cooperation or assistance be notable, the sin committed is mortal.

As Irish Bishops, in statement issued as IRA prepared for Border campaign. Whyte, J. H., *Church & State in Modern Ireland*, Gill & Macmillan, 1980, p. 321.

July 7, 1956
Liam Cosgrave

The Republic was not and could not be neutral in the issue between communism and democracy, usually described as the struggle between East and West.

As Minister for External Affairs, at Queen's University, Belfast. *The Irish Times*, July 9, 1956.

July 27, 1956
Dr Joseph Rogers

I also find it passing strange that...your Attorney-General should arraign in court an excellent priest of my diocese and the other loyal Catholics of Clonara Parish for their defence of the doctrine of the Blessed Trinity, a doctrine so nobly enshrined in our constitution. Are we to have legal protection in future against such vile and pernicious attacks on our faith?

As coadjutor Bishop of Killaloe, in letter to Taoiseach on trial of priest and others for assaulting Jehovah's Witnesses at Clonara, Co Clare. (Charges were dismissed and plaintiffs found guilty of blasphemy.) Coogan, Tim Pat, *De Valera*, Hutchinson, 1993, pp. 653-654.

December 12, 1956
IRA

[We seek] an independent, united, democratic Irish Republic. For this we shall fight until the invader is driven from our soil and victory is ours.

In statement issued after launching 'Harvest' campaign against Northern Ireland. Bardon, Jonathan, *A History of Ulster*, Blackstaff Press, 1992, p. 606.

December 17, 1956
Nat Minford

We Protestants are running this country, and are going to run it. We want to live in a country where peace will prevail. If we find that these attacks are going to continue, then we Protestants ourselves will have to determine what the future will be.

As Ulster Unionist MP, at Stormont, on IRA campaign. Coogan, Tim Pat, *The IRA*, Fontana, 1980, p. 389.

December 19, 1956
Anthony Eden

In the Ireland Act 1949 the Parliament of Westminster declared Northern Ireland to be an integral part of the United Kingdom. This is a declaration which all parties in this House are pledged to support. The safety of Northern Ireland and its inhabitants is therefore a direct responsibility of Her Majesty's Government which they will, of course, discharge.

As British Prime Minister, in House of Commons, on IRA border campaign. *HC Debates:* Vol. 562: Col. 1270.

December 29, 1956
Pravda

The Irish patriots cannot agree with Britain transforming the Six Counties into one of its main military bases in the Atlantic pact.

As Soviet Communist Party daily, explaining IRA campaign to readers. Coogan, Tim Pat, *The IRA*, Fontana, 1980, p. 387.

January 6, 1957
John A. Costello

Neither appeals for sympathy...nor natural sorrow for tragic deaths, should be allowed to betray anybody into an appearance of encouraging these actions... Three young Irishmen had been killed.

As Taoiseach, speaking on radio on deaths of IRA men Fergal O'Hanlon and Sean South, and a NI policeman, in IRA attack on Brookeborough RUC barracks. *The Irish Times*, January 7, 1957.

January 6, 1957
Eamon de Valera
The problem of partition cannot be solved by force... To allow any military body not subject to Dáil Éireann to be enrolled, organised and equipped is to pave the way to anarchy and ruin.

As Fianna Fáil leader, responding to Taoiseach John A. Costello, above. *The Irish Times*, January 7, 1957.

January 6, 1957
Brian Maginnis
I hope that Mr Costello's well-reviewed, courageous and statesman-like speech, particularly those parts which asked for discouragement of any signs of sympathy with men of violence, will have good effect on everybody.

As NI Attorney General, reacting to radio broadcast by Taoiseach John A. Costello condemning IRA. *The Irish Times*, January 7, 1957.

January 23, 1957
Justice Michael Lennon
I remember proclamations of this kind made in relation to myself [before 1921] and they always ended with the words 'God save the King'.

As judge, in sarcastic remark in Dublin court – which cost him his office – about proclamation bringing in Offences Against the State Act against IRA. Coogan, Tim Pat, *The IRA*, Fontana, 1980, p. 381.

February 15, 1957
Harry Midgley
All the minority are traitors and have always been traitors to the Government of Northern Ireland.

As NI Minister of Education, in Portadown Orange Hall. Farrell, Michael, *Northern Ireland: The Orange State*, Pluto, 1983, p. 221.

June 7, 1957
Sean O'Casey
Here we have bishops, priests and deacons, a censorship board, vigilant librarians, confraternities and sodalities, Duce Maria, Legions of Mary, knights of this Christian order and knights of that one, all surrounding the sinner's free will in an embattled circle... The banning of bombs is more to the point than the banning of books.

As playwright, on censorship. *The Irish Times*, June 8, 1957.

June 30, 1957
Dr Michael Browne
There seems to be a concerted campaign to entice or kidnap Catholic children and deprive them of their faith, against which non-Catholics had not protested. [The boycott] is a peaceful and moderate protest.

As Bishop of Galway, at Wexford Congress, on boycott of Protestant businesses in Fethard-on-Sea, Co Wexford, after Protestant woman left her Catholic husband and took their children to Belfast. Whyte, J. H., *Church & State in Modern Ireland*, Gill & Macmillan, 1980, p. 323.

July 4, 1957
Eamon de Valera
I regard this boycott as ill-conceived, ill-considered and futile for the achievement of the purpose for which it seems to have been intended; [and] I regard it as unjust and cruel to confound the innocent with the guilty...

As Taoiseach, in Dáil, condemning boycott of Protestant business in Fethard-on-Sea. Moynihan, Maurice, *Speeches and Statements by Eamon de Valera 1917-1973*, Gill & Macmillan, 1980, p. 580.

1958
Brendan Behan
My name is Brendan Behan, I'm the latest of the banned
Although we're small in numbers, we're the best banned in the land,
We're read at wakes and weddin's and in every parish hall,
And under library counters, sure you'll have no trouble at all.

As author of play, 'Borstal Boy', sung to the tune of 'McNamara's Band', when his play was banned by the censor. O'Sullivan, Michael, *Brendan Behan, A Life*, Blackwater Press, 1997, p. 243.

February 28, 1958
Rev Alfred O'Rahilly
[*The Irish Times* suffers] from chronic episcopophagy. It has an obsessional disease of bishop-baiting.

As priest, on paper's criticism of Archbishop of Dublin, Dr McQuaid, for causing withdrawal of O'Casey play in Dublin. *The Standard*, February 28, 1958.

c. June 1, 1958
Brendan Behan
A Protestant with a horse.

As playwright, in words of character defining an Anglo-Irishman, in 'The Hostage'. Fallon, Brian, *An Age of Innocence*, Gill & Macmilan, 1998, p. 33.

c. *June 1, 1958*
Brendan Behan
Sentenced to death in my absence – so I said, right, you can shoot me in my absence.

As playwright, in words of character in 'The Hostage'. Kiberd, Declan, *Inventing Ireland*, Jonathan Cape, 1995, p. 525.

July 21, 1958
Rev Andrea Maria Deksur
His Holiness felt that by reason of its geographical situation, the Irish television could be of great service to the Christian religion, provided that a transmitter be installed which would be sufficiently powerful to transmit its programmes to trans-oceanic territories.

As Monsignor based in Vatican, in Dublin, advising Irish Government on proposed television service. Coogan, Tim Pat, *De Valera*, Hutchinson, 1993, p. 658.

March 6, 1959
Harold Macmillan
Your Ministers have told me of their grave concern over the action of the Government of the Irish Republic in releasing the IRA terrorists they had interned in the Curragh. I may say at once that I fully share that concern.

As British Prime Minister, to Ulster Unionist Council in Belfast. Moynihan, Maurice, *Speeches and Statements by Eamon de Valera 1917-1973*, Gill & Macmillan, 1980, p. 595.

March 6, 1959
Eamon de Valera
I regard Mr Macmillan's statement as ill-advised and uncalled-for...the use or non-use of detention...is a matter for the Irish Government alone.

As Taoiseach, responding to criticism by British Prime Minister Harold Macmillan of release of internees in Republic. Moynihan, Maurice, *Speeches and Statements by Eamon de Valera 1917-1973*, Gill & Macmillan, 1980, p. 595.

March 7, 1959
Harold Macmillan
...there is no Greek or Turkish area in Cyprus. The villages are intermingled. It would have been quite impossible to make territorial partition work there, without mass or forced emigration.

As British Prime Minister, explaining at Belfast press conference why he supported partition in Ireland but not in Cyprus. Moynihan, Maurice, *Speeches and Statements by Eamon de Valera 1917-1973*, Gill & Macmillan, 1980, p. 595.

March 8, 1959
Eamon de Valera
...in about one half of the area of the Six Counties there is a nationalist majority... If the considerations which weighed with Mr Macmillan in arriving at the decision not to partition Cyprus would only be taken into account in the case of Ireland, a satisfactory solution could be arrived at.

As Taoiseach, at Fianna Fáil convention in Ennis, responding to Harold Macmillan, above. Moynihan, Maurice, *Speeches and Statements by Eamon de Valera 1917-1973*, Gill & Macmillan, 1980, pp. 596-597.

April 30, 1959
BBC
Strong feelings were aroused in Northern Ireland by the political statements made by Miss Siobhan McKenna...the Corporation has no wish to add to these feelings.

As British broadcasting body, on cancellation of second part of programme 'Small World' after actress had expressed sympathy for IRA and described Harold Macmillan as 'impertinent' for criticism of de Valera. *The Irish Times*, May 1, 1959.

June 3, 1959
Sean Lemass
The historic task of this generation is to secure the economic foundation of independence.

As incoming Fianna Fáil Taoiseach, in Dáil. *DÉ Debates*, June 3, 1959.

June 23, 1959
Sean Lemass
Personally I believe that national progress of any kind depends largely on an upsurge of patriotism... Patriotism as I understand it is a love of country, pride in its history, traditions and culture, and a determination to add to its prestige and achievements.

As Taoiseach, in first speech in Dáil after selection. Farrell, Brian, *Sean Lemass*, Gill & Macmillan, 1991, p. 98.

November 10, 1959
George Clark
It is difficult to see how a Catholic with the vast differences in our religious outlook, could be either acceptable within the Unionist Party as a member, or for that matter, bring himself unconditionally to support its ideals.

As Orange Grand Master, replying to suggestion from NI industrialist, Clarence Graham, that Catholics be permitted to join Unionist Party. Farrell, Michael, *Northern Ireland: The Orange State*, Pluto, 1983, p. 223.

November 12, 1959
Sean Lemass
The agreement...provides that the thirty-nine Lane pictures will be divided into two groups which will be lent in turn for public exhibition in Dublin, for successive periods of five years, over a period of twenty years.

As Taoiseach, announcing compromise over disputed Lane pictures between Commissioners of Public Works in Ireland and trustees of National Gallery in London (cf quote dated February 3, 1915). *The Irish Times,* November 13, 1959.

1960
Sean Lemass
Even the BBC service rarely if ever presents a play about Ireland without the characters moving about in clouds of alcoholic vapour.

As Taoiseach. Farrell, Brian, *Sean Lemass,* Gill & Macmillan, 1991, p. 99.

April 14, 1960
Brendan Behan
An author's first duty is to let down his country.

As author. *Guardian,* April 15, 1960.

November 10, 1960
Sean Lemass
Is it not plain common sense that the two existing political communities in our small island should seek every opportunity of working together in practical matters for their mutual and common good?

As Taoiseach, in Dáil, indicating new approach on Northern Ireland. Farrell, Brian, *Sean Lemass,* Gill & Macmillan, 1991, p. 115.

July 12, 1960
Brian Faulkner
When we in the Unionist Party defend ourselves against the political attacks of the Nationalist Party, we are perforce defending ourselves against the Roman Catholic hierarchy...until the hierarchy renounces its influence in politics, the Orange Order cannot renounce its influence in the Unionist Party.

As Ulster Unionist MP, at Orange demonstration in Comber, Co Down. Boyd, Andrew, *Brian Faulkner and the Crisis in Ulster Unionism,* Anvil, 1972, pp. 35-36.

September 30, 1960
Dr Thomas Morris
No dances on Saturday nights, eves of holy days, Christmas night or during Lent... Concern for the moral welfare of those who dance will surely be accepted as no more an interference with legitimate amusement than concern for their health and physical safety.

As Archbishop of Cashel and Emly, ordering dance promoters to cut back dances. Tobin, Fergal, *The Best of Decades,* Gill & Macmillan, 1996, pp. 19-20.

October 12, 1960
Nikita Khrushchev
[You are] evidently in sympathy with colonial domination... You will not be able to smother the voice of the peoples, the voice of truth, which rings aloud and will go on ringing. Death and destruction to colonial servitude! Away with it! We must bury it, and the deeper the better!

As Soviet leader, in shoe-banging exchange with Frederick Boland, Irish Representative at United Nations and President of UN General Assembly. *Official Records, UN General Assembly, 15th Session,* p. 683.

March 1961
Robert Babington
Registers of unemployed loyalists should be kept by the Unionist Party and employers invited to pick employees from among them.

As lawyer, addressing Ulster Unionist Labour Association. Tobin, Fergal, *The Best of Decades,* Gill & Macmillan, 1996, p. 92.

March 1961
Brendan Behan
There are three things I don't like about New York: the water, the buses and the professional Irishman. A professional Irishman is one who is terribly anxious to pass as a middle-class Englishman.

As author, in *New York Daily News,* after Irish-American judge upheld a ban on Behan from taking part in St Patrick's Day Parade. O'Sullivan, Michael, *Brendan Behan, A Life,* Blackwater Press, 1997, p. 276.

August 3, 1961
Basil Brooke (Lord Brookeborough)
Ulster has only room for one party.

As NI Prime Minister, speaking against Protestant support for the NI Labour Party because of unemployment. Arthur, Paul, *Government & Politics of Northern Ireland,* Longman, 1984, p. 78.

December 31, 1961
Eamon de Valera
I for one will find it hard to believe, for example, that a person who views the grandeurs of the heavens, or the wonders of this marvellous, mysterious world...will not find more pleasure in that than in viewing some squalid, domestic brawl or a street quarrel.

As President, recommending 'good, true and beautiful programmes' when launching Teilifís Éireann. *The Irish Times,* January 1, 1962.

December 31, 1961
Eamonn Andrews
Fortunately [*RTÉ* television] had come into being under a minister who refused to be stampeded into the final betrayal of Kathleen Ní Houlihan by depriving her of the classic 36-24-36, and containing her Celtic charms in a fourteen inch or a seventeen inch – or for the landed gentry – in a twenty-four-inch glass, so that she was in danger of becoming Cathode Ní Houlihan.

As Chairman of *RTÉ* Authority, launching Teilifís Éireann at ceremony in Shelbourne Hotel, Dublin. *The Irish Times*, January 1, 1962.

January 14, 1962
Sean Lemass
In this situation partition will become so obviously an anachronism that all sensible people will want to bring it to an end.

As Taoiseach, on effect of membership of Common Market, for which UK and Ireland (unsucessfully) applied. *The Irish Times*, June 15, 1962.

February 26, 1962
IRA
Foremost among the factors responsible for the ending of the campaign has been the attitude of the general public whose minds have been deliberately distracted from the supreme issue facing Irish people – the unity and freedom of Ireland.

Statement announcing end of Border campaign. Coogan, Tim Pat, *The IRA*, Fontana, 1980, p. 418.

June 1962
Sean Lemass
We recognise that a military commitment will be an inevitable consequence of our joining the Common Market and ultimately we would be prepared to yield even the technical label of our neutrality.

As Taoiseach, on possibility of joining NATO. Keogh, Dermot, *Twentieth-Century Ireland*, Gill & Macmillan, 1994, pp. 246-247.

1963
John Montague
Puritan Ireland's dead and gone,
A myth of O'Connor and O'Faolain.

As poet, on growing sexual licence in Ireland, in 'The Siege of Mullingar, 1963'. Kiberd, Declan, *Inventing Ireland*, Jonathan Cape, 1995, p. 581.

April 1963
Terence O'Neill
Our task will be literally to transform Ulster. To achieve it will demand bold and imaginative measures.

As NI Prime Minister, to Ulster Unionist Council, advocating more liberal attitude towards Catholic minority. Bardon, Jonathan, *A History of Ulster*, Blackstaff Press, 1992, p. 622.

June 4, 1963
Rev Ian Paisley
This Romish man of sin is now in hell.

As leader of Free Presbyterian Church, at Belfast rally to protest lowering of flag to half mast over Belfast City Hall on death of Pope John XXIII. Bardon, Jonathan, *A History of Ulster*, Blackstaff Press, 1992, p. 631.

June 27, 1963
John F. Kennedy
[Ireland's] sons and daughters are scattered throughout the world and they give this small island a family of million upon millions...in a sense, all of them who visit Ireland come home.

As US President, on arrival at Dublin airport for three-day visit to Republic. *The Irish Times*, June 28, 1963.

June 27, 1963
Eamon de Valera
We welcome you...as the representative of that great country in which our people sought refuge when driven by the tyrant's laws from their motherland, sought refuge and found themselves and their dependents a home in which they prospered, won renown and gave distinguished service in return.

As President, welcoming US President John F. Kennedy on three-day visit to Republic. *The Irish Times*, June 28, 1963.

June 28, 1963
John F. Kennedy
Lord Edward Fitzgerald did not like to stay in his family home because, as he wrote his mother, 'Leinster House does not inspire the brightest ideas.'

As US President, addressing Oireachtas in Leinster House, one-time home of Lord Fitzgerald. *RTÉ*, June 28, 1963.

June 28, 1963
John F. Kennedy
If this nation had achieved its present political and economic stature a century or so ago, my great-grandfather might never have left New Ross, and I might, if fortunate, be sitting down there with you. Of course, if your own President [Eamon de Valera] had never left Brooklyn, he might be standing up here instead of me.

As US President, addressing Oireachtas. *The Irish Times*, June 29, 1963.

June 28, 1963
John F. Kennedy
I'll be back in the springtime.

As US President, at end of Irish visit, four months before his assassination. *The Irish Times*, May 9, 1996.

c. *July 1, 1963*
William Craig
Far from apologising I would give them this piece of advice: grow up, or failing that, for the good of all, take a running jump off a great height.

As NI Home Affairs Minister, to trade unions who had asked for apology for his allegation that unemployed were lazy. Tobin, Fergal, *The Best of Decades*, Gill & Macmillan, 1996, p. 205.

October 18, 1963
Terence O'Neill
Let there be an end to public statements either in Ireland or abroad about 'ultimate unification of our country', the 'evil of partition', the 'Six-County area'... Talk will not of itself change things. There is more to the wind of change than hot air.

As NI Prime Minister, in Newcastle on new era in relations with Republic. *The Irish Times*, January 15, 1965.

October 20, 1963
Sean Lemass
We now see our task as reuniting the Irish people as well as reuniting the Irish territory.

As Taoiseach, in Boston, responding to call for 'mutual respect' by Terence O'Neill, above. *The Irish Times*, January 15, 1965.

1964
Richard Harris
The headline on one English paper read 'British Actor Wins Major Award'. Three days later I was arrested in a brawl in Covent Garden and the same paper had the headline 'Irish Actor in Brawl'.

As Limerick-born actor, after winning best actor award at Cannes Film Festival. *The Irish Times*, April 3, 1993.

January 1964
J. E. N. Barnhill
Charity begins at home. If we are going to employ people we should begin with unionists. I am not saying we should sack nationalist employees, but if we are going to employ new men we should give preference to unionists.

As NI Senator, in address to Rural Unionist Association in Derry. Tobin, Fergal, *The Best of Decades*, Gill & Macmillan, 1996, p. 93.

February 14, 1964
Terence O'Neill
The people of Londonderry and the people of Ulster would do very ill to exchange their hope

of prosperity for a tattered green banner and a snatch of old song, carried away by the wind.

As NI Prime Minister, speaking in Derry. *The Irish Times*, January 15, 1965.

March 20, 1964
Brendan Behan
Thank you sister, and may you be the mother of a bishop.

As author, to nun adjusting his pillows in Dublin hospital, on the day he died. O'Sullivan, Michael, *Brendan Behan, A Life*, Blackwater Press, 1997, p. 300.

April 12, 1964
Sean Lemass
There is among them [NI people] a growing desire to change the present image of that area from a place where time never seemed to move, where old animosities are carefully fostered, and where bigotry and intolerance seem to be preserved as a way of life, to one in closer conformity to the spirit of the age.

As Taoiseach, in Arklow. *The Irish Times*, January 15, 1965.

May 18, 1964
John Hume
[Nationalist] leadership has been the easy leadership of flags and slogans. Easy no doubt but irresponsible... It is the lack of positive contribution and the apparent lack of interest in the general welfare of Northern Ireland that has led many Protestants to believe that the Northern Catholic is politically irresponsible and therefore unfit to rule.

As Derry teacher in article headed 'The Northern Catholic'. *The Irish Times*, May 18, 1964.

May 26, 1964
Fine Gael
Most people in public life will state their acceptance of the teachings contained in the papal encyclicals. But two dangers exist. Firstly, such acceptance may amount merely to lip service, and secondly, these principles may be used as an excuse for inaction.

Announcing 'Just Society' proposals as party policy, involving economic and social planning to achieve progress. *Fine Gael: Winning through to a Just Society*, Fine Gael Party (undated), p. 3.

July 3, 1964
Sean O'Casey
The directors [of the Abbey Theatre] have been dead for years.

As playwright, in row with Abbey Theatre over cuts in London production of 'Juno and the Paycock'. Hunt, Hugh, *The Abbey*, Gill & Macmillan, 1979, p. 188.

July 5, 1964
Directors of Abbey Theatre
The directors of the Abbey theatre have read with great interest Mr Sean O'Casey's announcement that they have been dead for years. They would like to assure Mr O'Casey that, as in the case of Mark Twain, the rumour is greatly exaggerated.

As board members, responding to Sean O'Casey's remark, above. Hunt, Hugh, *The Abbey*, Gill & Macmillan, 1979, pp.188-189.

September 27, 1964
Rev Ian Paisley
If that flag is not removed tomorrow, I will organise a march and remove it myself.

As leader of Free Presbyterian Church, in Ulster Hall address, referring to Irish tricolour at Republican Party headquarters in Divis Street, Belfast. Marrinan, Patrick, *Paisley, Man of Wrath*, Anvil, 1973, p. 82.

September 28, 1964
James Kilfedder
Remove tricolour in Divis Street which is aimed to provoke and insult loyalists of Belfast.

As West Belfast Unionist election candidate, in telegram to Brian McConnell, NI Minister of Home Affairs, following which RUC removed flag from Republican Party headquarters in Divis Street, Belfast, causing a riot. Bardon, Jonathan, *Belfast*, Blackstaff Press, 1983, p. 271.

October 8, 1964
Patrick Smith
[They] could not lead their own grandmother.

As Fianna Fáil Minister for Agriculture, resigning in protest at lack of leadership from trade unions in pay bargaining. *The Irish Times*, October 9, 1964.

January 14, 1965
Sean Lemass
I shall get into terrible trouble for this.

As Taoiseach, in Stormont lavatory, after arriving for first meeting between Republic and NI Prime Ministers. O'Neill, Terence, *The Autobiography of Terence O'Neill*, Rupert Hart-Davis, 1972, p. 72.

January 14, 1965
Terence O'Neill
No, Mr Lemass, it is I who will get into trouble for this.

As NI Prime Minister, replying to Sean Lemass, above. O'Neill, Terence, *The Autobiography of Terence O'Neill*, Rupert Hart-Davis, 1972, p. 72.

January 14, 1965
Terence O'Neill
We both share the same rivers, the same mountains, and some of the same problems, and therefore I think it is reasonable that the two

premiers should meet and discuss matters of mutual interest, and that is actually what we did today.

As NI Prime Minister, in television interview after meeting Lemass at Stormont. Bardon, Jonathan, *Belfast*, Blackstaff Press, 1983, p. 273.

January 14, 1965
George Clark
One country lives beside another, and it is surely common sense that the two leaders meet to discuss ways of expanding their economies.

As Grand Master of Orange Order, reacting to Lemass-O'Neill meeting at Stormont. *The Irish Times*, January 15, 1965.

January 14, 1965
Sean Lemass
I think I can say a roadblock has been removed. How far the road may go is not yet known [but] it is better to travel hopefully than to arrive.

As Taoiseach, after meeting NI Prime Minister at Stormont. Tobin, Fergal, *The Best of Dcades*, Gill & Macmillan, 1996, p. 127.

January 15, 1965
Rev Ian Paisley
We as Protestant Unionists are not prepared to sit idly by and have our heritage bartered by you or anyone else. We declare that we...will act as the Ulster Volunteers acted to defend our rights.

As leader of Free Presbyterian Church, in protest letter to NI Prime Minister after Lemass-O'Neill meeting. *The Irish Times*, January 16, 1965.

January 30, 1965
Sean Lemass
I can think of nothing which would work more strikingly the great changes of our times, or the strengthening of our Republican self-respect, than to see a member of the British royal family coming to Ireland on a private visit, travelling freely round Ireland, without anyone paying special attention.

As Taoiseach, on demonstrations against visit to Republic by Princess Margaret. *The Irish Times*, January 30, 1965.

February 2, 1965
Nationalist Party
It is essential to enter into official opposition at Stormont to ensure that existing parliamentary machinery operates for the common good...our fidelity to the united Ireland ideal remains unaltered by this decision.

As NI anti-Partition party, in statement ending policy of non-cooperation in NI Parliament. *The Irish Times*, February 3, 1965.

February 2, 1965
Sinn Féin
The puppet regime is now accepted as permanent, and the object of a 32-County Republic is further away than ever, if not completely abandoned.

As Dublin-based party, in statement on NI Nationalist Party accepting role of official opposition at Stormont. *The Irish Times*, February 3, 1965.

February 12, 1965
John Hume
Many people in Northern Ireland have not yet realised the depth of feeling and anger in this city at the Government's decision. On Thursday they will see a whole city stand outside Parliament Buildings while the [Unionist] mayor hands the city's claim to the Prime Minister. We are not asking for favours for Derry. We want justice.

As chairman of University for Derry Action Committee, on NI Government's decision to site second NI university at Coleraine rather than Derry. *The Irish Times*, February 13, 1965.

February 12, 1965
Eddie McAteer
The Government might be able to slap down the men of Derry. They might even be able to slap down the men of Londonderry. But they cannot slap down the united men of Derry and Londonderry.

As Nationalist MP, on cross-community rejection in Derry of NI Government's decision to site second NI university in Coleraine rather than Derry. *The Irish Times*, February 13, 1965.

February 18, 1965
Albert Anderson
We are demonstrating the unanimous feeling in this city and in County Tyrone and I believe, in County Fermanagh, behind this claim. Derry has a flourishing university college. It should be developed immediately.

As Ulster Unionist Mayor of Derry, at Stormont, accompanied by Nationalist Party MP Eddie McAteer, on NI Government's decision that Derry should not get second university. *The Irish Times*, February 19, 1965.

c. April 1, 1965
Edmond Warnock
He has succeeded single-handed in doing within the last couple of months what all our enemies failed to achieve in twenty-five years of ceaseless endeavour, for he has thrown the whole Ulster question back into the political arena with consequences already apparent and with worse to come.

As Ulster Unionist MP, on meeting of NI Prime Minister, Terence O'Neill, with Taoiseach, Sean Lemass. Tobin, Fergal, *The Best of Decades*, Gill & Macmillan, 1996, p. 129.

June 30, 1965
John Hume
The plan stands clear. [It is] to develop the strongly unionist Belfast-Coleraine-Portadown triangle and to cause a migration from west to east 'Ulster', redistributing and scattering the minority so the Unionist Party will not only maintain but strengthen its position.

As Derry teacher, protesting at London meeting over NI Government's decision to site new NI university at Coleraine rather than Derry. Routledge, Paul, *John Hume*, Harper Collins, 1998, pp. 51-52.

December 10, 1965
Dr John Charles McQuaid
You may have been worried by much talk of changes to come. Allow me to reassure you. No change will worry the tranquillity of your Christian lives.

As Archbishop of Dublin, preaching in Dublin on return from Second Vatican Council in Rome. *The Irish Times*, April 17, 1973.

c. February, 1966
Eamon de Valera
It is my considered opinion that in the fullness of time history will record the greatness of [Michael] Collins and it will be recorded at my expense.

As President, refusing to become patron of Michael Collins Foundation. Coogan, Tim Pat, *Michael Collins*, Arrow Books, 1991, p. 432.

February 13, 1966
Dr Thomas Ryan
I am referring to certain morally – or rather immorally – suggestive parts of the show which were completely unworthy of Irish television, unworthy of Irish producers, unworthy of Irish audiences...

As Bishop of Clonfert, in sermon, on couple being asked on Late Late Show the colour of nightdress worn by woman on their wedding night. (She did not wear any.) McLoone, M., and MacMahon, J., *Television and Irish Society*, RTÉ/IFI, 1984, pp. 109-110.

February 16, 1966
Stephen Barrett
I understand that part of the entertainment offered to viewers of the Late Late Show on Saturday night consisted of questioning a husband and wife, in the absence of each other, about the colour of the nightdress worn by the lady on her honeymoon... In many homes, such a discussion is not usually engaged in, and to have it thrust into

the middle of family and friends can, to some of us at all events, appear to be in utter bad taste.

As TD, in letter to *The Irish Press*, February 16, 1966.

February 19, 1966
Sean Lemass

In later years it was common – and I also was guilty in this respect – to question the motives of those men who joined the new British armies formed at the outbreak of the war, but it must in their honour and in fairness to their memory be said that they were motivated by the highest purpose.

As Taoiseach, honouring – for first time by Fianna Fáil leader – the memory of Irish people who fought in the First World War. *Sunday Press*, February 19, 1966.

March 1966
Brian Trevaskis

I don't blame the people, I would rather blame the Bishop of Galway [who is a] moron.

As panelist on Late Late Show in remarks critical of new Galway Cathedral which provoked widespread objections. McLoone, M., and McMahon, J., *Television and Irish Society*, RTÉ/IFI, 1984, p. 116.

c. March 1, 1966
Oliver J. Flanagan

Sex never came to Ireland until Teilifís Éireann went on the air.

As Fine Gael TD, criticising the Late Late Show. (Often quoted as 'There was no sex in Ireland before television.') Collins, Pan. *It Started on the Late Late Show*. Ward River Press, 1981, p. 41.

May 1966
Micheál Ó Moráin

We all know that the *Irish Times* is the mistress of the Fine Gael party, and mistresses can be both vicious and demanding.

As Minister for Lands and the Gaeltacht, in speech favouring candidate for President, Eamon de Valera. Tobin, Fergal, *The Best of Decades, Ireland in the 1960s*, Gill & Macmillan, 1996, p. 144.

May 1966
T. F. O'Higgins

I do not know that the *Irish Times* is the mistress of our party, and I certainly do not know anything about the vicious demands of mistresses. On these questions I bow to the superior knowledge of Mr Moran (sic).

As Fine Gael candidate in presidential election replying to Micheál Ó Moráin, above. Tobin, Fergal, *The Best of Decades, Ireland in the 1960s*, Gill & Macmillan, 1996, p. 145.

May 21, 1966
Ulster Volunteer Force

From this day on, we declare war against the IRA and its splinter groups.

As loyalist group, in statement signifying re-emergence as paramilitary force. Deutsch and Magowan, *Northern Ireland, 1968-1973, A Chronology of Events*, Vol. I, Blackstaff Press, 1973, p. 4.

June 7, 1966
Gerry Fitt

The only sensible thing was to have him certified as a person insane. There could be no doubt in any person's mind that Mr Paisley was insane and an absolute lunatic.

As Republican Labour MP, at Stormont, after riots in Belfast's Cromac Square when Rev Ian Paisley's supporters marched through nationalist area carrying anti-Catholic slogans. *The Irish Times*, June 8, 1966.

June 15, 1966
Terence O'Neill

To those of us who remember the Thirties, the pattern is horribly familiar. The contempt for established authority; the crude and unthinking intolerance; the emphasis upon monster processions and rallies; the appeal to a perverted form of patriotism – each and every one of these things has its parallel in the rise of the Nazis to power.

As NI Prime Minister, at Stormont, on activities of Rev Ian Paisley. Marrinan, Patrick, *Paisley, Man of Wrath*, Anvil, 1973, p. 109.

June 26, 1966
Richard Leppington

I don't know why these men shot at us. We were doing nothing political.

As victim of shooting by UVF of 4 Catholic barmen in Malvern Street, Belfast, one of whom, Peter Ward, died. *The Irish Times*, June 27, 1966.

June 26, 1966
Paul Rose

Following this killing there could be retaliation and a spread of violence. Action must be taken before this happens. The situation is very dangerous.

As Labour MP and Chairman of Campaign for Democracy in Ireland, on UVF attack on Catholic barmen in Malvern Street, Belfast, on June 25, 1966. *The Irish Times*, June 27, 1966.

June 28, 1966
Hugh McLean

I am ashamed of myself. I am sorry I ever heard tell of that man Paisley or decided to follow him.

As UVF member, on being charged with murder of Catholic barman, Peter Ward, in Malvern Street, Belfast.

Marrinan, Patrick, *Paisley, Man of Wrath*, Anvil, 1973, p. 114.

June 28, 1966
Terence O'Neill
I flew back last night from France. The purpose of my visit was to honour the men of the 36th [Ulster] Division, many of whom were members of the original and authentic UVF. Let no one imagine that there is any connection between the two bodies; between men who were ready to die for their country on the fields of France, and a sordid conspiracy of criminals prepared to take up arms against unprotected fellow-citizens.

As NI Prime Minister, at Stormont, banning UVF. Bloomfield, Ken, *Stormont in Crisis*, Blackstaff Press, 1994, p. 95.

c. July 1, 1966
Albert Anderson
Those who pay the piper are entitled to call the tune. One man, one vote is not the law and is not a basic principle in local government elections.

As Ulster Unionist Mayor of Derry, opposing campaign against company and plural votes in local government. Routledge, Paul, *John Hume*, Harper Collins, 1998, p. 55.

July 3, 1966
Sunday Times
John Bull's Political Slum.

As London newspaper, in headline over article on Northern Ireland, echoing G.B. Shaw's play title, 'John Bull's Other Island'. Bardon, Jonathan, *A History of Ulster*, Blackstaff Press, 1992, p. 647.

September 10, 1966
Donogh O'Malley
I propose from the coming school year, beginning in September of next year, to introduce a scheme whereby up to the completion of the Intermediate Certificate course, the opportunity for free post-primary education will be available to all families.

As Education Minister, in speech in Dun Laoghaire, announcing free secondary education, without prior consultation with Cabinet. *Sean Lemass,* Gill & Macmillan, 1983, pp. 106-107.

October 12, 1966
Sean Lemass
Radio Teilifís Éireann was set up by legislation as an instrument of public policy and as such is responsible to the Government.

As Taoiseach, in Dáil, on complaint by Minister for Agriculture Charles Haughey that RTÉ news was not giving his statements more weight that those from Irish Farmers' Association. McLoone, M., and MacMahon, J., *Television and Irish Society*, RTÉ/IFI, 1984, p. 6.

c. January 1967
Peter Shore
When London gets a chill, Northern Ireland gets the 'flu and Derry gets pneumonia; it's that sort of relationship.

As British Economic Affairs Minister. Routledge, Paul, *John Hume*, Harper Collins, 1998, p. 56.

February 9, 1967
Donogh O'Malley
No one is going to stop me introducing my scheme next September. I know I am up against opposition, and serious organised opposition, but they are not going to defeat me on this.

As Minister for Education, in Senate, on scheme for free secondary education which he announced without consulting Cabinet, and succeeded in implementing. *The Irish Times*, February 10, 1967.

April 1967
George Colley
Do not be dispirited if at some time people in high places appear to have low standards.

As Fianna Fáil Minister, in comment to youth gathering in Galway, widely interpreted as criticism of Cabinet colleague, Charles Haughey. *The Irish Times*, May 11, 1967.

April 1967
Protestant Telegraph
[The Sinn Féin oath states] 'These Protestant robbers and brutes, these unbelievers of our faith, will be driven like the swine they are into the sea by fire, the knife or by poison cup until we of the Catholic Faith and avowed supporters of all Sinn Féin action and principles, clear these heretics from our land.'

As newspaper of the Rev Ian Paisley, quoting (bogus) version of Sinn Féin oath circulating among Orange Lodges. Coogan, Tim Pat, *The IRA*, Fontana, 1980, p. 322.

April 13, 1967
Frank Aiken
RTÉ [is] a semi-state body, and if they sent a team to [North] Vietnam, it would not be believed that they had done this without the approval of the Government... For a camera team it would be a conducted tour.

As Minister for External Affairs, in Dáil, on Government ban on RTÉ sending film crew to North Vietnam during Vietnam War. *The Irish Times*, April 14, 1967.

April 26, 1967
Terence O'Neill
The standards governing the conduct of Ministers are, and must be, more stringent than those which cover the conduct of private people. They must

stand above suspicion. They must not place themselves in the way of adverse comment.

As NI Prime Minister, dismissing Minister for Agriculture Harry West for urging Government to reopen St Angelo airport near Enniskillen in which he had (undeclared) interest. *The Irish Times*, April 27, 1967.

April 27, 1967
Paddy Harte
Which member of this Cabinet was going to go 'West'? The lobbies and corridors of the House were seething with rumours of corruption on housing in Dublin city, of men who had become very rich at the expense of the local authorities and the poor.

As Fine Gael TD, in Dáil, after sacking of Harry West from NI Government on previous day. *The Irish Times*, April 28, 1967.

May 9, 1967
Liam Cosgrave
When, as happened recently, a Government Minister considers it necessary to refer publicly to the apparently low standards of integrity of those in high places, it is clear that we are faced with something more than normal, irresponsible rumour-mongering. The only people in high places are Fianna Fáil.

As leader of Fine Gael, at party árd fheis, referring to remark in April by George Colley, Fianna Fáil Minister. *The Irish Times*, May 10, 1967.

March 1968
Derry Housing Action Committee
The formation of this committee marks the beginning of a mass movement away from the false political leaders and against the exploiting capitalist class who have left in their wake a trail of human misery, degradation and decay.

As civil rights group, announcing period of demonstrations. Bardon, Jonathan, *A History of Ulster*, Blackstaff Press, 1992, p. 650.

March 1968
Gerry Fitt
I am quite prepared to go outside constitutional methods.

As Republican Labour MP, on what he would do if constitutional methods failed to bring justice and democracy to Northern Ireland. Routledge, Paul, *John Hume*, Harper Collins, 1998, p. 57.

June 23, 1968
Austin Currie
If we cannot obtain justice through normal channels, then we should do so through the only other effective means at our disposal. There was

no danger of violence. Indeed, civil disobedience was a safety valve.

As Nationalist MP, at party conference, after squatting in council house in Caledon, Co Tyrone, allocated to 19-year-old single Protestant girl. *The Irish Times*, June 24, 1968.

August 14, 1968
Rev Ian Paisley
The Catholics have been interfering in Ulster affairs since 1641.

As leader of Free Presbyterian Church. *The Irish Times*, August 15, 1968.

August 24, 1968
Betty Sinclair
What we have done today will go down in history and in this way we will be more effective in showing the world that we are a peaceful people asking for our civil rights in an orderly manner.

As member of NI Civil Rights Association, persuading marchers from Coalisland to Dungannon to sit down rather than confront police. Bardon, Jonathan, *A History of Ulster*, Blackstaff Press, 1992, p. 652.

August 24, 1968
Gerry Fitt
My blood is boiling – only that there is a danger to women and children I would lead the men past that barricade.

As Republican Labour MP, as NI Civil Rights march was prevented by police from entering Dungannon. Bardon, Jonathan, *A History of Ulster*, Blackstaff Press, 1992, p. 653.

August 24, 1968
Albert Kennedy
The speech of Mr Gerry Fitt was most provocative when he announced from the platform that the ban imposed by the police made his blood boil, and called the County Inspector and District Inspector 'a pair of black bastards'.

As RUC Inspector General, in confidential report to Government of Gerry Fitt's speech at Dungannon Civil Rights Association march. *The Irish Times*, January 2, 1999.

October 3, 1968
NI Civil Rights Association
Situation inflammatory. People will not continue to suffer the indignity of second-class citizenship.

In telegram to British Home Secretary James Callaghan, protesting ban on Civil Rights Association march in Derry on October 5. Routledge, Paul, *John Hume*, Harper Collins, 1998, p. 64.

October 5, 1968
Gerry Fitt
I uttered a prayer of thanks as the blood spilled over my face and on my shirt... I knew that at last

Northern Ireland as she really was would be seen before the world.

As Republican Labour MP, after being batoned by RUC at Civil Rights Association march in Derry. *The Irish Times*, November 23, 1979.

October 5, 1968
Martin Cowley
He cut quite a dashing figure. He did the cutting and I did the dashing.

As *Irish Times* reporter, recalling how he was batoned by senior RUC officer at Civil Rights Association march in Derry. *The Irish Times*, October 8, 1988.

October 7, 1968
Terence O'Neill
We might get back to the situation of 1912 when a Liberal Government tried to interfere in Irish affairs.

As NI Prime Minister, warning of Unionist rebellion if British Government intervened after Derry riots of October 5, 1968. *The Irish Times*, October 8, 1968.

October 9, 1968
Eamon McCann
Middle-aged, middle-class and middle-of-the-road – it could give the kiss of death to the developing radical movement in Derry.

As left wing activist in Derry, on leadership of Derry Citizens' Action Committee. Routledge, Paul, *John Hume*, Harper Collins, 1998, p. 68.

October 9, 1968
People's Democracy
One man, one vote; fair boundaries; houses on need; jobs on merit; free speech; repeal of the Special Powers Act.

As student body formed at Queen's University, Belfast, in statement of aims. Bardon, Jonathan, *A History of Ulster*, Blackstaff Press, 1992, p. 656.

October 15, 1968
Nationalist Party
Being disappointed by Captain O'Neill's Government's failure to deal effectively with the root causes of unrest afflicting our society, we cease to function as official opposition until such time as the Government gives further concrete evidence of a sincere desire to remedy the situation.

As NI anti-Partition party, in statement protesting against both slow pace of reform and police action in Derry on October 5, 1968. *The Irish Times*, October 16, 1968.

October 16, 1968
William Craig
I believe the Londonderry disorder has brought the guns a step nearer.

As NI Home Affairs Minister, in Stormont debate on events of October 5, 1968, in Derry. *The Irish Times*, October 17, 1968.

October 21, 1968
Harold Wilson
...the feeling that he [Terence O'Neill] is being blackmailed by thugs who are putting pressure on him is something this House cannot accept.

As British Prime Minister, in House of Commons, about Unionist opposition to Terence O'Neill's reform programme. Deutsch and Magowan, *Northern Ireland, 1968-1973, A Chronology of Events*, Vol. I, Blackstaff Press, 1983, p. 11.

October 30, 1968
Basil Brooke (Lord Brookeborough)
How can you give somebody who is your enemy a higher position in order to allow him to come to destroy you?

As NI Prime Minister, asked why Catholics did not attain higher positions in Northern Ireland life. *The Irish Times*, October 30, 1968.

November 16, 1968
John Hume
I am not a law-breaker by nature but I am proud to stand here with 15,000 Derry people who have broken a law which is in disrepute. I invite Mr Craig to arrest the lot of us.

As organiser of Derry Citizens' Action Committee march in Derry which successfully defied ban by NI Home Affairs Minister, William Craig. Routledge, Paul, *John Hume*, Harper Collins, 1998, pp. 72-73.

November 28, 1968
William Craig
We face a reality: where you have a Roman Catholic majority you have lower standard of democracy...you remember when Dr Browne brought in a small measure of social reform, the Mother and Child Bill [in 1951], it was accepted by the Cabinet and Parliament but the Church authorities said this was not a matter for the people to decide because it was a matter of faith and morals... In the Republic [democracy] is subject to an overriding authority.

As NI Home Affairs Minister, in address at Loyalist Ulster Hall rally, later criticised for its anti-Catholic tone by NI Prime Minister Terence O'Neill. *The Irish Times*, November 29, 1968.

November 30, 1968
County Inspector Sam Sherrard
I have spared no effort in trying to keep your route clear... I must assure you of my sincerity.

As senior RUC officer, telling 6,000 civil rights marchers they could not go through Armagh city because of counter-demonstration organised by Rev Ian Paisley. *The Irish Times*, December 2, 1968.

December 9, 1968
Terence O'Neill

Ulster stands at the crossroads... There are, I know, today some so-called Loyalists who talk of independence from Britain – who seem to want a kind of Protestant Sinn Féin... Rhodesia, in defying Britain, at least has an air force and an army of her own. Where are the Ulster armoured divisions and the Ulster jet planes?... Unionism armed with justice will be a stronger cause than Unionism armed merely with strength... What kind of Ulster do you want? A happy and respected province in good standing with the rest of the United Kingdom? Or a place continually torn apart by riots and demonstrations?

As NI Prime Minister, in television address. *The Irish Times*, December 10, 1968.

December 10, 1968
William Craig

I will resist any effort by any Government in Great Britain...to interfere with the proper jurisdiction of the Government of Northern Ireland.

As NI Home Affairs Minister, in remarks to Bloomfield Unionists widely interpreted as support for NI independence. *The Irish Times*, December 11, 1968.

December 11, 1968
Terence O'Neill

I have known for some time that you were attracted by ideas of a UDI nature...clearly you cannot propose such views and remain in the Government.

As NI Prime Minister, in letter to William Craig, NI Home Affairs Minister, demanding his resignation for seeming to advocate a unilateral declaration of independence. *The Irish Times*, December 12, 1968.

December 19, 1968
Conor Cruise O'Brien

Ireland puts the portrait of that great enemy of imperialism, James Connolly, on its postage stamps, but in practice, in the routine conduct of its foreign policy, daily betrays everything that he, Connolly, stood for. This hypocrisy does not make us respected.

As new member of Irish Labour Party, in speech at Liberty Hall, Dublin. *The Irish Times*, December 20, 1968.

1969
Micheál Ó Moráin

[They are] left-wing political queers from Trinity College and Teilifís Éireann.

As Minister for Justice, on people running Labour Party. Browne, Vincent, *The Magill Book of Irish Politics*, Magill, 1981, p. 284.

January 1, 1969
Eddie McAteer

It is not good marching weather – in more senses than one.

As Nationalist Party leader, counselling against People's Democracy march from Belfast to Derry. Bardon, Jonathan, *A History of Ulster*, Blackstaff Press, 1992, p. 659.

c. January 1, 1969
Bogside Residents

You Are Now Entering Free Derry.

Slogan on gable wall in Derry after successful defiance of ban on civil rights marches. Routledge, Paul, *John Hume*, Harper Collins, 1998, p. 75.

January 3, 1969
Ronald Bunting

I have given a request to the loyal citizens of Ulster and, thank God, they have responded, to hinder and harry it, and I think they've hindered it and, I think you will agree, to a certain extent they have harried it.

As loyalist leader, on attacks by loyalists on People's Democracy march from Belfast to Derry, which culminated following day in ambush at Burntollet Bridge, Co Derry. Marrinan, Patrick, *Paisley, Man of Wrath*, Anvil, 1973, p. 162.

January 4, 1969
Bernadette Devlin

It is impossible to describe the atmosphere, but it must have been like that on V-day; the war was over and we had won; we hadn't lifted a finger but we'd won.

As leader of People's Democracy, on arrival in Derry of march from Belfast. Devlin, Bernadette, *The Price of My Soul*, Pan, 1969, p. 143.

January 5, 1969
Terence O'Neill

It is a short step from the throwing of paving stones to the laying of tombstones... Some of the marchers and those who supported them in Londonderry itself have shown themselves to be mere hooligans, ready to attack the police and others... We have heard sufficient for now about civil rights; let us hear a little about civic responsibility.

As NI Prime Minister, on march by People's Democracy and aftermath, during which police rioted in Derry. Bardon, Jonathan, *A History of Ulster*, Blackstaff Press, 1992, p. 661.

January 23, 1969
Brian Faulkner

It is, in my opinion, a political manoeuvre and to some extent an abdication of authority... The Government is better qualified to decide for itself what is to be done.

As NI Minister of Commerce, resigning over appointment of Lord Cameron to chair inquiry into disturbances. Boyd, Andrew, *Brian Faulkner and the Crisis in Ulster Unionism*, Anvil, 1972, p. 60.

January 24, 1969
Terence O'Neill

I am bound to say that if, instead of passively 'remaining', you had on occasions given me that loyalty and support which a Prime Minister has the right to expect from his deputy, some of these so-called crises might never have arisen.

As NI Prime Minister, replying to letter of resignation from Brian Faulkner. Boyd, Andrew, *Brian Faulkner and the Crisis in Ulster Unionism*, Anvil, 1972, pp. 61-62.

January 24, 1969
Brendan Corish

I am against coalition...this is a matter of conscience and...in such an eventuality, my continued support for socialism will be from the backbenches.

As leader of Labour Party, addressing party conference, four years before becoming Tánaiste in coalition government. *The Irish Times*, January 25, 1969.

January 25, 1969
Conor Cruise O'Brien

We should support the civil rights campaign in the North... There is a majority there that wants unity with Britain and we must respect that, but at the same time we must reject their right to oppress the minority.

As delegate to Labour Party conference. *The Irish Times*, January 27, 1969.

January 30, 1969
Terence O'Neill

I understand there are some in my Party who have stated they want a change of leadership. What they truly seek is a change of policy. I will not back down. I will not trim my sails. I will do my duty.

As NI Prime Minister, reacting to defection of 12 Ulster Unionist MPs to form 'O'Neill must go' faction. Deutsch and Magowan, *Northern Ireland, 1968-1973, A Chronology of Events*, Vol. I, Blackstaff Press, 1973, p. 19.

March 4, 1969
Jeremy Thorpe

Northern Ireland is still at the crossroads and the sky is overcast.

As Liberal leader, in House of Commons. Deutsch and Magowan, *Northern Ireland, 1968-1973, A Chronology of Events*, Vol. I, Blackstaff Press, 1973, p. 21.

April 23, 1969
Bernadette Devlin

If British troops are sent in I should not like to be the mother or sister of an unfortunate soldier stationed there...the one point in common among Ulstermen is that they are not fond of Englishmen who tell them what to do.

As Unity MP for Mid-Ulster, in House of Commons, in maiden speech. *Hansard*, April 23, 1969.

April 24, 1969
William Craig

The people of Ulster will not surrender their Parliament without a fight. What we see today on the streets of our Province – the disorders – will look like a Sunday school picnic if Westminster tried to take our Parliament away.

As former NI Minister, speaking at Stewartstown. Deutsch and Magowan, *Northern Ireland, 1968-1973, A Chronology of Events*, Vol. I, Blackstaff Press, 1973, p. 25.

April 28, 1969
Terence O'Neill

Ours is called a Christian country. We could have enriched our politics with our Christianity, but far too often we have debased our Christianity with our politics.

As NI Prime Minister, resigning because of lack of support in Ulster Unionist Party. Marrinan, Patrick, *Paisley, Man of Wrath*, Anvil, 1973, p. 178.

May 10, 1969
Terence O'Neill

It is frightfully hard to explain to Protestants that if you give Roman Catholics a good job and a good house, they will live like Protestants, because they will see neighbours with cars and television sets. They will refuse to have eighteen children, but if a Roman Catholic is jobless and lives in a most ghastly hovel, he will rear eighteen children on National Assistance. If you treat Roman Catholics with due consideration and kindness, they will live like Protestants in spite of the authoritative nature of their Church.

As former NI Prime Minister. *Belfast Telegraph*, May 10, 1969.

June 1969
Labour Party

The Seventies will be Socialist!

Slogan for general election. Keogh, Dermot, *Twentieth-Century Ireland*, Gill & Macmillan, 1994, p. 299.

June 1969
Conor Cruise O'Brien
The priest gave communism the expected treatment. Then he went on to socialism. 'Socialism,' he said, 'is worse than communism. Socialism is a heresy of communism. Socialists are a *Protestant* variety of communists.' Not only communists but Protestant communists!

As Labour Party member, retelling priest's sermon, delivered in Dingle. Cruise O'Brien, Conor, *States of Ireland*, Hutchinson, London, 1972.

June 16, 1969
Roy Bradford
Ask any of the thousands of visitors now enjoying the wonderful colours of June and they will tell you that the North of Ireland is essentially a peaceful place. The tourist has just about as much chance of being molested as he has of being knocked over by a runaway camel.

As NI Minister of Commerce, in London speech. Deutsch and Magowan, *Northern Ireland, 1968-1973, A Chronology of Events*, Vol. I, Blackstaff Press, 1973, p. 30.

July 8, 1969
Louis Boyle
I was due to address a Young Unionist meeting but it did not materialise because they held their meetings in the local Orange halls and were told they could not use it if I were to attend.

As Catholic member of Ulster Unionist Party, resigning on grounds it was sectarian. *The Irish Times*, July 9, 1969.

July 12, 1969
James Chichester-Clark
We have deeply resented the ambivalent and malicious picture of the Province which has been presented to the world. What we cannot accept is the way in which the British people themselves have been misled. Do they not understand even now who are the true friends of Britain in these islands?

As NI Prime Minister, at Orange demonstration at Moneymore. *The Irish Times*, July 14, 1969.

July 13, 1969
Rev Ian Paisley
I hate the system of Roman Catholicism, but, God being my judge, I love the poor dupes who are ground down under that system. Particularly I feel for their Catholic mothers who have to go and prostitute themselves before old bachelor priests.

As leader of Independent Orange Order, in speech at Loughall, Co Armagh. Marrinan, Patrick, *Paisley, Man of Wrath*, Anvil, 1973, p. 184.

July 14, 1969
Eddie McAteer
Unless we [Unionists and Nationalists] get together, there will be no city left for us to quarrel over.

As Nationalist Party leader, on rioting in Derry. *The Irish Times*, July 15, 1969.

July 15, 1969
Charles Haughey
This is something completely new in this country and indeed so far as I am aware in the world. We are entering a field in which there is no precedence of experience to guide us.

As Minister for Finance, in Dáil, on bill to exempt writers, sculptors and painters from income tax. *The Irish Times*, July 16, 1969.

July 31, 1969
Sean Bourke
I will have a few pints, and after that I will have a few more pints, and then I will have a jolly good booze-up and go for a holiday somewhere.

As ex-prisoner, after Supreme Court refused his extradition to Britain on charge of helping Soviet spy, George Blake, escape from Wormwood Scrubs in October 1966. *The Irish Times*, August 1, 1969.

August 6, 1969
Harold Wolseley
I would say the question of using troops here is very remote. After all, the RUC have this situation absolutely taped. We're in full control.

As Belfast Commissioner of Police, after serious rioting in city. *The Irish Times*, August 7, 1969.

August 6, 1969
Oliver J. Flanagan
Too much of our land has fallen into German hands... We have no liking for Nazis and there is no room in this country for Germans.

As Fine Gael TD, on purchase of Irish property by Germans. *The Irish Times*, August 7, 1969.

August 11, 1969
Eddie McAteer
If another hand than ours does embark upon the terrible work we all fear this week, be right sure this means the raising of the curtain on the last terrible act of the age-old Irish drama.

As Nationalist Party leader, on rising tension in Derry. *The Irish Times*, August 16, 1969.

August 12, 1969
Vincent McDowell
We urgently request that the [Irish] Government take immediate action to have a United Nations peacekeeping force sent to Derry...pending the

arrival of a United Nations force we urge the immediate suspension of the Six-County Parliament and the partisan RUC and B Specials and their temporary replacement by joint peace-keeping patrols of Irish and British troops.

As vice chairman of NI Civil Rights Association, after severe rioting in Derry. *The Irish Times*, August 13, 1969.

August 13, 1969
Northern Ireland Civil Rights Association

The Executive would like to make clear that at no time did it call for the intervention of Irish troops in Derry. This report was not authorised by the Executive and we expressly disassociate ourselves from this statement.

Statement issued after vice chairman Vincent McDowell called for joint British-Irish patrols. *The Irish Times*, August 14, 1969.

August 13, 1969
Jack Lynch

It is clear now that the present situation cannot be allowed to continue. It is evident that the Stormont Government is no longer in control of the situation. Indeed the present situation is the inevitable outcome of the policies pursued for decades by successive Stormont Governments. It is clear also that the Irish Government can no longer stand by and see innocent people injured and perhaps worse.

As Taoiseach, in television broadcast on situation in Derry. (His script said 'stand idly by' but 'idly' was omitted from teleprompter.) *The Irish Times*, August 14, 1969.

August 13, 1969
James Chichester-Clark

I must hold Mr Lynch personally responsible for any worsening of feeling which these inflammatory and ill-considered remarks may cause.

As NI Prime Minister, responding to broadcast by Taoiseach on Derry rioting. *The Irish Times*, August 14, 1969.

August 13, 1969
Eddie McAteer

I believe there must be intervention from somewhere. I would welcome a move from the United Nations or failing that from the Irish Republic. We must have protection.

As Nationalist Party leader, on Derry riots. *The Irish Times*, August 14, 1969.

August 14, 1969
Cardinal William Conway

I cannot understand why a parade, lasting five or six hours, and accompanied by dancing women singing party songs and firing off imitation cannon was allowed to take place in a city which was tinder-dry for an explosion.

As Primate of Ireland, on Apprentice Boys' parade which preceded rioting in Derry. *The Irish Times*, August 15, 1969.

August 14, 1969
British Home Office

The Government of Northern Ireland has informed the United Kingdom Government that as a result of the severe and prolonged rioting in Londonderry, it has no alternative but to ask for the assistance of troops at present stationed in Northern Ireland to prevent a breakdown of law and order...troops will be withdrawn as soon as this is accomplished.

As British Government ministry responsible for Northern Ireland, in statement announcing deployment of British Army. *The Irish Times*, August 15, 1969.

August 14, 1969
James Callaghan

By God, it is enjoyable being a minister. This is what I like doing, taking decisions, and I had to take the decision to put the troops in while I was in the plane on the way back from Cornwall.

As British Home Secretary, on how he took decision to send troops into Derry. Crossman, Richard, *The Diaries of a Cabinet Minister*, Vol. III, Hamilton and Cape, 1977, p. 619.

August 14, 1969
James Chichester-Clark

We must, and we will, treat the Government which seeks to wound us in our darkest hour as an unfriendly and implacable Government, determined to overthrow by any means the state which enjoys the support of a majority of our electorate.

As NI Prime Minister, at Stormont, on Irish Government. Deutsch and Magowan, *Northern Ireland, 1968-1973, A Chronology of Events*, Vol. I, Blackstaff Press, 1983, p. 39.

August 15, 1969
Frank Gogarty

For Christ's sake tell someone to intervene. Tell someone in Dublin. There will be another four hours of murder here.

As chairman of NI Civil Rights Association, at 2.00 a.m. in Belfast, after rioting had claimed five lives. *The Irish Times*, August 15, 1969.

August 15, 1969
Tomás MacGiolla

The only units in a position to make any defence last night in Belfast were the units of the IRA... The weapons are in this country. The weapons are in the FCA [army reserve] and in the Free State army – if you are not prepared to use them will you give them to us?

As President of Sinn Féin, at public meeting at GPO in Dublin. *The Irish Times*, August 16, 1969.

August 16, 1969
Paddy Devlin

We need money to feed and house people, but as we stand here talking there are people being shot down. The only way we can defend ourselves is with guns and we haven't got them. We need them.

As NI Labour Party representative, at public meeting at GPO in Dublin about situation in Northern Ireland. *The Irish Times*, August 18, 1969.

August 17, 1969
Richard Crossman

I fear that once the Catholics and Protestants get used to our presence they will hate us more than they will hate each other.

As British Minister, reflecting on introduction of troops into Northern Ireland conflict. Crossman, Richard, *The Diaries of a Cabinet Minister*, Vol. III, Hamilton and Cape, 1977, p. 620.

August 18, 1969
Lt-General Sir Ian Freeland

Honeymoons can be very short-lived.

As General Officer Commanding British Army in Northern Ireland, on warm reception given to troops brought in to stop rioting. *The Irish Times*, August 19, 1969.

August 18, 1969
Cathal Goulding

In response to urgent calls for help from an almost defenceless people...the Army Council has placed all volunteers on full alert and has already sent a number of fully equipped units to the aid of their comrades in the Six Counties.

As IRA leader, in interview in Dublin. *The Irish Times*, August 16, 1969.

August 18, 1969
Pravda

English imperialism is ready to use the powers of its bayonets to hold on to the Six Counties of Ulster which it tore by force from their native Ireland.

As Soviet Communist Party daily, commenting on events in Northern Ireland. *The Irish Times*, August 19, 1969.

August 18, 1969
British Government

Nothing which has happened in recent weeks in Northern Ireland derogates from the clear

pledges made by successive United Kingdom Governments that Northern Ireland should not cease to be a part of the United Kingdom...without the consent of the parliament of Northern Ireland. The Border is not an issue.

In statement describing use of British troops in Northern Ireland as a response to 'a breakdown of law and order'. McLoughlin, Michael, *Great Irish Speeches of the Twentieth Century*, Poolbeg, 1996, p. 273.

August 19, 1969
Bernadette Devlin

You're giving them tea now. What will you be giving them in six months?

As Unity MP for Mid-Ulster, addressing crowd in Bogside after British soldiers welcomed by residents. Arthur, Paul, *Government and Politics of Northern Ireland*, Longman, 1984, p. 129.

August 19, 1969
Jack Lynch

No group has any authority to speak or act for the Irish people except the lawful Government of Ireland.

As Taoiseach, challenging statement by IRA leader Cathal Goulding on August 18. *The Irish Times*, August 20, 1969.

August 19, 1969
Harold Wilson

We now want to see the B Specials phased out. Their disarming is entirely a matter for the GOC [General Freeland].

As British Prime Minister, during break in meeting in London with NI ministers, refering to all-Protestant Ulster Special Constabulary. *The Irish Times*, August 20, 1969.

August 20, 1969
Brian Faulkner

There is absolutely no suggestion that the USC [B Specials] will be disbanded. Let me make that crystal clear.

As NI Prime Minister, in interview following meeting in London between British and Northern Ireland ministers. Deutsch and Magowan, *Northern Ireland, 1968-1973, A Chronology of Events*, Vol. I, Blackstaff Press, 1983, p. 40.

August 20, 1969
Rev Ian Paisley

If you want to destroy a government you pull its teeth... Faulkner should tell the truth. The B Specials will be destroyed and our line of defence with it.

As leader of Free Presbyterian Church, on meeting in London of British and NI ministers. *The Irish Times*, August 21, 1969.

August 21, 1969
John Hume
The truth is that Ulster Unionists are not loyal to the Crown, but the half-crown.

As Derry civil rights leader. *The Irish Times*, August 23, 1969.

August 24, 1969
Raymond Wolseley
We are going to have another Cuba in Ireland in two months time... There are dark strangers from Europe in the Bogside.

As leader of Derry Chamber of Commerce delegation to Stormont, referring to foreign students. *The Irish Times*, August 25, 1969.

August 28, 1969
James Callaghan
I am not neutral. I am on the side of all people who are deprived of justice.

As British Home Secretary, addressing Bogside through megaphone from upstairs window of terraced house. *The Irish Times*, August 29, 1969.

August 28, 1969
James Callaghan
You know, Mr Paisley, we are all the children of God.

As British Home Secretary to Rev Ian Paisley in Conway Hotel, Belfast. Callaghan, James, *A House Divided*, Collins, 1973, p. 82.

August 28, 1969
Rev Ian Paisley
No, we are not, Mr Callaghan. We are all the children of wrath.

As leader of Free Presbyterian Church, replying to James Callaghan, above. Callaghan, James, *A House Divided*, Collins, 1973, p. 82.

August 29, 1969
Northern Ireland Tourist Board
Shooting is a popular sport in the countryside...the outstanding characteristic of the sport has been that it is not confined to any one class.

In advertisement. *New Statesman*, August 29, 1969.

September 11, 1969
Cameron Commission
Mr Gerry Fitt, MP, sought publicity for himself and his political views and must clearly have envisaged the possibility of a violent clash with the police as providing the publicity he so ardently sought. His conduct in our judgement was reckless and wholly irresponsible in a person occupying his public position.

In official report on disturbances in North, referring to Civil Rights march in Derry on October 5, 1968. *The Irish Times*, September 12, 1969.

September 11, 1969
Rev Ian Paisley
The Roman Catholic Church is getting nearer to communism every day.

As leader of Free Presbyterian Church. *The Irish Times*, September 11, 1969.

September 19, 1969
Denis Healey
The honeymoon period [is] coming to an end, but it has not ended in divorce or a stand-up fight between husband and wife. The troops have been accepted by both communities and a happy, comfortable married life [is] under way.

As British Minister for Defence, on visit to Northern Ireland. *The Irish Times*, September 20, 1969.

September 20, 1969
Jack Lynch
Let me make it clear too that in seeking reunification, our aim is not to extend the domination of Dublin. We have many times down the years expressed our willingness to seek a solution on federal lines.

As Taoiseach, speaking at Tralee. Lynch, John, *Speeches and Statements, August 1969-October 1971*, Government Information Bureau, 1971, pp. 10-11.

September 22, 1969
Cardinal William Conway
I personally would not shed a tear if the relevant sub-sections of Article 44 were to disappear.

As Primate of Ireland, on Article in Constitution recognising special position of Catholic Church. *The Irish Times*, September 23, 1969.

October 10, 1969
Lord Hunt
The protection of the Border and the State against armed attacks is not a role which should have to be undertaken by the police, whether they be regular or special.

As chairman of commission to reform RUC, in report announcing disbandment of B Specials. *The Irish Times*, October 11, 1969.

October 10, 1969
James Callaghan
Citizens of Bogside! I said I'd return. I have brought the new Inspector-General to see you...you'll have to look after him.

As British Home Secretary, introducing new RUC Inspector-General Sir Arthur Young to applauding crowd in Derry. *The Irish Times*, October 13, 1969.

October 19, 1969
Harry Sheehan
If the drink ban was introduced to prevent
drunkenness, then it was a complete flop. It had
in fact the opposite effect. Publicans had to deal
with more drunks than for many a long day.
As general secretary of Belfast Licensed Vintners'
Association, on Saturday night ban on serving drink after
7.00 p.m. because of rioting. *The Irish Times*, October 20,
1969.

October 22, 1969
Jack Lynch
We do not want to seek to impose our will on
anyone by force.
As Taoiseach, on Northern Ireland. Keogh, Dermot,
Twentieth-Century Ireland, Gill & Macmillan, 1994,
p. 305.

November 4, 1969
Rev Ian Paisley
I have information that the Government is
planning to have me certified by psychiatrists.
This is abominable and savours of the corruption
of the present regime.
As leader of Free Presbyterian Church. *The Irish Times*,
November 5, 1969.

November 18, 1969
Austin Currie
Some of the Opposition members showed
political courage in saying that members of the
minority should join the new force...members of
the minority should join the forces.
As Nationalist MP, advising Catholics to join Ulster
Defence Regiment and reserve police force. *The Irish
Times*, November 19, 1969.

November 20, 1969
Bernadette Devlin
For half a century it [Unionist Party
Government] has misgoverned us, but it is on the
way out. Now we are witnessing its dying
convulsions. And with traditional Irish mercy,
when we've got it down, we will kick it into the
ground.
As Unity MP for Mid-Ulster, in autobiography. Devlin,
Bernadette, *The Price of My Soul*, Pan, 1969, p. 206.

November 23, 1969
Eddie McAteer
Let those who seek to dance on our graves dance
lightly lest they waken the corpse.
As Nationalist MP, at party conference after being elected
President. *The Irish Times*, November 24, 1969.

December 8, 1969
Neil Blaney
If a situation were to arise in the Six Counties in
which the people who do not succumb to the
Unionist regime were under sustained and
murderous assault, then, as the Taoiseach said on
August 13th, we 'cannot stand idly (sic) by.'... The
Fianna Fáil Party has never taken a decision to rule
out the use of force if the circumstances of the Six
Counties so demand.
As Minister for Agriculture, speaking in Letterkenny, Co
Donegal. *The Irish Times*, December 9, 1969.

December 9, 1969
John Hume
The border is a sectarian border. To attempt to use
force to break it down would lead not only to civil
war but to a religious war. There are hostages in
Derry and hostages in Belfast. We are the ones
who would suffer.
As Derry civil rights leader, on speech of Neil Blaney,
above. *The Irish Times*, December 10, 1969.

December 28, 1969
IRA Provisional Army Council
[It] is a logical outcome of an obsession in recent
years with parliamentary politics, with the
consequent undermining of the basic military role
of the Irish Republican Army. The failure to
provide the maximum defence possible of our
people in Belfast is ample evidence of this neglect.
In statement signalling birth of Provisional IRA in protest at
IRA convention recognising governments in London,
Dublin and Belfast. *The Irish Times*, December 29, 1985.

c. January 1, 1970
Jimmy Young
We are now approaching Aldergrove Airport,
Belfast. Please put your watches back 300 years.
As NI comedian. Attributed.

February 17, 1970
Samuel Stevenson
I explained to them it was to be done on behalf of
the Big Man – the Rev Ian Paisley. When they
heard that, they were much more enthusiastic
about doing it.
As leader of UVF, giving evidence in court about how
fellow-conspirators carried out explosion at Dunadry in
1969 to topple NI Prime Minister Terence O'Neill. *The Irish
Times*, February 18, 1970.

February 18, 1970
Enoch Powell
A part of the process could well include the closer
constitutional and administrative identification of
these counties with the rest of the United
Kingdom.

As Conservative MP, advocating integration with UK at Unionist meeting in Enniskillen. *The Irish Times*, February 18, 1970.

March 11, 1970
Kevin Boland

I can understand that the consortium of belted earls and their ladies and left-wing intellectuals who can afford the time to stand and contemplate in ecstasy the unparalleled man-made beauty of the two corners of Hume Street and St Stephen's Green may well feel that the amateurish efforts of Mother Nature in the Wicklow Mountains are unworthy of their attention.

As Minister for Local Government, in Dáil, defending development in Georgian area of Dublin. *The Irish Times*, March 13, 1970.

March 12, 1970
John Hume

We have opted out of Northern Ireland for the last 50 years and we must involve ourselves now. Many people would not like to join the UDR because it was against their traditions but Catholics must move in to make it a neutral force and prevent it being taken over by the B Specials.

As Derry civil rights leader, speaking at Labour Party meeting in Birmingham. *The Irish Times*, March 26, 1970.

April 16, 1970
Rev Ian Paisley

Let me smell your breath!

As newly elected Stormont MP for Bannside, to reporter. *BBC*, April 16, 1970.

April 18, 1970
Stephen Coughlan

I remember when I was a very young boy...the problem of the Jews in Limerick... The Jews at that time, who are now gone, were extortionists... I remember an unfortunate woman was having a baby and they came getting their five shillings a week...they took the bed from under her.

As Labour Mayor of Limerick, to Credit Union League of Ireland, which immediately voted unanimously to disassociate itself from his remarks. *The Irish Times*, April 25, 1970.

April 19, 1970
Gerald Goldberg

Gentle Jesus, meek and mild, was absent [from Limerick] from January to July 1904, and as far as I can see, He has never bothered to return.

As Cork City alderman, on remarks about alleged Jewish extortion in Limerick in 1904 by Limerick Mayor, Stephen Coughlan, above. *The Irish Times*, April 25, 1970.

April 20, 1970
Peter Berry

I have come into knowledge of matters of national concern. I am afraid that if I follow the normal course the information might not reach the Government. Does my duty end with informing my Minister or am I responsible to the Government by whom I am appointed?

As Secretary of Department of Justice, asking advice of President de Valera when his minister, Mícheál Ó'Moráin, did not pass on to Taoiseach Jack Lynch information about arms plot involving other ministers. De Valera advised him to speak to Lynch. Walsh, Dick, *The Party*, Gill & Macmillan, 1986, p. 108.

April 25, 1970
Ben Briscoe

[Stephen Coughlan, Mayor of Limerick] is not and never has been anti-Semitic... I wish to express to the people of Limerick my own deep personal sorrow for the manner in which they have been made the scapegoat by Alderman Goldberg, a man with a very large chip on his shoulder.

As Jewish Fianna Fáil TD for Dublin South Central on Coughlan's remarks of April 18 about Jews in Limerick in 1904 and Gerald Goldberg's reply of April 19. *The Irish Times*, April 27, 1970.

May 5, 1970
Sean Flanagan

There is no crisis in Fianna Fáil, never was, and never will be.

As Fianna Fáil Minister for Lands, on rumours of Government crisis. *The Irish Times*, May 9, 1970.

May 7, 1970
Jack Lynch

I have requested the resignation as members of the Government of Mr Neil Blaney, Minister for Agriculture and Fisheries, and Mr Charles J. Haughey, Minister for Finance, because I am satisfied that they do not subscribe fully to Government policy in relation to the present situation in the Six Counties.

As Taoiseach, in statement from Government Information Service at 2.50 a.m. *The Irish Times*, May 8, 1970.

May 7, 1970
Jack Lynch

Prime facie, these reports involved two members of the Government... I felt it was my duty to request their resignations as members of the Government... I did so on the basis that not even the slightest suspicion should attach to any member of the Government in a matter of this nature.

As Taoiseach, in Dáil, on receiving reports of arms imports involving Charles Haughey and Neil Blaney. *The Irish Times*, May 8, 1970.

May 7, 1970
Liam Cosgrave
I considered it my duty in the national interest to inform the Taoiseach of information I had received and which indicates a situation of such gravity for the nation that it is without parallel in this country since the foundation of the State...that those who were drawing public money to serve the nation were in fact attempting to undermine it.

As Fine Gael leader, in Dáil, on why he had informed Taoiseach of suspected gun-running by ministers for IRA. McLoughlin, Michael, *Great Irish Speeches of the Twentieth Century*, Poolbeg, 1996, pp. 279-281.

May 8, 1970
Neil Blaney
Ireland has always had its British lackeys; you can pick them out in every generation, those hypocrites, those who for their own ends are always ready to play Britain's game in this country...where were these people who are so concerned now last August? Where were they when the people of the Six Counties cried out for help and moral support?

As Fianna Fáil TD, in Dáil, after resigning from Government in arms crisis. McLoughlin, Michael, *Great Irish Speeches of the Twentieth Century*, Poolbeg, 1996, pp. 288-289.

May 8, 1970
Neil Blaney
I have run no guns; I have procured no guns; I have paid for no guns, and I have provided money to pay for no guns.

As Fianna Fáil TD, after resigning from Government in arms crisis. McLoughlin, Michael, *Great Irish Speeches of the Twentieth Century*, Poolbeg, 1996, pp. 288-289.

May 8, 1970
Charles Haughey
I now categorically state that at no time have I taken part in any illegal importation or attempted importation of arms into this country.

As Fianna Fáil TD, in statement from his home after resigning from Government at request of Taoiseach. *The Irish Times*, May 9, 1970.

May 8, 1970
James Gibbons
I wish to deny emphatically any such knowledge or consent. In recent times [I] formed the opinion that Captain Kelly was becoming unsuitable for the type of work which he was employed at...

As Minister for Defence, in Dáil, denying knowledge of attempt by Captain Kelly of Irish Army to procure arms without proper legal authority. *The Irish Times*, May 9, 1970.

May 8, 1970
Captain James Kelly
Under privilege of the Dáil, Mr Gibbons has attacked me. The Army work which I did was brought to the knowledge of Mr Gibbons at any and every opportunity.

As Irish Army captain, on disclaimer by Minister for Defence of his role in arms procurement. *The Irish Times*, May 9, 1970.

May 8, 1970
Eddie McAteer
The screeching dove might well remember that Neil Blaney stood beside us in our hour of need...and if the midnight knock comes to our door, would not the gentlest of us love the feeling of security that a pike in the thatch can give?

As leader of Nationalist Party, on forced resignation of Neil Blaney in arms crisis. *The Irish Times*, May 9, 1970.

May 11, 1970
Official Sinn Féin
Republicans in many areas throughout the Six Counties were approached with offers of aid [by Irish Army intelligence officers] on two conditions, that they break with the Republican leadership in Dublin and set up a separate Republican movement for the North...there was intense Fianna Fáil activity in the Six Counties.

In statement on arms crisis. *The Irish Times*, May 12, 1970.

May 23, 1970
Charles Haughey
Every TD from the youngest or newest in the House dreams of being Taoiseach.

As Fianna Fáil TD, in interview after resigning from Government. *The Irish Times*, May 23, 1970.

May 28, 1970
Kevin Boland
This...constitutes felon-setting by the leader of the Irish Government...the greatest treachery of which an Irishman could be guilty.

As Fianna Fáil TD, on his resignation as Minister for Local Government in protest at sacking of ministers in arms crisis, following which he left Fianna Fáil on June 22. *The Irish Times*, May 29, 1970.

June 25, 1970
Cardinal William Conway
Nobody wanted to rake up old sores but...the bishops would like to stress their belief that it had

been amply justified in the past [but] account now had to be taken of changed circumstances.

As Primate of Ireland, announcing end of ban on Catholics attending Trinity College, Dublin. *The Irish Times*, June 26, 1970.

July 1, 1970
Reginald Maudling
For God's sake bring me a large Scotch. What a bloody awful country!

As British Home Secretary, in comment made on flight back to London after first visit to Northern Ireland. The Sunday Times Insight Team, *Ulster*, Penguin, 1972, p. 213.

July 6, 1970
Patrick Hillery
It would be an awful thing if we had to regard a visit by me to Northern Ireland as something to be embarrassed about. After all [Unionists] come to the Horse Show and we say nothing about it.

As Minister for External Affairs, after clandestine visit Belfast's Falls Road. *The Irish Times*, July 7, 1970.

July 7, 1970
Alec Douglas-Home
I should have expected him to have consulted Her Majesty's Government in advance if he wished to make a visit. Not to have done so, particularly in present circumstances, is a serious diplomatic discourtesy.

As Foreign Secretary, in House of Commons, about visit to Belfast's Falls Road by Minister for External Affairs. *The Irish Times*, July 8, 1970.

July 11, 1970
Peadar O'Donnell
The Protestant Ascendancy...has been overrun in part of Ireland, but a tricky, backward, largely Papist middle-class took its place... The middle-class for which Jack Lynch speaks and the feudal remnant...for which Chichester-Clark speaks could arrive at a careful accommodation, but the men napping stones North and South will still nap stones.

As veteran Republican leader, on troubles in North. *The Irish Times*, July 11, 1970.

July 23, 1970
James Anthony Roche
How do you like that, you bastards? Now you know what it's like in Belfast.

As visitor to public gallery of House of Commons, throwing two canisters of CS gas into chamber. *The Irish Times*, July 24, 1970.

August 9, 1970
Tom Barry
There has never been so much love-talk with British imperialism as of late, never so much sloppy talk and sloppy actions – particularly to the effect that Ireland can only be united by peaceful means.

As veteran IRA member, at commemoration of Kilmichael ambush in 1920, which he led and in which 17 Auxiliaries were killed. *The Irish Times*, August 10, 1970.

August 12, 1970
Conor Cruise O'Brien
I thought for a moment perhaps I ought to have clapped but then I felt I was going to be beaten up anyway and it would have been annoying if I had been beaten up and had clapped.

As Labour Party member, after being assaulted for not applauding speaker at Apprentice Boys' Rally in Derry. *The Irish Times*, August 13, 1970.

September 16, 1970
Eamonn McCann
Anyone who thinks that the events in Northern Ireland are a matter of laughter is a hypocrite.

As leader of Derry Labour Party, taking stage in Dublin's Peacock Theatre to protest portrayal of Northern Ireland in satirical revue, 'A State of Chassis'. *The Irish Times*, September 17, 1970.

September 16, 1970
Tomás MacAnna
All we can say is to echo the words of Byron; if we laugh at any mortal thing it is that we may not weep.

As co-author of satirical revue, 'A State of Chassis', replying from stage to remark by Eamonn McCann, above. *The Irish Times*, September 17, 1970.

October 5, 1970
President Nixon
I think politics are hard in our country, but in Ireland where you have to run against somebody who is Irish all the time, it must be impossible.

As US President, in speech at Dublin Castle during three-day visit to Ireland. *The Irish Times*, October 6, 1970.

October 15, 1970
Roy Bradford
When it comes to asserting the integrity of this Province against attack, moderation must go hand in hand with the mailed fist.

As NI Minister of Commerce. *The Irish Times*, October 16, 1970.

October 23, 1970
Justice Seamus Henchy
There was a flat contradiction between Mr
Haughey's version and Mr Gibbon's version, and
the difference seemed to be irreconcilable.

As judge, summing up at end of arms trial in which
Charles Haughey and Neil Blaney were acquitted. *The
Irish Times*, October 24, 1970.

October 24, 1970
Jack Lynch
No one can deny that there was this attempt to
import arms illegally. Blaney was involved too.

As Taoiseach, at press conference in New York after
hearing of not guilty verdicts in arms trial. *The Irish Times*,
October 26, 1970.

November 3, 1970
Garret FitzGerald
Either Mr Gibbons or Mr Haughey had perjured
themselves in court. The judge had made that
clear... How could the House have confidence in
a Government which was kept in office by the
vote of Deputy Haughey, one of the possible
perjurers, or Mr Gibbons?

As Fine Gael TD, in Dáil, during confidence debate after
arms trial. *The Irish Times*, November 4, 1970.

November 7, 1970
Neil Blaney
I feel a greater kinship with a Protestant from
Antrim than I do with a Catholic from Cork... I
don't necessarily mean Jack Lynch.

As Fianna Fáil TD, on being forced to resign by Taoiseach
Jack Lynch, in *Spectator*. *The Irish Times*, November 7,
1970.

December 4, 1970
Jack Lynch and Des O'Malley
A secret armed conspiracy exists in the
country...the Government have given
instructions that places of detention be prepared
immediately, and the Secretary General of the
Council of Europe is now being informed...as
these proposals will involve certain derogations
from the European Convention on Human
Rights.

As Taoiseach and Minister for Justice, in statement based
on information from gardaí. *The Irish Times*, December 5,
1970.

December 4, 1970
Eddie McAteer
Dear God, have they gone back to this? Only
near insurrection could justify such destruction
of civil rights.

As leader of Nationalist Party, on threat of internment in
Republic. *The Irish Times*, December 5, 1970.

December 5, 1970
Gerry Collins
The Labour Party is like the Widow Macree's dog
who will go a piece of the road with anyone.

As Fianna Fáil frontbencher, on possibility of Labour
adopting coalition policy. *The Irish Times*, December 5,
1970.

1971
F. S. L. Lyons
It was as if an entire people had been condemned
to live in Plato's cave, backs to the fire of life and
deriving their only knowledge of what went on
outside from the flickering shadows thrown on the
wall... When after six years they emerged, dazzled,
from the cave into the light of day, it was to a new
and vastly different world.

As historian, in celebrated lament on Irish neutrality. Lyons,
F. S. L., *Ireland Since the Famine*, Weidenfeld & Nicolson,
1971, p. 551.

January 13, 1971
Terence O'Neill
How could southern Ireland keep a bridal North
in the manner to which she is accustomed?

As former NI Prime Minister, on Republic's claims to North.
The Irish Times, January 16, 1971.

February 4, 1971
John Taylor
We are going to shoot it out with them [IRA]. It is
as simple as that.

As junior NI Home Affairs Minister. *The Irish Times*,
December 4, 1971.

February 7, 1971
James Chichester-Clark
Northern Ireland is at war with the Provisional
IRA.

As NI Prime Minister. Arthur, Paul, *Government and Politics
of Northern Ireland*, Longman, 1984, p. 125.

February 20, 1971
Patrick Hillery
Fianna Fáil will survive. You can have Boland but
you can't have Fianna Fáil.

As Minister for External Affairs, to hecklers supporting
former Cabinet colleague, Kevin Boland, in arms crisis
divisions, at Fianna Fáil árd fheis. *The Irish Times*, February
22, 1971.

February 20, 1971
Jack Lynch
Where it can be shown that attitudes embodied in
our laws and Constitution give offence to liberty
of conscience, then we are prepared to see what
can be done to harmonise our views so that,
without detracting from genuine values, a new

kind of Irish society may be created equally agreeable to North and South... We wish to extend an olive branch to the North.

As Taoiseach and Fianna Fáil leader, in speech to Fianna Fáil árd fheis. Lynch, John, *Speeches and Statements, August 1969-October 1971*, Government Information Bureau, 1971, p. 47.

March 9, 1971
Patrick Hillery

Legislators in a plural society should guard against considering matters solely from the standpoint of their personal religious practices.

As Minister for External Affairs, signalling Government rethink on law banning contraception. *The Irish Times*, March 11, 1971.

March 10, 1971
Oliver J. Flanagan

It is popular in...Europe to talk of sex, divorce and drugs. These things are foreign in Ireland and to Ireland and we want them kept foreign.

As Fine Gael TD, in Dáil debate on possible EEC membership. *The Irish Times*, March 11, 1971.

March 11, 1971
Catholic Hierarchy

The bishops fully share the disquiet...regarding pressures being exerted on public opinion on questions concerning the civil law on divorce, contraception and abortion... Civil law on these matters should respect the wishes of the people who elected the legislators and the bishops confidently hope that the legislators themselves will respect this important principle.

As Irish Bishops, on growing public pressure to legalise contraception. *The Irish Times*, March 12, 1971.

March 21, 1971
James Chichester-Clark

I have decided to resign because I see no other way of bringing home to all concerned the realities of the present constitutional, political and security situation...it would be misleading the Northern Ireland community to suggest that we are faced with anything but a long haul.

As NI Prime Minister, on his intention to resign after losing support of majority of Ulster Unionist MPs. *The Irish Times*, March 22, 1971.

March 25, 1971
Stephen Coughlan

With regard to contraception, abortion and all those nonsensical things, the Minister should put his two feet on top of them – if we wanted a healthy nation this was what the Minister should be doing or considering – not the ridiculous

suggestion that if you do not give up smoking you will die of cancer.

As Labour TD, in Dáil. *The Irish Times*, March 26, 1971.

March 28, 1971
Dr John Charles McQuaid

Any such contraceptive act is always wrong in itself...[Legalising contraceptives] would be an insult to our Faith...a curse upon our country.

As Archbishop of Dublin, in pastoral letter read in Dublin churches, following which some people walked out, shouting, 'Rubbish.' *The Irish Times*, March 29, 1971.

April 5, 1971
Irish Women's Liberation Movement

We shall not conceive.

As women's group, in words sung to tune of 'We shall overcome', as they invaded Dáil through window of men's lavatory to promote legalisation of contraception. Siggins, Lorna, *Mary Robinson*, Mainstream Publishing, 1997, p. 68.

April 23, 1971
Dr Noel Browne

Consciously or unconsciously many of them have chosen their celibate lives because they find the whole subject of sex and heterosexual relationships threatening and embarrassing. Their judgement then cannot be trusted on these issues.

As Labour TD, in speech referring to bishops, later disowned by Labour Parliamentary Party. *The Irish Times*, April 24, 1971.

May 1, 1971
Dr Cornelius Lucey

The people before us didn't rat on their children for the sake of Protestant schooling, land or soup. Surely we won't for the sake of easy sex.

As Bishop of Cork and Ross, in sermon on contraception. *The Irish Times*, May 1, 1971.

May 15, 1971
Rev Denis Faul

Celibacy is now being quoted by some doctors as a disease, and I am now waiting for some TDs or maybe senators to propose a law against it.

As Dungannon priest, responding to remarks on clerical celibacy made by Dr Noel Browne on April 23. *The Irish Times*, May 16, 1971.

May 15, 1971
Rev Michael MacGreil

Violence inevitably leads to the peace of the graveyard.

As Catholic priest, on Northern troubles. *The Irish Times*, May 15, 1971.

May 22, 1971
June Levine
She could blow them up to a huge balloon size and collapse with laughter as she let go of the end and the thing went shooting round the carriage. 'Mary, come on, what would your mother say?' I pleaded, and off she'd go again, blowing the condom up and holding it well out of reach.

As member of Irish Women's Liberation Movement, on journalist Mary Kenny's actions on Belfast-Dublin train when women challenged law by bringing contraceptives into Republic. Levine, June, *Sisters*, Ward River, 1982, p. 179.

May 23, 1971
Jack Lynch
I would not like to leave contraception on the long finger too long.

As Taoiseach, on plans for legislative reform. *The Irish Times*, May 23, 1971.

July 2, 1971
Bernadette Devlin
There are no illegitimate children, only illegitimate parents, if the term is to be used at all.

As Independent MP for Mid-Ulster, in interview about her pregnancy. *The Irish Times*, July 2, 1971.

July 3, 1971
Joanna Collins
I feel terribly upset about Arthur Griffith's being ignored. It's alright for Michael. He's a sort of hero. But poor Mr Griffith has been ignored.

As sister of Michael Collins, aged 91, about Arthur Griffith. *The Irish Times*, July 3, 1971.

July 7, 1971
Mary Robinson
If we are serious about the North we must change our attitudes. We must change our legislation and be able to say to the people of Northern Ireland that they can come into the south of Ireland and find the same tolerance of different moral attitudes...

As independent Senator, in Senate, on failure of Bill to legalise contraception. Siggins, Lorna, *Mary Robinson*, Mainstream Publishing, 1997, p. 70.

July 9, 1971
Cathal Goulding
When their answer to the just demand of the people are the lock-out, strike-breaking, evictions, coercions, the prison cell, intimidation or the gallows, then our duty is to reply in the language that brings these vultures to their senses

most effectively, the language of the bomb and the bullet.

As Chief of Staff of Official IRA, at graveside oration in Cork. *The Irish Times*, July 10, 1971.

July 11, 1971
Maire Drumm
The people of Derry are up now off their bended knees. For Christ's sake stay up. [People] should not shout 'up the IRA', they should join the IRA.

As Belfast Executive member of Sinn Féin, at Derry rally. *The Irish Times*, July 12, 1971.

July 11, 1971
John Hume
Their [British Army's] impartial role has now clearly ended...we cannot continue to give our consent to a continuation of the present situation...if our demand is not met by Thursday next we will withdraw immediately from parliament.

As SDLP deputy leader, demanding inquiry into shooting by British Army of two Derry men during rioting. *The Irish Times*, July 12, 1971.

July 12, 1971
Lord Balniel
I am satisfied from inquiries I have made there is no misconduct to be inquired into.

As British Minister, rejecting demand for inquiry from SDLP into shooting by British Army of two Derry men. *The Irish Times*, July 13, 1971.

July 18, 1971
John Taylor
I would defend without hesitation the action taken by the Army authorities in Derry against subversives during the past week or so when it was necessary in the end to shoot to kill. I feel that it may be necessary to shoot even more in the forthcoming months in Northern Ireland.

As NI Minister of State for Home Affairs, following shooting of two Derry men. *The Irish Times*, July 19, 1971.

July 29, 1971
Lt-General Sir Harry Tuzo
I have always attributed to the IRA a certain mild romance as patriots of a rather poetic and unusual nature, and Brady has effectively removed any starry-eyed attitude which I and others could have. These Provisionals [are] simply a straightforward gang of murderers, extortionists, intimidators, people of the worst possible kind.

As General Officer Commanding British Army in Northern Ireland, at press conference, referring to Ruairí Ó Brádaigh, President of Provisional Sinn Féin. *The Irish Times*, July 30, 1971.

August 5, 1971
Reginald Maudling
Lift some Protestants if you can.

As British Home Secretary, to NI Prime Minister Brian Faulkner, when discussing introduction of internment. Faulkner, Brian, *Memoirs of a Statesman*, Weidenfeld and Nicolson, 1978, p. 119.

August 6, 1971
John Bryans
We have no right to go into the EEC. We were never part of Europe and we never will be.

As Grand Master of Grand Orange Lodge. *The Irish Times*, August 8, 1971.

August 9, 1971
Brian Faulkner
I have decided...to exercise where necessary...the powers of detention and internment... We, quite simply, are at war with the terrorist... I want to say a word directly to my Catholic fellow-countrymen...we are now acting to remove the shadow of fear which hangs over too many of you.

As NI Prime Minister, announcing internment without trial, which applied only to Catholics. *The Irish Times*, August 10, 1971.

August 11, 1971
Charles Haughey
The cynical experiment of partitioning Ireland has ended in total, tragic failure... The Irish nation must now mobilise all its moral and physical resources, it must manifest without equivocation its concern for the people of the North.

As Fianna Fáil TD, on internment and subsequent violence in North. *The Irish Times*, August 12, 1971.

August 12, 1971
Jack Lynch
The Stormont regime, which has consistently repressed the non-unionist population and bears responsibility for recurring violence in the Northern community, must be brought to an end.

As Taoiseach, on introduction of internment. Lynch, John, *Speeches and Statements, August 1969-October 1971*, Government Information Bureau, 1971, p. 76.

August 13, 1971
Brigadier Marson Tickell
Operations by the security forces have virtually defeated the hard core of these gunmen...of course isolated gunmen remain and we must expect isolated attacks to continue and the people of the Province must not get over-excited if they do.

As British Army Chief of Staff in Belfast on aftermath of internment. *The Irish Times*, August 14, 1971.

August 13, 1971
Joe Cahill
The battle of the British Army hasn't been won, the losses of the IRA have been very slight...somewhat in the region of 30 men [two killed, the rest interned]. This is only a pinprick of the strength here.

As spokesman for Provisional IRA, at Belfast press conference, on aftermath of internment. *The Irish Times*, August 14, 1971.

August 14, 1971
Brian Faulkner
Internment has flushed out the gunmen.

As NI Prime Minister. *The Irish Times*, August 14, 1971.

August 19, 1971
Austin Currie
[I am] no longer, because of army action and the policy of the British Government, prepared to say to Catholics that they should join the UDR.

As SDLP MP, after meeting 31 Catholic members of the Ulster Defence Regiment in Belfast, 24 of whom stated they would resign because of internment. *The Irish Times*, August 20, 1971.

August 19, 1971
Jack Lynch
The events since the introduction of internment without trial on Monday, ninth of August, clearly indicate the failure of internment and of current military operations as a solution to the problems of Northern Ireland... I intend to support the policy of passive resistance now being pursued by the non-unionist population.

As Taoiseach in telegram to British Prime Minister Edward Heath. Lynch, John, *Speeches and Statements, August 1969-October 1971*, Government Information Bureau, 1971, pp. 77-78.

August 20, 1971
Edward Heath
I cannot accept that anyone outside the United Kingdom can participate in meetings to promote the political development of any part of the United Kingdom.

As British Prime Minister, replying to telegram from Taoiseach Jack Lynch, above. Lynch, John, *Speeches and Statements, August 1969-October 1971*, Government Information Bureau, 1971, pp. 78-79.

August 20, 1971
Jack Lynch
Mr Heath's assertion that what is happening in Northern Ireland is no concern of mine is not acceptable. The division of Ireland has never been,

and is not now, acceptable to the great majority of the Irish people who were not consulted in the matter when that division was made fifty years ago.

As Taoiseach in response to telegram from British Prime Minister Edward Heath, above. Lynch, John, *Speeches and Statements, August 1969-October 1971*, Government Information Bureau, 1971, p. 81.

c. *September, 1971*
Paddy McGuigan
Armoured cars and tanks and guns,
Came to take away our sons,
But every man will stand behind
The men behind the wire.

As songwriter. Popular ballad against internment in Northern Ireland. *100 Best Irish Songs and Ballads*, Mac Publications (undated), p. 29.

September 12, 1971
Cardinal William Conway
Who wanted to bomb a million Protestants into a united Ireland?

As Primate of Ireland, in statement with six other Catholic bishops condemning IRA. Deutsch and Magowan, *Northern Ireland, 1968-1973, A Chronology of Events*, Vol. I, Blackstaff Press, 1973, p. 126.

September 26, 1971
Rev Ian Paisley
God has been our help in 1641, 1688, 1690, 1798, 1912, 1920, and He will not fail us in the future.

As leader of Free Presbyterian Church. *The Irish Times*, October 2, 1971.

September 28, 1971
Jack Lynch, Edward Heath and Brian Faulkner
It is our common purpose to seek to bring violence and internment and all other emergency measures to an end without delay... Our discussions in the last two days have helped to create an atmosphere of greater understanding and it is our hope that the process of political reconciliation may go forward to a successful outcome.

As Taoiseach, and British and NI Prime Ministers, in statement after meeting at Chequers. Lynch, John, *Speeches and Statements, August 1969-October 1971*, Government Information Bureau, 1971, pp. 84-85.

October 1, 1971
Gerry Collins
[*RTÉ* should] refrain from broadcasting any matter calculated to promote the aims or activities of any organisation which engaged in,

promotes, encourages or advocates the attaining of any political objective by violent means.

As Minister for Posts and Telegraphs, in directive under Section 31 of Broadcasting Act banning interviews on Irish radio or television with IRA or Sinn Féin. *The Irish Times*, October 2, 1971.

October 6, 1971
Eamonn McCann
I am not certain how many of our speakers mesmerised the masses. Certainly the masses mesmerised the speakers.

As leader of Derry Labour Party, on events in the city since 1968. *The Irish Times*, October 6, 1971.

October 16, 1971
Edward Heath
If our troops were withdrawn and our efforts relaxed, we would be condemning the whole of Ireland to civil war and slaughter on a scale far beyond anything we have seen in recent years.

As British Prime Minister, on demands for British withdrawal from Northern Ireland. *The Irish Times*, October 18, 1971.

October 20, 1971
Edward Kennedy
[Northern Ireland] is becoming Britain's Vietnam... The Government of Ulster rules by bayonet and bloodshed...if only the cruel and constant irritation of the British military presence is withdrawn, Ireland can be whole again.

As US Senator, in Congress. *The Irish Times*, October 21, 1971.

October 26, 1971
John Hume
Today we do not recognise the authority of the Stormont Parliament and we do not care twopence whether this is treason or not.

As SDLP deputy leader, at meeting of 'alternative assembly' for Northern Ireland in Dungannon. Routledge, Paul, *John Hume*, Harper Collins, 1998, p. 106.

November 16, 1971
Edmund Compton
Our investigations have not led us to conclude that any of the grouped or individual complainants suffered physical brutality, as we understand the term.

As chairman of British Government inquiry into allegations of torture in NI, disclosing use of five techniques of 'in-depth' interrogation – hooding, wall-standing, use of 'white' noise and deprivation of food and sleep – on detainees. *The Irish Times*, November 17, 1971.

November 21, 1971
Cardinal William Conway
We condemn this treatment as immoral and inhuman. It is unworthy of the British people. It is the test of a civilised people that the methods of its elected government remain civilised, even under extreme provocation.

As Primate of Ireland, on disclosure in Compton Report of use of 'in-depth' interrogation on detainees. *The Irish Times*, November 22, 1971.

November 21, 1971
Neil Blaney
Give shelter to those who come to you, give them aid and money and anything else that might be useful to them. Let the people who are carrying on the struggle in the Six Counties know you are with them.

As independent TD, in speech in Letterkenny, after being expelled from Fianna Fáil for refusing to support Taoiseach Jack Lynch in vote of confidence. *The Irish Times*, November 22, 1971.

November 25, 1971
Harold Wilson
If men of moderation have nothing to hope for, men of violence will have something to shoot for.

As British Labour leader, in House of Commons, outlining blueprint for united Ireland. *Hansard*, November 25, 1971.

November 26, 1971
Graham Greene
'Deep interrogation' – a bureaucratic phrase which takes the place of the simpler word 'torture' and is worthy of Orwell's *1984*– is on a different level of immorality than hysterical sadism or the indiscriminate bomb of urban guerrillas. It is something organised with imagination, and a knowledge of psychology, calculated and cold-blooded, and it is only half-condemned by the Compton investigation.

As author, in letter to *Times* on Compton Report which claimed no brutality was used on detainees. *The Times*, November 26, 1971.

December 11, 1971
Edward Kennedy
The Alice-in-Wonderland logic of the Compton Report and the British Government's defence of it in Parliament would be laughable, were the implications of its cruel hypocrisy not so ominous for the prospects of peace in Ulster.

As US Senator, on disclosure in Compton Report of use of 'in-depth' interrogation on detainees. *The Irish Times* December 11, 1971.

December 13, 1971
Official IRA
On entering the house the officer in charge informed Senator Barnhill that his house was to be destroyed... [The Senator] then attacked the raiding party and in the ensuing struggle received wounds from which he died.

In statement on killing of Ulster Unionist senator near Strabane. *The Irish Times*, December 14, 1971.

December 13, 1971
Bernadette Devlin
Senator Barnhill was a bigot of first class order but he did not represent British imperialism and was not a threat to the IRA.

As independent MP for Mid-Ulster, on Official IRA killing of Ulster Unionist senator. *The Irish Times*, December 14, 1971.

December 15, 1971
Reginald Maudling
I don't think one can speak of defeating the IRA, of eliminating them completely, but it is the design of the security forces to reduce their level of violence to something like an acceptable level.

As British Home Secretary, on visit to Northern Ireland. *The Irish Times*, December 18, 1971.

December 16, 1971
David Thornley
If the present Dáil carried any flavour at all it was the smell of death and corruption in every sense of the word since the events of May 1970 [arms crisis]. So low is the status of politics that if every one of us was led off to internment in the Blasket Islands, in the words of Cromwell, not a dog would bark.

As Labour TD, in Dáil. *The Irish Times*, December 17, 1971.

December 20, 1971
Lt-General Sir Harry Tuzo
The IRA campaign has caused us to direct our energies in their [Catholics'] direction and inevitably this has caused us to collide from time to time with the Roman Catholic communities... I say to the Catholics of Northern Ireland...you have nothing to fear from the Army.

As General Officer Commanding British Army in Northern Ireland. *The Irish Times*, December 21, 1971.

c. January 1, 1972
Tommy Makem
I have four green fields, one of them's in bondage.

As songwriter, in 'Four Green Fields' about one of four provinces of 'mother' Ireland being partly under British rule. *100 Best Irish Songs and Ballads*, Mac Publications (undated), p.33.

January 2, 1972
Austin Currie
I say to Maudling, why the hell should we talk to you? We are winning and you are not.

As SDLP MP, at anti-internment rally in Belfast, referring to British Home Secretary Reginald Maudling. Bardon, Jonathan, *A History of Ulster*, Blackstaff Press, 1992, p. 686.

January 28, 1972
Garret FitzGerald
The diminishing importance of London as a centre of decisions affecting Northern Ireland, many of which would in future be taken in Brussels, might reduce northern unionists' sensitivities on the issue of whether the remaining powers were exercised in Westminster or in Dublin.

As Fine Gael TD, in Dáil, on benefits of EEC membership. *The Irish Times*, January 29, 1972.

January 30, 1972
Rev Edward Daly
I saw a young boy laughing at me. I'm not a very graceful runner. The next thing he suddenly gasped and threw his hands up in the air and fell on his face... He was very youthful looking, just in his seventeenth year, but he only looked about twelve.

As Derry priest, describing killing of one of 13 people shot dead by Paratroopers in Derry on what became known as Bloody Sunday. Bardon, Jonathan, *A History of Ulster*, Blackstaff Press, 1992, p. 688.

January 30, 1972
John Hume
Their action was nothing short of cold-blooded mass murder – another Sharpeville and another Bloody Sunday.

As SDLP deputy leader on shooting dead by British Army of 13 people in Derry. *The Irish Times*, January 31, 1972.

January 31, 1972
Bernadette Devlin
I have a right as the only representative who was a witness to ask a question of that murdering hypocrite...if I am not allowed to inform the House of what I know, I'll inform Mr Maudling of what I feel.
[Later] I am just sorry I didn't go for his throat.

As MP for Mid-Ulster, in House of Commons, pulling hair of Home Secretary Reginald Maudling in protest at shooting dead by British Army of 13 people in Derry. *The Irish Times*, February 1, 1972.

January 31, 1972
John Hume
Many people down there [in the Bogside] feel now that it's a united Ireland or nothing.

As SDLP deputy leader, in *RTÉ* interview on Derry walls after shooting dead by British Army of 13 people in Derry. White, Barry, *John Hume, Statesman of the Troubles*, Blackstaff Press, 1984, p. 120.

January 31, 1972
Derry Priests
We accuse the Commander of Land Forces of being an accessory after the fact. We accuse the soldiers of firing indiscriminately into a fleeing crowd, of gloating over casualties...these men are trained criminals. They differ from terrorists only in the veneer of respectability that a uniform gives them.

As group of Priests, in statement on shooting dead by British Army of 13 people in Derry, signed by Revs Edward Daly, Anthony Mulvey, George McLaughlin, Joseph Carolan, Michael McIvor, Denis Bradley and Tom O'Gara. *The Irish Times*, February 1, 1972.

February 1, 1972
Patrick Hillery
If Ireland received no help from the West, it might turn to the East. My orders are to seek help wherever I can get it... From now on my aim is to get Britain out of Ireland.

As Minister for External Affairs, at Kennedy airport, on way to speak at UN on Bloody Sunday killings. *The Irish Times*, February 2, 1972.

February 1, 1972
Lord Balniel
In each case soldiers fired aimed shots at men identified as gunmen or bombers, in self defence or in defence of comrades who were threatened.

As junior Defence Minister, in House of Commons, on Bloody Sunday killings in Derry. *The Irish Times*, February 2, 1972.

February 6, 1972
John McKeague
The troops did not shoot enough of them.

As Belfast loyalist leader, on David Frost Show on ITV, on Bloody Sunday killings in Derry. *The Irish Times*, February 7, 1972.

February 7, 1972
Lord Kilbracken
The time comes when one has to stand up and be counted... I don't want to retain the symbolic souvenir of my service in British uniform.

As Co Leitrim member of House of Lords, on returning his war medals to British Government in protest against Bloody Sunday killings. *The Irish Times*, February 8, 1972.

February 9, 1972
Maurice Hayes

The effect of the present security policy [is] alienating the whole Catholic community while at the same time failing to produce peace and security for any section of the population.

As Community Relations Commissioner in Northern Ireland, resigning over Bloody Sunday killings. *The Irish Times*, February 10, 1972.

February 12, 1972
William Craig

We are determined to preserve our British traditions and way of life, and God help those, ladies and gentlemen, who get in our way.

As leader of new loyalist group, Vanguard, at paramilitary rally in Lisburn. *The Irish Times*, February 14, 1972.

February 28, 1972
Edward Kennedy

Today the British troops in Ulster have become an army of occupation... Stormont is now defunct in all but name and it is time for Britain to deliver the *coup de grâce*...the goal of reunification is now too close for Ireland to turn back.

As US Senator, at Congress hearing on Northern Ireland. *The Irish Times*, February 29, 1972.

c. March 1, 1972
Jimmy Young

What I want to know is, where do we go from here?

As NI comedian, after bomb destroyed public toilets in centre of Belfast. Attributed.

March 2, 1972
Lord Parker

We have come to the conclusion that there is no reason to rule out these techniques on moral grounds and that it is possible to operate them in a manner consistent with the highest standards in our society.

As author of Parker Commission Report, commissioned by British Government, approving use of 'in-depth' interrogation on detainees: hooding, wall-standing, use of 'white' noise and deprivation of food and sleep. *The Irish Times*, March 3, 1972.

March 2, 1972
Lord Gardner

The blame for this sorry story...must lie with those who many years ago decided that in emergency conditions in colonial-type situations, we should abandon our legal, well-tried and highly successful wartime interrogation methods and replace them by procedures which were secret, illegal, not morally justifiable and alien to the traditions of the greatest democracy in the world.

As dissenting member of Parker Commission whose minority report was accepted by British Government as basis for banning 'in-depth' interrogation methods in Northern Ireland. *The Irish Times*, March 3, 1972.

March 13, 1972
Harold Wilson

The IRA truce had shown that they had a disciplined, tightly knit organisation.

As leader of British Labour Party, after meeting Provisional IRA secretly on visit to Dublin. *The Irish Times*, March 14, 1972.

March 18, 1972
William Craig

We must build up a dossier of the men and women who are a menace to this country because, if and when the politicians fail us, it may be our job to liquidate the enemy.

As leader of Vanguard, at Belfast rally of 60,000 loyalists. *The Irish Times*, March 20, 1972.

March 24, 1972
Brian Faulkner

Such a transfer is not justifiable and cannot be supported or accepted by us. It would wholly undermine the powers, authority and standing of this Government.

As NI Prime Minister, in letter to British Prime Minister Edward Heath, refusing demand that law and order powers be handed over to London, and announcing resignation of NI Government. *The Irish Times*, March 25, 1972.

March 24, 1972
Edward Heath

The transfer of security powers is an indispensable condition for progress in finding a practical solution in Northern Ireland. The Northern Ireland Government's decision therefore leaves us with no alternative to assuming full and direct responsibility for the administration of Northern Ireland.

As British Prime Minister, in House of Commons, announcing Direct Rule of Northern Ireland. *The Irish Times*, March 25, 1972.

March 24, 1972
Eddie McAteer

This is a day of sadness. I find no joy in being ruled from the remote, insensitive smokerooms of Westminster. Faced with the choice, I would in principle prefer to be ruled by a Protestant Irishman rather than by an Englishman.

As leader of Nationalist Party, on imposition of Direct Rule. Boyd, Andrew, *Brian Faulkner and the Crisis in Ulster Unionism*, Anvil, 1972, pp. 114-115.

March 25, 1972
William Whitelaw
One must be careful not to prejudge the past.
As first Secretary of State for Northern Ireland, on Irish history. Attributed.

March 27, 1972
Brian Faulkner
Northern Ireland is not a coconut colony and no coconut commission will be able to muster any credibility or standing.
As Ulster Unionist leader, in speech to Ulster Unionist Council rejecting British suggestion of advisory commission to assist Direct Rule. *The Irish Times*, March 28, 1972.

April 2, 1972
Seán Mac Stiofáin
If we become hesitant, the fight of this generation is lost. Concessions be damned. We want freedom.
As Provisional IRA Chief of Staff, in Derry. *The Irish Times*, April 3, 1972.

April 2, 1972
Cardinal William Conway
I have taken soundings of feelings of the Catholic community... Never before have I experienced the voice of the people coming through so loud and clear [for peace].
As Primate of Ireland, calling for an end to violence. *RTÉ*, April 2, 1972.

April 3, 1972
Ruairí Ó Brádaigh
In his excursion into politics, all the influence the Cardinal can command is being thrown behind direct British rule, just as his predecessors had urged successfully the acceptance of the disastrous Treaty of surrender of 1921.
As President of Provisional Sinn Féin, in response to Cardinal Conway's call for end to violence. *The Irish Times*, April 4, 1972.

April 19, 1972
Lord Widgery
There would have been no deaths in Londonderry on January 30 if those who organised the illegal march had not thereby created a highly dangerous situation... Some soldiers showed a high degree of restraint in opening fire, the firing of others bordered on the reckless.
As author of official report on Bloody Sunday killings in Derry. *The Irish Times*, April 20, 1972.

April 19, 1972
Eddie McAteer
This is a political judgement by a British officer and British judge upon his darling British Army. I suppose we are lucky he didn't also find that the thirteen committed suicide.
As leader of Nationalist Party, on Widgery Report on Bloody Sunday killings in Derry. *The Irish Times*, April 20, 1972.

April 20, 1972
Peter O'Toole
There is a war going on. There is a war that's been going on for years and years and years and can only and will only end when the British leave Ireland.
As film actor, in interview in Rome. *The Irish Times*, April 21, 1972.

May 5, 1972
Jack Lynch
The choice is between taking part in the great new renaissance of Europe or opting for economic, social and cultural sterilisation. It is like that faced by Robinson Crusoe when the ship came to bring him back into the world again.
As Taoiseach, in Cork, urging support for joining EEC. *The Irish Times*, May 6, 1972.

May 5, 1972
Brendan Corish
We are too small and our tiny voice in the organs of government of the EEC can and will be drowned out.
As Labour leader, at anti-EEC rally in Cork. *The Irish Times*, May 6, 1972.

May 7, 1972
Charles Haughey
I cannot understand how any patriotic Irishman or woman can oppose going into Europe... I can understand a northern unionist who wishes to keep Ireland divided hoping that Britain and the Six Counties of Northern Ireland will go into Europe while the Republic stays out, so that the Border may thereby be permanently entrenched.
As Fianna Fáil TD, at Edenmore, urging support for joining EEC. *The Irish Times*, May 8, 1972.

May 20, 1972
Liam Cosgrave
I don't know whether some of you do any hunting or not, but some of these commentators and critics are now like mongrel foxes; they are gone to ground and I'll dig them out and the pack will chop them when they get them.

As leader of Fine Gael, departing from script at party árd fheis to take issue with critics of his leadership. *RTÉ, May 20, 1972.*

May 21, 1972
Official IRA
Regardless of the calls for peace from slobbering moderates, while British gunmen are on the streets of the Six Counties the IRA will take action against them – in particular a British soldier from the Derry area who could remain in such a force after a massacre of 13 Derrymen by the British Army.

Statement issued after Official IRA killed Ranger William Best (19) at home on leave in Derry. *The Irish Times,* May 22, 1972.

May 29, 1972
Official Sinn Féin
The overwhelming desire of all the people of the North is for an end to military action by all sides.

Announcing Official IRA ceasefire, following outcry over killing of Ranger William Best of Derry. *The Irish Times,* May 30, 1972.

May 31, 1972
Joseph Cairns
[Ulster's] relegation to the status of a fuzzy wuzzy colony is, I hope, a last betrayal contemplated by Downing Street because it is the last that Ulster will countenance.

As retiring Lord Mayor of Belfast, on fall of Stormont. *Daily Telegraph,* June 1, 1972.

June 5, 1972
William Whitelaw
There can be no question of negotiations with people who are shooting at British troops. I cannot foresee negotiations with them even after the violence has stopped.

As NI Secretary of State, on possibility of meeting Provisional IRA. *The Irish Times,* June 6, 1972.

June 11, 1972
Colonel Muammar Gadafy
We support the Irish revolutionaries who are fighting Britain...we have strong ties with the revolutionaries to whom we have supplied arms.

As Libyan leader, at rally in Tripoli. *The Irish Times,* June 12, 1972.

June 22, 1972
Provisional IRA
The IRA will suspend offensive operations as and from midnight on Monday, June 26, 1972, providing that a public reciprocal response is forthcoming from the armed forces of the British Crown.

In statement offering ceasefire. *The Irish Times,* June 23, 1972.

June 22, 1972
William Whitelaw
As the purpose of Her Majesty's forces in Northern Ireland is to keep the peace, if offensive operations by the IRA cease on Monday night, Her Majesty's forces will obviously reciprocate.

As NI Secretary of State, in House of Commons, on IRA offer of ceasefire. *The Irish Times,* June 23, 1972.

July 6, 1972
Alwyn Williams
In terms of its educational system, Northern Ireland, to put it bluntly, is the Alabama of Europe.

As Pro-Vice Chancellor of Queen's University, Belfast, on segregated education in city. Deutsch and Magowan, *Northern Ireland, 1968-1973, A Chronology of Events,* Vol. I, Blackstaff Press, 1983, p. 193.

July 7, 1972
Provisional IRA
(1) A public declaration by the British Government that it is the right of all the people of Ireland acting as a unit to decide the future of Ireland.
(2) A declaration of intent to withdraw British forces from Irish soil by January 1, 1975.
(3) A general amnesty.

Demands at meeting of IRA and British ministers in London, as outlined in House of Commons by NI Secretary of State William Whitelaw. *The Irish Times,* July 11, 1972.

July 7, 1972
Seán Mac Stiofáin
Jesus, we have it!

As IRA leader, to comrades, in break during meeting of IRA and British ministers in London. Adams, Gerry, *Before the Dawn,* Heinemann, 1996, p. 205.

July 7, 1972
Gerry Adams
That means all bets are off, then.

As member of IRA delegation meeting British ministers in London, after NI Secretary of State William Whitelaw said all bets were off if news leaked out. Adams, Gerry, *Before the Dawn,* Heinemann, 1996, p. 205.

July 8, 1972
Provisional IRA
The truce between the Irish Republican Army and the British occupation forces was broken without warning by British forces at approximately 5.00 p.m. today at Lenadoon Estate, Belfast. Accordingly, all IRA units have been instructed to resume offensive action.

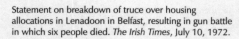

Statement on breakdown of truce over housing allocations in Lenadoon in Belfast, resulting in gun battle in which six people died. *The Irish Times*, July 10, 1972.

July 8, 1972
Dáithí Ó Conaill
We're on a new plane now and we won't need you next time. It'll be Heath and us next time.

As IRA leader, on telephone to SDLP deputy leader, John Hume, on breakdown of truce with British Government. White, Barry, *John Hume, Statesman of the Troubles*, Blackstaff Press, 1984, p. 131.

July 10, 1972
William Whitelaw
I arranged to see them because...any action that I could honourably take that would save lives or avoid further damage to property seemed to me should be taken.

As NI Secretary of State, in House of Commons, on why he met IRA in London. *The Irish Times*, July 11, 1972.

July 20, 1972
Paddy Devlin
If Mr Whitelaw thinks that Army behaviour will lead to our rejection of the Provisional IRA...he has grossly miscalculated. Military excesses create the need for a Provisional IRA.

As SDLP chief whip, after his Andersonstown home came under fire from British Army. *The Irish Times*, July 21, 1972.

July 21, 1972
Northern Ireland Office Spokesman
It looks like Bloody Friday.

As British official, commenting after IRA bombs in Belfast killed nine people and injured 130. *The Irish Times*, July 22, 1972.

July 23, 1972
Dr William Philbin
[Irish] ministers in Asia and Africa are being told to go home and make Christians of their fellow countrymen.

As Bishop of Down and Connor, in sermon at Muckamore. *The Irish Times*, July 24, 1972.

August 24, 1972
John Taylor
If we were not allowed to have our own parliament, then we must have an independent British Ulster.

As Ulster Unionist MP, in first public speech after being shot six months previously. *The Irish Times*, August 25, 1972.

September 2, 1972
Bob Cooper
Not since the worst excesses of Hitler and Stalin have so many suffered so much for the madness of so few.

As joint leader of Alliance Party. *The Irish Times*, September 2, 1972.

September 12, 1972
Paddy Devlin
Well, if we're not getting anything on internment, I'll have some of your scones.

As member of SDLP delegation, having tea at Chequers with British Prime Minister, Edward Heath. Devlin, Paddy, *Straight Left*, Blackstaff Press, 1993, p. 184.

October 7, 1972
Rev Martin Smyth
Integration would be a stepping stone to a united Ireland.

As Grand Master of Orange Order. *The Irish Times*, October 7, 1972.

October 19, 1972
William Craig
We are prepared to come out and shoot and kill. I am prepared to come out and shoot and kill. Let us put the bluff aside. I am prepared to kill, and those behind me will have my full support.

As leader of Vanguard, at meeting in London, in what became known as his 'shoot to kill' speech. *The Irish Times*, October 20, 1972.

October 20, 1972
William Craig
All I drink is an occasional glass of wine with a meal.

As leader of Vanguard, denying he was drunk when he said he was prepared to shoot and kill. *The Irish Times*, October 21, 1972.

October 22, 1972
Rev Ian Paisley
Let me make it perfectly clear that I and the Democratic Unionist Party are still dedicated to achieving total integration with Great Britain...legislative union must be absolute. On this as a party there can be no going back.

As leader of DUP. *The Irish Times*, October 23, 1972.

November 2, 1972
Jack Lynch
The specific list of Churches was neither desirable nor necessary and should be deleted...the proposed change would contribute to Irish unity.

As Taoiseach, on Bill to amend Constitution to remove special position of Catholic Church. *The Irish Times*, November 3, 1972.

November 2, 1972
Joseph Leneghan
Why should they change the Constitution to suit a crowd of thugs in the North of Ireland? God grant that we shall never see that crowd of thugs come in here. We have enough as we are without taking the risk of crossing the breed.

As independent TD, in Dáil, on Bill to amend Constitution to remove special position of Catholic Church. *The Irish Times*, November 3, 1972.

November 2, 1972
Conor Cruise O'Brien
The Bill was too little and too late. If this is an olive branch it is being extended with a very languid hand, almost contemptuous.

As Labour TD, in Dáil, on Bill to amend Constitution to remove special position of Catholic Church. *The Irish Times*, November 3, 1972.

November 16, 1972
Edward Heath
To those who urge that Northern Ireland should seize its own unilateral independence, I must say that not only would such an attempt bring about a blood bath, but that were it to succeed, the British Government would not pay one penny of the £200 million a year now provided.

As British Prime Minister, in Belfast. *The Irish Times*, November 17, 1972.

November 19, 1972
Kevin O'Kelly
Mr Seán Mac Stiofáin said, 'We believe that by armed struggle alone can we achieve our objectives.'

As RTÉ interviewer, broadcasting account of conversation with IRA leader, for which he was jailed and RTÉ Authority dismissed for breaching Section 31 of the Broadcasting Act. *The Irish Times*, November 20, 1972.

November 23, 1972
Conor Cruise O'Brien
Surely it was more dangerous to leave these people [IRA] in the shadows?... In a modern democracy, the autonomy of radio or television was as vital as the freedom of the press or of Parliament.

As Labour TD, in Dáil, opposing ban on IRA and Sinn Féin interviews on RTÉ. *The Irish Times*, November 24, 1972.

November 23, 1972
Garret FitzGerald
The Government was now using that interview as an excuse to destroy the independence on the [RTÉ] Authority and that was something that was totally unacceptable... The real threat to the country was not the IRA but the threat to freedom of speech.

As Fine Gael TD, in Dáil, opposing ban on IRA and Sinn Féin interviews on RTÉ. *The Irish Times*, November 24, 1972.

November 26, 1972
Seán Mac Stiofáin
I will be dead in six days. Live with that.

As Provisional IRA leader, in Dublin's Special Criminal Court, announcing hunger strike after receiving six month sentence for IRA membership. (The hunger strike lasted 57 days before being called off.) *The Irish Times*, November 27, 1972.

November 29, 1972
Patrick Cooney
How can [the Minister for Justice] come into this Parliament and ask it to support a Bill the like of which can only be found on the statute books of South Africa?

As Fine Gael spokesman on justice, opposing the Offences Against the State (Amendment) Bill, allowing wide Government powers against subversive organisations. Browne, Vincent, *The Magill Book of Irish Politics*, Magill, 1981, p. 266.

December 1, 1972
Neil Blaney
Not only did circumstances bring the freedom fighters into existence but so did the promised support of help not just by me but by a lot of other people as well. The blame lies on me and a whole lot of others.

As independent TD, on creation of Provisional IRA. *DÉ Debates*, Vol. 264: Col. 668.

December 1, 1972
Patrick Cooney
We have decided to put the nation before party and accordingly we withdraw the amendment.

As Fine Gael spokesman on justice, in Dáil, withdrawing opposition to Offences against the State Act, after bombs in centre of Dublin killed two people. *The Irish Times*, December 2, 1972.

December 9, 1972
John D. Stewart
Northern Ireland is like one of her great sons, George Best – on the transfer list but no rash of offers.

As NI writer and columnist. *The Irish Times*, December 9, 1972.

December 18, 1972
Dr Noel Browne
Yeats's 'Terrible Beauty' truly has become a sick and sectarian, angry and repressive old crone.

As Labour TD and former Minister for Health, writing in British left-wing weekly, *Tribune. The Irish Times*, December 19, 1972.

January 13, 1973
Captain James Kelly

The two bombs which exploded in Dublin at precisely the right time to bring a recalcitrant Opposition to heel were on a par with the burning of the Reichstag, used by Hitler in the 1930s to bring his Nazi party to power.

As former Irish Army officer, involved in arms crisis, on Fine Gael withdrawal of opposition to Offences against the State Act. *The Irish Times*, January 13, 1973.

February 6, 1973
Rev Ian Paisley

I utterly deplore the action of those leaders in Northern Ireland who are calling on people to jeopardise the whole economy of Ulster.

As leader of DUP, opposing United Loyalist Council strike against internment of loyalists. *The Irish Times*, February 7, 1973.

February 15, 1973
John Peck

I do not see what political interests would suffer if there were a single national orchestra, school of drama, school of ballet etc., just as there is a single rugby fifteen.

As retiring British Ambassador to Dublin. *The Irish Times*, February 15, 1973.

February 15, 1973
William Craig

Much though we wish to maintain the Union we should all be seriously thinking of an independent dominion of Ulster...if ever there is to be unification of Ireland...it is only neighbourly relations that can bring it about.

As leader of Vanguard, in Ulster Hall, Belfast. *The Irish Times*, February 17, 1973.

February 16, 1973
Gerry Fitt

The tired old rafters of the Ulster Hall must have been on the verge of collapse when Mr Craig enunciated breaking the link with Britain.

As leader of SDLP, on William Craig's speech on possible break with Britain. *The Irish Times*, February 17, 1973.

March 20, 1973
William Whitelaw

Her Majesty's Government believe that these proposals offer a reasonable deal for reasonable people and as such should be accepted.

As NI Secretary of State, in House of Commons, on White Paper to provide NI power-sharing and Council of Ireland. *The Irish Times*, March 21, 1973.

March 24, 1973
Frankfurter Rundschan

Summing it all up and considering what has happened, the Catholic side has won.

As West German journal, in comment on British Government proposals for power-sharing and Council of Ireland. *The Irish Times*, March 24, 1973.

March 29, 1973
Patrick Donegan

She'll get a boot up the transom and be told to get out of our waters fast.

As Minister for Defence, on action against Cypriot coaster, *Claudia*, apprehended off Helvick Head with arms for IRA. *The Irish Times*, March 30, 1973.

April 1, 1973
Rev Michael MacGreil

It is time that the Republic replaced its National Anthem with something more worthy of a civilised people, which would express sentiments of peace, justice and brotherhood, instead of the gun and the *bearna baoil* [gap of danger].

As lecturer in sociology at Maynooth Seminary. *The Irish Times*, April 2, 1973.

April 23, 1973
Pope Paul VI

Let the voice of violence become silent and let there be heard instead the voice of wisdom and guidance.

As Pontiff, expressing support for British proposal of NI power-sharing and Council of Ireland, during Easter message from balcony of St Peter's in Rome. *The Irish Times*, April 23, 1973.

May 8, 1973
Brian Faulkner

We are not opposed to power-sharing in Government, but we will not be prepared to participate in Government with any whose primary aim is to break the union with Great Britain.

As leader of Ulster Unionist Party, in policy statement which opened door to sharing power with SDLP. *The Irish Times*, May 9, 1973.

May 23, 1973
Liam Ahern

More guns we want, bags of guns.

As Fianna Fáil TD, in Dáil, on *Claudia* gun-running. *The Irish Times*, May 24, 1973.

June 8, 1973
Conor Cruise O'Brien
I intend to take out Section 31 of the Broadcasting Act and remove altogether, and deprive any future Minister of, the power to issue the kind of directions that we have.

As Minister for Posts and Telegraphs, at ITGWU conference, promising to end legislation banning IRA and Sinn Féin interviews on *RTÉ*. *The Irish Times*, June 9, 1973.

June 8, 1973
Rev Robin J. Williamson
In Ulster we have failed Christ miserably.

As outgoing Moderator of Non-Subscribing Presbyterian Church in Belfast. *The Irish Times*, June 9, 1973.

June 8, 1973
Justice Sean Breathnach
Why are you dressed up in those ridiculous garments?... I could sentence you for contempt wearing a scarf like that... I can warn you, you were lucky not to have been assaulted by a crowd. Any decent Irishman would object to this carry-on...my only regret [is] that I cannot have you locked up.

As Dublin District Court judge, addressing 5 members of Hare Krishna religious sect charged with using musical instruments in street and obstructing traffic by marching in single file along road. *The Irish Times*, June 9, 1973.

July 10, 1973
Dr Cahal Daly
Men still speak today of completing the unfinished business of 1916-1922. There is, after fifty years, much unfinished business still to do for Ireland. But the weapons of its completion are no longer rifles and grenades... The tools of Irish patriotism now are not the drill of war but the politics and economics of social justice and the structures of inter-community peace.

As Bishop of Ardagh and Clonmacnoise, during funeral of Lt-General Sean MacEoin, member of old IRA and former Justice Minister, at Ballinalee, Co Longford. *The Irish Times*, July 11, 1973.

July 15, 1973
George Colley
Some of the national newspapers right through the election campaign adopted a really outright campaign of vilification and distortion against us...there are journalists in some of the newspapers today writing regularly who are closely associated with...illegal organisations.

As former Fianna Fáil minister, on party's defeat in election. *The Irish Times*, July 16, 1973.

July 15, 1973
Erskine Childers
The violence in the North has postponed the day of reunification.

As President, on ABC network television in New York. *The Irish Times*, July 16, 1973.

August 7, 1973
Lord Carrington
Would I have gone back and slept happily in my bed knowing that there might be information which I was refusing to get which would save the lives of British soldiers in Ireland? I would never hold up my head again.

As British Defence Minister, on British Government connections with convicted armed robber Kenneth Littlejohn, who had offered to spy for Britain. *The Irish Times*, August 8, 1973.

August 7, 1973
Marcus Lipton
There is little doubt that the Government made a hard and fast deal with criminals.

As British Labour MP, commenting on British Government connections with convicted armed robber Kenneth Littlejohn, who had offered to spy in Ireland. *The Irish Times*, August 8, 1973

August 8, 1973
Kenneth Littlejohn
One of my main functions was to assassinate Shamus (*sic*) Costello who was the effective Number 1 of the Officials and who had been trained in Moscow. I was also to assassinate another high-up member in the officials, Sean Patrick Garland, who I believe was trained in Cuba... I was also told to assassinate Seán Mac Stiofáin.

As convicted armed robber claiming to be British spy, in statement in London magazine, *Time Out*. *The Irish Times*, August 9, 1973.

August 11, 1973
Jack Lynch
The IRA had accepted responsibility publicly for almost all the explosions it had caused. In the absence of such a claim, many people in Ireland believe that these explosions were the work of British intelligence agents.

As former Taoiseach, on bombs in Dublin on December 1, 1972, which killed two people. *The Irish Times*, August 13, 1973.

August 21, 1973
Major Hubert O'Neill
I would say without hesitation that it was sheer unadulterated murder. It was murder.

As Derry City Coroner and former British Army officer, at inquest on cause of death in Derry of 13 victims of Bloody Sunday shootings on January 30, 1972. *The Irish Times*, August 22, 1973.

August 28, 1973
Rt Rev A. H. Butler
He was convinced that Roman Catholics should be excluded from responsibility and participation in Government... It can be argued that if he had thought differently, if he had acted differently, Northern Ireland would not be in its present unhappy state.

As Church of Ireland Bishop of Connor, in eulogy for Lord Brookeborough in Belfast's St Anne's Cathedral. *The Irish Times*, August 29, 1973.

September 5, 1973
Rt Rev G. W. Tickle
Roman Catholics would do well to reflect that a significant proportion of these soldiers are Roman Catholics themselves... I am proud to be associated with an army which shows such restraint and compassion.

As Bishop to Catholic chaplains in British Army, on Derry City Coroner's finding of murder against British soldiers on Bloody Sunday. *The Irish Times*, September 6, 1973.

September 18, 1973
Edward Heath
If an Executive is not formed and functioning by the date laid down by the Act [March 1, 1974] there will be a situation of the utmost gravity. We cannot fall back on Direct Rule again... There are those who favour...total integration...Northern Ireland could no doubt be run fairly and efficiently under such a scheme.

As British Prime Minister, in remarks on integration which he withdrew following day. *The Irish Times*, September 19, 1973.

September 29, 1973
Major Hubert O'Neill
It was sheer, unadulterated, cold, calculated and fiendish murder.

As Derry City Coroner on cause of death of six people killed by IRA car bombs in Claudy. *The Irish Times*, September 29, 1973.

October 13, 1973
William Whitelaw
I have met more clergy of all denominations in the past eighteen months than in the whole of my previous life. Time will tell if it has done me any good.

As NI Secretary of State. *The Irish Times*, October 13, 1973.

October 30, 1973
Rona Fields
The analogy with the Nazis is real. The operating systems which have historically resulted in the destruction of a people are in operation in Northern Ireland.

As American sociologist and author of book on Northern Ireland, *Society on the Run*, speaking in Dublin. *The Irish Times*, November 1, 1973.

November 20, 1973
Brian Faulkner
Any time I had a horse running in a race, I was very content if he won by a neck. Mr Whitelaw will recognise a winner.

As leader of Ulster Unionist Party, after motion against power-sharing rejected by 374 votes to 362 by Ulster Unionist Council. *The Irish Times*, November 21, 1973.

November 22, 1973
John Hume
For the first time in any part of Ireland, Protestant, Catholic and Dissenter will be working together to build a new society.

As SDLP deputy leader, on power-sharing agreement with Ulster Unionist and Alliance parties. *The Irish Times*, November 23, 1973.

November 22, 1973
Brian Faulkner
I know enough of Mr Fitt and his colleagues to believe them to be men of their word, and I think he knows enough about me and my colleagues to believe us also to be men of our word...we will make a fairly formidable combination in Ulster.

As leader of Ulster Unionist Party, on power-sharing agreement. *The Irish Times*, November 23, 1973.

November 22, 1973
Rev Ian Paisley
The so-called settlement is nothing less than the first instalment and down payment on an eventual united Ireland scheme. That scheme will fail, for the unionist people are determined that they will never submit their necks to the heel of a Southern Parliament.

As leader of DUP, on power-sharing agreement and proposals for a Council of Ireland. *The Irish Times*, November 23, 1973.

November 22, 1973
Bernadette McAliskey (Devlin)
Paddy Devlin as Minister for Health?... Was this the same Paddy Devlin who stood...in the streets of Northern Ireland asking people not to pay rent, rates and other payments? Does the Government expect Mr Devlin to retain an ounce of credibility

with his own community when he plays the debt collector of the Tory Government?

As independent MP for Mid-Ulster, in House of Commons, on SDLP membership of power-sharing Executive. *The Irish Times*, November 23, 1973.

November 22, 1973
Gerry Fitt

Mr Devlin has helped more people...in one day than she would ever do in her lifetime. The days of the charisma of Bernadette Devlin are gone. We have found out what the little girl is capable of doing.

As leader of SDLP, in House of Commons, replying to attack on Paddy Devlin's membership of power-sharing Executive. *The Irish Times*, November 23, 1973.

November 25, 1973
Catholic Hierarchy

No change in state law can make the use of contraceptives morally right... It does not follow of course that the State is bound to prohibit the importation and sale of contraceptives.

As Irish Bishops, on private Bill to legalise sale of contraceptives, tabled in Senate by Labour member, Mary Robinson. *The Irish Times*, November 26, 1973.

December 1, 1973
Rev Ian Paisley

I have reason to believe that the fowl pest outbreaks are the work of the IRA.

As leader of DUP. *The Irish Times*, December 1, 1973.

December 2, 1973
Conor Cruise O'Brien

If the [contraceptives] Bill is defeated, Northern Ireland will point to it as final proof that Home Rule does indeed mean Rome Rule.

As Minister for Posts and Telegraphs, at Irish Humanist Association in Dublin. *The Irish Times*, December 3, 1973.

December 2, 1973
Cardinal William Conway

[Legalising contraceptives] would affect marital fidelity and mean a general extension of promiscuity... There is a contagion in these things. The effect seems to spread.

As Primate of Ireland, in radio interview. *The Irish Times*, December 3, 1973.

December 9, 1973
Sunningdale Communiqué

The Irish Government fully accepted and solemnly declared that there could be no change in the status of Northern Ireland until a majority of the people of Northern Ireland desired a change in that status.

The British Government solemnly declared that...if in the future, the majority of the people of Northern Ireland should indicate a wish to become part of a united Ireland, the British Government would support that wish.

In agreement signed by British and Irish Governments and three NI power-sharing parties at Sunningdale. *The Irish Times*, December 10, 1973.

December 9, 1973
Brian Faulkner

I wonder which of us has signed his own death warrant.

As leader of Ulster Unionist Party, paraphrasing Michael Collins in 1921, in exchange with British officials after signing of Sunningdale Communiqué. Bloomfield, Ken, *Stormont in Crisis*, Blackstaff Press, 1974, p. 193.

December 9, 1973
Rev Martin Smyth

I think the negotiators will get a welcome home in Northern Ireland similar to that given to Chamberlain when he returned from Munich.

As Grand Master of Orange Order, on Sunningdale Agreement setting up NI power-sharing executive and Council of Ireland (wrongly assuming that Chamberlain got hostile reception). *The Irish Times*, December 10, 1973.

December 12, 1973
Des O'Malley

If our right to unity, which follows from a desire of the majority of the Irish people for unity, is taken away, there can be no long-term solution to our problems. Ireland is one Ireland, one nation, one country, because God made it one.

As Fianna Fáil TD, reacting to Sunningdale Agreement. Walsh, Dick, *Des O'Malley, A Political Profile*, Brandon, 1986, p. 43.

December 12, 1973
Brian Faulkner

I come here to speak in the Assembly and I find that this crowd of disloyalist wreckers, led by a demon doctor who goes round the country preaching sedition, are preventing me. It is diabolical...the Unionist, SDLP and Alliance coalition will get good government going here.

As leader of Ulster Unionist Party, after NI Assembly adjourned because of loyalist protests against Sunningdale Agreement. *The Irish Times*, December 13, 1973.

December 12, 1973
Roy Bradford

I am totally convinced that the Sunningdale Agreement will be recorded in the history books as the first realistic and workable response to the Irish question mark, which has hung like a sword of Nemesis over Anglo-Irish relations.

As unionist member of NI power-sharing executive, to unionists at Ballyholme. *The Irish Times*, December 13, 1973.

December 15, 1973
Ulster Defence Association
Brian Faulkner, despite his acknowledged shrewdness, has been conned, just as Michael Collins was conned in the formulation of the Anglo-Irish Treaty in 1921.

Commenting on Ulster Unionist leader's support of Sunningdale Agreement. *The Irish Times*, December 15, 1973.

December 15, 1973
Tomás Mac Giolla
Mr Cosgrave has lived to confirm the work of his father, W. T. Cosgrave, who signed the partition Treaty of 1921 and the Boundary Agreement of 1925.

As President of Official Sinn Féin, on role of Taoiseach Liam Cosgrave in signing Sunningdale Agreement with British Government. *The Irish Times*, December 15, 1973.

December 27, 1973
Oliver Napier
Do you really want a Council of Ireland?...if you do nothing in the next few weeks, history will judge you and its judgement will be harsh and unforgiving.

As leader of Alliance Party, urging Republic to make concessions to Unionists on extradition, constitutional reform and security cooperation. *The Irish Times*, December 28, 1973.

January 2, 1974
Paddy Devlin
As far as I am concerned, sectarianism in Government employment is dead.

As SDLP member of NI power-sharing executive. *The Irish Times*, January 3, 1974.

January 7, 1974
Desmond Boal
[The Union] is in the process of being broken no matter how many hypocritical screams of horror come from people who have been blind to recent history... I would now consider a federal Irish parliament...with a provincial parliament possessing the powers recently held by Stormont.

As co-founder of DUP, whose leader, Rev Ian Paisley, disassociated himself from view expressed. *The Irish Times*, January 8, 1974.

January 8, 1974
Ruairí Ó Brádaigh
The proposal was a giant step...very courageous. He said that Protestants were concerned to

preserve their heritage. Very good. This is the type of solution that would satisfy the Republican movement.

As President of Provisional Sinn Féin, on proposal of Desmond Boal, above, for a federal Ireland. *The Irish Times*, January 9, 1974.

January 16, 1974
Justice James Augustine Murnaghan
[The acknowledgement] that Northern Ireland could not be reintegrated into the national territory until and unless a majority of the people of Northern Ireland indicated a wish to become part of a united Ireland [was] no more than a statement of policy.

As Judge in Dublin High Court ruling that Irish Government statement in Sunningdale Agreement was not repugnant to Constitution, as claimed by Kevin Boland, former Fianna Fáil minister. *The Irish Times*, January 17, 1974.

January 16, 1974
Hugh Logue
[The Council of Ireland is] the vehicle which would trundle the North into a united Ireland.

As SDLP member of power-sharing assembly, in sentence deleted from speech prepared for debate in Dublin at request of John Hume, to avoid angering unionists, but script had already been circulated to newspapers. White, Barry, *John Hume, Statesman of the Troubles*, Blackstaff Press, 1984, p. 156.

February 1, 1974
United Ulster Unionist Coalition
Dublin is just a Sunningdale away.

As anti-Sunningdale coalition, in slogan used in general election in which its candidates won 11 of 12 seats. Bardon, Jonathan, *A History of Ulster*, Blackstaff Press, 1992, p. 706.

February 16, 1974
Harry West
[We wish to] return to an Éire of peace, security and prosperity.

As leader of 'Official Unionist Party', as misquoted in *Daily Telegraph* which transcribed word 'era' as 'Éire'. *The Irish Times*, February 16, 1974.

February 21, 1974
Mary Robinson
We will be hypocrites with no right to the respect of the people of Northern Ireland or to self respect if we move a declaratory section [from Constitution] giving a particular Church a privileged position, while retaining the denominational moral outlook of that Church which is in conflict with the outlook of other Churches in the State.

As Labour member of Senate, proposing private Bill to legalise sale of contraceptives. *The Irish Times*, February 22, 1974.

February 27, 1974
Liam Cosgrave
The Council of Ireland would not be a threat to the interests or loyalties of the majority in Northern Ireland who now oppose any change in the status of the area. It is not a way of achieving unity by stealth.

As Taoiseach, in Dáil. *The Irish Times*, February 27, 1974.

March 2, 1974
Kevin Boland
Redmondism...has become rampant. The one-time Republican Party [Fianna Fáil] still dithers about openly embracing it...but the Coalition parties [Fine Gael and Labour] have grasped the nettle with both hands... Venal politicians with a vested interest in the status quo...have blasphemed the cause that dead generations of Ireland served.

As former Fianna Fáil minister, addressing árd fheis of his new party, Aontacht Éireann. *The Irish Times*, March 4, 1974.

March 9, 1974
Rev Denis Faul
Is it the Irish ideal for a bridegroom to fly out to Majorca with new wife and a pocketful of contraceptives, removing all the romance out of marriage?

As Dungannon priest, opposing legalisation of sale of contraceptives in Republic. *The Irish Times*, March 9, 1974.

March 9, 1974
Rev James Healy
I am proud to say I know happy, healthy couples, in love with each other, who have abstained from sexual intercourse for over twenty years.

As professor of moral theology, speaking against legalisation of sale of contraceptives. *The Irish Times*, November 9, 1974.

March 13, 1974
Liam Cosgrave
I now solemnly reaffirm that the factual position of Northern Ireland within the United Kingdom cannot be changed except by a decision of a majority of the people of Northern Ireland.

As Taoiseach, in attempt to reassure unionists about status of North under Sunningdale Agreement. *The Irish Times*, March 14, 1974.

March 13, 1974
Vivion de Valera
[Mr Cosgrave came] perilously near recognising without qualification a *de jure* right of a section of the Irish people to maintain partition.

As Fianna Fáil TD, responding to declaration on status of Northern Ireland by Taoiseach Liam Cosgrave, above. *The Irish Times*, March 14, 1974.

March 13, 1974
Brian Faulkner
For the first time a Government of the Republic has made a solemn declaration which accepts our right to remain part of the United Kingdom for as long as that is the wish of a majority of our people.

As 'NI Unionist Party' leader of NI power-sharing Executive, on declaration of March 13 by Taoiseach Liam Cosgrave on status of Northern Ireland. *The Irish Times*, March 14, 1974.

March 13, 1974
John Laird
Instead of being a step forward, it was more like a half-inch shuffle.

As unionist member of NI Assembly, on Dáil declaration by Taoiseach on status of Northern Ireland. *The Irish Times*, March 14, 1974.

March 17, 1974
John Kelly
Once upon a time the mention of Irishman suggested the pig in the parlour. We resented this ignorant smear...but it was at least better than the 'bomb in the boot' image that is now being wished on us by our own people.

As Fine Gael TD, addressing Irish Universities Club in London. *The Irish Times*, March 18, 1974.

March 25, 1974
Willie John McBride
I'm a rugby player, not a politician and as an Irishman I'm proof that rugby and politics are divorced.

As Irish international, justifying acceptance of captaincy of Lions team to tour apartheid South Africa. *The Irish Times*, March 26, 1974.

March 30, 1974
Joseph B. Murray
I have received pledges from 2,000 people and two Protestants.

As President of League of Decency. *The Irish Times*, March 25, 1974.

March 30, 1974
James Downey
We have got the pigs out of the parlour but we have not yet shifted the bishops out of the bedroom.

As political correspondent, referring to John Kelly's comments of March 17, 1974. *The Irish Times*, March 30, 1974.

April 1, 1974
Garret FitzGerald
It is South Africa which has brought politics into sport...the question which we as Irish people have to consider is whether we want to encourage this process of human degradation by involving ourselves in it.

As Minister for Foreign Affairs, appealing to Irish Rugby Football Union not to send Irish players on Lions tour of South Africa. *The Irish Times*, April 2, 1974.

April 13, 1974
P. C. Henry
To give the BBC the free run of Ireland, as suggested by the Minister of Posts and Telegraphs, is tantamount to reconquest.

As Professor of Old and Medieval English in University College, Galway, on proposal by Dr Conor Cruise O'Brien to relay BBC broadcasts throughout Republic. *The Irish Times*, April 13, 1974.

April 24, 1974
Roy Mason
Pressure is mounting on the mainland to pull out the troops; equally, demands are being made to set a date for withdrawal.

As British Defence Secretary, on NI troubles. *The Irish Times*, April 25, 1974.

April 25, 1974
Conor Cruise O'Brien
I am allowing the directive issued by my predecessor to stand... I am determined to ensure as far as I can that while armed conspiracies continue to exist in this country, their agents shall not be allowed to use the state broadcasting system for a systematic propaganda effort.

As Minister for Posts and Telegraphs, reversing earlier position on directive issued under Section 31 of Broadcasting Act forbidding IRA and Sinn Féin interviews. *The Irish Times*, April 26, 1974.

May 13, 1974
Harold Wilson
These documents reveal a specific and calculated plan on the part of the IRA by means of ruthless and indiscriminate violence to foment inter-sectarian hatred and a degree of chaos, with the object of enabling the IRA...to occupy and control certain predesignated and densely populated areas in the centre of Belfast...their intentions would have been to carry out a scorched-earth policy of burning the houses of the ordinary people as they were compelled to withdraw.

As British Prime Minister, informing House of Commons of contents of IRA documents found in house at Myrtlefield Park, Belfast. *The Irish Times*, May 14, 1974.

May 14, 1974
Ulster Workers' Council
This strike has been organised by the Ulster Workers' Council as a result of the decision by the Assembly to support the Sunningdale Agreement.

As loyalist strike committee, announcing start of general stoppage after NI Assembly voted 44-28 to ratify Sunningdale Agreement. *The Irish Times*, May 15, 1974.

May 15, 1974
Brian Faulkner
Where do they come from? Who elected them? What is their authority?

As 'NI Unionist Party' leader of NI power-sharing Executive, on Ulster Workers' Council, which had called strike to bring down Sunningdale Agreement. Fisk, Robert, *The Point of No Return*, Deutsch, 1975, p. 62.

May 16, 1974
Harry Murray
If that parrot beside you doesn't stop nodding, his head will fall off.

As chairman of Ulster Workers' Council, at Stormont Castle meeting with NIO Minister Stanley Orme, referring to Permanent Secretary Frank Cooper. *The Irish Times*, March 20, 1976.

May 17, 1974
Sammy Smyth
I am very happy about the bombings in Dublin. There is a war with the Free State and now we are laughing at them.

As UDA press officer, after UDA car bombs had killed 23 people in centre of Dublin. *The Irish Times*, May 18, 1974.

May 17, 1974
Harry West
Loyalist workers are prepared to plunge the country into chaos.

As leader of 'Official Unionist Party', on bid to bring down Sunningdale Agreement. *The Irish Times*, May 18, 1974.

May 19, 1974
Roy Bradford
...the Secretary of State should be encouraged to reopen lines of communication with the Ulster Workers' Council before the province is allowed to slide into chaos.

As unionist minister in NI power-sharing executive, opposing policy of colleagues not to negotiate with loyalist strikers. *The Irish Times*, May 20, 1974.

May 21, 1974
Seamus Mallon
I must remind this man that political treachery is not forgotten, no less than other forms of treachery. It is reprehensible for this man to act the Pontius Pilate on his colleagues.

As SDLP member in NI power-sharing executive, on remarks of Roy Bradford, above. *The Irish Times*, May 22, 1974.

May 21, 1974
Len Murray
It is not a strike. It is a stoppage of work imposed by an unrepresentative group of people on the vast mass of people in Northern Ireland who want to go to work today and tomorrow and next week and all the time.

As TUC General Secretary, during (unsuccessful) attempt to lead shipyard employees back to work during loyalist strike. Fisk, Robert, *The Point of No Return*, Deutsch, 1975, p. 109.

May 22, 1974
Brian Faulkner
We do recognise that for a long time there have been fears among a fairly large number of people on this matter of a Council of Ireland...we have called for a test of opinion at the next election.

As chairman of NI power-sharing executive, announcing decision to postpone Council of Ireland. *The Irish Times*, May 23, 1974.

May 22, 1974
Rev Ian Paisley
The Faulkner Unionists...are now preparing to force the people of Northern Ireland to swallow Sunningdale in two spoonfuls instead of one.

As DUP leader, on decision of power-sharing executive to postpone Council of Ireland. *The Irish Times*, May 23, 1974.

May 25, 1974
Harold Wilson
The people on this side of the water...see property destroyed by evil violence and are asked to pick up the bill for rebuilding it. Yet people who benefit from all this now viciously defy Westminster, purporting to act as though they were an elected government; people who spend their lives sponging on Westminster and British democracy and then systematically assault democratic methods. Who do these people think they are?

As British Prime Minister, in television broadcast to Northern Ireland on loyalist strike. *The Irish Times*, May 27, 1974.

May 25, 1974
Brian Faulkner
Today, I fear, we are the despair of our friends and the mockery of our enemies. Let us not plunge this country, which all of us love in our different ways, into a deepening and potentially disastrous conflict.

As chairman of NI power-sharing executive, appealing for end of loyalist strike. *The Irish Times*, May 27, 1974.

May 27, 1974
Hugo Patterson
The mind simply boggles at the thought of a whole community without electricity. Absolutely nothing will move...there'll be absolute chaos whenever we have this final shutdown. There's no question about that whatever.

As spokesman for NI Electricity Service, on threatened shut down of power by loyalist strikers. Fisk, Robert, *The Point of No Return*, Deutsch, 1975, p. 182.

May 27, 1974
Merlyn Rees
No parliamentary democracy...can accept that a gang of men, self-appointed and answerable to no one, should decide when and where and to whom the essentials of life should be distributed... Let us all work together... Give peace a chance.

As NI Secretary of State, in 5 a.m. statement announcing Government decision to use troops to take over petrol depots. *The Irish Times*, May 28, 1974.

May 27, 1974
Hugo Patterson
Let's be clear about this, this shutdown is on, it's complete, it's final, it's irreversible... We are past the point of no return.

As spokesman for NI Electricity Service, on 9.30 p.m. shutdown of power in Northern Ireland by loyalist strikers. Bardon, Jonathan, *A History of Ulster*, Blackstaff Press, 1992, p. 711.

May 28, 1974
Lord Hailsham
It's no good being or calling yourself Loyalist if you don't obey the law, and this is a conspiracy against the State. There is no doubt about it – in previous times, judges would have had no difficulty in describing it as high treason because it's an attempt to overthrow the authority of the Queen in Parliament.

As British Lord Chancellor, on loyalist strike. Fisk, Robert, *The Point of No Return*, Deutsch, 1975, p. 223.

May 28, 1974
NI Department of the Environment
The water and sewage situation is deteriorating.
Workers are now leaving the plants... Supplies
may now cease almost at once in some areas.

In news release on effect of loyalist strike. Office of
Information Services, NI Executive, May 28, 1974.

May 28, 1974
John Hume
I'll sit here until there is shit flowing up Royal
Avenue and then the people will realise what
these people are about and then we'll see who
wins.

As SDLP member of NI power-sharing executive,
speaking to colleagues at Stormont before fall of
executive. White, Barry, *John Hume, Statesman of the
Troubles*, Blackstaff Press, 1984, p. 170.

May 28, 1974
John Hume
[Edward Carson once said] that unionism's last
fight would be between the forces of the right
and the forces of the crown. That's it all started
now.

As SDLP member of power-sharing executive, speaking at
Stormont to colleagues after fall of executive. White,
Barry, *John Hume, Statesman of the Troubles*, Blackstaff
Press, 1984, p. 171.

May 28, 1974
Brian Faulkner
It is...apparent to us, from the extent of support
for the present stoppage, that the degree of
consent needed to sustain the Executive does not
at present exist. Nor, as Ulstermen, are we
prepared to see our country undergo, for any
political reason, the catastrophe which now
confronts it.

As chairman of power-sharing executive, announcing his
resignation because of effects of loyalist strike. Office of
Information Services, NI Executive, May 28, 1974.

May 30, 1974
Lord Arran
I loathe and detest the miserable
bastards...savage murderous thugs. May the Irish,
all of them, rot in hell.

As columnist, writing in *London Evening News* on
violence in Northern Ireland. *The Irish Times*, May 31,
1974.

May 31, 1974
Merlyn Rees
There is a strong feeling of Ulster nationalism
growing which will have to be taken into account
and which it would be foolish to ignore.

As NI Secretary of State, on success of loyalist strike in
bringing down power-sharing executive. *The Irish Times*,
June 1, 1974.

June 2, 1974
Paddy Devlin
There [was] massive concealed resistance within
the civil service...as part of the middle-class
Protestant swing behind the loyalists in its last few
days.

As former minister in power-sharing executive, on success
of loyalist strike. *The Irish Times*, June 3, 1974.

June 3, 1974
Reginald Maudling
Withdrawal of troops was a repugnant thought but
there comes a time when one must consider any
possibility no matter how repugnant.

As former Home Secretary, in House of Commons, on
aftermath of loyalist strike. *The Irish Times*, June 4, 1974.

June 4, 1974
Harold Wilson
I noticed that yesterday [Mr Paisley] was wearing a
small piece of sponge as a political symbol...all the
sponges in the ocean are not capable of washing
away the things for which he has been responsible
in Ulster over these past weeks.

As British Prime Minister, in House of Commons, on
aftermath of loyalist strike. *HC Debates:* Vol. 874: Col.
1045.

June 4, 1974
Edward Heath
We are facing the most ruthless group of urban
guerrillas the Western world has ever seen.

As Conservative leader, in House of Commons, on IRA. *The
Irish Times*, June 5, 1974.

June 8, 1974
Rev Michael Connolly
This is a fitting tribute to a great man. The price of
freedom has always been very high and Irishmen
have always been prepared to pay it in full.

As Wolverhampton priest, at paramilitary parade in London
for IRA hunger striker, Michael Gaughan. *The Irish Times*,
June 11, 1974.

June 9, 1974
Rev Michael Keane
England is always seen as our enemy. But we may
think how good a country it has been to us in the
past, giving us work, opportunity and money.

As priest, at requiem Mass in Ballina for IRA hunger striker,
Michael Gaughan, which prompted walk-out by IRA leader
Dáithí Ó Conaill, and others. *The Irish Times*, June 10,
1974.

June 9, 1974
Earl of Donoughmore
We did not talk politics with them but they
know a lot more about racing now.

As hostage of IRA, after release. *The Irish Times*, June 10,
1974.

June 13, 1974
Liam Cosgrave
Violence...is killing the desire for unity.

As Taoiseach, in Dáil. *The Irish Times*, June 14, 1974.

June 22, 1974
Micheál Mac Liammóir
What a paradise Ireland would be if it had as
much affection and respect for the living as it has
for the dead.

As leading Dublin actor and producer. *The Irish Times*,
June 22, 1974.

June 25, 1974
Bridget Rose Dugdale
I stand proudly here as the perpetrator of a calm
political act to change the corporate conscience
of a Cabinet.

As defendant in Special Criminal Court, on charge of
receiving 19 paintings stolen from Alfred Beit, for which
she received nine-year sentence. *The Irish Times*, June
26, 1974.

July 1974
John Hewitt
I was born an Ulsterman of planter stock. I was
born on the island of Ireland so secondly I'm an
Irishman. I was born in the British archipelago
and English is my native tongue, so I'm British.
The British are off shore to the continent of
Europe. So I'm European. That is my hierarchy
of values and as far as I'm concerned anyone
who omits one step in that sequence of values is
falsifying the situation.

As Ulster poet. *The Irish Times*, August 8, 1989.

July 1, 1974
Harry West
There are more ways, Dr FitzGerald, of killing a
dog than stuffing its mouth with butter.

As leader of 'Official Unionist Party', to Minister for
Foreign Affairs, Garret FitzGerald, at meeting in Belfast,
referring to Irish attempts to placate unionists. *The Irish
Times*, July 6, 1974.

July 11, 1974
Michael Kitt
He [Michael Kitt] never thought he'd live to see
the day when he'd be asked in an Irish
Parliament to betray that society which the great
Mr de Valera extolled in his celebration of the

delights and serenity of the peasant society of
comely maidens and athletic young men on the
village green.

As Fianna Fáil TD, in Dáil, on Bill to make contraceptives
available. *The Irish Times*, July 12, 1974.

July 11, 1974
Oliver J. Flanagan
...the availability of contraceptives will, in my
opinion, add more serious consequences to those
already there. You do not quench a fire by
sprinkling it with petrol.

As Fine Gael TD, in Dáil, on Bill to make contraceptives
available. *The Irish Times*, July 12, 1974.

July 11, 1974
Michael Kennedy
If in a small town or village one chemist applied
for a licence to sell contraceptives and another did
not, did the Minister not think that this would give
rise to a reaction within the community that so
and so is the man who handles the quare things?

As Fianna Fáil TD, in Dáil, on Bill to make contraceptives
available. *The Irish Times*, July 12, 1974.

July 20, 1974
David Thornley
The Taoiseach has behaved like an idiot, but one
thing he has succeeded in doing is getting himself
into the *Guinness Book of Records*.

As Labour TD, on decision of Taoiseach Liam Cosgrave to
vote against his own Government's Contraception Bill,
helping defeat it by 75 votes to 61. *The Irish Times*, July 20,
1974.

August 8, 1974
Lt-General Sir Frank King
...you can't go round shooting people because they
want to do a certain thing.

As General Officer Commanding British Army in Northern
Ireland on why army did not confront loyalist strikers. Fisk,
Robert, *The Point of No Return*, Deutsch, 1975, p. 152.

September 25, 1974
Conor Cruise O'Brien
In the event of a British withdrawal...it is virtually
certain civil war would break out in Northern
Ireland... It is reliably estimated that with its
present effective size [the Irish Army] could, if
called upon, hold one Border town, e.g. Newry...

As Minister for Posts and Telegraphs and Labour TD, in
party document leaked to *The Irish Times*. *The Irish Times*,
September 25, 1974.

October 14, 1974
Ivan Cooper
[Broadcasting the Angelus on *RTÉ*] was essentially
for Catholics and excluded a section of the

population...if people south of the Border wanted to move towards unity, they would have to get rid of it.

As Protestant member of SDLP, on *RTÉ*. *The Irish Times*, October 15, 1974.

October 18, 1974
Garret FitzGerald

The society that we have created here in the Republic is one which is unattractive not merely to bigoted loyalists but indeed to moderate and liberal Protestants in Northern Ireland.

As Minister for Foreign Affairs, in Dublin. *The Irish Times*, October 19, 1974.

October 27, 1974
Mary Robinson

[Dr Conor Cruise O'Brien] was using the weight of his office, the guaranteed publicity, speaking as a minister, to smear the liberal voice as having been in deliberate alliance with activists.

As independent Senator, responding to criticism by Dr O'Brien of her support for anti-internment rally. Siggins, Lorna, *Mary Robinson*, Mainstream Publishing, 1997, p. 93.

October 29, 1974
Conor Cruise O'Brien

Your school of liberalism is very vigilant to threats coming from parliament. You are so vigilant in that quarter that you don't notice other things creeping up from behind other quarters.

As Minister for Posts and Telegraphs, to Senator Mary Robinson, on her support for anti-internment rally. Siggins, Lorna, *Mary Robinson*, Mainstream Publishing, 1997, p. 94.

October 29, 1974
Rev Joseph Parker

I would be very concerned for the future of Christianity in Ireland because I think there is a grave danger that institutionalised Churches have been a hindrance towards reconciliation...[I am] a sad, lonely and disillusioned man.

As Church of Ireland founder of Witness for Peace movement, started when son Stephen was killed on Bloody Friday, on leaving Northern Ireland for good. *The Irish Times*, October 29, 1974.

November 17, 1974
Dáithí Ó Conaill

The consequences of war are not going to be kept solely in Ireland, they are going to be felt on the mainland of Britain.

As IRA leader, four days before 21 people killed in IRA Birmingham pub bombings (19 were killed outright; two died later). *The Irish Times*, November 23, 1974.

c. November 22, 1974
Queen Elizabeth II

We may hold different points of view but it is in times of stress and difficulty that we most need to remember that we have much more in common than there is dividing us.

As British monarch, after 21 people killed in IRA Birmingham pub bombings. Tomlinson, Richard, *Divine Right*, Little, Brown and Company, 1994, p. 292.

November 25, 1974
Roy Jenkins

These powers are draconian. In combination, they are unprecedented in peacetime. I believe they are fully justified to meet the clear and present danger.

As Home Secretary, introducing Prevention of Terrorism Act after Birmingham bombings which killed 21 people. *The Irish Times*, November 26, 1974.

November 28, 1974
Kevin McNamara

We in this House have a duty not only to pass this legislation to protect our own people but also to pause and think why it is that such a dreadful massacre as took place in Birmingham would suddenly precipitate a debate about Northern Ireland in this house this week.

As British Labour MP, in House of Commons. *The Irish Times*, November 29, 1974.

December 11, 1974
Dáithí Ó Conaill

The national leadership of the IRA did not order that attack... To the contrary, we condemn it. An attack like the one in Birmingham is murder.

As IRA leader, in German magazine. *The Irish Times*, December 12, 1974.

December 12, 1974
Rt Rev A. H. Butler

We were all most impressed with their attitude, with their fair-mindedness, and we were so pleased to find that they were talking seriously and deeply and with great conviction and had listened very carefully to what we had to say.

As Church of Ireland Bishop of Connor, on meeting IRA leaders at Feakle, Co Clare, prompting IRA ceasefire. *The Irish Times*, December 13, 1974.

January 1, 1975
William Shannon

Once again there is the shadow of the gunman and the crack of the sniper's rifle, once again Irish freedom fighters are interned without trial.

As Boston columnist writing in US journal *Annual of American Historical Society* (1975), quoted widely when appointed US Ambassador to Ireland four years later. *The Irish Times*, September 23, 1980.

c. January 15, 1975
J. J. McAuliffe

Mr Haughey is quite irresponsible in money matters. He cannot be controlled on a running account. His affairs can only deteriorate further.

As Allied Irish Banks general manager, in internal memo on Fianna Fáil TD Charles Haughey, published on February 16 1999 at Moriarty tribunal on payments to politicians . *The Irish Times*, February 17, 1999.

January 16, 1975
IRA

Principally due to a total lack of response to our peace proposals by the British Government, the Army Council cannot in conscience renew the order suspending offensive military actions.

Announcing end of brief ceasefire called after talks with Protestant churchmen. *The Irish Times*, January 17, 1975.

January 30, 1975
Jack Lynch

Mr Haughey had given a personal undertaking that he fully supported and was committed to the party's policy on Northern Ireland as enunciated by me as party leader.

As Taoiseach, restoring Charles Haughey to Fianna Fáil front bench for first time since 1970 arms trial. *The Irish Times*, January 31, 1975.

February 6, 1975
Justice Ambrose McGonigal

What appears before me today under the name of the UDA is gang law, a vicious and brutalising organisation. This is not an association of decent hard-working respectable people.

As judge in Belfast City Commission, in killing of Ann Ogilby in 'romper room', name taken by UDA from children's TV programme for place where sectarian victims were beaten to death. *The Irish Times*, February 7, 1975.

February 9, 1975
IRA

In the light of discussions which have taken place between representatives of the Republican movement and British officials on effective arrangements to ensure that there is no breakdown of a new truce, the Army Council of Óglaigh na hÉireann have renewed the order suspending military action.

Announcing renewed ceasefire after meeting British officials. *The Irish Times*, February 10, 1975.

February 9, 1975
Merlyn Rees

A genuine and sustained cessation of violence can be the basis for a more constructive and peaceful future for Northern Ireland.

As NI Secretary of State, in phrase he repeated frequently in following months. *The Irish Times*, February 10, 1975.

February 24, 1975
Seamus Costello

It had never been true, despite press and other rumours, that [the IRSP] had a military wing.

As Irish Republican Socialist Party leader at Belfast funeral of IRSP member shot by Official IRA. *The Irish Times*, February 25, 1975.

February 27, 1975
Cathal Goulding

By God, the threats of a few misguided and confused malcontents will not stop us now.

As Official IRA leader, at Belfast funeral of IRA member shot in 'war' with IRSP. *The Irish Times*, February 28, 1975.

April 12, 1975
Lt-General Sir Frank King

The Army was making such good progress that in another two or three months we would have brought the IRA to the point where they would have had enough.

As General Officer commanding British Army in Northern Ireland, condemning ceasefire agreed between IRA and British Government officials. *The Irish Times*, April 14, 1975.

April 14, 1975
Merlyn Rees

The General has expressed his regrets to me. The Government's actions with regards to the role of the Army...will be...directly related to a genuine and sustained cessation of violence.

As NI Secretary of State, in House of Commons, on Lt-General Sir Frank King's remarks, above. *The Irish Times*, April 15, 1975.

May 21, 1975
Rev Victor Griffin

Any society pledged to uphold democracy and freedom must be prepared to tolerate different views and practices in relation to moral questions.

As Dean of St Patrick's Cathedral, Dublin, calling for more pluralist society. *The Irish Times*, May 22, 1975.

May 23, 1975
Dr Eamonn Casey

We have never asked as a Church that our moral law be reflected in the civil law.

As Bishop of Kerry, on call by Church of Ireland Synod for more pluralist society and change in divorce and contraception laws. *The Irish Times*, May 24, 1975.

May 25, 1975
Rev William Arlow

The British...would do what the Americans call a Vietnam; they would pull out.

As Church of Ireland minister and intermediary, on what British officials told IRA in event of failure of NI Convention. *The Irish Times*, May 26, 1975.

June 7, 1975
Oliver Napier
Europe needs us as much as we need Europe.

As NI Alliance Party leader, on EEC membership. *The Irish Times*, June 7, 1975.

July 10, 1975
Seamus Heaney
Northern reticence, the tight gag of place
And times; yes, yes. Of the 'wee six' I sing
Where to be saved you only must save face
And whatever you say, you say nothing.

As poet, in 'North', about Northern Ireland. Heaney, Seamus, *North*, Faber and Faber, 1974, p. 59.

June 19, 1975
John Hume
An approach which seeks to exclude other traditions leads only to the grave, destruction, death and conflict. It may satisfy the bugles in the blood, it may satisfy the atavism in everyone, we may feel proud of it, but it will not succeed.

As SDLP deputy leader, in NI Convention. *The Irish Times*, June 20, 1975.

June 24, 1975
William Craig
Violence created violence. Sectarian killings...illustrated just how true that was and how depraved people had become...they must see to it that this sort of conduct could no longer be perpetuated.

As leader of Vanguard, in NI Convention. *The Irish Times*, June 25, 1975.

July 11, 1975
James Tully
Good luck, Bobby, and to hell with the begrudgers.

As Minister for Local Government, at launch of housing development in Kells, after TD withdrew allegation of improper relationship with developer, Bobby Farrell. *The Irish Times*, July 12, 1975.

August 2, 1975
Billy Mitchell
I may be a bad Christian but I'm a good Protestant.

As senior UVF leader, in interview. *The Observer*, August 3, 1975.

August 15, 1975
Justice Bridges
William Power, Hugh Callaghan, Patrick Joseph Hill, Robert Gerald Hunter, Noel Richard McIlkenny and John Walker, you stand convicted on each of 21 counts, on the clearest and most overwhelming evidence I have ever heard, of the crime of murder.

As judge, sentencing Birmingham Six to life for 1974 pub bombings which killed 21 people (on February 25, 1991 evidence was rejected as unsafe, and all six were exonerated). Mullin, Chris, *Error of Judgement*, Chatto & Windus, 1986, p. 206.

September 9, 1975
William Craig
Coalition government...cannot be equated with the ill-named concept of power-sharing.

As leader of Vanguard Unionist Party, resigning because members failed to support his suggestion of coalition with SDLP. *The Irish Times*, September 10, 1975.

October 2, 1975
Altiero Spinelli
Ireland had isolated itself. [I wonder] if it might not be a question of Catholic solidarity.

As EEC Commissioner, on Ireland's decision, alone among EEC countries, not to withdraw ambassador from Madrid after execution of five Basque separatists by Franco Government. *The Irish Times*, October 3, 1975.

October 29, 1975
Fianna Fáil
Fianna Fáil calls on the British Government to encourage the unity of Ireland by agreement, in independence and in a harmonious relationship between the two islands, and to this end to declare Britain's commitment to implement an ordered withdrawal from her involvement in the Six Counties of Northern Ireland.

As opposition party in Dáil, in new policy statement issued in Dublin. *The Irish Times*, October 30, 1975.

November 2, 1975
Gerry Fitt
Mr Lynch, whether he himself would agree or not, had put himself into the Provisional IRA camp in asking for a declaration from the British of their intention to withdraw from Northern Ireland.

As leader of SDLP, on call for British withdrawal by Fianna Fáil under leadership of Jack Lynch. *The Irish Times*, November 3, 1975.

November 8, 1975
Tiede Herrema
I have children of the same age and I see them as children with a lot of problems. I must say that if

they were my children I would do my utmost to help them.

As Dutch industrialist, after release by kidnappers, Eddie Gallagher and Marion Coyle, from house in Monasterevin. *The Irish Times*, November 10, 1975.

November 11, 1975
IRA Gunman
Christ, I'm in the wrong house.

As member of IRA, after shooting dead Belfast man in front of his family during Republican feud. *The Irish Times*, November 12, 1975.

November 12, 1975
Rev Denis Faul
If Senator Mary Robinson's Bill was passed, fornication, adultery and abortion would be on the rates.

As Dungannon priest, in TCD debate on Mary Robinson's Bill legalising sale of contraceptives. *The Irish Times*, November 13, 1975.

January 1, 1976
Phil Coulter
With their tanks and their guns,
Oh my God what have they done
To the town I loved so well.

As songwriter, in 'The Town I Loved So Well', about his native Derry. *100 Best Irish Songs and Ballads*, Mac Publications (undated), p. 38.

January 5, 1976
Cardinal William Conway
Those who take a life for a life are spitting in the face of Christ.

As Primate of Ireland, on sectarian killings of 5 Catholics and 10 Protestants in Co Armagh. *The Irish Times*, January 6, 1976.

January 8, 1976
Rev Robert Nixon
...those responsible for the murder of five Catholics in the families of Reavy's and O'Dowd's might as well have stopped the minibus at Kingsmills themselves... Those who murdered in those households sealed the fate of the ten who died on Monday.

As Presbyterian minister, at service for victims of massacre of 10 Protestants at Kingsmills, Co Armagh, after killing of 5 Catholics on previous day. *The Irish Times*, January 9, 1976.

January 12, 1976
Edward Heath
What I find intensely depressing...is that after six years of the most appalling civil strife, continuous bloodshed, and now one of the most brutal massacres of all, the parties in Northern Ireland are not able to come together...it is this

feeling that is bringing a majority of British people to say 'pull our forces out' and there comes a point where no political party can withstand that feeling.

As former British Prime Minister, in House of Commons, after sectarian killing of 5 Catholics and 10 Protestants in Co Armagh. *The Irish Times*, January 13, 1976.

January 12, 1976
Airey Neave
We must stand firm, resist voices of defeat, and not be intimidated, or beguiled into retiring to our tents to sulk.

As Conservative NI spokesman, in House of Commons, replying to Edward Heath, above. *The Irish Times*, January 13, 1976.

February 1, 1976
Maire Drumm
If they send Frank Stagg home in a coffin, I would expect the fighting men of Crossmaglen would send the SAS home in boxes.

As Sinn Féin Vice President, at Derry meeting in support of Frank Stagg, Republican prisoner on hunger strike in Wakefield Prison, England. *The Irish Times*, February 6, 1976.

February 21, 1976
George Wallace
My folks have been here from Northern Ireland and Scotland – it's so long ago now, it's now a foreign country in a sense – but we feel that we are kin... I side with the side of peace in the hope that it will come not only to Catholics but to Protestants as well. I'm gonna pray for y'all in Northern Ireland, Catholic and Protestant.

As Governor of Alabama, in interview. *The Irish Times*, February 21, 1976.

February 22, 1976
Joe Cahill
I pledge that we will assemble here again in the near future when we have taken your body from where it lies. Let there be no mistake about it, we will take it, Frank, and we will leave it resting side by side with your great comrade, Michael Gaughan.

As Belfast Republican, at Sinn Féin service in Leigue cemetery in Ballina, after hunger striker, Frank Stagg, was buried by State to prevent IRA funeral. (The body was reburied secretly some months later.) *The Irish Times*, February 23, 1976.

March 3, 1976
David Trimble
We should look for our brave men in prisons and for the fools among politicians.

As Vanguard member and future leader of Ulster Unionist Party, at close of NI Convention. *The Irish Times*, March 6, 1976.

March 3, 1976
Rev Ian Paisley
There is a story going round Queen's University that a well-known member of Vanguard and a lecturer in law at Queen's University was toying with his personal sidearm in a young lady's home. After seemingly unloading it he pulled the trigger and – surprise, surprise – it went off and the bullet embedded itself in a wall behind the girl missing her head by a mere inch. Our man from Vanguard very quickly filled in the hole with Polyfilla. One wonders how good Polyfilla is for holes in the head...

As leader of DUP, at close of NI Convention, referring to Vanguard member David Trimble. *The Irish Times*, March 6, 1976.

March 3, 1976
Eileen Paisley
A twister, a political Jesuit twister.

As wife of Rev Ian Paisley, in NI Convention, on John Hume. Routledge, Paul, *John Hume*, Harper Collins, 1998, p. 145.

March 25, 1976
Merlyn Rees
[I am] examining the action and resources required for the next few years to...achieve the primacy of the police.

As NI Secretary of State, announcing policy of putting RUC in front line against IRA. *The Irish Times*, March 26, 1976.

April 1, 1976
Merlyn Rees
Mrs Maire Drumm...boasted of sending British soldiers home in their coffins. She is rather like the women at the guillotine during the French revolution – she is knitting and enjoying what is going on.

As NI Secretary of State, about remarks of Sinn Féin Vice President on February 1, 1976. *The Irish Times*, April 2, 1976.

April 11, 1976
A. J. P. Taylor
I don't accept that withdrawal will necessarily lead in the end to a very bloody Civil War...the general tendency in these national conflicts is that the extremists are proven in the end to have taken the right line.

As British historian, interviewed on *RTÉ* about his advocacy of British withdrawal from NI. *The Irish Times*, April 12, 1976.

April 28, 1976
David Thornley
My presence was directed by my desire to defend free speech. If there are prosecutions, they will have to start with me.

As Labour TD, after appearing on Sinn Féin platform at GPO, Dublin, where banned meeting was held. He was later fined. *The Irish Times*, April 29, 1971.

May 5, 1976
Dr Cornelius Lucey
...if there is a dispute as to whether some particular thing such as divorce is a natural right or a religious right [and] if the minority demanding it is a religious one and a sizable one, the state may provide it for that particular group.

As Bishop of Cork and Ross. *The Irish Times*, May 6, 1976.

May 6, 1976
Thomas Passmore
Éire is more Romish than Rome itself. It would make no difference to us if birth pills were sold over the counter by the bucketful and Bills for divorce were available at ten minutes' notice. How dare he offer crumbs of civil rights to Protestants as though they were something less than human beings.

As Belfast Orange Grand Master, on comment by Bishop Lucey, above. *The Irish Times*, May 7, 1976.

August 9, 1976
Maire Drumm
When the first boy or girl is sentenced after the first of March, will you march after us until we pull the town down?...by God if it is necessary it will come down stone by stone, and if it is necessary other towns will come down, and some in England too.

As Sinn Féin Vice President, at Belfast rally about British Government proposal to refuse special category status to IRA prisoners after March 1, 1977. *The Irish Times*, October 29, 1976.

August 9, 1976
Gerry Fitt
I had a revolver in my hand and I pointed it at them... The thoughts that went through my head at that time all in the space of a few seconds were 'Gerry, this is how you die'; secondly, 'I hope to God I don't have to pull this trigger and kill someone myself.'

As leader of SDLP, on invasion of his bedroom in Belfast home by Republican crowd. *The Irish Times*, August 10, 1976.

August 29, 1976
Mairead Corrigan
[I] always thought that the people of the Falls and the people of the Shankill were just the same. Now I know.

As leader of Peace People, after march from Falls Road up Shankill Road, Belfast, following death of her sister's children when hijacked car crashed into them when driver shot dead by soldier. *The Irish Times*, August 30, 1976.

August 31, 1976
Liam Cosgrave
The Government believes the extent of violent crime by irregular, subversive, terrorist bodies…and the further threat to the institutions of the State implied by events, constitute a national emergency affecting the vital interests of the State.

As Taoiseach, proposing Declaration of Emergency which replaced that declared in 1939. *The Irish Times*, September 1, 1976.

September 2, 1976
European Commission of Human Rights
They constitute a breach of Article 3 of the Convention in the form not only of inhuman and degrading treatment but also of torture.

As Strasbourg-based body, finding breach of European Human Rights Convention by Britain in case brought by Republic on 'in-depth' techniques of interrogation used in 1971 on IRA suspects: hooding, wall-standing, use of 'white' noise and deprivation of food and sleep. *The Irish Times*, September 3, 1976.

September 2, 1976
Merlyn Rees
We regret the Irish Government's persistence in their raking over the events of five years ago…the only people who can derive any satisfaction from all this are the terrorists.

As British Home Secretary, on finding of European Commission of Human Rights, above. *The Irish Times*, September 3, 1976.

September 7, 1976
Paddy Donegan
The Government will never accept an acceptable level of violence.

As Minister for Defence in Dáil, on Criminal Law Bill (obliquely referring to celebrated remark of Reginald Maudling on December 15, 1971 on violence in Northern Ireland). *The Irish Times*, September 8, 1976.

September 26, 1976
Dr Edward Daly
Realistically, you can hardly expect the bishops to advocate a law legalising contraception, but I assure you, the door is open.

As Bishop of Derry, on debate in Republic on reform of contraceptive legislation. *The Observer*, September 26, 1976.

October 1, 1976
Allied Irish Bank Official
At this point Mr Haughey became quite vicious and told Mr Denvir that 'he would not give up his cheque book and he had to live' and 'that we were dealing with an adult and no banker would talk to him in this manner'. Furthermore he stated that if any drastic action were taken by the bank he could be a 'very troublesome adversary'.

As manager of account of Fianna Fáil TD Charles Haughey, in memo published on February 19, 1999, at Moriarty tribunal on payments to politicians. *The Irish Times*, February 19, 1999.

October 18, 1976
Paddy Donegan
It was amazing when the President sent the Emergency Powers Bill to the Supreme Court… In my opinion he is a thundering disgrace. The fact is that the Army must stand behind the State.

As Minister for Defence, to army officers at Columb Barracks, Mullingar, on decision of President Cearbhall Ó Dálaigh to refer Emergency Powers Bill to Supreme Court (reported by only journalist present, Don Lavery, who says 'thundering' was the actual word used, and that other, later, printed versions are misquotations). *The Irish Times*, October 19, 1976.

October 18, 1976
Joe Dowling
I consider today's remarks of the Minister for Defence to be a flagrant breach of both the spirit and the letter of the Constitution, compounded by the fact that they were delivered publicly before members of the Irish Army of whom the President is Commander-in-Chief.

As Fianna Fáil Defence spokesman, in Dáil, calling for resignation as Minister for Defence of Paddy Donegan for referring to President as 'thundering disgrace'. *The Irish Times*, October 19, 1976.

October 19, 1976
Cearbhall Ó Dálaigh
The gravamen of your utterance is, 'In my opinion, he is a thundering disgrace.' These words, I find, are followed by the sentence 'The fact is that the Army must stand behind the State.' Can this sequence be construed by ordinary people otherwise than as an insinuation that the president does not stand behind the State?

As President, responding in letter to speech given by Minister for Defence to army officers in Mullingar on October 18, 1976. *The Irish Times*, October 23, 1976.

October 19, 1976
Paddy Donegan
I hasten to make my apologies to you, sincerely and humbly, in this letter... I wish to tender to you my very deep regret for my use of the words 'thundering disgrace' in relation to you.

As Minister for Defence, in letter to President Cearbhall Ó Dálaigh concerning his speech of October 18, 1976. *The Irish Times*, October 23, 1976.

October 21, 1976
Liam Cosgrave
The Minister for Defence did not attack our institutions, he made what he and I regard as a serious comment on what the President did in a disrespectful way...the extent of his apology demonstrates his regret.

As Taoiseach, in Dáil, making clear Minister for Defence Paddy Donegan would not be asked to resign because of his description of President as 'thundering disgrace'. *The Irish Times*, October 22, 1976.

October 22, 1976
Cearbhall Ó Dálaigh
The only way now open to me to assert publicly my personal integrity and independence as President of Ireland – a matter of much greater importance for every citizen – to endeavour to protect the dignity and independence of the presidency as an institution is...to resign.

As President, following Dáil vote by 63-58 not to force resignation of Minister for Defence Paddy Donegan for referring to President as 'thundering disgrace'. *The Irish Times*, October 23, 1976.

October 26, 1976
Jimmy Carter
It is a mistake for our country's government to stand quiet on the struggle of the Irish for peace, for the respect of human rights and for unifying of Ireland.

As Democratic Party presidential candidate, speaking in Pittsburgh to Irish Americans. O'Hanlon, Ray, *The New Irish Americans*, Roberts Rinehart, 1997, pp. 174-175.

c. October 27, 1976
Lord Hailsham
Those bastards! Those Roman Catholic Bastards! How dare they interfere!

As Lord Chancellor, on attempts by Irish American politicians to influence British Government on Northern Ireland. To author, in interview.

October 27, 1976
James Molyneaux
The irresponsible opportunism of this peanut politician has undone much of what has been

achieved in persuading Americans to stop supplying arms to the IRA.

As leader of Ulster Unionist Party at Westminster, on Jimmy Carter's remarks, above. O'Clery, Conor, *The Greening of the White House*, Gill & Macmillan, 1996, p. 136.

October 28, 1976
Betty Williams
When I am abroad, I have my two feet firmly planted in Northern Ireland.

As leader of Peace People, in Germany, on criticism of frequent trips abroad. *The Irish Times*, October 29, 1976.

November 9, 1976
Edward du Cann
It is a matter of fury that the Government should have been saved by an MP who does not believe in the United Kingdom.

As Conservative MP, in House of Commons, on vote of independent MP for Fermanagh and South Tyrone, Frank Maguire, which prevented defeat of Labour Government. *The Irish Times*, November 10, 1976.

November 24, 1976
Bernadette McAliskey (Devlin)
When you marched in the United States, you were...a rebel against Authority. On Saturday you would be marching with Authority against the rebels.

As republican, in message to American singer, Joan Baez, on her decision to join Peace People march in London. *The Irish Times*, November 25, 1976.

November 27, 1976
Jane Ewart-Biggs
In Ireland I learned of its beauty and its sorrow, and its sorrow became my sorrow.

As widow of former British Ambassador to Ireland, Christopher Ewart-Biggs, assassinated by IRA in July, 1976, at Peace People rally in London. *The Irish Times*, November 29, 1976.

December 2, 1976
John Pardoe
A date should now be set for withdrawal and Northern Ireland politicians brought together in a constitutional conference and told that in two years the last British soldier and the last British subsidy will be gone.

As Liberal MP. *The Irish Times*, December 3, 1976.

December 6, 1976
Joan Baez
Bernadette has accused me of interfering in things I know nothing of. All I can say is that it would take her a long time to understand anything about my kind of politics.

As American folk singer, on claim by Bernadette McAliskey on November 24 that by associating with Peace People she was backing 'Authority'. *The Irish Times*, December 7, 1976.

January 6, 1977
Roy Mason
[The BBC] was disloyal, supported the rebels, purveyed their propaganda and refused to accept the advice of the Northern Ireland Office on what views to carry.

As NI Secretary of State, at dinner with BBC NI governors. *The Irish Times*, January 7, 1977.

January 9, 1977
Rev Des Wilson
I am blazingly angry when I see people traipsing up streets and over bridges. They had the opportunity to make changes in the Church but refused. What they want is peace without change.

As Belfast priest, on Catholic Church leaders who supported Peace People. *The Irish Times*, January 10, 1977.

January 23, 1977
Sean Garland
We have dismissed from our ranks, too often with bitter, even deadly consequences for ourselves, those who subscribed to militarism, opportunism and attitudes that tended towards sectarian conflict and the destruction of our class.

As national organiser of Official Sinn Féin, at party árd fheis in Dublin. *The Irish Times*, January 24, 1977.

January 27, 1977
Conor Cruise O'Brien
A new Constitution should be put before the people, omitting the present Articles 2 and 3 and freely declaring itself to be what it was…a Constitution for our actual present State consisting of 26 Counties.

As Minister for Posts and Telegraphs. *The Irish Times*, January 28, 1977.

February 8, 1977
Sam Silkin
…the five techniques will not in any circumstances be reintroduced as an aid to interrogation.

As British Attorney General, at European Court of Human Rights at Strasbourg, on use of wall-standing, 'white' noise, hooding and deprivation of food and sleep in NI interrogations. *The Irish Times*, February 9, 1977.

February 10, 1977
Roy Mason
Britain had recognised it was guilty of ill-treating fourteen persons. We admitted it and we have paid these fourteen compensation. I would think that was a first-class example of a mature democracy. Only the IRA can gain by this continuing.

As NI Secretary of State, in House of Commons, on Irish case against Britain before European Court of Human Rights. *The Irish Times*, February 11, 1977.

March 5, 1977
Charles Curran
A minister in Dublin told me once 'We in Ireland still have the whiff of gunpowder in our nostrils. That's why we have this Section.' We don't have the smell of gunpowder in Britain. That's why we don't have a Section 31 here.

As Director General of BBC, on ban in Republic on broadcasting IRA and Sinn Féin interviews. *The Irish Times*, March 5, 1977.

March 9, 1977
William Whitelaw
I shall admit that I was very wrong and that I made a major mistake when I was in Northern Ireland.

As former NI Secretary of State, on his decision to allow special category status to paramilitary prisoners. *The Irish Times*, March 12, 1977.

March 17, 1977
Tip O'Neill, Edward Kennedy, Daniel Moynihan and Hugh Carey
We appeal to our fellow Americans to embrace the goal of peace and renounce any action that promotes the current violence or provides support or encouragement for organisations engaged in violence.

As leading Irish American politicians, known as 'Four Horsemen', on Northern Ireland. *The Irish Times*, March 31, 1977.

May 2, 1977
Fred Mulley
We cannot let Northern Ireland just feel they can do what the hell they like and the British Army will always bail them out.

As British Defence Minister, on new loyalist strike. *The Irish Times*, May 14, 1977.

May 3, 1977
Rev Ian Paisley
When I consider the drunkenness, lewdness, immorality and filthy language of many of those Members, I care absolutely nothing for their opinion. Ulster Protestants are not interested in gaining the goodwill of these reprobates.

As leader of Ulster Action Council strike, in response to call from NI Secretary Roy Mason to condemn activities of his followers. *The Irish Times*, May 4, 1977.

May 3, 1977
Roy Mason
I took off in my helicopter from Stormont Castle that day, singing as I rose into the air 'Don't cry for me, Ballymena.' From the air it looked like high noon – in the streets Paisley's men, and 50 yards away, the RUC.

As NI Secretary of State recalling , in BBC interview, the failed 1977 loyalist strike in Northern Ireland. *The Irish Times*, October 15, 1988.

May 4, 1977
James Molyneaux
There is evidence that some people on the Action Council have a provisional government in mind, and are moving in that direction.

As leader of Ulster Unionist Party, at Westminster, announcing end of coalition with Rev Ian Paisley because of his organisation of loyalist strike. *The Irish Times*, May 5, 1977.

May 21, 1977
Liam Cosgrave
And remember, those people who comment so freely and write so freely – some of them aren't even Irish... Some of these are blow-ins. Now as far as we're concerned they can blow out or blow up.

As Fine Gael leader, at árd fheis, on political commentators. *The Irish Times*, May 23, 1977.

June 5, 1977
Dr Cornelius Lucey
They have to agree that the children will be brought up as Catholics. That's the second part – first they have to agree what is going to happen to their children. Then, only if their agreement is that the children will be brought up as Catholics, will they get a dispensation.

As Bishop of Cork and Ross, on conditions for dispensation for 'mixed' (Catholic and Protestant) marriages. *Sunday Press*, June 5, 1977.

June 8, 1977
Robert Muldoon
We are thinking of the people on the fringe, like the person who drove a car two years ago and now finds he can't get out of the organisation. Half the population of Northern Ireland have written to me asking 'why can't I come, I've done nothing,' but it's important to give the Peace People moral support for their work.

As New Zealand Prime Minister, on decision to allow 'converted terrorists' to settle in New Zealand. *The Irish Times*, June 9, 1977.

June 23, 1977
Airey Neave
Could not TV give our children more of the routine of danger experienced by the RUC? Is it not possible to create a series showing a Belfast Starsky and Hutch?

As Conservative NI spokesman, at Media Society dinner in London. *The Irish Times*, June 24, 1977.

July 6, 1977
James Molyneaux
They have agreed to a parliamentary pact with the Government under which they would not vote to bring it down, in return for progress on administrative devolution for Northern Ireland and an increase in the number of Northern Ireland seats at Westminster.

As leader of Ulster Unionist Party, at Westminster, on decision of unionist MPs to support minority Labour Government. *The Irish Times*, July 7, 1977.

July 31, 1977
Edward Kennedy
It is important for Irish Americans in the United States to do what we can to reassure the Protestants in Northern Ireland that they have nothing to fear from the Irish American community and that we are as concerned to reach a settlement that respects their basic rights as we are to secure the basic rights of the members of the Catholic community.

As US Senator. *The Irish Times*, August 1, 1977.

August 7, 1977
Aindrias O'Callaghan
We're telling Betty and we're telling Mairead, by all means go and sip champagne on the *Britannia*, but just tell Lizzie that as long as there's one British soldier in any part of Ireland, there will be always people who will struggle.

As Sinn Féin Ard Comhairle member, at Belfast rally, on invitation from Queen Elizabeth to Peace People leaders, Betty Williams and Mairead Corrigan, to visit her on royal yacht, *Britannia*. *The Irish Times*, August 8, 1977.

August 11, 1977
Queen Elizabeth
If this community is to survive and prosper, they must live and work together in friendship and forgiveness. There is no place here for old fears and attitudes born of history, no place for blame for what is past.

As British monarch, in speech at New University of Ulster. *The Irish Times*, August 12, 1977.

August 17, 1977
Hugh Leonard
The problem with Ireland is that it's a country full of genius but with absolutely no talent.
As author and playwright, in interview. *The Times*, August 17, 1977.

August 22, 1977
Dr Tomás Ó Fiaich
I believe that the day will come when Ulster Protestants will see that the best way to fulfil their aspirations and achieve happiness will be in the full Irish context.
As newly appointed Archbishop of Armagh. *The Irish Times*, August 22, 1977.

August 30, 1977
Jimmy Carter
The United States wholeheartedly supports peaceful means for finding a just solution that involves both parts of the community of Northern Ireland...a solution that the people in Northern Ireland as well as the Governments of Great Britain and Ireland can support.
As US President, in statement on US policy on Northern Ireland, promising investment aid if settlement reached. *The Irish Times*, August 31, 1977.

August 30, 1977
Edward Kennedy
My hope is that once a peaceful settlement is reached, the United States would undertake a Marshall-type programme of assistance to heal the wounds of the present conflict.
As US Senator, on President Carter's policy statement, above. *The Irish Times*, August 31, 1977.

September 17, 1977
Conor Cruise O'Brien
There is in fact more support for Irish unity in Britain than in [the whole] of Ireland... Goodwill to an imaginary Ireland is dangerous to people living in Ireland.
As Labour Party member, at Oxford conference, following which, in face of criticism from colleagues, he resigned party whip. *The Irish Times*, September 19, 1977.

October 3, 1977
George McGovern
A united Ireland can neither be secured nor sustained short of bloody civil conflict because Northern Ireland Protestants genuinely fear Catholicism and its influence on the Dublin Government.
As US Democratic presidential candidate. *The Irish Times*, October 4, 1977.

October 8, 1977
Irish Independence Party
We hear much talk about the use of violence to coerce a million unionists into a united Ireland. We hear too little talk about the use of force to compel half a million non-unionists to remain within a united British Kingdom.
As new NI political party, led by Fergus McAteer and Frank McManus. *The Irish Times*, October 9, 1977.

October 10, 1977
Betty Williams
The prize money would not belong to Mairead and me as some people will say. The Peace People have two and a half million pounds of projects on the table and this still would not be enough for what we have to do.
As leader of Peace People, on receiving jointly with Mairead Corrigan Nobel Peace Prize, worth £80,000, which they later decided to keep for themselves. *The Irish Times*, October 11, 1977.

October 14, 1977
Margaret Thatcher
It is a part of our country, our United Kingdom. Let the people of Ulster be assured of this – the Conservative Party stands rock firm for the Union of Great Britain and Northern Ireland.
As leader of Conservative Party, at conference in Blackpool. *The Irish Times*, October 15, 1977.

October 14, 1977
Amnesty International
Amnesty International is concerned that despite widespread allegations made public in Ireland earlier this year that persons under arrest have been maltreated, the Government of the time saw no necessity to instigate an impartial inquiry.
Report on activities in Republic of garda 'heavy gang'. *The Irish Times*, October 15, 1977.

October 19, 1977
Democratic Unionist Party
Save Ulster from Sodomy.
As party led by Rev Ian Paisley, in newspaper advertisement opposing reform of homosexual legislation. *The Irish Times*, October 20, 1977.

November 10, 1977
Rev Keith Walker
The crimes of Britain in Ireland during past centuries teach us that the moral justification of our presence in Ireland cannot be assumed, it can only be argued. We have taken from Ireland more than we have given.
As Church of England Canon, at synod in London. *The Irish Times*, November 11, 1977.

November 14, 1977
William van Straubenzee

The Republic of Ireland is a haven for terrorists and takes its place proudly alongside states like Libya who also do not recognise the obligations of civilisation.

As former Conservative Minister of State for Northern Ireland, on Republic's refusal to sign European Convention on Suppression of Terrorism. *The Irish Times*, November 15, 1977.

November 24, 1977
Roy Mason

Every terrorist would rig a complaint when in jail...prisoners were deliberately injuring themselves [and] even if they had been 'taken on', TV reporters didn't mind as long as it was good copy.

As NI Secretary of State, in House of Commons, on Thames Television programme alleging brutality against prisoners by RUC. *The Irish Times*, November 25, 1977.

December 4, 1977
Roy Mason

We are squeezing the terrorists like rolling up a toothpaste tube. We are squeezing them away from their supplies of money and explosives. We are squeezing them out of society and into prison.

As NI Secretary of State. *Daily Express*, December 5, 1977.

January 4, 1978
John McAuley

Pandering to the whim of those who wish to keep Ballymena's swimming pool open on Sundays would open the gates for a flood of godlessness such as Ulster has never seen.

As DUP Mayor of Ballymena, after using casting vote to close swimming pool on Sundays. *The Irish Times*, June 5, 1978.

January 8, 1978
Jack Lynch

If the British Government indicated that they would like to see the Irish people coming together and not continue to subsidise a small corner of Ireland, I believe the people of the North would be realistic and hard-headed enough to reach accommodation with the minority there and with ourselves.

As Taoiseach, calling for British declaration of intent to withdraw from Northern Ireland. *The Irish Times*, January 9, 1978.

January 8, 1978
Eddie McAteer

Molaim thú. Your voice is the true voice of Ireland. One more heave and we can all get some real peace.

As former Nationalist Party leader, to Taoiseach Jack Lynch, after Taoiseach called for British declaration of intent to withdraw from Northern Ireland. *The Irish Times*, January 9, 1978.

January 15, 1978
John Robb

...if the Protestants of Northern Ireland waited long enough they would either be spurned by Britain or outvoted by their Catholic fellow-Ulstermen into something they did not want.

As Co Antrim Presbyterian leader of New Ireland Movement, advocating federal Ireland at Fianna Fáil youth conference in Cork. *The Irish Times*, January 16, 1978.

January 16, 1978
Dr Tomás Ó Fiaich

I believe the British should withdraw from Ireland. I think it's the only thing that will get things moving.

As Archbishop of Armagh, in interview. January 16, 1978.

January 16, 1978
Rev Ian Paisley

[Dr Ó Fiaich] now could rightly be called the IRA's bishop from Crossmaglen.

As leader of DUP, on Archbishop of Armagh's call for British withdrawal. *The Irish Times*, January 17, 1978.

January 18, 1978
European Court of Human Rights

[The five interrogation techniques] did not occasion suffering of the particular intensity and cruelty implied by the word torture as so understood.

As Strasbourg-based body, finding UK guilty of 'ill-treatment' rather than torture in Northern Ireland. *The Irish Times*, January 19, 1978.

January 18, 1978
Michael Flannery

It's my experience from being in jail and on the [IRA flying] column in Tipperary that morale could be seriously affected by men worrying about their wives and children. If we help these people it will help the IRA to have contented men.

As leader of pro-IRA fundraising body, Irish Northern Aid (NORAID). *The Irish Times*, January 19, 1978.

January 22, 1978
Airey Neave
These actions of a neighbouring state are becoming intolerable. I invited...the Foreign Secretary to inform the Irish Government that we are no longer going to bear these insults with a stiff upper lip.

As Conservative NI spokesman, on Irish Government calls for British declaration of intent to withdraw from Northern Ireland. *The Irish Times*, January 23, 1978.

February 10, 1978
Mary Robinson
[The feminist movement] should demand a radical, planned alternative to the free enterprise society in which we live, and should examine the potential of a genuinely socialist Ireland.

As independent Senator, at University College, Galway Labour Party meeting. Siggins, Lorna, *Mary Robinson*, Mainstream Publishing, 1997, p. 212.

February 11, 1978
Garret FitzGerald
This is so partitionist a state that Northern Protestants would be bloody fools to join it.

As Fine Gael leader. *The Irish Times*, February 13, 1978.

February 18, 1978
Betty Williams
[He] has given the Provisional IRA the go-ahead to continue their campaign.

As leader of Peace People, at rally in Dublin, on Taoiseach Jack Lynch's comments on possible future amnesty for IRA. *The Irish Times*, February 21, 1978.

February 19, 1978
IRA
We accept condemnation and criticism...from the relatives and friends and from our supporters who have rightly and severely criticised us.

In statement on IRA fire-bombing of La Mon House restaurant in Co Down in which 13 people died. *The Irish Times*, February 20, 1978.

February 19, 1978
Jack Lynch
I have it from the highest authority, from the British authorities themselves, that only two percent of all violence in Northern Ireland is generated from this side of the Border.

As Taoiseach, on *RTÉ. The Irish Times*, February 20, 1978.

February 20, 1978
Roy Mason
I disagree absolutely and fundamentally with the statement that only two percent of incidents affect the Border. There has been a high attrition

rate against terrorists last year and now people are using the Border to operate from.

As NI Secretary of State, on Jack Lynch statement, above. *The Irish Times*, February 21, 1978.

April 4, 1978
Catholic Hierarchy
No change in state law can make the use of contraceptives morally right...it does not necessarily follow from this that the State is bound to prohibit the distribution and sale of contraceptives.

As Irish Bishops, in statement before meeting Minister for Health Charles Haughey. *The Irish Times*, April 5, 1978.

April 27, 1978
Harry West
Look at the birth rate. A majority of Roman Catholics will come in Northern Ireland. Not in my lifetime, but it will come. And it's inevitable that the majority will want to come into a united Ireland. It's inevitable that it will happen sometime.

As leader of Ulster Unionist Party, in interview. *The Irish Times*, April 27, 1978.

May 10, 1978
Tip O'Neill
The Protestants in Northern Ireland today have every right to be regarded as Irishmen. After all, if that were not the case, my family would not be entitled to call themselves Americans – for we have been in this country a far shorter time than those Protestants have been in Northern Ireland.

As Speaker of US House of Representatives, at Ireland Fund dinner in New York. *The Irish Times*, May 23, 1978.

May 28, 1978
Josie Airey
It's a strange thing that they could take Britain to the European Court on torture charges, while their laws have been torturing me for years.

As Cork woman, on ruling of European Human Rights Commission that she had been denied proper access to Irish courts to obtain legal separation, because of lack of legal aid. *The Irish Times*, May 29, 1978.

June 18, 1978
Rev Ian Paisley
It certainly does not become the Protestant cause, or anybody claiming to be Protestant, to act in the same way the IRA has acted, and I would appeal to those responsible to return this gentleman to his home in peace and quietness and in safety.

As leader of DUP, appealing (successfully) for release of Co Antrim priest, Rev Hugh Murphy, kidnapped by loyalists after RUC constable, William Turbot, had been abducted by IRA (and subsequently killed). *The Irish Times*, June 19, 1978.

June 19, 1978
Louis Hasrouni
If any Irish or other United Nations troops come in we will defend ourselves and shoot if necessary – unless of course they telephoned us first and let us know they are coming.

As pro-Israeli Lebanese militia leader, on deployment of Irish UN troops in south Lebanon. *The Irish Times*, June 20, 1978.

July 6, 1978
Rev Ian Paisley
I would like to solemnly protest in the name of the Lord, Jesus Christ, the great King and head of the Church. You can't reverse 400 years of history. The mass is a blasphemous fable and a dangerous deceit.

As leader of Free Presbyterian Church, to Cardinal Hume in Westminster Hall crypt where Mass was being celebrated for first time in four centuries. *The Irish Times*, June 7, 1978.

August 1, 1978
Dr Tomás Ó Fiaich
One would hardly allow an animal to remain in such conditions... The stench and filth in some of the cells, with the remains of rotten food and human excreta scattered around the walls was unbearable. In two of them I was unable to speak for fear of vomiting... No one could look on them as criminals. These boys are determined not to have criminal status imposed on them.

As Archbishop of Armagh, after visit to Maze Prison where Republican prisoners were engaged in 'dirty' protest in claim for political prisoner status. *The Irish Times*, August 2, 1978.

August 14, 1978
Daily Mirror
The Mirror believes that there is a policy – and only one – that can be carried through to success. And that is for Britain to announce its unshakable intention to withdraw altogether from Northern Ireland.

As British newspaper, announcing change in editorial policy. *Daily Mirror*, August 14, 1978.

October 13, 1978
Margaret Thatcher
If you wash your hands of Northern Ireland, you wash them in blood.

As Conservative Party leader, at party conference in Brighton, on calls for British withdrawal. *The Irish Times*, October 14, 1978.

December 15, 1978
Jack Lynch
The decision we have taken today...will add a further dimension to partition, although the ultimate benefits of membership of the system could outweigh the problems.

As Taoiseach, in Dáil, on decision to join European Monetary System which meant Irish pound would break with sterling. *The Irish Times*, December 16, 1978.

January 18, 1979
Rev Ian Paisley
These [cross-border EEC projects] are worked out by the Irish Government, our traditional enemy, and the British Government, which doesn't understand Ulster. No elected representative in Northern Ireland has any say. It gets our hackles up. We want to know what's going on.

As leader of DUP, on first visit to EEC headquarters in Brussels. *The Irish Times*, January 19, 1979.

February 28, 1979
Charles Haughey
The Bill seeks to provide an Irish solution to an Irish problem.

As Taoiseach, on Bill allowing availability of contraceptives on doctor's prescription. *Irish Independent*, March 3, 1979.

March 14, 1979
Robert Irwin
I have the records of one hundred and sixty patients...who have injuries I would not say were self-inflicted.

As Forensic Medical Officer, claiming ill-treatment of IRA and other suspects in Castlereagh Detention Centre by RUC. *The Irish Independent*, March 15, 1979.

March 16, 1979
Bennet Report
There can – whatever the precise explanation – be no doubt that the injuries were not self-inflicted and were sustained during the period of police detention at a police office.

As official report rejecting Northern Ireland Office claims that injuries received by prisoners at Castlereagh Detention Centre in Belfast were self-inflicted. *Irish Independent*, March 17, 1979.

March 28, 1979
Gerry Fitt
Because of what you have done in the last five years – disregarded the minority and appeased the blackmailers of the Northern Ireland Unionist majority – I cannot go into your lobby tonight.

As leader of SDLP, in House of Commons, on why he could not support Labour Government, which fell by vote of 311-310. *Irish Independent*, March 29, 1979.

March 28, 1979
Frank Maguire
You could say I came over to London to abstain in person.

As independent Fermanagh-South Tyrone MP, on refusing to vote to keep Labour in Government. To author.

March 30, 1979
Gerry Fitt
He said he would hold a most searching inquiry into these allegations and if he found any persons were responsible they would meet the full fury of his wrath, because he, as a prisoner of war, had suffered interrogation at the hands of the Gestapo – 'Gerry' [he said], 'it leaves its mark on you.'

As SDLP MP, on conversation with incoming NI Secretary of State, Airey Neave, on alleged ill-treatment of IRA suspects, 40 minutes before Neave was killed by INLA bomb in House of Commons car park. *Irish Independent*, March 31, 1979.

April 19, 1979
Tip O'Neill
We have been concerned that the problem has been treated as a political football in London.

As Speaker of US House of Representatives, in Dublin, on Northern Ireland. *The Irish Press*, April 20, 1979.

May 11, 1979
General James Glover
The Provisional IRA (PIRA) has the dedication and the sinews of war to raise violence intermittently to at least the level of early 1978, certainly for the foreseeable future...there is a strata of intelligent, astute and experienced terrorists who provide the backbone of the organisation...our evidence of the calibre of rank and file terrorists does not support the view that they are merely mindless hooligans drawn from the unemployed and unemployable.

As British Army strategist, in document 'NI – Future Terrorist Trends', leaked to IRA. *The Irish Press*, May 11, 1979.

July 18, 1979
Rev Ian Paisley
In the name of Ulster's dead, I indict you for harbouring their murderers.

As DUP leader, in European Parliament when Taoiseach Jack Lynch began address, in Irish, as incoming President of EEC Council. *The Irish Press*, July 19, 1979.

July 18, 1979
John Taylor
[He] started babbling away in Irish which is not even an official EEC language.

As Unionist MEP, on why he followed Rev Ian Paisley out of European Parliament chamber when Taoiseach Jack Lynch spoke in Irish. *The Irish Times*, July 19, 1979.

July 22, 1979
Rev Ian Paisley
[The Pope] is anti-Christ, the man of sin in the Church. Pope Benedict blessed the 1916 rebels...from that has flowed the IRA.

As leader of DUP, saying visit of Pope John Paul II to Northern Ireland was 'not on'. *The Irish Press*, July 23, 1979.

August 27, 1979
Prince Charles
I fear it will take me a very long time to forgive those people who today achieved something that two World Wars and thousands of Germans and Japanese failed to achieve.

As Prince of Wales, on killing of his uncle, Lord Mountbatten, by IRA. Dimbleby, Jonathan, *The Prince of Wales, A Biography*, Warner Books, 1995, p. 324.

August 29, 1979
Rev Romeo Panciroli
With deep regret, due to the dreadful murders of recent days, it has now been decided not to include a venue in Northern Ireland in the Papal itinerary.

As Director of Vatican Press Office, announcing that IRA killing of Lord Mountbatten and 18 British soldiers had caused cancellation of papal visit to Northern Ireland. *The Irish Times*, August 30, 1979.

August 30, 1979
John Taylor
If the leadership of the Loyalist paramilitaries find it absolutely impossible to refrain from renewed action on the ground, then in no way can that action occur on Ulster's soil. It should be directed to targets within the Republic of Ireland.

As unionist MP, after killing by IRA of Lord Mountbatten and 18 British soldiers. *The Irish Times*, August 31, 1979.

September 1, 1979
IRA
We will tear out their sentimental, imperialist heart.

In statement, referring to British establishment, after killing Lord Mountbatten. *The Republican News*, September 1, 1979.

September 2, 1979
Samuel Duddy
It's people like John Taylor...who have egged on loyalists with inflammatory speeches and then stepped back to allow the rank and file to take the rap.

As spokesman for Ulster Defence Association. *The Irish Times*, September 3, 1979.

September 9, 1979
Sile de Valera
If our political leaders are not seen to be furthering our republican aspirations through constitutional means, the idealistic young members of our community will become disillusioned...and turn to violence to achieve their aims.

As Fianna Fáil TD and granddaughter of Eamon de Valera, in speech at Liam Lynch commemoration at Fermoy, Co Cork, seen as challenge to leadership of Jack Lynch. *The Irish Times*, September 10, 1979.

September 23, 1979
Jack Lynch
We...have no wish to pressurise our Northern fellow-countrymen to take steps they are not ready for.

As Taoiseach, in Waterville, Co Kerry, replying to Sile de Valera, above. *The Irish Times*, September 24, 1979.

September 26, 1979
Martin Smyth and Walter Williams
While you and your predecessors have called for peace and justice, the reality is that your followers continue to destroy peace and deny the very basic right to life, and call forth counter atrocities from people who have suffered grievously. The full rites of the Roman Catholic sacramental system have been given to the IRA.

As Grand Master and Grand Secretary of Orange Order of Ireland, in open letter to Pope John Paul II on his visit to Ireland. *The Irish Times*, September 27, 1979.

September 30, 1979
Pope John Paul II
On my knees I beg of you to turn away from the paths of violence and to return to the ways of peace. You may claim to seek justice. I too believe in justice and seek justice. But violence only delays the day of justice. Violence destroys the work of justice...do not follow any leaders who train you in the ways of inflicting death.

As Pontiff, in Drogheda, in appeal to IRA on two-day visit to Republic. *The Irish Times*, October 1, 1979.

October 2, 1979
IRA
In all conscience we believe that force is by far the only means of removing the evil of the British presence in Ireland...we know also that upon victory, the [Catholic] Church would have no difficulty in recognising us.

Responding to Pope's appeal for peace at Drogheda. *The Irish Times*, October 3, 1979.

October 3, 1979
Patrick Hillery
It has come to my attention that there were rumours circulating as to the possibility of my resigning as President... I am not resigning... There is not a problem. There are difficulties for people living in public life but thank God we have a happy family life.

As President, denying rumours of domestic difficulties to political reporters summoned to Áras an Uachtaráin. *The Irish Times*, October 4, 1979.

October 13, 1979
Princess Margaret
The Irish, they're pigs. Oh, oh! You're Irish!

As sister of British monarch, in Chicago, in comment at dinner to Mayor Jane Byrne about death of Lord Mountbatten, as related by hostess of dinner. *The Irish Times*, October 17, 1979.

October 20, 1979
Governor Ronald Reagan
It's tragic that so much is being done in the name of God and it's the same God.

As Republican presidential candidate, in interview on Northern Ireland. *The Irish Times*, October 20, 1979.

November 10, 1979
Charles Haughey
Pearse's enemies claim that the Rising of 1916 denies him the right to be called a democrat. He is reviled as a militarist, a man who glorified in war. The truth, however, is that Pearse sought freedom in arms only because there was no other way open to him in the circumstances of the time.

As Minister for Health, in speech regarded as challenge to moderate policy on Northern Ireland of Taoiseach Jack Lynch. *The Irish Times*, November 12, 1979.

November 11, 1979
Jack Lynch
The paradox of Pearse's message for the Irish nation is that we must work and live for Ireland, not die, and most certainly not kill for it.

As Taoiseach, in Boston, after hearing reports of remarks by Charles Haughey, above. *The Irish Times*, November 12, 1979.

November 13, 1979
Bill Loughnane
He hid the thing from us at the parliamentary party meeting. He said there was going to be no infringement of our sovereignty...you can tell the truth some place and lie in the other place.

As Fianna Fáil TD, in comments about permitted but previously undisclosed British overflights along Border, which led to resignation of Jack Lynch as Taoiseach and party leader when Parliamentary Party refused to discipline Mr Loughnane.

November 14, 1979
Conor Cruise O'Brien

He was a manic, mystic nationalist with a cult of blood sacrifice and a strong personal motivation towards death. A nation which takes a personality of that type as its mentor is headed towards disaster.

As former Labour minister, on Padraic Pearse centenary. *The Irish Times*, November 15, 1979.

November 22, 1979
Gerry Fitt

I regard myself as representing the voice of sanity, the voice of concern, the voice that believes in political dialogue.

As leader of SDLP, resigning on grounds that party had become too 'Republican'. *The Irish Times*, November 23, 1979.

December 11, 1979
Garret FitzGerald

Deputy Haughey presents himself here seeking to be invested in office...but he comes with a flawed pedigree. His motives can be judged ultimately only by God but we cannot ignore the fact that he differs from his predecessors in that these motives have been and are widely impugned, most notably but by no means exclusively by people within his own party... They and others...have attributed to him an overweening ambition...a wish to dominate, even to own, the State.

As Fine Gael leader, on Charles Haughey taking office as Taoiseach. *The Irish Times*, January 14, 1979.

December 11, 1979
Jim Tunney

I don't buy my colours coming out of the stadium.

As Fianna Fáil TD, on his public backing for George Colley in Fianna Fáil leadership contest. Whelan, Ken, and Masterson, Eugene, *Bertie Ahern*, Blackwater Press, 1998, p. 29.

January 1980
Lord Denning

If the six men win it will mean the police were guilty of perjury, that they were guilty of violence and threats, that the confessions were involuntary and were improperly admitted in evidence and that the convictions were erroneous. That would mean the Home Secretary would either have to recommend they be pardoned or he would have to remit the case to the Court of Appeal. This is such an appalling vista that every sensible person in the land would say: 'It cannot be right that these actions should go further.'

As Master of the Rolls, dismissing appeals of Birmingham Six, serving life for 1974 pub bombings, and later exonerated. Mullin, Chris, *Error of Judgement*, Chatto & Windus, 1986, p. 216.

January 9, 1980
Charles Haughey

We have been living away beyond our means. We have been living at a rate which is just not justified by the amounts of goods and services we have been producing. To make up the difference we have been borrowing enormous amounts of money, borrowing at a rate which just can't continue.

As Taoiseach, addressing nation, at time when he had personal debts of £1.143 million. Smyth, Sam, *Thanks a Million Big Fella*, Blackwater Press, 1997, p. 53.

January 11, 1980
Yasser Arafat

I could challenge the Israelis or any British source for one single proof of an IRA connection. It is a big lie.

As leader of Palestinian Liberation Organisation, speaking to Irish TDs in Beirut on allegations PLO helped IRA. *The Irish Times*, January 12, 1980.

February 16, 1980
Charles Haughey

The situation is pretty desperate. It has gone on for too long... I am inviting the British Government to join with us in bringing forward a final and lasting solution.

As Taoiseach, at Fianna Fáil árd fheis, on situation in Northern Ireland. *The Irish Times*, February 18, 1980.

April 10, 1980
Vladimir Guncherov

We have a class approach. We do not hide the fact that our sympathies are with the oppressed people of Afghanistan, just as they are with the oppressed Catholic people of Northern Ireland.

As foreign editor of Soviet news agency, TASS. *The Irish Times*, April 11, 1980.

April 11, 1980
Patrick Cooney

The vast majority of Fine Gael TDs and Senators are opposed to any change in our laws [forbidding] divorce... The time and resources of Parliament would be better spent devising ways and means to prepare young people for marriage and its obligations.

As Fine Gael TD. *The Irish Times*, April 12, 1980.

April 28, 1980
Saad Haddad
Whoever will look at Mr Haughey's past will
find that the man himself was a gun-runner for
the IRA and is known for his good relations with
terrorists in Europe and the Middle East.

As leader of pro-Israeli militia in south Lebanon, after
criticism of his forces by Taoiseach Charles Haughey over
clashes with Irish UN soldiers. *The Irish Times,* April 29,
1980.

May 1, 1980
John Hume
Churchill's Dunkirk exhortation 'The situation is
serious but not desperate,' is said to have evoked
a somewhat bleary comment from an Irish
listener 'Over here the situation is always
desperate but never serious'.

As leader of SDLP, writing in US Journal *Foreign Affairs.*
The Irish Times, May 21, 1980.

May 20, 1980
Margaret Thatcher
[The constitutional affairs of Northern Ireland
are] a matter for the people of Northern Ireland,
this government and this parliament and no one
else.

As British Prime Minister, in House of Commons, before
meeting Taoiseach Charles Haughey. *The Irish Times,*
May 21, 1980.

June 9, 1980
Charles Haughey
If there is a prospect of moving to unity, to some
new arrangement, then we have no doubt
whatever that the wishes of the northern
unionists, particularly the Protestant people of
Northern Ireland, can be provided for both in
regard to divorce, contraception or any of these
other things about which they have strong
feelings.

As Taoiseach, on BBC, after meeting British Prime
Minister Margaret Thatcher. *The Irish Times,* June 10,
1980.

July 7, 1980
Neil Blaney
[Sean Donlon's] performance out there was such
that he was doing us no favours because of his
attitude towards those who were trying to bring
to the notice of the public the state of affairs in
Ireland.

As independent TD, on reports that Taoiseach Charles
Haughey planned to transfer Irish Ambassador to
Washington, Sean Donlon, as part of deal whereby
Blaney would return to Fianna Fáil. *The Irish Times,* July
8, 1980.

July 8, 1980
Daniel Patrick Moynihan
Sean Donlon is an outstanding ambassador. He is
knowledgeable, thoughtful and responsible. No
one has done more for Irish-American relations.

As US senator, objecting (successfully) with others to plans
by Taoiseach Charles Haughey to transfer Irish Ambassador
to Washington, Sean Donlon. *The Irish Times,* July 9, 1980.

July 27, 1980
Charles Haughey
There is a clear and conclusive evidence available
to the Government here from security and other
sources that NORAID has provided support for
the campaign of violence...on the basis of these
activities, it stands condemned.

As Taoiseach, on policy towards Irish Northern Aid
(NORAID) and other Irish-American organisations
sympathetic to IRA. *The Irish Times,* July 28, 1980.

July 27, 1980
Jim Gibbons
You can't go on indefinitely living with a lie. If you
attempt it you will be a miserable person.

As former Minister for Defence, in comment addressed to
Taoiseach Charles Haughey on his role in 1970 arms crisis.
The Irish Times, July 28, 1980.

October 28, 1980
Margaret Thatcher
There will be no concessions to those on hunger
strike. None at all.

As British Prime Minister, in House of Commons, on IRA
hunger strike in Maze prison for political status. *The Irish
Times,* October 29, 1980.

November 2, 1980
Sile de Valera
As a woman, I am deeply shocked by Mrs
Thatcher's lack of compassion on the issue of H
Blocks. [If] the situation is allowed to continue
and deteriorate, the British Government must
shoulder responsibility for further deaths, whether
it be in H Blocks or the streets or elsewhere
throughout the Six Counties.

As Fianna Fáil TD, in remarks on IRA hunger strikes in
Maze Prison 'H' Blocks which Fianna Fáil disowned. *The
Irish Times,* November 3, 1980.

November 11, 1980
Gerry Fitt
In 1972, I went to Willy Whitelaw, to every
corridor, to every tearoom in the House of
Commons and pleaded time after time to grant
political or special category status because I
believed it would in some way bring to an end the
terrible situation which had brought about by the

introduction of internment...I was wrong. It is a tragedy to have to admit it.

As Independent Socialist MP, on hunger strike by IRA prisoners in Northern Ireland for political status. *The Irish Times*, November 12, 1980.

November 16, 1980
Garret FitzGerald

We have always in this state rejected the demand for political status. We cannot urge another government to do what the Irish Government did not do.

As Fine Gael leader, on hunger strike by IRA prisoners in Northern Ireland for political status. *The Irish Times*, November 15, 1980.

November 25, 1980
Charles Haughey

The Government believe that if some adjustments could be made in the prison rules themselves, or in their interpretation, or in their application, a solution would be possible.

As Taoiseach, in Dáil, on hunger strike by IRA prisoners in Northern Ireland for political status. *The Irish Times*, November 26, 1980.

December 8, 1980
Charles Haughey and Margaret Thatcher

They...decided to devote their next meeting in London during the coming year to special consideration of the totality of relationships within these islands.

As Irish and British Prime Ministers, in joint communiqué after meeting in Dublin. *The Irish Times*, December 9, 1980.

December 8, 1980
Charles Haughey

[I am] hopeful [we are] in the middle of a historic breakthrough.

As Taoiseach, after meeting British Prime Minister Margaret Thatcher in Dublin. *The Irish Times*, December 9, 1980.

December 12, 1980
Brian Lenihan

As far as we are concerned, everything is on the table.

As Minister for Foreign Affairs, on meeting between Taoiseach and British Prime Minister. *The Irish Times*, December 13, 1980.

December 18, 1980
Republican Prisoners

In ending our hunger strike, we make it clear that failure by the British Government to act in a responsible manner towards ending the conditions which forced us to a hunger strike

will lead to inevitable and continual strife within H Blocks.

As prisoners, in Maze prison 'H' blocks, after 53 days on hunger strike. *The Irish Times*, December 19, 1980.

December 25, 1980
Robin Berrington

Ireland [is] pretty small potatoes compared to other countries of Europe...no great issues burn up the wires between Dublin and Washington...the high cost of goods, their unavailability, the dreary urbanscapes, the constant strikes and the long, dank and damp winters combine to gnaw away at one's enthusiasm for being here.

As US Embassy Cultural Affairs Officer, in circular letter to friends in Washington which was leaked to *The Irish Times*, as a result of which he was ordered to return to America. *The Irish Times*, January 28, 1981.

January 8, 1981
Enoch Powell

[Rev Ian Paisley is] the most resourceful, inveterate and dangerous enemy of Unionism...a greater threat to the Union than the Foreign Office and the Provisional IRA rolled into one.

As unionist MP. *The Irish Times*, January 9, 1981.

February 1, 1981
Andy Tyrie

The only way to beat terrorists is to terrorise them.

As leader of UDA. *The Irish Times*, February 2, 1981.

February 4, 1981
Yuri Ustimenko

If a person goes to bed late, he is Catholic, if early, a Protestant. Moreover, the Irish possess the astonishing ability of being able to determine the religion of people unknown to them from a first glance.

As correspondent of Soviet news agency, TASS, in book, *Ireland*, published in Moscow. *The Irish Times*, February 4, 1981.

February 5, 1981
Republican Prisoners

Our last hunger strikers were morally blackmailed... Where is the peace in the prisons which, like a promise, was held before dying men's eyes?

As prisoners in Maze and Armagh prisons, warning of further hunger strikes. *The Irish Times*, February 6, 1981.

February 6, 1981
Rev Ian Paisley

As elected leader of the Protestant people, I have entered into a compact with these men...with the help of God they and I...will yet defeat the most nefarious conspiracy that has ever been hatched against a free people.

As DUP leader, at midnight show of strength with men brandishing firearms certificates in Co Antrim in protest against Haughey-Thatcher communiqué of December 8, 1980. *The Irish Times*, February 7, 1981.

February 9, 1981
Rev Ian Paisley

All they want to do is kill, kill, kill Protestants... All they had to do is to go to their priest and get a pardon. Isn't it remarkable that all the worst crimes of republican violence have been committed immediately after Mass?

As leader of Free Presbyterian Church, on IRA, in sermon in Belfast. *The Irish Times*, February 10, 1981.

March 1, 1981
Dr Edward Daly

I do not believe that it is morally justified to endanger health or life by hunger strike in the present circumstances.

As Bishop of Derry, on new hunger strike by Republican prisoner, Bobby Sands and others for political prisoner status. *The Irish Times*, March 2, 1981.

March 4, 1981
Bobby Sands

If I die, God will understand.

As IRA hunger striker, in prison interview. *The Irish Times*, March 5, 1981.

March 5, 1981
Margaret Thatcher

There is no such thing as political murder, political bombing or political violence. There is only criminal murder, criminal bombing and criminal violence.

As British Prime Minister, in Belfast, vowing there would be no compromise on political status for prisoners. *The Irish Times*, March 6, 1981.

March 6, 1981
Dr Denis Hurley

Be quite clear about it, both the white South Africans and the oppressed majority of the people of South Africa clearly interpret the tour as an acceptance of apartheid.

As Archbishop of Durban on proposed Irish Rugby Football Union tour of South Africa. *The Irish Times*, March 7, 1981.

March 9, 1981
Charles Haughey

You know what I want – so what do you want?

As Fianna Fáil leader, asking independent TD Tony Gregory for support to form a government (cost of which amounted to £150 million). Whelan, Ken, and

Masterson, Eugene, *Bertie Ahern*, Blackwater Press, 1998, p. 35.

April 20, 1981
Neil Blaney

I felt that to try in any way to press him to give up his hunger strike would be futile. I do not think that this kind of torture should be added to his condition.

As independent TD after visit to hunger striker Bobby Sands after he was elected MP for Fermanagh-South Tyrone. *The Irish Times*, April 21, 1981.

April 27, 1981
Gerry Adams

Attempts to justify the British Government's ghoulish preoccupation with killing Bobby Sands flies in the face of all logic – either moral or factual. The H Blocks crisis did not have to come to death...efforts to project the political prisoners as criminal have floundered upon the rocks of the five years of passive protest by 400 Republican prisoners.

As Vice President of Sinn Féin, on hunger strike by Bobby Sands. *The Irish Times*, April 28, 1981.

April 30, 1981
Cardinal Basil Hume

Any hunger strike to death that includes within it the intention to die is suicide.

As Archbishop of Westminster, on IRA hunger strikes. *The Irish Times*, May 1, 1981.

April 30, 1981
Rev John Magee

All life is sacred and must be preserved as a gift from God. I therefore appealed, in the name of Christ and his vicar on earth, saying that violence of all kinds must be condemned in the clearest terms as being against the law of God.

As special envoy of Pope John Paul, after visits to Bobby Sands to ask him to give up hunger strike. *The Irish Times*, May 1, 1981.

April 30, 1981
Humphrey Atkins

Don't listen to the Provisionals. Don't believe lies and rumours. Do listen to your local clergymen... We will be making it our business to ensure that the news media gets the facts so listen to that too.

As NI Secretary of State, to people of Northern Ireland, as IRA hunger striker, Bobby Sands, slipped into coma. *The Irish Times*, May 1, 1981.

May 5, 1981
Margaret Thatcher
Mr Sands was a convicted criminal. He chose to take his own life, a choice that his organisation did not allow to many of their victims.

As British Prime Minister, in House of Commons, after death of hunger striker Bobby Sands. *The Irish Times*, May 6, 1981.

May 6, 1981
Republican Prisoners
You have got your pound of flesh, now give us our rights. Do not for one minute think that we are going to allow you to rob us of our principles. There are more Bobby Sands in these Blocks and we will continue to die if need be to safeguard these principles.

As prisoners in Maze prison, in statement directed to British Prime Minister, Margaret Thatcher, after death of hunger striker Bobby Sands. *The Irish Times*, May 7, 1981.

May 10, 1981
Dr Edward Daly
I would not describe Bobby Sands's death as suicide. I could not accept that. I don't think he intended to bring about his own death.

As Bishop of Derry, on Cardinal Hume's statement of April 30 on hunger strike deaths. *The Irish Times*, May 11, 1981.

May 15, 1981
Edward Kennedy
Unfeeling inflexibility will achieve nothing but more deaths.

As US senator, on death of second IRA hunger striker, Francis Hughes. *The Irish Times*, May 16, 1981.

June 3, 1981
Alexander Haig
If there were not Great Britain playing the role that it's playing there today, we might even have to create one to prevent a blood bath.

As US Secretary of State, on British presence in Northern Ireland. *The Irish Times*, June 4, 1981.

June 4, 1981
Garret FitzGerald
We are on the brink of a unique breakthrough in Irish politics, that is, the emergence of Fine Gael as the larger single party in the State... Should this assessment be correct, and should we require additional support in the Dáil, we are prepared to discuss with the Labour Party the formation of a strong alternative Government.

As Fine Gael leader, at Newbridge, Co Kildare, during election campaign. *The Irish Times*, June 5, 1981.

June 24, 1981
Charles Haughey
A shaky and uncertain coalition Government would be a sure recipe for a prolonged period of political instability.

As Taoiseach, appealing (unsuccessfully) for support of independent TDs to enable Fianna Fáil to remain in office after general election. *The Irish Times*, June 25, 1981.

July 6, 1981
Mother Teresa
I see people who are hungry because they haven't got food, but I've never dealt with people who are hungry because they chose to be hungry.

As visitor to Corrymeela reconciliation centre in Co Antrim, on IRA hunger strikes. *The Irish Times*, June 7, 1981.

August 10, 1981
Rev Michael Flanagan
[It was] disappointing when those who called the hunger strike did not end it when they achieved particular political-electoral victories in both North and South, and thus spare their own members and families and communities continued suffering.

As parish priest of Bellaghy, at funeral service for hunger striker, Thomas McElwee, prompting walk-out by Bernadette McAliskey and others. *The Irish Times*, August 11, 1981.

August 10, 1981
Bernadette McAliskey (Devlin)
What he was saying to those of us who have been trying to save the prisoners was that we've been playing with these young men's lives for electoral gain in Free State elections. The hunger strike was never called to achieve any electoral victory.

As republican activist, on remarks of Rev Michael Flanagan, above. *The Irish Times*, August 11, 1981.

August 22, 1981
John Kelly
[The State] is lying, panting, exhausted by her own weight, and being rent by a farrow of cannibal piglets.

As Fine Gael TD, on need to curb public expenditure, paraphrasing Joyce: 'Ireland is the old sow that eats her farrow.' *The Irish Times*, August 22, 1981.

August 26, 1981
Owen Carron
Dr FitzGerald's father was a gunman and nobody inquired into the legitimacy of that. So if a thing is legitimate in 1920, I don't see what makes it illegitimate in 1981.

As MP for Fermanagh-south Tyrone after winning by-election on death of Bobby Sands. *The Irish Times*, August 27, 1981.

August 30, 1981
Ken Livingstone
What I would say to everybody who's got arms and is carrying arms in Northern Ireland, whether they are in the British Army or the IRA, is to put those arms down and go back to your home... I think that there would be no greater move for peace than if the British forces just packed up and went home.

As leader of Greater London Council, on British Forces Broadcasting Service. *The Irish Times*, August 31, 1981.

September 6, 1981
Dr Cahal Daly
Your capacity for endurance, however misguided, is not so common in this materialistic age that Ireland can afford to be deprived of it.

As Bishop of Down and Connor, appealing to republican prisoners to call off hunger strike. *The Irish Times*, September 7, 1981.

September 19, 1981
Fidel Castro
The Irish patriots are in the process of writing one of the most heroic pages in human history.

As President of Cuba, on republican hunger strike. *The Irish Times*, September 19, 1981.

September 26, 1981
Edward Koch
If enough of us spoke out and urged the English to get out and let the Irish settle their differences, the English would return to England, as they should.

As Mayor of New York. *The Irish Times*, September 26, 1981.

September 27, 1981
Garret FitzGerald
What I want to do is to lead a crusade – a republican crusade – to make this a genuine republic on the principles of Tone and Davis... If I was a Northern Protestant today, I can't see how I could aspire to getting involved in a state which is itself sectarian.

As Taoiseach, on *RTÉ*. *The Irish Times*, September 28, 1980.

September 28, 1981
Charles Haughey
Davis had said, 'A free people can afford to be generous. A struggling people cannot and should not be so'...I cannot accept this self-abasement, this suggestion that we in the Republic have something to be ashamed of because of Partition.

As Fianna Fáil leader, responding to remarks by Taoiseach Garret FitzGerald, above. *The Irish Times*, September 29, 1981.

October 4, 1981
Republican Prisoners
...a considerable majority of the present hunger strikers' families have indicated that they will intervene and under these circumstances, we feel that the hunger strike must, for tactical reasons, be suspended.

As prisoners in Maze prison, calling off hunger strike for political status. *The Irish Times*, October 5, 1981.

October 10, 1981
Rev Denis Faul
It takes two glasses of whiskey to bring an Englishman up to the functional level of an Irishman.

As Dungannon priest, on dealings with British officials. *The Irish Times*, October 10, 1981.

October 11, 1981
Charles Haughey
Eamon de Valera and his comrades had at all times to fight against the remnants of that colonial mentality that still linger on in Irish life...we can see emerging once more in modern Ireland that mentality...we will not apologise to anyone for being what we are.

As Fianna Fáil leader, at unveiling of de Valera memorial at Ennis, Co Clare. *The Irish Times*, October 12, 1981.

October 11, 1981
Rt Rev Walton Empey
I happen to believe that on the whole we have a very fine constitution... It would I believe be a sad mistake to use any change as a means of wooing the Northern unionist...he will not be slow to see through it.

As Church of Ireland Bishop of Limerick, at synod in Tralee. *The Irish Times*, October 12, 1981.

October 31, 1981
Danny Morrison
Who here really believes we can win the war through the ballot box? But will anyone here object if, with a ballot paper in this hand, and an armalite in this hand, we take power in Ireland?

As Sinn Féin director of publicity, at party árd fheis in Dublin. *The Irish Times*, November 2, 1981.

November 6, 1981
Garret FitzGerald and Margaret Thatcher
Recognising the unique character of the relationship between the two countries, the Prime Minister and the Taoiseach have decided to establish an Anglo-Irish intergovernment council, through which institutional expression can be given to that relationship. This will involve regular meetings between the two Governments.

As Irish and British prime ministers, in communiqué after meeting at Downing Street. *The Irish Times*, November 7, 1981.

November 10, 1981
Charles Haughey
Britain will now proceed to deal with Northern Ireland as if it were an internal British problem [and] turn to the world and say all is well between her and Ireland.

As Fianna Fáil leader, in Dáil, criticising establishment of Anglo-Irish intergovernmental council. *The Irish Times*, November 11, 1981.

November 10, 1981
Margaret Thatcher
Northern Ireland is part of the United Kingdom – as much as my constituency is.

As British Prime Minister and MP for Finchley, in House of Commons (often misquoted as 'Northern Ireland is as British as Finchley'). *HC Debates*: Vol. 12: Col. 427.

November 10, 1981
Rev Ian Paisley
On behalf of the people of Ulster, I brand you a traitor and a liar.

As DUP leader, in House of Commons, to British Prime Minister, Margaret Thatcher, after her assurances that agreement with Garret FitzGerald did not affect Union. *The Irish Times*, November 12, 1981.

November 14, 1981
IRA
Armchair generals who whip up anti-nationalist murder gangs...cannot expect to remain forever immune from the effects of their evil work.

In statement on killing of unionist MP, Rev Robert Bradford. *The Irish Times*, November 21, 1981.

November 22, 1981
Cardinal Tomás Ó Fiaich
...participation in...murder, wounding, intimidation, kidnapping, destruction of property or any other form of violence is a mortal sin.

As Primate of Ireland, on IRA actions, after killing of unionist MP, Rev Robert Bradford. *The Irish Times*, November 28, 1981.

November 22, 1981
Dr Edward Daly
No member of our Church can remain a member, and at the same time remain a member of any organisation that decided of its own accord to perpetuate cold-blooded murder...whatever the motive, whatever the ideal.

As Bishop of Derry. *The Irish Times*, November 28, 1981.

December 27, 1981
Charles McCreevy
The Irish people need some leadership and it is not being supplied.

As Fianna Fáil TD, signalling opposition to party leader Charles Haughey, for which he was expelled from parliamentary party. *Sunday Tribune*, December 27, 1981.

January 11, 1982
Fred O'Donovan
Death on demand is what we are talking about.

As RTÉ chairman, referring to abortion. *The Irish Times*, January 14, 1983.

January 13, 1982
Lord Gowrie
The Border is an economic nonsense. Just look at the agriculture system – anyone with initiative can laugh all the way to the bank by fiddling.

As NI Minister of State. *Belfast Telegraph*, January 13, 1982.

January 27, 1982
Charles Haughey
It is a matter for the President to consider the situation which has arisen now that the Taoiseach has ceased to retain the support of the majority in Dáil Éireann. I am available for consultation by the President should he so wish.

As Fianna Fáil leader, after defeat of Fine Gael-led Government. Lenihan, Brian, *For the Record*, Blackwater Press, 1991, pp. 98-99.

January 27, 1982
Jim Kemmy
They took me for granted. That was the mistake they made last night. It might seem pompous for me to say it, but I feel I was entitled to influence the Government more than I did.

As independent TD, on withdrawal of support from Coalition Government because of budget measures, resulting in its defeat by 82-81 votes. *The Irish Times*, January 28, 1982.

February 2, 1982
Lt-General Carl O'Sullivan
We are not equipped to face even a minimum attack from outside. We haven't the ships, the planes, the artillery, the armour... Sovereignty is the ability to defend ourselves or to be defended. The 26-County State would do well to grow to such mature sovereignty before we think about other areas of sovereignty like Northern Ireland.

As retiring Chief of Staff of Irish Army. *The Irish Times*, February 2, 1982.

February 18, 1982
Fianna Fáil
We'll rise and follow Charlie!

From election song for supporters of Fianna Fáil leader, Charles Haughey. Attributed.

March 2, 1982
Mary Robinson
The task now is to build that socialist movement. We want banks nationalised, taxation reformed, building land controlled.
As Labour Party member. *The Irish Times*, March 2, 1982.

March 8, 1982
Graham Greene
It seemed to me that the new, Provisional, IRA was closer to the Chicago gangster than to the idealism of the men like Erskine Childers, and my friend Ernie O'Malley.
As author, after visit to Belfast. *The Irish Times*, March 8, 1982.

March 9, 1982
Mark Killilea
I caught them by the seat of the trousers and pushed them towards the press area and told them: 'In, quick, hard to your left, up on top of the Irish box, and jump for your lives.'
As Fianna Fáil TD, on how he got three Sinn Féin, Workers' Party TDs into locked Dáil chamber to vote support for formation of Fianna Fáil government. *The Irish Times*, March 10, 1982.

March 13, 1982
James Prior
Let's face it, it's the Catholics who have suffered more from the violence.
As NI Secretary of State. *The Irish Times,* March 13, 1982.

March 30, 1982
Charles Haughey
I have decided to take the unusual course of asking a member of the Opposition, in the national interest, to accept the appointment.
As Taoiseach, on his offer of EEC Commissioner to Fine Gael TD, Dick Burke, thus creating by-election which could have resulted in gain for his party, Fianna Fáil (but did not). *The Irish Times*, April 2, 1982.

March 30, 1982
Dick Burke
My acceptance was based on my perception of the national interest.
As Fine Gael TD, on his acceptance of offer from Fianna Fáil leader Charles Haughey of EEC Commissioner. *The Irish Times*, April 2, 1982.

May 3, 1982
Paddy Power
Britain themselves are very much the aggressors now.
As Minister for Defence, on sinking of Argentine aircraft carrier *Belgrano* by British submarine in Falklands war. *The Irish Times*, May 4, 1982.

May 6, 1982
Charles Haughey
As a neutral nation that has always refrained from military alliances of any kind, we have to take a clear view of any action, economic or otherwise, that would appear supportive of military action.
As Taoiseach, refusing British request to join EEC sanctions against Argentina in Falklands war. *The Irish Times*, May 7, 1982.

May 6, 1982
Nicanor Costa Mendez
Ireland has suffered injustice and has had to endure many attacks. So we were somewhat surprised by Ireland's first reaction. And now we are very happy with the change in your political position... We have learned from the Irish spirit of endurance.
As Foreign Minister of Argentina, on reversal of Ireland's decision to support British request for sanctions against Argentina in Falklands war. *The Irish Times*, May 7, 1982.

May 22, 1982
David Owen
Ireland has behaved with gross impertinence throughout.
As former British Foreign Minister on refusal of Fianna Fáil Government to back British sanctions against Argentina in Falklands war. *The Irish Times*, May 22, 1982.

May 25, 1982
Gerry Fitt
Ireland's stance on sanctions has led to a greater degree of anti-Irish feeling in Britain than at the time of the Birmingham bombings.
As Independent Socialist MP, on Irish refusal to back British sanctions against Argentina in Falklands war. *The Irish Times*, May 26, 1982.

June 10, 1982
Charles Haughey
Violence, evil in itself and appalling in its consequences, can only postpone the day of Irish unity.
As Taoiseach, in New York to Irish Americans. *The Irish Times*, June 11, 1982.

June 11, 1982
Padraig Flynn
There's one thing we have that they can never have, and that's a love of the four green fields of Ireland.
As Fianna Fáil Minister for Gaeltacht, referring to Fine Gael, at by-election meeting in Galway. *The Irish Times*, June 12, 1982.

June 18, 1982
Lord Gowrie
I don't think much of the 1921 settlement...
Northern Ireland is extremely expensive on the
British taxpayer...if the people of Northern
Ireland wished to join with the south of Ireland,
no British Government would resist for twenty
minutes.

As NI Minister of State, at Irish Club, London. *The Irish Times*, July 19, 1982.

June 21, 1982
Kenneth Walton
There is a common fallacy that the IRA is a
bunch of Barry Fitzgerald leprechauns. They
aren't. They are killers.

As deputy director of FBI in New York, on discovery of plan to smuggle surface-to-air missiles to IRA. *The Irish Times*, June 22, 1982.

July 29, 1982
Margaret Thatcher
No commitment exists for Her Majesty's
Government to consult the Irish Government on
matters affecting Northern Ireland.

As British Prime Minister, ending Anglo-Irish negotiations because of Irish attitude to Falklands war. *The Irish Times*, July 30, 1982.

August 15, 1982
James Prior
Mr Haughey's relations with the British
Government are supposedly not very good. In
fact, they are pretty awful at the moment.

As NI Secretary of State, on effects of Irish attitude to Falklands war. *The Irish Times*, August 16, 1982.

August 17, 1982
Charles Haughey
[It was] a bizarre happening, an unprecedented
situation...a grotesque situation...an almost
unbelievable mischance.

As Taoiseach, at Dublin press conference on resignation of Attorney General Patrick Connolly after man wanted for murder found at his home. *The Irish Times*, August 18, 1982.

August 24, 1982
Conor Cruise O'Brien
You've got to hand it to the man, you really
have. He is grotesque, unbelievable, bizarre and
unprecedented.

As political commentator, on remarks of Taoiseach, above, later shortened to 'GUBU'. *The Irish Times*, August 24, 1982.

September 1982
John Healy
If Charlie had ducks, they'd drown on him.

As *Irish Times* columnist, on Taoiseach Charles Haughey's run of bad luck. Smyth, Sam, *Thanks a Million Big Fella*, Blackwater Press, 1997, p. 56.

October 3, 1982
Charles Haughey
I will insist that the Cabinet stand firm behind me
with no shilly-shallying... The situation is going to
be dealt with. We are going to bring to an end the
simmering dissension and sniping.

As Fianna Fáil leader, on (unsuccessful) motion of no confidence in his leadership tabled by Fianna Fáil TD Charles McCreevy. *The Irish Times*, October 4, 1982.

October 6, 1982
Des O'Malley
You are aware of the reasons and I think in the
circumstances it is unavoidable.

As Minister of Trade, Commerce and Tourism, informing Taoiseach Charles Haughey of his resignation because of disagreements over Northern Ireland and economy. *The Irish Times*, October 7, 1982.

October 7, 1982
Mary Colley
He said they would blow his head off, and other
parts of his body as well...it was very frightening.

As wife of Fianna Fáil TD George Colley, on anonymous caller during 'night of long telephone calls' which preceded 58-22 vote of confidence in Charles Haughey as Fianna Fáil leader by parliamentary party. *The Irish Times*, October 8, 1982.

October 10, 1982
Conor Cruise O'Brien
If I saw Mr Haughey buried at midnight at a
crossroads, with a stake driven through his heart –
politically speaking – I should continue to wear a
clove of garlic round my neck, just in case.

As political commentator. *Observer*, October 10, 1982.

October 16, 1982
Garret FitzGerald
All life, whether of citizens or of people of other
nationalities, whether born or unborn, should be
protected by our Constitution.

As Fine Gael leader, promising support for anti-abortion amendment campaign. O'Reilly, Emily, *Masterminds of the Right*, Attic Press, 1991, p. 78.

October 29, 1982
Provisional Sinn Féin
Candidates in national and local elections must be
unambivalent in support of the armed struggle.

As political wing of IRA, in resolution passed at árd fheis in Dublin. *The Irish Times*, November 6, 1982.

c. *November 1, 1982*
Gerry Adams
The only complaint I have heard from
nationalists or anti-unionists is that he was not
shot forty years ago.

As Sinn Féin Vice President, on IRA killing of former NI
Speaker, Sir Norman Stronge. *Guardian,* November,
1982.

November 2, 1982
Michael O'Leary
The whole vocabulary of politics has been
debased...we have become a nation of alibis,
stratagems and veiled means... I didn't want to
be a scarecrow leader.

As leader of Labour Party, announcing resignation after it
had rejected his motion to inform electorate before
entering coalition. *The Irish Times,* October 29, 1982.

November 8, 1982
Gay Byrne
[That is] an interesting theological principle.

As host of Late Late Show on recommendation by priest
that viewers should withhold TV licence fees in protest at
his interview with retired brothel keeper, Madam Sin.
Cork Evening Echo, November 9, 1982.

November 13, 1982
Joan FitzGerald
It was my fault. I'm to blame, but he isn't
absent-minded about anything to do with his
work. He is very much on the ball.

As wife of Fine Gael leader Garret FitzGerald, on his
appearance wearing odd shoes. *The Irish Times,*
November 13, 1982.

November 23, 1982
Maureen Haughey
He's always Garret the Good. Garret has a halo,
and Haughey has horns.

As wife of Charles Haughey, on favourable press
treatment of Garret FitzGerald. *The Irish Times,*
November 24, 1982.

December 7, 1982
Chief Justice Tom O'Higgins
The Court is invited to assume that because of
the existence of widespread violence...any charge
associated with terrorist activity should be
regarded as a charge in respect of a political
offence... I am not prepared to make such an
assumption.

As judge, in ruling in Supreme Court which opened way
for extradition to Northern Ireland of republicans. *The
Irish Times,* December 8, 1982.

January 19, 1983
Charles Haughey
I want to make it crystal clear that the
Government as such and I as Taoiseach knew
absolutely nothing about any activities of this
sort... I think at this stage we're only dealing with
unfounded allegations and unsubstantiated
statements.

As former Taoiseach, on report by Peter Murtagh in *The
Irish Times* that telephones of two journalists were officially
tapped while Fianna Fáil were in Government. *The Irish
Times,* January 24, 1983.

January 21, 1983
Sean Doherty
The request to have the phones of two named
journalists put under surveillance resulted from
discussions between me and garda security chiefs,
when concern was being expressed that national
security was endangered through leaks of highly
confidential Government papers.

As former Minister for Justice, resigning from Fianna Fáil
front bench after disclosure in *The Irish Times* that he had
ordered tapping of telephones of two journalists. *The Irish
Times,* January 22, 1983.

January 23, 1983
Sean Doherty
Mr Haughey did not know that I was tapping
those journalists and indeed it was only shortly
before Christmas [after report in *The Irish Times*]
that Mr Haughey had a brief discussion with me
about the matter.

As former Minister for Justice, on tapping of journalists'
telephones when Charles Haughey was Taoiseach. *The Irish
Times,* January 24, 1983.

January 29, 1983
John Hume
As for the Unionists themselves, they have become
a petty people.

As leader of SDLP, addressing party conference. *The Irish
Times,* February 1, 1983.

February 3, 1983
Charles Haughey
...are [Fianna Fáil] policies to be decided for it by
alien influences, by political opponents, or worst
of all by business interests?

As leader of Fianna Fáil, before confidence vote in
parliamentary party which he survived by 40-33 votes. *The
Irish Times,* February 4, 1983.

March 17, 1983
Cardinal Cooke
The [British] don't belong there in the first place. I
am for a united Ireland for all the people.

As New York Primate, at St Patrick's Day parade in New York. *The Irish Times*, March 18, 1983.

March 17, 1983
Ronald Reagan

Those [in America] who support violence are no friends of Ireland.

As US President, in Irish Embassy in Washington. *The Irish Times*, March 18, 1983.

March 29, 1983
Catholic Hierarchy

Surely the most defenceless and voiceless in our midst are entitled to the fullest Constitutional protection.

As Irish Bishops, in statement backing referendum to insert anti-abortion amendment into Constitution. *The Irish Times*, March 30, 1983.

March 29, 1983
Anti-Amendment Campaign

The statement of the Catholic Hierarchy...reveals...the determination to enshrine Roman Catholic teaching on issues of private morality in the Constitution.

As group campaigning against anti-abortion amendment to Constitution, responding to Irish Hierarchy, above. *The Irish Times*, March 30, 1983.

April 4, 1983
Tomás MacGiolla

We are moving towards a Catholic Constitution for a Catholic people.

As leader of Workers' Party, on Catholic bishops' backing for anti-abortion amendment to Constitution. *The Irish Times*, April 5, 1983.

April 7, 1983
Major Sir Anthony Farrar-Hockley

The Malaysian terrorists were pretty good, but the most efficient terrorists that I have ever fought were the Israelis – the Irgun and Stern Gang...by God they were good, really good. Compared to them, the IRA are rank amateurs...they remain just a bunch of murderous thugs really.

As former British Army Commander of Land Forces in Northern Ireland. *The Irish Times*, April 8, 1983.

April 7, 1983
Proposed Constitutional Amendment

The State acknowledges the right to life of the unborn, and, with due regards to the equal right to life of the mother, guarantees in its laws to respect and, as far as practicable, by its laws to vindicate and defend that right.

Wording of anti-abortion amendment proposed by Fianna Fáil party and passed in Dáil by 87-13 votes. *The Irish Times*, April 28, 1983.

April 9, 1983
Most Rev J. W. Armstrong

This is the Mother and Child Act all over again. Can you...force a moral theology on a whole people which is symptomatic of only one church?

As Church of Ireland Archbishop of Armagh, on Government plans for anti-abortion referendum. *The Irish Times*, April 9, 1983.

April 27, 1983
Rev Victor Griffin

Can you imagine the old Stormont Parliament carrying through a law or bill against the united wishes of the Roman Catholic Church and people. Would there not be howls of 'sectarianism'?

As Church of Ireland Dean of St Patrick's Cathedral, Dublin, on backing of Catholic Bishops for anti-abortion amendment to Constitution. *The Irish Times*, April 28, 1983.

May 4, 1983
Michael Heseltine

Those countries which don't play a part in NATO should ask themselves why they should take advantage of the umbrella we provide.

As British Defence Minister, in comments on Republic, which prompted protest from Dublin. *The Irish Times*, May 6, 1983.

May 4, 1983
Mary Robinson

We are witnessing the forces of the Catholic Church moving in on a political debate, taking sides on it and using the resources of the Catholic Church to advance those sides.

As Senator, in Senate speech opposing anti-abortion amendment to Constitution. O'Leary, Olivia, and Burke, Helen, *Mary Robinson, the Authorised Biography*, Hodder & Stoughton, 1998, p. 99.

June 19, 1983
Gerry Adams

If Wolfe Tone were alive today...he would stand firmly with us...reviled...as an upstart, a subversive and the 1798 equivalent of the gunman.

As Vice President of Provisional Sinn Féin, at Bodenstown. *The Irish Times*, June 20, 1983.

June 28, 1983
John Hume

It is a commentary on the politics of the North of Ireland – or the fact that there is a problem there – that never before has someone with either my religious or political persuasion stood in the House to represent the city of Derry.

As leader of SDLP and newly elected MP for Derry, in House of Commons, in maiden speech. Routledge, Paul, *John Hume*, Harper Collins, 1998, pp. 189-190.

June 28, 1983
Anthony Kershaw

If we seem to be indifferent, it is because we are unable to decide what to do.

As Conservative MP, in House of Commons, on Northern Ireland. Routledge, Paul, *John Hume*, Harper Collins, 1998, p. 194.

July 13, 1983
John Hume

If you want the IRA to win, hang them.

As leader of SDLP, in House of Commons, in debate on capital punishment. *The Irish Times*, July 14, 1983.

July 13, 1983
Rev William McCrea

Give me a thousand dead IRA martyrs rather than a thousand IRA murderers any day.

As DUP MP, in House of Commons, in debate on capital punishment. *The Irish Times*, July 14, 1983.

August 16, 1983
Dr Kevin McNamara

There exists in Ireland a strong pro-abortion lobby, with powerful backing in the media and very substantial support from the international pro-abortion movement under the umbrella of the Anti-Amendment campaign.

As Bishop of Kerry. *The Irish Times*, August 16, 1983.

August 17, 1983
Justin Keating

The question at issue, as it was in the Mother and Child scheme in 1951 a quarter of a century ago...is what sort of country we are trying to build. Are we trying to build a 26-County Catholic green Republic?

As former Labour minister, at Labour Party meeting against anti-abortion amendment to Constitution. *The Irish Times*, August 18, 1983.

August 22, 1983
Catholic Hierarchy

There are people who are sincerely opposed to abortion and yet who feel that no referendum should take place at all...we recognise the right of each person to vote according to conscience.

As Irish Bishops, in statement on anti-abortion referendum. *The Irish Times*, August 23, 1983.

August 24, 1983
Malcolm Muggeridge

It is my opinion that the [anti-abortion] amendment as it is worded may in fact open the way to legalised abortion, rather than prevent it.

As English writer and anti-abortion campaigner, on why he decided to cancel plans to come to Ireland to support anti-abortion referendum campaign. *The Irish Times*, August 25, 1983.

August 29, 1983
Rev Victor Griffin

Where there is conflict, the rights of the mother to life and health must take precedence over the unborn child.

As Church of Ireland Dean of St Patrick's Cathedral, Dublin, on anti-abortion referendum. *The Irish Times*, August 30, 1983.

September 5, 1983
Nell McCafferty

If anyone doubted that the [anti-abortion] amendment was anti-woman, they had only to watch the performance on television of Mr Charles Haughey, who could not bring himself to mention woman, or pregnancy or mothers in the course of his broadcast.

As journalist and speaker at press conference held by Women Against the Amendment, in Dublin. *The Irish Times*, September 6, 1983.

September 5, 1983
Louise Asmal

This [anti-abortion] amendment contains within it the concept of revenge against sexually active women.

As speaker at press conference held by Women Against the Amendment, in Dublin. *The Irish Times*, September 6, 1983.

September 8, 1983
Anti-Amendment Campaigner

This referendum has been won with a Carmelite in one hand and a ballot box in the other.

As member of group opposing anti-abortion amendment, in comment at Dublin count in referendum, adopted from remark on October 31, 1981 by Danny Morrison about armelite and ballot box. *The Irish Times*, September 9, 1983.

October 22, 1983
Patrick Cooney

I think it's wrong to be critical of whatever flag they were fighting under. I thought we'd all grown up a bit.

As Minister for Defence, referring to Irish soldiers who fought in British Army in two World Wars, approving Irish Army participation in British Army Remembrance Day ceremonies in Dublin. *The Irish Times*, October 23, 1983.

October 22, 1983
Patrick Cahalane
There may be a few who are delighted to participate but there are others who regard it as a bad decision for the country... I do not feel the present British Army is a peace-keeping army.

As retired army officer, objecting to Minister for Defence Patrick Cooney's approval of Irish Army participation in British Army Remembrance Day ceremonies in Dublin. *The Irish Times*, October 23, 1983.

November 4, 1983
Maurice Dockrell
[I] told only one lie ever in the Dáil, when, quite unable to resist the temptation, [I] quipped 'I'm past it but I'm for it' in a debate about contraception.

As Fine Gael TD, in interview on his career. *The Irish Times*, November 5, 1983.

November 10, 1983
James Prior
What on earth would we do?...it might end with a Cuba off our western coast.

As NI Secretary of State, at meeting of Conservative MPs in London, on prospect of Sinn Féin electoral gains in Northern Ireland. *The Irish Times*, November 11, 1983.

November 26, 1983
Dominic McGlinchey
I am not going to be blackmailed by the grief of children. The only way to end repression in the North is through violence against the security forces and the State itself.

As leader of Irish National Liberation Army, who claimed involvement in 30 killings, in interview with Vincent Browne. *Sunday Tribune*, November 27, 1983.

November 29, 1983
Rev Des Wilson
Any solution would have to take into account that the Protestants of Northern Ireland were the best armed and best officially protected minority in Europe...

As Belfast priest, in individual contribution to New Ireland Forum of nationalist parties in Dublin. *The Irish Times*, November 30, 1983.

December 18, 1983
IRA
The Harrods bombing was not authorised by the Army Council of the Irish Republican Army. We have taken immediate steps to ensure that there will be no repetition of this type of operation again.

In statement after bomb at Harrods in London killed 5 people. *The Irish Times*, December 19, 1983.

December 18, 1983
Denis Thatcher
No damned Irish murderer is going to stop me shopping there.

As husband of British Prime Minister, on IRA bombing of Harrods in London. *The Irish Times*, December 24, 1983.

c. January 1, 1984
Bernard McLaverty
'But it is not like 1916.'
'It wasn't like 1916 in 1916.'

As author, in words spoken by characters in novel set in 1980s Northern Ireland. McLaverty, Bernard, *Cal*, Belfast, 1984, p. 73.

January 11, 1984
Conor Cruise O'Brien
I asked him whether the Rising of 1916 might not have been a mistake. He...replied, 'It might have been a mistake, but if so, it's a mistake I'm glad I was in.'

As son-in-law of former old IRA man and minister Sean MacEntee, who had died. *The Irish Times*, January 11, 1984.

January 15, 1984
Cardinal Tomás Ó Fiaich
If a person is convinced that he is joining for these reasons [community service] and that his positive reasons outweigh any interpretation that may be given his membership as condoning support for violence and crime, he may be morally justified.

As Primate of Ireland, on morality of Sinn Féin membership. *The Irish Times*, January 16, 1984.

January 19, 1984
Sylvia Meehan
A majority of women in the North, from both unionist and nationalist traditions, would not want to endure the present constraints in the South.

As Chairwoman of Employment Equality Agency in Republic, in individual submission to New Ireland Forum of nationalist parties in Dublin. *The Irish Times*, January 20, 1984.

January 24, 1984
Pastor Eric McComb
We don't need the Sinn Féin cardinal to be advocating votes for those who are out to murder these men.

As Superintendent of Elim Pentecostal Churches in Ireland, at funeral of UDR man, on comment of Cardinal Ó Fiaich on January 15, 1984. *The Irish Times*, January 25, 1984.

February 9, 1984
Dr Cahal Daly
The Catholic Church in Ireland totally rejects the concept of a confessional state. We have not

sought, and do not seek, a Catholic state for a Catholic people.

As Bishop of Down and Connor, in submission on behalf of Catholic bishops to New Ireland Forum of nationalist parties in Dublin. *The Irish Times*, February 10, 1984.

March 15, 1984
Garret FitzGerald

This moral obligation, to put Northern Ireland, its people and their interests first...can be fulfilled only by corresponding rejection of – revulsion against – the very idea of aid by way of money, or by way of weapons, or by way of moral support for those who are engaged in the acts of horrific violence.

As Taoiseach, calling on Irish Americans to ostracise pro-IRA groups in United States. McLoughlin, Michael, *Great Irish Speeches of the Twentieth Century*, Poolbeg, 1996, pp. 329-330.

April 2, 1984
Jesse Jackson

British troops cannot bring peace to Ireland any more than United States troops can bring peace to Lebanon, Grenada or Vietnam. No one seeking justice can rely on terror and no one seeking peace can tolerate injustice.

As US Democratic presidential candidate, in interview in USA. *The Irish Times*, April 3, 1984.

April 24, 1984
Rev James Shiels

He will be remembered among the saints in heaven. [He was] foremost in the campaign for the preservation of life...against abortion in the South.

As priest, at funeral of IRA volunteer killed in Derry by own bomb. *The Irish Times*, April 25, 1984.

May 2, 1984
New Ireland Forum

The Forum had identified...the desire of nationalists for a united Ireland in the form of a sovereign, independent Irish State...in addition, two structural arrangements were examined in detail, a federal/confederal state and joint authority... The parties in the Forum also remain open to discuss other views which may contribute to political development.

Report of New Ireland Forum of nationalist parties, meeting in Dublin. *The Irish Times*, May 3, 1984.

May 2, 1984
Garret FitzGerald

The ideal we would aspire to would be a unitary state...but we also recognise that we cannot achieve this ourselves and we have indicated an openness to other views.

As Taoiseach and leader of Fine Gael, at closing of New Ireland Forum of nationalist parties in Dublin. *The Irish Times*, May 3, 1984.

May 2, 1984
Charles Haughey

It [a unitary state] is not an 'option' – it is the wish of the parties of the Forum... Neither of these other two arrangements, federation or joint sovereignty, would bring peace and stability to the North.

As Fianna Fáil leader, at closing of New Ireland Forum of nationalist parties, meeting in Dublin. *The Irish Times*, May 3, 1984.

May 2, 1984
John Hume

To the unionists of the North with whom we share this piece of earth, Irish nationalism can today repeat de Gaulle's ringing affirmation of reconciliation to the Algerians: '*Je vous ai compris* – we understand your position.'...we accept that before now we might not have fully understood.

As leader of SDLP, at closing of New Ireland Forum of nationalist parties, meeting in Dublin. *The Irish Times*, May 3, 1984.

May 2, 1984
Colonel Muammar Gadafy

The Irish cause is a just one [but] in the last few years we've stopped our material support to the IRA in order to establish good relations with Britain.

As Libyan leader, on accusation that he supported terrorists. *The Irish Times*, May 3, 1984.

May 26, 1984
P. J. Mara

Uno duce, una voce.

As spokesman for Charles Haughey, leader of Fianna Fáil, on how party had 'one leader, one voice'. *The Irish Times*, December 29, 1984.

May 29, 1984
George Seawright

Fenian scum...taxpayers' money would be better spent on an incinerator and burning the whole lot of them. The priests should be thrown in and burned as well.

As DUP councillor, in remarks at Belfast Education and Library Board about Catholics who objected to playing of British national anthem at concerts, for which he was expelled from DUP. *The Irish Times*, June 1, 1984.

c. June 1, 1984
Mary McAleese

I don't want to ram rhythm down people's throats.

As Catholic lawyer, on contraceptive methods. *The Irish Times*, September 20, 1997.

June 2, 1984
James Prior
The Forum Report outlines three models. One is a unitary state, the second is a form of federation, the third is called joint authority...it is a dangerous fallacy to imagine that the unionist majority in Northern Ireland will agree. It is equally false to imagine that the Government or anyone else can engineer or induce such agreement.

As NI Secretary of State. *The Irish Times*, July 3, 1984.

June 2, 1984
Michael D. Higgins
It is wrong that the God of War should be getting a doctorate from the National University of Ireland.

As Chairman of Irish Labour Party, opposing conferring of NUI doctorate on US President Ronald Reagan. *The Irish Times*, December 29, 1984.

June 3, 1984
Ronald Reagan
I received a paper from Ireland that told me that in the clan to which we belong, those who said 'Regan' and spelt it that way were the professional people and the educators, and only the common labourers called it 'Reagan'. So meet a common labourer.

As US President, at Ballyporeen, Co Tipperary, his alleged ancestral home. *The Irish Times*, June 4, 1984.

June 4, 1984
Ronald Reagan
I can perhaps claim to be an Irishman longer than anyone here. I also have some other credentials. I am the great-grandson of a Tipperary man; I am the president of a country with the closest possible ties to Ireland; and I was a friend of Barry Fitzgerald.

As US President, addressing joint house of Oireachtas. *The Irish Times*, June 5, 1984.

June 5, 1984
Lord Justice Gibson
I regard each of the accused as absolutely blameless in this matter. That finding should be put in their record along with my own commendation for their courage and determination in bringing the three deceased men to justice, in this case to the final courts of justice.

As judge, at Belfast Crown Court, acquitting three RUC men of murdering one of three unarmed IRA members at roadblock. *The Irish Times*, June 6, 1984.

June 15, 1984
Cardinal Tomás Ó Fiaich
Such remarks, made in the context of a considered written judgement, seem to us inexplicable and inexcusable.

As Primate of Ireland, in statement signed by eight other NI Catholic bishops, on remarks of Lord Justice Gibson above. *The Irish Times*, June 16, 1984.

July 2, 1984
James Prior
The dangers for the people of Northern Ireland of sitting back and doing nothing are greater than the obvious risks of seeking to make some political advance.

As NI Secretary of State, in House of Commons, on report of New Ireland Forum. Bardon, Jonathan, *A History of Ulster*, Blackstaff Press, 1992, p. 753.

July 2, 1984
Rev Ian Paisley
I have followed too many funeral processions, I have held too many widows' hands and I have patted too many orphans' heads not to know the agony my people have gone through. They are not only Protestant but Roman Catholic bereaved ones.

As leader of DUP, in House of Commons. Bardon, Jonathan, *A History of Ulster*, Blackstaff Press, 1992, p. 753.

September 1984
Danny Morrison
Electoral politics will not remove the British from Ireland. Only armed struggle will do that.

As Sinn Féin candidate, speaking after defeat in European elections. *Magill*, September 1984.

September 2, 1984
Dr Kevin McNamara
...If we travel this road...we shall be settling the scene for an increase in venereal diseases, teenage pregnancies, illegitimate births and even abortion.

As Bishop of Kerry, in pastoral letter, on free access to contraceptives. *The Irish Times*, September 3, 1984.

September 13, 1984
Seamus Heaney
As a power group, they have never collectively yielded a damn thing and they have to learn to be a bit better-mannered towards their Catholic neighbours. But I think that anything that excluded them from being Irish, anything that makes them feel unwanted, is not called for...the writers should welcome them and the politicians should punish them.

As poet, on unionists. *The Irish Times*, September 13, 1984.

October 12, 1984
IRA
Today, we were unlucky, but remember we only have to be lucky once – you will have to be lucky always.
Statement to British Prime Minister, Margaret Thatcher, after bombing of Brighton hotel where she was staying. *The Irish Times*, October 13, 1984.

October 12, 1984
Margaret Thatcher
Now it must be business as usual.
As British Prime Minister, after Brighton bombing. *The Times*, October 13, 1984.

October 14, 1984
Margaret Thatcher
In church on Sunday morning – it was a lovely morning and we haven't had many lovely days – the sun was coming through a stained glass window and falling on some flowers, falling right across the church. It just occurred to me that this was the day I was meant not to see. Then all of a sudden I thought, 'There are some of my dearest friends who are not seeing this day.'
As British Prime Minister, at church service for victims of Brighton bombing. *The Spectator*, May 24, 1985.

November 3, 1984
Gerry Adams
The Brighton bombing was an inevitable result of the British presence in this country. Far from being a blow against democracy, it was a blow for democracy.
As President of Sinn Féin, at árd fheis. *The Irish Times*, November 5, 1984.

November 8, 1984
Alice Glenn
What man wants to have anything to do with a girl who had been used and abused by any man who comes along with condoms?
As Fine Gael TD, on legislation to make contraceptives available to people over 18. *The Irish Times*, November 9, 1984.

November 18, 1984
Chequers Communiqué
The identities of both the majority and the minority communities in Northern Ireland should be recognised and respected and reflected in the structures and processes of Northern Ireland in ways acceptable to both communities.
Joint statement by British Prime Minister Margaret Thatcher and Taoiseach Garret FitzGerald at Chequers. *The Irish Times*, November 20, 1984.

November 19, 1984
Margaret Thatcher
I have made it quite clear...that a unified Ireland was one solution. That is out. A second solution was confederation of the two states. That is out. A third solution was joint authority. That is out.
As British Prime Minister, at televised press conference in London, later remembered as her 'out, out, out' dismissal of New Ireland Forum options. *The Irish Times*, November 23, 1984.

November 20, 1984
Charles Haughey
Mount Everest has never seen such a mad scramble down from a summit as took place at Leinster House today... To the Taoiseach I say: you have led the country into the greatest humiliation in recent history.
As Fianna Fáil leader, in Dáil, on aftermath of meeting between FitzGerald and Thatcher. *The Irish Times*, November 21, 1984.

November 21, 1984
Garret FitzGerald
[Mrs Thatcher was] gratuitously offensive.
As Taoiseach, at Fine Gael meeting on British Prime Minister Margaret Thatcher's 'out, out, out' dismissal of New Ireland Forum options. *The Irish Times*, November 22, 1984.

November 21, 1984
Dr Kevin McNamara
It would be foolish to try to enforce it. It should be treated as a dead letter.
As Archbishop of Dublin, on legislation to make contraceptives available to people over 18. *The Irish Times*, November 21, 1984.

November 24, 1984
John Biggs-Davison
The search for a solution is part of the problem.
As Chairman of Tory NI Backbench Committee, on inadvisability of further Anglo-Irish negotiations. *The Irish Times*, November 24, 1984.

November 24, 1984
James Molyneaux
[It is like] a people walking in the darkness who had suddenly felt the sun in their faces.
As leader of Ulster Unionist Party, on British Prime Minister Margaret Thatcher's rejection of New Ireland Forum options. *The Irish Times*, November 26, 1984.

November 24, 1984
William Ward
How often I have been irritated as I'm sure you must be by that dreadful pronunciation 'haitch'. Give me the native Ulster 'h'... I'd like to point out

some of the names that have crept into the BBC and I make no apology, for reading them out.

As delegate at Official Unionist Party conference in Newcastle, on number of Catholics in BBC, allegedly recognisable by pronunciation of 'h' as 'haitch', and by their names. *The Irish Times*, November 26, 1984.

November 25, 1984
Dr Cahal Daly

Constitutional nationalism has received a humiliating setback. Alienation among nationalists is now shading over into anger and despair.

As Bishop of Down and Connor, on British Prime Minister Margaret Thatcher's rejection of New Ireland Forum options. *The Irish Times*, November 26, 1984.

November 25, 1984
John Hume

Not for the first time, the intransigence of Mrs Thatcher has fuelled the anger and bitterness upon which violence in Ireland is fed.

As leader of SDLP, on British Prime Minister Margaret Thatcher's rejection of New Ireland Forum options. *The Irish Times*, November 26, 1984.

November 27, 1984
Rev Ian Paisley

[Bishop Daly] is the Black Pope of the Republican movement.

As leader of DUP, on Dr Cahal Daly's warning of Catholic alienation in Northern Ireland. *The Irish Times*, November 24, 1984.

November 29, 1984
Charles Haughey

That sort of smug know-all commentator – I suppose if anything annoys me, that annoys me... I could instance a load of fuckers whose throat I'd cut, and push over the nearest cliff, but there's no percentage in that.

As Fianna Fáil leader, on political commentators, in interview. *Hot Press*, November 29, 1984.

December 4, 1984
Margaret Thatcher

I am afraid I have a weakness that when people ask me a direct question at a press conference, I give them a direct answer...I am anxious to get constructive talks going again.

As British Prime Minister, in Dublin, during EEC summit, on her 'out, out, out' dismissal of New Ireland Forum options. *The Irish Times*, December 5, 1984.

1985
Paul Durcan

We live in a Georgian, Tudor, Classical Greek, Moorish, Spanish Hacienda, Regency Period,

Ranch House, Three-Storey Bungalow
On the edge of the edge of town.

As poet, on new house styles in rural Ireland. Durcan, Paul, 'The Haulier's Wife meets Jesus on the road near Moone', *The Berlin Wall Cafe*, Harvill Press, 1995.

1985
US State Department

The naming of a special envoy [to Northern Ireland] would serve no useful purpose. Neither the British nor the Irish Government believes that such a diplomatic approach at this time would help in any way to promote reconciliation between the two communities and an end to the violence.

In communication to US Senate Foreign Relations Committee. O'Clery, Conor, *The Greening of the White House*, Gill & Macmillan, 1996, pp. 29-30.

February 5, 1985
Jack Marrinan

We certainly would not encourage our female members to think that this [pregnancy] is our normal condition for them to get into out of wedlock. We would expect our banghardai to be moral in every way.

As general secretary of Garda Representative Association, on disciplinary proceedings against unmarried police woman who became pregnant. *The Irish Times*, February 6, 1985.

February 13, 1985
John Robb

Are you going to vote to let us know once and for all that what you want is indeed a Catholic State for a Catholic people?

As Senator, on Bill to liberalise contraceptive legislation. *The Irish Times*, February 14, 1985.

February 13, 1985
Dr Joseph Cassidy

We do not want a Catholic state here for a Catholic people...we do not advocate a Catholic tyranny. It is not for bishops to decide if the law should be changed. This is a matter for the legislators after conscientious consideration of all the factors involved.

As Bishop of Clonfert, on Bill to liberalise contraceptive legislation. *The Irish Times*, January 14, 1985.

February 20, 1985
Des O'Malley

I am certain of one thing: we will never see a 32-county Republic on this island unless we establish a 26-county Republic... I stand by the Republic and accordingly I will not oppose this Bill.

As Fianna Fáil TD, defying party on Bill to liberalise contraceptive legislation. *The Irish Times*, February 21, 1985.

February 21, 1985
Tip O'Neill
I introduce the Prime Minister of the United Kingdom of Great Britain.

As Speaker of the House of Representatives, on presenting British Prime Minister Margaret Thatcher to joint session of US Congress. *The Irish Times*, February 22, 1985.

March 3, 1985
Bob Geldof
It used to be one of the prettiest in Europe and now it's a shambolical mess...not only is the city increasingly brutalised but the people in it have lost their old openness and that is a lot to do with the destruction of the city. Please stop destroying Dublin.

As pop singer, at civic reception in his honour in Mansion House, Dublin. *The Irish Times*, March 4, 1985.

March 8, 1985
Justice Declan Costello
[Holy Faith secondary school was] entitled to take into account that her association was carried on openly and publicly in a country town of quite a small population...and that they would regard her conduct as a rejection of the norms of behaviour and the ideals which the school was endeavouring to instil in and set for them.

As judge, ruling that schoolteacher had not been unfairly dismissed from New Ross school after going to live with local man whose wife had left him, and becoming pregnant. *The Irish Times*, March 8, 1985.

March 14, 1985
Rt Rev Howard Cromie
To call for a British withdrawal from Northern Ireland can only be regarded as a call for the withdrawal of all those who regard themselves as British... I hope and pray therefore that we have no more provocative and coat-trailing statements.

As Moderator of Presbyterian Church, on Cardinal Ó Fiaich's call for a British withdrawal, after meeting of church leaders at Dundalk to launch campaign for peace in North. *The Irish Times*, March 15, 1985.

March 25, 1985
Rev David Armstrong
In one word – bigotry.

As Presbyterian minister, when asked what forced him to leave Limavady, Co Derry, where he had been criticised by members of his congregation for visiting Catholic church. *The Irish Times*, March 26, 1985.

April 21, 1985
Charles McCreevy
Most people are aware of my current domestic situation but they haven't yet heard of the Parnellite lives of people from the top to the bottom in Fianna Fáil.

As Fianna Fáil TD, claiming his marital troubles had been used by opponents within party to block his political career. *The Irish Times*, April 22, 1985.

May 10, 1985
T. P. McKenna
You have not reflected the anger of the Irish people at that maladroit speech.

As London-based Irish actor, to Minister for Foreign Affairs Peter Barry at debate in London, referring to Margaret Thatcher's 'out, out, out' speech of November 19, 1984. *The Irish Times*, May 13, 1985.

May 10, 1985
Peter Barry
Mrs Thatcher's response offended me as well. I can afford to be offended provided I get the end result right.

As Minister for Foreign Affairs, responding to T. P. McKenna, above. *The Irish Times*, May 13, 1985.

May 19, 1985
Garret FitzGerald
...[the UDR] in its present form, in its composition and in its discipline and performance is a force that nationalists must and do fear. There have been just too many people murdered by the UDR, either on duty or off duty.

As Taoiseach. *The Irish Times*, May 20, 1985.

June 6, 1985
John Bjelke-Petersen
An Irish school wanted a guest speaker and asked the local university to supply a wit. The university replied that they had no one who was a wit but they had two halfwits.

As Premier of Queensland, Australia, at lunch in honour of President Hillery, and attended by Irish Ambassador Joe Small who had publicly complained about anti-Irish jokes. *The Irish Times*, June 7, 1985.

June 11, 1985
Pope John Paul II
Inevitably there occur discouraging moments in the dialogue for peace but the process must never be abandoned.

As Pontiff, in remarks on Northern Ireland to British Ambassador to Holy See, David Lane. *The Irish Times*, June 12, 1985.

June 11, 1985
Rev Ian Paisley
The Pope would be better off excommunicating those members of his Church who are butchering the Protestants of Ulster.

As leader of DUP, on Pope John Paul's support for reconciliation in Northern Ireland. *The Irish Times*, June 12, 1985.

June 18, 1985
Garret FitzGerald
Irish people had neither understood nor been able to accept the manner in which Israeli forces and militias, supported, armed and advised by the Israeli army, have harassed and at times physically attacked the UNIFIL force, including the Irish contingent.

As Taoiseach, at luncheon in Dublin in honour of President Herzog of Israel. *The Irish Times*, June 19, 1985.

July 12, 1985
Rev Ian Paisley
If they tried to stop us in Protestant Portadown, what would they do to us if we were ruled from Dublin?

As leader of DUP, on ban on Orange parade in Portadown. *The Irish Times*, July 13, 1985.

July 19, 1985
Cardinal Tomás Ó Fiaich
I think ninety percent of religious bigotry is to be found among Protestants, whereas the bigotry one finds among Catholics is mainly political.

As Primate of Ireland, in interview with *Universe*. *The Irish Times*, July 20, 1985.

July 21, 1985
Most Rev Donald Caird
We must record our deep regret and disappointment that such comments should be made... Remarks which attribute bigotry primarily to the Protestant community are not only unhelpful but inaccurate.

As Church of Ireland Archbishop of Dublin, in statement, signed by other Church of Ireland bishops, on Cardinal Ó Fiaich's remark, above. *The Irish Times*, July 22, 1985.

August 6, 1985
Dr Desmond Tutu
We must never say 'What can I do?' because here are young people who decided on a matter of principle to do what they thought was right and now they have become celebrities because of their moral stand.

As Protestant Bishop of Johannesburg, on Dunnes Stores anti-apartheid strikers in Dublin. *The Irish Times*, August 7, 1985.

September 2, 1985
James Prior
The Northern Ireland Office is always regarded as the dustbin.

As former NI Secretary of State, on Cabinet reshuffle. *The Irish Times*, September 3, 1985.

September 3, 1985
Dr Cahal Daly
Some Catholics have let the eyes of their souls become so darkened that they no longer recognise sin as sin.

As Bishop of Down and Connor, at mass for businessman shot dead by IRA. *The Irish Times*, September 4, 1985.

September 18, 1985
Eugene McCarthy
I wouldn't want to be extradited to the Republic of Ireland, but I'd rather go there than Northern Ireland.

As former Democratic presidential candidate, to US Senate Foreign Relations Committee on US-UK extradition treaty. *The Irish Times*, September 19, 1985.

September 30, 1985
Gusty Spence
I am the founder of the UVF. I've spent eighteen and a half years in prison and I am not proud of it. I am ashamed of it. I am against violence. I'd love to take Paisley by the scruff of the neck and rub his face in the blood and brains that have been spilt and make him smell them and taste them.

As founder of UVF, at fringe meeting at Labour Party conference in Bournemouth. *The Irish Times*, October 1, 1985.

October 1, 1985
John Hewitt
The important thing is never to hope. It is hope that brings turmoil, destruction. Acceptance, resignation, stoicism – yes! But never hope.

As Belfast poet, at conference on Northern Ireland troubles at Corrymeela. *The Irish Times*, October 1, 1985.

October 3, 1985
Justice Kevin Lynch
In support of the theory that Joanne Hayes had had twins, the gardaí resorted to unlikely, far-fetched and contradictory theories: first of one different father for the twins, not being Jeremiah Locke, and having blood group 'A'; second, superfecundation, or two separate fathers, one of each baby; thirdly, of Jeremiah Locke being the father of both babies but with bacterial contamination of the Cahirciveen baby's lung specimen...causing a true group 'O' to show as a group 'A'; and fourthly, that Joanne Hayes had had twins...but the Cahirciveen baby was not one

of those twins and accordingly there was a third
baby with injuries similar to those of the
Cahirciveen baby...portions of the garda report
display a want of logic.

As judge, summarising findings in inquiry in Kerry babies
case. *The Irish Times*, October 4, 1985.

October 6, 1985
Barry Desmond

...there was a campaign to get [me] out, and [I
have] no doubt that the Catholic Hierarchy are
involved at the highest level...the campaign had
been talked about at polite dinner parties.

As Minister for Health, about Catholic Church criticisms
of his proposed social legislation. *The Irish Times*,
October 8, 1985.

October 7, 1985
Catholic Hierarchy

The Hierarchy can only express amazement at
the statements attributed to Mr Desmond...that
they are involved in an alleged campaign aimed
at removing him from office. There is no
foundation whatever for this.

As Irish Bishops, responding to allegations from Barry
Desmond, Minister for Health, above. *The Irish Times*,
October 8, 1985.

October 28, 1985
Joe Cahill

The volunteers who did carry out those
operations are freely walking about today.

As senior IRA figure, admitting for first time IRA carried
out Birmingham pub bombings in 1974, killing 21
people. Granada TV, World in Action, October 28, 1985.

October 28, 1985
Roy Jenkins

The new evidence I have seen would be sufficient
to create in my mind what's sometimes called a
lurking doubt as to whether the convictions in
these cases were safe.

As Home Secretary, at time of conviction of Birmingham
Six in 1975 for pub bombings which killed 21 people.
Granada TV, World in Action, October 28, 1985.

October 30, 1985
James Molyneaux

On the day after betrayal by the British
Government and Parliament there is no good us
saying [to the paramilitaries], 'Tut, tut, be good
boys and put your guns away.' They would say,
'You are yesterday's men.'

As leader of Ulster Unionist Party, in London, after failing
to persuade British Prime Minister Margaret Thatcher to
break off Anglo-Irish negotiations. *The Irish Times*,
October 31, 1985.

November 9, 1985
Seamus Mallon

We cannot, will not and must not put this
aspiration [united Ireland] on the back-boiler. We
cannot make liars of ourselves, we cannot leave it
in suspended animation for any length of time, or,
like in County Armagh, the boys in the balaclavas
will come along and say 'We are the only people
pursuing this course.'

As SDLP deputy leader, at party conference in Belfast. *The
Irish Times*, November 11, 1985.

November 9, 1985
John Hume

They bomb factories and shout about
unemployment, they shoot a teacher in a
classroom, kill school bus drivers, kill people on
campuses and then lecture us about education...
They rob post offices leaving people without
benefit payments and then they preach to us about
defending the poor... One of these days Sinn Féin
will disappear up their own contradiction.

As leader of SDLP, at party conference in Belfast.
Routledge, Paul, *John Hume*, Harper Collins, 1998, p. 211.

November 10, 1985
Dr Jeremiah Newman

Unless we are careful to check this fanatical
politics, by the end of the century, genuinely
Catholic social expression will have been pushed
out of many areas.

As Bishop of Limerick, in sermon criticising Austin Deasy,
Minister for Agriculture, and Barry Desmond, Minister for
Health, for supporting social reforms. *The Irish Times*,
November 11, 1985.

November 12, 1985
Austin Deasy

To legislate solely as a Roman Catholic for Roman
Catholics would amount to political bigotry, and
that I will have no part in.

As Minister for Agriculture, on remarks of Dr Newman,
above. *The Irish Times*, November 13, 1985.

November 14, 1985
Enoch Powell

Does the right honourable lady not understand,
and if she does not yet she soon will, that the
penalty for treachery is to fall into public
contempt?

As unionist MP, in House of Commons, to British Prime
Minister Margaret Thatcher, on news of Anglo-Irish
Agreement. *The Irish Times*, November 15, 1985.

November 15, 1985
Anglo-Irish Agreement

The two Governments...affirm that any change in
the status of Northern Ireland would only come

about with the consent of a majority of the people of Northern Ireland... The United Kingdom Government accept that the Irish Government will put forward views and proposals on matters relating to Northern Ireland...in so far as these matters are not the responsibility of a devolved administration in Northern Ireland.

From Anglo-Irish Agreement signed at Hillsborough by Taoiseach Garret FitzGerald and British Prime Minister Margaret Thatcher. *The Irish Times*, November 16, 1985.

November 15, 1985
Garret FitzGerald

Tá sé mar chuspóir againn comh-aitheantas agus comh-urraim a bhaint amach don dá fhéiniúlacht i dTuaisceart Éireann. Féadfaigh náisiúnaithe anois a gceann a ardú agus a fhios acu go bhfuil seasamh acu atá ar comhchéim leis an seasamh atá ag comhaltaí an phobail Aontachtúil agus gur léir don saol go bhfuil an scéal amhlaidh.

As I have just said in Irish, our purpose is to secure equal recognition and respect for the two identities in Northern Ireland. Nationalists can now raise their heads knowing their position is and is seen to be, on an equal footing with that of members of the unionist community.

As Taoiseach, at signing of Anglo-Irish Agreement. *The Irish Times*, November 16, 1985.

November 15, 1985
Margaret Thatcher

I went into this Agreement because I was not prepared to tolerate a situation of continuing violence... I believe in the Union and that it will last as long as the majority so wish.

As British Prime Minister, at signing of Anglo-Irish Agreement. *The Irish Times*, November 16, 1985.

November 15, 1985
Charles Haughey

I believe that the concept of Irish unity has been dealt a very major blow... For the first time ever the legitimacy of the unionist position, which is contrary to unification, has been recognised by an Irish Government in an international agreement.

As leader of Fianna Fáil, on Anglo-Irish Agreement. *The Irish Times*, November 16, 1985.

November 15, 1985
Gerry Adams

Garret FitzGerald insults the long-suffering nationalist people of the Six Counties when he tells us in Gaelic that we can now raise our heads. It is because we have raised our heads and have struggled and made sacrifices for our civil and national rights that the running sore of British involvement in Ireland has been addressed at all.

As President of Sinn Féin, on remarks of Taoiseach after signing of Anglo-Irish Agreement. *The Irish Times*, November 16, 1985.

November 15, 1985
Ian Gow

I believe that...the involvement of a foreign power in a consultative role in the administration of the province will prolong, and not diminish, Ulster's agony.

As Minister of State, resigning from British Government in protest at Anglo-Irish Agreement. *The Irish Times*, November 16, 1985.

November 15, 1985
Margaret Thatcher

More money for these people? Look at their schools! Look at their roads! Why should they have more money? I need that money for my people in England who don't have anything like this.

As British Prime Minister, to Taoiseach Garret FitzGerald, on his suggestion of a joint approach to Europe for additional funding for the International Fund for Ireland. FitzGerald, Garret, *All in a Life*, Gill & Macmillan, 1991, p. 568.

November 16, 1985
Peter Robinson

We are on the window ledge of the Union.

As DUP deputy leader, in NI Assembly debate on Anglo-Irish Agreement. *The Irish Times*, November 19, 1985.

November 17, 1985
Michael Noonan

In effect we have been given a major and substantial role in the day-to-day running of Northern Ireland.

As Minister for Justice, on Anglo-Irish Agreement, on American television programme. *The Irish Times*, November 18, 1985.

November 18, 1985
Mary Robinson

I do not believe it can achieve its objective of securing peace and stability within Northern Ireland or on the island as a whole.

As Labour Party member, resigning from party in protest at Anglo-Irish Agreement. *The Irish Times*, November 19, 1985.

November 18, 1985
Merlyn Rees

The Orange card will no longer be a trump card.

As former NI Secretary of State, on unionist rejection of the Anglo-Irish Agreement. *HC Debates*: Vol. 87: No. 9: Col. 24.

November 18, 1985
Harold McCusker
The Prime Minister...will have ensured that I shall carry to my grave with ignominy the sense of the injustice that I have done to my constituents down the years – when, in their darkest hours, I exhorted them to put their trust in this British House of Commons... Is not the reality of this Agreement that they will now be Irish-British hybrids?

As unionist MP, in House of Commons, on Anglo-Irish Agreement. *HC Debates*: Vol. 87: No. 9: Col. 29.

November 19, 1985
Charles Haughey
In effect what is proposed in this Agreement is that the Irish Government, accepting British sovereignty over part of Ireland, will involve itself in assisting and advising the British Government to rule that part of Ireland more effectively, to help make it more amenable to the authority of the British Government.

As leader of Fianna Fáil, in Dáil debate on Anglo-Irish Agreement. *The Irish Times*, November 20, 1985.

November 21, 1985
Des O'Malley
If Eamon de Valera was a young man and sitting in the House with Frank Aiken, Sean Lemass, Sean MacEntee and the others, and they were asked to make up their minds and vote for this Agreement, does anybody think that they would not support it?

As independent TD, in Dáil, on Anglo-Irish Agreement. *The Irish Times*, November 22, 1985.

November 26, 1985
Margaret Thatcher
We shall not give way to threats or to violence from any quarter...the Agreement enforces the Union, and that should bring reassurance and confidence to the unionist majority.

As British Prime Minister, in House of Commons, in debate on Anglo-Irish Agreement. *HC Debates*: Vol. 87: No. 15: Col. 753.

November 26, 1985
Neil Kinnock
Zephaniah Williams, the Welsh Chartist, said: 'When prejudice blinds the eye of the mind the brightest truth shines in vain.' I do not address the bigots or the wallies on either side of the sectarian divide, when I plead with the majority of non-nationalists not to be blinded by prejudice.

As leader of British Labour Party, in House of Commons, on Anglo-Irish Agreement. *HC Debates*: Vol. 87: No. 15: Col. 755.

November 26, 1985
James Molyneaux
I have to say honestly and truthfully that in forty years in public life I have never known what I can only describe as a universal cold fury which some of us have thus far managed to contain.

As leader of Ulster Unionist Party, in House of Commons, on Anglo-Irish Agreement. *HC Debates*: Vol. 87: No. 15: Col. 769.

November 26, 1985
Clive Soley
The unionists are not stupid or blind to what is happening. They feel betrayed because they recognise that conditional unionism...is not a permanent solution for Northern Ireland.

As Labour MP, in House of Commons, on Anglo-Irish Agreement. *HC Debates*: Vol. 87: No. 15: Col. 823.

November 26, 1985
John Hume
In 1912 the Ulster Unionists defied the sovereign wish of Parliament to grant Home Rule... That taught them a lesson which they have never forgotten – that if one threatens a British Government or British Parliament and produces crowds on the streets from the Orange lodges, the British will back down.

As leader of SDLP, in House of Commons, on Anglo-Irish Agreement. *HC Debates*: Vol. 87: No. 15: Cols. 786-787.

November 26, 1985
John Hume
[Unionists] talk always of the past. Their thoughts are encapsulated in that marvellous couplet:
'To hell with the future and long live the past,
May God in his mercy look down on Belfast.'

As leader of SDLP, in House of Commons, quoting Maurice James Craig. McLoughlin, Michael, *Great Irish Speeches of the Twentieth Century*, Poolbeg, 1996, p. 356.

November 26, 1985
Ivor Stanbrook
[It is] a bad agreement, conceived in desperation, born out of fear of violence and foreign pressure, and confirmed in folly. It will make matters worse, not better, in Northern Ireland.

As Conservative MP, in House of Commons, on Anglo-Irish Agreement. Bardon, Jonathan, *A History of Ulster*, Blackstaff Press, 1992, p. 759.

November 27, 1985
Enoch Powell
When in the coming months the consequences of this understanding work themselves out and the Prime Minister watches with uncomprehending compassion the continued sequence of terrorism, murder and death in Northern Ireland which this Agreement will not prevent but will maintain and foment, let her not send to ask for whom the bell tolls. It tolls for her.

As unionist MP, in House of Commons, on Anglo-Irish Agreement. *HC Debates*: Vol. 87: No. 16: Col. 957.

November 27, 1985
Harold McCusker
The people of Northern Ireland whom I represent would prefer to be governed by a Catholic nationalist in Northern Ireland than a Minister from the Irish Republic who lives in Cork and who did not know where Northern Ireland was until five years ago.

As unionist MP, in House of Commons, referring to Irish Foreign Minister Peter Barry. *HC Debates*: Vol. 87: No. 16: Col. 919.

November 27, 1985
Rev Ian Paisley
There is a crisis in our land. [The House] will not hear from me again for some time, and perhaps never again.

As leader of DUP, in House of Commons, on Anglo-Irish Agreement. *HC Debates*: Vol. 87: No. 16: Col. 910-913.

November 27, 1985
Edward Heath
I confess that I have always found the Irish, all of them, extremely difficult to understand.

As former British Prime Minister, in House of Commons, on Anglo-Irish Agreement. *HC Debates*: Vol. 87: No. 16: Col. 900.

November 28, 1985
Mary Harney
Parnell's famous statement on impeding the march of a nation applied to his time, but did not address the realities of 1985... I believe this Agreement copperfastens nothing. I believe it should be seen as a step towards peace and reconciliation.

As TD, after being expelled from Fianna Fáil for defying party whip and voting for Anglo-Irish Agreement. *The Irish Times*, November 28, 1985.

December 3, 1985
Tom King
The Prime Minister of Ireland...has in fact accepted that for all practical purposes and into perpetuity there will not be a united Ireland.

As NI Secretary of State, at Brussels dinner. *The Irish Times*, December 4, 1985.

December 4, 1985
Merlyn Rees
Can I bring to the notice of the Secretary of State that wise old Ulster adage which has been put into a poem by Seamus Heaney which is, 'Whatever you say, say nothing.'

As former NI Secretary of State, in House of Commons, about Tom King's remark, above, which caused anger in Irish Government. (Correct quotation is 'whatever you say, you say nothing'.) *The Irish Times*, December 5, 1985.

January 1986
Ulster Unionist Party
Ulster Says No.

Slogan declaring opposition to Anglo-Irish Agreement for 15 Westminster by-elections. Bew, Paul, and Gillespie, Gordon, *Northern Ireland, A Chronology of the Troubles 1968-1993*, Gill & Macmillan, 1993, p. 195.

January 3, 1986
Pascal O'Hare
The Anglo-Irish Agreement has copperfastened the guarantee to the unionists.

As North Belfast Assembly member, resigning from SDLP in protest at party's support for Agreement. *The Irish Times*, January 4, 1986.

January 10, 1986
Tom King
They cannot go on saying 'no'. They must say 'yes' to something.

As NI Secretary of State, at Oxford conference, on unionists. *The Irish Times*, January 11, 1986.

January 14, 1986
Unionist Election Manifesto
1886 saw the introduction of Gladstone's first Home Rule Bill. One hundred years on, the conspiracy continues to deny the Ulster people the right to self-determination.

Issued by unionist parties prior to by-elections on issue of Anglo-Irish Agreement. *The Irish Times*, January 15, 1986.

February 1, 1986
Mairead Corrigan
It was the money that spoilt the whole thing.

As former leader of NI Peace People, on split between original founders after they decided to keep 1977 Nobel Peace Prize money for themselves. *Daily Mirror*, February 1, 1986.

February 1, 1986
Betty Williams
I didn't walk away from Ulster, I ran.

As former leader of NI Peace People, resident in United States, about break-up of organisation over personality differences between founders, and decision to keep 1977 Nobel Peace Prize money for themselves. *Daily Mirror*, February 1, 1986.

February 11, 1986
Peter Robinson
There is no point in saying on the Twelfth of July that we are prepared to die for Ulster when the music is in the background, if we are to give in now. Better to languish in jail, be removed from office or face financial penalty than to forsake principle and betray future generations.

As DUP deputy leader. *The Irish Times*, February 12, 1986.

February 12, 1986
Gay Byrne
[Ireland] is banjaxed and washed out...a man...stood up in the audience at the Late Late Show three or four years ago and said that if we had any manners we'd hand the entire island back to the Queen of England at 9 o'clock the following morning and apologise for its condition...as every week passes, I think that guy had something.

As broadcaster, in interview with *Hot Press*. *The Irish Times*, February 13, 1986.

February 20, 1986
Charles Haughey
The head of the Government has been shown to be unsound in his judgement, treacherous in his relationships, vacillating in his decisions, incompetent in the management of his party and his Government.

As leader of Fianna Fáil, in Dáil, on Taoiseach Garret FitzGerald's mishandling of dismissal of ministers of State. *The Irish Times*, February 21, 1986.

February 23, 1986
Harold McCusker
There is nothing that will satisfy the Gaelic, Roman Catholic Republic now on this island other than a total subjugation of the loyalist nation on this island... Unionists would have to defeat the threat posed to their position by latter-day Fenians.

As unionist MP, at Ulster Hall rally to mark the centenary of address by Lord Randolph Churchill at same venue against Home Rule. *The Irish Times*, February 24, 1986.

February 25, 1986
Andy Tyrie
I feel if we get into a violent confrontation, whether it's with the security forces or with the nationalist community here, it's going to lead to very little future for any of us...we live here and

it's not a matter of surrendering: it's a matter of just compromising for the sake of peace.

As leader of UDA, on agitation against Anglo-Irish Agreement. *The Irish Times*, February 26, 1986.

February 27, 1986
Margaret Thatcher
A strike ostensibly carried out in the name of the Union is all too likely to lead to erosion of support for the Union in the United Kingdom as a whole.

As British Prime Minister, in letter about planned protest against Anglo-Irish Agreement to Church of Ireland Archbishop of Armagh, Dr Eames. *The Irish Times*, March 1, 1986.

March 3, 1986
Peter Robinson
Marcos Thatcher...guilty or not guilty? I would like to have suggested the electric chair but unfortunately there are power cuts.

As DUP deputy leader, addressing loyalist rally in Belfast during day of action against Anglo-Irish Agreement and comparing British prime minister to Philippines dictator, President Marcos. *The Irish Times*, March 4, 1986.

March 12, 1986
House of Commons Environment Committee
The Irish sea is the most radioactive sea in the world.

From report criticising safety standards in British nuclear industry. *The Irish Times*, March 13, 1986.

March 14, 1986
Geoffrey Howe
Let them [Unionists] be in no doubt that the future of the Union, so far from being assured, would only be threatened by intransigence, inflexibility and shortsightedness of that kind.

As British Foreign Secretary, on unionist action against Anglo-Irish Agreement. *The Irish Times*, March 15, 1986.

April 14, 1986
Alan Wright
Left on their own after a British pull-out, loyalists would build a Berlin-type wall from Londonderry to Newry, with four border crossings and a 100-yard strip, mined and patrolled 24 hours a day. There would be conscription for the eighteen to twenty-one-year-olds whose sole duty would be to combat militant nationalism.

As head of Ulster Clubs, formed to resist Anglo-Irish Agreement. *The Irish Times*, April 14, 1986.

April 27, 1986
John Hume
[T]he Protestant boil had to be lanced. Mrs Thatcher is the right person in the right place in

the right time and they are recognising that she will not be broken.

As leader of SDLP, on unionist opposition to Anglo-Irish Agreement. *Observer*, April 27, 1986.

April 30, 1986
Seamus Mallon

We could see a new type of fascism emerging...accompanied by a bible in one hand and a petrol bomb in the other.

As SDLP deputy leader, on loyalist attacks on homes of Catholics and RUC members in Northern Ireland. *HC Debates*: Vol. 96: No. 104: Col. 978.

May 5, 1986
Dr Jeremiah Newman

I'm not sure if I'll be telling them how to vote...but they'll be under no illusions about the way I would like them to vote.

As Bishop of Limerick, in interview on divorce referendum. *The Irish Times*, May 5, 1986.

May 7, 1986
Eldon Griffiths

It is asking too much to require the police to stand there like sitting ducks while wild men throw petrol bombs at them.

As Conservative spokesman for Police Federation, in House of Commons, in debate on use of plastic bullets in Northern Ireland. *HC Debates*: Vol. 97: No. 108: Col. 151.

May 14, 1986
Alice Glenn

Any woman voting for divorce would be like a turkey voting for Christmas.

As Fine Gael TD, on divorce referendum. *The Irish Times*, May 15, 1986.

May 14, 1986
Michael Woods

Could it be that the Government have unwittingly created a constitutional Frankenstein which may sleep for a while and then rise and stalk the land?

As Fianna Fáil spokesman on justice, on divorce referendum. *The Irish Times*, May 15, 1986.

May 24, 1986
Rt Rev Walton Empey

Somehow we will have to nail the lie that permissiveness flows from the Church of Ireland and that morality is the sole possession of one Church in the land.

As Church of Ireland Bishop of Meath and Kildare, on divorce referendum. *The Irish Times*, May 24, 1986.

June 11, 1986
Patrick Magee

Tiocfaidh ár lá (our day will come).

As IRA member, convicted of bombing hotel in Brighton during Conservative Party conference in 1984, killing 5 people, after being sentenced in Old Bailey, London, to life imprisonment (released in 1999). *BBC*, June 11, 1986.

June 11, 1986
Catholic Hierarchy

While it would alleviate the pain of some, it would, we believe, release in society a force which would bring pain to a much greater number.

As Irish Bishops, in statement on divorce referendum. *The Irish Times*, June 12, 1986.

June 16, 1986
Proposed Constitutional Amendment

Where...a marriage has failed...the court may in accordance with law grant a dissolution of the marriage provided...proper provision...will be made for any dependent spouse and for any child...

From proposed amendment replacing article in Constitution prohibiting divorce. *The Irish Times*, June 16, 1986.

June 24, 1986
Rev Ian Paisley

You don't come crying to me if your homes are attacked. You will reap what you sow.

As leader of DUP, to RUC men who were ejecting loyalist politicians from Stormont after British Government had dissolved NI Assembly. *The Irish Times*, June 25, 1986.

June 25, 1986
John Hume

I hope that the people of the Republic will cast their votes for an Ireland that will respect the rights of conscience of all its people, Protestant, Catholic and dissenter.

As leader of SDLP, in message to voters in Republic on eve of divorce referendum. *The Irish Times*, June 26, 1986.

June 25, 1986
Garret FitzGerald

Ulster says 'no' to its minority. Can we say 'no' to our people whose marriages have failed?

As Taoiseach, in message to voters on eve of divorce referendum. *The Irish Times*, June 26, 1986.

June 29, 1986
Charles Haughey

If we were to elect the head of the Orange Order as President of this Republic, the Unionists would still find we are doing something dishonest, deceitful and totally unacceptable to them.

As Fianna Fáil leader, rejecting argument that allowing divorce would change unionist attitudes. *The Irish Times*, June 30, 1986.

July 8, 1986
Des O'Malley
Just as the 1925 Boundary Commission reinforced the geographical division of Ireland as negotiated in the 1922 Treaty, the result of the divorce referendum has underpinned the whole concept of partition.

As leader of Progressive Democrats, in Dublin, on rejection by electorate of Constitutional amendment to allow divorce. *The Irish Times*, July 9, 1986.

July 16, 1986
Eldon Griffiths
Here is an Irishman speaking about British territory. How dare he do such a thing.

As Conservative MP and Police Federation spokesman, on criticism by Minister for Foreign Affairs Peter Barry of RUC decision to allow Orange parade through Catholic area of Portadown. *The Irish Times*, July 17, 1986.

August 24, 1986
John Stalker
I am certainly not saying there was a conspiracy, but I think it would be a wise man who could say there was not.

As Deputy Chief Constable of Greater Manchester, on his removal from inquiry into alleged RUC 'shoot-to-kill' policy and three months' suspension on charges of misconduct which later proved to be unfounded. *The Irish Times*, August 25, 1986.

August 24, 1986
Cardinal Tomás Ó Fiaich
If we remain the last Catholic country in western Europe, that is because we have been remote, rural and poor: all these things are passing.

As Primate of Ireland, on rejection of Constitutional amendment to allow divorce. *The Guardian*, August 25, 1986.

August 31, 1986
Dr Edward Daly
You must make a choice between God and Satan, between Christ and the Devil.

As Bishop of Derry, condemning IRA murder of electrician working at British Army base. *The Irish Times*, September 1, 1986.

September 1, 1986
Martin McGuinness
Bishop Daly would have us believe that anyone who supported republican resistance to British rule in Ireland is to be damned for eternity. But by that logic, Tone was damned, as were Emmet, Mitchell, Pearse, Connolly and Mellowes, indeed also such worthies as de Valera and the father of Garret FitzGerald.

As Sinn Féin Vice President, on Bishop Daly's condemnation of IRA, above. *The Irish Times*, September 2, 1986.

September 11, 1986
George Seawright
I have a feeling that I am speaking for a lot of you when I say that if the streets of Ulster flow with blood through the Anglo-Irish Agreement, the streets of Dublin should flow with blood.

As independent councillor for Shankill (murdered on December 12, 1987) at Newtownards rally against Anglo-Irish Agreement. *The Irish Times*, September 12, 1986.

September 15, 1986
J. J. Walsh
When I play golf I get a caddy and Dr FitzGerald has plenty to do rather than push his wife around in a wheelchair.

As editor of *Munster Express*, after Dr FitzGerald cancelled a press conference to avoid meeting him because he wrote that it was unseemly for the Taoiseach to push his wife's wheelchair at functions. *The Irish Times*, September 16, 1986.

September 19, 1986
Alan Dukes
Accompanying this campaign there has been the suave, slick voice of Gerry Adams, protesting against the assassination of ordinary Catholics, while ignoring the IRA's assassination of ordinary Protestants... How can any sane person take him as other than a hypocrite.

As Minister for Justice, addressing the British Irish Association at Oxford. *The Irish Times*, September 20, 1986.

September 20, 1986
Gerry Adams
There haven't been any attacks by the IRA on Protestants.

As President of Sinn Féin, on allegation by Minister for Justice, Alan Dukes, above. *The Irish Times*, September 22, 1986.

October 11, 1986
Enoch Powell
One reason why America is so determined to get its hands on Ireland – or shall I say keep its hands on Ireland – is its desire to have a substitute in the event of bases and facilities being no longer available in Great Britain.

As Ulster Unionist MP for South Down. *The Irish Times*, October 11, 1986.

October 28, 1986
Colonel Muammar Gadafy
I consider him as a friend and I support him... If I were the leader of the south of Ireland I would consider that the North was colonised and I would fight to liberate that part of Ireland.

As Libyan leader, referring to Charles Haughey, in interview. *RTÉ*, October 28, 1986.

October 28, 1986
Peter Barry
Tonight Colonel Gadafy called on young people in this country, North and South, to support violence and to abandon their democracy. I consider Colonel Gadafy's statements as an outrageous intrusion into the affairs of this country.

As Minister for Foreign Affairs, replying to Colonel Gadafy's remarks, above. *The Irish Times*, October 29, 1986.

c. November 1, 1986
Tip O'Neill
Everyone thinks I'm dressing you down, Brian. I'm going to stare at you and look very stern. But don't worry. We'll look after the Irish.

As Speaker of US House of Representatives, to Congressman Brian Donnelly, signalling he would accept amendment, allowing visas for Irish, to Bill which required Donnelly's support. O'Hanlon, Ray, *The New Irish Americans*, Roberts Rinehart, 1998, p. 63.

November 2, 1986
Martin McGuinness
If you walk out of this hall today the only place you are going is home. Don't go, my friends. We will lead you to the Republic.

As Sinn Féin Vice President, at party's árd comhairle before vote of 429-161 ending abstentionist policy towards Dáil, which led to walk-out by dissident members who formed Republican Sinn Féin. *The Irish Times*, November 3, 1986.

November 3, 1986
Austin Currie
The decision to abandon abstention in Leinster House will lead to full participation in it and to full acceptance of its institutions, and will lead also to participation in a new Northern Ireland assembly, and eventually, though this will take a bit longer, attendance at Westminster.

As SDLP spokesman for trade and industry, on end of Sinn Féin abstention policy. *The Irish Times*, November 4, 1986.

November 4, 1986
Queen Beatrix
We Dutch greatly deplore the fact that this name, which to us has become symbolic of tolerance, should in a different setting be associated with intolerance.

As Queen of the Netherlands, on place of House of Orange in Irish history, at dinner in Royal Palace in Amsterdam for President Patrick Hillery. *The Irish Times*, November 5, 1986.

November 22, 1986
Paul Brady
We are still tryin' to reach the future through the past,
still tryin' to carve tomorrow through a tombstone.

As Strabane poet, quoted by SDLP leader John Hume at SDLP conference in Newcastle, Co Down. *The Irish Times*, November 24, 1986.

November 22, 1986
John Hume
Then there are the begrudgers, or as I prefer to call them, the whingers...they suffer from a massive inferiority complex which they constantly attempt to cover by talking tough about the need to stand up to the British. What they of course need is the self-confidence to sit down with the British, for that is the political way forward.

As leader of SDLP, in remarks directed at Sinn Féin in address to party conference in Newcastle, Co Down. *The Irish Times*, November 24, 1986.

November 28, 1986
Alice Glenn
We are now in a position to identify those who can clearly be classified as enemies of the people...these would be most of the political parties, the media, spokesmen for the trade unions...the Council for the Status of Women, all of the radical feminist organisations, the leadership of most of the Churches, apart from the Catholic Church...

As Fine Gael TD, in *The Alice Glenn Report*, in comment criticising alleged supporters of divorce, for which she had to resign from party. *The Irish Times*, November 29, 1986.

November 28, 1986
Donald Caird, William McDowell and Christopher Walpole
It is an undisputed matter of history that the Protestant citizens and their Church leaders have proved themselves to be loyal citizens of the state in which they live, and consequently it comes to them as a deeply hurtful insult to be identified as 'enemies of the people'.

As Archbishop of Dublin, Clerk of the Presbyterian Synod of Dublin and Chairman of the Dublin District of the Methodist Church respectively, replying to criticism of Protestant Church leaders by Alice Glenn TD over their role in divorce referendum. *The Irish Times*, November 29, 1986.

December 9, 1986
Rev Ian Paisley
Mrs Thatcher, I would like to indict you as a traitor of the loyalist people of Northern Ireland for denying them the right to vote on the Northern Ireland Agreement.

As leader of DUP, in intervention at European Parliament in Strasbourg, which forced British Prime Minister Margaret Thatcher to abandon delivery of her report on the EEC summit in London. *The Irish Times*, December 10, 1986.

January 13, 1987
John Brooke (Lord Brookeborough)
This happened, my Lords, a few days after that evil prelate Cardinal Ó Fiaich...said that Roman Catholics and nationalists should not join the Royal Ulster Constabulary. Ten percent of the Royal Ulster Constabulary are Roman Catholics. (He is) justifying the murder of these ten percent by the IRA.

As former NI cabinet minister, in House of Lords, on the killing of RUC member in Fermanagh on January 9. *The Irish Times*, January 15, 1987.

January 14, 1987
Cardinal Tomás Ó Fiaich
I am appalled by the personal attack made on me by Lord Brookeborough. My frequent and absolute condemnation of murder of RUC personnel by the IRA over the past decade are a matter of record.

As Primate of Ireland, on Lord Brookeborough's allegation, above. *The Irish Times*, January 15, 1987.

January 29, 1987
John McMichael, Tommy Little and Eddie Sawyers
If we are to break the deadlock, or if any proposed solution is to stand any serious chance of success, then it must attempt to ensure two things: (1) That Ulster Protestants no longer feel compelled to defend the Border; (2) That Ulster Catholics support and play a full role in society.

As members of Ulster Political Research Group of Ulster Defence Association, in policy document 'Common Sense'. *The Irish Times*, January 30, 1987.

February 13, 1987
Diarmuid Sheridan
What we have in mind is this. You put this book on an ordinary bookshelf. Imagine the effect it would have on a 13-year-old. There is all the difference in the world between adults and juveniles.

As chairman of the censorship board, on why it banned the book *The Joy of Sex*. *The Irish Times*, February 14, 1987.

February 22, 1987
Bruce Anderson
The only thing preventing Ireland from applying for membership of the Third World is its climate.

As UK columnist. *Sunday Telegraph*, February 22, 1987.

March 6, 1987
John Hume
If you took the word 'No' out of the English language, most of them would be speechless.

As leader of SDLP, on 'Ulster Says No' campaign against the Anglo-Irish Agreement. *The Irish Times*, March 7, 1987.

March 15, 1987
Coleman McCarthy
Economically and politically Ireland is becoming barren like a bogside with its turfbanks long stripped... An estimated 100,000 young people, their Irish eyes not smiling, have fled for new sods... In brief, Ireland's in hock and its people are in flight.

As US author and columnist. *Washington Post*, March 15, 1987.

May 9, 1987
Rev Denis Faul
We have a very strong feeling that the police acted contrary to law and contrary to morals and contrary to good politics. They are not allowed to act in the same way as the Provisional IRA, shooting people down.

As Dungannon priest, on killing of 8 IRA men and a passer-by by RUC and British Army when attacking police station in Loughgall, Co Armagh on May 8, 1987. *The Irish Times*, May 16, 1987.

May 16, 1987
Patrick Hurley
It is estimated that over 100,000 of us young Irish are now working and living illegally in the US. Our choice is...to return to poverty and hopelessness in Ireland, or remain on here...in apprehension of being hunted down and ultimately deported.

As founder of Irish Immigration Reform Movement, in New York. *Irish Echo*, May 16, 1987.

c. May 20, 1987
Joyce McCartan
I think it's about time women in Ireland took a stand with the way things are going, people getting murdered every week. And I don't care who they are, they're still somebody's son.

As resident of Ormeau district of Belfast, after son shot by UVF, one of 18 family members killed. *The Irish Times*, January 10, 1996.

May 29, 1987
James Molyneaux
...he explained that Members had been brought along in batches of about twenty and given glasses of whisky to fortify them. They were assured by NIO ministers that this would bring about the greatest breakthrough in Anglo-Irish relations in three hundred years.

As leader of Ulster Unionist Party on backbench MPs support for Anglo-Irish Agreement. *The Irish Times*, June 1, 1987.

June 10, 1987
Gerry Fitt (Lord Fitt)
The SDLP were only admitted to the Socialist International by my credentials. Now their support for a reactionary government brands them as class traitors.

As former leader of SDLP, on party's alleged desire to see Mrs Thatcher returned as British Prime Minister in June 11 election. *The Irish Times*, June 10, 1987.

July 7, 1987
Albert Reynolds
If we haven't got the razor-edged salesmen on the coal face, nobody's going to bring home the beef.

As Minister for Industry and Commerce, on need for export drive. *The Irish Times*, July 18, 1987.

September 2, 1987
Alan Dukes
Any other policy of opposition would amount to a cynical exploitation of short-term political opportunities for a political advantage which would inevitably prove to be equally short-lived. I will not play that game because it would not produce any real or lasting advantage for the Irish people.

As Fine Gael leader, at Tallaght, on decision, known as his 'Tallaght Strategy', not to oppose Fianna Fáil Government's economic policy. McLoughlin, Michael, *Great Irish Speeches of the Twentieth Century*, Poolbeg Press, 1996, p. 364.

September 12, 1987
Denis Anderson
I was almost physically sick. The whole place has been destroyed. No matter what road you go down, there are monstrosities, here, there and everywhere... From what I've seen in just one day's driving around, I wouldn't want to set foot in Connemara again, ever.

As Belfast-born housing architect, commenting on 'bungalow blitz' in Connemara. *The Irish Times*, September 12, 1987.

October 1, 1987
Hugh McLaughlin
This is not a secret society, although the membership is confidential; but then so also is the membership of Balmoral golf club, and they are not classified as a secret group.

As new Supreme Knight of the Knights of Columbanus. *The Irish Times*, October 3, 1987.

October 5, 1987
John Alderdice
As a psychologist, I do feel I have something to contribute.

As new leader of NI Alliance Party, on why he took post. *The Irish Times*, October 5, 1987.

October 6, 1987
Dr Alex Comfort
I have written 40 books on different subjects and there's only one *[The Joy of Sex]* anyone cares about. Maybe it's the illustrations.

As author of *The Joy of Sex*, visiting Dublin after the book was banned by censorship board. *The Irish Times*, October 7, 1987.

October 7, 1987
Dr Eamonn Casey
It is quite clear if a tradition of justice has not been established in a particular country, no Irish citizen should be extradited to that country.

As Bishop of Galway and acting chairman of Bishops' Commission on Emigrants, opposing extradition from Irish Republic to the United Kingdom. *The Irish Times*, October 8, 1987.

October 12, 1987
Brian Lenihan
We regard them as part of a global generation of Irish people. We shouldn't be defeatist or pessimistic about it. After all, we can't all live on a small island.

As Minister for Foreign Affairs, when asked in interview if emigration was defeat for Irish Republic. *Newsweek*, October 12, 1987.

October 12, 1987
Peter Barry
While the Government may not be worried the parents of these young people are. These people have made great sacrifices to educate their children and it is madness for the benefits of this to be made available to another economy.

As Fine Gael spokesman on foreign affairs, on remarks on emigration by Brian Lenihan, above. *The Irish Times*, October 13, 1987.

November 8, 1987
Gordon Wilson

Marie said, 'Is that you, Daddy?' I said 'Yes.' 'Are you all right, Daddy?' she asked. I said, 'I'm fine.' Three or four times I asked her if she was all right and each time she replied, 'I'm fine, how are you?' I said, 'Hold on, they will be coming to have us out soon.' Then she said, 'Daddy, I love you very much.' That was the last thing she said. I have lost my daughter and we shall miss her. But I bear no ill will. I bear no grudge. Dirty sort of talk is not going to bring her back to life.

As father, after losing his daughter in IRA bombing at Enniskillen war memorial which killed 11 people. McDaniel, Denzil, *Enniskillen, the Remembrance Day Bombing*, Wolfhound Press, 1997, p. 64.

November 8, 1987
Bono

I've had enough of Irish Americans, who...come up to me and talk about the resistance, the revolution back home and the *glory* of the revolution, and the *glory* of dying for the revolution. Fuck the revolution! They don't talk about the glory of *killing* for the revolution... Where's the glory in bombing a Remembrance Day parade of old age pensioners...? No more!

As lead singer in pop group U2, on hearing of Enniskillen bombing, in words recorded over track of Sunday Bloody Sunday and subsequently included in film *Rattle and Hum*. Bardon, Jonathan, *A History of Ulster*, Blackstaff Press, 1992, p. 777.

November 9, 1987
John Hume

I sincerely hope that no one will fall into the trap that has been laid by retaliating, because the doctrine of an eye for an eye leaves everyone blind.

As leader of SDLP, in House of Commons, on Enniskillen bombing. Routledge, Paul, *John Hume*, Harper Collins, 1998, p. 216.

November 13, 1987
Frank McGuinness

For the sins of their fathers, revenge has been taken against the children of Enniskillen... This is the legacy bestowed upon them. They in turn will bestow theirs on us, making us all children of Enniskillen, stumbling together through this island, crawling forward through the mess of our history, living and dying in a house that is now forever divided. All is changed after Enniskillen.

As playwright, writing on Enniskillen bombing. *The Irish Times*, November 13, 1987.

December 1, 1987
Garret FitzGerald

Harold Wilson came over...to meet a terrorist organisation which doesn't recognise this State and wishes to bring down this State. That was an appalling act of treachery to another democratic state.

As Fine Gael leader, recalling in BBC interview meeting between then British Prime Minister Harold Wilson and IRA. *The Irish Times*, December 2, 1987.

December 18, 1987
Anonymous

Belfast Says Noel.

Amended unionist banner which originally said 'Belfast Says No' to Anglo-Irish Agreement. *The Irish Times*, December 19, 1987.

January 28, 1988
Lord Chief Justice Lane

The court has no doubt the convictions were both safe and satisfactory.

As appeals judge, dismissing appeal in London by Birmingham Six, whose conviction for IRA bombings in 1974 which killed 21 people was later overturned. *The Irish Times*, January 29, 1988.

January 28, 1988
Dr Edward Daly

After the verdict, heading for Belfast, I thought of the people in graves in Derry and the six men in prison in England. I thought of all the obscene violences and injustices in our society and of the victims of those two evils. And I wept.

As Bishop of Derry, on dismissal of appeal of Birmingham Six. Callaghan, Hugh, *Cruel Fate*, Poolbeg Press, 1994, p. 175.

January 28, 1988
Gerry Collins

Anyone who believes there was a conspiracy to prevent justice but that there should be no prosecutions is not fit for public office... The British Attorney General has given a new lease of life to the IRA.

As Minister for Justice, on decision by British Attorney General, Sir Patrick Mayhew, not to bring prosecutions in alleged RUC shoot-to-kill cases in Northern Ireland. *The Irish Times*, January 30, 1988.

February 10, 1988
Martin Cahill

I don't know. Some army officer, maybe.

As Dublin underworld figure known as 'The General', on being asked by *RTÉ* reporter Brendan O'Brien who he thought the crime boss known as 'The General' was. Williams, Paul, *The General*, O'Brien Press, 1995, p. 124.

February 29, 1988
General Sir James Glover
In no way can, or will, the Provisional IRA ever be defeated militarily.

As former head of intelligence and commander of British troops in Northern Ireland. BBC, Panorama, February 29, 1988.

March 7, 1988
Geoffrey Howe
When challenged they made movements which made the military personnel operating in support of the Gibraltar police to conclude that their own lives and the lives of others were under threat. In the light of this response they were shot.

As British Foreign Secretary, in House of Commons, on shooting of 3 unarmed IRA members, Mairead Farrell, Danny McCann and Sean Savage, in Gibraltar. Hansard, March 7, 1988.

March 10, 1988
Eric Heffer
The recent shootings in Gibraltar are tantamount to capital punishment without trial. [It was] an act of terrorism.

As Labour MP, in House of Commons, sponsoring backbench motion condemning British Army shooting of 3 unarmed IRA members in Gibraltar. The Irish Times, March 11, 1988.

March 13, 1988
Peregrine Worsthorne
Terrorists are the enemies of the state, just as the Germans were during World War II. The primary aim therefore is not to bring them to justice. The primary aim is to defeat them.

As commentator in Sunday Telegraph, on British Army shooting of 3 unarmed IRA members in Gibraltar. Sunday Telegraph, March 13, 1988.

March 13, 1988
Auberon Waugh
If a majority of Britons feel like this – and my own soundings suggest that they do – what is to stop Mrs Thatcher setting up murder squads on the South American model?

As English author, on reaction to British Army shooting of 3 unarmed IRA members in Gibraltar. Sunday Telegraph, March 13, 1988.

March 13, 1988
Norman Tebbit
Personally I've had more than a bellyful of Mr Haughey, the Prime Minister of Southern Ireland. What is wrong with the man? Now he wants to pick on our men who killed three IRA terrorists before they could kill dozens of innocent civilians as well as decent and brave soldiers.

As member of British Government, on criticism by the Taoiseach, Mr Charles Haughey, of British Army shooting of 3 unarmed IRA members in Gibraltar. Sunday Express, March 13, 1988.

March 16, 1988
Michael Stone
There's a five second delay. Have one.

As loyalist attacker, throwing hand grenade at people attending funeral in Belfast of 3 unarmed IRA members shot by British Army in Gibraltar. The Irish Times, March 19, 1988.

March 19, 1988
Rev Alex Reid
Our parish is seen as dripping in the blood of the murders.

As Belfast priest, after giving last rites to two British Army corporals killed by nationalist crowd at funeral in Belfast of victims of loyalist attacker, Michael Stone. Bew, Paul, and Gillespie, Gordon, Northern Ireland, A Chronology of the Troubles 1968-1993, Gill & Macmillan, 1993, p. 213.

March 20, 1988
Margaret Thatcher
Are there no depths to which these people will not sink?

As British Prime Minister, on televised killing of 2 British soldiers at republican funeral in Belfast. The Irish Times, March 21, 1988.

April 5, 1988
Joseph Kennedy
You don't curse in front of a Catholic priest. In our country we aren't brought up to do that.
'Go back to your country.'
Go back to yours.
'This is ours.'

As US Congressman, accompanied by priest, in exchange with British soldier at roadblock in Belfast. The Irish Times, April 6, 1988.

April 18, 1988
Lord Denning
I'm afraid they, in that series called 'Rough Justice' and the like, going into this Birmingham bombers case and the like, are doing a great disservice to the system of British justice.

As former Master of the Rolls, dismissing television programmes about injustice done to Birmingham Six, whose convictions for IRA bombings in 1974 which killed 21 people were later overturned. The Irish Times, April 19, 1988.

May 18, 1988
Colin Morris
It is surely a novel view of democracy that the Government's version of an event in the public domain should go unchallenged – not since the abolition of the Divine Right of Kings have our rulers had that privilege.

As Controller of BBC NI, on restrictions on broadcasting sought by British Government after Gibraltar killings of 3 unarmed IRA members by British Army. *The Irish Times,* May 19, 1988.

May 22, 1988
Chaim Herzog
I would like to see what the Irish army or the Irish police would do if hundreds of kids, for whatever reason, say Protestant kids, came down from the North and hurled huge rocks and petrol bombs at cars on the main road running down from Belfast to Dublin. I have a feeling they wouldn't invite them in for a cup of coffee.

As Irish-born President of Israel, on criticism of Israeli reaction to Intifada in occupied West Bank. *The Irish Times,* May 23, 1988.

May 24, 1988
Gay Mitchell
The aide-de-camp has been used for every fair at every crossroads. The Taoiseach looks like head of government of a banana republic, having his ADC traipsing all over the country.

As Fine Gael TD, in Dáil exchanges on duties of Taoiseach's aide-de-camp. *The Irish Times,* May 25, 1988.

May 31, 1988
Charles Haughey
I don't think that anyone's office should be exempt, no matter what public propaganda they engage in on their own behalf.

As Taoiseach, in Dáil, on cost-cutting, and 50 percent reduction in staff of Ombudsman, Michael Mills. *The Irish Times,* June 1, 1988.

May 31, 1988
Michael Mills
I am shocked that Mr Haughey should suggest that I am engaged in public propaganda on my own behalf when I have reported on the damage done by reducing by half my investigation staff.

As Ombudsman, responding to remarks by Taoiseach Charles Haughey, above. *The Irish Times,* June 1, 1988.

June 9, 1988
Sonny Ramphal
The Commonwealth is now what Ireland would have wished pellucidly to be 40 years ago. And it has about it no hint of exclusivity. The tolerance

and understanding of differences which are among its hallmarks are ready to be extended where they are needed.

As Secretary General of British Commonwealth, in interview in Belfast. *The Irish Times,* June 10, 1988.

August 31, 1988
Star (British Edition)
SAS Rub Out Irish Rats.

As British tabloid, in headline for British readers on killing of 3 men in Northern Ireland by British Army. *The Irish Times,* September 3, 1988.

August 31, 1988
Star (Irish Edition)
SAS Shoot Dead Three IRA Men.

As British tabloid, in headline for Irish readers on killing of 3 men in Northern Ireland by British Army. *The Irish Times,* September 3, 1988.

September 16, 1988
Rhonda Paisley
I suppose the child of a chimney sweep never thinks of her father as dirty, even when he is covered in soot.

As daughter of Rev Ian Paisley, at launch of her book, *Ian Paisley, My Father*. *The Irish Times*, September 17, 1988.

September 30, 1988
Patrick McGrory
The blunders of MI5 and British intelligence in respect of this are simply incredible and I think after these mistakes it might be a good idea if the SAS changed its motto to the Spanish Civil War motto, *Viva la muerte, y bago la intelligencia* – long live death, down with intelligence.

As lawyer for the next-of-kin, on use of SAS to apprehend 3 unarmed IRA members in Gibraltar. *The Irish Times,* October 1, 1988.

October 7, 1988
Merlyn Rees
We didn't run Northern Ireland then, and we don't now. It's something that the English do not understand – the thin thread that now holds Northern Ireland and the rest of the UK together.

As former NI Secretary of State, recalling the Ulster Workers' Strike in 1974. *The Irish Times*, October 8, 1988.

October 19, 1988
Douglas Hurd
The terrorists themselves draw support and sustenance from having access to radio and television... The Government has decided that the time has come to deny this easy platform to those who use it to propagate terrorism.

As British Home Secretary, in House of Commons, announcing ban on broadcasting voices of representatives of the IRA, Sinn Féin, Republican Sinn Féin and the UDA. *The Irish Times*, October 20, 1988.

October 19, 1988
Seamus Mallon
How many hard-line activists in West Belfast and South Armagh will lay down their guns because they can't see Gerry Adams on television?

As SDLP deputy leader, on British Government ban on broadcasting direct statements by representatives of IRA, Sinn Féin, Republican Sinn Féin and the UDA. *The Irish Times*, October 20, 1988.

October 21, 1988
John Kelly
It is grossly undesirable that...the holder of Irish ministerial office should put himself under obligation to anyone, particularly a foreign potentate, by accepting any substantial gift, let alone of a value allegedly several times his own salary.

As Fine Gael TD, in Dáil, on acceptance by Taoiseach Charles Haughey of gift of a gold dagger and diamond necklace from Saudi Arabian crown prince. *The Irish Times*, October 22, 1988.

October 26, 1988
European Court of Human Rights
It was clear that the authorities had refrained in recent years from enforcing the law in respect of private homosexual acts between consenting male adults. There was no evidence that this had been injurious to moral standards in Ireland.

As Strasbourg-based body, ruling in case brought by gay rights campaigner Senator David Norris that Irish Government should decriminalise homosexual acts in private. *The Irish Times,* November 11, 1988.

November 11, 1988
Gennady Gerasimov
Soviet people ask when will the machine of police arbitrariness with regard to dissidents in Northern Ireland be stopped at last and when will justice as regards hundreds of political prisoners who were unlawfully thrown into Ulster jails be restored.

As Soviet Foreign Ministry spokesman, after UK refused to support Soviet-organised human rights conference in Moscow. *The Irish Times*, November 12, 1988.

November 29, 1988
Margaret Thatcher
Although the Government of the Republic makes fine-sounding speeches and statements, they do not seem to be always backed up by the appropriate deeds. It is no use having the government make great declarations about fighting terrorism if they lack the resolve to put them into practice.

As British Prime Minister, on refusal by Republic to secure extradition of Rev Patrick Ryan to Britain on charges relating to the IRA. *The Irish Times*, November 30, 1988.

November 30, 1988
Des O'Malley
We are no colonial outpost... We are committed to prosecuting terrorism through the due process of law. That process demands respect, and no amount of overheated rhetoric, seeking instant gratification, can set that process to one side.

As leader of Progressive Democrats, replying to Mrs Thatcher's criticism of Irish judicial process, above. *The Irish Times*, December 1, 1988.

December 13, 1988
Gerry Fitt (Lord Fitt)
One has only to think about the history of Ireland, every Republican myth and song, there was always a priest around everywhere. You have only to think of the Croppy Boy or Boolavogue.

As former leader of SDLP, criticising Irish Government's refusal to secure extradition of Rev Patrick Ryan on charges relating to the IRA. *The Irish Times*, December 14, 1988.

1989
Bernard Levin
The Irish [have given the USA], or at least the eastern part of it, many politicians and policemen, and a few crooked but successful nineteenth-century industrialists; but a comparison with the success of the Jews and the blacks, or for that matter the Poles, and now the Chinese, leaves the Irish far behind.

As chief columnist for *London Times*, in book, *A Walk up Fifth Avenue*. O'Hanlon, Ray, *The New Irish Americans*, Roberts Rinehart, 1997, p. 199.

January 17, 1989
Douglas Hogg
Certain solicitors in Northern Ireland are unduly sympathetic to one or another terrorist organisation in Northern Ireland.

As junior Home Office minister, in House of Commons, on NI solicitors who took IRA cases. *The Irish Times*, January 21, 1989.

January 17, 1989
Seamus Mallon
It will be on the Minister's head and on the head of this government if an assassin's bullet did what his words have done.

As SDLP MP, on remarks by British junior minister Douglas Hogg, accusing NI solicitors of terrorist sympathies. *The Irish Times*, January 18, 1989.

January 21, 1989
Dr Desmond Connell
Patience is the virtue of the lover, who seeks not the instant and transitory conquest, but the enduring relationship that grows with the strong intertwining roots of mutual knowledge.

As Archbishop of Dublin, on ecumenism. *The Irish Times*, January 21, 1989.

February 13, 1989
Geraldine Finucane
I wish to condemn a statement made by Douglas Hogg recently and we firmly believe that it was instrumental in Pat's death. I totally refute claims made by the UFF that Pat was a member of the IRA. Patrick was a solicitor who worked for human rights and civil liberties. He defended both Catholic and Protestant alike.

As wife of solicitor, Pat Finucane, shot dead by loyalists, on January 17 statement by British junior minister Douglas Hogg, accusing certain NI solicitors of terrorist sympathies. *The Irish Times*, February 14, 1989.

c. March 1, 1989
Gerry Adams
[The IRA has] to be careful, and careful again.

As President of Sinn Féin, at árd fheis, on 'mistakes' by IRA. Sharrock, David, and Davenport, Mark, *Man of War, Man of Peace*, Pan, 1988, p. 268.

March 3, 1989
Dr Cahal Daly
There have been calls from the IRA, from their political frontmen to 'refine' their operations, to be 'careful and careful again'. A simple translation is: 'Comrades, kill carefully.'

As Bishop of Down and Connor. *The Irish Times*, March 4, 1989.

April 2, 1989
Jim Kemmy
I never thought I'd live to see the day – and not an anti-communist bleat out of anyone.

As chairman of Democratic Socialist Party, on warm Irish welcome given at Shannon Airport to Soviet leader Mikhail Gorbachev. *The Irish Times*, April 3, 1989.

April 2, 1989
Mikhail Gorbachev
Not a stopover but a milestone.

As Soviet leader, characterising his visit to Shannon which lasted length of time it took to refuel his Canada-bound plane. *The Irish Times*, April 3, 1989.

May 26, 1989
Austin Currie
I don't think that meaningful devolution can occur as long as Dr Paisley and Mr Molyneaux are in control of their parties and adopt the attitude they do.

As new member of Fine Gael, explaining why he was leaving SDLP. *The Irish Times*, May 27, 1989.

June 29, 1989
Peadar Clohessy
Next week is another day.

As Progressive Democrat TD, on party's voting intentions in Dáil. *The Irish Times*, July 1, 1989.

July 12, 1989
Tony Gregory
When I got a deal for the homeless, medical cards for pensioners and attempted to have run-down areas of Dublin renovated, it was referred to as 'stroke politics'. When over the last few days deputies bartered for Mercs and high positions in the cabinet the media saw it as a new dawn and a move towards continental-style politics.

As independent TD, commenting on Fianna Fáil and PD post-election pact. *The Irish Times*, July 13, 1989.

August 1989
IRA Spokesman
There will be no ceasefire and no truces until Britain declares its intent to withdraw and leave our people in peace.

Republican News, August 1989.

August 5, 1989
John Donnellan
He would come out with a fork if it started raining soup.

As Fine Gael TD for West Galway, resigning from party in protest at leadership of Alan Dukes. *The Irish Times*, August 5, 1989.

August 7, 1989
Shane Paul O'Doherty
I came to the conclusion that injuring people and taking people's lives...created a society of massive injustice. We became part of the problem.

As former IRA member, in television interview before being released on licence from 30 life sentences imposed in 1976 for sending letter bombs. *The Irish Times*, August 8, 1989.

August 23, 1989
Dr Cahal Daly
The IRA and Sinn Féin...simply do not know how utterly peripheral they are to public opinion. They are living in a political past. They are politically yesterday's people.

As Bishop of Down and Connor, in interview. *The Irish Times*, August 23, 1989.

August 24, 1989
Alan Dukes
Only I had promised Garret that all I was going to do was sit and listen, I'd have been dug out of that bastard.

As Fine Gael leader, on meeting with unnamed Catholic bishop whom he claimed was 'utterly opportunistic' on marriage laws. *The Irish Times*, August 24, 1989.

September 22, 1989
Gerald Collins
We should never let the politics of the last atrocity to deflect or sidetrack us from achieving political progress and reform in Northern Ireland.

As Minister for Foreign Affairs, in telegram to NI Secretary Peter Brooke, after IRA bomb killed 10 at Royal Marines School of Music in Kent. *The Irish Times*, September 23, 1989.

October 19, 1989
Gerard Conlon
I'm an innocent man. I shouldn't have been in jail.

As member of Guildford Four, declared innocent after 14 years in prison for Guildford and Woolwich bombings. *The Irish Times*, October 20, 1989.

October 19, 1989
Tony Scrivener
Thank God we didn't have the death penalty in Britain.

As counsel for Gerard Conlon, declared innocent after serving 14 years for Guildford and Woolwich bombing. *The Irish Times*, October 20, 1989.

November 2, 1989
Peter Brooke
If in fact the terrorists were to decide that the moment had come when they wished to withdraw from their activities, then I think that government would need to be imaginative...in how it responded. Let me remind you of the move towards independence in Cyprus and a British Minister stood up and used the word 'never'...in two years there had been a retreat from that word.

As NI Secretary of State, opening door to talks with Sinn Féin. *The Irish Times*, November 4, 1989.

November 5, 1989
John Hume
They [Unionists] may forgive me for reminding them that they have always been a party of the '90s – the 1690s!

As leader of SDLP, at party conference, on Unionist Party claim to be the party of the '90s. Routledge, Paul, *John Hume*, Harper Collins, 1998, p. 235.

November 6, 1989
Gerry Adams
Mr Brooke's refusal to rule out future talks with Sinn Féin is a public admission of the inevitability of such talks. Sinn Féin is ready at any time to discuss the conditions in which justice and peace can be established.

As President of Sinn Féin, responding to Peter Brooke's statement of November 2. *The Irish Times*, November 7, 1989.

November 25, 1989
Rev William McCrea
It is not that the British cannot beat the IRA but it is that they do not want to do so. For if they defeated the Provos, they would have to stay, whereas they are determined to get out.

As DUP MP for Mid-Ulster, at party conference. *The Irish Times*, November 27, 1989.

November 28, 1989
Cardinal Tomás Ó Fiaich
I think what would be a good move in the North would be if, instead, the British said: Look, we're not going to stay here for all time.

As Primate of Ireland, on Peter Brooke's statement of November 2. *The Irish Times*, December 2, 1989.

1990
Seamus Heaney
History says, Don't hope
On this side of the grave,
But then, once in a lifetime
The longed-for tidal wave
Of justice can rise up
And hope and history rhyme.

As poet, from 'The Curse of Troy', 1990. Heaney, Seamus, *On Open Ground, Poems 1966-1996*, Faber and Faber, 1998, p. 330.

March 13, 1990
Margaret Thatcher
[This decision is] grossly offensive.

As British Prime Minister, on refusal of Supreme Court in Dublin to extradite two Republican prisoners to Northern Ireland because of alleged risk to their lives. Bew, Paul, and Gillespie, Gordon, *Northern Ireland, A Chronology of the Troubles 1968-1993*, Gill & Macmillan, 1993, p. 251.

March 13, 1990
Dr Joseph Duffy
We don't ignore the reality of condoms, but condoms in their proper place.

As spokesman for Catholic Hierarchy. *The Irish Times*, March 15, 1990.

March 16, 1990
George Bush
Once you've had a glass of Guinness with a man in Ireland, as I have with Brian Lenihan, why, you're friends.

As US President, welcoming Tanaiste Brian Lenihan, to White House. *The Irish Times*, March 17, 1990.

April 11, 1990
Garret FitzGerald
I do not want to spend the next 14 years saying only anodyne things.

As former Taoiseach, on why he would not run for president. *The Irish Times*, April 12, 1990.

April 28, 1990
Rev Denis Faul
The Catholic people in Northern Ireland, in the ghetto areas, live in a state of fear. They are in fear of the forces of law and order, and they are in greater fear of the IRA.

As Dungannon priest. *The Irish Times*, April 28, 1990.

April 28, 1990
Proinsias de Rossa
History has dealt a mortal blow to those who gave blind, uncritical support to the Eastern bloc. It is a valid criticism of my party that we did not more publicly criticise the defects we saw. But socialism is not dead... Stalinism is dead.

As President of Workers' Party, at árd fheis. *The Irish Times*, April 30, 1990.

May 1, 1990
Mary Robinson
I am looking forward to being a president for all the people, and that means for many who are under-represented or who have not got a voice in our very unequal society.

As independent candidate for president, launching campaign in Limerick. *The Irish Times,* May 2, 1990.

May 14, 1990
Rev Ian Paisley
Cardinal O'Fee (sic), so-called Prince of the Church, has gone to answer at the bar of Almighty God where his cardinal's cloak will bring him no favours.

As leader of Free Presbyterian Church, in leaflet after death of Cardinal Tomás Ó Fiaich. *The Irish Times*, May 15, 1990.

May 17, 1990
Brian Lenihan
Oh yeah, I mean I got through to him. I remember talking to him and he wanted us to lay off. There was no doubt about it in his mind.

As Minister for Defence, in response to question from academic researcher Jim Duffy on telephoning President Hillery on January 27, 1982, an answer which he changed when it became an issue in 1990 presidential election. Lenihan, Brian, *For the Record*, Blackwater Press, 1991, p. 110.

May 17, 1990
John Stevens
[Leakage of information] was restricted to a small number of members of the security forces and is neither widespread nor institutionalised.

As Cambridgeshire deputy chief constable, in report on collusion between NI security forces and loyalist paramilitaries. Bew, Paul, and Gillespie, Gordon, *Northern Ireland, A Chronology of the Troubles 1968-1993*, Gill & Macmillan, 1993, p. 234.

May 18, 1990
Richard Branson
The Irish Government hold the EC presidency and are a modern western democracy, but they appear to be treating their citizens with the same disregard as Ceauçescu did in Romania.

As chairman of Virgin Megastore, after conviction of Irish Family Planning Association for selling condoms at his Dublin store. *The Irish Times*, May 19, 1990.

June 29, 1990
Rev Michael O'Doherty
Reconciliation, tender loving care, and cash.

As representative of Catholic Marriage Advisory Council, on what soccer fans would need from their spouses on returning home after Ireland's long World Cup run in Italy. *The Irish Times*, June 30, 1990.

July 1, 1990
Sean Haughey
We may not have won the World Cup but we won the world!

As Dublin alderman, addressing crowds in O'Connell Street welcoming home Irish soccer team which reached quarterfinals of World Cup. *The Irish Times*, July 2, 1990.

July 2, 1990
Nelson Mandela
The outstanding Irish poet, William Butler Yeats, has written that too long a sacrifice can make a stone of the heart... We had to refuse that our long sacrifice should make a stone of our hearts.

As leader of African National Congress, addressing joint session of the Oireachtas shortly after his release from prison in South Africa. McLoughlin, Michael, *Great Irish Speeches of the Twentieth Century*, Poolbeg Press, 1996, pp. 374-375.

July 2, 1990
Nelson Mandela
What we would like to see is that the British Government and the IRA should adopt precisely

the line that we have taken to our own internal situation – settle down to resolve their problems in a peaceful manner.

As leader of African National Congress, at joint press conference with Charles Haughey in Dublin. *The Irish Times*, July 3, 1990.

July 6, 1990
Peter Brooke

We British are sometimes told we do not understand the Irish, but if this is so the failure to understand is a two-way street. Everything in which the IRA is currently engaged suggests that it does not understand us at all.

As NI Secretary of State. *The Irish Times*, July 7, 1990.

July 30, 1990
Margaret Thatcher

If he could speak to me now, he would say: 'You fight the battle against them. You bring them to justice and see that they are properly condemned and found guilty for what they have done.' And that's how we shall carry on.

As British Prime Minister, on killing of her former parliamentary private secretary and friend, Ian Gow MP, by IRA. *The Irish Times*, August 1, 1990.

August 17, 1990
Lord Denning

We shouldn't have all these campaigns to get the Birmingham Six released. If they had been hanged they would have been forgotten…the whole community would have been satisfied.

As former Master of the Rolls, on campaigns to free Birmingham Six, whose convictions for IRA bombings in 1974 which killed 21 people were later overturned. *Spectator*, August 17, 1990.

August 26, 1990
Sinead O'Connor

I didn't want to go on stage after the anthem of a country that's arresting people, harassing people, for expressing themselves on stage.

As singer, declaring she would not perform at New Jersey concert if 'Star Spangled Banner' was played (it wasn't). *USA Today*, August 27, 1990.

August 27, 1990
Frank Sinatra

I wish I could get her so I could kick her ass.

As American singer, after Sinead O'Connor refused to perform at New Jersey concert if 'Star Spangled Banner' was played. *The Irish Times*, August 28, 1990.

August 30, 1990
Brian Keenan

I'm going to visit all the countries in the world, eat all the food in the world, drink all the drink in the world, make love, I hope, to all the women in the world, and maybe I'll get a good night's sleep at the end of it all.

As Belfast teacher, in Dublin, after his release as a hostage for 1,600 days in Lebanon. *The Irish Times*, September 1, 1990.

September 19, 1990
Margaret Thatcher

They are at war with us and we can only fight them with the civil law. The question is whether we can do anything for protection, and also assure ourselves that the Republic of Ireland is doing all it can to track down terrorists and their store of weapons.

As British Prime Minister, after IRA shot and wounded Sir Peter Terry, Governor of Gibraltar, at time of killing of 3 unarmed IRA members there by SAS. *The Irish Times*, September 20, 1990.

October 4, 1990
Mary Robinson

Nobody gives a shit about them.

As independent candidate for president, in *Hot Press* interview, criticising Irish attitudes to emigrants. O'Leary, Olivia, and Burke, Helen, *Mary Robinson, The Authorised Biography*, Hodder & Stoughton, 1998, p. 190.

October 4, 1990
Mary Robinson

Yes. This is a very young country and I think it would be helpful to have a president who was in touch with what young people are doing.

As independent candidate for president, in *Hot Press* interview, when asked if she would open a stall in a Dublin record store selling condoms, in breach of Irish law. Siggins, Lorna, *Mary Robinson*, Mainstream Publishing, 1997, p. 135.

October 15, 1990
Austin Currie

I was born 20 miles North of the Border, but take Eamon de Valera – he was born in New York, his father was Spanish. But did anyone say to him he had no right to be president?

As Fine Gael candidate for president, responding to criticisms that he came from Northern Ireland. *The Irish Times*, October 16, 1990.

October 21, 1990
Garret FitzGerald

When I arrived at Áras an Uachtaráin about two hours after my Dáil defeat [on January 27, 1982], I found that the President had been besieged by senior Fianna Fáil TDs demanding that he refuse me a dissolution of the Dáil and require my resignation as a preliminary to inviting the Fianna Fáil leader to seek Dáil support for nomination as Taoiseach without an election. As I recall it the most persistent of these callers was the present presidential candidate, Brian Lenihan.

As Fine Gael leader, alleging Fianna Fáil TDs improperly pressurised President Hillery on forming a government in 1982. Lenihan, Brian, *For the Record*, Blackwater Press, 1991, p. 78.

October 23, 1990
Brian Lenihan

Other people may have rung the President about what was going to happen now, but I had nothing to do with it, good, bad or indifferent.

As Fianna Fáil candidate for president, responding to claim by *Irish Times* that it had corroborative evidence that he telephoned Áras an Uachtaráin during government crisis in 1982, which he had denied. *The Irish Times*, October 24, 1990.

October 25, 1990
Brian Lenihan

What I am saying to you now, Sean, and I am telling the Irish public now, is that, on mature recollection, and full reflection, I did not ring President Hillery on that night.

As Fianna Fáil candidate for president, in *RTÉ* interview with Sean O'Rourke, after emergence of tape recording of May 17, 1990 in which he said he did ring President Hillery on the night in question. *RTÉ*, October 25, 1990.

October 25, 1990
Jim Mitchell

Brian Lenihan should be hauled in here and hung,, drawn and quartered.

As Fine Gael director of elections, in Dáil debate on Fianna Fáil candidate's contradictory statements on telephone calls to President. *The Irish Times*, October 26, 1990.

October 26, 1990
Mary O'Rourke

Get back across the Shannon from whence you came. You come not in friendship but in guile.

As Fianna Fáil TD and sister of Brian Lenihan, to party colleague, Padraig Flynn, in Moate, on suspicion Flynn wanted to persuade Brian Lenihan to resign from Government over disputed telephone calls. Whelan, Ken and Masterson, Eugene, *Bertie Ahern*, Blackwater Press, 1998, p. 77.

October 30, 1990
Austin Currie

Harold Wilson said a week is a long time in politics. I can assure him, he being a stupid Englishman, things can change in two minutes.

As Fine Gael candidate for president, on sacking of Fianna Fáil candidate, Brian Lenihan, from Government by Taoiseach Charles Haughey. *The Irish Times*, October 31, 1990.

November 2, 1990
Padraig Flynn

Of course it doesn't always suit if you get labelled a socialist, because that's a very narrow focus in this country – so she has to try and have it both ways. She has to have new clothes and her new look and her new hairdo and she has the new interest in her family, being a mother and all that kind of thing. But none of you know, none of us who knew Mrs Robinson very well in previous incarnations ever heard her claiming to be a great wife and mother.

As Fianna Fáil representative, on *RTÉ* Saturday View, in much-criticised comment on presidential candidate Mary Robinson. Lenihan, Brian, *For the Record*, Blackwater Press, 1991, p. 191.

c. November 2, 1990
Mary Robinson

[He is] an aging movie queen.

As independent candidate for president, in statement challenging Brian Lenihan to debate in closing stages of presidential election campaign. O'Leary, Olivia, and Burke, Helen, *Mary Robinson, The Authorised Biography*, Hodder & Stoughton, 1998, p. 131.

November 6, 1990
Dick Spring

This debate is not about Brian Lenihan... It is a debate about how a once great party has been brought to its knees by the grasping acquisitiveness of its leader. It is ultimately a debate about the cancer that is eating away at our body politic – and the virus which caused that cancer, An Taoiseach, Charles J. Haughey.

As leader of Labour Party, in Dáil. Lenihan, Brian, *For the Record*, Blackwater Press, 1991, p. 173.

November 9, 1990
Mary Robinson

Even as I salute my supporters as Mary Robinson, I must also bid them farewell as President Elect... I was elected by men and women of all parties and none... And above all by Mna na hÉireann, who instead of rocking the cradle, rocked the system. I am not just a president of those here today but of those who cannot be here; and there will always be a light on in Áras an Uachtaráin for our exiles and emigrants.

As first woman president of Republic of Ireland, in acceptance speech. Finlay, Fergus, *Mary Robinson, A President with a Purpose*, O'Brien Press, 1990, pp. 8-9.

November 9, 1990
Peter Brooke

The British Government has no selfish strategic or economic interest in Northern Ireland.

As NI Secretary of State, in new initiative to try to end violence. *The Irish Times*, January 9, 1991.

November 18, 1990
William Trevor
A disease in the family that is never mentioned.
As author, on Northern Ireland. *Observer*, November 18, 1990.

December 2, 1990
Gerry Hunter
Remember Brian Keenan, well all the drink he couldn't finish, all the women he couldn't have, we'll help him finish.
As member of Birmingham Six, on eve of release from prison, referring to Brian Keenan's comments of August 30, 1990. *The Irish Times*, December 3, 1990.

December 3, 1990
Mary Robinson
May it be a presidency where I, the President, can sing to you, citizens of Ireland, the joyous refrain of the fourteenth-century Irish poet as recalled by W. B. Yeats: 'I am of Ireland, come dance with me in Ireland.'
As President, in inauguration speech. Siggins, Lorna, *Mary Robinson*, Mainstream Publishing, 1997, p. 151.

December 14, 1990
George Shields
Do they consider themselves officers and gentlemen that they dare to offer an apology.
As brother of David Shields, shot dead by IRA on basis of 'erroneous information'. *The Irish Times*, December 15, 1990.

December 17, 1990
Cardinal Cahal Daly
The longer you continue with your campaign of violence, the more ignominious in the end will be the memory you will leave behind you and the further away from attainment will be any of your aims and objectives.
As Primate of Ireland, on IRA, at installation. *The Irish Times*, December 22, 1990.

December 23, 1990
Most Rev Robin Eames
It's not a question of Brits Out, it's a question of Protestants Out.
As Church of Ireland Archbishop of Armagh, on IRA campaign. *The Irish Times*, December 24, 1990.

December 29, 1990
Monica Barnes
Quite a few male commentators are throwing cold water on the idea of the women's vote, but it is there and things will never be the same again.
As Fine Gael TD, on election of Mary Robinson as President. *The Irish Times*, December 29, 1990.

December 31, 1990
Charles Haughey
I like the company of poets. They take you away from the boring realities of life, if you like, and open up all sorts of exciting things, sometimes quite startling.
As Taoiseach, in interview. *The Irish Times*, December 31, 1990.

February 3, 1991
David Norris
The people in that building wouldn't recognise a civil right if it came up and pissed in their eye.
As member of Senate, and member of picket outside Sinn Féin árd fheis in Dublin. *The Irish Times*, February 9, 1991.

February 7, 1991
IRA
While the nationalist people of the Six Counties are forced to live under British rule, then the British Cabinet will be forced to meet in bunkers.
In statement after mortar bomb fired into garden of No 10 Downing Street during Cabinet meeting. Bardon, Jonathan, *A History of Ulster*, Blackstaff Press, 1992, p. 806.

February 25, 1991
Graham Boal
Having considered all the material, the respondent does not submit that the convictions are both safe and satisfactory.
As barrister, representing British Director of Public Prosecutions, rejecting evidence used to convict Birmingham Six of pub bombings which killed 21 people. *The Irish Times*, February 26, 1991.

February 25, 1991
Kate McIlkenny
Unsafe and unsound! I'm going to get that in print. Those words will be in my memory for the rest of my life.
As wife of Richard McIlkenny of Birmingham Six, after DPP in London rejected evidence used to convict her husband. *The Irish Times*, March 2, 1991.

February 26, 1991
Richard Branson
It is an utter disgrace that in the 1990s, the laws of Ireland would be responsible for the deaths of thousands of young people.
As chairman of Virgin Megastore, referring to AIDS victims, after Irish Family Planning Association was fined for selling contraceptives at his Dublin store. *The Irish Times*, February 27, 1991.

March 3, 1991
Cardinal Cahal Daly
A great deal of the present pressure is aimed at making condoms widely available, particularly at places where young people congregate, where they come for recreation, where they come – alas in too great numbers – for drink, where they come to dance, where they come for meals and so on.

As Primate of Ireland, opposing law liberalising contraceptive sales. *The Irish Times*, March 4, 1991.

March 5, 1991
Dr Brendan Comiskey
Today's rulers are attempting to do with condoms what their predecessors did with bread and circuses.

As Bishop of Ferns, opposing liberalising contraceptive sales. *The Irish Times*, March 6, 1991.

March 11, 1991
Dr Michael Smith
The way in which they affect behaviour could also have the consequence of spreading AIDS.

As Bishop of Meath, on condoms. *RTÉ*, March 11, 1991.

March 11, 1991
Rev Graham Hamilton
If [young people] are going to be sexually active, they at least might use safe sex or practice safe sex using a condom.

As Secretary of Methodist Board of Education, responding to claim by Bishop of Meath, Dr Smith, above, that the availability of condoms might encourage behaviour which would spread AIDS. *The Irish Times*, March 12, 1991.

March 14, 1991
Paddy Hill
I don't think the people in there have got the intelligence nor the honesty to spell the word [justice], never mind dispense it.

As member of Birmingham Six, on emerging from Court of Appeal after conviction overturned. *The Irish Times*, March 15, 1991.

March 14, 1991
Billy Power
The first fifteen years were the worst. It was all downhill after that.

As member of Birmingham Six, who spent 16 ½ years in prison, on emerging from Court of Appeal after conviction overturned. *The Irish Times*, March 15, 1991.

March 15, 1991
Des O'Malley
The disease [AIDS] kills in very painful circumstances, and to a lot of people that isn't irrelevant or a red herring.

As leader of Progressive Democrats, replying to Bishop of Limerick, Dr Newman, who said the issue of AIDS was a 'red herring' in the condom debate. *The Irish Times*, March 16, 1991.

March 15, 1991
Anne Maguire
You can be Irish in New York and you can be gay, but it hasn't been that you can be both.

As spokesperson for Irish Lesbian and Gay Organisation, in New York, after group excluded from St Patrick's Day parade. *The Irish Times*, March 16, 1991.

March 17, 1991
Edward Koch
Only in New York do you have a St Patrick's Day parade with a governor, Mario Cuomo, marching with invalids in wheelchairs, the mayor marching with gays and lesbians, and me, a Jewish boy, marching with the police department's Holy Name Society.

As former mayor of New York. *The Irish Times*, March 18, 1991.

March 28, 1991
Peter Brooke
We are setting out to achieve a new beginning for relationships within Northern Ireland, within the island of Ireland and between the peoples of these islands.

As NI Secretary of State, in House of Commons, announcing agreement on three-strand talks. *The Irish Times*, March 30, 1991.

March 31, 1991
Mary Holland
What do you get when you cross [NI Secretary] Peter Brooke with Don Corleone? Answer: An offer you don't understand but can't refuse.

As political columnist, relating anecdote told in Belfast political circles. *Observer*, March 31, 1991.

April 1, 1991
Bertie Ahern
In political life you have a hassle period of some difficulties. I'm neither separated nor the best family man in the world. I'm somewhere in between.

As Minister for Labour, on his private life. *The Irish Times*, April 6, 1991.

April 18, 1991
Combined Loyalist Military Command
[Our ceasefire is] a genuine and sincere move to bring about a peaceful and acceptable solution.

As body representing UDA and UVF, on limited ceasefire for duration of three-strand talks. *The Irish Times*, April 20, 1990.

April 24, 1991
IRA
Should these death squads become inactive, then the IRA will monitor the situation and act accordingly.

Responding to UDA and UFF ceasefire. *The Irish Times,* April 27, 1991.

April 24, 1991
Rev Ian Paisley
If we could get rid of Articles 2 and 3...the Berlin Wall which the Constitution built between North and South would be removed.

As leader of DUP, anticipating three-strand talks. *The Irish Times,* April 27, 1991.

c. May 1, 1991
Brian Lenihan
In health and mind I am a relatively young man. Years of involvement in politics at the highest level have not, in the immortal words of Patrick Kavanagh, 'flung a ditch on my vision of beauty, love and truth'.

As former Fianna Fáil Minister, in book on 1990 presidential campaign. Lenihan, Brian, *For the Record,* Blackwater Press, 1991, p. 226.

June 17, 1991
John Bruton
They [Fianna Fáil] still seem to see the office as a preserve...redolent of top hats, motorcades, museum openings and the odd distant wave from a passing limousine... Far from shutting our President up, we should be showing her off.

As leader of Fine Gael, on refusal by Taoiseach Charles Haughey to allow President Mary Robinson deliver Dimbleby lecture in London as 'not appropriate'. *The Irish Times,* June 22, 1991.

June 21, 1991
Colonel Muammar Gadafy
Ireland is a just cause. We support it, terrorism or not.

As Libyan leader, after UK refused to resume diplomatic relations. *The Irish Times,* June 22, 1991.

August 2, 1991
Rhonda Paisley
The Irish Republic now faces a dose of its own medicine as they harbour perpetrators of violence in Ulster.

As daughter of Rev Ian Paisley, on loyalist firebomb attacks in Republic. *The Irish Times,* August 3, 1991.

August 2, 1991
Michael Bell
It is people like her who have this country the way it is. The only way this country will be

united and be at peace is when people like her return to Britain.

As Labour Party TD and Justice spokesman, on comment of Rhonda Paisley, above. *The Irish Times,* August 3, 1991.

August 3, 1991
Steve McBride
There can be no place in the Ireland of the future for this sectarian rubbish.

As Alliance Party legal affairs spokesman, commenting on Michael Bell remark, above. *The Irish Times,* August 4, 1991.

August 6, 1991
Margaret Thatcher
Every Prime Minister needs a Willie.

As British Prime Minister, at farewell dinner for William Whitelaw, former NI Secretary of State. *Guardian,* August 6, 1991.

August 26, 1991
Dr Michael Murphy
It's a silly season for silly people.

As Bishop of Cork and Ross, dismissing claims of sighting of Virgin Mary at Ballytrasna, Co Cork. *The Irish Times,* August 31, 1991.

September 6, 1991
John Taylor
The harsh reality is that, as one walks down the street or goes into work, one out of every three Roman Catholics one meets is either a supporter of murder or, worse still, a murderer.

As unionist MP, on Sinn Féin electoral support among Catholics. *The Irish Times,* September 7, 1991.

October 4, 1991
Dr Eamonn Casey
It is the people who suffered most themselves who feel for others who suffer.

As Bishop of Galway and Chairman of Trocaire, on how Northern Ireland dioceses contributed most in Ireland to Third World. *The Irish Times,* October 5, 1991.

October 10, 1991
Gerry Collins
The old hard-line communist rump must never raise its ugly head again.

As Minister for Foreign Affairs, on Baltic Republics. *RTÉ,* October 10, 1991.

October 16, 1991
Charles Haughey
Hyped up and exaggerated by a massive campaign of vilification and character assassination of unprecedented intensity, without regard to evidence, proof or justification.

As Taoiseach, on alleged involvement in business controversies. *The Irish Times*, October 19, 1991.

October 16, 1991
John Bruton
The PDs are like Mao Zedong. He believed in perpetual revolution. They believe in perpetual negotiation.

As leader of Fine Gael, on lengthy PD-Fianna Fáil negotiations to remain coalition partners. *The Irish Times*, October 19, 1991.

c. October 16, 1991
Charles Haughey
He's the cleverest, the most cunning, the best of the lot.

As Taoiseach, describing Fianna Fáil TD Bertie Ahern to political correspondents after success of Ahern's negotiations with PDs. Whelan, Ken, and Masterson, Eugene, *Bertie Ahern*, Blackwater Press, 1998, p. 86.

October 16, 1991
Mary Robinson
It reminded me of a race meeting with tic-tac men. I was afraid to wave in case of implications.

As President, on visit to Chicago Mercantile Exchange. *The Irish Times*, October 19, 1991.

October 21, 1991
Boston Globe
As much as Mary Robinson would like to change Ireland's conservative, patriarchal, political culture...she often found herself surrounded by priests and politicians.

As US newspaper, on visit of President to Boston. *The Irish Times*, October 22, 1991.

October 21, 1991
Edward Kennedy
She is already a president for all seasons. Perhaps one day she will be a president for all Ireland.

As US Senator, welcoming President Mary Robinson in Boston. *The Irish Times*, October 22, 1991.

October 25, 1991
Belfast Taxi Driver
We are the softest of targets. All anyone has to do is look through the Yellow Pages, pick a likely taxi firm, and then dial a death.

As target of sectarian assassinations. *The Irish Times*, October 26, 1991.

November 7, 1991
Albert Reynolds
For some time now there has been considerable political instability which has led to an erosion of confidence in our democratic institutions. This uncertainty must not be allowed to continue.

As Minister for Finance, signalling withdrawal of support for Taoiseach Charles Haughey as leader of Fianna Fáil. *The Irish Times*, November 8, 1991.

November 7, 1991
Gerry Collins
It shows a frightful political immaturity...to vote Charles Haughey out of office and take it on for himself is going to wreck our party right down the centre. It's going to bust up Government.

As Minister for Foreign Affairs, on bid by Albert Reynolds for Fianna Fáil leadership. *The Irish Times*, November 8, 1991.

November 9, 1991
Charles Haughey
When Albert Reynolds talks about political stability, that seems to me very much like a bookie complaining about gambling.

As Taoiseach, on leadership challenge of Minister for Finance, Albert Reynolds. *RTÉ*, November 9, 1991.

November 14, 1991
James McDaid
In order to avoid the slightest suspicion, however unwarranted, attaching to the Minister for Defence, and in the broader national interest, I have requested the Taoiseach to withdraw my nomination... I have made it quite clear that I abhor the IRA.

As Donegal TD, declining Cabinet post after being accused of IRA sympathies for supporting constituent over extradition charge. *The Irish Times*, November 15, 1991.

November 14, 1991
Dick Spring
The arrogance, insensitivity and gross misjudgement he deployed yesterday proved once and for all...that Ireland deserves better... Taoiseach you must, today, consider your position. You must go, and go now.

As leader of Labour Party, calling for resignation of Taoiseach Charles Haughey in row over choice of Minister for Defence. *The Irish Times*, November 15, 1991.

November 14, 1991
Charles Haughey
I am tired, and the country is tired, of the hypocrites of virtue, ever ready with the instant moral judgement, the accusing finger.

As Taoiseach, replying to critics, including Dick Spring, above. *The Irish Times*, November 15, 1991.

November 22, 1991
Kenneth Baker
Those who live by terror will die by terror. Here the victims are the culprits.

As British Home Secretary, on two IRA members killed by own bomb in St Alban's. *The Irish Times*, November 23, 1998.

December 1, 1991
Roy Gillespie
The Roman Catholic Church is the problem in our province... Rome's aim is to destroy Protestantism, our children, our children's children, our way of life and the Bible.

As DUP councillor, at party conference. *The Irish Times*, December 7, 1991.

December 5, 1991
Gerry Adams
It should be clear by now that after two decades of failed initiatives, there is no partitionist solution.

As President of Sinn Féin, on resumption of talks between London and Dublin. *The Irish Times*, December 7, 1991.

December 6, 1991
Thomas Kenneally
For people in the South, the North is the great family denial, the unruly, deviant brother who's dying of AIDS.

As Australian author, visiting Dublin. *The Irish Times*, December 7, 1991.

December 20, 1991
Andrew Faulds
Taking a life is obscene, but damage to historic bits of culture, if that was their aim, is absolutely outrageous.

As British Labour MP, on IRA firebomb attack on National Gallery in London. *The Irish Times*, December 21, 1991.

January 15, 1992
Sean Doherty
There was a decision taken in Cabinet that...the leaking of matters from Cabinet must be stopped. I, as Minister for Justice, had a direct responsibility for doing that. I did that. I do feel that I was let down by the fact that people knew what I was doing.

As former Minister for Justice, revealing that Cabinet colleagues knew of telephone tapping of journalists in 1982. *The Irish Times*, January 16, 1992.

January 17, 1992
Charles Haughey
[This is] a total falsehood.

As Taoiseach, on suggestion that as Taoiseach in 1982 he was shown transcripts of phone taps on journalists. *The Irish Times*, January 18, 1992.

January 17, 1992
Gay Byrne
I imagine that singing that song will give a fair amount of ammunition to a fair number of people.

As host of *RTÉ's* Late Late Show, to NI Secretary of State Peter Brooke, after urging Brooke to sing 'Clementine' despite news of killing of seven Protestant construction workers by IRA near Cookstown. *RTÉ*, January 17, 1992.

January 17, 1992
Peter Brooke
I imagine it will.

As NI Secretary of State, replying to Gay Byrne, above. *RTÉ*, January 17, 1992.

January 20, 1992
Peter Brooke
[My decision to yield] to an unsignalled invitation to sing on the show was innocent in intent [but] it was politically in error.

As NI Secretary of State, offering to resign (not accepted) for singing on *RTÉ's* Late Late Show after killing of seven Protestant workers in North. *The Irish Times*, January 21, 1992.

January 21, 1992
Sean Doherty
I am confirming tonight that the Taoiseach, Mr Haughey, was fully aware in 1982 that two journalists' phones were being tapped and that he at no stage expressed a reservation about this action... As soon as the transcripts became available I took them personally to his office... I took the blame when Mr Haughey stated on *RTÉ* radio that he would 'not have countenanced' such an action, and described it as an 'abuse of power'.

As former Minister for Justice. *The Irish Times*, January 22, 1992.

January 22, 1992
Charles Haughey
I wish to state categorically that I was not aware at the time of the tapping of these telephones and that I was not given and did not see any transcripts of the conversations.

As Taoiseach, replying to Sean Doherty, above. *The Irish Times*, January 23, 1992.

January 31, 1992
Lt-Colonel Derek Wilford
I hear people say 'Troops out of Ireland.' It's like 'Troops out of Aden.' Then we made a positive decision, and I think we need to make a positive decision now about ending the war in Ireland.

As commander of Parachute Regiment in Derry on Bloody Sunday, 1972. *The Irish Times*, January 31, 1992.

February 11, 1992
Charles Haughey
'I have done the State some service, and they know't.
No more of that.'

As Taoiseach, in Dáil, quoting from Shakespeare's *Othello*, on resigning after disclosures by former Minister for Justice Sean Doherty about telephone tapping while he was Taoiseach. *The Irish Times*, February 12, 1992.

February 14, 1992
Triona Dooney
We have already seen the forced closure of pregnancy clinics, a legal witchhunt against students, the forced removal from library shelves of serious health publications, and now this court case. What will the next step be? The questioning or pregnancy testing of women leaving the country?

As Workers' Party women's affairs spokeswoman, on 14-year-old girl (known as Miss X) raped by neighbour, who was served with injunction to prevent her having an abortion in England. *The Irish Times*, February 15, 1992.

February 15, 1992
Sean Garland
There is nothing new in what the liquidators want to do. All over the world in the recent past, opportunists have emerged in progressive parties...singing the same song, the failure of socialism, the problems that democratic centralism cause.

As former General Secretary of Workers' Party, on attempt by Proinsias de Rossa at árd fheis to reconstitute party. *The Irish Times*, February 17, 1992.

February 15, 1992
Proinsias de Rossa
What is crucial for socialists now is to explore how new and renewed concepts of class and of power may serve to illuminate and transform this new situation.

As leader of Workers' Party, at árd fheis, in unsuccessful attempt to reconstitute party. *The Irish Times*, February 17, 1992.

February 16, 1992
Albert Reynolds
I will work day and night, go anywhere with any of my colleagues, to work out that new path for peace.

As newly elected Taoiseach, declaring at Longford Rally that his priority would be Northern Ireland. *The Irish Times*, February 17, 1992.

February 17, 1992
Miss X
It is hard at 14 to go through the nine months. It is better to end it now than in nine months time.

As rape victim, in words conveyed in court, when injunction granted at request of Attorney General preventing her travelling outside the Republic for an abortion. *The Irish Times*, February 18, 1992.

February 17, 1992
Dr Bernadette Bonner
Two wrongs don't make a right and you don't kill a child for the crime of the father.

As anti-abortion campaigner and chairwoman of the Responsible Society, on Miss X case. *The Irish Times*, February 18, 1992.

February 17, 1992
Clare Short
It is unforgivable to ask a 14-year-old to have a baby after she has been raped. I don't believe the people of Ireland want that.

As British Labour MP, on Miss X case. *The Irish Times*, February 18, 1992.

February 18, 1992
The Irish Times
What kind of state has it become that in 1992 its full panoply of authority, its police, its law officers, its courts are mobilised to condemn a 14-year-old girl to the ordeal of pregnancy and childbirth after rape at the hands of a 'depraved and evil man'. With what are we now to compare ourselves? Ceauçescu's Romania? The Ayatollahs' Iran? Algeria?

As Dublin newspaper, commenting on the Miss X case. *The Irish Times*, February 18, 1992.

February 19, 1992
Mary Robinson
We are experiencing as a people a very deep crisis in ourselves. I hope we have the courage, which we have not always had, to face up and look squarely and to say that this is a problem we have got to resolve.

As President, on case of 14-year-old rape victim restrained from travelling to England for an abortion. Siggins, Lorna, *Mary Robinson*, Mainstream Publishing, 1997, p. 177.

February 20, 1992
Rev Liam Mac An Sagart
Many of their actions, including the order that sent these young men to their deaths on Sunday night, can only be described as misconceived.

As priest, criticising IRA leaders at funeral service in Coalisland for two IRA men shot dead by British Army, which resulted in walk-out by many members of the congregation. *The Irish Times*, February 21, 1992.

February 22, 1992
Gerry Adams

Two or three or four years ago I would have seen it necessary to [state] the right of the IRA to engage in armed struggle. I don't feel the need to do that now. In fact I think my role now…is one of increasingly and persistently saying there's a need to end all acts of violence.

As President of Sinn Féin, in interview on peace process. *The Irish Times*, February 22, 1992.

February 22, 1992
Albert Reynolds

…here on the mainland…

As Taoiseach, outside No 10 Downing Street in London. Duignan, Sean, *One Spin on the Merry-Go-Round*, Blackwater (undated), p. 96.

February 23, 1992
Ben Dunne

I can blame no one, only myself. No, I am not a cocaine user. In a weak moment I took the goddamn stuff and in no way am I looking for pity.

As chairman of Dunnes Stores, in public statement after arrest on drug charges in Miami, Florida. *The Irish Times*, February 24, 1992.

February 23, 1992
Gerry Adams

Sinn Féin's position on the armed struggle is quite clear. We believe that the people have the right to use armed struggle in the context of seeking Irish independence. [And] Sinn Féin is not going to go away.

At President of Sinn Féin, at árd fheis in Dublin. *The Irish Times*, February 24, 1992.

March 3, 1992
John Hume

I am not asking you to disappear… I am asking you to lay down your arms and join the rest of us in facing up to this enormous task [of healing divisions].

As leader of SDLP, in remarks addressed to IRA. *Derry Journal*, March 3, 1992.

March 5, 1992
Justice Thomas Finlay

[The Supreme Court decided] if it is established as a matter of probability that there is a real and substantial risk to the life as distinct from the health of the mother, which can only be avoided by the termination of her pregnancy, that such termination is permissible, having regard to the true interpretation of Article 40.3.3 of the Constitution.

As Chief Justice, announcing four-to-one judgement of Supreme Court that abortions can be legal in some cases. *The Irish Times*, March 6, 1992.

March 6, 1992
Dr Michael Murphy

We don't want a get-rich-quick society, a grab-what-you-can society… Are we to find ourselves manipulated by vocal pressure groups into a society where life in certain circumstances becomes disposable?

As Bishop of Cork and Ross, in Lenten pastoral letter, on abortion. *The Irish Times*, March 7, 1992.

March 6, 1992
Colonel Muammar Gadafy

We do not approve of bomb explosions in London which is crawling with tourists and we are against those who terrorise peaceful cities. We have courageously said that all links will be broken with the IRA.

As Libyan leader. *The Irish Times*, March 7, 1992.

March 11, 1992
Don Lydon

[The judges] have in fact spat in the face of Christ.

As Fianna Fáil senator, on March 5 ruling by Supreme Court on abortion. *The Irish Times*, March 14, 1992.

April 5, 1992
Bill Clinton

I think sometimes we are too reluctant to engage ourselves in a positive way [in Northern Ireland] because of our long-standing special relationship with Great Britain and also because it seemed such a thorny problem. But…in the aftermath of the Cold War we need a governing rationale for our engagement in the world, not just in Northern Ireland.

As US Democratic candidate for president, making promises to Irish Americans in New York, including support for a visa for Sinn Féin leader, Gerry Adams. O'Clery, Conor, *The Greening of the White House*, Gill & Macmillan, 1996, p. 8.

April 13, 1992
Stuart Michael

We're live. We're running. They can't get us out of business. We've got the dealers up there working. They're suited and booted and they're dealing.

As commercial manager, on first day of trading after IRA bomb devastated London's financial centre. *Daily Telegraph*, April 14, 1992.

April 14, 1992
Catholic Hierarchy
[The right to life of the unborn] does not appear to be on the government's agenda at the present time.

As Irish Bishops, commenting on March 5 ruling by Supreme Court on abortion. Duignan, Sean, *One Spin on the Merry-Go-Round,* Blackwater, (undated), p. 25.

April 14, 1992
Albert Reynolds
Who the hell do they think they are? I'm not going to stand for it.

As Taoiseach, on statement from Catholic Hierarchy criticising Government, above, about which he rang individual bishops to protest. Duignan, Sean, *One Spin on the Merry-Go-Round,* Blackwater (undated), p. 25.

May 1, 1992
Albert Reynolds
There will be a return to state injunctions [on women travelling for abortions] if there is no vote on Maastricht. You might not like to know that but that is a reality.

As Taoiseach, in Dáil, promoting referendum on European Union. *The Irish Times,* May 2, 1992.

May 1, 1992
Alan Shatter
The Taoiseach's attempt to terrorise Irish women is an unacceptable and outrageous perversion.

As Fine Gael spokesman on justice, on remarks by Albert Reynolds, above. *The Irish Times,* May 2, 1992.

May 6, 1992
Dr Eamonn Casey
I intend to devote the remainder of my active life to work on the missions. In this way and with the help of God I will continue my life-long commitment to the church and its people.

As Bishop of Galway, resigning on disclosure in *Irish Times* that he had a son by Annie Murphy, living in the US. *The Irish Times,* May 7, 1992.

May 9, 1992
Annie Murphy
I just got on the phone and all the seventeen years of anger blew in his face. I told him you had your chances and no more chances, and I said I'm going to come up there (to Galway) at Easter and pull your damn hat off.

As mother of son by Bishop Eamonn Casey, on why she exposed him as father of her child. *The Irish Times,* May 11, 1992.

May 11, 1992
Dr Eamonn Casey
I acknowledge that Peter Murphy is my son and that I have grievously wronged Peter and his mother, Annie Murphy.

As former Bishop of Galway, in statement after leaving Ireland for exile in Central America. *The Irish Times,* May 12, 1992.

May 11, 1992
Peter Murphy
That's incredible. This is – my God – I couldn't have asked for anything more. I am dumbfounded but I am very proud.

As son of Bishop Eamonn Casey, reacting to news that Bishop had finally acknowledged he was his father. *The Irish Times,* May 12, 1992.

May 11, 1992
Judith Ward
Eighteen years, three months and five days I've been waiting for this. It's brilliant!

As ex-prisoner, on release pending quashing of her conviction for coach bombing in 1974 killing 12 people. *The Irish Times,* May 12, 1992.

May 15, 1992
Eamon Gilmore
[The Catholic Church's] statements on sexual matters will be taken with a pinch of salt from now on.

As Democratic Left TD, on Bishop Casey scandal. *The Irish Times,* May 16, 1992.

May 22, 1992
Alan Shatter
Are we now to deploy squads of gardaí at airports and ports to act as some sort of official censors of foreign publications? The opening of the iron curtain across Europe is now to be replaced by a curtain of shamrocks and leprechauns.

As Fine Gael spokesman on justice, on non-distribution of *Guardian* in Republic because of advertisement on abortion information. *The Irish Times,* May 23, 1992.

June 3, 1992
William FitzGerald
It's already done. It is a *fait accompli.* On June 18, the referendum was held and 65 percent of the people favoured it; 11 percent opposed it.

As 83-year-old US ambassador-designate to Ireland, when asked at US Senate confirmation hearing about the likely outcome of Maastricht referendum in Ireland, which had not then been held. (The referendum was passed two weeks later with 69 percent majority.) *The Irish Times,* June 17, 1992.

June 21, 1992
Irish Voice

In a week in which Americans discovered that their Vice President couldn't spell potato, Irish Americans discovered that their new ambassador to Ireland (a) didn't know what month it was and (b) couldn't tell the difference between loyalists, unionists and nationalists.

As New York newspaper, on mistakes made by ambassador-designate William FitzGerald at US Senate confirmation hearing. *The Irish Times*, June 24, 1992.

June 21, 1992
Jim Gibney

Sinn Féin is not standing in the airport lounge waiting to be flown to Chequers or Lancaster House;...idealists we are, fools we are not.

As Sinn Féin representative, speaking at Bodenstown, acknowledging that Britain would not leave Northern Ireland until after a 'sustained period of peace'. *The Irish Times*, June 23, 1992.

June 24, 1992
John Treacy

No blow is too low. No shot is too cheap. This is just a case of the Lilliputians firing their arrows at the emissary of Gulliver.

As US embassy spokesman, on Irish and Irish-American criticisms of US ambassador designate, William FitzGerald for mistakes at Senate confirmation hearing. *The New York Times*, June 24, 1992.

July 1, 1992
Dr Brendan Comiskey

I go to Maynooth for three days, three times a year, but I get very little support. You go to what is a business meeting with a three-page agenda but there is no one saying: 'Brendan, how are you? Are you hurting?'

As Bishop of Ferns, on private pressures facing bishops. *The Irish Times*, July 1, 1992.

July 8, 1992
Patrick Mayhew

[Their actions] would have disgraced a tribe of cannibals.

As NI Secretary of State, on triumphalist actions of Orange marchers passing site of loyalist killings on Ormeau Road, Belfast. Bew, Paul and Gillespie, Gordon, *Northern Ireland, A Chronology of the Troubles 1968-1993*, Gill & Macmillan, 1993, p. 268.

July 8, 1992
Mary Robinson

I had in mind all our exiles, all our emigrants – past and present – when I left the light in the window at Áras an Uachtaráin.

As President, in address to joint Houses of the Oireachtas. *The Irish Times*, July 9, 1992.

July 17, 1992
Catholic Hierarchy

The Health (Family Planning) (Amendment) Bill...has serious implications for moral behaviour... Casual and promiscuous sexual behaviour is always morally wrong. It is also acknowledged to be a major factor in the spread of AIDS.

As Irish Bishops, in statement on liberalisation of law on sale of condoms. *The Irish Times*, July 18, 1992.

August 10, 1992
Patrick Mayhew

I am satisfied that the UDA is actively and primarily engaged in the commission of criminal terrorist acts.

As NI Secretary of State, announcing proscription of Ulster Defence Association. Bew, Paul, and Gillespie, Gordon, *Northern Ireland, A Chronology of the Troubles 1968-1993*, Gill & Macmillan, 1993, p. 269.

August 18, 1992
Gerry Adams

My book is 'The Street and Other Stories'. I think you might enjoy it.

As President of Sinn Féin, and author, in advertisement submitted by Eason Advertising to *RTÉ*, but banned under Section 31 of Broadcasting Act because it used Adams's voice. *The Irish Times*, August 19, 1992.

August 22, 1992
Justice Thomas Finlay

The obligation to accept collective responsibility...involves, as a necessity, the non-disclosure of different or dissenting views held by members of the Government.

As judge, ruling in 3-2 Supreme Court decision on cabinet confidentiality, in case raised over how Government ministers took controversial decisions regarding the beef industry. *The Irish Times*, August 23, 1992.

September 18, 1992
Bono

We're an Irish band, Bill, and we come from Ireland, and we're not really up on the ins and outs of America's internal politics. But whoever sits in the White House affects all of us.

As lead singer of U2, talking to caller Bill Clinton on New York Rockline radio programme. *The Irish Times*, September 19, 1992.

September 18, 1992
Bill Clinton

You're from Ireland and one of the things I wish that the United States could do, not on its own but maybe through the United Nations, is finally play a constructive role in bringing an end to the historic tensions that still exist on that island.

As US Democratic presidential candidate, in conversation with Bono of U2 on New York Rockline radio programme. *The Irish Times*, September 19, 1992.

September 25, 1992
Pope John Paul II
There can be no justification from the moral point of view for disseminating information, the purpose of which is to facilitate the killing of the unborn.

As Pontiff, in address to Irish Bishops at Castle Gandolfo, Italy. *The Irish Times*, September 26, 1992.

September 25, 1992
Rev Ian Paisley
Some of the Unionist negotiators drink at the bar with these men [southern politicians], they sit at the table with them, they wine and dine with them, and are on Christian name-calling.

As leader of DUP, on Northern Ireland talks held in Dublin. *The Irish Times*, September 26, 1992.

September 26, 1992
John Hume
Northern Ireland is not a natural political entity...experience has shown that if an assembly controls the government of Northern Ireland, whether it's power-sharing or not, it won't work because any one party, by walking out, can wreck the whole thing.

As leader of SDLP, proposing group of commissioners to run Northern Ireland. *BBC*, September 26, 1992.

September 30, 1992
Padraig Flynn
Divorce is not for me personally, but a lot of marriages break down in this country and I am not going to stand in the way if the Irish electorate believes that people should have a second chance.

As Minister for Justice, on publication of White Paper on divorce. *The Irish Times*, October 3, 1992.

October 5, 1992
Mary Robinson
I felt shamed by what I saw, shamed, shamed on behalf of the European world and the American world and the developed world generally. What are we doing that we have not got greater conscience for it?

As President, at press conference in Nairobi, after visiting Somalia to highlight famine. *The Irish Times*, October 6, 1992.

October 9, 1992
Cardinal Cahal Daly
What is legally permissible rapidly comes to be seen as morally acceptable.

As Primate of Ireland, on divorce and abortion. *The Irish Times*, October 10, 1992.

October 10, 1992
Sinead O'Connor
Fight the real enemy!

As Irish singer, tearing up picture of the Pope as protest against Catholic social teaching, during live performance on US television. *The Irish Times*, October 10, 1992.

October 16, 1992
Proinsias de Rossa
We can no longer allow another state, Britain, to deal with the social problems that arise in Ireland.

As leader of Democratic Left, on Irish women travelling to England for abortions. *The Irish Times*, October 17, 1992.

October 20, 1992
Nelson Mandela
The IRA is conducting a struggle for self-assertion. They do not want Britain, a foreign country, to run a colony...we don't want any form of colonialism [and] we support those who fight it.

As leader of African National Congress, in interview with Bob Geldof. *Channel 4 Television*, October 20, 1992.

October 21, 1992
African National Congress
Mr Mandela described a situation which objectively is verifiable. His observations cannot be construed as support for the IRA.

As South African ruling party, responding to British criticisms of Nelson Mandela for remarks, above, about IRA struggle. *The Irish Times*, October 22, 1992.

October 23, 1992
Bill Clinton
I believe that the appointment of a special US envoy to Northern Ireland could be a catalyst in the effort to secure a lasting peace... We also believe that the British Government could establish more effective safeguards against the wanton use of lethal force and against further collusion between the security forces and Protestant paramilitary groups.

As US Democratic presidential candidate, in letter to former Congressman Bruce Morrison. O'Clery, Conor, *The Greening of the White House,* Gill & Macmillan, 1996, p 23.

October 29, 1992
Albert Reynolds
He [Des O'Malley] puffed up Goodman's claim for what I regard as cheap political gain. He was reckless, irresponsible and dishonest to do that here at the tribunal.

As Fianna Fáil Taoiseach, disputing account of coalition partner and leader of Progressive Democrats, Des O'Malley, at Beef Tribunal, of amount claimed from State by Goodman International. *The Irish Times*, November 6, 1992.

November 1, 1992
Bobby Molloy

The unprecedented action by the Taoiseach has had the effect of seriously destabilising the effective government partnership...put together by Charles Haughey and Desmond O'Malley... If we have not trust in one another we have nothing.

As Progressive Democrat Minister for Energy, on accusation by Taoiseach Albert Reynolds that PD leader Des O'Malley was 'dishonest'. *The Irish Times*, November 2, 1992.

November 2, 1992
Dick Spring

Not only has this government no effective life left, its senior members do not even have the ability to conduct themselves with dignity. The sooner it is swept out of the way, the better.

As leader of Labour Party, on dispute between leaders of Fianna Fáil-PD government over evidence to Beef Tribunal. *The Irish Times*, November 3, 1992.

November 3, 1992
Des O'Malley

It is very difficult...to remain in government if the leader of one party in effect charges the leader of the other party in the same government with perjury... We don't want to be in government for the sake of sitting at a desk.

As leader of Progressive Democrats, on charge of dishonesty by Taoiseach Albert Reynolds. *RTÉ*, November 3, 1992.

November 4, 1992
Albert Reynolds

I mean that, for the record. It's crap, total crap.

As Taoiseach, asked by reporter if it was true he did not speak to Des O'Malley outside Cabinet. Duignan, Sean, *One Spin on the Merry-Go-Round*, Blackwater (undated), p. 52.

November 5, 1992
Dick Spring

Given these [failings] it must surely be considered amazing that any party would consider coalescing with [Fianna Fáil]...we will not support any government with the track record of this one.

As leader of Labour Party, in debate of no confidence in coalition led by Fianna Fáil. *The Irish Times*, December 19, 1992.

November 8, 1992
Ruairi Quinn

Smash the remnants of Civil War politics for once and for all.

As Labour Party deputy leader, suggesting Fianna Fáil and Fine Gael form coalition. *The Irish Times*, November 9, 1992.

November 8, 1992
Proinsias de Rossa

We will not act as a crutch for conservative parties in decline.

As leader of Democratic Left, ruling out participation in government not dominated by left wing parties. *The Irish Times*, November 9, 1992.

November 9, 1992
Robert Kilroy Silk

Britain's interests abroad will be represented by a redundant, second-rate, politician from a country peopled by peasants, priests and pixies.

As British MP, protesting in *Daily Express* column at Irish farm commissioner, Ray MacSharry, representing EC in negotiations with US. *Daily Express*, November 9, 1992.

November 12, 1992
Nicholas Lloyd

Kilroy himself is by background and family Irish... I don't know quite what got into him. So I am saying sorry, and sorry in a big way, to everyone in Ireland.

As editor of *Daily Express*, apologising for column by Robert Kilroy Silk on November 9, 1992, above. *RTÉ*, November 12, 1992.

November 15, 1992
Albert Reynolds

Charlie McCreevy is looking at the whole system...to dehumanise it...

As Taoiseach, on plans by member of his cabinet to make the social welfare system less harsh. *RTÉ*, November 15, 1992.

November 16, 1992
Kathleen Reynolds

I just can't take it... I can't recognise the man I married in what's being said about him. In three weeks he's gone from being the best man around to someone none of us recognise.

As wife of Taoiseach, Albert Reynolds, on criticisms of her husband, in *Irish Press* interview on election campaign. Duignan, Sean, *One Spin on the Merry-Go-Round*, Blackwater (undated), p. 61.

December 4, 1992
Eamon Gilmore

Dick Spring has the media wind at his back. I used to call Morning Ireland 'Good Morning, Dick'. If there was a change in the weather, they rang him.

As Democratic Left TD, on Labour Party leader's exposure on *RTÉ*. *The Irish Times*, December 5, 1992.

December 13, 1992
Kieran Rose

By welcoming an often excluded and stigmatised community into the symbolic home of the Irish people, you are creating a powerful image which will work to heal the wounds of prejudice.

As representative of Gay and Lesbian Equality Network, to President Mary Robinson in Áras an Uachtaráin. *The Irish Times*, December 14, 1992.

December 16, 1992
Dr Moosajee Bhamjee

I hope my winning a seat will add colour and flavour to the [Dáil] proceedings, but that my professional expertise, psychiatry, will not be called on too often.

As South African-born Labour Party TD for Clare, upon winning seat. *The Irish Times*, December 19, 1992.

December 16, 1992
Ruairi Quinn

Surgeons' mistakes get buried, architects' mistakes get built.

As Labour Party deputy leader, at Dublin City Council meeting to award contract for phase two of civic offices at Wood Quay. *The Irish Times*, December 19, 1992.

January 4, 1993
Patrick Mayhew

If violence is abandoned, disavowed, forsworn, set behind them by the IRA and they give us sufficient time to see that it is for real, and that they mean it, then people will talk to them.

As NI Secretary of State, in radio interview. *The Irish Times*, January 5, 1993.

January 5, 1993
John Bruton

Now he wants to use this mandate to put back in office the same Taoiseach, the same ministers and the same party against whom he has campaigned with such self-conscious rhetoric for five years. Such a somersault diminishes not only his credibility but the credibility of all politicians.

As leader of Fine Gael, on Labour Party leader Dick Spring joining partnership government with Fianna Fáil. *The Irish Times*, January 6, 1993.

January 8, 1993
Herbert Ditty

As lord mayor from a foreign country I agreed to receive him just as I have received French [visitors] and people from every other country in the world.

As Lord Mayor of Belfast, on visit by Lord Mayor of Dublin Gay Mitchell. *The Irish Times*, January 9, 1993.

January 15, 1993
Dick Spring

This will be a government that will stand and fall on the issue of trust. Let me make no mistake about that. If it does not conform to the highest standards of accountability and openness, it will cease to exist. It is as simple as that.

As leader of Labour Party, entering government with Fianna Fáil. *The Irish Times*, January 16, 1992.

January 22, 1993
John Major

The Government made clear in 1974 that those who were killed on Bloody Sunday should be regarded as innocent of any allegation that they were shot while handling firearms or explosives.

As British Prime Minister, in letter to SDLP leader John Hume acknowledging for first time innocence of 13 civilians killed by soldiers on January 30, 1972, in Derry. *The Irish Times*, January 23, 1993.

January 28, 1993
Michael Mates

There would have been no murder of anybody if it hadn't been for the bloody riot organised by those very nationalists.

As NI security minister, in remarks on *RTÉ* documentary on Bloody Sunday in Derry, when paratroopers shot dead 13 people. *The Irish Times*, January 30, 1993.

January 30, 1993
Paddy Hill

There is only one way to send them home and that is in boxes.

As member of Birmingham Six, in remarks (later regretted) about British soldiers at Bloody Sunday rally in Derry. *The Irish Times*, February 6, 1993.

February 1993
Bill Clinton

When I met John Major the other night he slapped me on the shoulder and said, 'You know, you don't look like your passport photograph.' And I said, 'Well I really appreciate that John, and there's nothing personal in what you tried to do to me. Nothing. And next week I'll send you a note to that effect through [Irish-American columnist] Jimmy Breslin when I name him our envoy to Northern Ireland.'

As US President, in after-dinner speech in Washington, referring to British officials checking his passport application files during US election campaign. O'Clery, Conor, *The Greening of the White House*, Gill & Macmillan, 1996, p. 26.

February 2, 1993
Neil Jordan
If I make a good movie they say I'm a British director and if I make what they think is a bad one, they say I'm Irish.

As Irish film-maker. *Independent*, February 3, 1993.

February 5, 1993
Donald Pratt
If you substitute Protestant or Catholic or Jews or black, for women, then you have all the problems in the world, all the things that we abhor.

As former Irish squash champion, protesting at vote by Fitzwilliam Lawn Tennis Club in Dublin to retain ban on women members. *The Irish Times*, February 6, 1993.

February 10, 1993
Gordon Wilson
I do not claim to represent anyone. I can only reflect, in a very personal way, my hopes, feelings and thoughts about some of the many problems which confront the people of Northern Ireland at this time.

As father of Enniskillen bomb victim, on appointment to Senate. *The Irish Times*, February 11, 1993.

February 19, 1993
Krish Naidoo
Women who object to beauty contests are usually ugly. Men who object to beauty contests are usually married to ugly women.

As organiser of Miss Ireland contest. *The Irish Times*, February 20, 1993.

February 23, 1993
Edward Kennedy
We believe the hour has come for the United States to end its long tradition of silence on [human rights abuses in Northern Ireland].

As US Senator, in letter, co-signed by 11 senators, to President Clinton, prior to visit to US by British Prime Minister John Major. *The Irish Times*, February 24, 1993.

February 23, 1993
John Hume
Since Irish business people have made such an enormous contribution to America, it is not too much to ask them that they return the compliment. But I stress we are not looking for charity. We are offering a place in the biggest single market in the world – Europe.

As leader of SDLP, addressing US businessmen in Boston. *Belfast Telegraph*, February 24, 1993.

February 28, 1993
Dick Spring
The Irish Constitution is not cast in bronze.

As Tanaiste, on territorial claim to North. *BBC*, February 28, 1993.

March 9, 1993
Tom Foley
It is stupid and wrong-headed and wrongful to do a bad thing, a wrong thing, against the interests of those values and purposes that the campaign promise was given for, merely in order to say, 'I kept my campaign promise.'

As Speaker of US House of Representatives, asked in interview if President Clinton should keep his 'Irish' promises of appointing a peace envoy for Northern Ireland and granting a visa to Gerry Adams. *The Irish Times*, March 11, 1993.

March 17, 1993
Bill Clinton
The most significant thing I should be doing now is encourage the resumption of dialogue between the Irish and British governments.

As US President, in White House, after meeting Taoiseach Albert Reynolds. *The Irish Times*, March 18, 1993.

March 17, 1993
Albert Reynolds
[It was] way beyond my wildest dreams over what I thought was possible.

As Taoiseach, on meeting with US President Bill Clinton in White House and receiving promise of his full engagement in peace process. *The Irish Times*, March 18, 1993.

March 17, 1993
John Hume
I was astonished by the depth and detail of his knowledge. This is a major and positive development.

As leader of SDLP, after first meeting with US President Bill Clinton in Washington. *The Irish Times*, March 18, 1993.

March 17, 1993
Albert Reynolds
Welcome home!

As Taoiseach, to Jean Kennedy Smith, in White House, on announcement of her appointment as US Ambassador to Ireland. *The Irish Times*, March 18, 1993.

March 17, 1993
Irish Lesbian and Gay Organisation
Two, four, six, eight,
How do you know St Patrick's straight?

As pressure group, demonstrating at New York St Patrick's Day parade from which it was excluded. *The Irish Times*, March 18, 1993.

March 26, 1993
Wilfred Ball
There are no words can fit it for what they have done. They have taken my life away, my young

child. They should lay down their arms and stop right now. This should be the last tragedy of all.

As father of three-year-old Jonathan Ball, killed with Timothy Parry in IRA Warrington bombing. *The Irish Times*, March 27, 1993.

March 28, 1993
Rt Rev Michael Henshall

The courage and resilience of his parents stand in marked contrast to the white-feathered cowardice of that tiny minority of bigots, so untypical of the Irish people, whose lost cause is underscored by such desperate butchery.

As Bishop of Warrington, at funeral of 12-year-old Timothy Parry, killed by IRA bomb. *The Irish Times*, April 3, 1993.

March 28, 1993
Colin Parry

If my son becomes a symbol for peace, that would be Tim's unique achievement.

As father of 12-year-old Timothy Parry, killed by IRA bomb in Warrington. *The Irish Times*, April 3, 1993.

March 29, 1993
Gerry Adams

They would resent the fact that in a week in which six Catholics were killed, including a member of Sinn Féin, a man with a large young family, in which there were mass murder attempts on Sinn Féin and SDLP homes, there was no focus on this.

As President of Sinn Féin, on negative reaction of Sinn Féin supporters to anti-violence rally in Dublin following Warrington bombing. *The Irish Times*, March 30, 1993.

April 2, 1993
Gay Byrne

[Peter] will not be doing too badly if he turns out to be half the man his father is.

As host of *RTÉ* Late Late Show, to Annie Murphy, about her child by Bishop Eamonn Casey. *RTÉ*, April 2, 1993.

April 2, 1993
Annie Murphy

I'm not so bad myself, Mr Byrne.

Responding to Gay Byrne's remark on Late Late Show, above. *RTÉ*, April 2, 1993.

April 3, 1993
Nicholas Robinson

Friends are like fiddle strings. They must not be screwed too much.

As husband of President Mary Robinson, at fundraising event in Limerick. *The Irish Times*, April 3, 1993.

April 8, 1993
Gordon Wilson

I spoke as Marie Wilson's dad, as one who has suffered at their hands. They seemed unmoved. I left disappointed and indeed saddened.

As father of Enniskillen IRA bomb victim, on secret meeting with IRA to plead for peace. *The Irish Times*, April 10, 1993.

April 8, 1993
Dr Joseph McCarroll

Using [condoms] to stop the AIDS virus is ill-conceived.

As national secretary of Family Solidarity. *The Irish Times*, April 10, 1993.

April 9, 1993
Rev Pat Buckley

As for Gay Byrne's hope that young Peter should be half the man his father is, I don't know if I'd like a son of mine to break vows, commit adultery, live an 18-year-old lie, take seventy thousand pounds and then run and hide when the truth comes out.

As priest, in letter to newspaper, on remark by Gay Byrne on April 2 concerning Bishop Eamonn Casey's son. *The Irish Times*, April 9, 1993.

April 12, 1993
Annie Murphy

What the heck, if he thinks I'm evil, I'm evil. If you step into the wolves' ring, you don't expect love and flowers.

As mother of Bishop Eamonn Casey's son, on report that he called her evil. *The Irish Times*, April 13, 1993.

April 25, 1993
John Hume and Gerry Adams

We accept that an internal settlement is not a solution because it obviously does not deal with all the relationships at the heart of the problem.

As leaders of SDLP and Sinn Féin, in joint statement advocating national self-determination for Irish people as a whole. *The Irish Times*, April 26, 1993.

April 26, 1993
Michael McDowell

The talks would set back the inter-community peace process very significantly and were in any event doomed to failure.

As spokesman for Progressive Democrats, on talks between John Hume and Gerry Adams. *The Irish Times*, April 27, 1993.

April 30, 1993
John Hume

I apologise to no one for talking to Mr Adams. If I fail to achieve the objective of bringing violence to an end, the only damage will be that I have failed... But if the talks succeed, then the entire atmosphere will be transformed.

As leader of SDLP, reacting to criticism of talks with Sinn Féin leader Gerry Adams. *The Irish Times*, May 1, 1993.

April 30, 1993
Patrick Mayhew

Most people believe we would not want to release Northern Ireland from the United Kingdom. To be entirely honest, we would with pleasure. No, not with pleasure, I take that back. But we would not stand in the way of Northern Ireland, if that would be the will of the majority.

As NI Secretary of State, in interview with *Die Zeit*. *The Irish Times*, May 1, 1993.

May 3, 1993
Conor Cruise O'Brien

The Adams/Hume pact shows the SDLP up for what it has become under John Hume's leadership; a coldly sectarian party which is not above doing a deal with the accomplices of terrorism.

As political commentator, on talks between SDLP leader John Hume and Sinn Féin leader Gerry Adams. *The Irish Times*, May 4, 1993.

June 8, 1993
Mother Teresa

Let us pray that the leaders of this country will never allow divorce into this country.

As visitor to Knock shrine. *The Irish Times*, June 12, 1993.

June 12, 1993
Edward Heath

You have to be cleverer in intelligence, cleverer in action and cleverer politically. And to be perfectly blunt we have failed in all three.

As former British Prime Minister, on combating IRA. *The Irish Times*, June 12, 1993.

June 18, 1993
Mary Robinson

Gerry Adams greeted me in Irish and I said: 'It's nice to be in Belfast.'

As President, on shaking hands with Sinn Féin leader, against advice of British and Irish governments, at community reception in Belfast. *The Irish Times*, June 19, 1993.

June 18, 1993
Alan Shatter

If C. J. Haughey had visited Belfast and shaken hands with Gerry Adams, all hell would have broken loose... The chattering classes would have been outraged.

As Fine Gael TD, on President Mary Robinson's handshake with Gerry Adams in Belfast. Siggins, Lorna, *Mary Robinson*, Mainstream Publishing, 1997, p. 167.

June 18, 1993
Rev Alex Reid

The community has been vilified and misrepresented as violent, irrational almost, but you couldn't meet kinder people.

As Belfast priest, during President Mary Robinson's visit to Belfast. *The Irish Times*, June 19, 1993.

June 19, 1993
Reg Empey

We have a long-standing mountaineering tradition in our family. I have personally ascended Cave Hill.

As Lord Mayor of Belfast, at Dublin reception for successful Irish Everest expedition. *The Irish Times*, June 19, 1993.

June 20, 1993
Dr Chris McGimpsey

For Mary Robinson to be seen shaking hands with Gerry Adams would be like people in the South seeing the Queen shaking hands with one of the Shankill butchers.

As Belfast unionist, on President Mary Robinson's handshake with Gerry Adams. *The Irish Times*, June 21, 1993.

June 21, 1993
John Bruton

The President should not meet someone the Taoiseach or the Tanaiste would be unwilling to meet... It is possible to visit West Belfast without having contact with Sinn Féin.

As leader of Fine Gael, on President Mary Robinson's handshake with Gerry Adams. *The Irish Times*, June 22, 1993.

June 21, 1993
Gerry Adams

It is an indication of the arrogance of the British that they would dictate who would meet who and who would shake hands with who.

As President of Sinn Féin, on British criticism of President Mary Robinson for shaking his hand. *The Irish Times*, June 26, 1993.

June 26, 1993
Mary Harney

Trying to end prostitution by criminalising the prostitutes is like trying to end poverty by making it criminal to be poor.

As PD TD, in Dáil, on Bill decriminalising homosexual acts. *The Irish Times*, January 26, 1993.

June 26, 1993
David Norris
For the first time I feel I am a full citizen in my own country.

As Senator, on passing of Bill decriminalising homosexual acts. *The Irish Times*, January 26, 1993.

July 3, 1993
Patrick Mayhew
Well, nobody is dead. At the end of the opera, everybody is dead.

As NI Secretary of State, at performance of *Lucia di Lammermoor*, when asked about explosion in Belfast which injured 30 people. *The Irish Times*, July 3, 1993.

July 7, 1993
John Taylor
I have to say something which I thought I would never say and that is that the IRA are winning in Northern Ireland.

As unionist MP. *BBC*, July 7, 1993.

July 7, 1993
Patrick Mayhew
The IRA do not as yet realise that they are bound to fail, though upon many of them that truth is dawning.

As NI Secretary of State, responding to claim that IRA was winning. *The Irish Times*, July 8, 1993.

July 7, 1993
Seamus Mallon
When you have to blow people's houses, businesses and bodies apart in pursuit of a political objective, that cannot be seen as winning anything.

As SDLP deputy leader, responding to claim that IRA was winning. *The Irish Times*, July 8, 1993.

July 19, 1993
Alistair Hunter
I find it surprising, particularly in the light of the city's current preoccupation with terrorist incidents, that you would wish to call on a known terrorist.

As British consul-general in New York, referring to World Trade centre bombing, in letter to Mayor David Dinkins about his stated desire to visit IRA prisoner Joe Doherty in Belfast. *The Irish Times*, August 19, 1993.

July 19, 1993
Norman Tebbit
I suspect that the only things that will take [the territorial claim] out of the Irish Constitution is when the bombs begin to blow in Dublin.

As former Conservative minister. *Sky TV*, July 19, 1993.

July 20, 1993
John Hume
[This is] clear evidence that Lord Tebbit publicly encourages terrorism...issue an exclusion order against Lord Tebbit – send him to Northern Ireland.

As leader of SDLP, in House of Commons, on Norman Tebbit's comment, above. *The Irish Times*, July 21, 1993.

August 2, 1993
Paul O'Dwyer
We have had certain successes in other parts of the world, putting out flames. Why not try putting out the oldest fire of all?

As New York civil rights lawyer, calling for US intervention in Northern Ireland. *The Irish Times*, August 3, 1993.

August 5, 1993
Breege Granville
It's pagan and it should be stopped.

As spokeswoman for committee protesting against topless dancing in Teach Pheig pub in west Kerry Gaeltacht. *The Irish Times*, August 6, 1993.

August 5, 1993
Sylvie O'Connor
The west Kerry Gaeltacht does not exist in a time warp. Why not let a bit of light into the place?

As publican of Teach Pheig pub, rejecting protests about topless dancing. *The Irish Times*, August 6, 1993.

August 8, 1993
Martin McGuinness
We are the risen people.

As Sinn Féin Vice President, waving a tricolour at first major nationalist rally at Belfast city hall. *The Irish Times*, August 9, 1993.

August 10, 1993
David Dinkins
Mr Doherty's right to equal protection under the law was sacrificed in the interests of foreign policy and political expediency. I believe that Mr Doherty suffered a terrible injustice in this country.

As New York Mayor, in reply to July 19 letter from British consul-general criticising his stated desire to visit IRA prisoner Joe Doherty in Belfast after he was deported from United States. *The Irish Times*, August 19, 1993.

August 12, 1993
Louis Begley, John Irving, Susan Sontag, Allen Ginsberg
It seems little short of absurd to us that a brief advertisement, merely urging listeners to buy a book of short stories, should be judged a threat to Ireland's national security.

As American authors, in letter from PEN American centre to Irish Government about ban on use of Gerry Adams's voice to advertise his book. *The Irish Times*, August 13, 1993.

August 15, 1993
Douglas Gageby
Is there some terrible inhibition among our politicians or public people here that prevents them, once in a while, from saying loud and clear a kind word for that great city of Belfast? Green and Orange, Catholic and Protestant and non-believer, they are as much Yeats's indomitable Irishry as any.

As former *Irish Times* editor, opening Parnell Summer School at Avondale. *The Irish Times*, August 16, 1993.

August 24, 1993
Rev Brendan Hoban
We have too many priests in Ireland. Everywhere we go we are tripping over each other. Most of us seem to spend most of our time answering invitations to social functions, playing golf, breeding horses, training juveniles, celebrating jubilees, pricing cars and reading the death notices in desperation in case we can't find a funeral to attend.

As priest, writing in *Intercom* magazine for religious. *The Irish Times*, August 25, 1993.

September 8, 1993
John Taylor
In a perverse way this may be helpful because they are now beginning to appreciate more clearly the fear that has existed within the Protestant community for the past 20 years.

As unionist MP, on growing fear among Catholics following loyalist killings. *BBC*, September 8, 1993.

September 8, 1993
Bruce Morrison
Nothing that I have heard here suggested that Northern Ireland doesn't need help from outside the community to move forward.

As former US Congressman on need for US envoy, after leading delegation of Irish Americans to Ireland. *The Irish Times*, September 9, 1993.

September 18, 1993
John Hume
I don't give two balls of roasted snow what advice anybody gives me about those talks, because I will continue with them until they reach a positive conclusion.

As leader of SDLP, responding to criticism of his talks with Sinn Féin leader Gerry Adams. *The Irish Times*, September 19, 1993.

September 20, 1993
David Trimble
Meddling Mary...the physical embodiment of the aggressive territorial claim in the Irish Constitution.

As unionist MP, criticising President Mary Robinson for frequency of her trips to Northern Ireland. *News Letter*, September 21, 1993.

September 21, 1993
John Taylor
The term 'pan-nationalist front' was not introduced by [Unionists]. It was actually introduced by Gerry Adams in 1985 on a radio programme.

As Ulster Unionist MP, defending his use of term to claim that Sinn Féin, IRA, SDLP and Irish Government had formed anti-unionist alliance. (Adams had spoken of 'pan-nationalist interests' on radio programme). *The Irish Times*, September 25, 1993.

October 23, 1993
Samuel Drumgoole
A woman's arm went flying through the air and everyone started screaming. I started screaming too. My daddy had gone into the fish shop to get our dinner. Then someone said, it's OK, your Daddy left in time.

As 11-year-old, after premature IRA bomb in shop on Belfast's Shankill Road killed 10 people. *The Irish Times*, October 26, 1993.

October 24, 1993
Rt Rev Samuel Poyntz
We have had Bloody Sunday and Bloody Friday. Now you can add Bloody Saturday.

As Church of Ireland Bishop of Connor, on Shankill bomb. *The Irish Times*, October 30, 1993.

October 24, 1993
Michelle Williamson
I want to meet Gerry Adams face to face. I want to tell him what he put me through. They are nothing but scum. Evil bastards. Innocent people killed. Why? Why? Why?

As daughter who lost both parents in Shankill bomb. *The Irish Times*, October 30, 1993.

October 25, 1993
Bruce Morrison
We have been given a bigger mountain to climb.

As leader of Irish-American group, on effect of Shankill bomb. *The Irish Times*, October 26, 1993.

October 25, 1993
Patrick Mayhew
It must be understood that there will never be any bargaining with those who in this democracy are

being forced in arguments with bombs and bullets and the threat of violence.

As NI Secretary of State, in House of Commons, at time when secret talks were taking place between British Government and Sinn Féin. *The Irish Times*, May 27, 1998.

October 27, 1993
Gerry Adams

My attendance at the funeral of Mr Begley has been a matter of some controversy. My absence would have had the same effect.

As President of Sinn Féin, on helping carry coffin of IRA man killed planting Shankill bomb. *The Irish Times*, October 28, 1993.

October 28, 1993
John Hume

If we are to allow the politics of the last atrocity to stop the efforts for peace, then all we would keep talking about is atrocities.

As leader of SDLP, speaking in Strasbourg about Shankill bomb. *The Irish Times*, October 29, 1993.

October 29, 1993
Albert Reynolds

If we get a cessation of violence, all things are possible.

As Taoiseach, after meeting British Prime Minister John Major in Brussels. *The Irish Times*, October 30, 1993.

October 30, 1993
Bill Clinton

Credible evidence exists that Adams remains involved at the highest level in devising PIRA strategy... Neither the British nor the Irish Government favour granting Adams a visa.

As US President, in letter to New York Mayor David Dinkins. *The Irish Times*, November 11, 1993.

October 30, 1993
Loyalist Gunman

Trick or Treat!

As member of gang shooting down Hallowe'en customers in Rising Sun pub in Greysteel, Co Derry, 7 of whom died. *The Irish Times*, November 1, 1993.

October 31, 1993
William McKeown

They are sinful, they are wicked, they are absolutely depraved, and they acted really like animals here this evening.

As RUC chief superintendent, after loyalist Greysteel shooting which killed 7 people. *The Irish Times*, November 1, 1993.

October 31, 1993
Dr Edward Daly

'The gunmen are not dying for the people, the people are dying for the gunmen' – I think that summarises the week in Northern Ireland.

As Bishop of Derry, quoting from Sean O'Casey's 'The Shadow of a Gunman' (cf. April 23, 1923). *The Irish Times*, November 1, 1993.

November 1, 1993
John Major

If the implication of [these] remarks is that we should sit down and talk with Mr Adams and the Provisional IRA, I would only say that would turn my stomach and those of most honourable members. We will not do it.

As British Prime Minister, in House of Commons, as secret talks were taking place between British Government and Sinn Féin. *The Irish Times*, May 27, 1998.

November 4, 1993
John Hume

I think we would have peace within the next week in Northern Ireland if that were to happen.

As leader of SDLP, pleading for acceptance of Hume-Adams proposals for peace by two governments. *The Irish Times*, November 6, 1993.

November 4, 1993
Anthony Lake

This is not bullshit!

As National Security Adviser to President Clinton, at Capitol Hill meeting, to Congressman Joe Kennedy who used expletive when told President Clinton was serious about Northern Ireland. O'Clery, Conor, *The Greening of the White House*, Gill & Macmillan, 1996, p. 71.

November 6, 1993
Pauline Davey

For God's sake do not legalise abortion in Ireland, for you are killing not alone a baby, but you are killing the future voters of the Fianna Fáil government.

As delegate at Fianna Fáil ård fheis, in debate on abortion. *The Irish Times*, November 13, 1993.

November 7, 1993
Albert Reynolds

We have an opportunity for peace. Let's maximise it. History will never forgive us if we don't.

As Taoiseach, on negotiations between British and Irish Governments. *The Irish Times*, November 8, 1983.

November 10, 1993
Albert Reynolds

If it comes to it I will walk away from John Major... I am not prepared to let this opportunity pass.

As Taoiseach, in remarks on peace process to two reporters at Whitney Houston concert which later became known as the 'Houston Declaration'. Duignan, Sean, *One Spin on the Merry-Go-Round*, Blackwater Press (undated), p. 119.

November 11, 1993
Gerry Adams

I have no involvement in terrorist activity. This type of unfounded allegation is used by the British Government as a cover...to prevent any informed debate about its involvement in Northern Ireland.

As President of Sinn Féin, replying to US President Bill Clinton's decision to refuse him a US visa. *The Irish Times*, November 12, 1993.

November 16, 1993
Gerry Adams

Representatives of Sinn Féin have been in protracted contact and dialogue with the British Government...it was John Major who broke off that contact at the behest of his Unionist allies.

As President of Sinn Féin, revealing secret talks. *The Irish Times*, November 20, 1993.

November 16, 1993
Patrick Mayhew

No there hasn't. There has been no negotiating with Sinn Féin. No official as I see it is alleged to have been talking to Sinn Féin on behalf of the British Government. We have always made it clear there is going to be no negotiating with anybody who perpetrates or justifies the use of violence.

As NI Secretary of State, denying talks with Sinn Féin. *BBC*, November 16, 1993.

November 27, 1993
Angela McClurg

Bang goes the bomb, crash goes the glass
Why can't we have peace at last?

As 11-year-old, in Poems for Peace, launched in Ulster Museum by Women Together for Peace. *The Irish Times*, November 28, 1993.

November 28, 1993
Patrick Mayhew

If I receive a message by a well-established chain of communication coming from the leadership of the IRA that 'the conflict is over but we need advice on how to bring it to an end', I am not going to pass it up.

As NI Secretary of State, admitting secret contacts with Sinn Féin. *The Irish Times*, November 29, 1993.

November 29, 1993
Martin McGuinness

The text he read is counterfeit. No such communication was ever sent.

As Sinn Féin Vice President, on claim by Sir Patrick Mayhew on November 28 that IRA asked advice on how to end conflict. *The Irish Times*, November 30, 1993.

November 29, 1993
Rev Ian Paisley

You have rubbished any suggestion of any such talks. You have rubbished anyone who dared at a press conference put questions to you. And when we met you with the Prime Minister last week, you rubbished it again to us... It was a falsehood. It was worse. It was a lie.

As leader of DUP, in House of Commons, in remarks – for which he was ejected – directed to Sir Patrick Mayhew over his admission of contacts with Sinn Féin. *The Irish Times*, November 30, 1993.

November 30, 1993
Bill Clinton

Go the extra mile!

As US President, in telephone call to British Prime Minister John Major about Northern Ireland. *The Irish Times*, December 1, 1993.

December 1993
John Taylor

We in Northern Ireland are not Irish. We do not jig at crossroads, speak Gaelic, play GAA etc... It is an insult for Dubliners to refer to us as being Irish.

As unionist MP, in Dublin debate. *The Irish Times*, December 31, 1993.

December 1, 1993
Patrick Mayhew

In rechecking the documents some transcriptions and typing errors have come to light in the dossier of messages between the IRA and the Government.

As NI Secretary of State, when challenged by Sinn Féin about British version of contacts. *The Irish Times*, December 2, 1993.

December 9, 1993
Albert Reynolds

This is women now! You can't even give way to somebody who wants to give you information.

As Taoiseach, in exchange in Dáil with Fine Gael TD Nora Owen. (Often misquoted as 'There's women for you.') *The Irish Times*, December 10, 1993.

December 9, 1993
Una Claffey

No big deal, that's Albert!

As *RTÉ* political correspondent, on Albert Reynolds's remark, above. Duignan, Sean, *One Spin on the Merry-Go-Round*, Blackwater (undated), p. 43.

December 15, 1993
John Major
The Prime Minister...reiterates, on behalf of the British Government, that they have no selfish strategic or economic interest in Northern Ireland. Their primary interest is to see peace, stability and reconciliation established by agreement...which will embrace the totality of relationships. The role of the British Government will be to encourage, facilitate and enable the achievement of such agreement...

As British Prime Minister, in joint Downing Street Declaration on ways to end political violence in Northern Ireland. McLoughlin, Michael, *Great Irish Speeches of the Twentieth Century*, Poolbeg Press, 1996, p. 382.

December 15, 1993
Albert Reynolds
The Taoiseach...accepts on behalf of the Irish Government, that the democratic right of self-determination by the people of Ireland as a whole must be achieved and exercised with and subject to the agreement and consent of a majority of the people of Northern Ireland.

As Taoiseach, in joint Downing Street Declaration on ways to end political violence in Northern Ireland. McLoughlin, Michael, *Great Irish Speeches of the Twentieth Century*, Poolbeg Press, 1996, p. 383.

December 15, 1993
Rev Ian Paisley
You have sold Ulster to buy off the fiendish republican scum.

As leader of DUP, in House of Commons, to British Prime Minister John Major, after Downing Street Declaration. *The Irish Times*, December 16, 1993.

December 15, 1993
Dick Spring
We are talking about a permanent cessation of violence and we are talking about the handing up of arms.

As Tanaiste, in Dáil, on Joint Declaration. *The Irish Times*, December 16, 1993.

December 17, 1993
Jennifer Johnston
Peace would end the hopelessness. We should have something other than violence to talk about in the evening.

As Derry novelist, on Joint Declaration. *The Irish Times*, December 18, 1993.

December 20, 1993
James Molyneaux
The Joint Declaration is a recognition by both governments, for the very first time, jointly, that the will of the people of Northern Ireland, the

greater number of them, will prevail in all circumstances. That has never been said before.

As leader of Ulster Unionist Party, on Joint Declaration. *The Irish Times*, December 21, 1993.

December 21, 1993
Bill Clinton
US policy on Northern Ireland is made in the context of the deep ties of friendship and history the American people enjoy with the people of *both* Ireland and Britain.

As US President, on how 'special relationship' applied in future to both Britain and Ireland. *The Irish Times*, December 22, 1993.

January 11, 1994
John Major
I am not going to be drawn into negotiations by the back door by Mr Adams.

As British Prime Minister, on request by Sinn Féin President Gerry Adams for clarification of Joint Declaration. *The Irish Times*, January 15, 1994.

January 13, 1994
Edward Kennedy, Christopher Dodd, John Kerry and Daniel Patrick Moynihan
While no one can be certain that a visa for Mr Adams will result in the IRA's accepting the conditions established by Ireland and Great Britain for participation in the peace process, the United States cannot afford to ignore this possibility and miss this rare opportunity for our country to contribute to peace in Northern Ireland.

As US Senators, urging President Clinton to grant visa to Sinn Féin leader Gerry Adams. O'Clery, Conor, *The Greening of the White House*, Gill & Macmillan, 1996, p. 90.

January 13, 1994
Gerry Adams
I do not have a political package with which to approach the IRA.

As President of Sinn Féin, asking for clarification of Joint Declaration. *The Irish Times*, January 15, 1994.

January 18, 1994
James Molyneaux
One never ceases to be amazed by the gullibility of people who are otherwise intelligent, some of them in the ranks of the chattering classes, who are now being sucked into whining about clarification.

As leader of the Ulster Unionist Party, on Sinn Féin demands for clarification of the Joint Declaration. *The Irish Times*, January 22, 1994.

January 27, 1994
Albert Reynolds
No fundraising, short-term visa, send him home with a message, that you want him to join the peace train and leave violence behind, and that if he doesn't he'll never get another one.

As Taoiseach, in telephone call to US President Clinton recommending US visa for Gerry Adams. O'Clery, Conor, *The Greening of the White House*, Gill & Macmillan, 1996, p. 90.

January 28, 1994
Gerry Adams
I don't advocate violence. It is my personal and political priority to see an end to the IRA and an end to all other organisations engaged in armed violence.

As President of Sinn Féin, in statement to meet last-minute concerns of White House before granting US visa. O'Clery, Conor, *The Greening of the White House*, Gill & Macmillan, 1996, p. 97.

January 29, 1994
Gerry Adams
Does this mean I have to apologise every time an Irishman gets into a fight with an Englishman in a pub?

As President of Sinn Féin, on request by White House relayed via New York publisher Niall O'Dowd to condemn hoax bomb incident in San Diego before getting US visa. O'Clery, Conor, *The Greening of the White House*, Gill & Macmillan, 1996, p. 103.

January 31, 1994
Bill Clinton
I thought it was the appropriate thing to do because he's in a position to push this thing forward.

As US President, on decision to grant a visa to Gerry Adams to attend conference in New York. *The Irish Times*, February 1, 1994.

January 31, 1994
Albert Reynolds
Sinn Féin will pay a price for going on Capitol Hill. A lot of powerful people went out on a limb for Adams. If he doesn't deliver they'll have him back in the house with steel shutters [Sinn Féin headquarters in Belfast] so fast his feet won't touch the ground.

As Taoiseach, to Government press secretary, Sean Duignan. Duignan, Sean, *One Spin on the Merry-Go-Round*, Blackwater Press, (undated), pp. 139-140.

February 1, 1994
Michael D. Higgins
I find it difficult to be convinced that the existence of the orders and directions over the past 20 years has contributed in any meaningful way to the securing of peace in Northern Ireland.

As Minister for Arts, Culture and the Gaeltacht, on lifting Section 31 of Broadcasting Act banning IRA and Sinn Féin interviews on RTÉ. *The Irish Times*, February 2, 1994.

February 1, 1994
Tom Foley
It was premature to grant the visa at this time. As an exercise in dialogue it is self-defeating. He wants an opportunity to speak out on Sinn Féin.

As Speaker of US House of Representatives, on granting of US visa to Sinn Féin leader Gerry Adams. *The Irish Times*, February 2, 1994.

February 1, 1994
Edna O'Brien
Where [Michael] Collins was outgoing and swashbuckling, Gerry Adams is thoughtful and reserved, a lithe, handsome man with a native formality. Given a different incarnation in a different century one could imagine him as one of those monks transcribing the gospels into Gaelic.

As London-based Irish author, in profile of Gerry Adams published in *The New York Times*. *The New York Times*, February 1, 1994.

February 1, 1994
John Hume
The only sign of a border left in a unified Europe are British military checkpoints on the Irish Border. What are they there for? To deal with people who want rid of the Border.

As leader of SDLP, at New York conference for NI party leaders. *The Irish Times*, February 2, 1994.

February 1, 1994
Gerry Adams
I come here with a message of peace. We're going to have peace, not in forty or fifty years time, but in our time.

As President of Sinn Féin, in speech to Irish Americans in New York. *The Irish Times,* February 3, 1994.

February 3, 1994
Robin Renwick
When I listen to Gerry Adams, I think, as we all do, it's reminiscent of Goebbels. It's an extraordinary propaganda line. The line is – I want peace but only after we've won.

As British Ambassador to Washington. *CNN*, February 3, 1994.

February 6, 1994
The New York Times
The lion whines about Mr Adams.

As leading US newspaper, in headline on British complaints over Gerry Adams's visit to New York. *The New York Times*, February 6, 1994.

February 10, 1994
Jim Mitchell
He seems to have what I call a charismatic deficit.

As Fine Gael TD, challenging party leadership of John Bruton. *The Irish Times*, February 12, 1994.

February 12, 1994
Sam McAughtry
If I go into a pub in England and say, 'I am not Irish, I am a Belfast Protestant,' I'll be told, 'Right, Paddy, whatever turns you on.'

As writer and broadcaster, in debate in Belfast on Northern Protestant identity. *The Irish Times*, February 21, 1994.

February 24, 1994
Anthony Lake
I am also a senior official, and he is wrong.

As US National Security Adviser to President Clinton, on report in British newspapers that a senior US official in London had said it was a mistake to grant Gerry Adams a US visa. *The Irish Times*, February 25, 1994.

March 9, 1994
Roy Bradford
Behind the fine words, ordinary decent unionists, not the 'kick-the-pope' type, believe that there is an unrelenting pressure on them to capitulate.

As former unionist member of NI executive. *The Irish Times*, March 10, 1994.

March 10, 1994
Daniel Patrick Moynihan
Have we been had?

As US Senator, in full text of letter sent to Senator Edward Kennedy on their support for Gerry Adams's visa campaign, after IRA mortar bombs fired at Heathrow Airport. O'Clery, Conor, *The Greening of the White House*, Gill & Macmillan, 1996, p. 126.

March 14, 1994
IRA
There is a responsibility on the British Government to move from its negotiating stance. The people of Britain and Ireland deserve better.

In statement after mortar bomb attack on Heathrow Airport. *The Irish Times*, March 15, 1994.

March 17, 1994
Bill Clinton
It's difficult to know what to make of the latest attacks at Heathrow. As in Hebron, reactionary forces will always attempt to kill the peace.

As US President, addressing guests at White House St Patrick's Day party. O'Clery, Conor, *The Greening of the White House*, Gill & Macmillan, 1996, p. 131.

March 17, 1994
Niall O'Dowd
John F. Kennedy never did anything like this for the Irish. The American Irish have always had their noses pressed against the window, looking into the White House from the outside. Now they are inside, and nothing will ever be the same again.

As New York publisher and intermediary in NI peace process, at first ever White House St Patrick's Day party. O'Clery, Conor, *The Greening of the White House*, Gill & Macmillan, 1996, p. 129.

March 31, 1994
John Hume
No stone should be left unturned to advance the cause of peace.

As leader of SDLP, paraphrasing James Craig comment of March 29, 1922. *The Irish Times*, April 2, 1994.

March 31, 1994
Nancy Soderberg
One of the things we were concerned about was that the unionist community didn't trust us. They thought that we had a secret agenda to get a united Ireland in our back pocket. The truth is we don't, and...I don't really care whether there is a united Ireland or not.

As special adviser to President Clinton, on inviting unionists to Washington. O'Clery, Conor, *The Greening of the White House*, Gill & Macmillan, 1996, p. 138.

April 1994
James Molyneaux
I never thought I'd see the day that Senator Edward Kennedy would sit across a table from me and ask: 'Mr Molyneaux, what can we do for you?'

As leader of Ulster Unionist Party, after meeting US Congress leaders in Washington. O'Clery, Conor, *The Greening of the White House*, Gill & Macmillan, 1996, p. 138.

April 3, 1994
Martin McGuinness
I am not a member of the IRA but I have in the past been involved in the defence of a community which has suffered greatly at the hands of British occupation forces.

As Sinn Féin Vice President, in radio interview. *RTÉ*, April 4, 1994.

April 11, 1994
Rev Sean McManus
Dr Paisley, this may not do you much good at home but I have to confess to having respect and regard for you as a person, as a political leader.

As organiser of Irish National Caucus in US, greeting Rev Ian Paisley at Washington Press Club. *The Irish Times*, April 12, 1994.

April 11, 1994
Rev Ian Paisley
Some people will interpret what you say as the kiss of death to me.

As leader of DUP, responding to effusiveness of greeting from Rev Sean McManus at Washington Press Club. *The Irish Times*, April 12, 1994.

April 12, 1994
Patrick Mayhew
The ending of the conflict which has so affected the lives of so many in Northern Ireland over the last 25 years – that's not going to require any surrender.

As NI Secretary of State, in New York speech. *The Irish Times*, April 14, 1994.

April 13, 1994
Rev Ian Paisley
Isn't it a good thing we can all laugh, Ulster people and those from the South. We can laugh, and laugh at one another. It's our salvation.

As DUP leader, addressing Irish Americans in New York. *The Irish Times*, April 14, 1994.

April 29, 1994
Patrick Mayhew
Any rational person must know that violence is the road to nowhere… I am referring to people with something between their ears except bone and prejudice.

As NI Secretary of State. *The Irish Times*, April 30, 1994.

May 15, 1994
Albert Reynolds
As he said, we have a friend in the White House every day of the year.

As Taoiseach, after discussing peace process with US President Clinton in Indianapolis. *The Irish Times*, May 16, 1994.

May 19, 1994
British Government
Constitutional issues are among those eligible to be addressed in the talks process… The British Government accepts the validity of all electoral mandates, including Sinn Féin.

Responding to Sinn Féin requests for clarification of Joint Declaration of December 15, 1993. *The Irish Times*, May 20, 1994.

May 19, 1994
Patrick Mayhew
[Sinn Féin] have got the key. They can turn it.

As NI Secretary of State, after clarification of Joint Declaration of December 15, 1993. *The Irish Times*, May 20, 1994.

May 20, 1994
Dr Desmond Connell
If, under the influence of the contraception culture, society accepts a view of marriage that releases the married couple from all commitments to procreation, it opens the way to the final debasement of marriage, the recognition of so-called homosexual marriages.

As Archbishop of Dublin. *The Irish Times*, May 21, 1994.

May 21, 1994
Mary Banotti
Unless it changes course quickly, Fine Gael will lose the battle for voters' minds…because it has become considerably more conservative than the vast majority of those who want to vote for us.

As Fine Gael candidate in European Elections. *The Irish Times*, May 21, 1994.

May 21, 1994
Jim Mitchell
Fine Gael is choking on an overdose of the liberal agenda.

As Fine Gael running mate for Mary Banotti in European Elections. *The Irish Times*, May 21, 1994.

May 22, 1994
Mel Gibson
When I first heard of the Minister for the Arts and Culture I thought, 'Boy, what a stupid idea that is!' But this guy is more like an artist than a politician. He's a good guy. I think he really cares.

As Hollywood star, filming 'Braveheart' in Ireland, on Michael D. Higgins. *The Irish Times*, May 23, 1994.

May 26, 1994
Jack Charlton
People all over Ireland are always giving me presents. If I step out of a car, someone will put a pint in my hand. It has become so bad I have had to buy a second house to put the presents in.

As manager of Republic of Ireland soccer team, on being made Freeman of Dublin. *The Irish Times*, May 27, 1994.

June 9, 1994
Sam Beattie
Any hint of amnesty while violence is still in progress is the green light to those who think that murder today will go unpunished in the years to come.

As chairman of the NI Police Federation. *The Irish Times*, June 11, 1994.

June 10, 1994
Jeremy Hardy
I think [telling Irish jokes] is completely different from joking that the Scots are mean, because nobody seriously believes that the Scottish people are unfit to handle money, yet the view that the Irish are 'too stupid' to be governed is reinforced by British troops.

As English comedian, approving London court decision that Irish jokes were racist. *The Irish Times*, June 11, 1994.

June 19, 1994
Patrick Mayhew
[She will ask] 'What did you do in the so-called war, Daddy?' And you will say: 'I killed a man of 87.'

As NI Secretary of State, posing question daughter might ask of loyalist gunman after 6 Catholics, including 87-year-old man, were shot dead in O'Toole's Bar in Loughinisland, Co Down. *The Irish Times*, June 20, 1994.

June 19, 1994
Albert Reynolds
What savagery! The time has come for everyone to accept that peace can no longer be delayed.

As Taoiseach, on being told in New York of 6 Catholics shot dead in O'Toole's Bar in Loughinisland, Co Down. *The Irish Times*, June 20, 1994.

July 5, 1994
Nora Bennis
What the liberal agenda has done is to create a culture of death in Ireland. It led to the contraception mentality and contraception is anti-life. Abortion of course is death for unborn babies...as well as emotional death for women.

As leader of conservative Catholic movement, Family Solidarity. *The Irish Times*, July 6, 1994.

July 5, 1994
Hugh Annesley
I believe that those within the Provisional movement who are interested in the peaceful way are probably – just probably – in the majority.

As RUC chief constable. *The Irish Times*, July 9, 1994.

July 12, 1994
Philip McGarry
If this is part of the IRA's much vaunted peace process, one can only wonder what their war process is like.

As chairman of Alliance Party, on IRA killing of UDA member Ray Smallwoods. *The Irish Times*, July 16, 1994.

July 26, 1994
Lord Holme
They are not so much 'Gerry and the Peacemakers' as 'Gerry and the Prevaricators.'

As spokesman for British Liberal Democrats, after Sinn Féin meeting in Letterkenny failed to endorse Joint Declaration. *The Irish Times*, July 30, 1994.

July 29, 1994
Sean Duignan
The Taoiseach has been totally vindicated and the tribunal repeatedly emphasises that he at all times acted in the national interest.

As Government Press Secretary, on Taoiseach Albert Reynolds's response to the still-unpublished findings of tribunal inquiring into beef processing industry. *The Irish Times*, July 30, 1994.

July 29, 1994
Dick Spring
If Mr Duignan is purporting to act on behalf of the Government, he is not acting on my behalf and it must be a misunderstanding by him.

As Tanaiste, on claim by Sean Duignan, Government Press Secretary, that Beef Tribunal report vindicated Taoiseach Albert Reynolds. *The Irish Times*, July 30, 1994.

August 1, 1994
Sinn Féin Official
We have to have something that the dead can live with.

As intermediary in peace process, in remark to New York publisher, Niall O'Dowd, on wording of possible IRA ceasefire announcement. Attributed.

August 2, 1994
Mary Harney
Certain people in Government took the opportunity offered by their early access to the [beef tribunal] report to badly mislead the public and the media as to its real thrust. The claim that he was totally vindicated and that his decisions were objectively in the national interest is wholly false.

As leader of Progressive Democrats, on Taoiseach Albert Reynold's claim to be vindicated by the Beef Tribunal report. *The Irish Times*, August 3, 1994.

August 4, 1994
Ernest Bryll
Like me, Irish people are lazy. They are not very formal and everything is a bit late.

As Polish Ambassador, at Kerry summer school. *The Irish Times*, August 5, 1994.

August 15, 1994
Dr Desmond Connell
Every so often he seems to come back and tear open the wounds again. He does not seem to have any concept of the damage, the injury, which has been caused particularly to the young people.

As Archbishop of Dublin, on Bishop Eamonn Casey, in exile for conduct over fathering a child. *The Irish Times*, August 16, 1994.

August 19, 1994
Gerry Adams
We acknowledge the hurt that we have inflicted. We wish to set all that behind us, all of the last 25 years.

As President of Sinn Féin. *The Irish Times*, August 20, 1994.

August 19, 1994
Gay Mitchell
Some of these people couldn't find Ireland with a compass.

As Fine Gael spokesman on justice, on Irish passports given to 11 Saudi and Pakistani nationals who invested in Ireland. *The Irish Times*, August 20, 1994.

August 22, 1994
Niall O'Dowd
You basically have three choices. If you are rich enough you can pay $500a year at the Waldorf Astoria Hotel at some fancy dinner, or you can grab your placard and march with NORAID outside the British embassy, or you can try to take a positive, activist role.

As New York publisher and intermediary in NI peace process. *The Irish Times*, August 23, 1994.

August 25, 1994
Albert Reynolds
Permanent. No pussy-footing. I haven't devoted two years of my life to this to be insulted with a temporary ceasefire. And another thing. I want their announcement to be written in language that an 11-year-old can understand.

As Taoiseach, speaking to Irish-American delegation on way to meet Sinn Féin about proposed IRA ceasefire. Finlay, Fergus, *Snakes & Ladders*, New Island Books, 1998, p. 237.

August 26, 1994
Rev Martin Smyth
If these conditions are met, then Unionists will have to learn to deal with Sinn Féin whether they like it or not.

As unionist MP, on demand for permanent ceasefire and hand-over of weapons. *The Irish Times*, August 27, 1994.

August 26, 1994
David Ervine
Unionists, including the paramilitaries, have accepted for years that they will have to sit down and talk to the other great monolith in this country, nationalists and republicans. Mr Paisley is standing in the way of that.

As leader of Progressive Unionist Party. *The Irish Times*, August 27, 1994.

August 26, 1994
Robert Ballagh
The sun is at last setting on the Northern conflagration. A quarter of a century later the government has belatedly, nervously, but none the less thankfully, returned to its responsibilities.

As artist, supporting 'Time for Peace' campaign. *The Irish Times*, August 27, 1994.

August 26, 1994
William Ross
There are always a lot of fools around prepared to believe good of evil people.

As unionist MP, on rumours of IRA ceasefire. *The Irish Times*, August 27, 1994.

August 28, 1994
Ruairí Ó Brádaigh
Once the southern state was accepted by the Provos, it was only a matter of time before its twin sister, the northern statelet, would be accepted also.

As leader of Republican Sinn Féin. *The Irish Times*, August 29, 1994.

August 29, 1994
Gerry Adams
I am satisfied that Irish nationalism, if properly mobilised and focussed, at home and internationally, now has sufficient political confidence, weight and support to bring about the changes which are essential to a just and lasting peace. This is the considered position I put to the IRA.

As President of Sinn Féin, on eve of IRA ceasefire. *The Irish Times*, August 30, 1994.

August 30, 1994
Albert Reynolds

I know you're a quarter Irish and I want you to have that part of your brain working... You'll have to break every rule in the book to get this one.

As Taoiseach, in (successful) plea to Nancy Soderberg, special adviser to President Clinton, to get President to issue US visa to veteran IRA man Joe Cahill and secure IRA ceasefire. O'Clery, Conor, *The Greening of the White House*, Gill & Macmillan, 1996, p. 153.

August 31, 1994
IRA

Recognising the potential of the current situation and in order to enhance the democratic peace process...the leadership of Óglaigh na hÉireann have decided that as of midnight, Wednesday August 31, there will be a complete cessation of military operations. All our units have been instructed accordingly.

RTÉ, August 31, 1994.

August 31, 1994
John Major

We need to be clear that this is indeed intended to be a permanent renunciation of violence, that is to say, for good.

As British Prime Minister, on IRA ceasefire. *The Irish Times*, September 3, 1994.

August 31, 1994
Jonathan Stephenson

[This is] Jesuitical nit-picking. The Collins National Dictionary defines the word 'complete' as 'entire', 'finished', 'perfect', 'with no part lacking'.

As SDLP Vice President, on British Prime Minister John Major's doubts about permanence of IRA 'complete' cessation of violence. *The Irish Times*, September 1, 1994.

September 2, 1994
Bill Clinton

We want all elements in Northern Ireland...to feel that there is a peace dividend.

As US President, at Martha's Vineyard vacation home, promising benefits would follow from IRA ceasefire. *The Irish Times*, September 3, 1994.

September 2, 1994
Michael Flannery

They have stopped their hostilities without any guarantees whatsoever. I see pictures in the papers of celebrations in Belfast, but I have to wonder, what are they celebrating?

As 92-year-old co-founder of Irish Northern Aid (NORAID), in New York, on IRA ceasefire. O'Clery,

Conor, *The Greening of the White House*, Gill & Macmillan, 1996, p. 172.

September 2, 1994
Charlie McCreevy

Asking the *Irish Times* and certain commentators in the *Irish Times* to be fair to the Fianna Fáil party would be like saying that Hitler's policies were fair to the Jews.

As Minister for Trade and Tourism, on *Irish Times/MRBI* poll unfavourable to Fianna Fáil. *The Irish Times*, September 3, 1994.

September 2, 1994
Des O'Malley

If Ms O'Keefe is the only person to end up in the dock, then Irish public administration will have shown all the logic and fairness of the Mad Hatter's Tea Party.

As PD TD, on warrant issued for journalist Susan O'Keefe to disclose sources at Beef Tribunal. *The Irish Times*, September 3, 1994.

September 8, 1994
Rev Ian Paisley

[He told me] 'Get out of this room and never come back until you accept that I speak the truth.'

As leader of DUP, on abrupt end to meeting with British Prime Minister John Major at Downing Street. *The Irish Times*, September 10, 1994.

September 14, 1994
Albert Reynolds

We live in a changing world. We are all pooling sovereignty in Europe for the benefit of an enlarged community. Surely it is illogical to argue against that process taking place in Ireland, where there will have to be a pooling of sovereignty.

As Taoiseach, in interview. *The Daily Telegraph*. September 14, 1994.

September 19, 1994
John Hume

My dream is to see Ireland regarded as an off-shore island both of the United States of America and the United States of Europe, and given special treatment by both because it has played a major role in both.

As leader of SDLP, in interview in Washington. *The Irish Times*, September 20, 1994.

September 22, 1994
David Trimble

It is appreciated now in Washington that there are two sides to this.

As unionist MP, after meeting Vice President Al Gore and members of US Congress. *The Irish Times*, September 23, 1994.

September 23, 1994
Jack Boothman
I don't accept the claim of Unionists that they are British. And I know that in their hearts and souls they don't believe it either. They are just Irish of a different tradition and upbringing.

As President of GAA. *The Irish Times*, September 24, 1994.

September 24, 1994
Gerry Adams
None of us can say, two or three years up the road, that if the causes of conflict aren't resolved, another IRA leadership won't come along, because this has always happened.

As President of Sinn Féin, in interview. *Boston Herald*, September 26, 1994.

September 24, 1994
Gerry Adams
I'm not coming here to make war or look for guns. I'm coming here with an argument.

As President of Sinn Féin, at rally in gun-making town of Springfield, Massachusetts. *The Irish Times*, September 26, 1994.

September 26, 1994
Douglas Hurd
There's a tendency in some places to put him on some kind of level with Nelson Mandela. We know – because it's measured in free elections – exactly what support Gerry Adams and Sinn Féin have in Northern Ireland. It's ten percent. He's Mr Ten Percent. He's a minority within the minority in Northern Ireland.

As British Foreign Secretary, on US television. *The Irish Times*, September 27, 1994.

September 27, 1994
Fionnuala Flanagan
Of course we sang Irish songs, and of course we sang rebel songs; half of our songs are rebel songs for a very good reason. I make no apology for that.

As Hollywood film actress, on reports in British press that rebel songs were sung at party she gave for Sinn Féin President Gerry Adams in Los Angeles. O'Clery, Conor, *The Greening of the White House*, Gill & Macmillan, 1996, p. 166.

September 28, 1994
Rudi Giuliani
As US attorney I carried out my responsibilities faithfully. I agreed with the decision of my government, just as I agree with the decision of my government now.

As Mayor of New York, on his welcome for Sinn Féin leader Gerry Adams, despite his former role as prosecutor of IRA man Joe Doherty. *The Irish Times*, September 29, 1994.

September 30, 1994
Boris Yeltsin
I'm going to tell you the truth. I slept. The journey was 18 hours and I slept. That's what happened. My security guards should have woken me but they didn't. They were afraid to. I'll give them a kick for that.

As Russian President, on his non-appearance at Shannon Airport while Taoiseach Albert Reynolds and Army Band waited for him at steps of plane. *The Irish Times*, October 1, 1994.

October 2, 1994
Paul O'Dwyer
I want the phones to ring off the walls so that the President of the United States will say: 'What's happening here?'

As veteran Irish-American activist, asking Irish Americans to call White House to demand it receive Sinn Féin leader Gerry Adams. O'Clery, Conor, *The Greening of the White House*, Gill & Macmillan, 1996, p. 169.

October 3, 1994
Bob Dole
And I'll bring you in the front door, not the back door.

As Republican Senator, to Sinn Féin leader Gerry Adams, in Washington, on how he would welcome him to White House if elected president. O'Clery, Conor, *The Greening of the White House*, Gill & Macmillan, 1996, p. 174.

October 4, 1994
Gerry Adams
What we need is a de Klerk to persuade the unionists their future lies on the island of Ireland. They don't have to forgive. We seek to forgive and move forward.

As President of Sinn Féin, in address at Washington Press Club. *The Irish Times*, October 5, 1994.

October 4, 1994
Ken Magennis
No, I most certainly do not trust Gerry. I don't know who Gerry is. I don't think he knows who he is. We know him as the leader of the IRA/Sinn Féin. But sometimes he tells us he is not that person. So I wonder who he is. He is someone who fronts for a vicious organisation that killed almost 2,000 people during the last 20 years.

As unionist MP, asked on US Larry King Show if he trusted Gerry Adams. O'Clery, Conor, *The Greening of the White House*, Gill & Macmillan, 1996, p. 176.

October 13, 1994
Combined Loyalist Military Command
In all sincerity we offer to the loved ones of all innocent victims over the past 25 years abject and true remorse. No words of ours will compensate for the inevitable suffering.
As body representing UDA and UVF, announcing ceasefire. *The Irish Times*, October 14, 1994.

October 13, 1994
Gusty Spence
We have clawed our way up from the abyss, and we want to ensure that other young fellows do not make the same mistakes – if they were mistakes – as we did.
As loyalist leader, who took part in first UVF attack on Catholics in Malvern Street, Belfast, in 1966, announcing Combined Loyalist Military Command ceasefire. *The Irish Times*, October 14, 1994.

October 13, 1994
David Ervine
The politics of division see thousands of people dead, most of them working class, and the headstones on the graves of young men. We've been fools. Let's not be fools any longer. All elements must be comfortable within Northern Ireland... You can't eat a flag.
As leader of Progressive Unionist Party, on loyalist ceasefire. *The Independent*, October 14, 1994.

October 14, 1994
John Bruton
If the Air Corps has a frequent flyer programme, government ministers could probably get to the moon and back on their accumulated points.
As leader of Fine Gael, alleging abuse of the government jet. *The Irish Times*, October 15, 1994.

October 21, 1994
John Major
I am now prepared to make a working assumption that the IRA ceasefire is intended to be permanent...if the IRA continues to show that it has ended terrorism, then we shall be ready to convene exploratory talks before this year is out.
As British Prime Minister, in Belfast. *The Irish Times*, October 22, 1994.

October 22, 1994
Martin McGuinness
The representatives of the British Government...said to us that the eventual outcome of all that the British were trying to do would be that the island would be as one.
As Sinn Féin Vice President. *BBC*, October 22, 1994.

October 24, 1994
David Ervine
We don't want to get up in the morning and say 'Am I British or Irish today?' We want to get up and say, 'My God, I'm late for work.'
As leader of Progressive Unionist Party, in New York speech. *The Irish Times*, October 25, 1994.

October 24, 1994
Gary McMichael
I have less reason to sit down with Sinn Féin than many people, but I recognise that we have to sit down and we have to put the past behind us. It's going to be difficult to do so. I will have a lump in my throat when I sit across the table from Gerry Adams.
As leader of Ulster Democratic Party whose father was killed by IRA, speaking in New York. *The Irish Times*, October 25, 1994.

October 25, 1994
Billy Hutchinson
I can't wait for the day Sinn Féin puts forward a social policy in a council and we say, 'I second that.'
As loyalist leader, addressing meeting in Boston College. *The Irish Times*, October 26, 1994.

November 1, 1994
Bill Clinton
In the Middle East and in Northern Ireland we can't let the people who have been the pawns of war wait too long to see the benefits of peace.
As US President, announcing investment conference for Northern Ireland. *The Irish Times*, November 5, 1994.

November 8, 1994
Hugh Smyth
I want to offer the hand of friendship. I might even offer the players from Dublin a couple of drinks because we need the three points more than they do.
As Belfast Lord Mayor, on Republic-NI soccer match in Belfast. *The Irish Times*, November 12, 1994.

November 13, 1994
Dick Spring
We have allowed a child abuser to remain at large in our community, when we had it in our power to ensure he was given up to justice. Is no one to take responsibility?
As Tanaiste, on delay by Government in acting on extradition request from Northern Ireland for paedophile priest, Rev Brendan Smyth. *The Irish Times*, November 14, 1994.

November 16, 1994
Dick Spring
The key issue, throughout this entire episode, has been accountability – the right of the public to secure adequate explanations and the responsibility of the holders of high office to take responsibility for their actions.

As Tanaiste and leader of Labour Party, in Dáil, stating he could not enter new government with Fianna Fáil as he was misled by Fianna Fáil leader Albert Reynolds in extradition case. McLoughlin, Michael, *Great Irish Speeches of the Twentieth Century*, Poolbeg Press, 1996, p. 392.

November 17, 1994
Albert Reynolds
Had my colleagues and I been aware of these facts last week, we would not have proposed or supported the nomination of Harry Whelehan as President of the High Court. I now accept that the reservations voiced by the Tanaiste were well-founded and I regret the appointment.

As Taoiseach, on revelations about delay in extradition request for paedophile priest, Rev Brendan Smyth. *The Irish Times*, November 18, 1994.

November 17, 1994
Harry Whelehan
The judiciary must at all times enjoy total and unquestioned public support and its reputation for absolute public independence and integrity is of paramount importance under the Constitution. The vindication of my own good name in the light of recent unjust attacks...must yield to those considerations to prevent the office of the President of the High Court being further embroiled in public controversy.

As President of High Court, announcing his resignation. *The Irish Times*, November 18, 1994.

November 17, 1994
Albert Reynolds
It's amazing. You cross the big hurdles and when you get to the small ones you get tripped.

As Taoiseach, in final words in resignation speech in Dáil. *The Irish Times*, November 18, 1994.

November 17, 1994
Sammy Wilson
Yet another tacky episode in the history of what must be one of the most corrupt states in Europe. It emphasises the reasons why unionists want nothing to do with that scandal-ridden country, which is noted for graft, church interference and corruption.

As DUP press officer, on political crisis in Dublin. *The Irish Times*, November 19, 1994.

November 25, 1994
Rev Brendan Smyth
I'm sorry I'm in prison but I'm glad that I was caught.

As paedophile priest, in *RTÉ* interview in Magilligan Prison. *The Irish Times*, December 3, 1994.

November 29, 1994
Cardinal Cahal Daly
There has not been for many years any cover-up and there will not be any cover-up. We're humbled by the whole experience.

As Primate of Ireland, on child abuse by clergy. *The Irish Times*, November 29, 1994.

December 1, 1994
George Mitchell
The chance to work in Northern Ireland at this hopeful time means a great deal to me [as] my father was the orphaned son of an Irish immigrant.

As former US Senator, in White House, after being appointed presidential economic adviser on NI. *The Irish Times*, December 2, 1994.

December 2, 1994
Rev Matthew Ring
It would seem to me that the show is over, the game is up, the media have blown the whistle and the hypocrisy, corruption and double standards have finally come to light.

As priest, on child abuse by Catholic clergy. *The Irish Times*, December 2, 1994.

December 6, 1994
Gerry Adams
One couldn't have a political settlement if there were still armed groups or weapons floating around. At the same time those that do have weapons are unlikely to decommission them short of a political settlement.

As President of Sinn Féin, in interview in Washington. *The Irish Times*, December 7, 1994.

December 9, 1994
Rev William McCrea
We are hard-headed and clear-minded Ulstermen and women gathered in conference today resolving together and before the world that Six into Twenty-Six will not go.

As DUP MP, at party conference. *The Irish Times*, December 10, 1994.

December 15, 1994
John Bruton
The Government must go about its work...as transparently as if it were working behind a pane of glass.

As newly elected Taoiseach. *The Irish Times*, December 7, 1996.

January 7, 1995
Patrick Mayhew
If the hard men say 'What did Gerry Adams do? We have called a ceasefire but have got nothing sufficient in return,' – then Mr Adams would take a long walk on a short plank and be replaced by someone harder.

As NI Secretary of State, to students in London, on why British must give Gerry Adams some support. *Observer*, January 8, 1995.

January 12, 1995
Rev Enda McDonagh
A sense of darkness, of winter darkness, of the darkness of death, has surrounded recent revelations. In Ireland it is said the old Church is dying.

As Maynooth professor of moral theology, on scandals in Catholic Church. *The Irish Times*, January 14, 1995.

January 22, 1995
Cardinal Cahal Daly
I wish to ask forgiveness from the people of this island for the wrongs and hurts inflicted by Irish people upon the people of this country during that shared history, and particularly the last 25 years.

As first Irish Roman Catholic Primate to speak in Canterbury Cathedral. *The Irish Times*, January 23, 1995.

January 30, 1995
Peter Brooke
In my view he [Gerry Adams] was a brave man and I hope he will be justified...he led them [IRA] across the Rubicon. In my view that was a courageous step. The whole world is grateful to him for having done it.

As former NI Secretary of State. *BBC* Panorama, January 30, 1995.

February 1, 1995
John Major
Let me say this to you tonight – nothing is going to be imposed on Northern Ireland. Peace cannot be secured by coercion.

As British Prime Minister, in radio address to reassure unionists after British newspapers claimed British-Irish Framework Document brought united Ireland closer. *BBC*, February 1, 1995.

February 6, 1995
Bill Clinton
I've always been conscious of being Irish. I mean, I'm sort of – I look Irish. I am Irish. It means a lot to me.

As US President, in interview with *Boston Globe*. *The Irish Times*, February 6, 1995.

February 14, 1995
Quentin Thomas
Like General [Ulysses] Grant, think not only what the enemy can do *to* you, but what you can do *for* the enemy.

As chief British negotiator in Northern Ireland, explaining, in New York speech, tactics used with Sinn Féin. *The Irish Times*, February 15, 1995.

February 23, 1995
John Major
I am not going to be a persuader for a united Ireland. I am a unionist who wants peace for the unionists, peace for the nationalists, and a rational, sane future for Northern Ireland.

As British Prime Minister, on Framework Document on future government of Northern Ireland. *The Irish Times*, February 25, 1995.

February 23, 1995
Edward Kennedy
If we expect Sinn Féin to act like a legitimate political party, we must treat it like one.

As US Senator, in letter asking President Clinton to lift fundraising ban on Sinn Féin leader Gerry Adams. O'Clery, Conor, *The Greening of the White House*, Gill & Macmillan, 1996, p. 188.

February 23, 1995
Peter Robinson
Ulster has been served an eviction notice to leave the United Kingdom.

As DUP deputy leader, on Framework Document. *The Irish Times*, February 25, 1995.

February 27, 1995
Mary Robinson
The fear is genuine. The fear of the ground shifting, the fear of a takeover, is undermining a sense of identity. If someone tried to undermine our sense of identity, if someone said to us Ireland should join the Commonwealth tomorrow, think of the ripples of fear that would produce.

As President, in interview in Japan, on Framework Document. *The Irish Times*, February 15, 1995.

February 28, 1995
Justice Rory O'Hanlon
If I remained silent...I would be betraying a trust God has imposed upon me, just as if I had been a judge in Nazi Germany in the 1930s and 1940s and had remained silent when the Jewish holocaust was being planned and put into effect.

As judge, opposing abortion information bill before Dáil. *The Irish Times*, March 1, 1995.

March 7, 1995
Patrick Mayhew
Fifty million British people would not like to see Mr Adams shaking hands with the president of the world's greatest democracy.

As NI Secretary of State, in Washington, opposing meeting between Gerry Adams and President Clinton. *The Irish Times*, March 10, 1995.

March 7, 1995
Nancy Soderberg
They thought we had lost our minds. They made entreaties, 'Don't do it,' and then we'd do it.

As special adviser to President Clinton, on rejection of British appeals to White House concerning Sinn Féin. O'Clery, Conor, *The Greening of the White House*, Gill & Macmillan, 1996, p. 192.

March 7, 1995
Niall O'Dowd
I suppose what the British never understood was that you could throw ambassadors and ministers into it, but at the end of the day there were no votes in the British position.

As New York publisher and intermediary in NI peace process, on why Irish Americans had more influence on White House on Irish issues than British diplomats. O'Clery, Conor, *The Greening of the White House*, Gill & Macmillan, 1996, p. 193.

March 9, 1995
Catholic Hierarchy
Anybody who acts in a way calculated to facilitate abortion, anybody who helps a mother identify or contact those who will destroy the life of her child, is participating in the violation of that child's most basic right.

As Irish Bishops, opposing abortion information bill before Dáil. *The Irish Times*, March 9, 1995.

March 9, 1995
Liz O'Donnell
[This] is basically a snub to the House, a snub to the decision of the Supreme Court, and a snub to all compassionate Irish people, practicing Catholics or non-practicing Catholics.

As PD spokesperson on justice, in Dáil, on Bishops' opposition to abortion information. *The Irish Times*, March 10, 1995.

March 9, 1995
Sean Haughey
A Fianna Fáil TD who sincerely opposes the bill is now branded right-wing, a fundamentalist Catholic, a conservative, narrow minded, a backwoodsman, anti-woman, opportunistic, and more recently, a hypocrite.

As Fianna Fáil TD, in Dáil, on abortion information bill. *The Irish Times*, March 11, 1995.

March 9, 1995
Lady Olga Maitland
[This is] a slap in the face for John Major.

As Conservative MP, on President Clinton's decision to allow Gerry Adams to raise funds in US. *The Irish Times*, March 10, 1995.

March 12, 1995
Gerry Adams
Mrs Windsor can come and go as she wants.

As President of Sinn Féin, on visit to Belfast by Queen Elizabeth II. *The Irish Times*, March 12, 1995.

March 12, 1995
John Hume
Irish people today are now one of the most powerful people in the world, if we relate everything to people and not to territory. If we harness this there is no doubt that the next century will not only be the first century without violence but the first without emigration.

As leader of SDLP, interviewed while leading St Patrick's Day parade in Washington. *The Irish Times*, March 13, 1995.

March 13, 1995
Pat Hale
Something is happening in Ireland that we have long prayed for. A flame has been lit, a flame that grows stronger every day. That flame is peace.

As leader of Ancient Order of Hibernians, in US, presenting award to Gerry Adams in Albany, NY. *The Irish Times*, March 14, 1995.

March 14, 1995
Peter Hitchens
Will it have a military attaché?

As *Daily Express* correspondent and critic of Sinn Féin, at press conference held by Gerry Adams to open Sinn Féin 'diplomatic mission' in Washington. [Adams replied by asking Peter Hitchens to 'decommission himself'.] *The Irish Times*, March 15, 1995.

March 15, 1995
Richard Holbrooke
Decommissioning must be mutual, balanced and across the board, and must begin now and not await the end of talks.

As Assistant US Secretary of State, on Northern Ireland. *The Irish Times*, March 16, 1995.

March 16, 1995
Bill Clinton
I'm catching more shit because of you Irish. It's too bad! I don't care.

As US President, to Congressman Peter King, on British anger at decision to allow Sinn Féin leader Gerry Adams to raise funds in US. O'Clery, Conor, *The Greening of the White House*, Gill & Macmillan, 1996, p. 200.

March 16, 1995
Bill Clinton
This is going to work!

As US President, waving fist in air, in company of John Hume and Gerry Adams at US House Speaker's St Patrick's Day lunch. *The Irish Times*, March 17, 1995.

March 17, 1995
John Bruton
I was wrong Mr President, you were right.

As Taoiseach, on his belief that a US visa for Sinn Féin leader Gerry Adams would not lead to IRA ceasefire. O'Clery, Conor, *The Greening of the White House*, Gill & Macmillan, 1996, p. 203.

March 17, 1995
Bill Clinton
To those who have laid down their arms, I would ask you to take the next step and begin to seriously discuss getting rid of those weapons.

As US President, addressing loyalist and republican politicians in White House. *The Irish Times*, March 18, 1995.

March 17, 1995
Dr Paddy Leahy
What I would do is quietly finish up my affairs. I would go to the Far East... I would write a few letters. And then I would take my tablets. It might be lonely but I wouldn't have to cry or die every time my children or my friends come to see me.

As euthanasia advocate, who later took his life in Thailand. *The Irish Times*, March 18, 1995.

March 17, 1995
Mo Mowlam
I accept that a Labour Government, when in office, would not act as a persuader to a united Ireland... We would instead act as a persuader to a balanced political settlement.

As British Labour Party's NI spokesperson. *New Statesman*, March 17, 1995.

March 31, 1995
Albert Reynolds
Historically you didn't hand in your armoury, you returned the pike to the thatch. That is the culture and you might as well recognise that.

As former Taoiseach, at Oxford Union. *The Irish Times*, April 1, 1995.

April 3, 1995
John Taylor
Why are people unionists? There are three reasons. One is some have a very strong loyalty to the crown. The second is that a lot of us have a very strong loyalty to the half crown... And the third reason is an in-built fear of the Church of Rome.

As unionist MP, at Dublin Rotary Club, on importance of pluralism in Republic. *The Irish Times*, April 4, 1995.

April 5, 1995
Richard Holbrooke
I always talk about Northern Ireland because there is real progress being made after decades, though it takes an awful long time and we're not at the end of the road. That's the message for south-eastern Europe.

As Assistant US Secretary of State. *The Irish Times*, April 6, 1995.

c. April 15, 1995
John Bruton
[I am] sick of answering questions about the fucking peace process... I am the Taoiseach. My job is to run the country.

As Taoiseach, in interview with Cathy Farrell of Cork Radio 96FM. *The Irish Times*, April 20, 1995.

April 18, 1995
Mary Robinson
I had no expectation that I was going to meet Pinochet, and it was with great dismay that I saw that he was attending the dinner... I did not show any pleasure in meeting him.

As President, on shaking hands with former dictator on visit to Chile in March. *The Irish Times*, April 22, 1995.

April 25, 1995
Patrick Mayhew
What we have said very consistently is that before...Sinn Féin can enter the conference room along with the constitutional parties, substantial progress on the decommissioning of arms has got to have taken place.

As NI Secretary of State. *The Irish Times*, April 29, 1995.

April 27, 1995
John Hume
Would the Secretary of State please advise his backbenchers to keep their negative mouths shut, because all they are doing is undermining that great new atmosphere among the people.

As leader of SDLP, in House of Commons, on Conservative MPs attacks on peace process. Routledge, Paul, *John Hume*, Harper Collins, 1998, p. 273.

April 28, 1995
Margaret Thatcher
You can imagine how we felt when President Clinton received Gerry Adams. What would you think he would have felt if we received the people responsible for the Oklahoma bombing?

As former British Prime Minister, speaking in Arkansas. *The Irish Times*, April 29, 1995.

April 28, 1995
Marion Gibson
What binds us together is the common tears. There are no Catholic tears or Protestant tears, only tears of people.

As speaker at conference of Irish Association of Victim Support. *The Irish Times*, April 29, 1995.

May 17, 1995
Rev Ian Paisley
There is going to be political skullduggery and shenanigans going on and I will have no part in that.

As leader of DUP, refusing invitation to White House investment conference for Ireland. *The Irish Times*, May 20, 1995.

May 18, 1995
Gerry Adams
Decommissioning [of all weapons] has to happen, there's no doubt about that, as part of the entire process. The only people who can disarm the IRA are the IRA. Who else can do it? Now when and how and if they do depends on us winning their confidence.

As President of Sinn Féin, in interview in Philadelphia. *The Irish Times*, May 20, 1995.

May 19, 1995
Anthony Lake
The peace process is like a bicycle. It topples over if it goes too slowly.

As US National Security Adviser to President Clinton. Attributed.

May 19, 1995
Dan Burton
For the life of me I can't figure out why we are sending $29.6 million to Ireland. It is an English province. They can handle it.

As US Congressman for Indiana, on America's contribution to International Fund for Ireland. *The Irish Times*, May 20, 1995.

May 24, 1995
Michael Keane
The fabric of Irish society has been badly damaged. The death of *Irish Press* newspapers is not just the end of an era in Irish journalism, it is a tragedy for those who sought an alternative voice and those who provided it.

As editor of *Sunday Press*, in statement on demise of *Irish Press* (established by Eamon de Valera in 1931), *Sunday Press* and *Evening Press*. May 24, 1995.

May 24, 1995
Glen Barr
If Gerry Adams is shaking my hand he'd better look at what's in the other one.

As loyalist leader, at White House investment conference. *The Irish Times*, May 25, 1995.

May 24, 1995
Patrick Mayhew
Let nature take its course...let copulation thrive!

As NI Secretary of State, borrowing quote from Shakespeare's King Lear, in address to forum of Irish and US business people at White House investment conference on Northern Ireland. O'Clery, Conor, *The Greening of the White House*, Gill & Macmillan, 1996, p. 216.

May 25, 1995
Robert Coulter
Three days ago I would have preached that we should have established some relationship with the Ulster Scots here. Now I don't think so, as there is a hand of friendship here from Irish Americans and we should be there letting our voice be heard in a friendly manner.

As unionist Mayor of Ballymena, at White House investment conference on Ireland. *The Irish Times*, May 26, 1995.

May 25, 1995
Peter Robinson
[President Clinton's speech was] a side salad of sentimentality. Who's he to tell us the Framework Document is synonymous with peace – it's not.

As DUP deputy leader, at White House investment conference on Ireland. *The Irish Times*, May 26, 1995.

May 25, 1995
Bill Clinton
I know I speak for all Americans when I say those who take risks for peace...will always be welcome at the White House.

As US President, at White House investment conference on Ireland. *The Irish Times*, May 26, 1995.

May 25, 1995
Ron Brown
Northern Ireland is open for business.

As US Commerce Secretary, at White House investment conference on Ireland. *The Irish Times*, May 26, 1995.

May 25, 1995
Al Gore
Threads are being woven, one stitch at a time, into the shimmering cloak of peace.

As US Vice President, at White House investment conference on Ireland. *The Irish Times*, May 26, 1995.

May 31, 1995
Prince Charles
We are all deeply conscious of what has gone wrong over the centuries. There has been so much misunderstanding, sorrow and personal tragedy.

As Prince of Wales, making first visit by a Prince of Wales to Dublin Castle in 84 years. *The Irish Times*, June 1, 1995.

May 31, 1995
John Bruton
Your courage and initiative in coming here has done more to sweep away the legacy and fear and suspicion which has lain between our two peoples than any other event in my lifetime.

As Taoiseach, welcoming Prince Charles to Dublin Castle. *The Irish Times*, June 1, 1995.

June 19, 1995
Nelson Mandela
When we made a statement suspending armed struggle we totally rejected a demand from the South African Government that we would hand in our arms, and we said that is a decision that we ourselves will take at an appropriate time.

As South African President, on meeting Gerry Adams in Johannesburg. *The Irish Times*, June 20, 1995.

June 25, 1995
Phyllis Hamilton
Michael explained that, in the time before Jesus, there was no marriage ceremony, and that this is all that was required for a man and woman to become husband and wife... Michael warned me that this was to be our secret and that no one was to know.

As companion of 'singing priest' Rev Michael Cleary, who died 18 months previously, on their private marriage vows. *Sunday World*, June 25, 1995.

June 25, 1995
Cardinal Cahal Daly
Personal opinions which depart from communion with the world-wide college of bishops or are at variance with the teachings of the Holy Father are just that, personal opinions.

As Primate of Ireland, on call by Bishop Comiskey of Ferns to consider options to priestly celibacy. *The Irish Times*, June 26, 1995.

June 28, 1995
Dr Brendan Comiskey
My listening tells me that our priests are greatly disturbed, and in some instances demoralised, by a series of sexual scandals involving the clergy and by the legitimate, if extremely painful, questions coming from a confused and bewildered laity.

As Bishop of Ferns, rejecting view of Cardinal Daly, above. *The Irish Times*, June 28, 1995.

July 3, 1995
Sean Reilly
How can I go and tell her that her killer is free, that her life meant nothing, that if you're Catholic and working class and from West Belfast, you're treated like dirt.

As father of Karen Reilly, and daily visitor to her grave, on release of British soldier, Private Lee Clegg, convicted of her 1990 murder. *The Irish Times*, July 4, 1995.

July 4, 1995
Hugh Grant
Maybe you'll feel different now [after Oklahoma bomb] about rewarding a terrorist like Gerry Adams.

As British film actor, heckling White House aide, George Stephanopolous, at Washington dinner. *The Irish Times*, July 6, 1995.

July 19, 1995
Dr Brendan Comiskey
The Cardinal is behind all this. Otherwise why should Brendan Comiskey be called to Rome? The Cardinal started all this by attacking me. This has all to do with the type of Church we have in Ireland, and all I was trying to do was formulate a debate.

As Bishop of Ferns, on summons to Vatican after outspoken statements on priestly celibacy. *The Irish Times*, July 20, 1995.

August 13, 1995
Gerry Adams
They haven't gone away, you know.

As President of Sinn Féin, replying to heckler who shouted 'Bring back the IRA' at Belfast rally against Orange marches. *The Irish Times*, August 14, 1995.

August 22, 1995
John Hume
When he said the IRA's not gone away...my own interpretation was that he was simply telling the truth. They have stopped their campaign, that's what matters.

As leader of SDLP, on Gerry Adams's remark, above. *BBC*, Breakfast with Frost, August 22, 1995.

August 23, 1995
Rev William Hoey

We have so many of our church leaders caught up with a false ecumenism that they are afraid of saying the wrong thing, for fear of giving offence to the red-hatted weasel in Armagh...

As Church of Ireland clergyman, in Belfast parish newsletter. *The Irish Times*, August 24, 1995.

September 20, 1995
Anthony Lake

When I see [Gerry] Adams I try to convince him of the merits of baseball as a metaphor for politics. He sent me a video of hurling, which looks like a game with no rules.

As National Security Adviser to President Clinton. O'Clery, Conor, *The Greening of the White House*, Gill & Macmillan, 1996, p. 224.

September 27, 1995
Michael Heseltine

We should do absolutely nothing. We shall pursue our right to fight terrorism, to protect innocent people, wherever we have jurisdiction.

As British Deputy Prime Minister, on British response to finding of European Court of Human Rights that British soldiers acted in breach of European Convention on Human Rights in killing 3 unarmed IRA members in Gibraltar. *The Irish Times*, September 28, 1995.

September 28, 1995
Ali Alatas

[It was] almost like a declaration of war.

As Foreign Minister of Indonesia, on pro-East Timor article written by Minister for Foreign Affairs Dick Spring in *The Irish Times*. *The Irish Times*, September 29, 1995.

September 29, 1995
IRA

Given...that [the British Government] and their loyalist death squad allies hold the largest stocks of licenced and unlicenced weapons, the demand for an IRA handover of weapons is ludicrous.

The Irish Times, September 30, 1995.

October 13, 1995
Cardinal Cahal Daly

To all victims...we express in the name of the church our most humble apology for the hurt caused to them.

As Primate of Ireland, on sexual abuse by clergy. *The Irish Times*, October 14, 1995.

October 19, 1995
Michael Farrell

Many Northern Protestants harbour a deep-seated fear of the Republic as a predatory, Catholic-dominated society. Ending the ban [on

divorce] could make a real contribution to easing tension between the communities on this island.

As chairman of Irish Council for Civil Liberties. *The Irish Times*, October 21, 1995.

October 26, 1995
Catholic Hierarchy

In marriage a husband and wife give and receive an unconditional promise to be a husband and wife as long as they live. If remarriage is recognised by civil law, then, even as they speak these solemn words, the State will effectively say – if either of you wishes to repudiate this promise, the courts will act on the basis that you do not mean what you say.

As Irish Bishops, in statement of which one million copies were circulated urging 'no' vote in divorce referendum. *The Irish Times*, October 21, 1995.

October 30, 1995
Irish American Unity Conference

A welcome to David Trimble, the David Duke of Ireland.

As Irish-American pressure group, in advertisement in *The New York Times* comparing unionist leader to former leader of Ku Klux Klan on grounds both supported provocative parades. *The New York Times*, October 30, 1995.

October 30, 1995
David Duke

I think this is a cheap shot on both of us.

As former KKK leader, on reaction to statement, above. *The Irish Times*, October 21, 1995.

October 31, 1995
Proinsias de Rossa

The bishops' perspective is predicated on a view of the Irish people as fickle, inconstant creatures, who unlike Roman Catholic bishops and priests, need to be locked into their vows for life.

As leader of Democratic Left, on divorce campaign. *The Irish Times*, November 1, 1995.

November 1, 1995
Mary Robinson

What has happened since the issue [of divorce] was last before the people is a whole structure of reform of our marriage law...a very thoughtful infrastructure has been developed.

As President, in US television interview. *The Irish Times*, November 4, 1995.

November 1, 1995
Justice Rory O'Hanlon

With regard to the 'thoughtful infrastructure', I would describe it as a massive, hastily cobbled-together body of law, designed for the purpose of bolstering up a divorce campaign.

As chairman of anti-divorce campaign, responding to President Robinson, above. *The Irish Times*, November 4, 1995.

November 10, 1995
Dr Thomas Flynn

Any Catholic who gets divorced and who then remarries may not receive the sacraments while living as husband and wife.

As spokesman for Catholic Hierarchy. *The Irish Times*, November 13, 1995.

November 12, 1995
Dr Laurence Ryan

In a real-life situation, a priest would not be in a position to refuse holy communion to somebody who approaches him in the normal way at mass.

As Bishop of Kildare and Leighlin, contradicting Dr Flynn, above. *The Irish Times*, November 13, 1995.

November 26, 1995
Úna Bean Mhic Mhathúna

G'way, ye wife-swapping sodomites.

As representative of 'no' vote campaign, at counting centre, to victorious pro-divorce campaigners. *The Irish Times*, November 27, 1995.

November 29, 1995
Bill Clinton

Now, whenever we have the most minor disagreement, I walk out on the Truman balcony and I look at those burn marks [made when British forces laid siege to US capital], just to remind myself that I dare not let this relationship get out of hand again.

As US President, in speech to joint Houses of Parliament in London, on strains in special relationship between US and UK over Northern Ireland. O'Clery, Conor, *The Greening of the White House*, Gill & Macmillan, 1996, p. 233.

November 30, 1995
Bill Clinton

You must stand firm against terror. You must say to those who still would use violence for political objectives – you are the past; your day is over.

As US President, at Mackie factory in Belfast. *The Irish Times*, December 1, 1995.

November 30, 1995
Catherine Hamill

My first daddy died in the Troubles. It was the saddest day of my life. I still think of him. Now it is nice and peaceful. I like having peace and quiet for a change instead of people shooting and

killing. My Christmas wish is that peace and love will last in Ireland for ever.

As 8-year-old schoolgirl, reading letter to President Clinton at Mackie factory, Belfast. *The Irish Times*, December 1, 1995.

November 30, 1995
Hillary Rodham Clinton

Many women, perhaps because of children, have a link to the future that keeps giving us the hope and energy to try and make things better, no matter how dark they seem.

As wife of President Clinton, on meeting Joyce McCartan of Belfast who lost 18 relatives in the Troubles. *The Irish Times*, December 1, 1995.

November 30, 1995
Bill Clinton

This day...will long be with us as the most remarkable day of our lives.

As US President, to crowd at Belfast City Hall. *The Irish Times*, December 1, 1995.

November 30, 1995
Bill Clinton

I got a letter from 13-year-old Ryan from Belfast. Now Ryan, if you're out in the crowd tonight, here's the answer to your question. No, as far as I know, an alien spaceship did not land in Roswell, New Mexico, in 1947. And Ryan, if the United States air force did discover alien bodies, they didn't tell me about it, and I want to know.

As US President, to crowd at Belfast City Hall. O'Clery, Conor, *The Greening of the White House*, Gill & Macmillan, 1996, p. 236.

December 1, 1995
Bill Clinton

In the last century it was often said that the Irish who fled the Great Hunger were searching for *caislean oir* – castles of gold. I cannot say that they found these castles of gold in the United States, but I know they built a lot of castles of gold for the United States... Now we seek to repay that in some small way by being a partner with you for peace.

As US President, addressing joint session of Oireachtas. *Great Irish Speeches of the Twentieth Century*, Poolbeg Press, 1996, p. 421.

December 1, 1995
Mandy Grunwald

My God, what pictures. You can't buy this stuff. You can't invent it. It's the real thing. Ireland. Peace. Unfortunately these people don't live in America. Maybe their relatives do.

As media director of US President Clinton's election campaign, on large crowds cheering President in Dublin.

O'Clery, Conor, *The Greening of the White House*, Gill & Macmillan, 1996, p. 237.

December 1, 1995
Finola Bruton
There is a vital place beyond the work place; many women choose to be there. They should be applauded and acknowledged.

As wife of Taoiseach, John Bruton, introducing Hillary Rodham Clinton to meeting of women in Dublin. *The Irish Times*, December 2, 1995.

December 1, 1995
Marie Geoghegan-Quinn
[It was] deeply offensive and an attempt to upstage the First Lady.

As Fianna Fáil TD, on Finola Bruton's remark, above. *The Irish Times*, December 2, 1995.

December 3, 1995
Bill Clinton
The power of the United States goes far beyond military might. What you saw in Ireland for example had not a whit to do with military might. It was all about values.

As US President, speaking in Madrid after visit to Ireland. *The Irish Times*, December 4, 1995.

December 8, 1995
Bill Clinton
I never dreamed when it all started and I was a young man living in England and just fascinated by it and heartbroken by it, that I'd ever have a chance to do anything to help it. I hope I have. I hope I'll have more. You know, I've been fascinated by it for 25 years...from the day the Troubles began.

As US President, in White House interview. *The Irish Times*, December 9, 1995.

December 8, 1995
Anthony Lake
One of the reasons the visit succeeded was because of the exquisite choreography that made the third act of any Mozart opera seem easy.

As National Security Adviser to President Clinton, on equal treatment given to both sides during President Clinton's visit to Northern Ireland. *The Irish Times*, December 11, 1995.

December 29, 1995
US State Department
Many embassy employees saw the embassy under Ambassador Smith as more attuned to Irish rather than US interests...she also expressed an appreciation for Irish culture.

In report on dissent in embassy over decision by US Ambassador Jean Kennedy Smith to approve visa for Gerry Adams. *The Irish Times*, March 6, 1996.

December 31, 1995
Dr Desmond Connell
We are experiencing a revolution of values within our country. The intrusion of the mass media, the impact of mass global tourism, the communications explosion, unemployment or fear of losing a job, divorce, all these things affect and haunt many families today...some are damaged beyond their control.

As Archbishop of Dublin. *The Irish Times*, January 1, 1996.

January 11, 1996
South Armagh Tourism
A welcome smile,
A country mile,
Stay awhile.

Slogan adopted to lure tourists back after IRA ceasefire. *The Irish Times*, January 12, 1996.

January 11, 1996
Bertie Ahern
If the British Government was going to insist on the early surrender of weapons...they should have said so loudly, clearly and repeatedly before the ceasefire. Of course if they had insisted on an early arms surrender, the ceasefire would in all probability not have happened.

As leader of Fianna Fáil, speaking in Belfast. *The Irish Times*, January 12, 1996.

January 19, 1996
Jack Charlton
I am as happy as a pig in muck.

As former trainer of Irish Republic soccer team, on news he would become honorary Irish citizen. *The Irish Times*, January 19, 1996.

January 28, 1996
Martin McGuinness
The Unionists want their new assembly. The British Government wants to give them their assembly. We are not going to give them their new Stormont. We are not going to be part of their new assembly.

As Sinn Féin Vice President, on announcement of elections to new assembly. *The Irish Times*, January 29, 1996.

January 30, 1996
Catholic Hierarchy
In all cases where it is known or suspected that a child has been or is being sexually abused by a priest or religious, the matter should be reported...without delay to the senior ranking police officer for the area.

As Irish Bishops, ending practice of internal investigation and silence in cases of child abuse. *The Irish Times*, January 31, 1996.

February 9, 1996
IRA

The British Government acted in bad faith, with Mr Major and the Unionist leaders squandering this unprecedented opportunity to resolve the conflict.

Announcing end of 17-month ceasefire, before bomb exploded at Canary Wharf in London. *The Irish Times*, February 10, 1996.

February 9, 1996
Gusty Spence

For heaven's sake and for the sake of the people of Northern Ireland, hold anything that you may anticipate doing until such time as the situation becomes clear. I am going down on my knees, begging.

As loyalist leader, urging loyalist paramilitaries not to breach ceasefire after end of IRA ceasefire. *The Irish Times*, February 10, 1996.

February 10, 1996
Bill Clinton

The terrorists who perpetrated this attack cannot be allowed to derail the efforts to bring peace to Northern Ireland.

As US President, on IRA bombing of Canary Wharf in London. O'Clery, Conor, *The Greening of the White House*, Gill & Macmillan, 1996, p. 241.

February 12, 1996
John Major

No one – no one – took more risks for peace. But we never lost sight of the fact that the IRA commitment had not been made for good.

As British Prime Minister, on end of IRA ceasefire. *The Irish Times*, February 13, 1996.

February 12, 1996
George Mitchell

It would be compounding the tragedy if we let the peace process die in the rubble of bombed buildings in London.

As special economic adviser on Ireland to President Clinton. *The Irish Times*, February 13, 1996.

February 16, 1996
John Freeman

Well, we haven't gone away either.

As Irish Congress of Trade Unions President, to 4,000-strong peace rally in Belfast, paraphrasing Gerry Adams's comment of August 13, 1995 about IRA. *The Irish Times*, February 17, 1996.

February 18, 1996
Dr Brendan Comiskey

Pedestals are the loneliest places in Ireland, good breeding grounds for present and future alcoholics.

As Bishop of Ferns, on return to Enniscorthy after treatment for alcoholism. *The Irish Times*, February 19, 1996.

March 1, 1996
IRA

We sued for peace. The British wanted war. If that's what they want we will give them another 25 years of war.

In meeting with John Hume and Gerry Adams, as related later by Adams. Routledge, Paul, *John Hume*, Harper Collins, 1998, p. 285.

March 6, 1996
Rev Roy Magee

The loyalist paramilitaries see themselves as British and any attack on anything that's British is an attack on their ethos and identity.

As broker of loyalist ceasefire on IRA statement that it would not attack loyalist targets. *The Irish Times*, March 7, 1996.

March 9, 1996
Jean Kennedy Smith

They said I did charity work, but if I were a man, they would have said I ran an international organisation.

As US Ambassador to Ireland and founder of 55-nation Very Special Arts Programme. *The Irish Times*, March 9, 1996.

March 11, 1996
Bill Clinton

We must not allow those who have been hardened by the past to hijack the future of the children of Northern Ireland.

As US President, accepting Irish American of the Year award from New York publisher Niall O'Dowd. *The Irish Times*, March 12, 1996.

March 11, 1996
Bill Clinton

Her commitment was tireless. So was her willingness to pick up the phone and call the President.

As US President, on US Ambassador to Ireland, Jean Kennedy Smith. *The Irish Times*, March 12, 1996.

March 12, 1996
Combined Loyalist Military Command

Have no lessons been learned from the past; are our people, all our people, to be subjected to interminable warfare, must we listen to the cries of our women and children for another lifetime?

As body representing UDA and UVF, reacting to end of IRA ceasefire. *The Irish Times,* March 13, 1996.

March 14, 1996
Mo Mowlam
I am not going to spend my evening hiding behind potted palms.

As Labour NI spokesperson, on prospect of meeting Gerry Adams at Washington dinner. *The Irish Times,* March 15, 1996.

March 15, 1996
Bill Clinton
You don't have to all of a sudden start trusting people. You just have to show up, start, go to work...reach an agreement in good faith.

As US President, in words directed to IRA. *The Irish Times,* March 16, 1996.

March 15, 1996
David Trimble
St Patrick was a Brit who went to Ireland to tell the natives what to do.

As leader of Ulster Unionist Party, on why he was celebrating St Patrick's Day at party in White House. *The Irish Times,* March 16, 1996.

March 21, 1996
Seamus Mallon
This is a monster, raving looney proposal and a sop to the Unionists.

As SDLP deputy leader, in House of Commons, on British proposal for NI elections. *The Irish Times,* March 22, 1996.

March 26, 1996
David Trimble
Once the Dublin Government realises it can no longer export bombs along with its social problems to England, it will become as helpful as a Tory backbencher in search of a knighthood.

As leader of Ulster Unionist Party, calling for travel restrictions between UK and Republic of Ireland. *The Irish Times,* March 30, 1996.

March 27, 1996
John Bruton
I think they belong to some leprechaun's book of unusual Irish statements.

As Taoiseach, in Dáil, on David Trimble's remarks, above. *The Irish Times,* March 30, 1996.

April 4, 1996
John Hume
Consider the bitterness of the European conflict over the centuries, and the 35 million dead in 1945; yet fifty years later there is a European Union. But the Germans are still German and the French are still French. How did they do it?

Exactly as I am trying to do here, by building institutions that respect their differences, gave no victory to either side, but allowed them to work together in their common interest, to spill their sweat not their blood, and thereby break down the barrier of centuries.

As leader of SDLP, in interview. Routledge, Paul, *John Hume,* Harper Collins, 1998, p. 155.

April 14, 1996
Brian Eggins
A tom cat marks out its territory with an indescribable obnoxious spray. Orangemen do just the same...with spray-type paint on the kerbstones.

As delegate at Alliance Party conference. *The Irish Times,* April 15, 1996.

April 20, 1996
James Simmons
It has been one of my lifelong ambitions to help release Ulster people from guilt and furtiveness over sex. The poem...describes a happily married couple making love – triumphing over the filth and dirtiness of a Northern Ireland railways toilet.

As poet, on decision by Larne councillors to ban his poetry in schools because of his poem 'Rainbow', after matter arose during discussion of planning application submitted by Simmons. *The Irish Times,* April 21, 1996.

April 26, 1996
Fergus Finlay
They will, but they won't be worth a penny candle.

As Labour Party negotiator, on whether all-party talks could start without Sinn Féin. *The Irish Times,* April 27, 1996.

May 1, 1996
Rev Roy Magee
[Business-type unionists] believe the process is leading to a united Ireland and they are trying to goad the loyalist paramilitaries into doing their dirty work for them.

As Presbyterian intermediary with loyalists, on call by clandestine elements for end to loyalist ceasefire. *The Irish Times,* May 8, 1996.

May 2, 1996
Seamus Smith
I admire Harvey Keitel and Quentin Tarantino, and I'm not saying everyone in Ireland would be affected by this film, but even if one person were affected, I wouldn't like to have it on my conscience.

As film censor, on banning film 'From Dusk Till Dawn' because of 'extraordinary violence' on the screen. *The Irish Times,* May 3, 1996.

May 2, 1996
Conor Cruise O'Brien
I'm pursuing a unionist agenda insofar as I want to help moderate non-sectarian unionists [in] resisting the pressure that is forcing them to go in a direction in which they do not want to go.

As former Labour Minister in Dáil, on decision to stand as UK Unionist Party candidate in NI elections. *The Irish Times*, May 3, 1996.

May 9, 1996
Conor Cruise O'Brien
They told me to nail my colours to the mast. Now I can wrap them round my neck.

As UK Unionist Party candidate in NI elections, on donning Ulster tie at nomination. *The Irish Times*, May 10, 1996.

May 15, 1996
John Major
I want Sinn Féin to be part of the negotiations. They have an important contribution to make. But they cannot make it while there is no IRA ceasefire in place.

As British Prime Minister, writing in *The Irish Times*. *The Irish Times*, May 15, 1996.

May 29, 1996
David Trimble
The little Hitlers in the Department of Foreign Affairs [must know] that this attitude will produce failure... The Department of Foreign Affairs must resign itself to losing the illegitimate power to stretch its fingers into the nooks and crannies of Northern Ireland which the careless and deluded Thatcher government conceded.

As leader of Ulster Unionist Party, writing in *The Irish Times*, claiming Foreign Affairs sought preordained conclusion to NI talks. *The Irish Times*, May 29, 1996.

May 31, 1996
Pat Doherty
We are in an era of conflict resolution... I do think it's the end game.

As Sinn Féin Vice President, on peace process. *The Irish Times*, June 1, 1996.

June 5, 1996
Mary Robinson
Children of the Irish heritage are learning to negotiate the past images of the Famine – the evictions, the workhouse, the coffin ship – into the facts of present-day hunger in developing countries.

As President, at dinner in London's Guildhall. *The Irish Times*, June 6, 1996.

June 7, 1996
Terry Dicks
I am appalled and ashamed that an American, a foreigner, has been chosen for the task which involves a part of the United Kingdom.

As Tory MP, on appointment of former US Senator George Mitchell as chairman of NI talks. *The Irish Times*, June 8, 1996.

June 19, 1996
IRA
We are still prepared to enhance the democratic peace process.

In statement after bombing centre of Manchester. *The Irish Times*, June 20, 1996.

June 20, 1996
Gerry Adams
Sinn Féin is not involved in armed struggle. Sinn Féin does not advocate armed struggle. We are truly and absolutely committed to democratic and peaceful means of resolving political problems.

As President of Sinn Féin, writing in *The Irish Times*. *The Irish Times*, June 20, 1996.

June 26, 1996
Dick Spring
That she should be shot down in this fashion is an attack on all of us, and on the values that democracy and democratic parties are based on.

As Tanaiste, on murder of journalist Veronica Guerin. *The Irish Times*, June 27, 1996.

June 26, 1996
Mary Harney
We all know who they are, with their holiday homes, their fast cars and their yachts. And we all have had enough of it. It is time they were put down.

As leader of Progressive Democrats, on murder of journalist Veronica Guerin. *The Irish Times*, June 27, 1996.

July 7, 1996
Harold Gracey
It is a siege of Portadown and of Ulster. If we fail in this we are finished.

As District Grand Master of Portadown Orange Order, on ban on Orange Parade at Drumcree, Portadown. *The Irish Times*, July 8, 1996.

July 10, 1996
Patrick Mayhew
Cheer up for heaven's sake.

As NI Secretary of State, to *BBC* interviewer on widespread disorders coinciding with Orange protests at Drumcree, Portadown. *BBC*, July 10, 1996.

July 11, 1996
Cardinal Cahal Daly
This has been a bleak day in the history of Northern Ireland... The State has been seen to capitulate before lawless violence and the threat of violence.

As Primate of Ireland, after police forced Orange Parade through nationalist protestors on Portadown's Garvaghy Road. *The Irish Times*, July 12, 1996.

July 11, 1996
Hugh Annesley
I have got to say I am sick, and so are my colleagues, sick to death, of being stuck in the middle of an unwinnable situation.

As RUC Chief Constable, on criticism of police after reversal of RUC decision to block Orange marchers from marching along Garvaghy Road, Portadown. *The Irish Times*, July 12, 1996.

July 12, 1996
John Bruton
I said to the Prime Minister what I am saying to you now... A democratic state cannot afford to be partial in the way it upholds the law... The lack of firmness of the British Government was a very big mistake.

As Taoiseach, on reversal of police decision to block Orange marchers from marching along Garvaghy Road, Portadown. *BBC*, July 12, 1996.

July 15, 1996
David Trimble
We were in a very volatile situation...we were very anxious that the paramilitaries would not break their ceasefire.

As leader of Ulster Unionist Party, on why he met Billy Wright of UVF during Orange protests at Garvaghy Road, Portadown. *BBC*, July 15, 1996.

July 16, 1996
Seamus Mallon
The authority of the State and the policing of the State was challenged... Mr Trimble led that challenge.

As SDLP deputy leader, on crisis at Drumcree, Portadown. *The Irish Times*, July 17, 1996.

July 26, 1996
Mary O'Rourke
There's women for you.

As deputy Fianna Fáil leader, on Michelle Smith winning three gold medals for Ireland in Olympic Games, paraphrasing Albert Reynolds's comment 'This is women now!' of December 9, 1993. *The Irish Times*, July 27, 1996.

July 26, 1996
John White
I am here to ensure that incidents like I was involved in do not happen again.

As loyalist convicted for 1973 murder of SDLP Senator Paddy Wilson and companion, after meeting British Prime Minister John Major in Downing Street as part of loyalist peace delegation. *The Irish Times*, July 27, 1996.

August 16, 1996
James Baker
We have also seen a representative of the IRA hosted in the White House just prior to the resumption of terror bombings in London. The result has been the worst relationship with our closest ally, Britain, since the Boston Tea Party.

As former US Secretary of State, in speech backing presidential campaign of Bob Dole. *The Irish Times*, August 17, 1996.

September 4, 1996
Rev Padraig Standun
When I dodder back here in 25 or 50 years time, I don't want to look out on serried ranks of male clerics on a one-legged church that denies women equality at the altar. I would rather that there wouldn't stand a stone upon a stone in this building [than] we carry on as we are, complacent, self-indulgent, misogynist.

As priest, in homily at Maynooth College. *The Irish Times*, September 5, 1996.

September 6, 1996
Gerry Adams
It is a very peaceful, legitimate and democratic tactic. Some people quite legitimately said to Orange business people that you can't expect to treat me as you did over July and August and then expect me to come to your business and put money in your till.

As President of Sinn Féin, on nationalist boycott of some unionist businesses. *The Irish Times*, September 7, 1996.

September 15, 1996
Ian Paisley Jr
You can only poke a community in the eye so often before they kick you on the ankle.

As son of Rev Ian Paisley, on loyalist picketing of Catholic churches. *The Irish Times*, September 21, 1996.

September 15, 1996
David McAllister
As Protestants we refuse to consent to Roman Catholics coming into a Protestant village to worship, until those same Roman Catholics give back to Protestants their civil and religious liberties to parade the streets of Ulster.

As DUP councillor, leading loyalist blockade of Catholic Church in Bushmills, Co Down. *The Irish Times,* September 16, 1996.

September 17, 1996
Dr Harry Allen
[They] are denying the religious liberty that those protesting are demanding.

As Presbyterian Moderator, condemning loyalist picketing of Catholic churches. *The Irish Times,* September 18, 1986.

October 4, 1996
Rev Ian Paisley
You might as well discuss with Hitler about better terms for the annihilation of Jews, as discuss with southern Ireland the way forward for Northern Ireland.

As leader of DUP, at NI Forum. *The Irish Times,* October 5, 1996.

October 8, 1996
David Ervine
This is the work of a group of people who have no interest in Republicanism, in uniting Catholic, Protestant and Dissenter. Wolfe Tone must be spinning in his grave. These people are fascists.

As leader of Progressive Unionist Party, on IRA bombing of British Army barracks in Lisburn. *The Irish Times,* October 9, 1996.

October 11, 1996
John Major
Warrant officer Bridwell was aged 43, with a wife and children, Mr Adams. I sent him there, Mr Adams, so spare me any crocodile tears. Don't tell me this has nothing to do with you. I don't believe you, Mr Adams.

As British Prime Minister, to Conservative Party conference, on soldier killed by IRA bomb in Lisburn. *The Irish Times,* October 12, 1996.

October 11, 1996
John Bruton
The strategy of a ballot box in one hand and a gun in the other was first originated by the Nazis.

As Taoiseach, on IRA bomb in Lisburn, paraphrasing Danny Morrison's comment of October 31, 1981, on ballot box and armalite. *The Irish Times,* October 12, 1996.

October 20, 1996
David Brewster
He has gone seventy-five miles to be offended in Londonderry, forty-five miles to be offended in Dunloy, forty miles to be offended in Bellaghy, and thirty miles to be offended in Newry. I hear he has gathered enough air miles to be offended at the Orange parade in Canada next summer.

As delegate to Ulster Unionist Party conference, on nationalist who said he was offended by Orange parades. *The Irish Times,* October 21, 1996.

October 20, 1996
David Trimble
Events have enhanced our credibility and diminished the credibility of Irish Americans. The clearest symbol of the change was to be found at this year's White House St Patrick's Day reception. Remember 1995, Gerry Adams was a privileged guest; 1996, he was outside, and John Taylor, Jeffrey Donaldson and I were on the inside.

As leader of Ulster Unionist Party, addressing party conference. *The Irish Times,* October 21, 1996.

October 22, 1996
Most Rev Walton Empey
I find it difficult to understand how Christ is in any way glorified by means of bands and parades, especially those of an offensively triumphalist nature.

As Church of Ireland Archbishop of Dublin, addressing Dublin and Glendalough Synod. *The Irish Times,* October 23, 1996.

December 1, 1996
Sammy Wilson
We have Gerry [Adams] going about like a pop star – Gerry and the peacemakers. They have taken it to London, they have taken it to Washington, they wanted to take it to Australia but Australia wouldn't let them in. We used to send convicts to Australia. Now they're sending them back... And I know a fair number of boys who would like to send him down under.

As DUP speaker at party conference. *The Irish Times,* December 2, 1996.

December 2, 1996
Rev Ian Paisley
In the ethos of Protestantism, there is no place for those that attack anybody going to their desired place of worship.

As leader of Free Presbyterian Church, on attack on Catholic worshippers at church in Harryville. *The Irish Times,* December 3, 1996.

December 11, 1996
Robert Saulters
[Mr Blair] has already sold his birthright by marrying a Romanist and serving communion in a Roman Catholic church. He would sell his soul to the devil himself.

As Grand Master of Orange Order of Ireland, on British Labour leader, Tony Blair. *The Irish Times*, December 12, 1996.

December 12, 1996
Tony Blair

I married my wife because I love her.

As British Labour leader, replying to Robert Saulters, above. *The Irish Times*, December 13, 1996.

c. December 12, 1996
Michael Lowry

I did not make a secret of the fact that Dunnes Stores paid me for professional services by way of assistance towards my house. If someone were trying to hide income, would he or she not be more likely to put it in an offshore account?

As Fine Gael TD, in Dáil, later revealed to have had money paid to him into two off-shore accounts. Smyth, Sam, *Thanks a Million Big Fella*, Blackwater Press, 1997, p. 136.

December 13, 1996
Sean O'Callaghan

The peace process has been a disaster for Ireland because constitutional nationalism has been hijacked by Gerry Adams and the IRA. People need to wise up, otherwise there will be civil war.

As former IRA member and informer. *The Irish Times*, December 14, 1996.

December 21, 1996
John Hume

Political leadership is like being a teacher. It's about changing the language of others. I say it, and I go on saying it, until I hear the man in the pub saying it back to me.

As leader of SDLP. *Irish Independent*, December 21, 1996.

January 16, 1997
Edward Kennedy

Day after day, week after week, month after month, the British Government refused to build on the opportunity for peace and the refusal was a grave and profound mistake. Instead of a historic opportunity for peace the seventeen-month ceasefire became a historic missed opportunity.

As US Senator. *The Irish Times*, January 17, 1997.

January 24, 1997
Rev Gerard Moloney

These soaps show people having one-night stands, committing adultery, or engaged in lesbian affairs as if they were perfectly acceptable and normal patterns of behaviour.

As priest, protesting about TV series 'Brookside', in Catholic magazine, *Reality*. *The Irish Times*, January 25, 1997.

January 24, 1997
Mary Halpin

We get criticised when we deal with these issues and criticised when we don't for not reflecting real life patterns. The other end of the spectrum from Brookside is Coronation Street which...reflects a world that doesn't exist any more.

As senior *RTÉ* scriptwriter, replying to Rev Gerard Moloney, above. *The Irish Times*, January 25, 1997.

January 24, 1997
Charles (Chuck) Feeney

I simply decided I had enough money. It doesn't drive my life. I'm a what-you-see is what-you-get kind of guy.

As Irish-American multi-millionaire, on giving away his fortune, much of it to Irish projects. *The Irish Times*, January 25, 1997.

January 27, 1997
Maire Geoghegan-Quinn

When politics demands – and wrongly demands – that a TD's family members serve as expendable extensions of the elected member, I will not serve.

As former Fianna Fáil minister, announcing retirement from politics after media reports on her son's expulsion from school. *RTÉ*, January 27, 1997.

January 27, 1997
George Mitchell

In Northern Ireland there is a deep sense of history there, with reliance on the past as justification for current grievances. In this country [United States] it's much more like – here's the problem, how do we solve it?

As chairman of NI talks. *The Irish Times*, January 28, 1997.

February 3, 1997
The News Letter

The News Letter says today the events of Bloody Sunday are unforgivable and that those who lost innocent loved ones deserve nothing less than a heartfelt, unambiguous apology from the highest source.

As pro-unionist newspaper, on killing of 13 unarmed Catholic civilians by British Army in Derry on January 30, 1972. *The News Letter*, February 3, 1997.

February 4, 1997
John Bruton

The people who were shot were entirely innocent of any wrongdoing and they deserve an unambiguous apology.

As Taoiseach, in Dáil, calling for a new inquiry into killing of 13 unarmed civilians by British Army in Derry on January 30, 1972. *The Irish Times*, February 5, 1997.

February 20, 1997
Edward Heath
There was a crisis in Tiananmen Square after a month in which the civil authority was being defied, and they took action about it. Very well. We can criticise it exactly the same way as people criticise Bloody Sunday in Northern Ireland, but that isn't by any means the whole story.

As former British Prime Minister, in BBC discussion on death of Chinese leader Deng Xiaoping. *BBC*, February 20, 1997.

February 20, 1997
Seamus Mallon
It seems incredible that the murder of people in Tiananmen Square, and by association the murder of people in Derry on Bloody Sunday, was a necessary part of good government.

As SDLP deputy leader, on remarks of Edward Heath, above. *The Irish Times*, February 21, 1997.

February 20, 1997
John Hume
Now, after a quarter of a century of bloodshed, agony and destruction, they tell us that the armed struggle is stalemated and that neither they nor the British Army can win. What a tragedy for all of Ireland that they couldn't see this blindingly obvious truth 25 years ago, when we told them.

As leader of SDLP, rejecting electoral pact with Sinn Féin in absence of IRA ceasefire. *The Irish News*, February 20, 1997.

March 7, 1997
Pro-Choice Campaigner
Keep your rosaries off our ovaries.

As demonstrator, on placard at pro-choice demonstration in Dublin. *The Irish Times*, March 8, 1997.

March 11, 1997
Rita Restorick
I feel he responded as one person to another, not as a politician. It was quite a pleasant surprise. But there is a large hole in our lives now... You can never justify gaining your aims through violence.

As mother of IRA victim Lance Bombardier Stephen Restorick, on receipt of a letter of condolence from Gerry Adams. *The Irish Times*, March 12, 1997.

March 14, 1997
David Maclean
When the day comes that the evil scum of the IRA are no longer murdering the innocent...when I no longer need all my compassion for the innocent, I shall be able to spare some for the perpetrators.

As British junior Home Office minister, in letter to constituent who had complained about treatment in Britain of Irish remand prisoner, Roisin McAliskey. *The Irish Times*, March 15, 1997.

March 20, 1997
Dr Noel Browne
Under our constitution it is a glass box, glass cage or even a goldfish bowl. It is our House of Lords, our *Legion d'Honneur*; simply an honour from the people and no more.

As former Minister for Health, on presidency. *The Irish Times*, March 20, 1997.

March 23, 1997
Lord Alderdice
You would never have seen James Molyneaux dancing a jig hand-in-hand with Ian Paisley down the Garvaghy Road. You wouldn't have seen James Molyneaux consorting with scoundrels like Billy Wright.

As Alliance Party leader, at party conference, comparing unionist leader David Trimble unfavourably with his predecessor James Molyneaux. *The Irish Times*, March 24, 1997.

April 1, 1997
Seamus Mallon
When you strip away the verbiage from the Sinn Féin position all we are talking about is Sunningdale for slow learners.

As SDLP deputy leader. *The Irish Times*, April 2, 1997.

April 8, 1997
Rev David O'Hanlon
It was not until I saw photographs of [Mary Robinson] with the Pope, bedizened in Kelly green, showy jewellery and – to boot – a sprig of vegetation, that I realised what the President of Ireland truly is – cheap.

As Rome-based priest, in letter to *The Irish Times*. *The Irish Times*, April 8, 1997.

April 10, 1997
Pamela Conroy
If I recall rightly she wore a refined plain wool two-piece which was perhaps a shade simple when compared with the extravagant, bejewelled and embroidered ensemble favoured by the Pope.

As letter-writer to *The Irish Times*, replying to Rev David O'Hanlon, above. *The Irish Times*, April 18, 1997.

April 18, 1997
Brother Edmund Garvey
For those who did have hurtful experiences, I apologise and ask forgiveness.

As Congressional leader of Christian Brothers, on sexual abuse of children in their care. *The Irish Times*, April 19, 1997.

April 21, 1997
Ben Dunne
I said at the time, 'I think Haughey is making a huge mistake, trying to get six or seven people together. Christ picked twelve apostles and one of them crucified him.'

As businessman, giving evidence at Dunne Tribunal on his reaction when asked to become one of a group to help then Fianna Fáil leader Charles Haughey financially. *The Irish Times*, April 22, 1997.

April 21, 1997
Charles Haughey
As no money has been paid, no repayment arises.

As former Taoiseach, denying in letter to solicitor for Dunne Settlement Trust that he received money from businessman Ben Dunne. *The Irish Times*, April 22, 1997.

April 22, 1997
Ben Dunne
[I said] 'Look, here's something for yourself.' [He replied] 'Thank you, big fella.'

As businessman, describing to Dunne Tribunal how he gave three bank drafts worth £70,000 each to Charles Haughey in 1991. *The Irish Times*, April 23, 1997.

May 4, 1997
Mo Mowlam
The ball is in the IRA's court. The goals have shifted.

As NI Secretary of State, in Belfast, after Labour victory in British general election. *The Irish Times*, May 5, 1997.

May 4, 1997
Gerry Adams
Where is Margaret Thatcher? Where is John Major? They have gone away, you know.

As President of Sinn Féin, on Labour victory in British general election, recalling his own often-criticised comment of August 13, 1995 about the IRA. *The Irish Times*, May 5, 1997.

May 6, 1997
Dr Willie Walsh
If one is apportioning blame for the hurt and pain inflicted, I believe that the principle fault was on our side. To our eyes today the Roman Catholic *ne temere* decree was indeed contrary to the spirit of Christian generosity and love. I feel many of us would want to apologise to and ask forgiveness from our non-Roman brethren.

As Bishop of Killaloe, writing in *The Furrow*. *The Irish Times*, May 7, 1997.

May 14, 1997
Moosajee Bhamjee
The only thing I've found out is that there is a lot of blackmail in politics, in getting elected. For example, one man phoned me and said, 'If you could get me that planning permission, there's ten votes in my family for you.'

As Labour TD for Clare, on retiring from politics after one term. *The Irish Times*, May 15, 1997.

May 19, 1997
Gerry Adams
Britain might have once ruled the waves, now it is reduced to waiving the rules.

As President of Sinn Féin, on refusal of House of Commons to grant privileges of membership to himself and Martin McGuinness after they had been elected as abstentionist MPs. *The Irish Times*, May 20, 1997.

May 20, 1997
Tony Blair
My message is simple. I am committed to Northern Ireland… My agenda is not a united Ireland… I value the Union.

As British Prime Minister, on first visit to Belfast. *The Irish Times*, May 21, 1997.

May 23, 1997
Rev William McCrea
Two out of three of the nationalist community voted for murder and they will live to regret it.

As former MP, on his general election defeat by Martin McGuinness of Sinn Féin, on Sinn Féin poll in Tyrone. *The Belfast Telegraph*, May 23, 1997.

June 1, 1997
Tony Blair
The fact that one million people should have died in what was then part of the richest, most peaceful nation in the world is something that still causes pain as we reflect on it today. Those who governed in London at the time failed their people through standing by while a crop failure turned into a massive human tragedy.

As British Prime Minister, in statement on Irish Famine. *The Irish Times*, June 2, 1997.

June 2, 1997
Alban Maginness
The political mould has been broken.

As SDLP councillor, on becoming first nationalist Lord Mayor of Belfast. *The Irish Times*, June 3, 1997.

June 4, 1997
Jean Kennedy Smith
I know there will be peace. I'm an American.
That means I'm an optimist.

As US Ambassador to Ireland. *The Irish Times*, June 5, 1997.

June 16, 1997
Bertie Ahern
They have ransacked the dictionary to find new words in order to avoid condemning this brutal murder.

As Taoiseach, on Sinn Féin reaction to IRA killing of 2 RUC men in Lisburn. *The Irish Times*, June 17, 1997.

June 25, 1997
Tony Blair
My message to Sinn Féin is clear. The settlement train is leaving. I want you on that train. But it is leaving anyway. You cannot hold the process to ransom any longer. So end the violence and end it now.

As British Prime Minister, giving IRA five weeks to call new ceasefire. Routledge , Paul, *John Hume*, Harper Collins, 1998, p. 307.

July 6, 1997
Robert McCartney
This is about setting up a *de facto* section of the Republic of Ireland in Northern Ireland. The symbols of it – the tricolours on every lamp post – are there the length of Garvaghy Road.

As UK Unionist Party leader, after Orange parade was forced by police through nationalist protestors. *The Irish Times*, July 7, 1997.

July 6, 1997
Ronnie Flanagan
I had to take a course of action that would result in less violence, and I'm talking about serious violence. I'm talking about the risk of loss of life.

As RUC chief constable, on his decision to bow to loyalist threats of mass violence if Orange parade not allowed to march along Garvaghy Road, Portadown. *The Irish Times*, July 7, 1997.

July 9, 1997
Charles Haughey
I now accept that I received the £1.3 million from Mr Ben Dunne and...that he handed me £210,000 in Abbeville in November 1991.

As former Taoiseach, reversing earlier evidence to Dunne Tribunal. *The Irish Times*, July 10, 1997.

July 15, 1997
Charles Haughey
My private finances were purely peripheral to my life. I left them to Mr [Des] Traynor to look

after. I didn't have a lavish lifestyle. My work was my lifestyle and when I was in office I worked every day, all day. There was no room for any sort of an extravagant lifestyle.

As former Taoiseach, when asked at Dunne Tribunal about sum of £705,000 received to defray living expenses. *The Irish Times*, July 16, 1997.

July 15, 1997
Charles Haughey
I think an accountant often makes a very bad minister for finance.

As former Taoiseach, in exchanges at Dunne Tribunal. Smyth, Sam, *Thanks a Million Big Fella*, Blackwater Press, 1997, p. 161.

July 20, 1997
IRA
The IRA is committed to ending British rule in Northern Ireland. It is the root cause of divisions and conflict in our country. We want a permanent peace and therefore we are prepared to enhance the search for a democratic peace settlement through real and inclusive negotiations.

Announcing ceasefire from midday on July 20. *The Irish Times*, July 21, 1997.

July 20, 1997
Bill Clinton
As NI leaders begin to shape their future, I urge them to do so on the basis of the principles of fairness and compromise that underpin all democratic systems.

As US President, on IRA ceasefire announcement. *The Irish Times*, July 21, 1997.

July 20, 1997
Xabier Arzallus
Unfortunately Spain does not have a Tony Blair nor does the Basque country have a Sinn Féin or a Gerry Adams.

As President of Basque National Party, on NI peace process. *The Irish Times*, July 21, 1997.

July 22, 1997
Rev Brendan Smyth
Long ago, I have made my peace with God.

As paedophile priest, apologising in court to victims. *The Irish Times*, July 23, 1997.

July 25, 1997
Paedophile Victim
Rot in hell, Smyth!

As victim, as paedophile priest Rev Brendan Smyth was sentenced by Dublin court to 12 years in jail, where he died four weeks later. *The Irish Times*, July 26, 1997.

August 6, 1997
Rosemary Brown (Dana)
There's nothing in the Constitution says I can't sing as president.

As singer and candidate for president, asked if she would still sing if elected. *The Irish Times*, August 7, 1997.

August 7, 1997
Ray Burke
Mr [James] Gogarty told me that JMSE [Murphy Structural Engineers Ltd] wished to make a political contribution to me and I received from him in good faith a sum of £30,000 as a totally unsolicited political contribution. At no time during our meeting was any favour sought or given.

As Minister for Foreign Affairs. *The Irish Times*, August 8, 1997.

August 11, 1997
Albert Reynolds
I said to John Major: 'How can I go to the Republican leadership and ask them to give up their guns, when Fianna Fáil never handed over any guns?'

As former Taoiseach, speaking after lecture in Belfast, recalling Fianna Fáil's entry into Dáil in 1927. *The Irish Times*, August 12, 1997.

August 19, 1997
John Taylor
More people speak Chinese to each other in Northern Ireland than speak Irish.

As unionist MP, welcoming decision by Fair Employment Agency that Irish language signs at Queen's University Students' Union were incompatible with a neutral working environment. *The Irish Times*, August 20, 1997.

August 25, 1997
Justice Brian McCracken
It is quite unacceptable that a member of Dáil Éireann, and in particular a Cabinet Minister and Taoiseach, should be supported in his personal lifestyle by gifts made to him personally... If such gifts were to be permissible, the potential for bribery and corruption would be enormous... By allowing himself to be put in a position of dependency, Mr Charles Haughey...indeed devalued some of the undoubtedly valuable work which he did when in office.

As judge, delivering report on Dunne Tribunal. *The Irish Times*, August 26, 1997.

August 25, 1997
Bertie Ahern
We owe it to the least fortunate of our citizens to ensure that public decisions affecting everyone's welfare are taken only on grounds of equity and the public good, and to ensure that possession of wealth can never purchase privately political favours.

As Fianna Fáil leader, on findings of Dunne Tribunal. *The Irish Times*, August 26, 1997.

September 2, 1997
Continuity IRA
The logical outcome is a new Stormont and the copper-fastening of partition. The only way forward [is] the armed struggle.

As breakaway group from IRA, in statement through spokesman, on peace process. *The Irish Times*, September 3, 1997.

September 8, 1997
John Hume
My adult life...has been devoted to resolving the very serious crisis in the North. It is now at a very crucial stage and therefore I feel it is my duty to stay with my colleagues in the SDLP and to continue to devote all my energies towards achieving a new and agreed Ireland, based on a lasting settlement and a lasting peace.

As leader of SDLP, declining Fianna Fáil offer of nomination as presidential candidate. *The Irish Times*, September 9, 1997.

September 15, 1997
Peter Robinson
The cruellest cut of all is that the leadership of the Ulster Unionist Party know that if they had followed the DUP and the UK Unionists in abandoning the talks it would have resulted in the collapse of the pan-nationalist talks process, which would have permitted a unionist outcome.

As DUP deputy leader. *The Irish Times*, September 16, 1997.

September 15, 1997
Ray Burke
It is the first time since the Treaty that we have the possibility of moving into substantive talks.

As Minister for Foreign Affairs, on NI talks. *The Irish Times*, September 16, 1997.

September 16, 1997
Mitchell McLaughlin
Those who planted that bomb today are the enemies of the peace process.

As Sinn Féin chairman, on bomb which destroyed centre of Markethill. *The Irish Times*, September 17, 1997.

September 16, 1997
Adi Roche
This is going to be a fun campaign.

As aid organiser and Labour candidate for president. *The Irish Times*, September 20, 1997.

September 17, 1997
National Conference of Priests in Ireland
The lesson of history about scapegoating particular categories such as Jews or alleged witches may not have been learned in responding to the current issue of child sex abuse.

As representative body of Catholic clergy, on scapegoating of priests over paedophile clergy. *The Irish Times*, September 18, 1997.

September 17, 1997
David Trimble
Those who walk out leave the Union undefended.

As leader of Ulster Unionist Party, on entering talks which included Sinn Féin. *The Irish Times*, September 18, 1997.

September 17, 1997
Ray Burke
If Mr Gogarty is indeed the source of these allegations then he is the author of a campaign of lies against me.

As Minister for Foreign Affairs, after retired company executive James Gogarty offered to testify at tribunal that construction companies gave Ray Burke £40,000 each in political contributions. *The Irish Times*, September 18, 1997.

September 19, 1997
Mary McAleese
...my sense of who I am as a person was also shaped by the stereotyping and pigeonholing of people as Catholic, as nationalist... At its core I am an Irishwoman – simple as that. I love the entire island.

As Fianna Fáil candidate for president. *The Irish Times*, September 20, 1997.

September 19, 1997
Clare Boylan
Boys are born knowing, and girls soon find out, that possession of a penis is all the label you need for life.

As author. *The Irish Times*, September 20, 1997.

September 22, 1997
Fergus Finlay
Who has been sent to the *gulag*? Who has been locked up in the Lubyanka?

As joint campaign manager for Labour presidential candidate, Adi Roche, on charges by critics that her work style was 'Stalinist'. *The Irish Times*, September 23, 1997.

September 24, 1997
John O'Donoghue
It is no exaggeration to say that a ray of light shines across the entire island of Ireland and will lift the hearts of all its inhabitants.

As Minister for Justice, after all-party talks opened at Stormont. *The Irish Times*, September 25, 1997.

September 24, 1997
T. C. G. O'Mahony
I felt it was the opening of the sluice gates to the liberal agenda, and I don't think I was far wrong.

As spokesman for Christian Community Alliance, on election of Mary Robinson as president in 1990. *The Irish Times*, September 26, 1997.

September 25, 1997
Mary McAleese
Many people ask why I use words like embrace, love and hope for the presidency... I make no apology for using such words. Ireland needs them.

As Fianna Fáil candidate for president. *The Irish Times*, September 27, 1997.

September 25, 1997
Adi Roche
Sometimes people like you. Sometimes they don't. Sometimes people work out. Sometimes they don't. There have been times when I've had to make tough decisions.

As Labour candidate for president, answering critics of her work style. *The Irish Times*, September 27, 1997.

September 30, 1997
Mo Mowlam
Unemployment is still twice as high among Catholics as Protestants in Northern Ireland. This imbalance must be addressed. It is unacceptable in any civilised society.

As NI Secretary, at Labour Party conference. *The Irish Times*, October 1, 1997.

c. *October 1, 1997*
Rosemary Nelson
The worst threat is that I am going to be killed. They [RUC interrogators] told one guy, 'You're going to die when you get out. And tell Rosemary she's going to die too.'

As lawyer representing nationalist residents of Garvaghy Road, Portadown, in complaint to US special investigator, 18 months before being killed in NI car bomb. *The Irish Times*, March 17, 1999.

October 2, 1997
Derek Nally
I have to shave in the morning.

As independent presidential candidate, when asked what single characteristic set him apart from other four candidates for presidency (all women). *The Irish Times*, October 3, 1997.

October 5, 1997
Martin McGuinness

Sinn Féin is not going to the negotiating table to strengthen the Union. We are going to smash the Union.

As Sinn Féin Vice President, at rally in Coalisland. *The Irish Times*, October 6, 1997.

October 6, 1997
Rosemary Brown (Dana)

I am very proud to be a Roman Catholic. I am not going to keep my head down. The penal days are over.

As independent candidate for president. *The Irish Times*, October 7, 1997.

October 7, 1997
Bertie Ahern

In the case of Deputy Ray Burke, I see a much more sinister development, the persistent hounding of an honourable man to resign an important position on the basis of innuendo and unproven allegations.

As Taoiseach, on forced resignation of Minister for Foreign Affairs Ray Burke over accepting money from construction company. *The Irish Times*, October 8, 1997.

October 9, 1997
Ruby Cooling

We are not against the Gaelic Athletic Association as such. But what we are against is the offensive rule they have to exclude members of the security forces from the organisation.

As Mayor of North Down, on her decision to ban Bushmills whiskey from official receptions in Bangor town hall after manufacturers sponsored a Co Antrim GAA team. *The Irish Times*, October 10, 1997.

October 9, 1997
Alan Clarke

The only solution for dealing with the IRA is to kill six hundred people in one night. Let the United Nations and Bill Clinton and everyone else make a scene, and it's over for twenty years.

As Conservative MP. *The Irish Times*, October 10, 1997.

October 12, 1997
UFF prisoners

If the DUP and the UK Unionists won't take on the enemies of the Union at Stormont Castle, they certainly won't take them on in conflict. Actions speak louder than words. Stop living in the past, McCartney and Paisley.

As loyalist prisoners in Maze prison, in statement read out at loyalist rally in Belfast city hall. *The Irish Times*, October 13, 1997.

October 13, 1997
Tony Blair

We can either carry on with the hatred and despair and the killings, treating people as if they were not part of humanity, or we can try and settle our differences by negotiation, discussion and debate.

As British Prime Minister, on meeting Sinn Féin leader Gerry Adams for first time. *The Irish Times*, October 14, 1997.

October 16, 1997
Eoghan Harris

Mary McAleese is clearly…an unreconstructed northern nationalist who will drag all sorts of tribal baggage with her when she is elected President of Ireland… I think she will make a very dangerous and tribal president.

As writer and media adviser, who helped campaign of former president Mary Robinson. *The Irish Times*, October 17, 1997.

October 16, 1997
Gerry Adams

Personally I would vote for Mary McAleese if I had a vote… I think she is a victim of smear and dirty tricks.

As President of Sinn Féin, on presidential election in Republic. *The Irish Times*, October 17, 1997.

October 21, 1997
Mary McAleese

I am a board member of Channel 4. I'm a member of Northern Ireland Electricity. I, along with Sir Rupert Smith, the officer commanding troops in Northern Ireland, was invited to a very private luncheon with Her Majesty the Queen, which I was delighted to attend.

As Fianna Fáil candidate for president, on allegations quoted in leaked Foreign Affairs memos that she sympathised with Sinn Féin. *The Irish Times*, October 22, 1997.

October 21, 1997
Brid Rodgers

The fundamental question is the serious undermining of the important and effective work of the Department of Foreign Affairs. I am disgusted that a person or persons unknown have now put that work at risk for narrow political advantage.

As SDLP member, on leaking of Foreign Affairs memos on confidential conversations with northern figures, designed to damage Fianna Fáil candidate Mary McAleese. *The Irish Times*, October 22, 1997.

October 22, 1997
Mary McAleese
It is a mistake to believe that we can build
bridges from mid-stream to no-man's land.
Nationalists need to make peace and build
confidence with unionists, and vice versa.

As Fianna Fáil candidate for president, speaking in
Dublin. *The Irish Times*, October 23, 1997.

October 22, 1997
Ken Maginnis
I hope you win, Mary. Corporate Ireland needs
you and deserves you. Your election will help
unionists to explain why any meaningful
relationship with the Republic is becoming
increasingly improbable.

As unionist MP, on Fianna Fáil presidential candidate
Mary McAleese. *The Irish Times*, October 24, 1997.

November 3, 1997
Noel Dempsey
If [Mary McAleese] wears the poppy at her
inauguration she can legitimately be asked at a
later stage to wear the Easter lily... Nationalists
in Northern Ireland would regard the wearing of
the poppy as a symbol similar to the sash that the
Orangeman wears.

As Minister for the Environment, in interview. *RTÉ*,
November 3, 1997.

November 4, 1997
Dick Spring
I will arise and go now... I think I will put it in
John B. Keane's words – when you are from
Kerry and when you are as ignorant as us, you
have to be fierce clever.

As leader of Labour Party, announcing his resignation.
The Irish Times, November 8, 1997.

November 9, 1997
Ruairí Ó Brádaigh
English rule in Ireland is modernising itself these
days, trying to make itself more acceptable
internationally by involving as large a section as
possible of the nationalist population of the Six
Counties, and it's working. What is available is
Sunningdale number two.

As President of Republican Sinn Féin, at árd fheis in
Dublin. *The Irish Times*, November 10, 1997.

November 11, 1997
Mary McAleese
Our dancers, singers, writers, poets, musicians,
sportsmen and women...are giants on the world
stage. Our technologically skilled young people
are in demand everywhere. There are those who
absorb the rush of newness with delight. There

are those who are more cautious, even fearful... I
want to point the way to a reconciliation of these
many tensions.

As President, in inaugural address. *The Irish Times*,
November 12, 1997.

November 14, 1997
Christopher Bland
Governing the BBC is in many ways very much
like governing Ireland. Both combine creativity
with unpredictability, and present similar problems
in terms of divine obstinacy.

As chairman of BBC. *The Irish Times*, November 15, 1997.

November 15, 1997
Francie Molloy
This phase of negotiations may fall apart, it may
not succeed. And whenever that does happen, then
we simply go back to what we know best.

As Sinn Féin negotiator, addressing republicans in south
Armagh. *The Irish Times*, November 22, 1997.

November 28, 1997
Justice Hugh Geoghegan
The amended Constitution does not now confer a
right of abortion outside of Ireland. It merely
prevents injunctions against travelling for that
purpose.

As judge, in High Court ruling allowing pregnant
13-year-old rape victim to travel to England for abortion.
The Irish Times, November 29, 1997.

November 28, 1997
Dr Desmond Connell
I had hoped the decision would be...one which
would cherish the welfare of each of the children
involved, one 13 years old, the other 13 weeks in
the womb.

As Archbishop of Dublin, criticising High Court ruling
allowing 13-year-old rape victim travel for abortion. *The
Irish Times*, November 29, 1997.

November 30, 1997
Rev Ian Paisley
No Unionist should be at talks negotiating the
Union with Bertie Ahern, John Hume or anyone
else. The Union is not negotiable.

As leader of DUP, at party conference in Portrush, Co
Antrim. *The Irish Times*, December 1, 1997.

November 30, 1997
Sammy Wilson
This party will never get a beard rash from making
up to Gerry Adams.

As DUP speaker at party conference in Portrush. *The Irish
Times*, December 1, 1997.

December 9, 1997
Gearoid Ó Cairealláin
There is a disease after breaking out in the North among Irish speakers. [It is how] to make Irish attractive to the Protestant community... Be careful, this disease is contagious.

As President of the Gaelic League, warning that encouraging Protestants to learn Irish could lead to favouring unionist principles. *The Irish Times*, December 10, 1997.

December 11, 1997
Gerry Adams
For the first time in my life a British Prime Minister was able to hear from an Irish republican that the relationship between our two islands, which has meant so much suffering and death and pain and agony, can be put to one side – can become part of our history [for] a new relationship between the people of these islands.

As President of Sinn Féin, after meeting British Prime Minister Tony Blair at 10 Downing Street. *The Irish Times*, December 12, 1997.

December 12, 1997
Rev James McEvoy
[It would be] repugnant if she should ever again abuse the august office which she occupies in a way which would once more embarrass the Catholic Church by giving scandal to its members.

As Professor of Philosophy at St Patrick's College, Maynooth, on President Mary McAleese, a Catholic, receiving communion at Church of Ireland Christ Church Cathedral. *Irish News*, December 12, 1997.

December 16, 1997
Hugh Leonard
Why, oh why did Mary McAleese do it? It isn't the rights or wrongs of her taking communion at Christ Church Cathedral that bother me. What is sheer torture is the hellish prospect of the resultant letters to *The Irish Times*.

As author and playwright, in letter to *Irish Times*. *The Irish Times*, December 16, 1997.

December 17, 1997
Dr Desmond Connell
[To be courteous] you will not engage in the deception that is involved in taking communion...it is profoundly insulting to the Church of Ireland.

As Archbishop of Dublin, on President Mary McAleese receiving communion at Church of Ireland Christ Church Cathedral. *The Irish Times*, December 17, 1997.

December 18, 1997
Proinsias de Rossa
If the Three Wise Men arrived here tonight, the likelihood is they would be deported.

As leader of Democratic Left, calling for amnesty for asylum seekers. *The Irish Times*, December 19, 1997.

December 18, 1997
Pat Rabbitte
Of all the cubs being suckled by the Celtic Tiger, by far the fattest, sleekest and best nurtured are the lawyers.

As Democratic Left TD, on work of tribunals. *The Irish Times*, December 20, 1997.

December 21, 1997
Jean Kennedy Smith
Religion after all is about bringing people together.

As US Ambassador to Ireland, and a Catholic, after taking communion in Church of Ireland Christ Church Cathedral despite criticism by Catholic bishops of those who did so. *The Irish Times*, December 22, 1997.

January 9, 1998
Bertie Ahern
Isn't it ironic, I'm out there, with many more people, trying to stop people from different religions shooting each other, and others are getting wound up about how they participate in each other's religious services.

As Taoiseach, on controversy over Catholics taking communion in Christ Church Cathedral. *The Irish Times*, January 10, 1998.

January 9, 1998
Bernadette Sands McKevitt
Bobby did not die for cross-border bodies with executive powers, he did not die for nationalists to equal British citizens within the Northern Ireland state.

As sister of hunger-striker Bobby Sands, denouncing peace process as 'deception'. *The Irish Times*, January 11, 1998.

January 19, 1998
Lt-Col Derek Wilford
What are they going to apologise for? Are they apologising for the government of the day, the military political machine of the day? Are they trying to apologise on my behalf and my soldiers? I would have to warn them not to do so. They cannot apologise for me.

As commander of Parachute Regiment in Derry on Bloody Sunday, 1972. *The Irish Times*, January 20, 1998.

January 19, 1998
Raymond Seitz
London even stopped passing sensitive
intelligence to the White House because it often
seemed to find its way to the IRA.

As former US Ambassador to UK, in memoirs, about
White House dealings with Sinn Féin in 1994-5. Seitz,
Raymond, *Over Here*, Weidenfeld & Nicolson, 1998,
p. 286.

January 19, 1998
Raymond Seitz
She was both wilful and skittish, a dangerous
mix. Ambassador Smith told everyone...that I
was intentionally subverting President Clinton's
policy in Ireland, that I was in the pocket of the
British Government; and that I was anti-Irish.
Even from London I could smell my goose
cooking.

As former US Ambassador to UK, in memoirs, on US
Ambassador to Ireland, Jean Kennedy Smith. Seitz,
Raymond, *Over Here*, Weidenfeld & Nicolson, 1998,
pp. 286-287.

January 19, 1998
Jean Kennedy Smith
Let the peace process speak for itself. The fact is
that the all-party talks are under way and the
outlines of a political settlement are being
discussed.

As US Ambassador to Ireland, replying to criticisms by
former US Ambassador to UK, Raymond Seitz, above.
The Irish Times, January 20, 1998.

January 23, 1998
Michael Smith
I'm faced with the kind of bill for soldiers, in
terms of compensation for deafness, that hasn't
happened in any other country in the world,
even those that were at war.

As Minister for Defence. *The Irish Times*, January 24,
1998.

January 27, 1998
Sean McColgan
Why did they kill my Daddy? I loved him. He
was big and he brought me everywhere.

As 11-year-old son of taxi-driver John McColgan, killed
by loyalists. *The Irish Times*, January 28, 1998.

January 30, 1998
David Trimble
We're perfectly capable, should the need arise, of
saying 'No'. After all, it's going back to what we
know best.

As leader of Ulster Unionist Party, mimicking Sinn Féin
speaker's comment of November 15, 1997. *The Irish
Times*, January 31, 1998.

February 7, 1998
Joe Higgins
In the 1980s, tens of thousands of our people were
illegal in the United States. We had politicians
crossing the Atlantic every month begging for
them to be made legal. The very least we can do is
to afford the same to people who have sought
refuge here.

As leader of Socialist Party, at anti-racism rally outside
Department of Justice in Dublin. *The Irish Times*, February
9, 1998.

March 6, 1998
Rev Brian Hackett
Are you scared about the integrated pubs and
businesses about the place? Are you scared that
there are other Damiens and Philips all over
Northern Ireland? Maybe we are all dreaming in
Poyntzpass, but I say it is all over bar the shouting
and do these men realise that?

As priest, officiating at funeral of Damien Trainor, shot with
Protestant friend Philip Allen in Dessie Canavan's Railway
Bar in Poyntzpass, addressing his remarks to loyalist killers.
The Irish Times, March 7, 1998.

March 17, 1998
Bill Clinton
This is the decision of a lifetime for peace in
Ireland. You must get it done. You must do it for
yourselves and for your children.

As US President, at White House, addressing Irish political
leaders. *The Irish Times*, March 18, 1998.

March 25, 1998
Charles Haughey
Farcical, absurd, grossly unfair and iniquitous.

As former Taoiseach, in High Court challenge to Moriarty
Tribunal investigating his finances. *The Irish Times*, March
26, 1998.

March 25, 1998
Maureen Haughey
I asked myself what country was I living in. Was I
living in Russia after the revolution?

As sister of former Taoiseach, Charles Haughey, on learning
Moriarty Tribunal was to examine her bank account in
investigation of her brother's finances. *The Irish Times*,
March 26, 1998.

March 29, 1998
Christian Brothers
We, the Christian Brothers of Ireland, wish to
express our deep regret to anyone who suffered
ill-treatment in our care, and we say to you who
have experienced physical or sexual abuse by a
Christian Brother, and to you who complained of
abuse and were not listened to, we are deeply
sorry.

As religious order, in advertisement in national newspapers. *The Irish Times*, March 30, 1998.

March 30, 1998
Monica McWilliams
John Taylor described us as the 'WC' and we told him 'Yes, and we'll flush away your certainties.'

As leader of Women's Coalition in Northern Ireland, on insults from male political rivals. *The Irish Times*, March 30, 1998.

April 1, 1998
Billy Hutchinson
In some ways – almost in a biblical or a spiritual way I suppose – I am repenting by trying to make this a better place for people.

As former loyalist paramilitary, on why he took up politics after serving 15 years for murdering two Catholics. *The Irish Times*, April 1, 1998

April 2, 1998
Martin McGuinness
Castlereagh interrogation centre, with coffee.

As Sinn Féin Vice President, describing conditions at Castle Buildings venue for NI talks. *The Irish Times*, April 2, 1998.

April 7, 1998
Tony Blair
I feel the hand of history upon our shoulders.

As British Prime Minister, arriving in Belfast for conclusion of NI talks. *The Irish Times*, April 8, 1998.

April 8, 1998
Rev Ian Paisley
If Mr Trimble signs up with Sinn Féin-IRA, and they go together down the road, Republican violence is going to break out. If Sinn Féin do not go with the agreement, then the IRA would turn on its violence. So no matter what happens at these talks, there is not going to be peace. There is going to be war.

As leader of DUP, at press conference, objecting to talks process. *The Irish Times*, April 9, 1998.

April 9, 1998
Pastor Alan Campbell
Trimble is selling us out like de Klerk sold out the white South Africans.

As Protestant minister, protesting in Belfast against unionist leader David Trimble's role in talks. *The Irish Times*, April 10, 1998.

April 10, 1998
David Trimble
I have risen from this table with the Union stronger than when I sat down.

As leader of Ulster Unionist Party, on achievement of Good Friday Agreement incorporating a new Assembly and cross-border bodies, changes in the Constitution of the Republic, and eventual decommissioning of paramilitary weapons. *The Irish Times*, April 11, 1998.

April 10, 1998
John Hume
Today we can take a collective breath and begin to blow away the cobwebs of our past. Only once in a generation does an opportunity like this come along, an opportunity to resolve our deep and tragic conflict.

As leader of SDLP, on Good Friday Agreement. *The Irish Times*, April 11, 1998.

April 10, 1998
Gerry Adams
These negotiations and the new arrangements which result from them are part of our collective journey from the failures of the past and towards a future of equals.

As President of Sinn Féin, on Good Friday Agreement. *The Irish Times*, April 11, 1998.

April 10, 1998
Bertie Ahern
This is a day we should treasure, when agreement and accommodation have taken the place of differences and division.

As Taoiseach, on Good Friday Agreement. *The Irish Times*, April 11, 1998.

April 10, 1998
President Clinton
I was talking to people up to eight, nine and even later this morning Washington time. They sat, talked, fought, argued and got back together, and for some of them they put their political lives on the line. Others may have put even more on the line as you well know.

As US President, on his role in Good Friday Agreement. *The Irish Times*, April 11, 1998.

April 10, 1998
Larry Butlin
Hell just froze over. There's going to be peace in Ireland.

As White House aide, asked why people in White House were watching CNN. *The Irish Times*, August 28, 1998.

April 10, 1998
Seamus Heaney
For once, and at long last, the language of the Bible can be appropriated by those with a vision of the future rather than those who sing the battle hymns of the past.

As Nobel poet laureate, on Good Friday Agreement. *The Irish Times*, April 11, 1998.

April 10, 1998
Robert McCartney

TV interviewers, with humiliating deference, hang on to the ambiguous utterings of former terrorists, posing as democrats, in three-piece suits.

As leader of UK Unionist Party, on aftermath of Good Friday Agreement. *The Irish Times*, April 11, 1998.

April 17, 1998
Rev Ian Paisley

When treachery takes the stage, secrecy is always its garment.

As leader of DUP, at NI Forum. *The Irish Times*, April 18, 1998.

April 17, 1998
Francie Mackey

My only 'crime' is that I have challenged the illegal British claim to my country. We disagreed with the leadership and now they are trying to silence us and stop us making our case at the [Sinn Féin] árd fheis.

As district councillor from Omagh, speaking after his expulsion from Sinn Féin for joining 32-County Sovereignty Committee, which backed 'Real IRA'. *The Irish Times*, April 18, 1998.

April 17, 1998
Joe Dillon

The IRA exists to challenge the foreign occupation of our country. It is not and should never be used as a militia to sort out internal discussions in the Republican movement.

As representative of 32-County Sovereignty Committee on possibility of IRA move against republicans who opposed IRA ceasefire. *The Irish Times*, April 18, 1998.

April 18, 1998
George Mitchell

There are people on both sides who want to disrupt the process, who are committed to the way of violence and who will step up their activities now...

As chairman of NI talks. *The Irish Times*, April 18, 1998.

April 18, 1998
Loyalist Protestor

The Union is safe. So was the Titanic!

As demonstrator, on placard held up outside meeting of Ulster Unionist Party council which endorsed Good Friday Agreement. *The Irish Times*, April 20, 1998.

April 18, 1998
Gerry Adams

We have just heard that David Trimble won the vote in the Ulster Unionist Party meeting today and we welcome that. Well done, David!

As President of Sinn Féin, addressing árd fheis in Dublin on Good Friday Agreement. *The Irish Times*, April 20, 1998.

April 18, 1998
Martin McGuinness

There is now no absolute commitment (by Britain), no raft of parliamentary acts, to back up an absolute claim, but only one agreement, to stay until the majority decide otherwise. This is a long way from being as British as Finchley.

As Sinn Féin Vice President, addressing árd fheis in Dublin on Good Friday Agreement and recalling Margaret Thatcher's claim of November 10, 1981 that Northern Ireland was as much part of the UK as her constituency of Finchley. *The Irish Times*, April 20, 1998.

April 24, 1998
Michael Longley

I was born in Belfast of English parents. My father served in two world wars. I was educated at the Royal Belfast Academical Institution, and Trinity College, Dublin. Sometimes I feel British. Sometimes I feel Irish. Often I feel neither. This Agreement allows me to feel more Irish, more British, and just as importantly, more 'neither'.

As Belfast poet, commenting on Good Friday Agreement. *The Irish Times*, April 24, 1998.

April 25, 1998
Gary McMichael

When he says 'no', he means 'no future'. He has no alternative and no answers.

As leader of Ulster Democratic Party, referring to the Rev Ian Paisley, at meeting to endorse Good Friday Agreement. *The Irish Times*, April 27, 1998.

April 25, 1998
Sir Kenneth Bloomfield

We had so many other things on our agenda, that we forgot about the victims, who in a sense were yesterday's news.

As NI Victims' Commissioner and former head of NI Civil Service, in Glencree, Co Wicklow, with relatives of victims of Dublin and Monaghan bombings. *The Irish Times*, April 27, 1998.

April 26, 1998
Bertie Ahern

The British Government are effectively out of the equation and neither the British parliament nor people have any legal right under this agreement to impede the achievement of Irish unity if it had the consent of the people North and South... Our nation is and always will be a 32-county nation. Antrim and Down are, and will remain, as much a part of Ireland as any southern county.

As Taoiseach, at 1916 Easter Rising commemoration at Arbour Hill, Dublin. *The Irish Times,* April 27, 1998.

April 27, 1998
Monica McWilliams
The sectarian conflict here will be solved sooner than the patriarchal issue.

As leader of Women's Coalition in Northern Ireland, on male-dominated NI politics. *The Irish Times,* April 27, 1998.

April 30, 1998
IRA
Let us make it clear that there will be no decommissioning by the IRA. This issue, as with any other matters affecting the IRA, its functions and objectives, is a matter only for the IRA, to be decided upon and pronounced upon by us.

In statement following Good Friday Agreement. *The Irish Times,* May 1, 1998.

April 30, 1998
William Ross
People who vote yes are voting for Gerry Adams running the hospitals or controlling the education of our children.

As unionist MP, urging voters not to support Good Friday Agreement in referendum. *The Irish Times,* May 1, 1998.

May 3, 1998
Conor Cruise O'Brien
I am glad to be an ally of Paisley's in the defence of the Union.

As UK Unionist, on Good Friday Agreement. *Sunday Independent,* May 3, 1998.

May 4, 1998
Bertie Ahern
This is the first time since 1918, in an act of self-determination, that everyone on this island, on the one issue, has had the opportunity to pass their verdict.

As Taoiseach, urging support for 'yes' vote in referendum on Good Friday Agreement. *The Irish Times,* May 9, 1998.

May 10, 1998
Gerry Adams
When we call for an end of the British presence in Ireland we do not mean our unionist neighbours. You have as much right to a full and equal life on this island as any other section of our people.

As President of Sinn Féin, at árd fheis in Dublin. *The Irish Times,* May 11, 1998.

May 10, 1998
Michael O'Brien
These men are our Mandelas. They are fit and strong, unbowed and unbroken, humorous, politically astute, and they still believe in unity after twenty-three years in the belly of the beast.

As temporarily released IRA prisoner, welcoming members of IRA's 'Balcombe Street Gang' to Sinn Féin árd fheis in Dublin. *The Irish Times,* May 25, 1998.

May 11, 1998
John Flannery
Travellers expect to have everything done for them and do nothing for themselves. They are able-bodied men who should be able to go out and do FÁS courses like everybody else, but instead are lying out in the sun like pedigree dogs.

As Fine Gael councillor in Mayo, in remarks at meeting for which he was charged and acquitted under Prohibition of Incitement to Hatred Act. *The Irish Times,* March 2, 1999.

May 11, 1998
Robert McCartney
They will be going out to the pro-Union people of Ulster, shoulder-to-shoulder with the representatives of Sinn Féin-IRA and the SDLP, and asking the pro-Union people to commit political suicide. Political suicide, like the human variety, is irreversible.

As UK Unionist leader, on Ulster Unionists advocating a 'yes' vote in referendum on Good Friday Agreement. *The Irish Times,* May 12, 1998.

May 14, 1998
Tony Blair
From now on the future of Northern Ireland rests with the principle of consent. At the same time we are offering new ways for the nationalist community to find and express their identity, and to ensure fairness and equality to all.

As British Prime Minister, in Belfast, supporting 'yes' vote in referendum on Good Friday Agreement. *The Irish Times,* May 15, 1998.

May 14, 1998
Sam McGrory
The war is over.

As head of UDA prisoners in Maze prison, in radio interview, following Good Friday Agreement. *BBC,* May 14, 1998.

May 15, 1998
Hugh Smyth
When are you going to say 'yes' to anything?

As former Progressive Unionist Mayor of Belfast, interrupting Robert McCartney and Rev Ian Paisley as they publicly signed pledge to oppose Good Friday Agreement. *The Irish Times,* May 16, 1998.

May 16, 1998
Loyalist Protestor
What's the difference between David Trimble and Wolfe Tone? 200 years.

As demonstrator, on poster in Belfast opposing Good Friday Agreement. *The Irish Times*, May 16, 1998.

May 17, 1998
Peter Robinson
The mooring ropes have been loosened and we have been set adrift and pushed towards a united Ireland.

As DUP deputy leader, opposing Good Friday Agreement. *The Irish Times*, May 18, 1998.

May 17, 1998
President Clinton
If I were an Irish Protestant, which I am, living in Northern Ireland instead of the United States, I would be thinking about my daughter's future and her children's future... I believe a lot of undecided people will go and vote with their hopes instead of their fears.

As US President, in London, urging 'yes' vote in referendum on Good Friday Agreement. *The Irish Times*, May 18, 1998.

May 19, 1998
Bono
I would like to introduce you to two men who have taken a leap of faith out of the past and into the future.

As U2 lead singer, raising hands of John Hume and David Trimble together in the air at concert in Belfast promoting 'yes' vote in referendum on Good Friday Agreement. *The Irish Times*, May 20, 1998.

May 20, 1998
Gerry Adams
Sinn Féin is not the IRA. That is a matter of fact. I don't go off and get permission from men in a back room or from people in balaclavas about how we develop the party.

As President of Sinn Féin, in *Irish Times* interview. *The Irish Times*, May 20, 1998.

May 24, 1998
Bernadette Sands McKevitt
The Real IRA did not need a mandate to continue its war, as the men of 1916 did not need a mandate to go out and fight on Easter Monday.

As vice chairwoman of the 32-County Sovereignty Committee, in interview rejecting Good Friday Agreement. *Ireland on Sunday*, May 24, 1998.

May 28, 1998
Maureen Dowd
Gerry Adams in Armani from Macy's with all the New York society babes chasing after him...as he makes his US victory lap this week...now Washington, New York and Hollywood are caught up in Irish terrorist chic.

As *The New York Times* columnist, on visit by Sinn Féin leader to United States. *The New York Times*, May 28, 1998.

May 30, 1998
Rev Ian Paisley
She has become a parrot.

As leader of DUP, criticising Queen Elizabeth for her support for Good Friday Agreement. *The Irish Times,* May 30, 1998.

May 30, 1998
Joe McDonagh
[The motion] adopted by the conference, that the GAA 'pledges its intention to delete Rule 21...when effective steps are taken to implement the amended structures and policing arrangements envisaged in the British-Irish peace agreement,' reflected the thinking of the conference.

As GAA chairman, on decision by GAA to defer repeal of rule banning membership by RUC members. *The Irish Times*, June 1, 1998.

May 31, 1998
Dr Brendan Comiskey
I wish to bring healing and closure to this sad period in our history by expressing my deep sorrow and my promise to do whatever I can to make amends... I ask forgiveness and healing from God, from all within the Church of Ireland community, and from all who have suffered in any way then or since.

As Bishop of Ferns, in presence of Church of Ireland Bishops, on 1957 Catholic boycott of Protestant businesses in Fethard-on-Sea. *The Irish Times*, June 1, 1998.

June 7, 1998
Dr Dermot Clifford
They have said that they are going to wait until the RUC is totally reformed and then they will delete Rule 21 but they are taking no risks for peace...there was something bordering on intimidation around.

As Archbishop of Cashel and Emly, on decision by GAA to defer repeal of rule banning membership by RUC members. *The Irish Times*, June 8, 1998.

June 16, 1998
Con Houlihan
The GAA inhibits Catholics from joining the 'unacceptable' RUC. Rule 21 is catch 22.

As national sports columnist, in letter to *The Irish Times*, on GAA's decision to defer repeal of rule barring membership by RUC members until RUC was reformed. *The Irish Times*, June 16, 1998.

June 22, 1998
David Trimble
We can now get down to the historic and honourable task of this generation; to raise up a Northern Ireland in which pluralist unionism and constitutional nationalism can speak to each other with the civility which is the foundation of freedom.

As leader of Ulster Unionist Party, in speech to business and community leaders in Belfast. *The Irish Times*, June 23, 1998.

June 29, 1998
Alistair Graham
Drumcree has become, to use all the clichés, the touchstone, the litmus test, the line in the sand, the landmark event in the whole parading issue in Northern Ireland. And yet we all know that this one is not simply about the parade itself, is not just about getting Orange feet on, or keeping them off the Garvaghy Road.

As chairman of NI Parade Commission, announcing restriction on Orange march in Drumcree which led to confrontation between Orange Order and security forces. *The Irish Times*, June 30, 1998.

July 1, 1998
David Trimble
We are not saying, nor have we ever said, that simply because someone has a past they can't have a future.

As First Minister of NI Assembly, on former paramilitary members in Assembly. *The Irish Times*, July 2, 1998.

July 1, 1998
Seamus Mallon
We don't always agree, and there will be times when we disagree, but we will disagree face to face, and what disagreements we have we will sort them out face to face. [David Trimble's] back was sore enough at the present time that he wouldn't appreciate it any other way.

As deputy First Minister of NI Assembly. *The Irish Times*, July 2, 1998.

July 3, 1998
President Clinton
I think it would be tragic indeed if either side felt so aggrieved by the ultimate resolution of the marching issue that they lost the bigger picture in the moment. Give this new assembly a chance to work.

As US President, at press conference in Hong Kong, referring to confrontation at Drumcree. *The Irish Times*, July 4, 1998.

July 6, 1998
Land Vey
Everywhere I go I am insulted. A man slaps me at the bus stop. Someone throws a used nappy at me from his window. The policeman sees it but he does nothing. Truly this is a very hard place to live in.

As black immigrant, on racist attacks in Dublin. *The Irish Times*, July 11, 1998.

July 6, 1998
Rev Ian Paisley
Only God can deliver us from this situation.

As DUP leader, on confrontation at Drumcree. *The Irish Times*, July 8, 1998.

July 7, 1998
News Letter
God may have more important things to do and is unlikely to make a personal appearance at Garvaghy Road.

As Belfast newspaper, replying to Rev Ian Paisley's comment, above. *News Letter*, July 7, 1998.

July 7, 1998
Rev Ian Paisley
The Twelfth of July. That will be the settling day.

As leader of DUP, referring to confrontation at Drumcree. *The Irish Times*, July 11, 1998.

July 9, 1998
David McNarry
[If Orangemen protesting at Drumcree] are to be treated so scantily, then I've got to say that we can, if we wish, put our minds to paralyse this country in a matter of hours.

As member of strategy committee of Orange Order, in radio interview on confrontation at Drumcree. *BBC*, July 9, 1998.

July 9, 1998
Rev William Bingham
The Orange Order does not want to see the country paralysed. We're not in the business of bringing the province to rack and ruin.

As Armagh Grand Chaplain of Orange Order, on warning by David McNarry, above. *The Irish Times*, July 10, 1998.

July 10, 1998
Chechnya
The foreign ministry of the Chechen Republic of Ichkeria calls on the opposing sides in the conflict to show restraint and put an end to violence.

As breakaway Russian Republic, in statement on confrontation at Drumcree. *The Irish Times*, July 11, 1998.

July 12, 1998
Rev William Bingham
After last night's atrocious act, a 15-minute walk down the Garvaghy Road by the Orange Order would be a very hollow victory, because it would be in the shadow of three coffins of little boys who wouldn't even know what the Orange Order is.

As Armagh Grand Chaplain of Orange Order, on death of 3 Catholic children in loyalist fire bomb attack on their home in Ballymoney, Co Antrim. *The Irish Times*, July 13, 1998.

July 12, 1998
David Trimble
I must say to the Portadown brethren that the only way in which they can clearly distance themselves from these murders...the only way they can repudiate that, is now to leave the hill at Drumcree parish church and return home.

As First Minister of NI Assembly, on death of 3 Catholic children in loyalist fire bomb attack. *The Irish Times*, July 13, 1998.

July 14, 1998
Christine Quinn
I don't know whether I can pick up the pieces. I don't have many pieces left in my life.

As mother of 3Catholic children killed in loyalist fire bomb attack in Ballymoney. *The Irish Times*, December 29, 1998.

July 21, 1998
Rev Gordon McCracken
My resignation came in the wake of attacks on the security forces [at Drumcree], in particular the sight of the policeman's helmet that had suffered from a bullet impact. That, for me, was just the final straw.

As deputy Grand Chaplain of the Orange Order in Scotland, on why he was resigning. *The Irish Times*, July 22, 1998.

July 23, 1998
Most Rev Robin Eames
I saw hatred and viciousness. I saw bewilderment on the faces of people who had never before had to question what membership of the Order involved in a time of crisis. For them traditional membership of the Order was a family matter – an expression of what they believed to be their cultural and religious ethos. At Drumcree 1998 they found they had choices to make. I believe they have reached a crossroads.

As Church of Ireland Primate, writing in English Catholic weekly on confrontation at Drumcree. *The Tablet*, July 23, 1998.

August 5, 1998
Gerry Adams
The war will be over when all of those who have engaged in war – and some are still engaging in war – stop; when the British Army of occupation which still maintains a huge military presence in republican areas begins demilitarising instead of remilitarising; when all the prisoners are free; when there is justice and equality and we have a proper policing service.

As President of Sinn Féin, on calls to say the war was over. *Irish News*, August 5, 1998.

August 6, 1998
Sean Gordon
The people of Ireland have been led a merry dance. Not all by accident. Irish national radio and television and elements of the Irish media, purporting to have superior swimming knowledge to the rest of us, have blissfully ignored the obvious and unpalatable in favour of the feel-good factor.

As Irish Amateur Swimming Association's recording officer, on four-year international ban on Irish Olympic triple-gold medal winner Michelle de Bruin for manipulating drug test. *The Irish Times*, August 7, 1998.

August 7, 1998
Michelle de Bruin [Smith]
I have always represented my country with pride. I have never cheated or lied and I haven't lied in this case either.

As winner of three Olympic gold medals, on four-year international ban for manipulating drug test. *The Irish Times*, August 8, 1998.

August 8, 1998
Loyalist Volunteer Force
Irrespective of whether or not Republicans recognise the English dictionary, for LVF personnel the meaning of the word 'complete' is quite clear. The word means: entire, whole, brought to an end, perfect, absolute, utter, finished.

As breakaway loyalist group, in statement announcing 'complete' Loyalist Volunteer Force ceasefire after two year campaign in which it killed 16 Catholics. *The Irish Times*, August 10, 1998.

August 14, 1998
Mary Kotsonouris
'Parnell loved a lass and the bishops condemned' (Yeats). A bishop loved a lass and the bishops forgave. Now in view of the happy outcome in the latter case, will the Roman Catholic hierarchy at

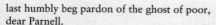

last humbly beg pardon of the ghost of poor, dear Parnell.

As former district court judge, in letter to *Irish Times* regarding bishops' willingness to forgive Bishop Eamonn Casey, in exile after disclosure he had fathered a child. *The Irish Times*, August 14, 1998.

August 15, 1998
Gerry Adams
I condemn it without any equivocation whatsoever.

As President of Sinn Féin, on 'Real IRA' explosion in Omagh which claimed 28 lives. *The Irish Times*, August 17, 1998.

August 15, 1998
Omagh Resident
If this is peace, what is war?

As victim, on *BBC*, after Omagh bomb. *BBC*, August 15, 1998.

August 16, 1998
Mary McAleese
I think we have, unfortunately, a posse of what you might describe as serial killers on the loose on this island... They're off the scale, off the Richter scale of decency.

As President, on Omagh bomb. *The Irish Times*, August 17, 1998.

August 16, 1998
John Hume
They are undiluted fascists. These murderers are the enemy of the people of Ireland.

As leader of SDLP, on Omagh bomb. *The Irish Times*, August 17, 1998.

August 17, 1998
Ed Winters
They were clearly so much in love. They couldn't stop looking at each other. They girl wanted me to take a photograph of her fiancée for her locket... I heard just this morning that her body was identified by finding the locket.

As Omagh photographer, recalling visit to his studio by couple on day before Omagh bomb. *The Irish Times*, August 18, 1998.

August 17, 1998
Michael McNally
I wasn't able to drive fast because people were screaming in pain. I was only able to go at about thirty miles per hour. As we went over the ramps at the hospital I could hear the roars of pain.

As bus driver, on taking injured to hospital in his bus after Omagh bomb. *The Irish Times*, August 18, 1998.

August 17, 1998
Francis Mackey
I am saying that I and the 32-County Sovereignty Movement are not involved in any military activity or involved in any way in what took place on Saturday.

As Omagh District councillor and member of 32-County Sovereignty Committee, politically linked with the 'Real IRA', on Omagh bomb. *The Irish Times*, August 18, 1998.

August 18, 1998
'Real IRA'
Despite media reports it was not our intention at any time to kill any civilians. It was a commercial target, part of an ongoing war against the Brits. We offer apologies to the civilians.

As breakaway group from IRA, admitting responsibility for Omagh bomb. *The Irish Times*, August 19, 1998.

August 18, 1998
Prince Charles
I remember only too well feeling deeply angry when my great uncle Mountbatten and other relations were blown to small pieces. [I hope] this time it will be the end of all the horrors that poor Ireland has had to suffer.

As Prince of Wales, talking to people in Omagh in aftermath of bomb. *The Irish Times*, August 19, 1998.

August 19, 1998
Bernadette Sands McKevitt
I don't agree with violence such as we've witnessed. I don't agree with that at all... What I'm saying to you is there are always, and have always been, people who have been engaged in violence from whatever quarter, be it from Irish republicanism, be it from the British or whatever, and I said this before, if we don't address the problem, how are we going to solve it?

As vice chairwoman of the 32-County Sovereignty Committee, politically linked with the 'Real IRA', in radio interview after Omagh bomb. *RTÉ*, August 19, 1998.

August 22, 1998
Seamus Heaney
What was brutally and incomprehensibly an act of destruction has attained the status of a great divide. It has marked time. It may even be said to have marked the soul in that it has left everybody chastened, more tender, even a little afraid. Afraid *for* rather than afraid *of* – afraid for our society, for fundamental human bonds.

As Nobel poet laureate, on Omagh bomb. *The Irish Times*, August 22, 1998.

August 22, 1998
Irish National Liberation Army
We acknowledge and admit faults and grievous errors in our prosecution of the war. Innocent people were killed and injured and at times our actions as a liberation army fell short of what they should have been. For this we as republicans, as socialists and as revolutionaries do offer a sincere, heartfelt and genuine apology.

As left-wing Republican group, declaring ceasefire after 23-year campaign. *The Irish Times*, August 24, 1998.

August 22, 1998
Gus Macdonald
Dublin is a great place for a stag night, but not for an economic policy.

As Minister in Scottish Office, replying to Scottish National Party leader Alex Salmond's claim that Scotland could learn from Ireland's economic success. *Sunday Tribune*, August 23, 1998.

August 23, 1998
Tony Blair
In a world dominated by terror we could, to use the parlance, 'take them out'. But our country is built on the values of democracy. We are winning the argument, which is why more and more people are opting for peace.

As British Prime Minister, rejecting calls for reintroduction of internment in wake of Omagh bomb. *The Observer*, August 23, 1998.

August 23, 1998
Francis Coyle
The devil came to Omagh that day.

As Omagh resident injured in Omagh bomb on August 15. *Sunday Independent*, August 23, 1998.

September 1, 1998
Gerry Adams
Sinn Féin believe the violence we have seen must be for all of us now a thing of the past – over, done with and gone.

As President of Sinn Féin, responding to calls to say the war was over. *The Irish Times*, September 2, 1998.

September 3, 1998
President Clinton
[Gerry Adams's] words, and I quote: 'the violence must be a thing of the past – over, done with, gone' – those words were music to ears all over the world and they paved the way for the progress still to come. Thank you, Sir.

As US President, on visit to Belfast, paying tribute to Sinn Féin President. *The Irish Times*, September 4, 1998.

September 4, 1998
Patricia McKenna
Mr Clinton blows up people without knowing or caring who they are, just like the 'Real IRA'.

As Green Party MEP, on US bombing of targets in Sudan and Afghanistan in response to explosions at US embassies in Nairobi and Dar es Salaam. *The Irish Times*, September 5, 1998.

September 4, 1998
President Clinton
The Celtic tiger is roaring and you should be proud.

As US President, addressing workers at Gateway computer plant, Dublin. *The Irish Times*, September 5, 1998.

c. September 4, 1998
David Trimble
The origin of the handshake is to show that there is no weapon in one's hand. I am not going to shake his hand until I am absolutely certain that he is not holding weapons in reserve.

As First Minister of NI Assembly, on meeting Gerry Adams but refusing to shake his hand. *The Irish Times*, September 10, 1998.

September 5, 1998
President Clinton
Because of what you have done in Ireland you have made it possible for me on behalf of the United States and the cause of peace in the world to tell every warring, feuding, hating group of people trapped in the prison of their past conflicts to look at Ireland and know there can be a better day.

As US President, addressing people in Limerick. *The Irish Times*, September 7, 1998.

September 5, 1998
President Clinton
You know Frank, you made a lot of money writing about the old Limerick, but I like the new one better.

As US President in Limerick, in remarks during speech directed at Frank McCourt, author of *Angela's Ashes*. *The Irish Times*, September 7, 1998.

September 12, 1998
Chris Patten
Northern Ireland politically has been in the past like the Grand National without a finishing line. Every time you get over one fence, people say, 'Ah, think that was clever, do you?' And you've got a bigger one just coming up. And one day what is going to happen, people in Northern Ireland are going to wake up and realise there hasn't been a fence for some time.

As chairman of Independent Commission on RUC reform. *The Irish Times*, September 12, 1998.

September 14, 1998
David Trimble

I want this to be a pluralist parliament for a pluralist people.

As First Minister of NI Assembly, at first formal sitting, redefining James Craig's ideal of November 21, 1934 of a Protestant Government for a Protestant people. *The Irish Times*, September 15, 1998.

September 14, 1998
Sammy Wilson

The Women's Coalition wish to be all things to all men.

As DUP spokesman. *The Irish Times*, September 15, 1998.

September 15, 1998
Jiang Zemin

I would say that the Irish are a genius people for literature. Why, most of them seem to have won the Nobel Prize for Literature.

As President of People's Republic of China, on meeting Taoiseach Bertie Ahern in Beijing. *The Irish Times*, September 16, 1998.

September 20, 1998
Martin Bell

You Irish have many advantages – you have no colonial past, you never persecuted anyone – and you speak an international language, English, in a way that almost everyone can understand.

As MP and former foreign correspondent, on role of Irish soldiers in UN peace-keeping missions. *The Irish Times*, September 21, 1998.

September 21, 1998
Dr Richard Clarke

[Many believe] that the reputation and standing of the Church of Ireland in the southern part of this island has been severely damaged by events at Drumcree during July... Further afield again, the image of Christianity before Muslims, Hindus and those of other faiths has clearly been damaged as far away as Africa and Asia.

As Church of Ireland Bishop of Meath and Kildare, addressing diocesan synod. *The Irish Times*, September 22, 1998.

September 29, 1998
Tony Blair

Even in the final hours of the Good Friday talks, with the deadline passing, black coffee on tap, tables being thumped, exhausted bodies on sofas strewn with drafts and redrafts...even then I could feel the will of that vast, decent majority of

people urging us on. The only road they want to march down is the road to the future.

As British Prime Minister, addressing Labour Party conference in Blackpool. *The Irish Times*, September 30, 1998.

September 29, 1998
Rosemary Nelson

These difficulties have involved RUC officers questioning my professional integrity, making allegations that I am a member of a paramilitary group, and at their most serious making death threats.

As lawyer representing nationalist residents of Garvaghy Road, Portadown, testifying to US Congressional hearing on human rights, five months before being killed in NI car bomb. *The Irish Times*, March 20, 1999.

September 30, 1998
Gerry Adams

Don't kick the dog to see if it is still sleeping.

As President of Sinn Féin, on IRA, at fringe meeting of British Labour Party in Blackpool. *The Irish Times*, October 10, 1998.

October 1, 1998
Paddy MacKernan

I do believe it is my duty as secretary-general, in view of the deep unhappiness and concern expressed in writing by the majority of the officers involved, respectfully to request that you inform the Taoiseach of their reaction to the transfers envisaged.

As secretary-general of the Department of Foreign Affairs, in letter to Minister for Foreign Affairs David Andrews, on appointments of ambassadors. *The Irish Times*, October 2, 1998.

October 1, 1998
David Andrews

I received a letter from the secretary-general advising me to see the Taoiseach, to be a good boy and take on board the concerns expressed about the locations to which people were to be sent... I am the Minister. I am not a rubber stamp, and I refuse to be a rubber stamp.

As Minister for Foreign Affairs, in Dáil, on letter from department secretary-general Paddy MacKernan. *The Irish Times*, October 2, 1998.

October 6, 1998
Dr Wan Azizah

Someone wrote in my year book: 'She is well known on the Dublin buses as the gentle Chinese nun who wouldn't cross herself going past churches.'

As Muslim Malay wife of imprisoned Malaysian politician, Anwar Ibrahim, on how she was perceived during her days as a medical student in Dublin in the 1970s. *The Irish Times*, October 6, 1998.

October 7, 1998
David Jones
Unfortunately when you are standing up for liberties, sometimes the cost of those liberties can be very high.

As spokesman for Portadown Orange Order, on the death of RUC constable Frank O'Reilly, killed by blast bomb thrown by protesting Orangemen. *The Irish Times*, October 30, 1998.

October 16, 1998
Nobel Committee
John Hume has throughout been the clearest and most consistent of Northern Ireland's political leaders in his work for a political solution... David Trimble showed great political courage when at a critical stage of the process, he advocated solutions which led to the peace agreement.

As judges of Nobel Peace Prize, making award to John Hume and David Trimble. *The Irish Times*, October 17, 1998.

October 16, 1998
John Hume
I always kept repeating myself – it's the old teacher in me – that I hope that, in the future, the symbol of our patriotism will be the spilling of our sweat and not the spilling of our blood.

As leader of SDLP, on *RTÉ*'s Late Late Show, on being awarded the Nobel Peace Prize. *RTÉ*, October 16, 1998.

October 16, 1998
David Trimble
Everyone will take pleasure in this prize to John Hume and me. My only concern is that I hope it doesn't prove to be premature.

As First Minister of NI Assembly, in Denver, Colorado, on being awarded Nobel Peace Prize. *The Irish Times*, October 17, 1998.

October 16, 1998
Peter Robinson
Better by far to be scorned by the world, 'the great and the good', and hold on to one's principles, than to be lavished with praise and applauded by the movers and shakers for having truck with terrorists.

As DUP deputy leader, on award of Nobel Peace Prize to John Hume and David Trimble. *The Irish Times*, October 17, 1998.

October 17, 1998
Seamus Heaney
There is a parable about the fox and the hedgehog... The hedgehog, according to the story, knows one big thing; the fox knows many things. In terms of this story, John Hume is the hedgehog, who knew the big truth that justice had to prevail. David Trimble is the fox, who has known many things but who had the intellectual clarity and political courage to know that 1998 was the time to move unionism forward...

As Nobel poet laureate, on award of Nobel Peace Prize to John Hume and David Trimble. *The Irish Times*, October 17, 1998.

October 20, 1998
Most Rev Robin Eames
We in the Church of Ireland have a long and proud record of loyalty to our country and respect for law and order. How tragic it is that the name of one of our parishes now has worldwide connotations of disloyalty and lawlessness.

As Church of Ireland Primate, in address to diocesan synod in Armagh, referring to confrontation at Drumcree. *The Irish Times*, October 21, 1998.

October 22, 1998
David Jones
We would have difficulty with these pledges. One of the pledges is to obey the law but regrettably...we don't accept the authority of the Parades Commission.

As Orange Order spokesman in Portadown, in remarks for which he had to resign. *The Irish Times*, October 23, 1998.

October 24, 1998
David Trimble
After more than a quarter of a century out of power, unable to control our destiny, we are now on the verge of taking power back into our own hands. Power it is true that must be shared with others... But is there not also a sense of excitement about taking responsibility, about beginning anew, about a real chance to do what Craig and Carson wanted to do then? Build a Northern Ireland at peace with itself and its neighbour.

As First Minister of NI Assembly, addressing Ulster Unionist Party conference in Derry. *The Irish Times*, October 26, 1998.

October 24, 1998
Elaine McClure
Women have as much chance of occupying those [seats] as I have of being Bill Clinton's next conquest.

As delegate from Newry to Ulster Unionist Party conference in Derry, pointing to male-occupied leaders' seats on platform. *The Irish Times*, October 26, 1998.

October 24, 1998
David Brewster
The present Stormont is not a city on a hill, it is not a new Jerusalem [but it might give us] freedom to achieve freedom.

As delegate to Ulster Unionist Party conference in Derry. *The Irish Times*, October 26, 1998.

October 25, 1998
Conor Cruise O'Brien
Many unionists would presently see inclusion in a united Ireland...as so outlandish as not to deserve serious consideration. Yet events may show that, in the conditions of the late 20th century, no other way to safeguard the vital interests of the Protestant community in Northern Ireland is available. Within the United Kingdom the Ulster Protestants, about a million people in a society of more than fifty million, are currently without political clout. In a united Ireland, with a total population of less than six million, the ex-unionists would be a formidable voting *bloc*, for whose support the other parties would compete.

As UK Unionist, in memoirs, *My Life and Themes*, which brought about his resignation from UK Unionist Party. *Observer*, October 25, 1998.

October 26, 1998
Rev Gerard Moloney
The Church suddenly found itself on the defensive, its weaknesses and sinfulness glaringly exposed to an often gleeful media and a shocked and confused public. Clergy and people alike looked to the bishops for leadership and guidance, only to find that the bishops themselves seemed confused and uncertain.

As editor of *Reality*, the Redemptorist magazine, on effect of sex scandals on Catholic Church. *The Irish Times*, October 26, 1998.

October 26, 1998
Rev Kevin Hegarty
[He said] 'There. That's one of the men I'm warning you about.'

As editor of *Ceide* magazine, in wake of court cases involving paedophile priests, recalling overheard remark by father pointing out priest to his son in hotel in west of Ireland. The Irish Times, October 26, 1998.

October 27, 1998
Reg Empey
It is now obvious that Mr McCartney has brought a cuckoo into the Unionist nest. It is perfectly clear by Dr O'Brien's remarks that the UKUP has a defeatist attitude to maintaining the Union.

As member of Ulster Unionst Party, on suggestion by Conor Cruise O'Brien that a united Ireland might best serve unionist interests. *The Irish Times*, October 28, 1998.

October 28, 1998
Tom Parlon
Taoiseach, there are 150,000 farm families telling you today – wake up to the alienation of rural Ireland.

As Irish Farmers' Association President, addressing 40,000-strong farm protest in Dublin. *The Irish Times*, October 29, 1998.

October 30, 1998
David McWilliams
We are in danger of moving from the Celtic Tiger to the Celtic Ostrich.

As economist, credited with first use of phrase 'Celtic Tiger'. *The Irish Times*, November 2, 1998.

October 31, 1998
Seamus Mallon
I was struck by the coincidence of timeframe of Havel's painful political journey from the Prague uprising of 1968 and the path of people from the launch of the Northern Ireland civil rights movement's marches in the same year through to the present day...there is also a more profound parallel, of utter adherence to the political path of consent.

As deputy First Minister of NI Assembly, on visit to Stormont by Czech President Vaclav Havel. *The Irish Times*, October 31, 1998.

November 2, 1998
David Trimble
There is a certain irony, is there not, in the IRA's constant litany of 'Not an inch!' and 'What we have we hold!'

As First Minister of NI Assembly, on IRA's refusal to decommission arms. *The Irish Times*, November 3, 1998.

November 4, 1998
Rev Dominic Johnson
A few years ago I acted as resident's chaplain to Mrs Mary Robinson at an evening prayer service. Our photograph was taken. Today I removed that framed photograph from my office and tore up the negative as an act of silent protest at the viewpoint expressed in her authorised biography, that abortion should be available 'in limited circumstances' in Ireland.

As priest in Glenstal Abbey, Co Limerick. *The Irish Times*, November 4, 1998.

November 8, 1998
Ruairí Ó Brádaigh
The Stormont Agreement simply updates and strengthens English rule here by including nationalist representatives in executive positions. They sit in the old Stormont parliament which has been refurbished after the fire – just like British rule itself.

As leader of Republican Sinn Féin, at party árd fheis in Drogheda. *The Irish Times*, November 9, 1998.

November 10, 1998
Duke of Edinburgh
I think any initiative which can overcome these rather artificial differences [in Ireland] can only be good.

As husband of British monarch, at Dublin Castle, presenting youth awards. *The Irish Times*, November 11, 1998.

November 11, 1998
Mary McAleese
The men of the 36th Ulster Division and the 16th Irish Division died here. They came from every corner of Ireland. Among them were Protestants, Catholics, unionists and nationalists, their differences transcended by a common commitment not to flag but to freedom. Today we seek to put their memory at the service of another common cause...the reconciliation of Protestant Ulster with Ireland and the reconciliation of Ireland with Great Britain.

As President, opening Island of Ireland Peace Park near Ypres in France to commemorate Irish fallen of First World War. *The Irish Times*, December 12, 1998.

November 11, 1998
Susan Phillips
For the first time in my life the two strands in me came together

As Wicklow councillor and southern Protestant, at opening of Island of Ireland Peace Park near Ypres in France to commemorate Irish fallen of First World War. *The Irish Times*, December 12, 1998.

November 11, 1998
Ivan Hunter
At home republicans and unionists don't meet. Here we have a common ground. It's marvellous.

As unionist councillor from Newtownabbey, at opening of Island of Ireland Peace Park near Ypres in France to commemorate Irish fallen of First World War. *The Irish Times*, December 12, 1998.

November 13, 1998
Bertie Ahern
Was this 'isolated Republic' a bridge too far?...To what extent have the Troubles modified our self-understanding as a nation?... Has it made us more pluralistic and not just more tolerant?...Why is even a pluralist Ireland foreign to unionists?...Is there such a thing as a sane nationalism, and do we have it now?

As Taoiseach, opening conference on nationalism. *Sunday Independent*, January 17, 1999.

November 17, 1998
Peig Ní Mháille
We were all uplifted by Mary Robinson's words in her inaugural speech, 'I am of Ireland – come dance with me in Ireland.' Sadly many of mná an Áras were not included in that invitation.

As former personal secretary to Presidents Ó Dálaigh and Hillery, in letter to *Irish Times* on dismissal of long-serving staff of Áras an Uachtaráin by President Mary Robinson. *The Irish Times*, November 17, 1998.

November 21, 1998
Jim McDaid
The Ireland in which Fianna Fáil was founded in 1926 has been irrevocably changed. The new Republic must be for everyone. It must be for the unemployed, it must be for people with disabilities, it must be for single parents, for gay people, for small farmers.

As Minister for Tourism, Sport and Recreation. *The Irish Times*, November 23, 1998.

November 25, 1998
Niall O'Dowd
In such a scenario we could have the spectacle of the British Prime Minister arguing in parliament that it is OK to negotiate while the IRA hangs on to ninety tonnes, but not to ninety-five tonnes of weaponry.

As New York publisher and intermediary in NI peace process, on unionist calls for some decommissioning by IRA. *The Irish Times*, November 25, 1998.

November 26, 1998
Seamus Pattison
As he [Gladstone] wound up his speech to the Commons before the vote on the first Home Rule Bill in 1886, he reflected, and I quote: 'This is one of the golden moments of our history – one of those opportunities which may come and may go, but which rarely return or, if they return, return at long intervals...' That aspiration has a particular meaning for us today.

As Ceann Comhairle, welcoming British Prime Minister Tony Blair to Oireachtas to address joint session. *The Irish Times*, November 27, 1998.

November 26, 1998
Tony Blair
Down through the centuries, Ireland and Britain have inflicted too much pain, each on the other... We have both grown up now. A new generation is in power in each country.

As British Prime Minister, addressing joint houses of Oireachtas in Dublin. *The Irish Times*, November 27, 1998.

November 28, 1998
Rev Ian Paisley
Daniel O'Connell, a man who married his cousin and was rightly accused of all kinds of sexual deviancy – no surprise that the Prime Minister, with a Cabinet of many self-confessed homosexuals and partnerships without marriage, should find a place for him.

As leader of DUP, at party conference, on British Prime Minister Tony Blair's praise for Daniel O'Connell in address to Oireachtas. *The Irish Times*, November 28, 1998.

November 28, 1998
Ian Paisley Jr
Imagine doing your bathroom in those. It would give a whole new meaning to the Relief of Derry.

As delegate at DUP conference, on sale of 'King Billy' tiles. *The Irish Times*, November 30, 1998.

December 1, 1998
Louis Smith
Having not the slightest connection with the celebration of two thousand years of Christianity, the spike in O'Connell Street is quite pointless.

As letter writer to *Irish Times*, on plans to erect 394-foot spike in centre of Dublin. *The Irish Times*, December 1, 1998.

December 10, 1998
Rev Cecil Cooper
It is even more remarkable that the Roman Catholic Church, until recently the staunch defender of public morality in this country, has been so silent in this instance... We may feel a certain sympathy or even pity for Mr Ahern as an individual. But he is not just an individual. He is the leader of the Government. He is a role model. He represents the nation abroad.

As editor of *Church of Ireland Gazette*, in editorial on 'astonishing' fact that Taoiseach Bertie Ahern travelled with his partner Celia Larkin. *The Irish Times*, December 11, 1998.

December 10, 1998
Chief Emeka Anyaoku
I can promise you that if Ireland should ever decide to [rejoin the Commonwealth] you can be sure of a very warm welcome, a *céad míle fáilte* in fact.

As Secretary General of British Commonwealth. *The Irish Times*, December 11, 1998.

December 10, 1998
John Hume
European Union is the best example in the history of the world of conflict resolution and it is the duty of everyone, particularly those who live in areas of conflict, to study how it was done and to apply its principles to their own conflict resolution.

As leader of SDLP, accepting joint Nobel Peace Prize in Oslo. *The Irish Times*, December 12, 1998.

December 10, 1998
David Trimble
[Edmund] Burke is the best model for what might be called politicians of the possible...because he is the philosopher of practical politics, not of visionary vapours.

As First Minister of NI Assembly, accepting joint Nobel Peace Prize in Oslo. *The Irish Times*, December 12, 1998.

December 12, 1998
Ruairi Quinn
It is not the end of the journey. It is the commencement of a wonderful radical voyage.

As leader of Labour Party, on merger with Democratic Left. *The Irish Times*, December 13, 1998.

December 12, 1998
Brian Fitzgerald
Democratic Left has absolutely no principles. They went from Sinn Féin to Official Sinn Féin/IRA to Sinn Féin the Workers' Party, the Workers' Party, New Agenda and Democratic Left, leaving a trail of destruction in every party they have been a part of. They have no home now so they are prepared to crawl to us.

As Labour Party delegate, at meeting on merger of Labour and Democratic Left. *The Irish Times*, December 13, 1998.

January 13, 1999
Bertie Ahern
[I am] as prepared to acknowledge the greatness of Michael Collins as Fine Gael politicians are prepared to acknowledge the tremendous achievements of Sean Lemass.

As Taoiseach and first Fianna Fáil leader to pay tribute to Collins, speaking at UCD. *Sunday Independent*, January 17, 1999.

January 14, 1999
James Gogarty
They're laughing at me and they're getting
£1300, or £1350 a day, for laughing at me. I am
here at this tribunal to tell the truth, warts and
all.

As witness at Flood Tribunal, on tribunal lawyers. *Sunday
Independent*, January 17, 1999.

January 15, 1999
Padraig Flynn
I never asked or took money from anybody to do
favours for anybody in my life.

As European Commissioner, on *RTÉ*'s Late Late Show, on
money he received from property developer Tom
Gilmartin. *RTÉ*, January 15, 1999.

January 19, 1999
James Gogarty
I don't think there was a whole lot said, but I
said, 'Will we get a receipt for this money?' and
Bailey said, 'Will we fuck!'

As witness in Flood Tribunal, describing journey in car
with Michael Bailey of Bovale Developments to give cash
to Fianna Fáil politician Ray Burke. *The Irish Times*,
January 20, 1999.

January 22, 1999
Seamus Mallon
There may be heavy cloud, there may be flak,
there may even be hijackers on board. But we
can see the lights of the runway.

As deputy First Minister of NI Assembly. *The Irish Times*,
January 23, 1999.

January 23, 1999
David Trimble
If it is necessary to park the process for a while
so as to tackle the obstacles created by the
paramilitaries, so be it. What we don't want is
for the process to have a crash-landing where it
is seriously damaged.

As First Minister of NI Assembly. *BBC*, January 23, 1999.

February 5, 1999
Bertie Ahern
If what I say here leads to people ringing Mr
Gilmartin and he says x, y or z, and then I have
to come back to say he said x, y or z, or if
someone rings him and says a, b and c, and I
must come back here and say a, b and c, I will be
here for the rest of my life.

As Taoiseach, on contacts with property developer Tom
Gilmartin, potential witness in Flood Tribunal
investigating payments to politicians. *The Irish Times*,
February 6, 1999.

February 7, 1999
John Bruton
I wanted to give a straight and full and final
answer to the media query. So I checked it out
with the only person who could definitely confirm
my own view that I had never met Tom Gilmartin
– Tom Gilmartin himself.

As Fine Gael leader, on why he contacted potential witness
to Flood Tribunal investigating payments to politicians. *The
Irish Times*, February 8, 1999.

February 10, 1999
Brendan Solan
He did the State – some service!

As letter-writer to *The Irish Times*, paraphrasing Charles
Haughey's farewell words to Dáil on February 11, 1992: 'I
have done the State some service...' *The Irish Times*,
February 10, 1999.

February 14, 1999
Bertie Ahern
Our view is that decommissioning in one form or
another has to happen. I am on record in recent
weeks as saying that this is not compatible with
being a part of government – I mean part of an
executive – that there is not at least a
commencement of decommissioning.

As Taoiseach, in interview published on *Sunday Times*
website. *The Irish Times*, February 15, 1999.

February 15, 1999
Martin McGuinness
We were never told anything by a single member
of the Irish Government or the civil service which
would indicate that the Irish Government was of a
view that Sinn Féin should be barred from
positions on an executive unless there was IRA
decommissioning.

As Sinn Féin Vice President, on remarks by Taoiseach
Bertie Ahern, above. *The Irish Times*, February 16, 1999.

February 17, 1999
Pleurat Sejdiu
We don't want a Gerry Adams because then we
would have an IRA. We do not want to have an
IRA. The KLA is a regular army and is supported
by the people. It is not a terrorist organisation.

As London representative of Kosovo Liberation Army, after
US Secretary of State Madeleine Albright suggested at Paris
peace talks that KLA leaders should model themselves on
Sinn Féin leader. *Reuters*, February 2, 1999.

February 17, 1999
James Gogarty
From the dock? Oh Jesus! I didn't know that.
Putting me in the dock? Oh Mother of God!

As witness at Flood Tribunal on payment to politicians,
when accused by barrister Garrett Cooney of making long

rambling speeches from the 'dock' rather than witness stand. *The Irish Times*, February 18, 1999.

February 18, 1999
Justice Michael Moriarty

[Bankers believe] 'If you owe us one thousand pounds, it's your problem. If you owe us one million pounds, it's our problem.'

As chairman of Moriarty tribunal, on payments to politicians. *The Irish Times*, February 19, 1999.

February 18, 1999
Gerry Scanlan

This dream account, or dream relationship, turned into what I would describe as a banker's nightmare.

As former chief executive of Allied Irish Banks, on bank account of Charles Haughey, in evidence to Moriarty Tribunal on payments to politicians. *The Irish Times*, February 19, 1999.

March 2, 1999
Dr Desmond Connell

A profound alteration in the relationship between parent and child may result when the child is no longer welcomed as a gift but produced as it were to order... No child can be happy as a product.

As Archbishop of Dublin, in lecture at Maynooth, criticising 'contraceptive culture'. *The Irish Times*, March 3, 1999.

March 3, 1999
Tony O'Brien

To suggest that children who have been planned are not intrinsically loved by their parents is a fantasy, gratuitously offensive and without any basis.

As chief executive of Irish Family Planning Association, on remarks of Dr Desmond Connell, above. *The Irish Times*, March 4, 1999.

March 5, 1999
Jenni Murray

You have in the past been very outspoken in your views and you've been very controversial in your views, and, I think, comments about your nationalist background. How do you keep your mouth shut for a seven-year term?

As *BBC* interviewer, in question to President Mary McAleese for which *BBC* apologised. *The Irish Times*, March 6, 1999.

March 15, 1999
George Mitchell

Until just about a few years ago, I was as Irish as a shish kebab.

As former US Senator of Lebanese and Irish origin, receiving Irish-American of the Year award in New York for chairing NI talks. *Newsweek*, March 29, 1999.

March 16, 1999
Bertie Ahern

Normally when you park something it gets vandalised.

As Taoiseach, on David Trimble's suggesion of 'parking' Good Friday Agreement. *The Irish Times*, March 17, 1999.

March 16, 1999
Mo Mowlam

We are within a hair's breadth of a settlement.

As NI Secretary of State, receiving peace award in Washington. *The Irish Times*, March 17, 1999.

March 17, 1999
Stella O'Leary

We need the strength of a Gore presidency to ensure that all the elements of the Good Friday Agreement are fully implemented.

As President of Irish-American Democrats in Washington, at St Patrick's Day breakfast for Vice President Al Gore. *The Irish Times*, March 18, 1999.

March 17, 1999
Bill Clinton

They must see that distant horizon where children will grow up in an Ireland trouble-free and not even remember how it used to be.

As US President, on vision required by NI politicians. *The Irish Times*, March 18, 1999.

March 23, 1999
Geralyn McNally

The ill-disguised hostility to Mrs Nelson on the part of some police officers was indicative of a mindset which could be viewed as bordering on the obstructive.

As member of NI Independent Commission for Police Complaints, in report on police harassment claims by solicitor Rosemary Nelson, killed by car bomb on March 15. *The Irish Times*, March 24, 1999.

March 25, 1999
Most Rev Richard Clarke

There is, I am delighted to say, a rising generation which will, I believe, refuse to tolerate the brutal fantasies and monstrous stereotyping of other religious traditions by which all our Churches, and not least the Church of Ireland, have sought to bolster up their own membership since time immemorial.

As Church of Ireland Bishop of Meath and Kildare, in Christ Church Cathedral, Dublin, at service in which many prominent Roman Catholics took communion in defiance of prohibition by Catholic Hierarchy. *The Irish Times*, March 26, 1999.

March 30, 1999
Tony Blair
On my mother's side were very strong Irish Protestants. I married a Catholic although I am Church of England. We are about to enter the 21st century. Do these things really have to pull people apart?

As British Prime Minister, arriving in Belfast for crisis talks on Good Friday Agreement. *The Irish Times*, March 31, 1999.

March 31, 1999
IRA
We wholeheartedly support efforts to secure a lasting resolution to the conflict...IRA guns are silent.

In Easter statement. *The Irish Times*, April 1, 1999.

April 1, 1999
Rough Guide to Ireland
[Ireland] is shamefully intolerant of minority groups. If you are black you may well experience a peculiarly naive brand of ignorant racism.

As guide book for young people visiting Ireland. *The Irish Times*, April 24, 1999.

April 1, 1999
Tony Blair
These are the people who...have never had anything constructive to offer. These people literally are the past in Northern Ireland.

As British Prime Minister, at Stormont talks, on loyalist protesters. *The Irish Times*, April 2, 1999.

April 4, 1999
Most Rev Walton Empey
It is difficult to see the Risen Christ in the abominable attitude of the Government in its treatment of refugees and asylum-seekers. There is little evidence there of God's love for these people.

As Church of Ireland Archbishop of Dublin, speaking in Christ Church Cathedral. *The Irish Times*, April 5, 1999.

April 17, 1999
David Andrews
You mean a man is being murdered?

As Minister for Foreign Affairs, at meeting with Bishop Carlos Belo in Dili, East Timor, after independence leader came to say his son was being killed 500 yards away by pro-Indonesian militias. *The Irish Times*, April 19, 1999.

April 17, 1999
Justice Hugh O'Flaherty
I accept that the appearance of detachment must be the most important thing for a judge and there cannot be a scintilla of suspicion to call in question his impartiality.

As Supreme Court judge, resigning over his role in judiciary's handling of case of drunk driver who had prison sentence remitted in controversial circumstances. *The Irish Times*, April 18, 1999.

April 22, 1999
William Geary
I left the country branded a scoundrel and a traitor and now my name is cleared after all these years.

As 100-year-old former garda superintendent, in New York, on winning case for wrongful dismissal in 1928 for allegedly accepting bribe from IRA. *The Irish Times*, April 23, 1999.

April 22, 1999
Pope John Paul II
You're British, aren't you?

As Pontiff, greeting Ulster Unionist leader, David Trimble, in the Vatican in first ever meeting between a Pontiff and a Unionist Party leader. *The Irish Times*, April 23, 1999.

April 22, 1999
David Trimble
I think the Ulster Unionist electorate is remarkably mature in these matters and it much prefers to see a confident face of unionism and our willingness to carry our message to anyone in the world.

As Ulster Unionist leader, on meeting Pope John Paul II in the Vatican. *The Irish Times*, April 23, 1999.

April 30, 1999
Sinead O'Connor [Mother Bernadette Mary]
I don't need publicity. If I fart I get it.

As former singer, after ordination as Tridentine priest. *The Irish Times*, May 1, 1999.

May 8, 1999
Gerry Adams
By the same token it is amazing how tonnes of bombs dropped in the Balkans are morally and politically acceptable while the silent guns of the IRA, we are told, are a threat to peace.

As President of Sinn Féin, at árd fheis in Dublin, referring to NATO air strikes against Yugoslavia. *The Irish Times*, May 10, 1999.

May 11, 1999
Bertie Ahern
On behalf of the State and of all citizens of the State, the Government wishes to make a sincere and long overdue apology to the victims of childhood abuse for our collective failure to intervene, to detect their pain, to come to their rescue.

As Taoiseach, announcing commission of inquiry into child sexual abuse in institutions, exposed in *RTÉ* programme, States of Fear. *The Irish Times*, May 12, 1999.

May 14, 1999
Terry Keane
He layered me with Irishness. To him I was Terry O'Donnell, whose clan was from Donegal, and he would recount stories about what the O'Donnells said to the O'Neills. There was an element of Lady Chatterley and her lover about it.

As journalist, describing her 27-year affair with Charles Haughey on The Late Late Show. *RTÉ*, May 14, 1999.

May 14, 1999
Terry Keane
Charlie always had the uncomplicated belief that the greater good was served by him getting what he wanted.

As journalist, describing her 27-year affair with Charles Haughey. *RTÉ*, May 14, 1999.

May 18, 1999
David Trimble
No guns, no government.

As First Minister of Northern Ireland Assembly, demanding IRA decommissioning before forming an executive with Sinn Féin. *The Irish Times*, May 19, 1999.

June 1, 1999
Mick McCarthy
There is no question that the controversy affects their [Irish players'] preparations. On the other hand, I don't know what else can happen to the lads in the Yugoslav team to affect their preparations. If the situation was reversed and we were going to Yugoslavia and my granny's chippie in Waterford was bombed, I think I'd be going there with a point to prove.

As Irish football team manager, on preparations for European Cup soccer international between Ireland and Yugoslavia, later abandoned. *The Irish Times*, June 2, 1999.

June 1, 1999
Rev Joe Young
How can anyone stand under a flag and play football when ethnic cleansing is taking place? No three points are worth endorsing Milosevic.

As chairman of Limerick Football Club, threatening to resign if European Cup soccer international between Ireland and Yugoslavia took place. *The Irish Times*, June 2, 1999.

June 21, 1999
David Ervine
If we do fail, people will never, ever, forgive the politicians. Failure is not an option.

As leader of Progressive Unionist Party, on negotiations to implement Good Friday Agreement by June 30 deadline. Hard Talk, *BBC* World Service, June 21, 1999.

June 25, 1999
Sinead O'Connor (Mother Bernadette Mary)
I was warned by Sinn Féin that I shouldn't mention punishment beatings. I'm a priest for fuck's sake. What do they expect?

As former singer, after cancelling her appearance at the West Belfast Community Festival. *Sunday Business Post*, June 27, 1999.

June 30, 1999
Gerry Adams
It is a case of jumping together into the future or lurching backwards into the past.

As Sinn Féin President, during negotiations on decommissioning at Stormont Castle in attempt to conclude peace process. *RTÉ*, June 30, 1999.

July 1, 1999
Ken Magennis
We are walking through a hall of mirrors and we see reflections and when we move towards them there is nothing there.

As Unionist Party spokesman, during negotiations on decommissioning at Stormont Castle in attempt to conclude peace process. *RTÉ*, July 1, 1999.

July 1, 1999
Tony Blair
I believe what we have witnessed in the last few days are literally historic, seismic shifts in the history of Northern Ireland...the entire civilised world will not understand if we cannot put this thing together and make it work.

As British Prime Minister, during negotiations on decommissioning at Stormont Castle in attempt to conclude peace process. *RTÉ*, July 1, 1999.

July 1, 1999
Bertie Ahern
There is an awful lot to gain and a frightening amount to lose.

As Taoiseach, during negotiations on decommissioning at Stormont Castle in attempt to conclude peace process. *RTÉ*, July 1, 1999.

QUOTE OF THE CENTURY

October 16, 1998
John Hume
I always kept repeating myself – it's the old teacher in me – that I hope that, in the future, the symbol of our patriotism will be the spilling of our sweat and not the spilling of our blood.

As SDLP leader, on *RTÉ*'s Late Late Show, on being awarded the Nobel Peace Prize. *RTÉ*, October 16, 1998.

INDEX

Numbers in bold denote quote. Numbers not in bold denote reference.